THE ESSENTIAL
BATHROOM
DESIGN GUIDE

THE ESSENTIAL
BATHROOM
DESIGN GUIDE

NATIONAL KITCHEN & BATH ASSOCIATION

JOHN WILEY & SONS, INC.

New York / Chichester / Weinheim / Toronto / Singapore / Brisbane

Library of Congress Cataloging-in-Publication Data
The essential bathroom design guide / National Kitchen & Bath
   Association.
     p.   cm.
    Includes index.
    ISBN 0-471-12673-X (cloth : alk. paper)
     1. Bathrooms—Remodeling. I. National Kitchen and Bath
   Association.
   TH4816.3.B37E84   1997
   747.7 ' 97—dc21   96-47467

Printed in United States of America

10 9 8 7 6 5 4 3 2 1

Preface

The kitchen/bathroom industry has grown significantly since its genesis, and today is a well regarded design specialty. It is also a lucrative business. Remodeling and new construction projects of kitchens and bathrooms total over $40 billion annually and continues to grow each year. Bathrooms are the second most frequently remodeled rooms in the home. They are becoming relaxation centers, private havens, even spas -- stylish, comfortable, beautiful and functional.

The bathroom -- the indoor bathroom that is -- is a relatively new concept when compared to all other spaces in a residential dwelling. Private indoor bathrooms have been standard in new homes for less than 100 years. Though homeowner attitudes about bathroom spaces have changed in recent years, their creation was borne of necessity, not design. And in including them in homes, the goal of architects and builders was to fit the fixtures in the smallest space possible. Comfort and aesthetics were not priorities. Thus the 5' x 7' bathroom so typical of many homes.

The lack of attention and priority first attached to indoor bathrooms really isn't surprising when you consider the history of the room's primary activities -- bathing and waste elimination. Through the Dark Ages and Renaissance, the first was considered improper and dangerous. The second was taken care of outdoors or "out doors" where it was tossed. People, including 13th century kings and queens, bathed only occasionally at best. And it took a 19th century cholera epidemic to convince even medical professionals that water-borne sewage systems were needed.

Though Americans in the 1800s increased bathing frequency to as often as once per week, taking a bath meant dragging a wooden tub into the kitchen and filling it with hot water. The outhouse was a backyard fixture. Metal tubs and toilets, and the infamous John Crapper's automatic flushing system didn't come on the scene until the late 19th century. The first vitreous china water closet wasn't introduced until 1907.

If the concept of the bathroom is new, the idea of bathroom design is even newer. Minimum standards for bathrooms were set by the Department of Housing and Urban Development in the 1940s. The first book on functional bathroom design wasn't written until 1976. In 1992 the **National Kitchen & Bathroom Association** released its *27 Guidelines for Bathroom Planning*, along with the first-ever comprehensive resource bathroom design and planning, **The Bathroom Industry Technical Manuals**. As a result of industry research, the NKBA updated its bathroom guidelines in 1995, increased them in number to 41, and incorporated Universal Design principles.

The bathroom has come of age. The 5' x 7' cramped spaces are disappearing -- replaced in new homes and through remodeling with more spacious layouts, featuring beautiful fixtures, surfaces and accessories.

This book covers the foundations of the bathroom design business as outlined by NKBA. Bathroom planning guidelines and safety criteria, equipment and materials, mechanical systems and accepted drawing and presentation standards are all incorporated in this one-of-a-kind, all-encompassing text.

Today, NKBA is the leading organization for the kitchen and bathroom industry, known for its quality education programs and materials, and its exceptional promotion of the bathroom profession to consumers. We applaud your entrance into the bathroom design field, and congratulate you for beginning or expanding your education with the widely recognized and respected information included herein.

Nick Geragi, CKD, CBD, NCIDQ
Director of Education and Product Development
National Kitchen & Bath Association

About NKBA Membership

NKBA membership is the first step toward building close, powerful working relationships with other NKBA members as well as with clients. You'll benefit from:

- **Networking with the best and brightest.** Exchange ideas, insights and strategies you can use immediately to build business.

- **Consumer advertising and publicity programs.** NKBA consumer marketing programs are designed to link you with qualified prospects pursing kitchen and bathroom projects. Advertising, publicity, our own quarterly consumer magazine, and our exclusive consumer referral program, Direct to Your Door™ make NKBA a powerful enhancement to your existing marketing program.

- **Business management tools.** Supplies that streamline your day-to-day operation, reduce costs, and enhance your professionalism.

- **Certification.** Certified Kitchen Designer (CKD) and Certified Bathroom Designer (CBD) designations bring you added professional recognition, prestige and credibility.

- **Nationally acclaimed trade shows.** Where you can be among the first to see the latest in design and technology.

- **Prestigious design competitions.** Creating valuable publicity for NKBA members only.

Consumer research confirms that NKBA membership creates credibility and confidence among homeowners who plan to remodel their kitchens or bathrooms. It evokes a powerful image of stability and security. A feeling of confidence that delivers business!

Take advantage of the opportunities NKBA affiliation can create! **Call 1-800-THE-NKBA** for a free brochure and membership application, email educate@nkba.org, or write to:

NKBA
687 Willow Grove Street,
Hackettstown, New Jersey 07840.

Contents

CHAPTER **1**

Bathroom Mechanical Systems

The success of your bathroom plan will be based on how well you can plan the plumbing system, the heating/cooling/ventilation system, the lighting system and the electrical system.

Each one of the fixtures depends on the plumbing system to operate efficiently. You must know when you can economically rearrange the fixtures in a renovation project or suggest additional fixtures for a new home plan.

Because people use the bathroom without clothing on, the heating and/or cooling of that space is important to their comfort. Bathroom odors and surface material deterioration caused by water condensation can be controlled and/or eliminated by your design of an effective ventilation system.

Your clients' personal grooming time will be enhanced by a well-engineered lighting layout that takes into account the importance of a shadowless environment.

And, with electrical appliances and other types of equipment so common today, your ability to properly place electrical outlets that are safe to use in a moist water environment is as important as the other systems previously mentioned.

In this chapter you will be introduced to each one of these systems so that you understand how they work and what practical and affordable changes you can make for a bathroom project you are designing. Once you've mastered this material, you'll be prepared to continue on to study the specific equipment and materials used in well-designed bathroom spaces.

SECTION **1**

Plumbing

Experienced bathroom planners know that behind (and underneath) every successful bathroom is a sound plumbing system. Knowing what parts of the plumbing system are buried beneath the floor and hidden in walls will help you design and price your jobs competitively.

In this section, we will review the two basic parts of a plumbing system - the water supply system and the drain/waste/vent system.

Contemporary bathrooms require water to be brought to many fixtures within the room. It's no longer just the bathtub, toilet and lavatory that need to be connected to the plumbing system. Laundry equipment, jetted bathtubs, steam rooms, saunas, multiple showerheads and bidets all need water and drainage systems.

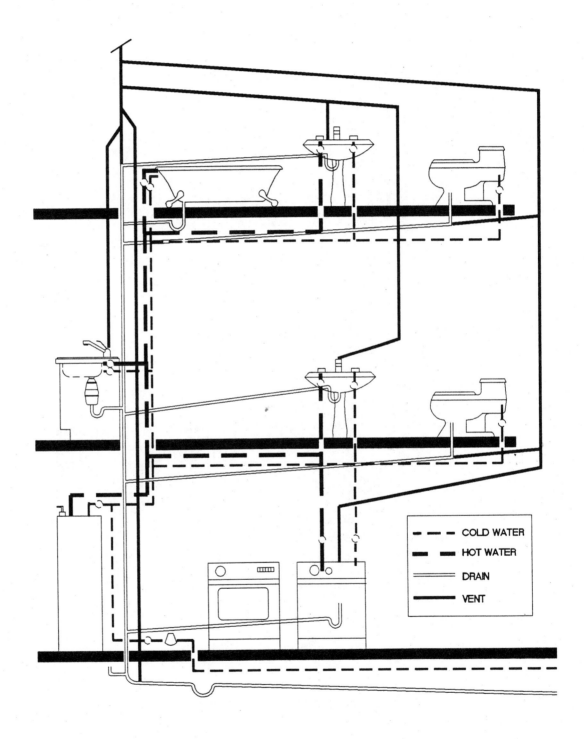

Figure 1 Typical Residential Plumbing System. The home's plumbing system is made up of plumbing lines to deliver water and drain/waste/vent lines that take wastewater away.

CODES AND REGULATIONS

Building codes vary from community to community. The most widely used plumbing code is the **Uniform Plumbing Code**, a model code written by IAPMO (International Association of Plumbing and Mechanical Officials). However, model codes are also produced by ASME (the American Society of Mechanical Engineers), BOCA (Building Official and Code Administrators), whose code is called the **Basic Plumbing Code**, the SBCCI (Southern Building Code Congress International), producers of the **Southern Standard Plumbing Code**, and the PHCC (National Association of Plumbing Heating Cooling Contractors), the National Plumbing Code.

Major cities such as Chicago have their own plumbing codes. The CABO (Council of American Building Officials), **One and Two Family Dwelling Code** bases its plumbing code provisions on three other model codes - BOCA, SBCCI and ICBO (International Conference of Building Officials), but IAPMO does not participate in the CABO code. A local government could use parts of the CABO code having to do with structures, but use the IAPMO code for plumbing.

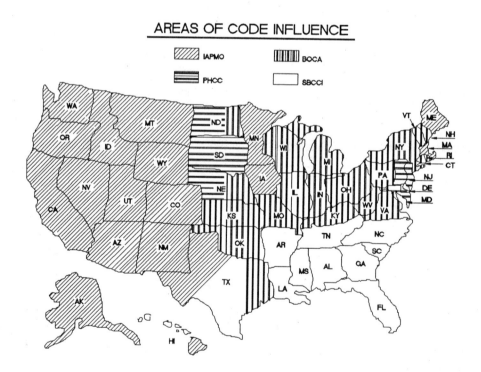

AREAS OF CODE INFLUENCE

Figure 2   Plumbing codes have been created by many model code bodies. Here are the general regions of four of the major codes.

Typical Areas of Difference

Plumbing codes are more similar than they are different. All are designed to ensure a safe and functional plumbing system. Each provides regulations to make sure that plumbing odors will be vented to the outdoors and that the fixtures will have an adequate water pressure. The codes can be very different in the details, however. Watch for differences in these areas:

- The minimum dimensions of a shower pan;

- The minimum curb height of a shower pan;

- A maximum number of gallons per minute a showerhead can produce;

- The number of gallons per flush for a toilet (especially important in drought-stricken states);

- The kinds of plumbing materials that are allowed (some plastics are not allowed);

- The minimum size (diameter) of water supply lines to fixtures;

- Anti-scald requirements, such as pressure and/or temperature balancing valves on showers and bathtub fixtures, now appear in all codes.

The plumbing inspector will be knowledgeable about local code requirements, such as those that might limit the use of plastic pipe or that might require water supply lines of a certain size.

Responsibility for Fixtures

The plumbing contractor is generally not responsible for fixtures you specify. Suppose you choose a volume control valve and overhead showerhead (from a foreign source) with a 12 gallon-per-minute (gpm) flow rate. These large showerheads are illegal at the factory level in the United States. If you specify a valve and/or showerhead with a flow rate higher than 2.5 gpm, the plumber is not liable for the code official turning down the installation.

You might also request an acrylic shower unit that does not meet the minimum size requirements of the local code. Or, you could choose a European plumbing fixture that has not been approved by the regional codes and standards.

The plumbing contractor will argue that you should have checked on code approval before writing your specifications. The plumbing contractor will not agree to absorb the cost of fixtures that do not meet codes and standards. To be sure that your products meet codes, check with the governing body in your area.

Locating Technical Data

The performance of toilets and other plumbing fixtures is governed by ANSI **(American National Standards Institute)**. Compliance with ANSI standards is voluntary. Because the standards often become part of the plumbing codes, manufacturers conform in order to get their products approved for the market. Different standards apply to different fixtures. If you are choosing an unusual fixture that you have never used before, you need to find out if it meets ANSI standards.

Finding information about fixtures and standards requires a little extra effort. You will need to call the company and request technical information, especially any test results produced by independent testing laboratories. The technical data will list various ANSI and ASTM **(American Society for Testing and Materials)** standards. If you find that the fixture has been approved, you should present the technical information to the local plumbing inspector before ordering. Point out the test data and ask if this meets local code requirements.

When you call the company for technical data, you should also ask for a copy of their installation instructions. This information is usually contained in a manual. The manual shows plans and elevations and gives all critical dimensions and centerlines.

Certified Bathroom Designer (**Lou Hall**) photocopies these plans directly from the manual onto a transparent sheet of plastic. He then peels off the backing paper and superimposes the plans or elevations on his own vellum drawings. This approach eliminates having to redraw dimensions for each fixture. If the plumbing contractor calls with a question about the unusual fixture, you can point to the page on the plans where these dimensions can be found.

A better alternative to having the installation manual in hand before giving plans to the plumbing contractor is to order the fixture early, before the plumbing contractor begins work. Fixtures include installation instructions in the box. These instructions include the di-

mensions needed to **rough-in** the plumbing. (Rough-in plumbing is completed when the house is still in the framing stage - before wall finishes have been installed.) Such early ordering also allows you to inspect all fixtures and fittings for damage before the job begins.

The job must have a secure area where all the fixtures can be stored without getting damaged. And the fixtures must all arrive early in the construction sequence. It is quite common for delivery delays to occur. The safest approach is to order the technical and installation manuals and have the material in your files, as well as the fixtures, fittings and other pieces of equipment on the jobsite.

Water Conservation

Many states and communities have laws regarding water conservation. Codes are minimum requirements. In any situation, local residential and commercial projects may require installation of fixtures even more water-conserving than the 1.6 gpm limit for toilets and the 2.5 gpm limit for showerheads. A showerhead with a flow rate less than 2.5 gpm will save water and still might provide comfortable bathing by mixing air and water to keep pressure high. Pulsating showerheads can provide comfortable showers and still fall within water-conserving requirements.

Understanding the plumbing system will help you avoid unnecessary costs. Installing plumbing in new construction or changing fixtures in existing construction can be done economically - if you understand how the pieces of the plumbing system go together. The easiest way to think of the plumbing system is to visualize two different parts:

- The **water supply system**, which carries water from the municipal water system or well into the house and around to fixtures and appliances;

- The **drain/waste/vent system**, (DWV), which carries wastewater and sewer gases out of the house.

To understand the function of each part of the plumbing network, it is easiest to separate each part by its function.

WATER SUPPLY SYSTEM

Water enters the house through a main supply pipe connected to a water utility main or to a well. If the house is served by a utility, the water arrives through a main pipe which will vary according to demand. If the water comes from a private well, it is also carried to the house via a pipe, which is connected to a pump that moves the water through the system. Where the water supply enters the house, you will find a shutoff valve. This main shutoff valve cuts off the water supply to the whole house.

The supply main delivers the water through the meter to the water heater, where it splits into two branches. One supplies the water heater, the other branches off, along with a twin hot line from the water heater, to supply fixtures in the house.

The **supply branches** run horizontally through the floor joists or concrete slab. Where the supply branches run vertically in the wall to an upper story, they are called **supply risers**. In a two-story house, more branch lines could be found in the second-floor joists. In some houses, branch lines are found in the attic.

At the termination of each hot and cold water line, a **tee** (a T-shaped pipe) sticks out of the wall. A shutoff valve is attached to the tee and allows water to be cut off from just one fixture. Repairs can be made without cutting off the water supply to the entire house. Every fixture should have shutoff valves. Supply tubing is used to connect the shutoff valve to the fixture.

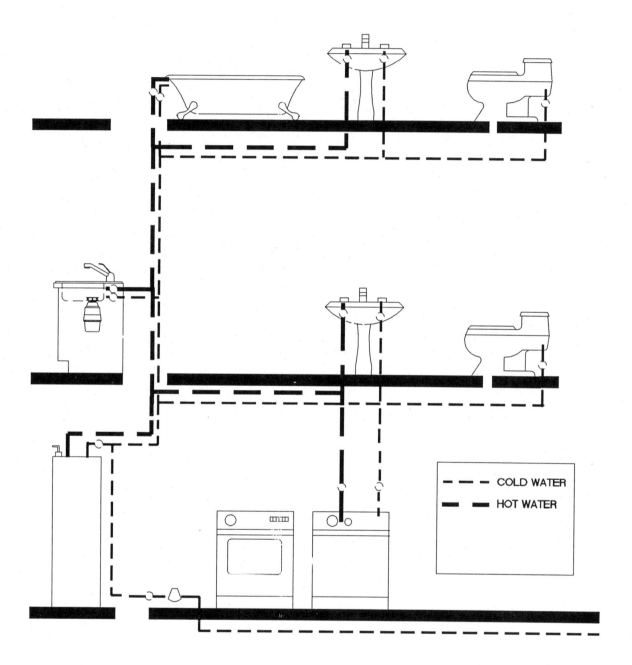

COLD WATER

HOT WATER

Figure 3 A schematic diagram shows a simplified version of the water supply side of the plumbing system.

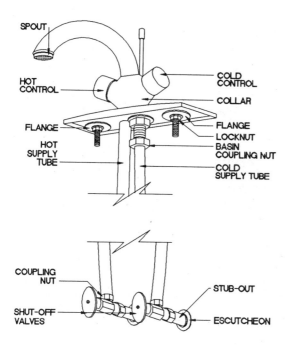

Figure 4 Lavatory water supply connections with shut-off valve.

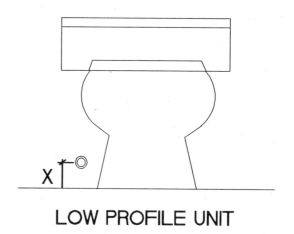

LOW PROFILE UNIT

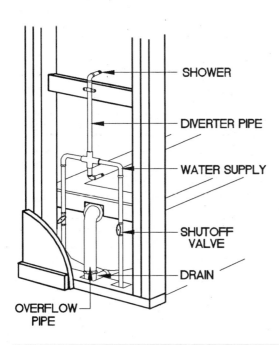

Figure 5 Bathtub/shower water supply connections with shut-off valve.

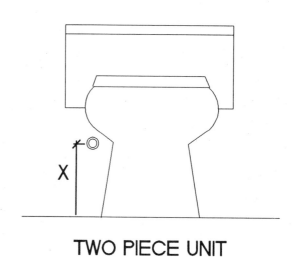

TWO PIECE UNIT

Figure 6 Supply line placement comparison between close-coupled and one-piece toilet.

Water Pressure

Water coming into the house is under pressure. On municipal water systems, pressures of 50 to 60 pounds per square inch (psi) are common. The pressure should not be lower than 30 psi or higher than 80 psi.

Pressure can be affected by the number of outlets being served (and how often they are used at the same time), the distance the piping must travel to those outlets, the number of turns in the piping and other variables.

EXTERNAL USAGE DEMANDS

A drop in pressure can be created by low pressure of the water entering the house. For instance, if a community waters its lawns at 5:00 p.m. every night, the pressure drop would be felt by anyone taking a shower. Cities in drought areas might also have inadequate water pressure.

FIXTURE DISTANCE FROM THE MAIN

Pressure drop can also occur when a fixture is too far from the water main and when the fixture requires a high volume of water.

PIPING CONFIGURATION

A pipe run with many turns and bends will reduce the available water pressure.

Water Volume/Velocity

Multiple showerheads and fillers for jetted bathtubs require high water pressure and a high volume of water to function effectively. A later section will discuss the special plumbing arrangements necessary for these fixtures.

CORROSION IN THE PIPES

Corrosion or scale that builds up on the inside of water supply lines will decrease water flow. This is most common with galvanized pipe. Corrosion decreases the inside diameter of the pipe and water flow can be reduced to a trickle.

PIPE SIZE

Pipe size also governs volume. The normal size of pipe from the city water lines to the house is 1" in diameter. However, in older houses you might find a pipe size of only 5/8" to 3/4". If you wanted to use a jetted bathtub or large shower, a 5/8" to 3/4" main would not supply enough water for the fixture. The plumbing contractor would have to dig a trench through the yard and install a new main of the proper size.

The plumbing lines in a house become smaller the closer they are to the fixtures. The 1" main drops to 3/4" branch lines. The lines supplying individual fixtures are smaller yet - 1/2". *What happens if you have a large bathtub or a shower with a 12 gallon per minute flow which require greater water volume?* A 1/2" supply pipe simply will not provide enough water. In these cases, the plumbing contractor should provide a home run supply line. This is a supply line that goes all the way back to the main and the water heater.

The supply lines for these water consuming fixtures must be 3/4". The faucets must also be capable of delivering a high volume flow. You cannot put a standard faucet meant to be connected to a 1/2" supply line on a bathtub or shower that requires a high volume of water. Check the pipe diameter before ordering.

Using the correct pipe size is especially important with multi-head showers or body sprays. In *Figure 7,* **Roland A. Franco**, CBD, shows how a 1/2" pressure balancing loop is connected to 3/4" supply lines using thermostatic controlled valves. The pressure balancing loop is needed to keep one showerhead from having low pressure at one head and high pressure at another.

Height and locations of the sprays are determined by the person bathing, and are not necessarily the same for each installation. It is wise to discuss these heights with your client, noting their physical size. Chapters 2 and 3 provide detailed information about fittings available and the accepted planning guidelines for fitting placement. However, remember that pipes hidden in the wall are what make such a system successful.

Supply Pipe Materials

The plumbing code in your area will spell out which materials can be used for supply pipe. The plumbing contractor will normally decide which type of supply pipe to use. Copper is generally considered to be the most durable supply pipe. However, in agricultural areas where nitrate levels in the drinking water are relatively high, copper can corrode. Galvanized pipe gives better performance in these cases.

The chart on page 13 shows the most common types of pipe materials as well as their advantages and disadvantages.

CUSTOM SHOWER WITH MULTIPLE SHOWER HEADS AND BODY SPRAYS.

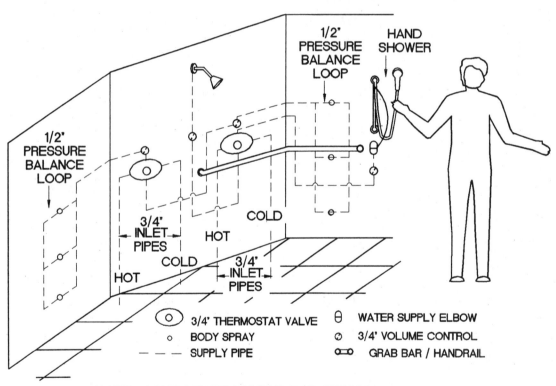

* NOTE : CONSULT WITH CLIENT FOR SPECIFIC
VALVE AND HEAD DIMENSION LOCATIONS,
WHICH WILL VARY WITH EACH CLIENTS HEIGHT.

Figure 7   Correct piping for a multiple-head shower and multiple body sprays.

SUPPLY PIPE MATERIALS		
MATERIAL	**PROS**	**CONS**
Copper Pipe	Lightweight Easy to Assemble Corrosion resistant with most water supplies	Not good with very hard or very soft water Joints can be damaged by water hammer Damaged if frozen
Copper Tubing (flexible)	Easy to use in cramped spaces Bends easily around corners Can use flare fittings which can be disassembled Can withstand a few freeze/thaw cycles	Pipe walls become thinner if frozen Same cautions as above
Galvanized Pipe	Strong & resistant to water hammer Good for alkaline water	Time consuming to install Corroded by soft water Scale can reduce inside pipe diameter Need a dialectic fitting when joined to copper
CPVC (Chlorinated Polyvinyl Chloride)	Lightweight Can be used for hot or cold Resists damage from freezing	Must have support clamps 3' o.c. Keep away from heat ducts & flues Noisy
Polyethylene (PE)	Can be used for supply main from well to house Low working temperature (-67°F to 112°F) Used in ground; even at low temperatures Will not corrode	Cannot be used for hot water lines

Protecting Pipes from Freezing

In parts of the country with severe winter temperatures, protecting pipes from freezing is a major concern. Because pipes will be enclosed in walls, they will get colder than room temperature. Here are some things you can do to keep pipes from freezing:

- Place fixtures so that supply pipes are placed in inside walls.

- Make sure the walls of the crawl space or basement are insulated and foundation vents blocked during winter.

- Place insulation on top of any supply lines in attics.

If fixtures must be on outside walls, bring supply lines through the bottom of the vanity instead of the wall in the back of the vanity. It is also a good idea to place a heating supply duct in the bottom of the vanity. The residual heat can help offset cool temperatures inside the vanity.

Access Panels

Showers and bathtubs should include access panels to make future plumbing repair easier. An access panel for a bathtub/shower should allow room to repair the bathtub drain as well as room to work on the shower mixing valve. Shutoff valves should be located on the supply lines.

In the case of back-to-back showers, however, an access panel is not possible. To provide shutoff control for a shower, choose a shower mixer valve that has a built-in shutoff. These valves

feature a moveable escutcheon (a protective plate or flange). Screws behind the escutcheon shut off the supply of water and allow repair of the mixing valve.

Preventing Water Hammer

A washing machine, shower or lavatory valve that turns the water supply off quickly can send a shock wave through the supply system. This shock wave is called **water hammer** because it sounds like a hammer banging on the pipes. Water hammer is easy to prevent. Coiled air chambers can be attached to the supply pipes at each fixture. The air chamber allows room for the initial surge of water when the fixture closes down. The plumbing contractor can also provide water hammer protection by extending the supply line 24" above the tee. The extension will normally be filled with air, except when the valve sends a surge of water through the pipe.

Renovating the Supply System

Working with existing plumbing is more difficult than planning bathrooms for new construction. Here are some of the things to watch for in existing construction.

PIPE DIAMETER

The diameter of supply pipes may be too small to allow another fixture to be added. Different fixture arrangements are served by different pipe sizes. Codes only allow two fixtures to be connected to 1/2" branch lines. For three fixtures, a 3/4" branch line is adequate. You would need to increase the branch line to 1" if you wanted a bidet, a toilet, a shower and a separate bathtub in the same bathroom.

The codes also require supply lines of a certain size for each fixture. The following chart details these pipe sizes. In older homes, risers to lavatories and standard toilets could be as small as 3/8". Today, supply pipe for low-profile toilets, standard bathtubs and showers must be 1/2".

If you intend to replace the old toilet with a low-profile model, the diameter of the supply line will have to be changed. Your plumbing contractor will also have to move the tee or stop for the shutoff valve down, so that it will fit under the tank on the low-profile toilet.

Recommended Pipe Sizes

House Main .... 1"
House Service .... 3/4"
Supply Riser .... 3/4"
Toilet (close coupled) ...... 3/8"
Toilet (one piece) .... 1/2"
Bathtub .... 1/2"
Bathtub (High Volume) ... 3/4"
Shower .... 1/2"
Shower (High Volume) .... 3/4"
Lavatory .... 3/8"
Bidet .... 3/8"
Clothes Washer .... 1/2"

SUPPLY PIPE COMPATIBILITY

If a plumbing system has already been remodeled, you may see two different kinds of supply pipe used. Copper pipe may be joined to galvanized pipe. These two pipe materials react chemically with each other and cause corrosion.

A **dielectric union** should be used to join these two pipe materials. A dielectric union does not react with either of the metals and will prevent corrosive buildup on the inside of the pipes around the transition.

ACCESS FOR REPAIR

If a home is built on a crawl space, it may be difficult for the plumber to reach the work area without crawling the length of the house. To make future repair easier, find a nearby closet and ask the general contractor to prepare an access hatch. The contractor may have to add headers to any joists that need to be cut. The floor will also have to be repaired. But the added convenience for current and future work will save money in the long run.

Alternatively, the craftsmen might open up the floor in the bathroom being remodeled. This works particularly well in a home that has limited crawl space. By stripping the walls of old plaster or drywall and completely opening the floor, the workmen have access to the chaseways between floor joists or wall studs. This makes the retrofit of existing piping much easier, and therefore less costly.

Heating Water

With an increasing number of bathtubs and other appliances hungry for hot water, the water heater must be large enough to meet the demand. The size of the storage tank and its recovery rate are extremely important if a large amount of hot water will be required for a jetted bathtub or high volume showerhead.

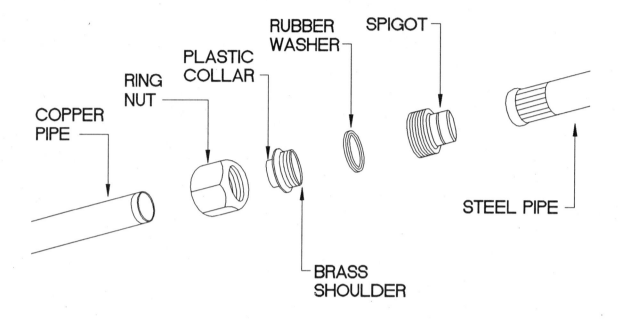

Figure 8   *Dielectric unions should always be used when joining galvanized steel to copper pipe. The plastic collar and rubber washer separate the two metals and prevent corrosion.*

STORAGE TANK WATER HEATERS

Storage tank water heaters consist of a storage tank with 1" or 2" of tank insulation and a heat source. A thermostat monitors the water temperature and activates the heat source when the temperature drops below a desired setting.

Cold water enters the water heater through the dip tube and releases the water near the bottom of the tank, just above the heat source. As the cold water is heated, it rises to the top of the tank where it is ready for use.

Water Heater Capacity: The average family uses 20 gallons of hot water per person per day. This figure includes water used for dishes, showering and

bathing. A rule of thumb is that a family of four needs a 50 gallon tank.

Therefore, you might think that an 50 gallon water heater would be adequate in all cases. But a 50 gallon water heater set at 120°F does not provide 50 gallons of 120°F water at one draining. As a rule, with either gas or electric water heaters, the tank will provide between 65% an 70% of its listed capacity at the temperature set on the temperature control dial. This is because incoming water mixes with and cools the remaining hot water.

Recovery Rate: The recovery rate of a water heater is far more important than the water heater's capacity. **Recovery rate** means the length of time required for the water heater to bring the temperature of the cold, stored water up to the temperature set on the dial. Since the temperature of cold water can vary widely, manufacturers state recovery rates on the basis of rise in temperature. Electric water heaters have significantly slower recovery rates than gas or oil units. To compensate for this recovery rate difference, a larger storage capacity electric tank should be specified. *For example,* experts suggest that a 40 gallon gas heater will provide as much hot water as a 52 gallon electric unit.

However, even the 40 gallon gas or 52 gallon electric hot water tank may not be adequate. *For example,* if you are specifying fixtures that require a large volume of water, and these fixtures will be used concurrently, you should recommend that the client buy two water heaters, or a large commercial tank.

Alternatively, the client should be willing to balance their water patterns with the heater's capacity and therefore, stagger their use of fixtures to accommodate the tank's capability.

For example, if the client is a professional couple who spend all day at work, they may plan to use the jetted tub for joint relaxation in the evening. Because no one was home during the day, and no hot water was being used, a single electric water heater should have adequate capacity. But if the client is a family with a jetted bathtub in the master suite and four teenagers who shower twice a day, a single electric water heater will not be adequate.

To be on the safe side, a quick recovery water heater should be specified when a jetted bathtub is used.

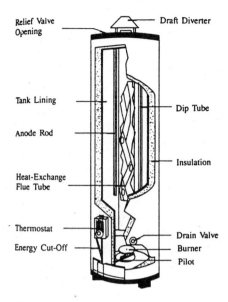

Gas Water Heater

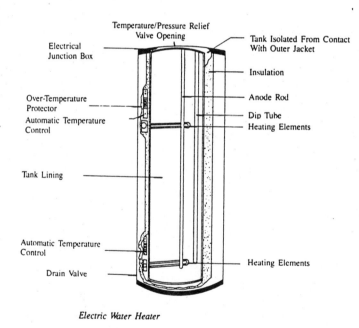

Electric Water Heater

Figure 9   How gas and electric water heaters work.

The following chart can help you select an approximate size and recovery rate for the water heater. The numbers illustrate the recovery rate difference between electric and gas water heaters.

SIZING WATER HEATERS

Bathrooms →		1		2		3	
↓ Bedrooms		gal.	R	gal.	R	gal	R
2	gas	40	30	50	35	50	45
	elec	66	18	66	28	82	28
3	gas	40	35	40	45	50	63
	elec	82	18	82	28	82	28
4	gas	50	35	50	45	50	63
	elec	66	28	82	28	2/66	18
5	gas	40	45	50	63	75	63
	elec	82	28	82	28	2/66	18

R = recovery rate based on gallons of water raised 100° F per hour. Storage capacity and recovery rate are based on supplying enough hot water for three automatic washer loads of clothing at 25 gallons per load over a two hour peak period. An additional 9 gallons per hour in either storage capacity, recovery rate, or combination thereof has been added for each additional bathroom or two bedrooms. If a high volume bathtub or showerhead is used, these sizes should be increased accordingly.

BOOSTER HEAT

If you believe that the waiting period for water to reach the fixture may be too long, you and the plumbing contractor should discuss other ways to provide supplementary heat.

Consider installing a separate water tank in the problem area. Of course, you will have to plan storage room for the water tank plus a vent for flue gas and combustion air if the water heater is gas.

A second option is to install a continuously recirculating line between the fixture and the water heater. The pump location and electrical requirements must be determined during planning and estimating, and you should consider the energy loss. As the hot water travels through the loop, it loses heat. Heat loss will be continuous, even though the fixture only needs hot water a few minutes each day.

A third option is to install a small in-line heater. These do not raise the temperature of the water. They just keep the pipes from cooling off.

DEMAND WATER HEATERS

Instant or **demand** water heaters do not have storage tanks. A gas burner or electric element heats water only when there is a demand for hot water. Hot water never runs out, but the flow rate (gallons of hot water per minute) is low.

The largest gas-fired demand water heater supplies only 3 gallons of hot water per minute. Most models can supply less than 2 1/2 gpm at that temperature rise. This flow rate is only enough for a low-flow showerhead.

Temperature control on these units can also be a problem because they raise the water temperature a set number of degrees. If the water coming in is

60°F, the demand heat can produce scalding hot water. Be sure the unit you choose is thermostatically controlled.

Unless your clients are extremely concerned about energy conservation and are willing to use low-flow shower-heads, the hot water supplied by a demand heater will not be adequate. These heaters are appropriate for vacation homes where the home will only be used occasionally. They could also be used for a half bathroom in a remote part of the house, far from the main water heater, where someone washing their hands at the lavatory must run the water for a period of time before clearing the line of cool water. Here, an instant water heater would give heat as the faucet was turned on.

WATER QUALITY

Your clients may be concerned about water quality in their homes. Designing a bathroom or upgrading one is the right time to discuss the water quality issue. Water quality is a problem because of contaminants in the water supply.

There are two types of water contamination: one affects the water's purity for drinking (lead, nitrates, bacteria) and the other affects the water's function (hardness, iron).

Protecting the clients' health by providing safe drinking water is always an issue that a design professional must consider when planning a bathroom project. You should also find out if there are any function contaminants because this will limit the products and surfaces you specify.

Contaminants

LEAD

Lead is a dangerous contaminant. **The National Sanitation Foundation** estimates that 16% of the nation's households have unacceptable high drinking water lead levels. A person's health can be affected by even low lead levels. If the clients' drinking water contains more than 10 micrograms of lead per liter of water, they should consider changing the piping in the plumbing system, flushing the lines on a regular basis or installing a treatment system that removes the lead.

TRIHALOMETHANES (THM)

A second contaminant is trihalomethanes (THM). These are a group of chemicals that cause cancer in laboratory animals. The group includes chlorine when found in excessive amounts. Most communities add chlorine to their drinking water. This keeps down the growth of taste- and odor-producing organisms in water. But chlorine, in addition to making water taste like a swimming pool, can also be a contaminant.

Because of this, the **Environmental Protection Agency** will be requiring local water companies to reduce the amount of chlorine in their water. Utilities may soon turn to other ways of treating their water.

Current regulations require a THM concentration of 100 micrograms per liter. If your clients' water supply exceeds this level, or if chloroform is a concern, they should consider water treatment equipment.

In agricultural areas, in addition to bacteria, two contaminants are a problem.

NITRATES

Nitrates which are by-products of fertilizer, can leach into ground water. If the water company draws water from an underground aquifer or from a river or lake with agricultural runoff, nitrate levels may be seasonally high. However, water companies test for nitrate levels and keep it within safe levels (10 micrograms per liter). If your clients' water supply comes from a well, they should have their water tested regularly, and they might want to consider water treating equipment.

PESTICIDES

Pesticides are also of concern in rural areas. Those who obtain water from their own well should have their wells tested. Or a local utility will provide information about which contaminants are present in the groundwater near the well.

Monitoring/Testing Water Quality

If you or your client have questions, you can request additional information from the **EPA's water quality hotline - 800/426-4791**.

The co-operative extension service in your local or state government is a valuable source of information on water quality problems and water treatment equipment as well.

Testing laboratories can be used to obtain information about tap water. The following labs send instructions and a mail order kit:

- **National Testing Laboratories;** 6555 Wilson Mills Rd., Cleveland, OH 44143

- **Suburban Water Testing;** 4600 Kutztown Rd., Temple, PA 19560

- **Beland Water Lab;** 548 Donald St., Bedford, NH 03110

Water Treatment

If you discover that your client's water quality exceeds the EPA standards, you can obtain test data on water treatment equipment from the **National Sanitation Foundation**, 3475 Plymouth Rd., Ann Arbor, MI 48105. Ask for the *"listing book"* of drinking water treatment units. **Consumers Union** also tests water treatment devices. See **Consumer Reports** January 1990 at your local library.

CARBON FILTER SYSTEM

The best way to remove excess chlorine (one of the THMs) is to install a whole house carbon filter system. This removes the chlorine from all the fixtures in the house. And it is large enough to have sufficient flow of water through the system. It also removes some pesticides, **VOCs (Volitile Organic Compounds that emit toxins including chemicals such as paint thinner, dry cleaning fluid and spot remover etc.)** This treatment system removes contaminants by passing the water through a filter containing particles of carbon. The carbon **absorbs** the contaminants. **(This means the contaminants attach to the surface of**

the carbon.) After a time, the surface area of the carbon particles fills up. The filter needs to be changed every couple of months.

REVERSE OSMOSIS

To remove other contaminants, your client will need a different type of treatment equipment. Lead and nitrate, for example, are best removed with a **reverse-osmosis** unit. These units are not a good choice for water conserving areas because about 75% of the incoming water goes down the drain. They are best used beneath a kitchen sink or bathroom lavatory to filter drinking water, they are compact enough to fit in a cabinet. You certainly wouldn't choose this for a shower. Lead and nitrate are not a problem for bathing - only for drinking.

DISTILLER

Another option for removing lead and nitrate is a **distiller. (A distiller is like a still used to make alcohol.)** A heating element boils the water and, as the steam condenses, some impurities are removed. A distiller is not effective against THMs.

Lead in Plumbing

Not all houses and apartment buildings have lead problems. It depends on when they were built, what kind of plumbing pipes they have and what types of water mains connect the building to the water supply system. The significant doses of lead do not come from water in underground aquifers and reservoirs, but from pipes - both lead pipes and lead solder used to connect copper pipes that carry water.

Contamination can start with a corrosive reaction between lead and water in large lead pipes of municipal water-delivery systems and in smaller lead pipes, called service connections, that link large mains to the pipes in buildings. The service connections in Brooklyn, New York, for example, are still lead. Through the early 1900s, it was common practice to use lead pipes for interior plumbing as well.

You are most likely to find lead pipes in systems installed prior to 1930. Only the water supply pipes are of concern because they deliver drinking water. Many homes also had lead waste pipes but these are not a cause for concern. Lead water supply pipes should always be removed when remodeling a bathroom. However, this causes us to ask other questions such as; *how far back should the pipes be removed? Will it be necessary to replace the pipes all the way back to the street?* It may be costly to change the whole supply system in the home, but this should be brought to the attention of the homeowner. Replace the pipes with copper, galvanized pipe or plastic. Additions or repairs to copper pipes should not be made with lead solder. The plumber will be familiar with alternatives.

If changes to the system cannot be made, tell your client to run the water for half a minute before drinking, this will flush lead-containing water out of the supply pipes.

Softening Water

In addition to making water safe to drink, the water may need further treatment to prevent it from damaging household surfaces. **Hard water is water that contains scale-forming miner-**

als, such as calcium and magnesium. Hard water is a major problem in rural areas. When hard water mixes with soap, nonsoluble fatty acids are formed. These coat bathroom fixtures and are difficult to remove. Water softening equipment will reduce these problems. The softener removes calcium and magnesium and replaces it with sodium. Unfortunately, added sodium is a health concern for many, and it leaves drinking water tasteless.

To avoid taste problems in drinking water, many homes only soften hot water. The softening system is attached to the water line leading to the water heater. Because heat intensifies scale buildup, treatment to prevent this buildup in hot water pipes is a critical first step. Untreated cold water lines then are used throughout the rest of the system. The ideal installation has both hot and cold lines softened. A special second (cold water only) line is then run to sinks and lavatories for drinking water only.

Two primary tanks comprise a softening system. In the exchange tank incoming water passes over a granular substance to remove calcium and magnesium. A salty solution is kept in the brine tank for the periodic process of regenerating the exchange tank.

THE DRAIN/WASTE/VENT (DWV) SYSTEM

The **drain/waste/vent (DWV) system carries water and waste to the city sewer or septic tank**. Unlike the water lines, the drain/waste lines are not pressurized. Water and waste drain by gravity. Fixtures should be grouped around a central core where the main soil stack is located.

To keep waste flowing through the lines, drain/waste lines slope downhill. The slope must be 1/4 inch per foot. This means that the pipe must slope 1/4 inch downhill for every horizontal foot.

All of the drain/waste lines in the house eventually end up in a single large sewer line that carries waste to a city sewer system or a septic tank. The city sewer system carries waste away from the property. A septic tank treats waste in an enclosed tank right on the property. Septic tanks are watertight receptacles that receive the discharge of the drainage system. The solids in the waste biodegrade in the septic tank and sink to the bottom of the tank. The liquids are discharged into the soil outside the tank.

If you are adding fixtures to the home, you should check the size of the septic system. Tanks are sized according to the family's water consumption patterns, such as the number of bedrooms and types of fixtures. Adding large, water-using fixtures may mean the septic system should be made larger.

You'll find it easier to remember what the various parts of the DWV system do if you can remember three key concepts.

- The drain system relies on a trap to prevent sewer gas from backing up into the house.

- The system needs drain lines to carry waste away.

- And, finally, the DWV system needs atmospheric pressure to keep the waste flowing downstream.

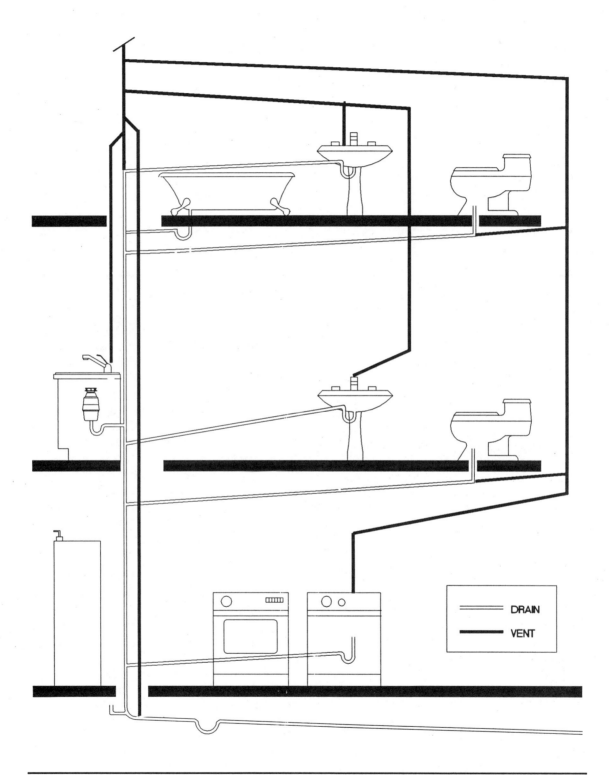

Figure 10   Details of the DWV System. Waste and vent lines are grouped around the central soil stack.

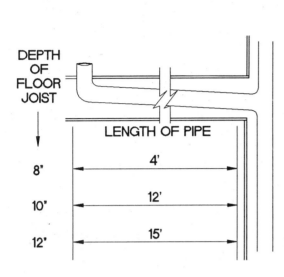

Figure 11   *Watch out for the depth of the floor joists when you plan fixture placement. Waste pipe must always flow 1/4 inch per foot downhill.*

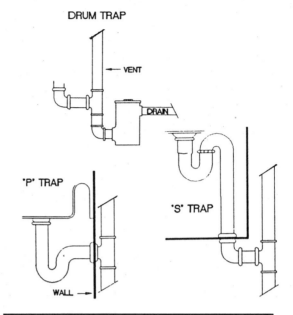

Figure 12   *Types of traps you might encounter in remodeling.*

The Trap

The trap is a P-shaped pipe connecting the fixture and the drain pipe. It provides a water seal against sewer gases which could otherwise enter the house through the fixture. When the fixture drains, water flows through the trap and into the drain pipe. However, the trap never empties completely, it holds enough water to maintain the seal. Usually, you will find a P-trap inside the cabinet under a bathroom lavatory, or exposed underneath a console or wall-hung lavatory. Pedestal lavatories may have more specific location requirements to ensure that the trap and water supply lines are properly located and centered behind the pedestal support. Because some pedestal supports are not completely hollow or may include a support bar, to ensure fixture integrity, these planning considerations must be detailed on the elevations so that the plumbing contractor can properly locate the pipes during the rough-in stage of the project.

Toilets have traps built in. You can sometimes see the outline of the trap on the surface of the toilet. Fixtures, such as bathtubs or showers, that do not have built-in traps, must have room under the floor for the trap as well as the drain line. In old houses, the bathtub may have had a cleanout visible on the floor. This is actually the top part of a drum trap. Because the seal on the drum trap is not reliable (and can allow odor to enter the room) the plumbing contractor should change the trap during a remodel.

Another type of trap still found in existing construction is the S-trap, which is no longer permitted by building codes. Most often found under sinks, the S-trap was rarely connected to a vent. It goes straight through the floor. When the sink full of water suddenly empties, the suction from the moving slug of water can clear the trap. Sewer gas would then back up into the room. These traps should be changed during a remodel. A new vent will be required, the use of a P-trap is suggested.

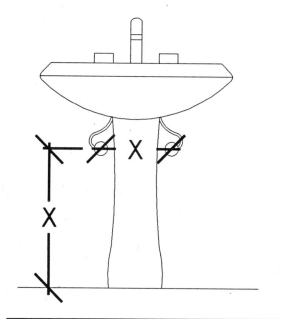

Figure 13   Carefully specify the drain location for a pedestal lavatory.

The Waste Lines

The waste lines are identified by function and configuration. The toilet discharge pipe is known as a soil line or stack. Lines are the horizontal runs. Stacks are the vertical components of the system. The size of the soil or waste pipe is determined by the intended use of the fixture. Because pipe sizes vary, interchanging or substituting fixtures may require changes in the waste lines. Waste pipes 1 1/2 inches in diameter will serve standard bathtubs and lavatories. Waste lines 2 inches in diameter are needed for stall showers and large Roman tubs. Showers with body sprays or multiple heads may need a 3-inch waste line to prevent overflowing. For the toilet, soil pipes are a minimum of 3 inches in diameter and often 4 inches in diameter.

Pipe measurements always refer to the inside diameter. The outside dimensions of pipe materials vary tremendously. Cast iron, for example, is much thicker than plastic pipe.

The following chart lists common fixture drain sizes.

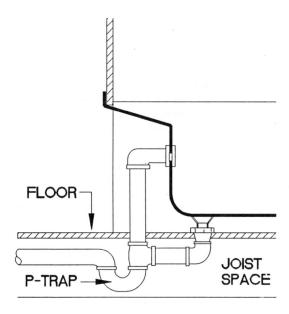

Figure 14   A P-trap must be installed under the bathtub drain.

DWV Waste Line Sizes		
FIXTURE	FIXTURE UNITS	MINIMUM DRAIN SIZE
Bathtub	2	1 1/2"
Bidet	2	1 1/2"
Toilet	4	3"
Wall Urinal	2	1 1/2"
Single Lavatory	1	1 1/4"
Double Lavatory	2	1 1/2"
Shower Stall	2	2"
Showers per Head	1	2"
Laundry Tub	2	1 1/2"
Clothes Washer	2	2"
Floor Drain	2	2"
Drinking Fountain	1	1 1/4"
Kitchen Sink	2	1 1/2"
Bar Sink	1	1 1/2"
Sink and Dishwasher	3	1 1/2"

Vent Lines

The vent lines admit air into the system to allow a free flow of liquid waste. The vent pipe also provides an exit for sewer gases which would otherwise build up in the system and force their way through the fixture trap into the house.

Each trap installed must be vented. Common vents can be shared between fixtures, as long as the lowest fixture is the one with the highest flow. The vent extends from the fixture to the house exterior through the roof. The designer can often determine the concealed vent pipe location by observing the roof line from the house exterior or by inspecting the attic.

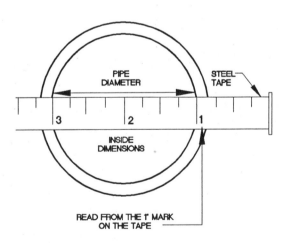

Figure 15   Pipe sizing and nomenclature.

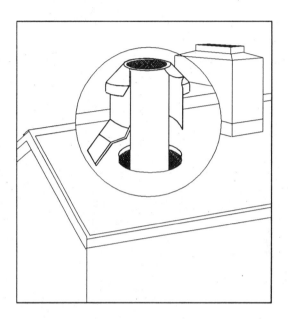

Figure 17   The vent terminates above the roof line.

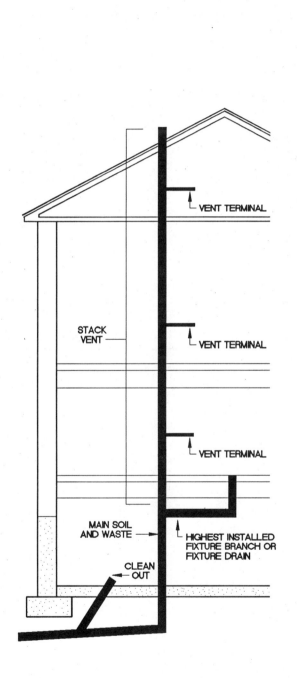

VENT TERMINAL

STACK VENT

VENT TERMINAL

VENT TERMINAL

MAIN SOIL AND WASTE

HIGHEST INSTALLED FIXTURE BRANCH OR FIXTURE DRAIN

CLEAN OUT

Figure 16   A typical stack vent. This layout shows how all vent lines tie into a central stack.

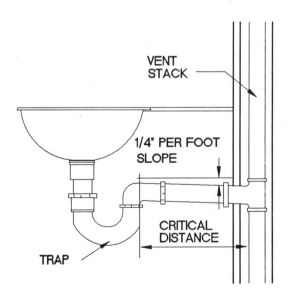

VENT STACK

1/4" PER FOOT SLOPE

CRITICAL DISTANCE

TRAP

Figure 18   The size of the drain pipe is determined by its distance from the vent stack.

Special attention should be paid to the existing vent path, or a new vent pipe location under consideration if the bathroom will feature an operable skylight.

Vent Pipes and Skylights: Bathroom vent ducts (both from the plumbing waste vent and the fan duct) must be far enough from the skylight to avoid odors or moist air from being drawn indoors - which would occur if the skylight were open. **CABO** code has specific requirements for the distance between plumbing vents and skylights. This code states that a vent must be 5 feet (measured horizontally) from an operable skylight. It must also be at least 2 feet above the top of the opening. *Remember, local codes may differ from the* **CABO** *model code* - so check any local requirements before specifying an operable skylight in a bathroom project.

Waste Line Distance from Vent: Limits established for the distance between trap and vent in continuous waste and vent systems include the following for residential applications:

Pipe Size	Distance to Vent
1 1/4" (3cm)	60"
1 1/2" (4cm)	72"
2" (5cm)	96"
3" (7.6cm)	144"
4" (10cm)	192"

NOTE: Local codes may specify different requirements. Always check local codes.

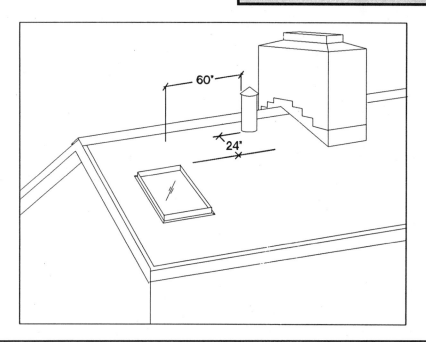

Figure 19   The vent stack must be located away from an operable skylight in a bathroom.

When the distance from the trap to the vent is extended, larger drain lines are needed. The plumbing contractor should be consulted before plans are finalized.

Bathroom planners must consider the costs required to relocate or modify a vent pipe concealed in a wall. This should be an expected expense when recessing medicine cabinets in a wall above the lavatory or the toilet.

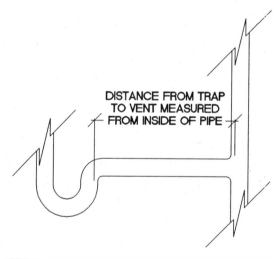

DISTANCE FROM TRAP
TO VENT MEASURED
FROM INSIDE OF PIPE

Figure 20   The vent must be located so that the length from the fixture trap to the vent does not exceed the distance given.

DWV Materials

According to the National Association of Home Builders, cast iron is the most widely used pipe for drain/waste/vent systems. Plastic pipe is second in preference, followed by copper. Plastic pipe is noisier than cast iron. If plumbing waste lines are placed above a room where sound transmission could be distracting (e.g. a dining room), be sure to have the plumbing contractor insulate the waste line.

Reference the chart on page 30 for typical materials.

The terms used to describe fittings in the DWV system are generally named for letters of the alphabet - wyes (Y), tees (T), etc. Male fittings are those that fit inside female fittings. These same descriptive terms are used for supply fittings as well.

Rough-In Dimensions

Rough-in dimensions for typical plumbing fixtures are shown in each manufacturer's manual. Note how the rough-in dimensions relate to the plumbing pipes in the walls. New toilets feature a soil pipe rough- in 12 inches from the wall. Older toilets may have a rough-in dimension of 10 inches or even 14 inches. When a 10-inch rough-in must be reused, a special-order toilet will be needed or an "off-set hurkle ring" can be used to change the 10-inch dimension to a 12-inch or a 14" diameter to a 12".

Changing the DWV System

When plumbing changes are planned in the DWV system, the bathroom planner should consider how the change will affect the size of the drain pipe.

- *What is the water usage of the fixture?*

- *Will relocation plans affect the drain pipe's relationship to the vent stack?*

- *Will existing construction constraints hamper the required 1/4 inch slope per foot for all residential drainage systems?*

DWV Pipe Materials

MATERIAL	PROS	CONS
Cast Iron (Hubless)	Durable Easy to assemble Resistant to chemicals	Heavy Expensive Must be supported at joints
Cast Iron (Bell & Spigot)	Durable Resistant to chemicals Joints rigid	Requires skill to assemble Workers exposed to lead vapor Expensive Time consuming to install
ABS (Acrylonitrile-butadiene styrene)	High range of temperatures (-40°F to 180°F) Easy to assemble with solvent welding or threaded fittings Lightweight Inexpensive	May not be approved by some codes Not resistant to industrial chemicals
PVC (Polyvinyl Chloride)	Light Weight Easy to assemble	May not be approved by some codes Not resistant to industrial chemicals

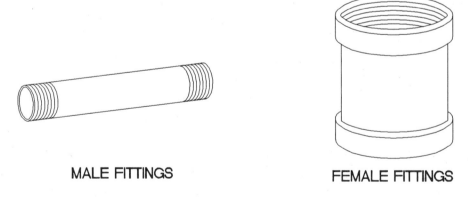

MALE FITTINGS   FEMALE FITTINGS

Figure 21   DWV fittings have names, which reflect whether the threading is on the inside or the outside of the pipe.

CASE STUDY #1

Existing Bathroom Plan

Martha Kerr, CKD, CBD, has suggested the following simple, yet effective, plumbing changes in a small utilitarian bathroom. Each one of these changes is generally feasible with North American 2x4 framing, and with available crawl/basement space below and/or attic space above the room.

In this typical bathroom, one enters from the hallway and first passes by a rather small, 48" vanity. Between the vanity and the bathtub/shower combination fixture is the toilet. This is a typical common plumbing wall installation for a small bathroom sandwiched between two bedrooms. Note the window on the back wall behind the combination bathtub/shower.

Option #1 - Adding a Second Lavatory

The first change Martha suggested was to convert the 48 inch single lavatory vanity to one which has two lavatories. Extending the countertop across the low-profile, one-piece toilet tank is an excellent way to expand the limited countertop available in such a double-bowl arrangement. Typically, the single lavatory waste line and trap can remain inside the cabinet. The two lavatories can be plumbed to this single DWV system pipe, much like a double sink in a kitchen is plumbed. Therefore, no additional piping in the wall will be required. The existing vent will work as well. Water lines on the supply side of the system will need to be fed to both lavatory bowls in this new installation. The advantage to this plan is that in such a small bathroom, the double lavatories make personal grooming easier and more convenient for people using the space at the same time. The disadvantage is that the amount of available counter space is limited.

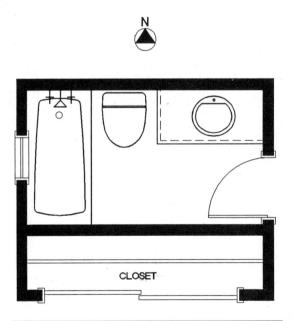

Figure 22   *The existing bathroom.*

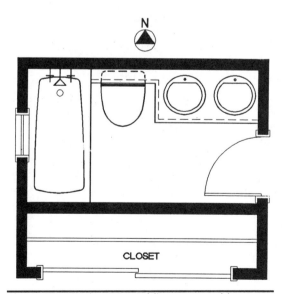

Figure 22   *Option #1 - Adding a second lavatory.*

Option #2 - Switching the Bathtub to a Shower

In the second solution, the lavatory and toilet remain in the same location. Martha now suggests a change in the bathing/showering facility, omitting the standard 60-inch bathtub and replacing it with a luxurious, large, well-planned 60-inch stall shower. This is an excellent renovation consideration for a client living in a home which features a bathtub in another bathroom.

Realtors will generally say that if the house has one bathtub, stall showers are acceptable in other bathrooms. Based on our North American preference for daily showers over soaking in the bathtub, this real estate resale recommendation makes sense.

Switching the bathtub to a shower has a major effect on the DWV system. Whereas a bathtub requires a 1 1/2" drain, a stall shower calls for a 2 inch drain. Therefore, the plumbing contractor must remove and replace the bathtub drain with a larger one during the demolition phase of the project. The existing vent pipe location will be acceptable for the shower. The water supply lines currently servicing the combination bathtub/shower will also be adequate, but will be raised up to a more convenient height for the user.

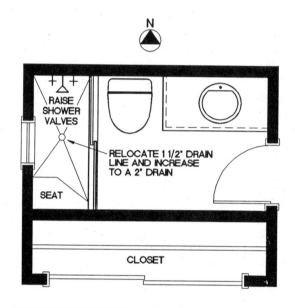

Figure 22   Option #2 - The plumbing changes required to exchange a bathtub for a stall shower.

Option #3 - Relocating the Shower Valve

Martha's third idea is an excellent alternative to the standard approach of locating the shower valve directly below the showerhead (which you'll learn more about in Chapters 2 and 3). She suggests locating the valve on the end wall directly opposite the showerhead.

To do this, the plumbing contractor routes the water lines across the back wall, underneath the window and over to the new wall location. In colder climates, these water supply lines may require insulation along the outside wall.

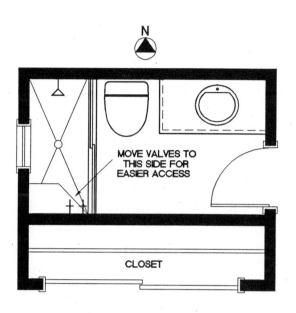

Figure 22   Option #3 - The plumbing changes required to relocate the shower valve location.

Option #4 - Adding a Shower

In Martha's fourth bathroom alternative, construction changes have been
planned to increase the overall square
footage devoted to the bathroom by partially incorporating space from a closet
that adjoins the bathroom. Although the
bedroom closet gets smaller, the double
poles provide the same amount of pole
length for the users.

Shortening the closet provides
enough extra space in the bathroom to
install a stall shower and small soaking
bathtub. This change means that the
combination bathtub/shower unit can re-
vert back to a fixture reserved for bathing. Therefore, no enclosure (which
would visually minimize the size of the
space) is needed. It will be a more pleasant spot for the bather, and will help
make the bathroom look larger. Because
closets are only 24" deep and a shower

should be a minimum of 32" - 34" deep,
the shower extends beyond the wall and
the bathtub is changed to a shorter soaking bathtub.

This plumbing alteration is completely different from the other three suggested earlier, because an entirely new
fixture unit is being added to the space.
Here an additional shower vent may
have to be added and connected into the
existing vent stack. This can be accomplished by routing the new vent up the
wall, above and across the ceiling and
tieing it in using a loop vent.

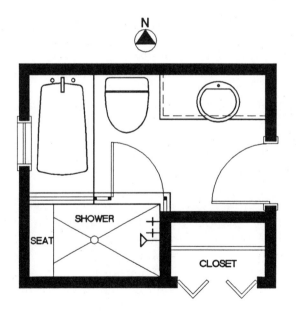

Figure 22   Option #4 - The plumbing changes required to add a stall shower in a modified closet
area.

New hot and cold water lines must be run to the new fixture. Because the bathtub and shower are not used concurrently, these new water lines can be added to the existing water supply lines. The slope for the required 2" drain for the shower can be accommodated within the floor joist system as it travels from the common plumbing wall to the new shower. To facilitate the supply, drain and vent pipe installation the plumber should be allowed to open up the floor of the bathroom.

Case Study #2

On projects where only a minor amount of structural work will be done, **Kent Barnes**, CKD, CBD, has developed a trick for avoiding major wall demolition.

If storage cabinetry is planned between the two lavatories, replacing a single vanity with a double vanity will require changes in the DWV lines. Each bowl in the vanity top then should have its own waste line and be connected to the vent.

By pulling the vanity forward a few inches, Mr. Barnes provides room for a trap beneath each lavatory. But each trap can share a common drain and still meet the distance and slope requirements of the code. This saves a major amount of wall demolition and speeds up job completion.

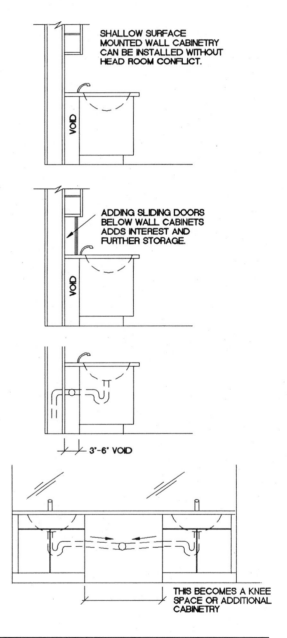

Figure 23   Innovative ways to modify plumbing lines to the bathroom vanity.

Heating Systems

No matter how sharp you make a bathroom look, if it's not warm, it's not comfortable. Because a bathroom is a space for sedentary activity, the room may even need to be 3°F to 5°F warmer than rooms in the rest of the house. The activity level of the person using the room and the amount of clothing they are wearing affect how much heat is required.

Today's bathrooms are larger than in the past. Large master bathrooms adjoin master suites. Keeping both rooms at a comfortable temperature can be difficult. You need to know how much heat to provide and where to place the registers. If the bathroom is part of a room addition, you should know what effect distance from the central heating unit will have on comfort. The farther from the furnace, the less heat available for the room.

Heating equipment has changed a great deal in the last few years. You need to know when a particular system might be troublesome. Heat pumps, for instance, deliver heated air at lower temperatures (90° F) and higher velocities than forced air furnaces. Air at this temperature feels chilly to someone just stepping from the bathtub.

THE COMFORT ZONE

Many years ago, when mechanical engineers and physiologists began studying the human response to heat and cold, they coined a phrase that has been a cornerstone of HVAC **(Heating, Ventilating, Air Conditioning)** design ever since - **the comfort zone**. Research has shown that humans are comfortable over a rather narrow range of temperatures and humidities.

The activity level and age of the person also affect comfort. For instance, as people age, their metabolic rate slows down. Temperatures that are comfortable for active young adults feel cold to the elderly. People also feel chilled when an air current, or a draft, blows air past their body. Air currents, even when the air is warm, blow heat away from the body. When the human body is wet, the chilling effect of a moving air stream is similar to the "*wind chill effect*" of winter weather.

Heating systems are designed to keep the human body in the comfort zone. The heating system must be able to provide enough heat so that the indoor temperature remains in this narrow band that we experience as "*comfortable*".

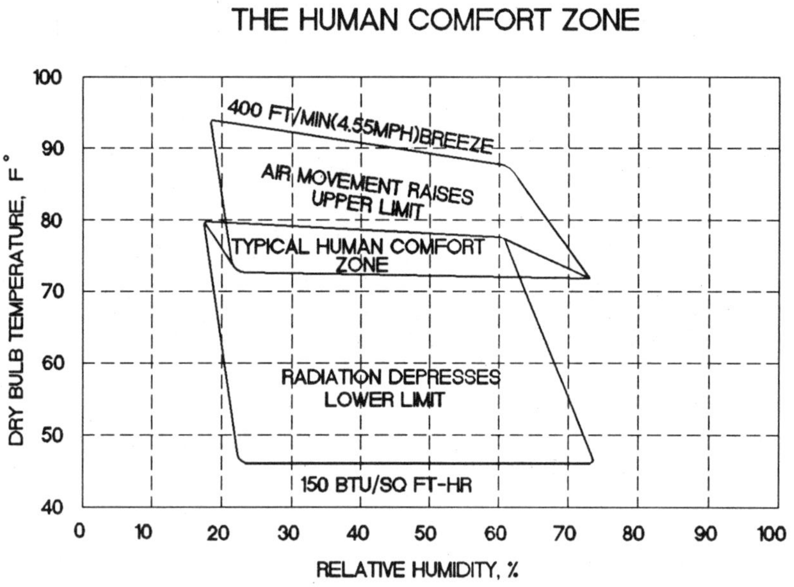

THE HUMAN COMFORT ZONE

Figure 24   The human comfort zone is a narrow range of temperatures and humidities.

HEAT LOSS

A heating system replaces heat that is lost through the shell of the house. How much energy the heating system requires to replace that lost heat depends on four factors:

- Where the house is located.

- How large the house is.

- The energy-efficiency of the house.

- The energy-efficiency of the heating system.

The efficiency of the existing furnace may play a role in whether to extend ducts or buy a larger furnace. Any time you add space to the house, you add more volume. *Will the existing furnace be able to heat the added volume? Is this the right time to replace an inefficient old furnace?*

The only way to accurately answer these questions is to do a heat loss analysis. An energy auditor or HVAC contractor can do a heat loss analysis of the house. The analysis will include measurements of wall, ceiling, floor and window areas. The auditor will also measure insulation levels and infiltration around doors and windows.

You may find that the existing furnace will be large enough if you make the bathroom extremely energy efficient. This might mean using less glass than you would like. Glass areas are the biggest sources of heat loss in a building. Or you might find that adding insulation to the attic would give you a little more leeway in using glass.

In California, bathroom designers working under the constraints of the state's energy code make these trade-offs all the time.

The very practical requirements of heating systems and the home's energy requirements may seem like the least glamorous part of bathroom design. But remember that you are designing for comfort. If you know your way around heating systems, your knowledge becomes one more design tool you can use to insure satisfied customers.

HEAT DISTRIBUTION

Central Heat

In most climates, central heating systems are necessary to keep a house warm. Steam, hot water, forced warm air and electric heating systems all function in the same basic way with the same basic set of components to provide heat.

Each central heating system is equipped with a control, a heat producer, a heat exchanger and a heat distributor. The control, called a thermostat, signals a need for heat. The signal turns on the heat producer, an oil or gas burner or an electric heating element. The heat produced warms the transfer medium (air, water, or steam) in a heat exchanger.

The transfer medium moves by gravity or is forced through ducts (warm air) or pipes (water or steam) to the heat distributors (convectors, registers, or radiators) located in living areas. Return ducts (or pipes) carry the medium back to the heat exchanger. When the temperature of the living area reaches the level set

on the thermostat, the thermostat automatically shuts down the system. In addition, heating systems that use natural gas or oil as a fuel must be vented. When heat is provided by electricity, there are no venting requirements.

Zoned Heat

Central heat refers to a heat source that heats the whole house. *But what if the house is long and sprawling? What if people only live in half their house and want temperatures in the other half to remain cooler except on special occasions?* Another kind of heat, called **zoned heat**, divides the house into two or more parts.

Typically associated with hot water and steam, (hydronic heating systems), zoned heat provides the client with greater control of temperatures in large homes or living spaces. Essentially, heat is produced from a single source and distributed through separate loops (pipes), which are each controlled by their own thermostats located in separate sections of the home or space. However, the concept of zoning can apply to the addition of a second heat source designed to heat a separate area or "zone" of the home. Zoned heat is an especially useful concept for bathroom designers to remember. It can be used to keep a room addition comfortable, and it can be less expensive than completely reworking the original heating system.

Consult an HVAC contractor early in the planning process whenever you are adding space. Consider zoned heat if the added space is far from the heat source. For instance, if the central heating unit, such as a forced air furnace, is more than 40 feet from a new room addition, the furnace may not be able to adequately heat the new addition. Another example is an L-shaped addition that would serve as a master suite and bathroom. Because the addition is far from the central heating source, it makes more sense to add a second furnace to provide heat. The need for a second source of heat may affect your plans.

Perhaps the HVAC contractor sees space you have designated as a linen closet as a potential spot for a furnace closet. You must understand the space needs of central heating systems in order to incorporate this mechanical equipment into your space planning and it is best to discuss space needs before you finalize your plans.

In the following sections we are going to discuss the heating systems you are likely to find in your projects. The discussion will focus on the kinds of problems that can affect the comfort level of your clients.

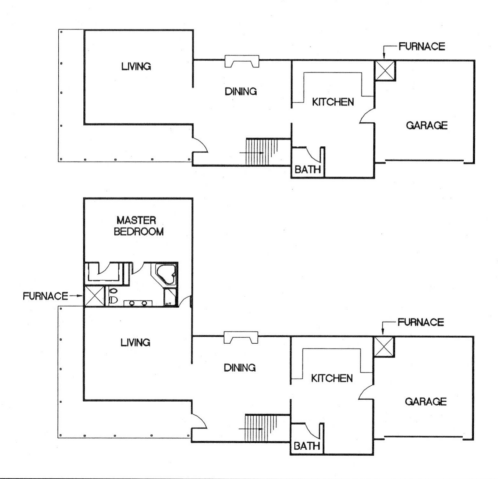

Figure 25   A secondary heat source is added for a room addition that is far from the original furnace.

FORCED AIR FURNACES

Low installation cost, rapid heat delivery and reliability make forced warm-air systems a popular heating choice. Forced air furnaces can use either natural gas or oil as a fuel. Electric forced air furnaces also exist, but are less common except in areas where the cost of electricity is low.

All forced air systems use heating ducts to distribute heat from the furnace to the rooms. In a forced warm air system, a blower pulls air from the rooms into the return air intake and return duct, through a filter, and into the furnace. There the air is heated. It then flows back to the rooms through the warm-air **supply ducts** and **supply registers** or **diffusers**.

Efficiency

Furnaces and boilers are rated for their Annual Fuel Utilization Efficiency (AFUE). The AFUE number allows you to compare furnaces. A furnace's efficiency

Federal Energy Efficiency Standards	
Product	**NAECA Minimum**
Gas Furnaces	78% AFUE
Gas Furnaces (Mobile home use)	75% AFUE
Heat Pumps and Air Conditioners (Split Systems)	10.0 SEER 6.8 HSPF
Heat Pumps and Air Conditioners (Single Package)	9.7 SEER 6.6 HSPF

HSPF: Heating Season Performance Factor.
SEER: Seasonal Energy Efficiency Rating.

has to do with how much heat escapes up the chimney. In a 100% efficient furnace, 100% of the fuel is available to heat the home. In a 78% efficient furnace, 78% of the fuel burned would theoretically be available to heat the home. These are laboratory test values, however. When a furnace is installed, the installed efficiency can be quite a bit lower than the advertised efficiency. Installing a more efficient heating system does not always yield the savings people expect.

New standards for energy efficiency in furnaces went into effect in 1992. These standards require furnaces to be at least 78% efficient. Furnaces and heat pumps must now meet requirements of the **National Appliance Energy Conservation Act**.

Forced air furnaces that burn oil are also more efficient today than in the past. They use high speed, flame retention heads. This technology ensures a better mix of air (which is needed for combustion) and oil. A similar range of efficiencies is available with oil-fired, forced-air furnaces.

Venting

Any heat-producing appliance that uses a fossil fuel must be vented to the outdoors. Combustion of fossil fuels (such as oil, gas, or propane) produces toxic gas. This gas is called **flue gas** because it was vented into flues, or chimneys.

Furnaces that are already installed are probably vented into a flue - either a masonry chimney or a double-walled flue pipe. Furnaces with high AFUE ratings may not need a flue pipe. It is possible to vent them through a side wall.

This knowledge may help you advise your clients about furnace selection. Perhaps they want to choose a new furnace anyway. Choosing one that can be vented through a sidewall might give you greater freedom in siting the furnace closet.

Heating Ducts

Up to this point, this section has focused on the workings of the central heating source, its efficiency and venting. *But once heat is created, how does it get distributed?*

The air that is heated by the furnace goes to a plenum. The **plenum** is a

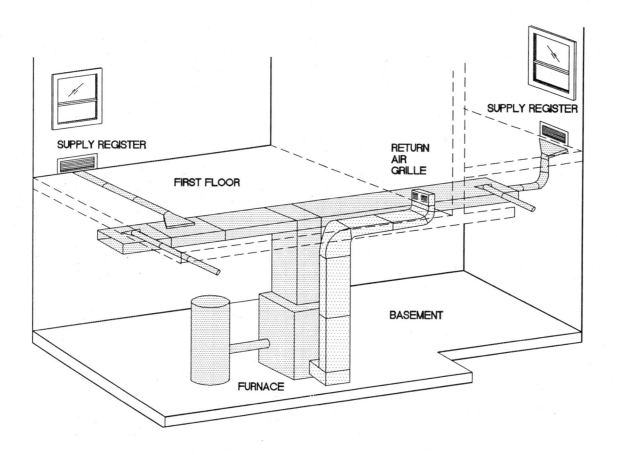

Figure 26   A forced-air system has a plenum and branch ducts that deliver heated air to registers or diffusers. Cool air is returned to the furnace through the return air intakes.

large, sheet-metal enclosure, either above or below the furnace. The plenum is designed to distribute heated air coming from the furnace. A second plenum may be located in the attic. Rectangular **trunk ducts** take off from the plenum.

Branch ducts, which are smaller, branch out from the trunk duct. In homes built on crawl spaces or over basements, these branch ducts lead to registers or baseboard diffusers. Registers or diffusers are placed along outside walls, usually below windows. Warm air currents rising from the registers counteract cold air currents that cascade down the windows.

Slab houses usually have a different forced warm air duct layout. In slab homes, a duct system may be embedded in the concrete slab. Warm air in the ducts is discharged into rooms through registers placed near outside walls, usually below windows. However, the registers are fed by a perimeter loop that goes around the perimeter of the slab. Perimeter heating systems are designed to eliminate cold floors.

Most forced, warm-air heating systems can support another register or two if the furnace is centrally located. However, if the furnace is in an attached garage of a ranch house and a new master suite is being added to the opposite end of the house, the long duct runs will make adequate heating difficult. Further considerations will be needed before requiring an existing heating system to heat additional space, such as the size of the system, the size of the duct work and the distance of the new space from the furnace.

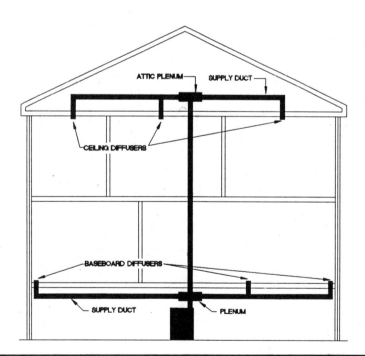

Figure 27   In two-story houses, ductwork is often hidden in interior or exterior walls. It may even be in the attic.

Also, it is not easy to add new registers to a slab house. Adding registers means jack hammering holes in sections of the floor. Even then, the central heating unit may be too small to heat the added space. If the central heating unit is not large enough, you may need to add a separate furnace to the new space.

Where to Place Supply Registers

Supply registers (or outlets) or diffusers in a forced air system should be placed so that the air does not blow directly on the occupants. Moving air makes a damp person feel chilly.

Supply registers should not be placed so close to the side of a toilet that a

seated person would feel the warm air on his/her skin. Most supply registers have movable vanes that can be adjusted.

Supply registers can be placed high or low on the wall. Low wall outlets are better in cold climates because heated air rises, and if registers are low on the wall, the heat has a chance to spread across the floor before it rises to the ceiling. This keeps the floor at a comfortable temperature.

In the warmer climates, however, high wall locations might be better. This is because heat is required for only short periods. Most of the year, the air conditioner is turned on. In such situations, high wall outlets are best because cool

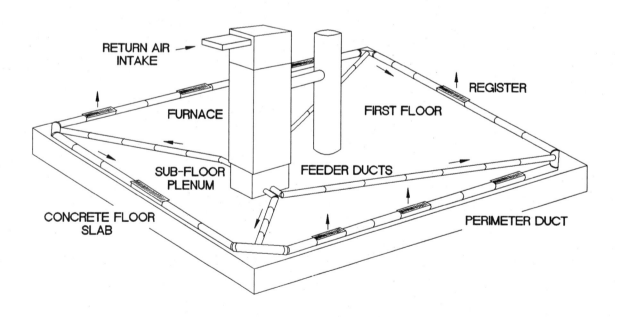

Figure 28   Crawl space houses can have forced air systems. The ducts are buried in concrete. Registers are located along the outside walls of the house.

air falls. If registers are close to the floor, a band of cool air hovers above the floor, while the ceiling level temperature remains warm. Unfortunately, high wall outlets are more visible. Plan their location with the HVAC contractor to avoid conflicts with the design. In climates with equally long heating and cooling seasons, the low wall location is better.

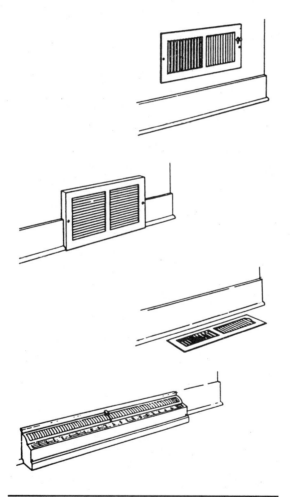

Figure 29 Registers and diffusers distribute heat. They have directional vanes to project heat into the room. Return air grilles collect air and do not have adjustable vanes.

In small bathrooms, it is difficult to find a good place to put the register. The toekick is a good location, or place registers high on the wall, perhaps above the vanity mirror. Make sure, however, that the HVAC contractor uses a register with adjustable vanes.

This allows the client to adjust the air stream. A high velocity air stream aimed toward the opposite wall might strike the wall and cause annoying air movement in the room.

Return-Air Grilles

Return-air intakes in bathrooms are not absolutely necessary. Small bathrooms do not require return air intakes, but large bathrooms may need them. If there is no good place to put a return air intake, the bathroom door should not be tightly sealed. It should have a 1/4" to 1/2" space below it. This is to prevent negative pressure that can occur when the bathroom vent fan is turned on.

Negative pressure can suck combustion gases from the furnace into the bathroom.

Placement of the return air grille is not as critical as placement of the supply registers. Return air grilles only have detectable air movement 6" from the face of the grille. The air flow is not likely to chill your clients. If the bathroom has a return air grille, it can be placed high or low on the wall.

COMBINATION SPACE/WATER HEATERS

Combination heaters work on the same principle as an automobile heater, but instead of an engine, the heat source is a gas- or oil-fired water heater. The theory behind the system is simple: since the water already is using energy to stay warm, heat can be drawn off and circulated to the living area. By capturing the heat that ordinarily would be lost, the efficiency of the system is increased.

When heat is needed, a wall thermostat triggers a small pump, which circulates hot water from the water heater to a coil in an air handler. Air is blown over the coil to absorb the heat and then is distributed through ducts by fans. Meanwhile, slightly cooled water is circulated back to the water tank for reheating.

These combination heaters are best used where heating demands are low. However, you might consider using them in a well insulated master bedroom and bathroom addition because they provide both hot water and heat. Space must be planned for the storage tank and air handler.

HYDRONIC HEAT

Hydronic heat is another form of central heat. It uses no ducts, but carries its heat in water, which circulates in pipes. (**Hydronic** comes from **hydro**, - meaning water.) One pipe supplies heated water to the room heating units through a supply main. The other pipe returns the cooled water to the boiler through a separate return main (or pipe).

A hydronic heating system may include any of the following; baseboard radiators, cast iron radiators, floor or ceiling coil system, "Hide-A-Vectors" and convectors.

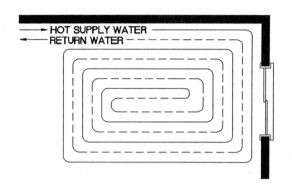

Figure 30 With hydronic heat, one pipe supplies heated water and the other returns cool water to the boiler.

Hot-Water Panels: Houses with concrete slab floors may have hydronic hot-water heat in the floor. A boiler heats water and circulates it through water lines embedded in the slab. You cannot add on to this kind of heating system. Any demolition that requires cutting holes in the concrete should be done very carefully to avoid cutting into water lines.

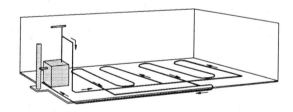

Figure 31 Hot-water panel heat can be used in slab houses.

Forced Hot Water: In a forced hot water system, a boiler heats water that circulates through pipes. The pipes lead to radiators or convectors. These units transfer heat to the room air.

Convectors consist of a core and "*fins*". Hot water heats the core and the fins, which, in turn, warm the air passing over them. The core and fins are enclosed in a cabinet, causing a more effective air flow over the heating surfaces than if they were exposed. Fan-coil units are similar, but they use small fans to push the heated air out into the room. Fan-coil units can also be used for cooling.

The HVAC contractor is most knowledgeable about what can and cannot be done to move or rearrange parts of the heating system. It can be difficult to move radiators, convectors or fan-coil units to a different location because that involves changing piping. If you are working in a bathroom with this type of heating system, work closely with the HVAC contractor during the planning stage. Also, on your first walk-through, carefully trace the path of pipes. Check any walls to be removed to make sure no pipes are embedded in them.

From a heating standpoint, the best location for these devices is below a window. An alternate location is the toe-kick area beneath a vanity. Temperatures are not hot enough to burn peoples' toes.

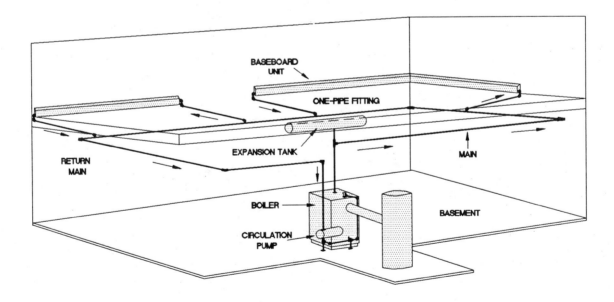

Figure 32 In a forced-hot-water system, the water is heated in a boiler and pumped through pipes to radiators, fan-coils or convectors.

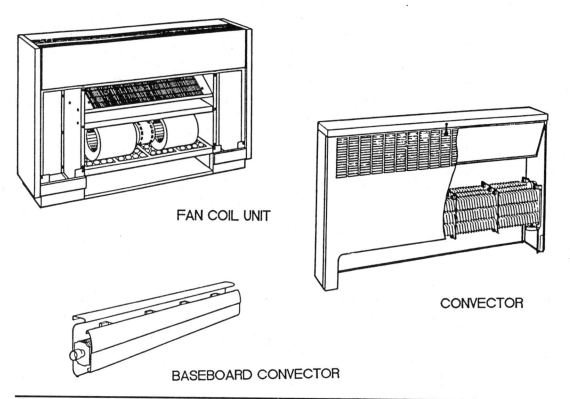

FAN COIL UNIT

CONVECTOR

BASEBOARD CONVECTOR

Figure 33   In hot water systems, room air is heated as it circulates around fan-coil units or convectors. Baseboard convectors are the most common in homes.

Steam Heat: Old-fashioned steam-heat systems circulated steam instead of hot water. Steam systems also used radiators. Both one-pipe and two-pipe systems were once common. If you are remodeling a home with steam heat, it is best to leave the radiator in its current location.

These systems should not be rearranged. Because of their age, they can also be difficult to disassemble. Fittings may be partially rusted, and trying to remove a radiator may loosen connections elsewhere in the system.

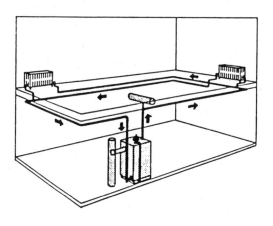

Figure 34 Steam systems circulate steam, produced by a boiler, to radiators.

ELECTRIC HEAT

There are two common types of electric heat: electric resistance heat and electric heat pumps. Electric heat is not as common as it was in the days of cheap electricity. But heat pumps, which also use electricity, are becoming more popular because they can be used for heating and cooling. Because heat pumps are also used for cooling, we will discuss them as a separate system after we finish heating and cooling.

Electric Forced Air

Electric forced air systems are not common today because the cost of electricity has risen and made this form of heat more expensive. In an electric furnace, heat is provided by air moving across heating elements. The heated air circulates through supply ducts and is returned to the furnace through return intakes. No vents are necessary because no combustion takes place in the furnace.

Resistance Heat

Electric resistance heat works by directly converting electric current into heat. Almost all of the energy in the electric current ends up as usable heat. Electric resistance heat usually is the most expensive form of heat, but it is the least expensive to install and allows the user to control the temperature of each room separately.

Electric resistance heat can also be provided by heating panels. These heating panels are a special kind of drywall, with wiring embedded in them. This eliminates expensive duct work. And, electric resistance heat requires no fur-

nace. You might think of using this heating system in a small bathroom or room addition to provide supplementary heat. Your drywall contractor will need to order special drywall with wiring embedded in it. The electrical contractor will also have to add a circuit to handle the heating load. A disadvantage is that resistance heat takes time to warm up. If a person wishes to take the chill off a bathroom, this system will not respond quickly.

Electric resistance heat can be provided by baseboard units. The baseboards look much like hot water baseboards. Instead of having hot water passing through them, however, they are manufactured with an electric heating element similar to that used in an electric range. Units installed in each room or area are controlled by a separate thermostat mounted on the wall or installed as part of the baseboard unit.

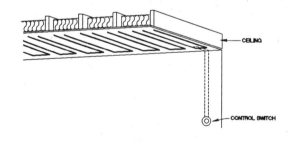

Figure 35 Electric radiant heat can be provided by wiring that is embedded in drywall.

hydronic heating and can be connected to a boiler, water heater, heat pump or solar heating system.)

Another newcomer to the market is thermal mass heat storage. Unlike most conventional heaters, mass heat storage systems can store heat and have controls to regulate when and how much heat is released. This feature allows the homeowner to take advantage of lower electric rates during off-peak hours.

AUXILIARY HEATING

There are few worse feelings than rising from bed on a chilly morning and stepping on a cold tile floor in a 65°F bathroom. This situation calls for a quick secondary source of heat to raise the temperature.

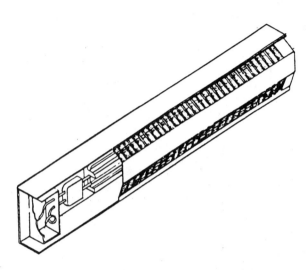

Figure 36 An electric resistance baseboard heater has a heating element much like the element in an electric range.

Other Types of Electric Heating

Electric radiant heating installed in flooring is popular in Europe and beginning to make headway in the United States. In this system, electric coils are attached to the subfloor and covered with a lightweight concrete or installed with built-up subflooring. A thermostat connected to a heat sensor inside the flooring regulates the temperature of the system.

Because these systems heat the floor itself instead of warming air, the heat is more evenly distributed and comfortable for cold feet. Although expensive, these systems are an alternative worth considering for "cold" flooring such as tile, wood, marble and granite. (Radiant flooring systems also work with

Auxiliary bathroom heaters generally use electricity to provide heat. Electricity can create two forms of heat-radiant heat or heat that is transferred by convection.

Radiant heat is transferred through invisible electromagnetic waves from an infrared energy source such as a heat lamp. When the infrared energy strikes an object or person, the radiation is absorbed and converted into heat. Radiant heaters provide heat in two ways: first, by using infrared heat lamps. These lamps are coated inside to create a reflective surface that directs the heat rays downward to the floor. The second type of heater incorporates a metal-type heating element. These units provide greater heat output than the lamps. Radiant heaters are quieter than fan-forced systems, and the heat produced is also much more localized. These units are ideal for spot heating.

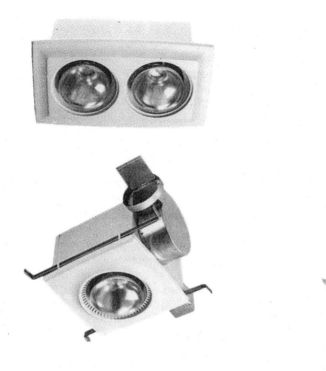

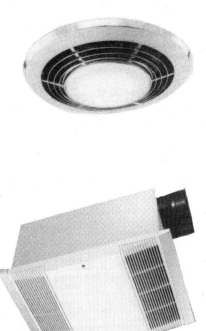

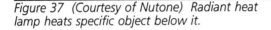

Figure 37 (Courtesy of Nutone) Radiant heat lamp heats specific object below it.

Figure 38 (Courtesy of Nutone) A combination heater, vent and ceiling light.

Convection refers to air heated by an element that then naturally, or assisted by a fan, moves to cooler objects or people to equalize temperatures. Fan-forced heaters distribute the warmed air evenly throughout the space in a matter of seconds.

These types of heaters are excellent for general room heating in spaces other than shower or bathtub areas. Whenever air blows across the body, a "wind chill" effect takes place. The air, regardless of how warm, feels cold to the skin and will chill the person. Fan-forced heaters can also be noisy. The high motor speed, together with excessive air turbulence, creates a clatter which can be most unpleasant. Some of the better units overcome the noise factor by using a fan which moves the necessary volume of air at a very low motor speed.

Ceiling-mounted convection heaters are also an option. These can be combined with a room light and ventilation fan. Make sure the ventilation fan has adequate capacity. *(See Section 5, "Ventilation".)* Be sure also, to check the sones rating on the fans. The sones scale is used to approximate the sound level heard by the human ear. The sound level is rated from 1 to 10, with 1 being the quietest.

Both convection heat and radiant heat are also available in wall heaters. They should not be installed on the side of a vanity or next to a toilet where someone could accidentally bump against the heater. They should not be used in bathrooms for children or the elderly because of the possibility of burns. Finally, do not place them under towel racks where they could ignite a towel.

To determine the correct heat size for a space, figure 1 1/2 watts per cubic foot. Heaters less than 1,500 watts usually are 120-volt models. Over 1,500 watts, the model will require a 240-volt line.

THERMOSTATS

Thermostats are like switches, except they control the operation of a boiler, furnace or electric heater. In most houses, one thermostat is used to control the temperature in several rooms. However, the thermostat can only sense the temperature in the room where it is located. For this reason, it is important that the thermostat be located either where the temperature is representative of the whole house or where temperature control is most important.

Locate the thermostat at a height of 48" above the floor. Avoid placing the thermostat on outside walls or near outside doors. Likewise, do not place it near heat outlets, behind doors, or on walls that receive heat from the sun, a fireplace, or lamp.

Ask the heating contractor to make sure the thermostat location will not cause the bathroom to be cold. If the bathroom tends to be colder than other rooms in the house, move the thermostat so that it turns on the heat more often. You can also provide auxiliary heat as described previously.

SOLAR HEATING

Homeowners frequently ask bathroom designers to bring natural light into their homes. Most homeowners have experienced how comfortable a warm sunlit room can become, even on a cold winter day. If a bathroom is on the south facing side of the house, and your clients have seen pictures of glass atriums, they may ask about this option for their bathroom.

Passive solar heating principles are the easiest to incorporate into a bathroom design. **Passive solar** means that the building itself is designed to capture the sun's heat. In **active solar**, collectors and pumps that distribute heat are needed. A bathroom designer must learn about solar design to use the sun's heat effectively. Make sure the solar option is right for your climate and the building's orientation.

Rooms must be oriented so that window areas face south. To prevent summer overheating, windows must have a shading overhang to exclude the high arc of the summer sun, which would overheat the room. In the winter, the sun's arc is lower and closer to the horizon, so its rays come in below the overhang.

If you do decide to incorporate some aspects of passive solar design, provide auxiliary heat for sunless periods and nightime. (A publication that gives details of passive solar design is **Solar Orientation**; also see **Sunspaces & Greenhouses**. Both are available from the **Building Research Council**, 1 East St. Mary's Road, Champaign, IL 61820.)

RENOVATION CONSIDERATIONS

Most heating systems can be revamped to fit your design. Warm-air and heat pump duct work can often be extended. If a new bath is located in an addition, it is often possible to extend the duct work to provide for heating and cooling. Before this is done, however, the existing furnace should be checked to be sure there is sufficient heating and/or cooling capacity. The fan on the unit should be checked to see that it is capable of delivering additional air. It may be necessary to replace the fan motor or fan assembly to increase the air-handling capacity of the system, even though the furnace burner has sufficient heating capacity.

When you are working on existing buildings, always check the following items:

- The location of floor registers, diffusers, radiators, etc.

- The location of duct work or pipes.

- The location of the central heating system.

Always check walls that you intend to move or remove for duct work. Experi-enced bathroom designers draw details of the existing vent locations and gas pipes on their plans. The drawings show how the mechanical systems relate to the space above.

Remember, ducts can be located in the basement or the attic. If the heating system uses radiators or convectors, make sure you know where pipes are located in the walls.

When adding a bathroom and master suite, consider adding a second furnace, or one of the hot water/furnace combination units. This will allow your clients to "zone" their heat. They can turn heat down in the part of the house they are not using.

A second furnace can often be a better "comfort" solution because the heating unit is closer to the rooms to be heated. Make sure to provide a furnace closet on your plans. The furnace closet should be placed to minimize noise for the occupants.

SECTION 3

Cooling

Nearly 58 million American households (60%) use some type of air conditioning system. In regions where air conditioning is common, you should be familiar with how the equipment works and how any changes you make affect it.

Instead of using energy to create heat, air conditioners use energy to remove heat, or more correctly, humidity. The energy source for air conditioning is electricity.

There are four types of air conditioners:

- Room Air Conditioners

- Central Air Conditioners

- Ductless Air Conditioning

- Electric Heat Pumps

Evaporative coolers and fans can also be used to provide summer comfort. But neither one removes humidity, which is the real cause of discomfort.

Because heat pumps are also used for heating, we will discuss this system separately in Section 4.

ROOM AIR CONDITIONERS

As the name implies, room air conditioners are sized to cool just one room. Therefore, a number of them are required for a whole house. Standard room air conditioners are noisy and can produce uncomfortably wide fluctuations in temperature from room to room.

CENTRAL AIR CONDITIONERS

Central air conditioners are designed to cool the entire home and they have a number of advantages. They are out of the way, quiet and convenient. If the home already has a forced air heating system, a central air system can easily be tied into the existing duct work. Adding an air conditioner to an existing forced air system is the least expensive way to provide summer cooling.

SIZING THE COOLING SYSTEM

Bigger is not better when it comes to cooling systems. Proper sizing is critical to efficient operation. Oversized systems not only cost more initially but will cycle on and off frequently. This increases electricity use and decreases overall energy efficiency of the unit.

Most air conditioners are rated in BTUs per hour. Central air conditioners and heat pumps may also list cooling capacity by tons. One ton is equivalent to 12,000 BTUs. Capacity ratings of most air conditioners are certified under a program administered by the **Air Conditioning and Refrigeration Institute**.

With air conditioning systems, equipment cost is more proportional to size than it is with heating equipment. Therefore, doubling the cooling output nearly doubles the cost of the cooling unit.

EFFICIENCY

Efficiency is just as important in an air conditioning system as it is in a heating system. Efficiency of room air conditioners is measured by the energy efficiency rating (EER). This is the ratio of the cooling output in BTUs divided by the power consumption (in wattage). The EER does not factor in performance over the cooling season. A room air conditioner with an EER over 9.5 is considered efficient.

Central air conditioners and heat pumps operating in the cooling mode are rated according to their Seasonal Energy Efficiency Rating (SEER). This rating is the seasonal cooling output in BTUs divided by the seasonal energy input in watt hours for an average U.S. climate.

UPFLOW FURNACE-MOUNTED SYSTEM

DOWNFLOW FURNACE-MOUNTED SYSTEM

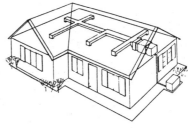

INDEPENDENT HORIZONTAL-FLOW SYSTEM

Figure 39 Central air conditioning systems have ductwork installed below the floor or in the attic. The ductwork may limit changes you're considering for the new room.

The national appliance efficiency standard for central air conditioners, which was first effective in 1992, required a minimum SEER of 10.

Central air conditioners are almost always more efficient than room air conditioners. Energy-saving features to look for include:

- A fan-only switch (which allows the unit to operate for ventilation and can substantially reduce air conditioning costs);

- A filter check light that acts as a reminder to check the filter after a predetermined number of operating hours;

- An automatic delay fan switch to turn the fan off a few minutes after the compressor turns off.

Central air conditioners are purchased from local HVAC contractors. Your clients can gather product and energy information before making their final choice.

DUCT SYSTEMS

Since warm air rises to the ceiling and cool air falls towards the floor, it is preferable to introduce heated air into a room at a low level and cooled air at a high level.

In a combined system, the best compromise is a floor or baseboard outlet that directs the air flow upward with sufficient velocity to reach the ceiling. Otherwise cool air may pool at the floor level.

In small bathrooms where wall space is limited, the HVAC contractor may wish to install the supply outlet in the toe-kick area of the vanity. While this location works well for heating, it does not work well for cooling.

In this case it's better to place the supply outlet high on the wall. Be sure the register does not blow directly on the occupants. The vanes in registers are adjustable for different angles, one of the final items you should check as you walk through the job.

OTHER COOLING SYSTEMS

Swamp Coolers

Evaporative coolers are most practical in dry climates, such as the Southwest. Sometimes called *"swamp coolers"*, they work by blowing house air over a damp pad or by spraying a fine mist of water into the household air supply. The dry air evaporates the moisture and cools off. These cooling systems cannot be used in humid areas because they do not dehumidify the air.

Window Fans

Window fans for cooling and ventilation are a reasonable option for cooling temperate climates if they are used properly. They should be located on the leeward (downwind) side of the house facing out. A window should be open in each room. Interior doors must remain open to allow air flow. Window fans will not work as well in houses with long, narrow hallways or those with small rooms and many interior partitions. Window fans can be noisy, especially on high settings, but they are inexpensive.

Whole-House Fans

Whole-house fans are more convenient than window fans. Mounted in a hallway ceiling on the top floor, the fan pulls air from the house and blows it into the attic. The fan usually is covered on the bottom by a louver vent. Installing a whole-house fan in the hallway during a bathroom remodeling project might be part of the work you specify.

The fan should have at least two speeds, with the highest one capable of changing the entire volume of air in the house every 3 minutes. *For example,* a 1,500 sq. ft. house with 8-foot ceilings contains 12,000 cubic feet. The fan thus should be rated at 4,000 cubic feet per minute (cfm). Because the fan blows air into the attic, the attic must have sufficient outlet vents. The free vent area, including soffit vents, ridge vents and gable-end vents, should be twice the free vent area of the fan opening. (Free vent area is a measure of the area of the vent opening minus the area blocked by screening and louvers.) For safety reasons, the fan should have manual controls. It should also have a fusible link, which automatically shuts the fan down in case of fire.

Attic Fans

Attic fans, also called roof fans, can substantially reduce the temperature of attic air. Although most attics have openings for ventilation, the vents are usually not large enough to prevent the attic temperature from reaching 140°F or higher on a hot day. This heat is transferred into the living areas below. Mounted as high as possible in a gable or roof surface, an attic fan exhausts hot attic air and pulls in cooler outside air through vents in the eaves or soffits. These fans can reduce the attic temperature 20% or more.

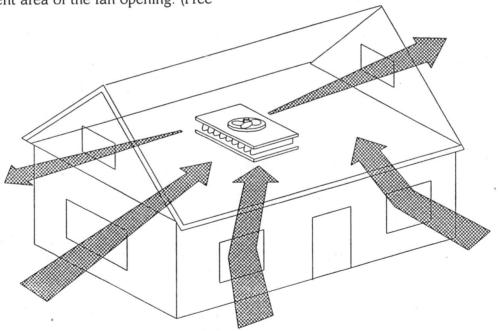

Figure 40 In climates where humidity is not a problem, whole-house fans can be used to cool the house at night.

Ceiling Fans

Ceiling fans are another popular option but are not ideal for bathrooms because the cool air currents will blow past the client's wet body, causing a "*wind chill*" phenomenon which will be uncomfortable for the bather.

RENOVATION CONSIDERATIONS

When conducting your jobsite inspection, look for registers in floors and walls. Be especially alert for ducts that might be hidden in walls you plan to remove. If the house has a second story, check rooms above to be sure there are no registers in these rooms. If you are in doubt, check the attic, basement or crawl space to see where ducts turn down or up into the wall cavities.

In existing buildings, you may need to pre-plan new duct and register locations with your subcontractor. The old register may not be in the right place for a new bathroom. Your contractor may need to split ductwork and bring in an additional register.

Find out how much additional demolition will be required. Perhaps you can find a different location that suits the design and requirements for the duct.

If you are adding a bathroom to a house, find out whether the existing air conditioner system can handle the added volume. You may need to add a small room unit for a new master suite/bathroom.

Adding duct work to cool new space is easier if the ducts are not embedded in a concrete slab. Duct work located in an attic, crawl space or basement gener-

ally can be extended if the new space is not too distant from the cooling equipment. Jackhammering out a concrete slab to add duct work might not be cost effective. Again, discuss the options with the HVAC contractor.

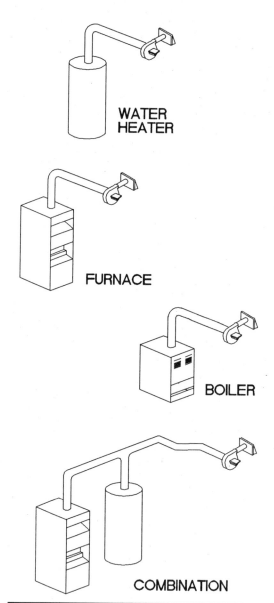

Figure 41 Add-on power venters (centrifugal blowers) can be used to provide induced draft venting for furnaces and water heaters.

Air Cleaners

Clients who are sensitive to indoor pollutants should consider installing an air cleaner in their heating/cooling system. Air cleaners can be used with most brands and styles of forced-air furnaces, heat pumps, and central air conditioners.

According to the **Air Conditioning and Refrigeration Institute (ARI)** electronic air cleaners are 10 to 20 times more efficient than standard air filters. Electronic air cleaners trap large particles with a screen pre-filter and smaller particles with a form of static electricity.

Another form of air cleaner is the self-charging mechanical filter. This filter is made of polypropylene or polystyrene. These materials are able to hold a static charge across their surface to trap particles. Self-charging mechanical filters are less efficient than electronic air cleaners. Consult an HVAC contractor before specifying an air cleaner. The air cleaner must be compatible with the main heating/cooling system.

Heat Pumps

HOW THE SYSTEM WORKS

Used for both Heating & Cooling

Electric heat pumps operate on a different principle. Instead of directly producing heat from the electric current, they use electricity to move heat from one place to another. They work in the same way as a refrigerator, using a special refrigerant fluid (HCFC-22) that changes back and forth between liquid and vapor. In the heating mode, the heat pump extracts heat from outside the house and delivers it to the house. In the cooling mode, it extracts heat from the house and takes it outside.

Geo-Thermal Units

Most consumers are acquainted with air-source heat pumps. In recent years, ground-source (geo-thermal) heat pumps have become more popular because they are effective all year, regardless of outside temperature. This is because ground temperature at about six feet underground is a constant 55°F whether outside air temperature is zero or 100°F or more.

The underground heat exchanger is a continuous loop of polyethylene tubing in which the heat-transfer solution travels to and from the geo-thermal unit in the house. The loop may be laid horizontally at a depth of about 6-8 feet, or vertically in a well 100-200 feet deep. There can be multiple loops in the well. The unit in the house has a variable-speed compressor, an evaporator coil, a blower fan and a reversing valve that moves the heat either into or out of the unit to heat or cool the home. Incoming warm air is 90°F -105°F, even in winter. The variable-speed compressor eliminates the rush of cool air and the noise often associated with air-source heat pumps.

Geo-thermal units are being promoted extensively in the United States and Canada by electric utilities. While they can cut heating/cooling costs by 40%, they might be difficult or impossible for retrofit because of lawn space needed for excavation or drilling. Many utilities offer rebates to help offset higher installation cost.

Ideal for Temperate Climates

Air-source heat pumps work most efficiently when there is a small difference between inside and outside temperature. For instance, when the outdoor temperature is 55°F, it is relatively easy for the heat pump to capture heat from the air. But when the outside temperature drops below 40°F, there is relatively little heat left. At freezing, which is 32°F, the air contains no excess heat. Therefore, air-source heat pumps are not widely used in climates where winter temperatures are below 32°F more than 20% of the heating season. For the colder days, air-source heat pumps have electric coils (like the heating coils on a range) that provide supplementary heat when the temperature outside drops below 32°F.

Air Temperature Concerns

One complaint that has been lodged against heat pumps is that the heated air coming from the register is not as warm as heat from warm air furnaces. A heat pump may deliver air only at about 90°F. To compensate, the heat pump delivers the air at a higher velocity. The air movement may be especially noticeable to a partially clothed person using the bathroom.

Sizing the System

Sizing can be difficult because the same unit is used for both cooling and heating. A heat pump sized for heating loads in a cold climate will be considerably oversized when it comes to cooling. A heat pump sized for cooling loads in a warm climate will tend to be oversized when it comes to heating.

A good heat pump technician should be able to help your clients choose the best compromise between cooling and heating capacity.

Locating the System

Heat pumps are among the most flexible home cooling or heating equipment because they can be mounted almost anywhere. This may be helpful if space is tight, and you have no place to put a utility closet for mechanical equipment. However, these units are again somewhat noisy, so don't plan an exterior location just below the master bedroom window.

Ventilation

Ventilating a bathroom eliminates moisture, mold growth and a variety of problems that cause materials in the bathroom to degrade. Moisture loosens tiles, encourages mildew, traps dirt on surfaces and makes drywall soggy. It makes fixtures rust, doors swell to unclosable proportions and paint peel inside and outside the house. Moisture problems also can show up in the attic in the form of wet roof framing, or in insulation, where condensation diminishes the insulating value.

A typical family of three produces 20 pounds of water vapor in a day (equivalent to 2 1/2 gallons of water). Showering and bathing account for only five percent of the total, but all of this water vapor is produced in an hour or less in an enclosed space. A shower can push the relative humidity in a bathroom from normal levels (40% or less) to 99% in less than 10 minutes.

Bathrooms need ventilating fans, even if there's a window. And it's a challenge to the designer to specify the right ventilation system - one that will adequately and quietly exhaust air.

WINDOW AREA

Operable windows are the most basic form of bathroom ventilation. The CABO **One and Two Family Dwelling Code** requires that bathrooms and toilet compartments have operable windows with a minimum of 3 square- feet. Half of this space must be operable.

Windows are not required when a bathroom vent fan is used. But recent research suggests that a vent fan should be used - even if a bathroom has the required operable window area.

VENTILATING FANS

What will the correct ventilation accomplish in a bathroom? Research suggests that a ventilating fan lowers relative humidity in a bathroom to outside conditions within about half an hour after a 10-minute shower.

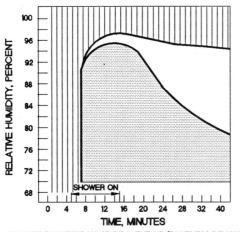

EXHAUST FAN KEEPS MOISTURE IN THE AIR (DAMPNESS DEMONS)
LOWER DURING SHOWER AND RAPIDLY REDUCES IF AFTER SHOWER

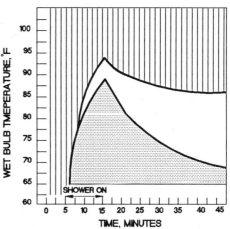

GRAPH SHOWS HOW EXHAUST FAN HELPS TO CONTROL BATHROOM
TEMPERATURE DURING AND AFTER SHOWER.

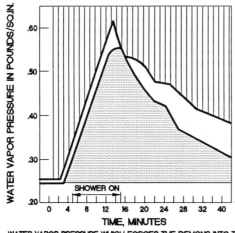

WATER VAPOR PRESSURE WHICH FORCES THE DEMONS INTO THEIR
'HIDING PLACES,' IS QUICKLY REDUCED BY EXHAUST FAN AFTER
A SHOWER.

|||||||| UNVENTILATED BATHROOM

:::::::: BATHROOM WITH EXHAUST FAN PROVIDING
8 AIR CHANGES PER HOUR

Figure 42   (Courtesy of The Home Ventilating Institute) Bathroom ventilation comparison charts.

Moreover, the drop in humidity generated by a ventilating fan makes it less likely that moist air will be carried into the wall cavities or attic space. In cold climates, water vapor can cause serious moisture damage. The water vapor condenses into liquid water and will cause wood to decay.

ASHRAE Guidelines

Concern over the quality of indoor air and the potential for moisture problems indoors has been growing. After the big push in the late 1970s to insulate houses and improve energy efficiency, homes could be built so tightly that indoor air quality dropped.

ASHRAE **(American Society of Heating, Refrigerating and Air Conditioning Engineers,** 1791 Tuille Circle, NE, Atlanta, GA 30329**)** has created a **ventilation standard**. The title of this standard is **Ventilation for Acceptable Indoor Air Quality**.

The ASHRAE standard requires a minimum of 0.35 air changes per hour for living areas of the house. One air change per hour means that all of the air in the house is replaced with fresh air - once an hour. The ASHRAE standard says that about a third of the home's air should be replaced hourly. As we have seen, air exchange is particularly important in bathrooms, where humidity levels can be high.

To correctly compute the number of air changes required, you need to know how many cubic feet of air the house contains. The volume of air in the house is measured in cubic feet.

What if we want to know how many air changes are needed in a minute? ASHRAE did these calculations. Their standard says that a house must have at least 15 CFM **(cubic feet per minute)** of fresh air per person. Bathrooms must have 50 CFM of intermittent outdoor air or 20 CFM of fresh air if a fan operates continuously.

What does this standard mean for a bathroom designer? The most important number is 50 CFM. This is a starting point to think about how much ventilation you need to provide in the bathroom.

Friction Affects Fan Performance

If you have already specified bathroom fans, you know that each fan has a CFM rating. This rating tells how many CFM the fan is capable of moving. What you may not realize is that the fan manufacturer also gives specific instructions on how the fan should be installed and what installation accessories you should use to maximize the efficiency of the system. *Figure 43* details the variety of ductwork accessories typically used.

These instructions cover details such as:

● The length of duct run.

● The duct material.

● The diameter of the duct.

● Angle and number of turns in the duct.

All of these things affect how hard the fan has to work to move air out of the bathroom.

INSTALLATION ACCESSORIES

INSTALLATION ACCESSORIES ARE USUALLY NEEDED TO COMPLETE A VENTILATION JOB. THEY INCLUDE THE FOLLOWING:

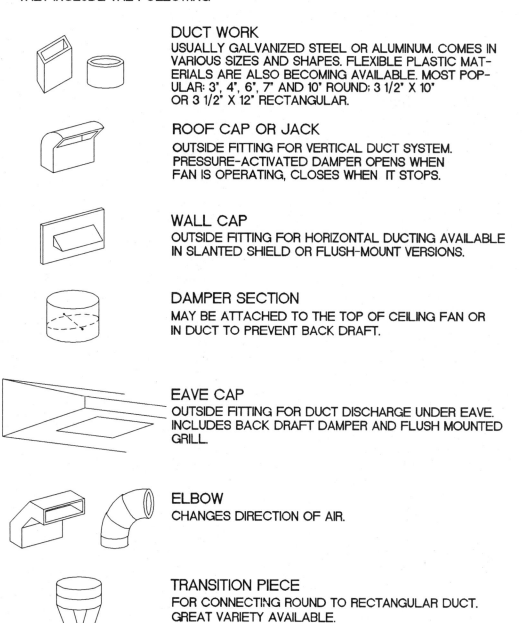

DUCT WORK
USUALLY GALVANIZED STEEL OR ALUMINUM. COMES IN VARIOUS SIZES AND SHAPES. FLEXIBLE PLASTIC MATERIALS ARE ALSO BECOMING AVAILABLE. MOST POPULAR: 3", 4", 6", 7" AND 10" ROUND; 3 1/2" X 10" OR 3 1/2" X 12" RECTANGULAR.

ROOF CAP OR JACK
OUTSIDE FITTING FOR VERTICAL DUCT SYSTEM. PRESSURE-ACTIVATED DAMPER OPENS WHEN FAN IS OPERATING, CLOSES WHEN IT STOPS.

WALL CAP
OUTSIDE FITTING FOR HORIZONTAL DUCTING AVAILABLE IN SLANTED SHIELD OR FLUSH-MOUNT VERSIONS.

DAMPER SECTION
MAY BE ATTACHED TO THE TOP OF CEILING FAN OR IN DUCT TO PREVENT BACK DRAFT.

EAVE CAP
OUTSIDE FITTING FOR DUCT DISCHARGE UNDER EAVE. INCLUDES BACK DRAFT DAMPER AND FLUSH MOUNTED GRILL.

ELBOW
CHANGES DIRECTION OF AIR.

TRANSITION PIECE
FOR CONNECTING ROUND TO RECTANGULAR DUCT. GREAT VARIETY AVAILABLE.

Figure 43 Ductwork installation accessories allow the system to accommodate existing construction constraints without limiting the system's efficiency.

The length of the duct run affects fan performance because of friction. Friction slows down moving objects. Air moving down a duct slows down because of friction from the duct walls. The longer the duct, the more friction affects the air flow rate.

It makes sense that the material the duct is made of might increase or decrease the friction. Three types of duct are commonly used to vent bathroom fans - sheetmetal, plastic plumbing pipe or flexible plastic dryer duct. Air travels much faster down the smooth surfaces of the metal or plumbing pipe. Friction in the corrugated plastic duct slows air flow.

The diameter of the duct also affects air flow. The narrower the duct, the less air that can get through, and the harder the fan has to work to push the air. Turns in the ductwork add greatly to friction. If duct must turn, two 45 degree turns are better than one 90 degree turn.

A research project in Canada found that bathroom fans, as typically installed, delivered only 45% of their advertised air flow. The most commonly used 50 CFM bathroom fans were only delivering 24 CFM. In the state of Washington, where the 1991 Washington State Ventilation Code requires that fans meet the 50 CFM minimum, the **Puget Sound Power & Light Company** recommends "a fan rated for 70 or 80 CFM."

Make-up air is essential to the performance of a vent fan. A 50 CFM fan cannot remove that much air unless the make-up air is available in the bathroom with the door closed. It is common to provide up to an inch of space at the bottom of the door to admit make-up air. This problem can be abetted by use of a heat recovery ventilator (HRV), formerly known as an air-to-air heat exchanger, but this can add to the cost in both dollars and space.

Figuring Ventilation Needs

Fans in the United States are tested by **The Home Ventilating Institute**, the trade association supported by residential fan manufacturers. The tests are conducted at Georgia Tech, an independent testing body. HVI-certified ventilating equipment will be labeled with the number of cubic feet the fan will ventilate.

A real convenience for the designer is the **Home Ventilating Institute's Certified Products Directory**. It lists all certified fans by the number of cfms and their noise level. (Write to **HVI**, 30 West University Drive, Arlington Heights, IL 61312.)

If the fan does not have the HVI label, determine the proper CFM rating for the bathroom with this formula: multiply the length and width of the bathroom by 1.07 (assuming an 8-foot ceiling). For a 6' x 8' foot bathroom, the calculation would be as follows:

$$6 \times 8 \times 1.07 = 51.36$$

The multiplier that you use for rooms with other ceiling heights is as follows:

Cubic Feet of Room (L x W x H) x 8 Air Changes Per Hour divided by 60 Minutes = The Required Fan CFM Rating.

Tight Houses and Loose Houses

You may need to go beyond the minimum requirements if the house is tightly constructed, extremely energy efficient, has a jetted tub or indoor spa, or many people showering or using the bathtub at one time. **Charles Blodgett**, CBD, recommends a fan with up to 400 CFM capacity in these cases.

The **University of Minnesota, Dept. of Extension Home Economics**, has also published a report that provides specific information on fan sizing under "*loose house*" and "*tight house*" conditions. (**University of Minnesota, Minnesota Extension Service**, 1420 Eckles Ave., St. Paul, Minnesota, 55108). For "loose houses" the report recommends the following:

- Use a bathroom vent fan for each bathroom with a shower or bathtub.

- Operate the vent fan when humidity levels are too high.

- Provide bathroom supply air in the bathroom.

- Operate the forced air system whenever showers are turned on.

For "*tight houses*" the recommendations go much further:

- Provide minimum ventilation air through an HRV with a means of distributing ventilation air throughout the structure.

- Place controls on the heat exchanger so that it operates automatically and continuously when the temperature is above 55°F .

- Provide bathroom supply air (and preferably return air too) with the forced air heating system.

- Use a bathroom vent fan for each bathroom containing a shower or bathtub.

- Operate the forced air system whenever showers are on.

- Operate the vent fan when humidity levels are too high.

The study found that showers were one of the largest sources of moisture in a residence. A bathroom fan was not sufficient protection against moisture buildup and poor indoor air quality in tight houses.

With tight houses, some sort of mechanical ventilation must be provided. Heat exchangers or whole house ventilation systems should be used with tight houses, as we will see in a later section. For the moment, however, return to the single bathroom fan and the problem of noise.

Noise

Noise is the chief drawback of any fan. The noisier the fan, the less it will be used.

Household fans are rated in sones. One sone approximates the noise a quiet refrigerator makes in a quiet kitchen. All fans bearing the **Home Ventilating Institute** label are certified for cfm ratings, while some are certified for sone ratings as well. Although a bathroom fan can be HVI certified with a sone limit of 6.5

sones, find one that produces less than 3 sones at high speed so that the homeowner won't be tempted to shut if off permanently. You may need to compromise on sound to get the ventilation you need, but look for the quietest products possible.

Testing the accuracy of sones ratings was also part of the Canadian study. The investigation found that the sones ratings did not always predict the installed sound level. They attributed differences to variability of the installation, room size, and reverberation characteristics. Sones ratings, then, can give you a pretty good idea of how quiet the fan will be. But you should also check the installation against the manufacturer's technical literature.

Through product selection and quality control over the installation, you can make sure the customer gets the quietest operation possible.

REMOTE FANS

If you need a fan with a high **CFM** rating, but find that the sones rating is climbing, consider specifying a remote fan. Roof mounted fans have higher CFM ratings but are farther from the bathroom. Vibration is less of a problem. Sound damping rubber pads can be used to reduce vibration between the ducts and the framing. The advantage of a remote fan is that two bathrooms can be connected to the same fan. Continuous ventilation might also be an option with a remote fan. This would lower the re-

quired ventilation rate to 20 CFMs of outdoor air.

Some remote fan units are also so lightweight and quiet that they can be mounted on brackets and attached to framing in the attic or basement. The fans are mounted "*in line*" with the duct work. The duct must still continue all the way through the roof or be vented out a side wall.

In addition to being quieter, remote fans are more durable than ceiling-mounted units. This is because they are designed to operate for longer periods. They are also more expensive.

A QUIET INSTALLATION

For the quietest fan installation, minimize the length of duct runs. The fan should be placed as close to the exit point as possible. But it will have to be near the source of moisture - the shower or bathtub. With a remote fan, consider placing one intake grille above the shower and another above the mirror. This prevents fogging of the mirror. Some mirrors also have a healing feature which prevents the mirror from fogging over.

Try to route the duct to minimize the number of elbows or turns. Elbows cause friction and make the fan noisier and less effective. Use smooth duct rather than flex duct. If you do use flex duct, however, make it a larger diameter. The following chart can help you plan the duct sizing, length and layout.

EXHAUST DUCT SIZING					
Fan Tested CFM @ 0.25" W.G.	Flex Diameter	Maximum Length Feet	Smooth Diameter	Maximum Length Feet	Maximum Elbows *
50	4"	25	4"	70	3
50	5"	90	5"	100	3
50	6"	Over 100	6"	Over 100	3
80	4"	Not Allowed	4"	20	3
80	5"	15	5"	100	3
80	6"	90	6"	Over 100	3
100	5"	Not Allowed	5"	50	3
100	6"	45	6"	Over 100	3
125	6"	15	6"	Over 100	3
125	7"	70	7"	Over 100	3

* For Each Additional Elbow Subtract 10 Feet from Length.

Rubber mounts can be used to cut down vibration from the fan. Not all electricians are familiar with sound-damping techniques. However, HVAC contractors or suppliers are familiar with ways to reduce noise. By reducing vibration, you will reduce fan noise.

Fan Controls

In a children's bathroom, you can force occupants to take advantage of the ventilation system by connecting the fan operation to the light switch. If there is no outside window, this may save the bathroom from early decay. You could also use a timed fan/light switch. With such a device, the fan turns on when the light is switched on and remains on for several minutes after the light is turned off. Without it, the fan may not be turned on when it should be or, more commonly, will be shut off before it thoroughly vents humidity.

A more sophisticated and logical way of controlling bathroom fans is to use a humidistat, which shuts down ventilation when humidity falls to a set point, whether that be 10 or 45 minutes later. The desirable humidity level is set at 40% or less.

Many residential customers, however, want control over the fan switch. A good compromise is to put a vent fan on a timer switch in residential work, but separate the light switch and fan timer. The fan should run for at least 15 minutes after a shower. Your client can set the switch then forget about it.

Since the noise of the fan can be disturbing, "*audition*" the equipment before you specify it if possible. Most bathroom fans are one-speed, though fans with more than one speed are available. These allow the client to keep the fan on at a slow speed (which is always quieter) if soaking in the bathtub. For showering, the speed can be increased for better moisture removal. Educate your clients about the need for ventilation and quality differences between low-end and high-end products.

INSULATING THE DUCTWORK

What the fan does with all that moisture-laden air is important. The fan should be ducted, with minimal twists and turns, to the outside of the house, not to the attic or to the space between the joists above the bathroom ceiling. The duct should run through heated or insulated space, or else moisture will condense and pool within it. Condensation may also drip from the fan housing if it is uninsulated and below an unheated space.

While it might seem that the logical solution is to pile insulation over the fan housing, that is not allowed by the electrical code. The fan housing and technical literature will give required clearances. Combination fan/light equipment should not be covered with insulation because of the danger of heat build-up.

The **National Electrical Code** recognizes that condensation can be a problem. Two solutions are possible. The code allows a "plastic bubble" which is designed to fit over electrical equipment like a dome. Insulation can then be placed over this. The second option is for the builder to construct a drywall

box, which could be covered with insulation. This is the more time-consuming option.

Be sure to have the contractor insulate the duct on all sides. A thickness of 4 inches would be adequate. The duct should slope downward so that any small amount of condensation that might occur will drip to the outside. Also, try to use only one elbow. Where aesthetics is not a consideration, vent directly through a wall instead of the roof. You could also consider venting the fan through a basement or crawl space. But don't do this if it makes the path to the outdoors longer.

Make sure the general contractor finishes the installation with the wall cap or roof jack provided by the manufacturer to prevent cold drafts blowing over your clients as they step from the bathroom.

HEAT RECOVERY VENTILATION

To keep air quality high and heat loss low in a tight house, fresh air can be brought in through a heat recovery ventilator. In this piece of equipment, available in one-room or whole-house sizes, a pair of fans push outgoing air and incoming air past each other in adjacent but separate channels so that the heat in the outgoing air can preheat the incoming air (or vice versa). These devices typically recover 60% to 85% of the heat which would otherwise be lost when warm inside air is replaced with cold outside air.

These units can be cost-effective in northern climates, especially those with 5,000 degree days or more. (A degree day is a unit of measure used in estimating the energy needs for heating and

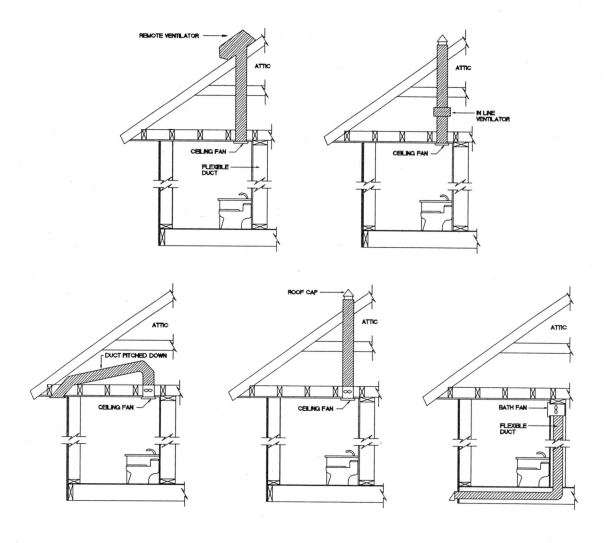

Figure 44   Typical ventilation system ducting methods.

cooling a building.) In Canada, where some areas have a lot of baseboard electric heat, they are mandated by the 1995 National Building Code in new homes with no-duct heating systems. The energy used to power the fans should be much less than the energy that would be required to heat the same amount of air entering a house, but whole-house systems need an experienced designer to get adequate air flow, properly-sized ducts and quiet operation.

The effectiveness of an HRV in removing pollutants from a house is affected by the amount and location of the mixing of fresh and room air. The rotary core on some HRVs has a desiccant coating that transfers moisture between the air streams. This is useful for large homes in cold climates where not enough moisture is generated inside to maintain humidity levels. But it is also important in hot, humid climates where the desiccant removes moisture from incoming air and precools it to lessen the cooling load.

SKYLIGHTS

One often overlooked method of venting baths is the open skylight, which will vent the room if the operable skylight is open. Because hot air rises, an open skylight will allow heated room air and moisture to escape. When used for venting, a skylight that operates by electric motor is more convenient to use than one that opens manually. Even when operable skylights are available, however, clients may not always use them. The cold draft created by an open skylight is least desirable when ventilation is needed most - right after a

shower. A ventilating fan is a more reliable option.

RENOVATION CONSIDERATIONS

When you do your initial pre-design inspection, be sure to check for ventilation. Many homes have no bathroom ventilation. In others, the vent may terminate in the attic. Even if your job entails only a minor change, such as choosing a new vanity and floor covering, be sure to inform your client about the need for adequate ventilation.

To determine if the bathroom is vented to the outside, check the roofline and walls of the house. Look for a roof jack or wall cap. If you do not find any evidence that the fan has been vented outdoors, search the attic. Also, look for evidence of attic moisture damage if the fan terminates in the attic.

Check the function of the fan.

- *Does it look rusty?* If so, condensation may be a problem. You may need to think about rerouting duct work as well as replacing the fan.

- *Is it noisy?* If it is, no wonder the clients aren't using it. Replace it with a quieter model.

- *Does it have a good damper that keeps cold winds from whistling down the duct?* If not, investigate dampers. Choose one with a spring-loaded control. Plan to insulate the duct to keep condensation from occurring.

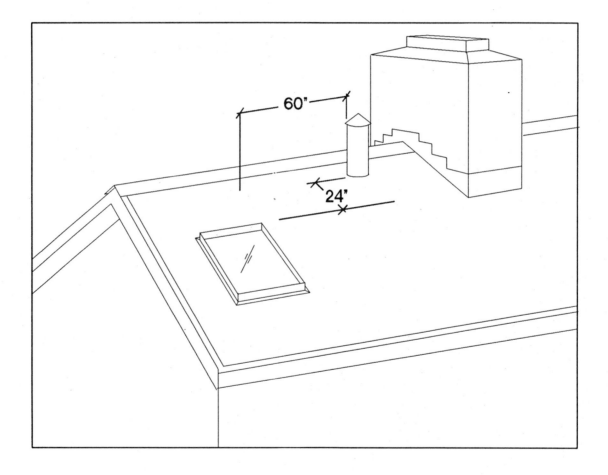

Figure 45   The vent stack must be located away from an operable skylight in a bathroom.

SECTION **6**

Lighting

Good bathroom lighting should first and foremost provide adequate illumination for the task at hand, be it shaving, applying make-up or providing general lighting to the space. It can be designed to be unnoticed or the fixtures can be selected for their decorative nature, becoming part of the bathroom motif. It should create a feeling of spaciousness in a cramped bathroom or provide adequate brightness in the far reaches of a luxury bathroom suite.

A well-designed lighting plan can create a romantic mood for a jetted bathtub for two or simply brighten the mirror to make the morning shave easier. The main purpose of lighting is to compensate for absence of natural light, however, designing the lighting to augument any natural daylight present. To complete your design, you will also help your client select fixtures and lamps. In the lighting industry, **fixtures** are also called **luminaires**. **Bulbs** are called **lamps**.

LIGHTING TERMINOLOGY

To begin our discussion of lighting, the following lighting facts from the **American Lighting Association** will help you become familiar with lighting terms.

Basic Kinds of Lighting

- **General or Ambient Lighting:** Lighting that radiates a comfortable level of brightness, enabling one to see and walk about safely. A basic form of lighting that replaces sunlight, it can be achieved with chandeliers, ceiling or wall-mounted fixtures, recessed or track lights, and with lanterns outside the home.

- **Task Lighting:** Lighting that is focused on a specific task such as reading, sewing, grooming or cooking. Task lighting should be bright enough to prevent eyestrain and can be accomplished with track and recessed lighting and pendant lighting.

Figure 46   A small bathroom features an attractive and functional lighting system.

Figure 47   A large bathroom has an unusual but attractive lighting system above the vanity.

- **Accent Lighting:** A decorative form of lighting that spotlights treasured objects such as paintings and houseplants or highlights the texture of a wall, drapery or outdoor garden. This type of lighting is usually provided by track, recessed or wall-mounted fixtures.

General Lighting Terms

- **Ballast:** A device that limits the electric current flowing into a fluorescent or high intensity discharge lamp.

- **Candle Power:** Intensity of light measured at the lamp. Used for task and accent lighting.

- **Compact Fluorescent Tube:** A smaller type of fluorescent lamp which, with special adapter, can fit easily into incandescent screw-type sockets.

- **Dimmer Control:** A device which is used to vary the light output of an electric lamp.

- **Fluorescent Light:** Light emitted by the electrical stimulation of mercury vapor molecules inside a tubular lamp with an interior coating of phosphors. Saves energy by using one-fifth to one-third as much electricity as incandescents of the same wattage.

- **Footcandle:** The measure of light falling onto a surface. The number is used to determine the amount of light required for a visual task.

- **Halogen (Tungsten-Halogen) Lamp:** An incandescent lamp containing a halogen gas that burns bright white when ignited by a tungsten filament.

- **High-Intensity Discharge Light:** Light emitted by a high-intensity electric lamp containing either mercury vapor, high pressure sodium or metal halide. Generally used in street lighting and for other industrial and commercial purposes, they should not be used for residential applications.

- **Incandescent Light:** Light emitted by an electric lamp in which a metallic (tungsten) filament is burned to incandescence by an electric current.

- **Lamp:** An artificial light source, such as an incandescent bulb or fluorescent tube.

- **Low Voltage Lighting:** The lighting system that utilizes 12-volt current instead of regular 120-volt household current. Requires transformer to reduce current. Produces superior accent lighting when used with tungsten-halogen lamp with built-in reflector. Also useful for under cabinet task lighting and cabinet interiors.

- **Lumens:** The amount of light measured at the light source.

- **Parabolic Reflector Lamp:** Projector type lamp with maximum light output for use in floodlighting and long light throws. Light output is about four times that of a regular incandescent lamp.

- **Reflector Lamp:** Lamp with built-in reflector that either floods or concentrates spotlight on a subject, giving it twice the light output of a regular incandescent lamp.

- **Transformer:** A device which is used to reduce standard 120-volt household current to the 12-volts used in low-voltage lighting systems.

- **Wattage:** The amount of electricity consumed by a light source.

- **Work Plane:** The surface at which an activity to be illuminated takes place. In a bathroom, the work plane would be 29" - 34" above the floor. In a living room, the work plane is assumed at 30".

Lighting Design Terms

- **Cross Lighting:** Lighting objects such as a tree or statue from two or more sides to soften shadows and reveal more detail.

- **Downlighting or Area Lighting:** Lights mounted in ceilings to cast broad illumination over wide areas and in soffit boards to illuminate vanity areas.

- **Grazing:** Lighting objects such as tile or masonry walls up close to throw light across their surface and highlight their texture.

- **Lightscaping:** The effective, creative use of outdoor lighting for security, recreation, convenience and decorative purposes.

- **Shadowing:** Lighting an object from the front and below to create intriguing shadows on a wall or other vertical rear surface.

- **Moonlighting:** Lights are aimed downward among tree branches to recreate moonlight filtering through branches, casting attractive shadow.

- **Silhouetting:** Lighting an object from behind and below to create a striking silhouette of the object against a solid backdrop.

- **Spread or Diffused Lighting:** Circular pattern of light cast downward to illuminate a focal point.

- **Spotlighting:** Lights focus a controlled intense beam to highlight an object, open shelf area or art.

- **Uplighting:** Lights aimed upward creating a highly dramatic effect akin to the theatre.

NATURAL LIGHT

Nothing beats natural light for warmth and area lighting and there may be another reason to maximize natural light as well. Researchers are discovering a growing link between lighting and health.

Health Concerns

Ultraviolet light is necessary for our bodies to synthesize vitamin D, which in turn is necessary for calcium absorption. Windowless offices, air pollution and long winters indoors all reduce our exposure to natural light.

No one knows exactly how much light we need to stay healthy. Estimates in the scientific community range from 15 minutes to two hours or more. However, it generally is agreed that the more natural light we get, the better.

Research conducted at the **Massachusetts Institute of Technology** and the **National Institute of Mental Health** report other links between light and health. Studies there suggest a link between inadequate light and increased fatigue, decreased performance, diminished immunological defenses and possibly impaired fertility.

These are significant considerations to keep in mind for bathroom planners, since homeowners spend a great deal of their time indoors. It is particularly critical in areas with lengthy winters.

Window Placement

Window placement is the most obvious area where planners can make a difference in designing a healthy, warmly lit home. Not only do they provide light, but windows provide ventilation, views and emergency exits as well.

Windows primarily intended for lighting should be wide and high on the wall. A warm diffuse light will spread from the window and reflect off the light-colored ceiling. North-facing windows, which do not get sunlight, should be lower, closer to the floor and larger.

Skylight Planning

Skylights and roof windows also bring light, air and even heat. In cooler, cloudy climates, it's best to place the skylight so that it faces to the south and west. Low-E glazed skylights should be considered if the skylight faces north. In warmer climates, north- and east-facing skylights are preferred. This orientation has less heat build up than windows facing south and west. If you are not taking advantage of a view, avoid clear roof windows. Clear glass projects a "hard" beam of light, shaped like the skylight opening, onto the floor. Bronze-colored skylights aren't much better. They simply cast a dimmer version of the same shape. White opal acrylic skylights, however, diffuse and soften the natural light, producing a gentle light that fills the whole room.

If you are dealing with a remodeling with pre-existing skylights that are clear or bronze, consider installing a white acrylic panel at or above the ceiling line to soften the light they cast. The shaft of the skylight can also house light fixtures. This keeps the light shaft from becoming a black hole after dark. Skylights and roof windows should have ultraviolet filters to prevent the sun from bleaching natural fabrics and rugs. Low-E glazed skylights are available from manufacturers.

ARTIFICIAL LIGHTING

Successful bathrooms have a balance of all three lighting types. They are:

- General lighting

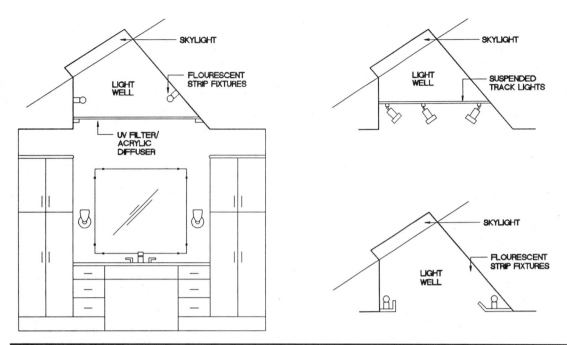

Figure 48   A skylight's light well is also a good place to install lighting fixtures.

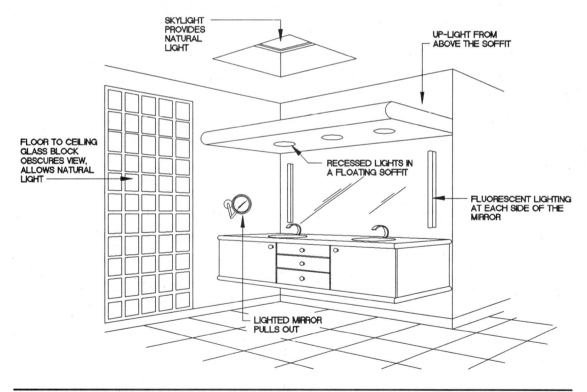

Figure 49   A well-designed vanity area which employs several types of light source.

- Task lighting

- Accent lighting

General lighting provides eye-pleasing illumination of an entire room and protects against accidents.

Task lighting concentrates light at specific locations, such as at a vanity top or above a soaking bathtub (for reading).

Accent lighting is used for interest and for highlighting objects. It can dramatize focal points in a space and add sparkle to the overall lighting scheme. In a bathroom, for example, you might want to accent artwork or highlight a decorative bathtub faucet.

Lighting Effects

General, task and accent lighting are achieved by any one, or a combination of, three different lighting effects. These include the following:

- **Downlight**

- **Indirect light**

- **Uplight**

DOWNLIGHT

A downlight shines straight down on the area it illuminates. Recessed, semi-recessed and surface-mounted downlights appear to blend with the ceiling, making them the most unobtrusive light source available. Recessed downlights are round or square metal canisters installed in the soffit or ceiling between the joists.

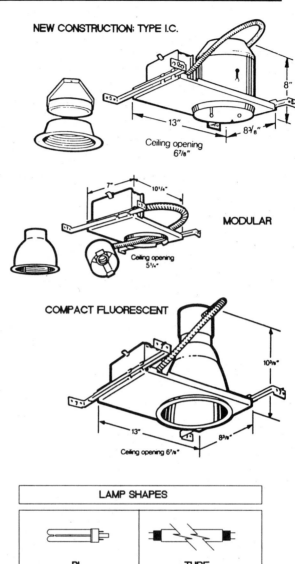

NEW CONSTRUCTION: TYPE I.C.

MODULAR

COMPACT FLUORESCENT

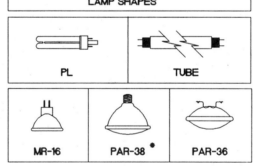

LAMP SHAPES	
PL	TUBE
MR-16	PAR-38 *	PAR-36

* NOTE: VERSIONS OF SOME LAMPS NO LONGER MEET E-PACT STANDARDS. HOWEVER, HALOGEN VERSIONS OF MANY PAR LAMPS DO MEET THE NEW STANDARDS

Figure 50   Recessed ceiling lights are mounted in brackets that are hidden above ceiling level. Recessed fixtures can trap light. Make sure you select the best lamp and fixture design to maximize the beam spread and the amount of light which will reach the surface below the fixtures. Non-Halogen, PAR-38, R-30 and R-40 lamps are now banned from manufacture in the United States by federal law.

Downlights create pools of light and are best used over counter space and general floor area. Beam width depends on the distance between the light and receiving surface and on the beam angle of lamp.

Avoid placing incandescent downlights directly above seating locations. The hot beam of light feels uncomfortable, even if the lamp's illumination is needed for reading. You should also avoid placing a single downlight above a working surface because it could put the worker in his/her own shadow. Two downlights above, placed side by side, would avoid this problem with spillover light. In cold climates, if the recessed canister is placed in a cathedral ceiling without proper insulation, water vapor can condense on the cold metal. Drops of water from the recessed fixture may

drip on occupants. Recessed lights also provide perfect pathways for moisture to enter the attic. This is not desirable because the moisture may condense on the underside of the roof sheathing. A special vapor barrier housing is made for recessed canister fixtures.

Another form of downlighting can be created by building a light box out of a decorative material or standard North American construction 2x4 framing, and installing fluorescent tubes within this enclosure. A frosted or eggcrate diffuser is then installed in the bottom of this *light box*. In the past, many designers have avoided using fluorescent lights in a bathroom design. As you will learn later, excellent color rendition is possible with fluorescent lamps; therefore, they are a viable option for bathroom areas.

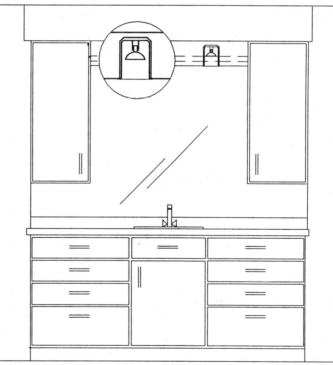

Figure 51   A 3/4" valance panel above the vanity can house a low-voltage, halogen light fixture.

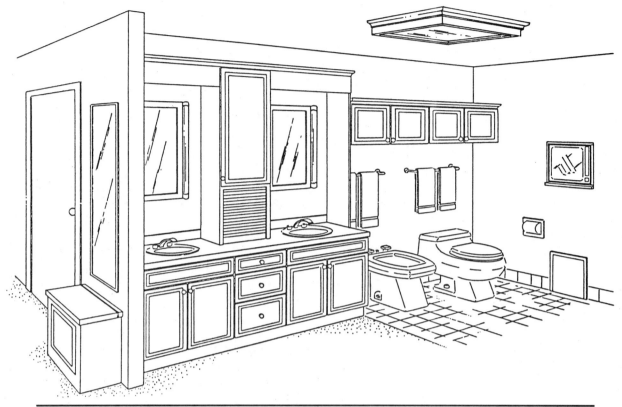

Figure 52 A custom built light box above a toilet area houses color-corrected fluorescent lights.

INDIRECT LIGHT

Indirect light is light beamed toward a ceiling or wall. The light bouncing off that surface illuminates the room. More restful to the eyes, indirect lighting reduces the useful light in the room because some of that light is absorbed by the wall surface. Indirect lighting can be concealed in soffits or by valances.

UPLIGHT

Uplighting is a form of indirect lighting. It is often used to make a room look more intimate. Uplighting can be concealed behind a crown molding. For an even wash of light, fixtures should overlap behind the molding rather than being placed end to end. Otherwise, pools of light will be created. Uplights can also be placed near planters to throw dra-

matic shadows of leaves against the wall or ceiling.

Be careful when using uplighting however. Any imperfections in the wall surface or ceiling will be highlighted by the subtle shadows created by light that skims the wall surfaces. (Flat paints minimize imperfections.) Never plan such a system for a bathroom with a glossy ceiling surface.

Uplights can also be unflattering to people's faces and in fact can create a ghoulish appearance. Reserve their use for areas where people's faces will not be illuminated by the uplight.

MEASURING LIGHT

There are many ways to measure light. Manufacturer's specifications list

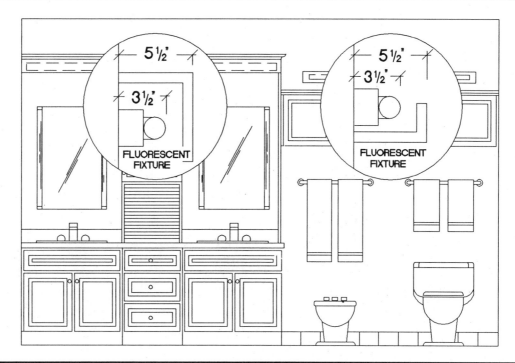

Figure 53 An indirect lighting system can be created by concealing a fixture behind a custom molding in a grooming area.

similar information in a variety of ways. This makes it confusing for the bathroom planner to determine just what is appropriate.

The factors that measure light and that can be used to determine the proper amount of illumination are:

- **Lumen:** The light intensity or raw lighting horsepower of a lamp. Every light source has a lumen value, measured at the lamp.

- **Candle Power:** The directional light intensity of a lamp. A spotlight will have a higher candle power than a floodlight, although the lumen value is the same. Only directional lamps (i.e. floodlight, spotlight, narrow spotlight etc.) are given a candle power value. Candle power is measured at the lamp and is expressed in candelas.

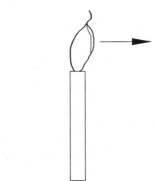

Figure 54 The candela is the light produced by one candle in one direction.

- **Footcandle:** The unit of measurement used to indicate the amount of light falling on a given surface. The goal of all functional lighting design is to provide a certain footcandle level to a surface adequate for the intended task. For bathrooms, the recommended foot candle level is 30 - 50 footcandles depending on the age of the user and the colors used in the room.

Light Source Efficiency

Measuring energy efficiency is less complicated than measuring light output. It is calculated by the measure of how much light is produced - measured in lumens - in relation to the amount of energy used - measured in watts.

Lumens-per-watt ratings are similar to the miles per gallon rating of cars. Some light sources convert electricity into light much more efficiently than others. This means they can deliver more light for the same amount of electricity.

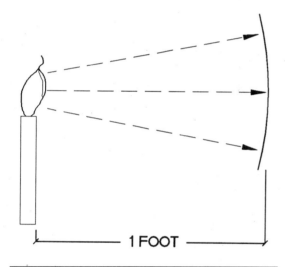

── 1 FOOT ──

Figure 55   A footcandle is the amount of light thrown on a 1 square foot surface, 1 foot away, by an ordinary wax candle.

The Continuing Impact of EPACT

November 1, 1995 was the deadline for full impact of the Energy Policy Act of 1992 (EPACT) as it was written, although the act mandates further revisions (with deadlines) that will change lamps and fixtures until at least the year 2005, and probably beyond. EPACT requires state governments to incorporate all energy efficiency standards into building codes.

The legislation sets standards for incandescent reflector lamps and general service fluorescent lamps. These standards cover lumens per watt (LPW) and color rendering. They encourage use of halogen PAR lamps over conventional incandescent lamps. In general, full wattage (40W, 75W and 110W) fluorescent lamps have been eliminated to encourage energy saving 34W, 60W and 95W types. This rules out use of commonly used 4' medium bi-pin tubes, 2' U-shaped tubes, 8' slimline and 8' high output tubes.

Color rendering standards allow the cheaper halophosphor colors (such as warm white and cool white) only in reduced-wattage or energy-saver types. Full-wattage types will be available only in rare earth (triphosphor) colors which are more efficient and render color better.

The designer should be aware that lamp performance standards will become stricter, so relamping to today's minimum standards may require further retrofitting in the future. The safest course is to invest in the most energy-efficient technologies available when the job is being done.

INCANDESCENT LIGHTING

Efficiency

The incandescent lamp is the most common lighting source in American homes. It produces a gentle warm light in most applications. Incandescent lamps are widely available and inexpensive. Unfortunately, it is also the least energy efficient light source available. Many of which have been discontinued due to EPACT. Ninety percent of the energy consumed by an incandescent lamp is given off as heat rather than visible light. This is because incandescents do not directly convert electricity to light. Rather, they use electricity to heat a coiled tungsten filament in a vacuum or inert gas-filled bulb until the filament glows.

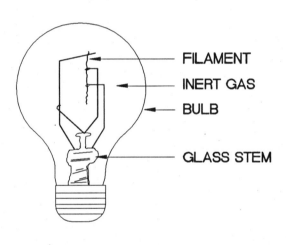

FILAMENT

INERT GAS

BULB

GLASS STEM

Figure 56 How an incandescent lamp produces light.

Lamps

There are hundreds of types, sizes and finishes of incandescent lamps. Their shape and size are designed by a code consisting of one or more letters and a number. The letters designate the shape; and the number indicates the di-

ameter of the bulb in eighths of an inch. *For example,* an A-19 lamp is of the standard "A" shape and is 19/8ths of an inch, or 2 3/8 inches, in diameter. (Lamps also are being manufactured in compact sizes, with A lamps in 25, 40, 50, 60, 75 and 100 watts all having the same diameter.) Many of these lamps now come in halogen, but none qualify under EPACT.

In addition to standard lamps, there are decorative lamps that can be used in fixtures where the lamps are exposed. The CA, F and B bulbs are flame-shaped lamps with different bases and slightly different shapes.

Most of the bases on incandescent lamps are screw-type. Bases vary in size according to the wattage and use of the lamp.

Lamp Lifespan

A lamp's lifespan is measured in hours and is printed on the packaging. Incandescent lamps have the shortest life span of all available lamps. In addition, before the end of the bulb lifetime, the light output decreases to 20% of its original level. This is because the heated coiled tungsten filament evaporates with use, releasing molecules of the metal which coat the surface of the bulb and slowly cause the bulb to darken. As it darkens, the lamp consumes almost the same amount of energy it did when it was new, yet it emits less light. In addition, because the filament becomes thinner with use, it also has increasingly higher electrical resistance. This further reduces the lamp's efficiency. The bulb eventually burns out when the filament ruptures.

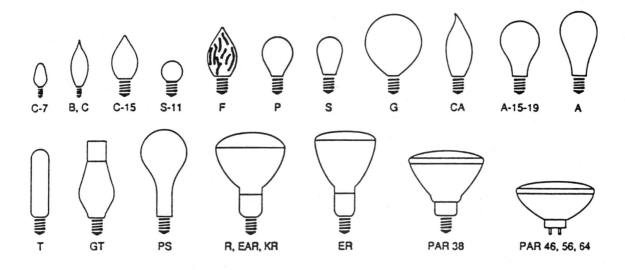

Figure 57   Each lamp shape has its own letter code. The number associated with the lamp is its diameter.

Long-life lamps (which last from 1,500 to 3,500 hours) are less energy efficient than regular life incandescent lamps because the filament is operated at a lower temperature to extend its life. Energy-conscious bathroom planners should specify long-life bulbs only where replacement is difficult, or should consider replacing or converting incandescent lamps to fluorescent lamps (which have a life of more than 10,000 hours).

Attempts to increase the efficiency and extend the life of incandescent lamps have led to the development of a number of energy-saving incandescent lamps for limited residential use.

Reflector Lamps: Reflector or R-lamps are incandescent lamps with an interior coating of aluminum that reflects light to the front of the bulb. Certain light fixtures, such as recessed or directional fixtures, trap light inside. Reflector lamps reduce this loss by projecting light out of the fixture and into the room, so that more light is delivered

where it is needed. In these fixtures, a 50-watt reflector bulb provides equivalent lighting and uses less energy than a 100-watt standard incandescent bulb.

Reflector lamps are appropriate for accent and task lighting and are available in 25, 30, 50, 75 and 100 watts. While they have a lower initial efficiency (lumens per watt) than regular incandescents, the ability to control the direction of light at the task makes them more effective.

Projector lamps (known as PAR, for their "*Parabolic*" shape) are another directional light source. They are used to produce spot or floodlighting. However, they differ from the reflector lamps in shape and can be used indoors or outdoors since rain, snow or temperature changes will not crack the glass.

An eventual aim of EPACT is to replace all R and PAR incandescent lamps with halogen equivalents.

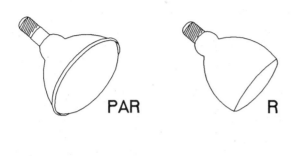

Figure 58 *Typical reflector and PAR lamps.*

FLUORESCENT LIGHTING

Light Output

Because of the energy efficiency advantage that fluorescent lighting offers over incandescent lighting (almost three times more energy efficient), it is becoming more popular with bathroom planners. More options are available than ever before too, thanks, in part, to a prod by regulatory officials to use fluorescents. California, for example, requires that general lighting in the kitchen and bathroom be fluorescent.

Lamps

Fluorescent lamps convert electric power to visible light by using an electric charge to "*excite*" gaseous atoms. These atoms emit ultraviolet radiation which is absorbed by the phosphor on the tube walls. The phosphor coating produces the visible light. These lamps require a ballast, a small transformer that provides the high voltage necessary to initiate the charge. The ballast also regulates the current that flows through the tube. Fluorescent lamps convert elec-tricity to visible light up to five times more efficiently than incandescent lamps and last up to 20 times longer.

Fluorescent lamps require special fixtures, but there are many more lamp shapes and sizes than in the past. The fixture for the standard, straight fluorescent tube consists of a metal channel that contains the ballast. Most fluorescent lamps with a 40-watt rating or less require a small device to start the lamp called a starter. The start-up delay associated with this type of fluorescent lamp is brief; the lamp will flicker when first turned on. "*Rapid start*" fluorescent lamps go on immediately without flickering. This is the type of fixture you should use. Clients might be annoyed by the flicker of standard fluorescent tubes.

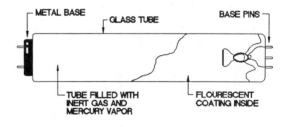

Figure 59 *How a fluorescent lamp produces light.*

New electronic ballasts have been introduced in fluorescent fixtures to replace the old "wire windings" ballasts. Essentially a transformer, the new ballast uses electronic components to produce the amount of current necessary to excite the lamp. These new ballasts use less wattage, are more energy efficient, produce less heat and will last longer than the old windings ballasts.

Relatively new are lightweight, straight fixtures without the traditional magnetic core-coil ballast. These fixtures use a resistor to limit the current flow. Though this type of fixture is smaller, the resistor ballast is much more efficient than the standard magnetic fixtures.

U-shaped and circular fluorescent tubes are also available. With adapters, circular fluorescent lamps can be used in conventional incandescent sockets. The adapter contains the ballast and holds the fluorescent tube. This system could be considered if you find a fixture of a particular design that appeals to your client.

Compact fluorescent lamps (CFs) are gaining in popularity. Some look similar to incandescent lamps. Some have screw bases (designated as SP) to replace incandescents; others (PL) plug

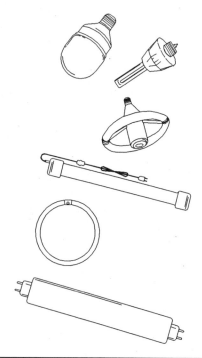

Figure 60 Fluorescent lamps now come in compact sizes for greater flexibility in fixture design.

into adapters with integral electronic ballasts. The adapters screw into conventional sockets. Some are "short fluorescents" with an integral starter, for operation with preheat electromagnetic ballasts. Most have a 10,000-hour average life, although a few are rated at 8,000 hours and some high-lumen CFs last 20,000 hours. Integral electronic ballasts are instant-start and have eliminated the hum and flicker that used to be associated with CFs.

Dimming Fluorescent Lights

Many designers are under the incorrect assumption that fluorescent lights cannot be dimmed. If a special ballast is purchased and installed in a fluorescent fixture, a fluorescent rheostat switch can be used to offer multiple levels of fluorescent light within a bathroom space. Many new fluorescent lamps have dimmable ballasts in the base. This can enhance a master suite you might be planning. They are however expensive and sometimes difficult to obtain.

LOW-VOLTAGE LIGHTING

Halogen lamps have been used for decades in car headlights and slide projectors. They are now speeding into the home as a major new light source alternative. They are replacing the more inefficient incandescent A, R and PAR lamps. They consume about half the power and last up to seven times longer than standard light bulbs. The light quality from halogen is whiter, lacking the typically yellowish color produced by ordinary incandescent bulbs.

The halogen lamp, like its forerunner, has tungsten wire filaments that are heated until they give off light. In a standard incandescent lamp, the burning tungsten particles are gradually deposited on the inside of the glass bulb, which wears away the elements, darkens the glass and eventually reduces the light. In the new halogen lamp, halogen gas surrounds the filament, offering a regenerative life by redepositing the burning tungsten particles on the filament. That is why the bulb lasts longer (about 2,000 hours) and provides a consistently higher light output.

Low-voltage lighting uses less energy and can be an especially effective light source for indirect or spot lighting. Standard 120-volt current is passed through a transformer. The voltage drops down to 12 volts. Smaller light fixtures can then be run on this stepped-down, low-voltage. For concealed lighting in valances or for recessed soffit lighting, the small low-voltage lamps could be perfect. Or, for a single, subtle spotlight on a bathroom planter or artwork, a low-voltage spot can provide the perfect accent. The small lamp and bulb sizes make low-voltage lighting increasingly popular.

Light levels with low-voltage lighting are relatively easy to figure. Each lamp is rated for both wattage and beam spread. The rating stamp will tell you whether the lamp is a flood (FL), a spot (SP), a narrow spot (NSP), or a very narrow spot (VNSP). The beam spread depends on the lamp's height above the floor or countertop. Technical data on illumination levels can be ordered from the manufacturer. Add more fixtures or more powerful lamps to raise the illumination level.

Note: There are now many **halogen lamps** in larger sizes that work on standard voltage.

BRIGHTNESS RELATIONSHIPS

Understanding the types of light sources available will not guarantee a successful lighting plan unless brightness relationships also are figured into the equation. Lighting designers use the following terms to describe brightness relationships:

- **Brightness** is the intensity of light from an object or surface that directly reaches they eye of the viewer.

- **Contrast** is the brightness difference between surfaces in the field of view. When little contrast exists, the lighting plan provides shadowless illumination. *For example,* indirect light plans which provide light through reflection (ambient illumination) eliminate any shadows within the space. Remember however, that some shadowing is necessary to perceive an object as a three dimensional form. Shadows can add depth and interest.

- **Glare** is the unwanted brightness that annoys, distracts or reduces visibility.

- **Sparkle** or **glitter** are the small areas of high brightness which are desirable to provide sensory stimulation. The interplay of light attracts the eye, alerts the mind and brings sparks of life in the room. Often called a **focal glow**, the highlighted area can be an effective part of any plan.

Regardless of size or shape, every bathroom needs general and task lighting. Accent lighting with a decorative fixture also adds sparkle. The relationship between these various light sources forms the brightness pattern of the system.

The human eye responds to reflected light. Extreme contrast between high and low areas of brightness can strain the eye and cause visual discomfort. *For example*, a bathroom with black fixtures and a white laminate countertop would be challenging to light effectively. However, some contrast is essential if vision is to be comfortable.

While a soft, diffused light minimizes shadows, it can be dull and unpleasant. Dropped ceilings with panels of fluorescent fixtures provide an even, but monotonous, light. The artful use of hard light provides highlights that emphasize texture and shape. The challenge is to control reflected light for optimum effect.

- To provide the proper brightness relationships in a bathroom, each area should be divided into three zones.

- The first is the task area itself (such as the makeup mirror).

- The second zone is the area immediately surrounding the task area. The lighting level in the second zone (the area adjacent to the mirror) should be no greater than in the first zone and no less than one-third of the level in the first zone.

- The third zone is the general surrounding space, allow about one third the light level of task lighting or zone one.

The light level relationship between these areas is critical to preventing brightness contrasts that can be tiring to the eyes.

COLOR RENDITION

Brightness relationships are only one of the factors in designing a lighting plan. Color rendition, which is measured by a **Color Rendition Index (CRI)** is just as important in lighting aesthetics, particularly with fluorescent lamps. Color rendition is difficult to evaluate objectively. The color that our eyes "*see*" is the effect of light waves bouncing off, or passing through, various objects. The color of a given object, therefore, is determined in part by the characteristics of the light source under which it is viewed.

Color rendition, then, is a relative term; it refers to the extent to which the perceived color of an object under a light source matches the perceived color of that object under another source (such as daylight or incandescent lighting). On a scale of 1 to 100, with 100 being the color rendition closest to daylight, incandescent light typically has a CRI of about 95. Fluorescent lamps can range from 50 - 90 CRI.

Formerly, fluorescent lamps made clients look pale in the bathroom mirror. However, in response to criticism of poor color rendition, most manufacturers of fluorescents have introduced lamps that use color-correcting phosphors. The newer compact fluorescents also contain special phosphors needed to light skin well.

If your clients are hesitant about choosing a fluorescent fixture, you may want to suggest trying out several different lamps in a lighting store or your

EPACT at a Glance—Substitution Options

Special Note: Applications subject to the following conditions require use of full wattage lamps (*) from the "Minimum Compliance" column.

- Ambient temperatures below 60° F
- Dimming ballasts
- Cold temperature ballasts
- Low power factor ballasts in shoplights, residential fixtures, etc. (check with ballast manufacturer)

F96T12 SLIMLINE — Effective May 1, 1994

Non-Complying Lamps	Most Efficient System (Ballast change required)	Good Retrofit (See Note above)	Minimum Compliance (See Note above)	Exempt Lamps (Still available)
F96T12/CW (75W, COOL WHITE)	FO96/841 (4100K, 85CRI, OCTRON) FO96/741 (4100K, 75CRI, OCTRON)	F96T12/D841/SS (60W, 4100K, 80CRI) F96T12/D41/SS (60W, 4100K, 70CRI)	F96T12/CW/SS (60W, COOL WHITE, 62CRI) F96T12/D841* (75W, 4100K, 80CRI) F96T12/D41* (75W, 4100K, 70CRI)	F96T12/CWX (89CRI, COOL WHITE DELUXE) F96T12/DSGN50 (90CRI, DESIGN 50) F96T12/N (86CRI, NATURAL) F96T12/GO (GOLD) F96T12/GRO (GRO-LUX) F96T12/GRO/WS (GRO-LUX WIDE SPECTRUM)
F96T12/W (75W, WHITE)	FO96/835 (3500K, 85CRI, OCTRON) FO96/735 (3500K, 75CRI, OCTRON)	F96T12/D835/SS (60W, 3500K, 80CRI) F96T12/D35/SS (60W, 3500K, 70CRI)	F96T12/W/SS (60W, WHITE, 57CRI) F96T12/D835* (75W, 3500K, 80CRI) F96T12/D35* (75W, 3500K, 70CRI)	
F96T12/WW (75W, WARM WHITE)	FO96/830 (3000K, 85CRI, OCTRON) FO96/730 (3000K, 75CRI, OCTRON)	F96T12/D830/SS (60W, 3000K, 80CRI) F96T12/D30/SS (60W, 3000K, 70CRI)	F96T12/WW/SS (60W, WARM WHITE, 52CRI) F96T12/D830* (75W, 3000K, 80CRI) F96T12/D30* (75W, 3000K, 70CRI)	
F96T12/D (75W, DAYLIGHT)		F96T12/D865/SS (60W, 6500K, 80CRI)	F96T12/D865* (75W, 6500K, 80CRI)	

F96T12/HO HIGH OUTPUT — Effective May 1, 1994

Non-Complying Lamps	Most Efficient System	Good Retrofit	Minimum Compliance	Exempt Lamps
F96T12/CW/HO (110W, COOL WHITE)		F96T12/D41/HO/SS (95W, 4100K, 70CRI)	F96T12/CW/HO/SS (95W, COOL WHITE, 62CRI) F96T12/LW/HO/SS (95W, LITE WHITE, 48CRI) F96T12/D41/HO* (110W, 4100K, 70CRI)	F96T12/CWX/HO (89CRI, COOL WHITE DELUXE) F96T12/DSGN50/HO (90CRI, DESIGN 50) F96T12/N/HO (86CRI, NATURAL) F96T12/GO/HO (GOLD) F96T12/GRO/HO/WS (GRO-LUX WIDE SPECTRUM)
F96T12/W/HO (110W, WHITE)		F96T12/D35/HO/SS (95W, 3500K, 70CRI)	F96T12/D35/HO* (110W, 3500K, 70CRI)	
F96T12/WW/HO (110W, WARM WHITE)		F96T12/D30/HO/SS (95W, 3000K, 70CRI)	F96T12/WW/HO/SS (95W, WARM WHITE, 52CRI) F96T12/D30/HO* (110W, 3000K, 70CRI)	
F96T12D/HO (110W, DAYLIGHT)			F96T12/D865/HO* (110W, 6500K, 80CRI)	

F40T12 — Effective November 1, 1995

Non-Complying Lamps	Most Efficient System	Good Retrofit	Minimum Compliance	Exempt Lamps
F40CW (40W, COOL WHITE)	F032/841 (4100K, 85CRI, OCTRON) F032/741 (4100K, 75CRI, OCTRON)	F40/D841/SS (34W, 4100K, 80CRI) F40/D41/SS (34W, 4100K, 70CRI)	F40CW/SS (34W, COOL WHITE, 62CRI) F40/D841* (40W, 4100K, 80CRI) F40/D41* (40W, 4100K, 70CRI)	F40CWX (89CRI, COOL WHITE DELUXE) F40/DSGN50 (90CRI, DESIGN 50) F40N (86CRI, NATURAL) F40G (GREEN) F40GO (GOLD) F40B (BLUE) F40GRO (GRO-LUX) F40GRO/WS (GRO-LUX WIDE SPECTRUM)
F40W (40W, WHITE)	F032/835 (3500K, 85CRI, OCTRON) F032/735 (3500K, 75CRI, OCTRON)	F40/D835/SS (34W, 3500K, 80CRI) F40/D35/SS (34W, 3500K, 70CRI)	F40W/SS (34W, WHITE, 57CRI) F40/D835* (40W, 3500K, 80CRI) F40/D35* (40W, 3500K, 70CRI)	
F40WW (40W, WARM WHITE) F40WWX (40W, WARM WHITE DELUXE) F40WWX/SS (34W, WARM WHITE DELUXE)	F032/830 (3000K, 85CRI, OCTRON) F032/730 (3000K, 75CRI, OCTRON)	F40/D830/SS (34W, 3000K, 80CRI) F40/D30/SS (34W, 3000K, 70CRI)	F40WW/SS (34W, WARM WHITE, 52CRI) F40/D830* (40W, 3000K, 80CRI) F40/D30* (40W, 3000K, 70CRI)	
F40D (40W, DAYLIGHT) F40D/SS (34W, DAYLIGHT)	F032/750 (5000K, 75CRI, OCTRON)	F40/D865/SS (34W, 6500K, 80CRI)	F40/D865* (40W, 6500K, 80CRI)	

FB40/6 CURVALUME "U-Lamp" — Effective November 1, 1995

Non-Complying Lamps	Most Efficient System	Good Retrofit	Minimum Compliance	Exempt Lamps
FB40/CW/6 (40W, COOL WHITE)	FB032/841/6 (4100K, 85CRI, OCTRON) FB032/741/6 (4100K, 75CRI, OCTRON)	FB40/D41/6/SS (34W, 4100K, 70CRI)	F40/CW/6/SS (34W, COOL WHITE, 62CRI) FB40/D41/6* (40W, 4100K, 70CRI)	FB40/CWX/6 (89CRI, COOL WHITE DELUXE)
FB40/W/6 (40W, WHITE)	FB032/835/6 (3500K, 85CRI, OCTRON) FB032/735/6 (3500K, 75CRI, OCTRON)	FB40/D35/6/SS (34W, 3500K, 70CRI)	F40/W/6/SS (34W, WHITE, 57CRI) FB40/D35/6* (40W, 3500K, 70CRI)	
FB40/WW/6 (40W, WARM WHITE) FB40/WWX/6 (40W, WARM WHITE DELUXE)	FB032/830/6 (3000K, 85CRI, OCTRON) FB032/730/6 (3000K, 75CRI, OCTRON)	FB40/D30/6/SS (34W, 3000K, 70CRI)	FB40/WW/6/SS (34W, WARM WHITE, 52CRI) FB40/D830* (40W, 3000K, 80CRI) FB40/D30* (40W, 3000K, 70CRI)	

INCANDESCENT REFLECTOR LAMPS — Effective November 1, 1995

Non-Complying Lamps	Best Complying Retrofit	Suitable Substitute	Exempt Lamps (Still available)
75PAR38	45PAR/CAPSYLITE	50PAR30/CAPSYLITE	COLORED TYPES ROUGH SERVICE ER SHAPED BR SHAPED
100PAR38	75PAR/CAPSYLITE	75ER30	
150PAR38	90PAR/CAPSYLITE	75PAR/CAPSYLITE	
75/65PAR38	45PAR/CAPSYLITE	50PAR30/CAPSYLITE	
100/80PAR38	75PAR/CAPSYLITE	75ER30	
150/120PAR38	90PAR/CAPSYLITE	75PAR/CAPSYLITE	
75R30	50PAR30LONGNECK/CAPSYLITE	50ER30	
75R40	45PAR/CAPSYLITE/VERY WIDE FLOOD	50ER30	
100R40	75PAR/CAPSYLITE	75ER30	
150R40	90PAR/CAPSYLITE	120ER40	
200R40	150PAR/CAPSYLITE	120ER40	

Figure 61 (Courtesy of Sylvania)   Identifying light sources and substitution options based on the energy policy act of 1992 (EPACT).

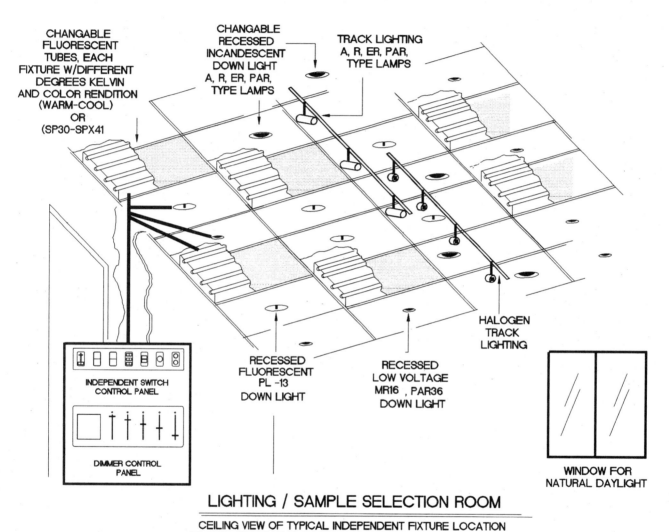

CHANGABLE
FLUORESCENT
TUBES, EACH
FIXTURE W/DIFFERENT
DEGREES KELVIN
AND COLOR RENDITION
(WARM-COOL)
OR
(SP30-SPX41

CHANGABLE
RECESSED
INCANDESCENT
DOWN LIGHT
A, R, ER, PAR,
TYPE LAMPS

TRACK LIGHTING
A, R, ER, PAR,
TYPE LAMPS

INDEPENDENT SWITCH
CONTROL PANEL

DIMMER CONTROL
PANEL

RECESSED
FLUORESCENT
PL -13
DOWN LIGHT

RECESSED
LOW VOLTAGE
MR16 , PAR36
DOWN LIGHT

HALOGEN
TRACK
LIGHTING

WINDOW FOR
NATURAL DAYLIGHT

LIGHTING / SAMPLE SELECTION ROOM

CEILING VIEW OF TYPICAL INDEPENDENT FIXTURE LOCATION
ON GRID SYSTEM FOR EASY LAMP AND FIXTURE CHANGE OUT

Figure 62 Preparing a multi-light area in the showroom.

showroom to find a lamp that gives acceptable skin color. Samples of wallpaper, countertop material, tile and paint should also be checked so they can see if the colors are acceptable under the light source. **Nick Geragi**, CKD, CBD, NCIDQ certified (NKBA Director of Education and Product Development) recommends setting up an area of the showroom to preview different fixture and lamp combinations.

Different options in switches and dimmers can also be part of the preview package.

COLOR TEMPERATURE

Color temperature describes whether a light source has warm or cool tones. Color temperature is different from color rendition. The latter describes how accurately a light source represents an object's color. Color temperature, on the other hand, is related to aesthetics rather than accuracy.

Light from an incandescent-filament source is warm in color quality and imparts a friendly feeling. Under this light source, warm colors (oranges, reds and browns) are enhanced, while cool colors (blues and greens) are subdued. Generally when the overall atmosphere of a room is on the warm side, the full values of the warm colors will be enhanced when lighted with filament lamps. Blues and greens in fabrics, wallcoverings and paint will be muted or changed in color. The inverse is true of cool lamps in a cool color scheme. Neutral lamps affect the colors in a room the least.

Low color temperatures emit warm or redder tones, while high color temperatures emit cool or blue tones. The low color temperatures (warm tones) generally are preferred for residential use as they are more flattering.

Some labels describe the color temperatures by numerical degrees. Cool color temperatures range between 3,800°- 5,000° Kelvin, while warm color temperatures generally are less than 3,500°K. For the best color rendition, pick lamps with a color temperature between 3,000° Kelvin and 4,000° Kelvin. For the best color rendition choose lamps with a color temperature between 3,000° Kelvin and 4,000° Kelvin.

Above this range, skin starts looking too green; below this, it starts looking too yellow. The following chart shows the variation in lamp temperature, color rendition and light output.

CHOOSING THE CORRECT LAMP

Lamps with the same color temperature may have different CRIs and different efficiencies. The CRI of the fluorescent lamp is determined by the bulb's phosphor coating. Do not confuse color temperature with the CRI. Most package labels provide the color temperature but do not provide the lamp's CRI, and yet both are needed to fine tune color rendition. The manufacturer or electrical supply outlet usually will have this information.

Characteristics of Common Lamps (Sylvania)

Color Type	Lamp	Color Temp K	CRI	Lumens	Watts
Compact Fluorescent	Dulux S	2700, 3500, 4100, 5000	82	230, 400, 580, 800	5, 7, 9, 13
	Dulux S/E	2700, 4100, 3000	82	230, 400, 580, 800	5, 7, 9, 13
	Dulux D	2700, 3000, 3500, 4100	82	525, 780, 1250, 1825	9, 13, 18, 26
	Dulux D/E	2700, 3000, 3500, 4100	82	600, 900, 1250, 1825	10, 13, 18, 26
	Dulux EL Quad	2700	82	600, 900, 1200, 1500	11, 15, 20, 23
	Dulux EL R	2700	82	600, 900	11, 15
	Soft White Dulux EL G	3000	82	725, 1000	15, 20
Linear Fluorescent	T-12 F40CWX/SS	Deluxe Cool White	100	1925	34
	T-12 F40/D835	Designer 800	100	3300	40
	T-12 F40WW/SS	Warm White SuperSaver	100	2750	34
Incandescent	A-19 25A	Inside frost	100	210	25
	A-19 40A/RP	Clear	100	460	40
	A-21 50/150/ DLSW/SP	Double Life Soft White, 3-way	100	580, 1400, 1980	50, 100, 150
	A-19 60A/W/ DLSW/RP	Double Life Soft White	100	800	60
Tungsten Halogen	MB-19 Halogen A-Line	Inside Frost	100	1300	75
	MB-19 A-Line	Inside Frost Capsylite	100	960, 1850	60, 100
	75PAR 30	Flood Capsylite	100	1100	75
	60PAR 38	Flood Capsylite	100	900	60
	20MR16	Reflector Rim Mount (12v)	100	5000 CBCP	20

These are selected household lamps from hundreds in the 1996 Sylvania Product Catalog. Color temperature is listed only for compact fluorescent lamps. EL=Dimmable, electronic ballast. G=Globe shape. CBCP=Center Beam Candle Power. SuperSavers not to be used in fixtures with starters.

REFLECTION AND COLOR

Reflection from walls and ceilings affects the overall lighting scheme in a bath. Choose paints carefully.

Semigloss paint reflects more light than flat paint and should be used sparingly because its reflectance will highlight imperfections in the surface of the wall. You can check the reflectance level of paint by obtaining a fan-deck sample from the paint company. The fan deck contains a chart that lists reflectance levels.

Bathroom task lighting recommendations usually assume that certain reflectance levels are present in a residential bathroom. Ceiling reflectance levels are higher than counters and cabinets because ceilings are frequently painted white. If you are using dark, non-reflective surfaces, such as black matte counters, you should raise the light level to compensate for reduced reflectance.

Refer to the chart to become familiar with the recommended levels for bathroom surfaces.

Light colors, because of reflection, spread light throughout the room. Colors with shorter wave lengths (green, blue, and violet) create an impression of cold. In comparison, colors with longer wave lengths (yellow, orange and red) appear warm. A lighting source should render the color scheme at its best.

Reflectance Levels of Paints

Paint Color	Light Reflected
Warm Colors	
White	80-90%
Pale Yellow,	
Yellow, Rose	80%
Pale Pastels	70%
Cool Colors	
(Blue, Green Pastels)	70-85%
Full Yellow Hue	
(Mustard)	35%
Medium Brown	35%
Blue, Green	20-30%
Black	10%

Reflectance Levels from Room Surfaces

Surface	Light Reflected
Ceilings	60-90%
Walls	35-60%
Floors	15-35%
Countertops	30-50%
Cabinets	35-60%

LIGHTING THE VANITY

Task lighting for the vanity should be designed carefully. Using a single recessed light centered above the vanity, or one surface-mounted light above the mirror, creates dark shadows under the eyes, nose and chin.

Lighting from the Side

Lighting experts note that the best task lighting is provided by **cross lighting**. Cross lighting provides even illumination from side to side and top to bottom.

The first, and preferred, method is to provide two vertical light strips on either side of the bathroom mirror. This light can be provided by "*theater lighting*", or by strip fluorescent, lincandescent or single incandescent wall sconce fixtures. Theater lighting is created by light bars with visible globes, an imitation of dressing room mirrors in stage productions.

These light bars have been slimmed down from a bulky 4" to a more attractive 2 1/2". The globe-shaped bulbs (called G-lamps) are available in smaller sizes. The "G-14", for example, is only 1 3/4" in diameter. However, these bright little lamps are harsh and can create glare. Elderly clients and others with sensitive eyes may prefer a traditional wide bar and oversized G-bulbs, such as round G-40 lamps. Regardless of bulb size, always use a white frosted bulb when the bulb in the light fixture is exposed. Clear bulbs produce too much glare to provide good task lighting.

The center of the light bars or wall sconce fixture should be placed at eye level. Usually the fixture is centered 60"

or 64" off the floor. For a single lavatory vanity, at which the user will stand approximately 22" away from the mirror, the fixtures should be spaced about 30 inches apart. The size of the lamps depends on the brightness of the room. The more reflectance off the walls, vanity top and fixtures, the less illumination you need. One additional design hint: install the fixture with a dimmer switch so your client can apply make-up in low light to simulate a night time setting.

Although standard bathroom recommendations suggest that the proper placement for two side mounted lights is approximately 30" apart, recent research suggests this may be too far apart for a person who stands close to the mirror. The IES recommended standard for residential lighting specifies a primary task plan located 16" from the mirror for both standing and sitting applications. This standard is based on research conducted from the **Illuminating Engineering Society**, which identified how close people stood to a mirror in a bathroom when shaving or performing grooming tasks.

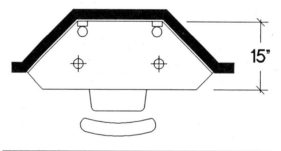

Figure 63   Reducing the make-up counter depth to 15" is a consideration for ease of use, while not requiring the user to bend over in an unhealthy manner.

What this tells us is that the user may lean over the 22" vanity top to get closer to the mirror. As soon as you move closer to the mirror, the distance separating the two lights is reduced. The IES standard goes on to say that luminaries should be mounted outside the 60 degree visual cone, the center of which coincides with the line of sight.

Robern Manufacturing Company recently worked with the **University of Pennsylvannia** to determine where lights should be spaced according to this standard. Robern, a manufacturer of fine medicine cabinets with integral built-in lighting systems, then designed their product based upon this academic research. The research found that the optimum spacing is between 15 1/4" to 23 1/4" depending on the distance the user stands from the mirror.

Fluorescent or halogen strip lighting can also be used on either side of a decorative mirror. Designer **R.B. Davis** used glass rod light fixtures on either side of a two-layered mirror. Two downlights in the soffit provided extra illumination. (Floating glass shelves were stepped back to allow elbow room around the lavatory.)

Another option is to use fluorescent fixtures filtered through a louvered baffle. The baffle diffuses the glow and reduces the glare of the fluorescent bulbs.

Cross illumination can also be provided by wall-mount translucent fixtures at eye level on either side of the sink. These can flank a small mirror or be floated on the surface on a full wall mirror. Sidelights can be close to the mirror, but don't position them so that they shine directly on the mirror itself. This will produce a harsh glare. Use the client's height and leaning posture as a guide when positioning sidelights.

If the vanity is placed in an alcove or between tall cabinets, a fourth option could be used. Provide cross lighting with light mounted on the side cabinets. For an indirect light effect, consider using a lighted mirror. A lighted mirror casts an even light on the client's face, without producing glare.

Figure 64 (Courtesy of Robern)   A small vanity features lincandescent lighting on each side of mirror.

amount of light up toward the bottom of the face. This form of cross lighting can be effective, but it is not as effective as lighting the mirror from both sides.

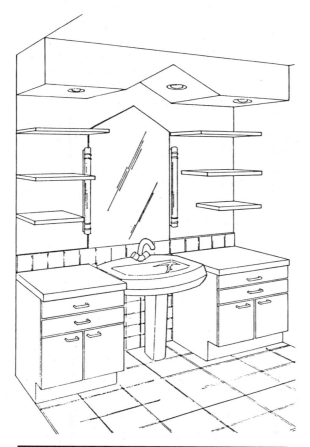

Figure 65   Vertical rod light fixtures combined with two downlights provide lighting. Note the stepped-back floating glass shelves to allow elbow room around the lavatory.

Lighting from Above the Mirror

If there is no room for lighting on either side of the mirror, you can still use the crosslighting concept. Place the light fixture above the mirror at a height of 78". Make sure the light source is as long as the mirror. Use a light colored countertop to reflect the maximum

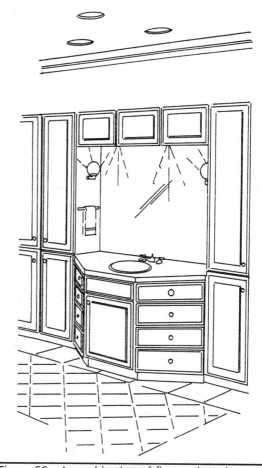

Figure 66   A combination of fixtures have been used in this lavatory area.

GENERAL LIGHTING

While the task area at the vanity is the most critical to light correctly, the bathroom as a whole needs adequate light as well. The typical installation is a single ceiling fixture with white opal diffusers that project a few inches below the ceiling. These fixtures are bright, glaring and produce unpleasant shadows.

Multiple fixtures that are flush or recessed into the ceiling often is a good option. This also works well for elderly clients and others with sensitive eyes. Recessed fixtures reduce glare even with high wattage bulbs.

Recessed fixtures do present some problems in bathrooms, however. These lights generate heat that must be allowed to dissipate. Recessed fixtures cannot be covered with insulation because a 3" clearance must be provided to meet code requirements. This can create a hole in the insulation, allowing moisture from the bathroom to rise into the attic. And, recessed fixtures are also difficult to use near outside walls. The roof slope over outside walls may not allow enough clearance for recessed fixtures. When planning bathrooms, vapor proof housings should always be considered.

If roof slope and condensation are not likely to be a problem, recessed fixtures can be very effective for general lighting. Light levels for general lighting depend on whether the fixture is recessed or surface mounted.

SHOWER LIGHTING

Recessed fixtures work well for showers. Use a flat lensed unit to get the greatest beam spread.

The fixture must tolerate high moisture levels. Fixtures marked *Suitable for Damp Locations* or *Suitable for Wet Locations* should be chosen. These fixtures are sealed to keep moisture out of the wiring - a safety plus in any bathroom. All circuits used near a bathtub or shower should have GFCI (Ground Fault Circuit Interupter) protection against accidental shock.

NIGHT LIGHTS

Since the bathroom space will probably be used by family members or guests at night, a *"night light"* is an excellent addition to the lighting plan. This safety item can be as simple as a small lamp that plugs in to a duplex outlet.

Alternatively, you may plan a low-voltage lighting system built-in to the cabinet toe-kick, underneath the countertop overhang, or as part of a ledge or shelf behind the vanity that provides soft illumination. Late night bathroom users can then find their way into the space without being blinded by a bright, glaring overhead light. The light may be also provided by the general bathroom lighting placed on a rheostat switch.

For frequent late night bathroom users or elderly clients, consider installing a three-way switch to the night light system, with the second switch close to the bed. This allows the user to turn the light on before getting out of bed. The person can then find the way to the bathroom without stumbling, or waking anyone else sleeping in the same room.

BATHTUB LIGHTING

For bathtub/shower combinations, lighting can be handled just as for shower lighting. However, large jetted tubs or soaking tubs are more than just utilitarian bathing fixtures. Your customers will want greater control over lighting. They may want lighting on a dimmer. And you should certainly provide light for reading.

Check the location of light fixtures from the vantage point of your customer. Make sure the customer will not see a glaring lamp while relaxing in the bathtub.

Because of the amount of moisture generated, lighting above bathtubs should also be *"Suitable for Damp Locations"*. The **National Electrical Code** also requires that the fixtures be totally enclosed, protected by a GFCI circuit, and not less that 6' above the water line. Switches must be a minimum of 5' from the edge of the bathtub or shower.

CLOSET LIGHTING

Lighting should also be provided inside bathroom linen or storage closets. A recessed fixture or a fluorescent strip mounted above the door is the best kind of closet lighting.

The electrical codes are specific about closet lighting. The codes do not permit open or partially enclosed lamps, such as a porcelain fixture with a bare bulb. This is because the lamp can become hot and ignite stored items.

The **CABO** code establishes certain distances from storage, depending on the type of light fixture:

- Surface-mounted incandescents above the door or on the ceiling must be 12" (305 mm) from storage.

- Surface-mounted fluorescents above the door or on the ceiling must be 6 "(152 mm) from storage.

- Recessed, completely enclosed incandescents above the door or on

the ceiling must be 6" (152 mm) from storage.

- Recessed fluorescents above the door or on the ceiling must be 6" (152 mm) from storage.

By specifying the right fixture, you can give your clients an additional 6" of storage.

LAUNDRY LIGHTING

When a laundry is part of the bathroom, light is needed for sorting and folding clothes. Ceiling-mounted task lighting should be centered over appliances, the sink, and sorting table.

For ironing, a light fixture should be angled in front of the ironing board so that wrinkles are clearly visible. Use ceiling-mounted adjustable recessed can lights, 20" to 24" apart and 24" ahead of the front edge of the board for maximum beam spread.

LIGHTING TIPS

Avoid using theatrical lighting in hot climates. The heat from the exposed bulbs can feel uncomfortable to clients. Consider using low-voltage lighting instead. Low-voltage lighting generates less heat.

As you draw your elevations, think about the swing of medicine cabinet doors and doors on storage closets. Make sure doors will not swing into light fixtures. Check the location of wall-mounted fixtures on your elevations. They should not block access to the mirror or become a safety hazard.

SECTION **7**

Electrical

ELECTRICAL CODE CONSIDERATIONS

Like plumbing, electricity is a mystery to many bathroom planners. It's easy to understand why. Nearly everything is behind walls. In an increasingly technological age, electrical know-how is becoming critical.

A wave of new electric-powered bathroom equipment means that you must have a firm grasp of the basics of home wiring. Home automation and "integrated systems", such as the **Smart House™**, use electricity for every function from security to heat controls.

Electrically controlled plumbing makes it possible for the homeowner to call home and have the bathtub start filling before they arrive. The bathtub's computer memory can be preset to the right temperature and fill level. This new technology presents an extra challenge for the designer who must understand the new design possibilities.

Because of the danger of fatal shock when water and electricity mix, safety is one of the most important considerations in designing bathroom electrical layouts. Safety is the goal of the **National Electrical Code**. Most local codes are based on this national model code. The N.E.C.'s code provisions are designed to make a bathroom safe. Local units of government may have added their own additions to the code.

The details of an electrical installation, such as grounding requirements and the type of outlet boxes, will be handled by the electrical contractor. Electrical contractors are well aware of local code provisions and can tell you whether code requirements will have an impact on your project's budget. The major added expense that could occur is if the local code requires all wiring to be run in conduit. **(Conduit is a hollow metal tube that contains electrical wiring.)** Most residential work in the United States is not required to run in conduit. Conduit is required for apartment or condominium buildings over three stories and for all commercial work.

Even though you can rely on your contractor to know the day-to-day code provisions, it is still a good idea to discuss anything out of the ordinary, such as toilets with electronic controls. Go over potential trouble spots, such as unusual locations for receptacles, with the general contractor or electrical subcontractor before work begins. You should also make a special note of nonstandard dimensions or locations on your plans. The task of communicating switch and outlet locations is not difficult if your drawings are clear.

Plumbing fixtures with electronic controls could also be questioned by local code officials. You should check the product literature to make sure the product has received approval from **Underwriters Laboratories**. (All electrical products sold in the U.S. must have U.L. approval.) If the product has been approved, you will be safer if you discuss your fixture choice with both the plumbing and electrical inspectors before ordering. Because the danger of shock increases when electricity and water are in close proximity, local inspectors may need to be educated about new elec-

tronic plumbing products.

THE ELEMENTS OF THE ELECTRICAL SYSTEM

Part of the reason that electricity seems so complex is the extensive terminology, much of which will be explained here. The basic concept, however, is straight forward. Many compare it to the flow of water. **(Electric current is, after all, a flow of electrons.)** Think of it this way: where water pressure is measured in pounds per square inch (psi), electrical pressure is measured in **volts**. Where the rate of flow of water is measured in gallons per minute (gpm), the rate of flow of electricity is measured in amperes, abbreviated as **"amps"**. Power is measured in watts. The wattage tells you the amount of power available. The electrical bill from the utility company is based on the total watts consumed within a given time frame,

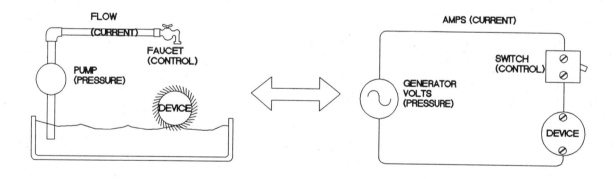

POWER FORMULA

$$V \times A = W \qquad W / V = A$$

$$V = VOLTAGE \qquad A = AMPERAGE \qquad W = WATTAGE$$

Figure 67   Electricity is easy to understand if you compare it to water. The power formula allows you to convert watts to amps. Either wattage or amperage ratings are found on all household appliances.

(Power [watts] x Time Used = Energy Consumed). The power (wattage) level of a particular fixture or appliance dictates the required capacity of the electrical circuit. The more wattage present, the bigger the electrical wire required.

If you understand how the system works, you will be able to find the service panel on the house and decide whether additional wiring will be needed. To find the service panel, stand outside and look to see where the wires from the utility connect to the house, this is called the service drop. Standing outside, you will also see the electric meter. After passing through the meter, which measures energy in watt hours, wires feed into a service box.

The service box is located on the inside of the house near the electric meter, or may be in the basement directly below the electric meter. This is the control center for the home's electrical service.

Inside the service box is an electrical service panel. The service panel is where the circuit breakers or fuses are located.

Most homes have what is called "three wire service" that feeds into the service panel. Three wires - two "hot" (which means they have voltage) and one "ground" (zero voltage) - connect to the box from outside.

The service panel channels the electrical power into branch circuits. Branch circuits run to lights, switches, receptacles, and permanently wired equipment, such as jetted bathtubs or spas. Branch circuits use smaller wires than main service wires because electrical appliances and devices don't need the full

power that's available. Let's back up for a moment and look at each part of the electrical system in greater detail.

Service Entrance

Electricity is brought into the house via cable that is dropped into a mast. This mast looks a bit like the periscope of a submarine. The wiring may also enter the house underground. (If you are thinking of changing the location of the service entrance, you should talk with the power company first. They determine where this drop line can enter the house.)

As mentioned previously, the cable is brought to a service panel. In remodeling, the service panel may need to be upgraded. The panel may not have enough room for additional circuits. Or, the number of electrical appliances being added might overload the capacity of the main cable.

The minimum service entrance permitted by most local codes is a 100 amp, 240 volt service. A service with only two wires - one hot and one neutral - is inadequate for modern household demand. Generally speaking, homes that do not have 240-volt service should be upgraded to it. Jetted bathtubs and saunas require 240-volt service.

In houses over 1400 square feet, a 200 amp service is recommended. A 200 amp service is adequate for most needs, but may not be adequate for very large homes or homes with a large number of major electrical appliances. In any residential bathroom remodeling project, a 200 amp service should be considered for present and future needs.

Branch Circuits

The electric current in the service panel is distributed through branch circuits. Each circuit can only carry a limited amount of current. If it is overloaded, the wiring will overheat. Each circuit is protected by a fuse or circuit breaker. These are the weak points of each circuit, the safety devices that keep the branch circuits and anything connected to them from overheating and catching fire. If there is an overload or a short circuit, a fuse will blow or a circuit breaker will trip, shutting off the flow of current.

Fuses have a thin metal strip through which current passes into a circuit. If too much current starts to flow, the metal melts and cuts off the current.

Circuit breakers are heavy-duty switches that serve the same purpose as fuses. When a circuit is carrying more current than is safe, the breaker switches to RESET. On most breakers, the switch has to be pushed to OFF and then to ON after the circuit trips.

Although most people think of fuses as old fashioned, they are actually more reliable than circuit breakers. Circuit breakers sometimes malfunction. When a fuse burns out, it must be replaced by a new fuse. This provides absolute protection against overheating.

Unfortunately, this absolute protection created a problem. If the fuse kept burning out, the occupants of the house became irritated. They were tempted to put in a larger fuse, substituting a 20-amp fuse for a 15-amp fuse. Or, they might have been tempted to put a penny in the fuse holder. This also prevented fuse burnout.

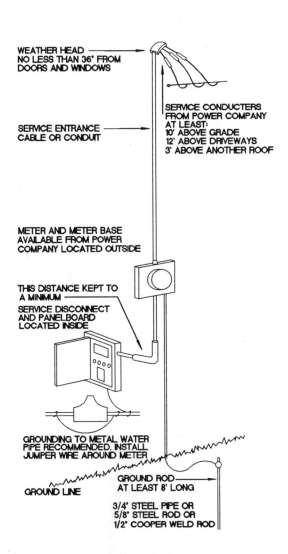

WEATHER HEAD
NO LESS THAN 36" FROM
DOORS AND WINDOWS

SERVICE CONDUCTERS
FROM POWER COMPANY
AT LEAST:
10' ABOVE GRADE
12' ABOVE DRIVEWAYS
3' ABOVE ANOTHER ROOF

SERVICE ENTRANCE
CABLE OR CONDUIT

METER AND METER BASE
AVAILABLE FROM POWER
COMPANY LOCATED OUTSIDE

THIS DISTANCE KEPT TO
A MINIMUM

SERVICE DISCONNECT
AND PANELBOARD
LOCATED INSIDE

GROUNDING TO METAL WATER
PIPE RECOMMENDED. INSTALL
JUMPER WIRE AROUND METER

GROUND LINE

GROUND ROD
AT LEAST 8' LONG

3/4" STEEL PIPE OR
5/8" STEEL ROD OR
1/2" COOPER WELD ROD

Figure 68   Electricity enters the house through the service mast. It passes through the electrical meter into a service box. Inside the service box, a service panel with circuit breakers or fuses distributes power to the branch circuits. The system is grounded to a cold water pipe.

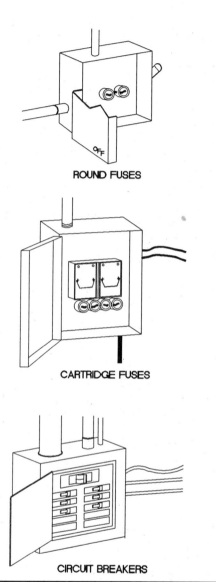

ROUND FUSES

CARTRIDGE FUSES

CIRCUIT BREAKERS

Figure 69   Three types of service panels might be found on a home. The service panel will contain circuit breakers, cartridge fuses or round fuses.

When homeowners substituted larger fuses, the old knob and tube wiring in their home could overheat. Insulation on the wire would become crisp, or even burn off completely. Thus, if you are doing a jobsite inspection at a house, and you see that the service panel contains fuses, you should investigate the condition of knob and tube wiring

Knob and tube wiring used separate wires spaced a few inches apart. Wherever the wires pass through framing members, they are threaded through porcelain tubes or supported by porcelain knobs. Look in the attic or in the basement where the wiring is exposed. The system could be in good condition if it has not been abused. But if it is not in good condition, a simple bathroom remodel could become more complicated, requiring a whole house electrical inspection. If the inspector finds unsafe wiring, he or she will require that it be upgraded, whether that is in the original budget or not. Knob and tube wiring was most often used with fuses, but you could find it even in houses with circuit breakers if the homes have been partially rewired.

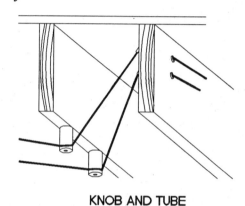

KNOB AND TUBE

Figure 70   Knob and tube wiring used porcelain knobs and tubes to protect framing members from wiring.

Circuit breakers are generally more convenient because they can be reset quickly. If the circuit overloads, the switch on the circuit breaker trips. If a circuit breaker trips continuously, that is an indication the circuit breaker is overloaded or defective. Like fuses, all circuit breakers are rated for a specific amperage. Circuits today typically are rated for 20 amps for convenience outlets and lighting.

Wiring Options

Wire size depends on how many amps the circuit is carrying. The wire size is expressed as a gauge number; the smaller the number, the larger the wire. The wire size for a 20 amp circuit is #12 wire. Houses with older wiring (and 15 amp circuits) typically used #14 wire. If you are remodeling a bath with knob and tube wiring, you must update the wiring for receptacles to the #12 wiring used today. However the lighting could remain as the original knob and tube. Otherwise, the electrician might have to cut out portions of the wall or ceiling surface to run new wiring. If you are installing fixtures, such as a spa, jetted bathtub or sauna, the electrical contractor may use a larger wire size.

In most parts of the country, the electrical contractor will use non-metallic-sheathed cable (Type NM) for lighting and most appliance circuits. This is the least expensive kind of wiring and the simplest to install. The wiring part of the project will be less expensive if NM cable can be used.

NM cable, popularly known as Romex, contains three wires.

- One is the current carrying wire, or **hot wire**. It carries current to the receptacle. **(The hot wire is black or red.)**

- A second current carrying wire is the **neutral wire**, which completes the loop back to the service panel. **(The neutral wire is white.)**

- The third wire, which does not carry current, is the **ground wire**.

(It can either be bare copper wire or a coated green wire.)

The individual wires in NM cable are protected by a tough, thermoplastic covering. In new construction, the electrician drills holes in the framing members and pulls the cable through the holes.

Armored cable (Type AC) is similar to non-metallic-sheathed cable except it has a flexible steel cover replacing the plastic covering. (It is also called BX cable.) Armored cable is installed in the same way as nonmetallic-sheathed cable. Because it is flexible, it is easier to install than conduit, which is rigid.

Conduit is used where additional protection from mechanical damage is needed and where required by building codes. (Chicago's code, for instance, requires conduit as a result of sensitivity to the Chicago fire.) Conduit is a special grade of aluminum or steel pipe, either galvanized or enameled, or nonmetallic pipe, usually polyvinyl chloride (PVC) or polyethylene (PE).

A final alternative to consider in remodeling is surface-mounted raceway. This is similar to conduit, in that it has its own connectors and boxes. However, the boxes and raceway are mounted to the surface of walls, not inside them. Some raceway is low-profile and relatively inconspicuous. Other products are purposefully large and designed to duplicate the profile of baseboards. This type of raceway is large enough to carry television cable or phone wiring as well as non-metallic sheathed cable.

If you design bathrooms in an area where the code requires conduit, ask the electrician if armored cable is an acceptable substitute. You will usually save money with armored cable rather than conduit if just a small amount of additional wiring is needed. In new work, using conduit may be just as cost-effective. Electricians find it easy to pull wire through conduit once the conduit has been installed. Working with armored cable and connecting it to boxes is, comparatively, time consuming. Armored cable must be carefully cut with a hacksaw each time it enters a junction, switch, or receptacle box.

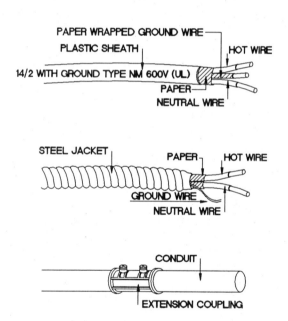

Figure 71 Non-metallic-sheathed cable (NM) contains three wires surrounded by a tough, thermoplastic sleeve. Armored cable, known as AC or BX cable, surrounds its current carrying wires with a flexible steel covering. Conduit is rigid, hollow tubing made of metal or plastic. Individual wires are pulled through the conduit after it is installed.

Junction Boxes

Connections between wires are made inside plastic or metal **boxes**. Switches, receptacles, and wall or ceiling-mounted light fixtures must each have their own box. The boxes are rectangular, octagonal or circular, and are made of plastic or metal. The boxes are nailed or screwed to the studs, but if the nearest stud is not where you want the box to be, the installer can also attach the box to a mounting bar.

After snaking wiring through the framing, the electrician may ask to go over the location of the switch and receptacle boxes before he or she installs them. Switch boxes normally are installed with the box bottom exactly 48" below the finished ceiling surface (for a ceiling height of 8'). If the ceiling is to be 5/8" drywall, the bottom of the box would be 48 5/8" from the ceiling joists. As you recall from a previous section, drywall can be hung horizontally. Drywall is 48" wide. Putting the switch at a 48" height makes it easier for drywallers to do a good job. They merely have to cut a notch around the box and slide the drywall over it.

The next best location for the switch is with the **top** of the box at a 48" height. The drywall contractor can then notch the bottom sheet of drywall.

For universal considerations, NKBA recommends that all outlets and switches be placed within 15" - 48" above the finished floor.

If the box is installed near the edge of the drywall, the drywaller could have difficulty making an accurate cut. The edges of the drywall are fragile. A 3/4" or 1" strip is likely to break off. This causes problems because the drywall taper must fill this large gap with joint compound. The joint compound may take a long time to dry. Or, it might not be as smooth as the surrounding wall. A standard switch or receptacle plate might not completely cover the patched hole. This problem is so common in construction that many contractors use oversized cover plates around their switches as a matter of course. Gaps around receptacles are not as much of a problem because receptacles are not placed near the edges of drywall panels.

Bathroom planners doing custom work may request that their clients reach out and touch the wall. The planner would then specify this height for the switch. This is a subtle improvement, but one that is appreciated by clients who are very tall, very short, or who have impaired mobility.

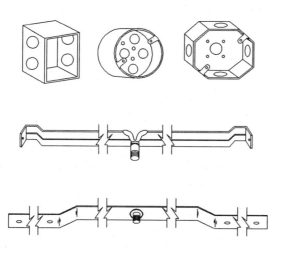

Figure 72 Boxes can be rectangular, octagonal or circular. Bar hangers can be used to position boxes between studs.

The electrician may also ask that you check the location of receptacle boxes. Make sure you compare your plans with the actual locations proposed. An electrician sometimes overlooks a receptacle or puts it some place other than where you have specified. If you have a higher than average backsplash, the electrical box might end up behind the backsplash and have to be raised. Also be sure to tell the electrician if you want the receptacle turned horizontally rather than vertically.

When your design calls for solid surfacing or a backsplash that is higher than normal, make sure the receptacle boxes are set before the solid surfacing subcontractor takes measurements. This allows the solid surfacing subcontractor to accurately measure for cutouts. You should also mark the thickness of the solid surfacing material, tile or paneling in your specifications and list the height locations on the plans and elevation drawings. This tells the electrical contractor where to set the boxes. **The face of the electrical box must always be flush with the finished wall surface. This is a code requirement.**

Boxes are also important in remodeling, especially if knob and tube wiring is to be joined to new wiring. Connections between existing wiring and new wiring must always be made inside electrical boxes. The box protects the flammable parts of the building from sparks in the event of an electrical fire or overheating. The box must always be accessible. This may require a junction box with a blank cover plate in the middle of a wall.

Be sure to ask the electrician if he or she plans to include any junction boxes that are not shown on your plans. Make sure the box is moved out of sight or new wiring is used if the location of the junction box will interfere with your design.

PLANNING FOR ELECTRICAL NEEDS

An easy way to organize your electrical layout is to use the four kinds of circuits the **National Electrical Code** requires in a residence:

- Lighting and general purpose;

- Small appliance;

- Individual appliance;

- And ground fault circuit interrupter (GFCI).

Circuits

General purpose circuits supply energy to light fixtures and outlets throughout the house and receptacles everywhere except in the kitchen, dining area, and laundry.

Small appliance circuits provide power for equipment in the bathroom and laundry. A separate circuit is required for laundry receptacles. The same circuit can be used for a washing machine and the plug of a gas dryer. An electric dryer will have its own 240-volt receptacle. No lighting may be installed in these circuits.

Individual appliances draw enough current to warrant individual circuits. A motor for a spa or jetted bathtub should be on its own circuit. Be sure to check the wiring requirements for these fixtures and use correct symbols on your plans for all equipment and required switches. The recognized industry stand-

ards for all symbols are included for you in Chapter 4. Also, be sure to include locations for switches that turn the equipment on and off.

Amperage

When you are planning your bathroom layout, you will select certain fixtures and appliances based on your clients' needs. For instance, they may want a bathroom vent fan combined with a heat lamp. Or you may be adding a spa or jetted bathtub. All of these appliances or fixtures require electricity.

Appliances that have motors (such as a vent fan or whirlpool pump) require a surge of electricity when they first turn on. This is because it takes power to start the motor. Once the motor is running the power needed drops back.

Each circuit in a house, as mentioned previously, also has an amperage rating. The normal household circuit used for receptacles and lighting is a 20-amp circuit. The **National Electrical Code** contains a chart that will tell you how many receptacles or lights can go on a given circuit. A 20-amp circuit cannot have more than 16 amps loaded onto it.

Permanently installed equipment, such as a bath vent fan combined with a resistance heater and room light, may require its own 20-amp circuit. And jetted bathtubs and spas, because of their larger motors, may require a separate 15 to 20-amp circuit.

Larger motors, such as those on jetted bathtub, "*pull*" more electricity than small motors, such as hair dryers. Every appliance that uses electricity has a rating that tells how much electricity it uses. The rating is given in amps. These ratings can be found on the name plate of the appliance or in the technical literature.

It would help your general contractor and electrical subcontractor if you can provide this information early. They will be able to accurately bid the job and have the right circuit breakers and wiring on hand.

As a bathroom planner, you do not have to know how to lay out circuits. However, you should be aware that the electrical contractor may need to do additional work to add enough circuits for the fixtures or appliances you specify.

Safeguards

Another requirement of the **National Electrical Code** is that every circuit have a grounding system. Grounding ensures that in the event of a stray current, all metal parts of the wiring system or of lamps or appliances connected to it, will be maintained at zero volts. The ground wire for each circuit is connected to the distribution center (service panel) and then is run with the hot and neutral wires in the branch circuits.

A special type of circuit breaker - the **Ground Fault Circuit Interrupter (GFCI)** - is installed in bathrooms. The GFCI monitors the balance of electrical current moving through the circuit. If an inbalance occurs because of stray current, the GFCI circuit opens the circuit, instantly, cutting off the electricity. An electrical shock as short as 2/100 of a second can be fatal. The GFCI receptacle is designed to sense a short-circuit within 5/1000 of a second. Although this will not prevent a shock, it can prevent

a fatality. All bathroom outlets must be protected by a GFCI circuit breaker. Or, each outlet can use a GFCI receptacle instead of a normal receptacle.

It is generally less expensive in new construction to protect all bathroom outlets by using a GFCI circuit breaker. In a small scale remodeling project, it may be more cost effective to use a single GFCI outlet. One GFCI receptacle can be installed to protect lights or other receptacles further down the line. This can be a good solution in remodeling because the electrical panel may not have room for the oversized GFCI circuit breaker.

GFCIs are extremely "*user-friendly*". When a GFCI has tripped, it is reset like a regular circuit breaker. For a receptacle GFCI, a reset button is pushed.

As a final note on safety, check the electrician's work to make sure he/she is protecting wiring from possible nail penetration. The N.E.C. requires all wiring to be placed 1 1/4" from the edge of framing members. Cables run in notches in the studs or joists must be protected by metal plates 3" long. These rules are designed to prevent drywall nails from penetrating the cable. Drywall installers are not going to pay attention to the location of wiring. If a nail happens to strike wire embedded in the wall, it could create a short circuit. Tracking down the problem would be a nightmare.

Switches

There are dozens of switch types available. In many cases, selection is based on style. But function is just as important. In addition to choosing switches that accent your design, consider using specialty switches to improve convenience.

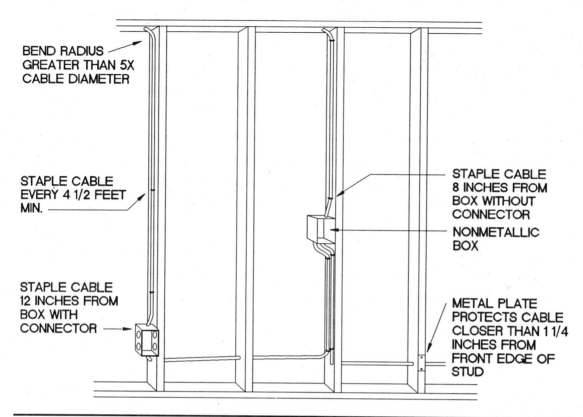

BEND RADIUS
GREATER THAN 5X
CABLE DIAMETER

STAPLE CABLE
EVERY 4 1/2 FEET
MIN.

STAPLE CABLE
12 INCHES FROM
BOX WITH
CONNECTOR

STAPLE CABLE
8 INCHES FROM
BOX WITHOUT
CONNECTOR

NONMETALLIC
BOX

METAL PLATE
PROTECTS CABLE
CLOSER THAN 1 1/4
INCHES FROM
FRONT EDGE OF
STUD

Figure 73   Check to make sure holes for wiring are at least 1 1/4" from the face of the framing. Also, make sure wiring installed in notches is protected by a 3" metal plate.

Most switches in a home are called *"single-pole"* or *"two-way"*. **Single-pole** switches control a light or receptacle from one location only. Another type, a **three-way switch**, operates in pairs to control a light or receptacle from two lo-cations. They are used for rooms with two entrances. In most cases, you would use a **single pole switch** near the door of the bathroom. However, you might want a three-way switch at either end of a long hall or at two places in a master suite.

Some switches operate with a touch on a plate or button. Others have lighted handles which glow when the switch is off to serve as locators. Lighted switches can take the place of a bathroom night light.

Another switch to remember for bathroom linen closets is the **contact switch**. These switches are installed on the door frame. They are a good choice for a linen closet light because they turn on automatically when the door opens. Because they are installed out of sight, you may find they give your room a less cluttered look. A bank of six or eight switches not only looks cluttered: it is not functional. Clients cannot remember which switch to flip.

In **low voltage** switching systems, the wall switches control a special low-voltage circuit. This circuit connects to a relay that operates the line voltage switch. This allows the use of inexpen-sive switches and doorbell-type wire on the switching circuit. This system can be expanded so that all the lights in the house can be controlled from one or more master panels, usually located in the master bedroom and/or at the main entrance.

Low voltage lighting is becoming more common in residential work. New low voltage lighting systems and an increasing selection of attractive fixtures are used to accent bathroom features and provide light or switch control when clearances are tight. Low voltage fixtures generate less heat, so the boxes they are installed in can be smaller.

One good place to consider using a low voltage switch is near a pocket door. The switch box is small, and will fit in the wall space in either side of the door's "pocket". If you use a low voltage switch, you must also use low voltage lights. You cannot mix and match standard fixtures and low voltage switches.

Placing your lighting on a **rheostat switch** will also give the bathroom extra personality. While a dimmer may not be necessary for a small bathroom, if the bathroom is part of a master suite or is a luxury relaxation center, control of light level is essential. Dimmer switches allow the client to vary the light level with the activity. A switch must have 125% of the capacity of the total light load connected to it. Rapid start fluorescent fixtures can be dimmed if you ask the electrical supplier to install a special dimming ballast in the fixture. This is easiest to do before installation.

Some switches are linked to receptacles, such as a wall switch used to turn on the receptacle for a floor lamp. Never use a dimmer on a switch connected to a receptacle. Turning down the dimmer could ruin an appliance plugged into the outlet.

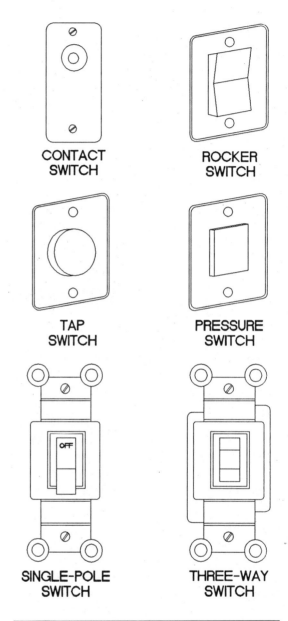

CONTACT SWITCH

ROCKER SWITCH

TAP SWITCH

PRESSURE SWITCH

SINGLE-POLE SWITCH

THREE-WAY SWITCH

Figure 74 Switches that light up at night and dimmer switches can be used to give clients greater control of their lighting. Other switches, such as tap, pressure and rocket switches, are chosen for aesthetic reasons. A contact switch on the door frame of a linen closet will keep wall space uncluttered. The light will switch on when the closet door opens.

Some switches are designed to save space. *For example,* two switches can fit in the space of one standard-sized box.

If your plan calls for a special lighting system or unusual switch arrangements, you should consult your local lighting store or electrical contractor to see if any special switches would enhance the project.

Receptacles

Most receptacles are "duplex receptacles" because they have two outlets. Duplex receptacles are rated for 15 or 20 amps, and they carry 120-volt current. One or both outlets may be electrically live at all times, or one or both may be controlled by a wall switch. Switch-controlled receptacles are usually used to turn on a floor lamp from a remote location. A switch near the room entrance could turn on a floor lamp. This might be appropriate for a master suite.

On remodeling projects, you will find receptacles that are both grounded and non-grounded. Grounded receptacles accept three-prong plugs. The third prong connects the frame or housing of the appliance to the grounding system.

Electrical codes require that all new residential receptacles must be grounded. Your electrical contractor will be required to bring all receptacles in the bathroom up-to-code at the time of remodeling, even if just one bathroom is being redone. The code may require additional ground wires, and it will mean the installation of GFCI receptacles or circuit breakers. This is an added expense you should anticipate.

Other special forms of outlets are available. These include receptacle and switch combinations, clock outlets, and radio and television outlets which also supply antenna and ground connection. Among the most useful receptacles are child-proof models that require an adult's grip to uncover them.

Bathrooms require outlets for equipment such as hair dryers and electric shavers. Enough receptacles should be provided to avoid the use of an extension cord in the bathroom.

For minimum quality electrical service, no point along a wall, as measured along the floor, should be more than 6 feet from a receptacle. Every wall space more than 2' wide must have a receptacle. If an open entry door (not a closet door or cabinet door) makes a wall space inaccessible, it does not have to have a receptacle. Thus, it may be important for you to plan your door swings before laying out the receptacle locations.

Plan where your clients will need receptacles. For instance they may need a receptacle for a television on a recessed cabinet. They certainly will need a receptacle for shaving or hair care. And there should be a receptacle convenient for a vacuum cleaner and a night light. At least one receptacle must be installed in each bathroom.

As discussed in the section on heating, you may be providing an additional heat source in the bathroom. If you choose an electric resistance heater that is installed at floor level or low on the wall, you cannot place a receptacle above it. Otherwise, wiring from an appliance plugged into the outlet might hang down and overheat.

To meet the code requirement for receptacles, you could select a resistance heater with built-in receptacle. The receptacle would be wired to a separate circuit.

ELECTRICAL EQUIPMENT

A New Water Heater

After the furnace, the water heater is the largest energy user in the house. If you are adding a bath or adding a large fixture that requires an additional water heater, you will need space for the tank and enough electrical capacity for the water heater circuit.

If the home has an existing electric water heater, chances are you will not have the option of installing a gas water heater, even though a gas water heater would be a preferable heat source for a jetted tub. Some homes are not piped for natural gas. The option, then, is to plan carefully for another electric water heater.

Television and Telephone Wiring

Clients today may wish to have a television or telephone in the bathroom. Include the location for a cable jack in the bathroom and a shelf that can hold a television. In addition to finding a good location for the phone, you should also plan to put the phone jack as far from electric outlets and switches as possible. Household wiring can cause static on phone lines.

RENOVATION CONSIDERATIONS

In remodeling jobs, electricians refer to "new work" and "old work". "New

work" refers not so much to new construction as to jobsites where the framing is exposed and running wire is relatively easy. Wiring a renovation with gutted walls, for example, is new work.

"Old work" refers to locations where small holes are cut in the walls and wiring is fished through the covered wall cavities. Boxes are then mounted to finished surfaces.

You will be in good graces with electrical contractors if you think through the location of outlets. When designing, ask yourself:

- *What is the closest live outlet with power?*

- *What studs, joists, or other framing might be in the way en route?*

To locate the nearest live outlet, think spatially. The outlet may be on the other side of a partition wall. You may find an electrical circuit just above the ceiling.

Discussing circuit locations with the electrical contractor before drawing your wiring plan may save you money. The electrical contractor may be able to draw power from a nearby, pre-existing source.

To bring new wiring to a remodeled room without doing major demolition, you may be able to ask the carpentry contractor to remove baseboard so that wiring can be run in a notch behind the baseboard.

Wiring to an upstairs bathroom may be snaked through chases, or voids, around duct work or plumbing pipes.

In some cases the electrical contractor may need to cut small holes at the tops and bottoms of walls. The electrical contractor will use **fish tape** to pull new wiring from hole to hole. **Fish tape is a stiff wire used to probe wall cavities.** Electrical wiring can then be tied to one end and pulled to the other hole.

Because switches, receptacles and junction boxes must be flush with the finished surface, the electrician may need to add a **box extension** to an existing box to make it the correct depth. Also, if additional wires need to be brought into the box, the box may have to be changed to a larger one. This may require more demolition to the finished surface around the box.

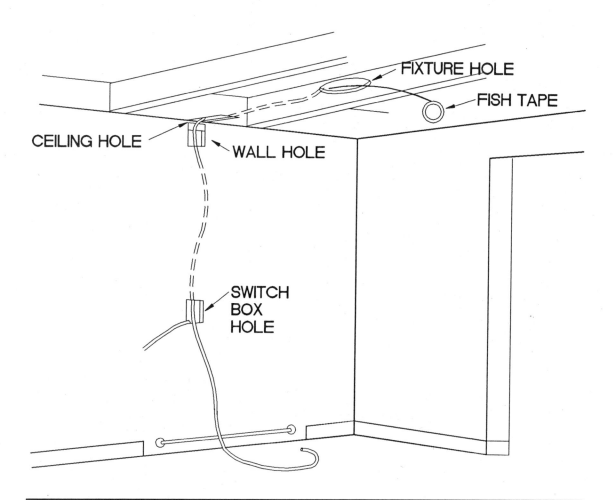

Figure 75 Wiring in remodeling can be fished through wall cavities. Only small holes are needed. Fish tape is used to pull the wire through to the new location.

If the local code requires conduit, the electrical contractor will have to open up a channel. The electrician may cut out such a channel in the course of his or her work. However, it is better to have the person responsible for repairing the channel make the cuts. A crew member of the general contractor's should cut back lath and plaster (or drywall) along a straight line at the center of adjoining studs or joist spaces, or wherever boxes are needed. When the electrician is finished, the area will be easier to patch. If demolition is done carefully, holes can be patched with drywall or they can be replastered.

To avoid demolition, you could also consider using a surface-mounted raceway. Wiring can be run inside the raceway. This solution might be suitable for an inexpensive remodel job or a commercial job where design is not the main consideration.

By working with the electrical contractor you can plan how to provide needed wiring without opening large holes in walls.

One other problem that is rare, but can occur, is to find that a house has been wired with aluminum wiring. Aluminum wiring requires one larger wire size than copper wire. If the electrician finds aluminum wiring, expect added expense.

As a quick reminder of problem areas, remember to check for the following:

- *Is there knob and tube wiring?*

- *Are there open splices in the wiring in the attic?*

- *Is the insulation on the wiring still in good condition?*

- *Is the location of the service box or service mast in conflict with your plan?*

- *Is the service box in a wall that is going to be removed?*

- *Is the service box in a wall that will have a door or window placed in it?*

- *Will the service box still be accessible after the remodel?*

- *Is there an undersized service panel, (100 amps or less)?*

- *Do you see fuses rather than breakers?*

- *Are there subpanels spun off the main panel or scattered throughout the house?*

These are just a few of the problems you can encounter in remodeling. Wiring and electrical work in new construction is infinitely easier than in existing buildings. Team up with a good electrical contractor - one who is experienced in sorting out existing wiring - and your job will be a lot easier.

S	SINGLE POLE SWITCH
S_2	DOUBLE POLE SWITCH
S_3	THREE WAY SWITCH
S_4	FOUR WAY SWITCH
S_{DM}	SINGLE POLE SWITCH w/ DIMMER
S_{3DM}	THREE WAY SWITCH w/ DIMMER
S_{LM}	MASTER SWITCH FOR LOW VOLTAGE SWITCHING SYSTEM
S_L	SWITCH FOR LOW VOLTAGE SWITCHING SYSTEM
S_{WP}	WEATHERPROOF SWITCH
S_{RC}	REMOTE CONTROL SWITCH
S_D	AUTOMATIC DOOR SWITCH
S_P	SWITCH AND PILOT LAMP
S_K	KEY OPERATED SWITCH
S_F	FUSED SWITCH
S_T	TIME SWITCH
Ⓢ	CEILING PULL SWITCH
	DUPLEX OUTLET
GFCI	DUPLEX OUTLET WITH GROUND FAULT CIRCUIT INTERRUPTER
S	SWITCH AND SINGLE RECEPTACLE OUTLET
S	SWITCH AND DUPLEX OUTLET
Ⓑ	BLANKED OUTLET
Ⓙ	JUNCTION BOX
Ⓛ	OUTLET CONTROLLED BY LOW VOLTAGE SWITCHING WHEN RELAY IS INSTALLED IN OUTLET BOX
	SINGLE RECEPTACLE OULET
	TRIPLEX RECEPTACLE OULET
	QUADRUPLEX RECEPTACLE OULET
	DUPLEX RECEPTACLE OUTLET-SPLIT WIRED
	TRIPLEX RECEPTACLE OUTLET-SPLIT WIRED
Ⓒ	CLOCK HANGER RECEPTACLE
Ⓕ	FAN HANGER RECEPTACLE
	INTERCOM
	TELEPHONE OUTLET
Ⓣ	THERMOSTAT
	SMOKE DETECTOR

TV	TELEVISION OUTLET
C	CABLE OUTLET
T_L	LOW VOLTAGE TRANSFORMER
	HANGING CEILING FIXTURE
	HEAT LAMP
	HEAT/LIGHT UNIT
	HEAT/FAN LIGHT UNIT
	RECESSED CEILING DOWN LIGHTING
	RECESSED CEILING VAPOR LIGHT
	BUILT-IN LOW VOLTAGE TASK LIGHT
	BUILT-IN FLUORESCENT LIGHT
	CONTINUOUS ROW FLUORESCENT LIGHTS
	SURFACE MOUNTED FLUORESCENT LIGHT
	WALL SCONCE
DW	DISHWASHER
GD	FOOD WASTE DISPOSAL
TC	TRASH COMPACTOR
R	REFRIGERATOR OUTLET
H	HOOD
M	MICROWAVE OVEN
R	ELECTRIC RANGE/COOKTOP
WO	ELECTRIC SINGLE/DOUBLE OVEN
G	GAS SUPPLY
CT	GAS COOKTOP
WO	GAS SINGLE/DOUBLE OVEN
CW	CLOTHES WASHER
CD	CLOTHES DRYER
SA	SAUNA
ST	STEAM
WP	WHIRLPOOL
TW	TOWEL WARMER
	HEAT REGISTER

ANY STANDARD SYMBOL GIVEN ABOVE W/ THE ADDITION OF LOWERCASE SUBSCRIPT LETTERING MAY BE USED TO DESIGNATE A VARIATION OF STANDARD EQUIPMENT.

WHEN USED THEY MUST BE LISTED IN THE LEGEND OF THE MECHANICAL PLAN.

Figure 76 (Adapted from Architectural Graphic Standards) Electrical Symbols.

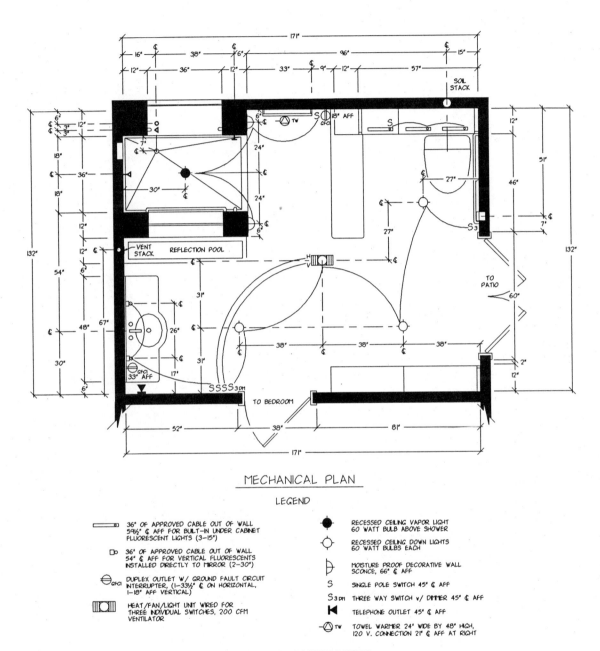

MECHANICAL PLAN

LEGEND

36" OF APPROVED CABLE OUT OF WALL
59½" ₡ AFF FOR BUILT-IN UNDER CABINET
FLUORESCENT LIGHTS (3-15")

36" OF APPROVED CABLE OUT OF WALL
54" ₡ AFF FOR VERTICAL FLUORESCENTS
INSTALLED DIRECTLY TO MIRROR (2-30")

DUPLEX OUTLET W/ GROUND FAULT CIRCUIT
INTERRUPTER, (1-33½" ₡ ON HORIZONTAL,
1-18" AFF VERTICAL)

HEAT/FAN/LIGHT UNIT WIRED FOR
THREE INDIVIDUAL SWITCHES, 200 CFM
VENTILATOR

RECESSED CEILING VAPOR LIGHT
60 WATT BULB ABOVE SHOWER

RECESSED CEILING DOWN LIGHTS
60 WATT BULBS EACH

MOISTURE PROOF DECORATIVE WALL
SCONCE, 66" ₡ AFF

S   SINGLE POLE SWITCH 45" ₡ AFF

S₃ᴰᴹ   THREE WAY SWITCH W/ DIMMER 45" ₡ AFF

TELEPHONE OUTLET 45" ₡ AFF

TOWEL WARMER 24" WIDE BY 48" HIGH,
120 V. CONNECTION 21" ₡ AFF AT RIGHT

NOTE: PRIMARY HEAT SOURCE IS RADIANT
FLOORING TO BE INSTALLED BY OTHERS.

Figure 77 A bathroom mechanical plan.

Chapter **2**

Bathroom Equipment and Materials

*A*t the heart of any bathroom design are the fixtures and fittings you specify. The rapid growth and development of the fixtures and fittings industry has been phenomenal. Especially when you consider that less than a century ago the typical bathroom consisted of a wooden tub pulled in front of the fireplace on Saturday night, a pitcher and basin on a washstand in the bedroom, and a "privy" out back. Today, more than 95% of all American homes have at least one bathroom, and more than 50% have two or more bathrooms.

The three major domestic fixture and fitting manufacturers that serve our industry today were the founding fathers of the plumbing business in the mid and late 19th century.

HOW AMERICAN STANDARD BEGAN

The American Standard plumbing business as we know it today, is a result of successive mergers by a number of companies between 1857 and 1929. The oldest was Ahrens and Ott Manufacturing of Louisville, which began producing cast iron soil pipes in 1857. Another firm produced enameled cast iron bathtubs exclusively. A

third, Thomas Maddock's Sons Company, produced ceramic sanitary ware such as toilets and lavatories. These three companies, plus several more, combined their efforts under the heading American Standard Inc. here in North America. American Standard is affiliated with the Ideal Standard companies which are suppliers in other parts of the world.

THE FIRST KOHLER BATHTUB

In 1883, John Michael Kohler, founder in 1873 of the Kohler Company, sold his first bathtub to a local farmer in exchange for one cow and 14 chickens. As a manufacturer of cast iron agricultural implements, Kohler used a staple in his line, a combination hog scalder/horse trough, for the mold. After adding a layer of enamel and four legs, the trough became a bathtub.

THE ELJER TOILET TANK

Eljer Plumbingware was the first to introduce the vitreous china tank toilet in the United States in 1907. Until then, the tanks were commonly wood, lined with copper, zinc or galvanized steel. Eljer's round china tanks solved the problem of leakage and sediment buildup. However, initial sales were slow because a skeptical public worried that the vitreous china was too fragile to hang on a wall and support the weight of 6 1/2 gallons (24.60 liters) of stored water. To prove the strength of his vitreous china tank, *Raymond Elmer Crane* (founder of Eljer Plumbingware) staged a demonstration talked about for years. A tank was placed on its side on the ground, then two rails, a plank and the entire work force of the Eljer plant - 27 men weighing a total of 4,748 pounds (2155 Kilograms) - piled on top of the plank. The tank didn't break and plumbing history was made.

EARLY BATHROOMS FOR THE WEALTHY

In the late 1800s as these novel fixtures designed for indoor use were introduced, the wealthy began retrofitting their spacious mansions. Upper class interest in the bathroom continued through the gilded age of building, which lasted until the Great Depression. Typically, bedrooms - called "chambers" - were sectioned off to include a bathroom. These new bathrooms were generally sprawling spaces with a free-standing lavatory, bathtub and pull-chain toilet placed around the perimeter of the space.

INDOOR PLUMBING FOR EVERYONE

For the general public, private indoor bathrooms became a standard for new homes in the early 1920s. In these modest dwellings well-designed space was not a priority for architects or builders. Rather, the major focus was squeezing three separate fixtures - bathtub, toilet, and wall-hung lavatory - into the smallest space possible. Consequently, a cramped 5' x 7' (152.4cm x 213.36cm) area became the standard space reserved for the bathroom. Early bathrooms in both luxury and more modest homes, had no sense of cohesive design or organization.

SPECIFYING BATHROOM PRODUCTS TODAY

That approach doesn't work today. The challenge facing contemporary, bathroom designers is to select the best fixtures and fittings for the project under consideration and then to arrange them efficiently and attractively in a total room environment. Once these component parts are specified, the storage system must be planned and all the surrounding systems selected.

This chapter familiarizes you with all the engineering details of the fixtures and fittings used in the bathroom, from both domestic and international sources, as well as the details of other types of bathroom equipment and surfaces used. Chapter 3 teaches you how to use these tools of bathroom design to create a room that functions well and is a pleasure to look at.

Fixture Materials

Before we discuss the materials used for fixtures and fittings, let's define some key words:

- **Fixture:** A bathtub, shower, lavatory (bathroom sink), toilet (water closet), bidet or urinal that receives water.

- **Fitting:** A lavatory, shower or bathtub faucet, bathtub filler spout, showerhead, body spray, body mist or other finished piece through which water passes and then enters a fixture. For simplicity, we'll use the word "fitting" to refer to all of these types of water delivering devices.

- **Accessory:** Towel bars, handrails, toilet paper holders and various other items that complement the fixtures and fittings and are an important part of each bathroom center of activity.

Your company may have specific terminology policies. So ask how you should refer to the various fixtures in your specifications.

When speaking with a client, use terms that are familiar to the average homeowner, or explain a new name to the client the first time you use it.

FIXTURE CONSTRUCTION

Vitreous China

Vitreous china is used in the manufacture of lavatories, toilets, bidets and urinals. Vitreous china is a form of ceramic/porcelain that is vitrified or "glass-like." It is used for lavatories and toilets because of its formability and sanitary characteristics. Vitreous china has less than .5 moisture absorption compared to other types of ceramics, such as wall tile, that may have as much as 10% moisture absorption.

Figure 78   (Courtesy of American Standard Inc.)
Vitreous china is a popular fixture material for bathroom lavatories.

A MOLDED PRODUCT

Vitreous china fixtures are a pottery product. To begin the manufacturing process, flint, feldspar and water are mixed with different types of clays. Once combined, the mixture is poured into a Plaster of Paris mold, where it remains during the curing process. The Plaster of Paris mold is cast from a "master mold" which is reused. These molds consist of two sections which form the inside and outside profile of the piece. In solid casting, the mixture is poured into the area between these mold sections. This mixture, called a "slip," then conforms to the interior profile of the mold. For thicker elements of vitreous china fixtures such as the rim of a pedestal lavatory an alternative method called "drain casting" is used. This permits the forming of a hollow section without the use of an interior mold.

QUALITY STANDARDS

When the fixture is removed from the mold, it is inspected for imperfections. Different manufacturers have different definitions of acceptable quality. Generally it pays to stay with reputable brands and deal only with firms that have a good reputation for service.

The number of times a Plaster of Paris mold is used affects the incidence of imperfections in the fixture. To maintain a high quality product, first class manufacturers use the molds fewer times. Some fixture imperfections are repairable. Others are not, which then requires that the fixture be destroyed. Therefore, an unacceptable flaw in the tank of a one-piece unit will require destruction of the entire fixture. This is one reason why these fixtures cost more than two-piece toilets.

Figure 79 (Courtesy of Kohler Co.) Vitreous china is also used for toilets and bidets. In this example, a wall-hung lavatory has a shroud to conceal the plumbing pipe.

THE GLAZE

After a fixture passes inspection, a glaze is applied. The fixture is fired in a kiln for an average of 24 hours at temperatures reaching up to 2,250° Fahrenheit (1232°C). Once the fixture is removed from the kiln, it is again inspected for imperfections in the glaze surface. Fixtures that meet all standards are boxed and shipped.

Decorated Vitreous China

Some vitreous china fixtures are enhanced with the application of a decorative decal, the addition of striping in a precious metal, or the application of an accent color and/or pattern. A decal or decorative stripping is applied after the china fixture has been glazed and fired. The fixture is then refired a second time. If this additional firing is at 800° Fahrenheit (426°C), the decoration is "on-glaze." If the firing is at a higher temperature, the decoration is "in-glaze." If the decorative detail is "on-glaze" it will require more care than a typical fixture. If the decoration is "inglaze" it will be as durable as a standard fixture. To determine just how careful your client must be when using or cleaning the fixture, find out at what temperature the final firing took place.

Enameled Steel

Bathtubs and lavatories can be constructed out of enameled steel. This material is fabricated by forming steel in a cold state, then applying a coating of enamel, and finally firing the finished piece in an oven.

To fabricate an enameled steel fixture a sheet of metal is pressed into a die so that it forms the desired shape. This process is called "drawing" because the process results in creating a shape that has depth. The fixture is also subject to mechanical operations, called "stamping" to cut or form the fixture or individual parts of the fixture. Some enameled steel fixtures also require sections to be welded together. After the form and shape have been finalized, an enamel coating is sprayed onto the fixture. It is then fired in a furnace.

In the showroom, an enameled steel fixture looks quite similar to a cast iron one. However, there are dramatic differences between these two types of fixtures. Enameled steel fixtures are more susceptible to damage than some other fixture materials because when an object is dropped on the fixture, the smooth formed steel will flex on impact. Because of the smooth nature of the enameled finish, it does not follow the movement of the steel, and may therefore chip.

Enameled steel bathtubs are also noisy and good heat conductors, causing the bath water to cool quickly. On the plus side, they're the least expensive fixture you can specify and they're easy to handle because of their light weight.

Figure 80   (Courtesy of Kohler Co.) Decorated vitreous china fixtures add a touch of elegance to guest bathroom spaces.

Proprietary Materials

In an effort to maintain the weight benefits and the cost savings of enameled steel in fixtures, yet overcome the material's susceptibility to damage, major manufacturers have introduced proprietary fixture materials over the last several years. To learn more about the benefits of these special products, read the manufacturer's literature or consult with the company representative.

Cast Iron

You may have heard the term cast iron, but have never known what the term really means. "Cast iron" actually describes a manufacturing process used for more than a century to produce bathtubs.

The difference between the mechanical operations used to form sheetmetal fixtures and the cast iron manufacturing process is that the metal in this second process is formed by molding it when it is so hot it is a liquid.

A CAST PRODUCT RECYCLED

Sand is used to create the shape of the mold. The molten iron, at 2,700° Fahrenheit (1482°C), is poured into a channel, filling the cavity. After the molten iron has cooled and solidified, the sand cast is removed (the sand is recycled) and the exposed product is ready for finishing. The exterior surface must be smoothed to a uniform finish. Once this is done, the final enamel finish coat is added. This finish is a combination of clay, frit, color oxides and opacifiers. It's applied to the exposed surfaces of the fixture in powder form, and then fired at 1,250° Fahrenheit (695°C) which melts the powder uniformly into a smooth coating which fuses to the cast iron base material.

The enamel coating on iron is much thicker, and the cast iron more resistant to movement than is the case with an enameled steel fixture. Therefore, a cast iron product is more chip-resistant.

Figure 81 (Courtesy of Kohler Co.) A relatively small 60" whirlpool is often used in smaller bathrooms. This has five fully-adjustable jets and integral heater to maintain water temperature.

HEAT TRANSFERENCE

Cast iron fixtures are cool to the touch and therefore may be momentarily uncomfortable for the bather as he/she reclines against the back rest above the water line. Because the cast iron is a good conductor of heat, the bath water will cool more rapidly in a cast iron bathtub than it will in one made out of a plastic material, which has better insulating properties.

WEIGHT FACTOR

Cast iron bathtubs are heavy, and therefore generally limited to sizes up to 72" x 36" (182.88cm x 91.44cm) and 60" x 42" (152.4cm x 106.68cm). Attention to this weight factor is important if you're designing a bathroom that's accessible only up a long flight of stairs. It can easily require four strong men to wrestle a cast iron bathtub up to a second floor location. Check the manufacturer's specifications to verify the exact weight of the fixture.

Stainless Steel

Stainless steel fixtures are generally formed following the same process described for enameled steel fixtures. However, no surface coating is applied to a stainless steel fixture.

Stainless steel quality is generally judged by the steel gauge, the nickel content of the fixture and the finishing technique.

Figure 82   (Courtesy of Kohler Co.) A stainless steel lavatory adds an interesting texture to the bathroom space.

The higher the gauge number, the thinner the steel. 18 gauge steel is considered the best product for an upscale residential project. 20 gauge steel may also be acceptable. 22 gauge steel

should only be used in very low budget projects.

Nickel in the steel increases the corrosion and stain-resistant qualities of the fixture. European products typically have a higher nickel content than U.S. stainless steel products. Lastly, a brushed finish is easier to care for than a mirror-like surface.

Cast Polymers

Cultured marble, cultured onyx, cultured granite and solid-colored polymer-based materials are all used for cast mineral filled polymer fixtures. Although generally referred to as "cultured marble," a better term for you to use when describing all of these materials is "cast polymer." The term is recommended so you can discuss this potential fixture and surfacing material without limiting yourself to describing a product that looks like synthetic marble.

Regardless of the use, cast polymer surfaces are created by pouring a mixture of ground marble and polyester resin into a treated mold, where the curing process takes place at room temperature or in a curing oven.

GEL COAT APPLICATION

The process begins by spraying a gel coat onto a mold. Because most residential fixtures are sprayed by hand, the gel coat thickness ranges from 12 to 20 mil (1 mil = 1/1000th of an inch). Research by the **Cultured Marble Institute** has proven that a 12 mil gel coat is the minimum acceptable gel coat thickness. A 20 mil gel coat is more durable. However, gel coats thicker than 20 mil do not add wearability. Quite the opposite - thicker gel coats that are applied unevenly lead to a common problem associated with cast polymer fixtures called "crazing." Crazing is the presence of tiny fractures within the gel coat resulting from the thermal shock caused by repeated exposure of the material to alternating hot and cold water. This problem typically shows up around the drain in a lavatory if the gel coat is not thick enough, if the fixture is improperly installed by the plumber, if water stands in the lavatory, or if the incorrect cleaner is used.

Figure 83   (Courtesy of The Cultured Marble Institute) Cultured marble combines beautifully with other materials, and offers the advantage of a bathtub as an integral part of the deck.

A Molding Process

The gel coat is first allowed to cure. A semi-liquid material which consists of polymer resins, a catalyst to promote curing, and highly filled, inorganic particulates of pulverized calcium carbonate, hydrated alumina and, in some instances, glass bubbles is then poured into the mold.

If the cast polymer material will have a solid color, no further steps are taken. If the material will have a marbleized pattern throughout, the second color is swirled into the mixture. The mixture is then allowed to cure. After which it is removed from the mold, inspected, finished, boxed and shipped.

Patterns and Designs

- **Cultured Marble and Onyx:** Traditionally, cast polymers have attempted to duplicate the look of marble or onyx.

- **Granite:** A granite-like pattern is available.

- **Solid colors** are also on the market.

The durability properties of solid colors and granites are the same as standard cultured marble. However, new types of cast polymers, such as granite-look materials, are generally equal in expense to solid surface materials because of the additional cost of materials and the need for more careful mold handling.

The difference between the marble, onyx and granite look in cast polymer materials is caused primarily by the type of raw materials used.

- Cultured marble is 20% to 30% polymer resin by weight.

- Cultured onyx is 30% to 35% polymer resin by weight.

- Cultured granite is 35% to 45% polymer resin by weight.

- Cultured marble and cultured granite are opaque.

- Cultured onyx is translucent.

QUALITY STANDARDS

Because the material is fabricated with a gel coat finish, the benefits of machining in the field are not present in a cast polymer product.

This polyester gel coat finish is also not as durable as other surfacing materials. However, a skilled craftsman can repair damage to a cast polymer fixture on the jobsite, and the cultured marble patterns are generally the least expensive finish available.

The cast polymer industry is typically made up of small shops spread throughout North America. Therefore, the quality of fixtures varies dramatically.

The best way to ensure a quality fixture is to specify only products which are certified under the joint **Cultured Marble Institute** (CMI) - **National Association of Home Builders Research Center** (NAHB RC) Certification Program (435 North Michigan Ave., Suite 1717, Chicago, IL 60611).

Under this program, manufacturers of cast polymer products are subject to unannounced plant inspections. Additionally, randomly selected products are periodically put through a series of stringent tests related to stain resistance, wearability, thermal shock and structure properties according to standards of the **American National Standards Institute** (ANSI).

Manufacturers of products meeting the requirements of the ANSI standards are permitted to affix CMI-NAHB RC cer-

tification labels to their products. These labels provide consumers with a guide to quality among cast polymer products.

Solid Surfacing

Solid surfacing materials are excellent products for bathroom wall panels and countertops, as well as fixtures. Manufactured from acrylic, polyester or a combination of acrylic and polyester base materials, these homogeneous (color all the way through) materials can be machined by a skilled fabricator and are repairable if damaged. The hard, non-porous surfaces are stain and burn resistant.

Figure 84 Solid surfacing material is beautifully combined with laminate, ceramic tile and mirror in this attractive bathroom. Note how the solid surfacing is used as countertop material, as well as a cap to frame the tambour laminate and to finish the bathtub.

There are differences between acrylic-based and polyester-based materials. A more detailed discussion of solid surfacing materials follows in *Section 7 - Surfacing Materials*.

Natural Stone

Granite or marble slabs may be used to create custom, one-of-a-kind lavatories. Typically, these natural stone products are reserved for wall, counter or floor surfacing in slab or tile format.

A detailed discussion of their application appears in *Section 7 - Surfacing Materials*.

Natural Wood

In recent years, several manufacturers have offered wood bathtubs and lavatories. They were beautiful, but the bathtubs never gained market acceptance and are no longer available from major manufacturers. Wood lavatories, however, are still on the market.

Wood fixtures are generally constructed from solid strips of teak or oak. Teak wood is considered more desirable than any other species because of its oily composition, which minimizes its expansion and contraction properties. This is why teak is used so extensively in marine applications. Once constructed, the fixtures are finished with a marine varnish to protect and enhance the beauty of the wood.

Wood fixtures should not be exposed to constant, direct sunlight and they should be wiped down after each use. If damaged, the finish can be repaired.

Man-made Plastics

Novice bathroom designers are often confused by all the terms that relate to bathroom fixtures made from man-made materials. Some fixtures are identified by the reinforcing material used: fiberglass. Other fixtures are identified by the exterior finish material used: acrylic. And still others are identified by the manufacturing process employed to fabricate the fixture: injection molded.

To understand the differences among these fixtures you need to understand the differences between a reinforcing material and a finishing one. Plus, you should be familiar with the different attributes of each one of the popular finishing materials.

Figure 85   (Courtesy of American Standard Inc.)
Large bathtubs are typically made from man-made plastics because of the material's moldability and its lightweight attributes.

FIBERGLASS

Fixtures that are generally referred to as "fiberglass" refer to the backing material used to reinforce a polyester gel coat finishing surface. A mold receives a layer of gel coat and then fiberglass strands immersed in a polyester resin is sprayed on or placed on top of the mold in mat form. Additional reinforcing, in the form of wood or metal strips or braces, is attached at this stage of the manufacturing process.

The polyester gel coat is not as durable as other finish surface layering materials in use today. However, it is generally the least expensive. Much like cultured marble (cast polymer) products, such fixtures are widely produced by small factories. Therefore, quality levels can vary widely.

ACRYLIC

Another manufacturing approach is to create the fixture by forming it out of a 1/8" - 1/10" (.32 - .25cm) sheet of acrylic or acrylonitrile-butadiene styrene (ABS). In this thermo-forming method the temperature of a thermoplastic material, such as acrylic or ABS, is elevated to a level which makes it pliable and workable; it is then vacuum formed into a mold, creating the desired shape. All fixtures requiring structural support are sprayed with resin and chopped strands of glass in much the same manner as the fiberglass spray-up method of construction detailed above. The application of reinforcement boards or braces is also the same for both materials.

Acrylic and ABS thermal plastics are harder materials than polyester gel coat and the color goes all the way through the material. They also offer deeper

color tones and are more resistant to abrasion, high heat scarring and sun fading. Although acrylic can be scratched, it is repairable. As you might expect, acrylic fixtures are also more expensive than gel coat finished fixtures. Acrylic bathtubs are reinforced on the underside, usually with fiberglass.

INJECTION MOLDING

Injection molding is the third method of manufacturing plastic fixtures. The plastic material is heated until it reaches a liquid state, at which time it's injected into the cavity of a mold. With this process, the color you see on the surface goes all the way through the material. All plastic fixtures are warm to the touch, and therefore are comfortable for the bather to lean against. These fixture materials act as insulators so that the water in the bathtub does not cool too rapidly. Noise can be reduced by including a sound-deadening undercoating.

Figure 86   (Courtesy of Kohler Co.) One-piece, two-piece and three-piece stall showers and bathtub/shower combination units are available in man-made materials.

REFINISHING EXISTING FIXTURES

To minimize the cost of a bathroom renovation project, the client may consider resurfacing rather than replacing one or all of the fixtures. If the bathtub or enclosure is worn or is an outdated color, this might be a practical alternative to completely replacing the fixture and surrounding material. However, refinishing is not recommended for the lavatory or toilet as they can be damaged easily in these high use areas.

The products used and the installation methods employed vary, so the durability of a refinished product is entirely dependent on the company selected to complete the work.

Paint products are used by some resurfacing companies. After the fixture is cleaned and prepared, polyurethanes and enameled paints are sprayed onto the fixture. These materials flake, chip and peel quite easily. Simulated porcelain is more chip-resistant and not as prone to fading and yellowing. This simulated porcelain is applied to the fixture after it has been cleaned and etched and then treated with a bonding agent. This type of simulated porcelain is chemically cured, rather than being fired in a furnace.

Whatever method of refinishing is selected, the client must be aware that the bathtub will not be usable for two to four days during the curing process and that the finish should be considered delicate.

Section **2**

Fixture Design and Construction

LAVATORY FIXTURES

The bathroom sink is called a lavatory, basin or bowl. Throughout this manual they are identified as "lavatories."

There are generally five types of lavatories:

- **Pedestal:** A free-standing fixture. The water supply lines are visible. The trap is partially concealed by the base.

Figure 87   Pedestal lavatory.

- **Wall-hung:** A fixture that hangs from the wall. Plumbing lines and trap are visible unless a shroud is used to cover them.

Figure 88   Wall-hung lavatory.

- **Integral:** A fixture that is fabricated from the same piece of material as the countertop material. Plumbing is concealed in the cabinetry.

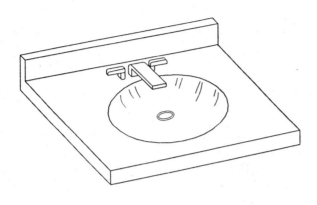

Figure 89   Integral lavatory.

- **Countertop:** A separate fixture installed above or below the level of the countertop material. Plumbing lines are concealed in the cabinetry.

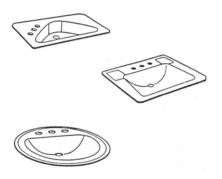

Figure 90
Countertop lavatory.

- **Console Table:** A separate or integral fixture that is installed above or below a countertop material that is supported by decorative legs, creating a console piece of furniture. Plumbing lines are partially concealed by the front

edge of the console furniture piece.

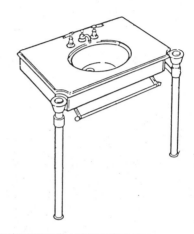

Figure 91   Console Table lavatory.

Types of Lavatory Fixtures

PEDESTAL LAVATORY

A variety of sizes is available. The smallest pedestal lavatory is little more than a bowl on a base. Larger pedestal lavatories offer a generous bowl and counter space on each side of the lavatory.

Plumbing specialists suggest the following checklist for you to think through when you specify a pedestal lavatory:

- **Open Pedestal Base:** The pedestal base may be open all the way down the back, may be solid up to 16" off a finished floor, or may have a horizontal support bar connecting both sides of the pedestal base somewhere along the back. These last two fixture designs may interfere with the drain location. Therefore, read the manufacturer's specifications to verify what the back of the pedestal base looks like and where the drain line should be roughed in.

- **Finishing the Pipes:** Because the pedestal base is at least partially open, do not install a mirror behind the unit. To maintain continuity, remember to consider the

Figure 92   Carefully study the manufacturer's rough-in dimensions. Here are two pedestal lavatories that vary in width from 22" to 38".

decorative finish on the shut off valves, P-trap, box flange and supply lines as you select the other fittings in the bathroom.

- **Connecting Two Pieces:** The pedestal lavatory and base are two separate pieces. Some companies provide mounting brackets to connect these two pieces. Many do not, which will require that you bolt the lavatory to the wall.

- **Vertically Align the Pedestal Base:** Because the plumbing lines are exposed behind the vertical pedestal base, it is critical that the drain and supply lines are dimensionally balanced behind the pedestal. This is far less critical inside a vanity cabinet, where the supply lines can be anywhere within the open cabinet space. For a pedestal lavatory, the rough-in dimensions must be perfectly centered on the pedestal - make sure your plans are accurate.

- **Selecting the Right Faucet:** Your choices of faucet handle style and escutcheon plate diameter may be limited if the pedestal lavatory has a small back deck, or if there is an integral splash along the back of the fixture. If you are specifying a fitting that has not been designed to fit on the pedestal lavatory by the fixture manufacturer, verify that these two items are compatible by reviewing the dimensional information from both companies.

- **Specifying the Height:** Shut-off valves are typically 22" (55.88cm) off the finished floor for both countertop and pedestal lavatories. The design of some pedestal lavatory bases limits the shut-off valves to about 16" (40.64cm) off the finished floor. This height dimension is as important as the vertical arrangement mentioned above.

Exact specification for the rough-in plumbing lines is critical in bathrooms that will feature a pedestal lavatory. The pedestal base offers little height flexibility. Although some manufacturers do offer two heights, if the base is not available in the right height for your client, you may want to consider building a platform directly beneath the pedestal.

- **A Storage System:** Pedestal lavatories do not provide built-in storage. They can be surrounded quite attractively by a storage system. To add shelf storage, plan to install a ledge on the wall directly behind the pedestal. Alternatively, or in addition, consider a recessed or surface- mounted shallow wall cabinet behind or adjacent to the pedestal fixture.

A pedestal lavatory can dramatically increase the visual space of a small bathroom. Pedestal lavatories are particularly appropriate in small powder rooms where drama and beauty is of importance. Pedestals are functional in a family bathroom if the users complete grooming activities at a dressing table or center elsewhere in the bath or in an adjacent bedroom.

Figure 93   (Courtesy of American Standard and Wilsonart International) This pedestal lavatory has an interesting storage system designed around it.

Figure 94 (Courtesy of Kohler Co.) Side-by-side pedestal lavatories have extra storage space created with a shelf behind them and a ledge treatment created out of natural stone.

WALL-HUNG LAVATORY

Square, round and corner wall-hung units are available with both centered and off-set fittings. Wall-hung lavatories are particularly appropriate in a bath designed for a handicapped user.

- **Supporting the Fixture:** The wall-hung fixture literally "hangs" off the wall on brackets that cantilever away from support blocking secured inside the wall between the studs.

Figure 95 (Courtesy of Kohler Co.) A unique wall-hung lavatory with faucets attached to a mirror cistern.

- **Adjustable Heights:** Some European manufacturers have introduced wall-hung lavatories that are adjustable in height. Do not specify any fixture that moves in any direction until you have verified local code acceptability.

Many wall-hung lavatories leave the supply lines exposed below the lavatory. However, some lavatories offer the option of a shroud or cover which conceals the piping below the lavatory.

INTEGRAL LAVATORY

Integral lavatories are usually cast polymer or solid surface material. By definition, they are all one piece, although in solid surfaces these often are customized by under-mounting a countertop lavatory of the same material but in a different color. These are two pieces technically, but are integral in effect.

Integral bowls are the easiest to clean because of their seamless configuration. Be forewarned - they are also typically the shallowest types of bowls available. Therefore, in a shallow integral bowl, a high arched spout might cause a splash-back problem that the client finds unacceptable. If you are dealing with an integral bowl that is shallow, stick with standard type faucets to minimize the splash-back problem. Additionally, it is a good idea for clients to understand that splashing may occur until they grow accustomed to using the faucet at the lavatory.

The drawback to the integral bowl is that damage to either the bowl or the countertop may necessitate replacement of the entire unit. Clients may question whether the entire top needs to be replaced if the integral lavatory is damaged. They may ask: *"Can't the lavatory just be cut out, so that I can drop in a new lavatory?"* This is rarely possible because of the potential destruction of the top as one attempts to cut the old bowl out while the top is in place. Additionally, if you attempt to cut the bowl out you will interfere with the drilled hole placement, which will prohibit its reuse.

COUNTERTOP LAVATORY

In high-end design some of these fixtures sit entirely above the countertop, bowl and all, or extend beyond the front of the countertop. However, most are fitted into a countertop cut-out, either dropped in from above or under-mounted below.

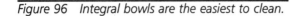

Figure 96   Integral bowls are the easiest to clean.

Figure 97   (Courtesy of Kohler Co.)   Some lavatories are mounted completely above the countertop, draining through it. The example above shows a conical form lavatory.

Figure 98   (Courtesy of Allmilmo) The countertop lavatory above protrudes beyond the countertop and cabinetry in this storage wall.

- **Self-rimming:** If the lavatory is designed to hang from its own rim atop the counter, it is called "self-rimming". The lavatory features a bowl that fits into a cut-out, with a rim around the edge of the bowl from which it is suspended from the countertop. A bead of sealant between the rim and the countertop prevents water seepage. The weight of the fixture, the sealant, the supply lines and the trap hold the lavatory in place.

  Edge Detailing: Self-rimming lavatories allow the edge detail of the bowl to enhance the design of the fixture. Before the lavatory is installed and the plumbing connected, the installer should inspect the edges of the fixture to make sure that there are no chips or areas of damage that will be unacceptable to the consumer.

Figure 99   (Courtesy of American Standard Inc.) A self-rimming lavatory sits on top of the counter surface.

Warpage: Self-rimming lavatories are also susceptible to warpage. Large lavatories, and particularly oval designs, may not fit flush on the countertop. Because they do not rest perfectly on the countertop surface, they will require a larger caulking line. The client must understand this and must be willing to accept the fixture with this installation.

Selecting the Caulking: Several major manufacturers supply color matched caulking to complete the installation. If not available, you, as the designer, must determine what color sealant or bead is required. Alert the installer so that the proper materials are on the jobsite. For example, there is nothing more unsightly than a teal laminate counter surface and a teal lavatory separated by a bead of white caulking.

Templates: For some hand-made china self-rimming bowls, no template will be available. In a bathroom with more than one lavatory, do not allow the installer to use one bowl as a template for all. There may be slight differences. Each lavatory should be used for its own template. As a general rule, make sure the self-rimming lavatory is on the job when the countertop is cut. That way there will be no mistakes.

Cleaning Concerns: The client must be made aware that the raised lip of the self-rimming fixture will require that a towel or sponge be used to wipe the counter surrounding the rimmed lavatory.

Ledge Drilling: The drilling location for a self-rimming lavatory must be verified before the cabinetry is ordered. Most standard, self-rimming lavatories have one hole, a 4" (10.16cm) center set drilling, or a 8" (20.32cm) to 12" (30.48cm) widespread drilling as part of their back ledge. Therefore, no special dimensioning is required because the overall depth of the lavatory will accommodate the bowl, the overflow and the plumbing lines to the faucet.

However, pay particular attention to the number and diameter of the holes drilled in the lavatory. As you will learn when we talk about lavatory faucets, a mini-widespread faucet does not use an escutcheon plate and has rigid piping so that there is no flexibility in the distance separating the valves from the spout. Therefore, if there is any discrepancy between the drilling holes on the lavatory and the faucet drilling it won't work.

Another compatibility problem may occur when you attempt to specify a single hole faucet with an escutcheon plate on a lavatory faucet that has been drilled with three holes. Sounds simple enough - you're going to use the escutcheon plate to cover the two unused holes. The problem is the diameter of the hole. On many lavatories that are drilled for a standard 4" (10.16cm) center set, that center hole will only be 1-1/8" (2.8cm) in diameter. For a single hole faucet, you need 1-1/4" (3.18cm). It is difficult, and expensive, to drill a cast iron lavatory. The potential for damage is great as well.

Figure 100   (Courtesy of Eljer Plumbingware) An example of a single hole faucet.

Figure 101   (Courtesy of American Standard Inc.) A lavatory which features a Hudee rim.

- **Rim Type:** Cast iron, vitreous china, as well as enameled steel lavatories, can be installed with a stainless steel rim called a "Hudee rim". The lavatory is dropped into a cut-out and then secured in place by the rim and retaining clips installed underneath. The stainless steel rim may detract from the finish on the lavatory, the faucet and the adjacent counter surface. Additionally, the rim tends to collect soil, making this type of installation more difficult to clean than others. This is also a rather dated look and style in bathroom design.

- **Under-Mounted:** In this case, the lavatory is installed from below the counter surface. The countertop extends over the edge of the lavatory and facilitates cleaning. This type of lavatory should always be ordered with a glazed rim. The bowl then becomes strictly utilitarian providing no opportunity for the edge or the shape of the bowl to act as an accent in the design. This type of installation is particularly successful in a natural stone and solid surface or cast polymer material.

Although rarely done, lavatories can be under-mounted in decorative laminate. Special care must be taken when under-mounting a lavatory in a decorative laminate top to insure that no water seeps between the laminate edging material and reaches the plywood or particleboard substrate below. One way to protect against this is to laminate the underside of the top near the lavatory.

Make sure that the laminate self-rimming material is also seamed at the front of the bowl so that the joint is concealed. Lavatories are also sometimes under-mounted in a ceramic tile installation if an experienced tile setter is available to install the small 1/4" round tile pieces that will be used to complete the transition from the tile deck surface to the lavatory profile. Regardless of what type of material is used, the bathroom designer should always specify a lavatory with a glazed

rim for an under-mounted installation so that any exposed edge of the lavatory will be finished.

- **Flush Mounted Type:** In some areas of the country mounting a square-edged lavatory flush with the surrounding ceramic tile deck is popular. The rim and outside edge of the lavatory must be glazed, and the unit must have square corners to facilitate the flush installation. Additionally, the client must accept the possibility of a slight height difference between the lavatory and the adjacent tile caused by the natural tendency for these large bowls to warp. Offered by a few makers, these are either colored glass or fancy ceramic. Glass units are conical, others are bell-shaped or hexagonal. This type also goes well as a console lavatory

Figure 102   (Courtesy of Kohler Co.) An under-mounted lavatory facilitates cleaning.

Figure 103   (Courtesy of American Olean Tile Co.) A surface-mounted lavatory is attractively combined with ceramic tile.

CONSOLE LAVATORY

Another type of lavatory is called a "console." The integral lavatory and countertop are supported by two to four decorative legs. No cabinet storage system is installed below. This approach combines the sense of space a pedestal lavatory creates with the functionality of adjacent surface space for grooming aids. However, a cabinet storage system should be designed elsewhere in the room.

FAUCET DRILLING POINTERS FROM THE PRO'S

For a self-rimming lavatory with no faucet drilling, or an under-mount lavatory, drilling for the faucets in the countertop is the normal installation. Because you must specify the exact placement of the drilling holes, plan this area carefully.

- **Locate the Overflow:** Make sure you and the installer understand where the overflow is supposed to be located. The most typical installation has the overflow at the front of the bowl. However, a few specialty lavatories are designed with the overflow in the back. Improperly installing this lavatory bowl will prohibit the lift rod from reaching the drain, because it will now be in the wrong location. Check the manufacturer's specifications!

Figure 104   (Courtesy of Kohler Co.) A console lavatory adds a decorative element in this bathroom space.

- **Identify the Overall Dimensions of the Lavatory:** The lavatory size listed in the manufacturer's specifications may refer to the interior diameter of the lavatory. However, to properly locate the countertop drilling, you must work with the overall or outside dimension of the fixture.

- **Verify Required Cabinet Depth:** The drilling may be placed in the counter surface behind the fixture or off to one side of the unit.

Generally 6" (15.24cm) plus the front-to-back dimension of the lavatory will be sufficient. For some fixtures, this may require a cabinet deeper than the industry standard of 21" (53.34cm). The overall depth must be calculated in such a situation.

Figure 105 and the chart below detail what calculations you must complete to verify that the lavatory and faucet will fit in the cabinet.

- **A"** Backsplash material thickness.

- **B"** Cleaning room from the edge of the deck mounted faucets to the front edge of the splash material.

- **C"** Diameter/width of faucet escutcheon plate.

- **D"** Cleaning room from the edge of the deck mounted faucet to the back edge of the lavatory

- **E"** Overall depth of the lavatory (including clip space if necessary)

- **F"** Additional lavatory space requirement for front overflow channel.

- **G"** Space required from lavatory front to the inside of the cabinet.

- **H"** Cabinet face frame thickness.

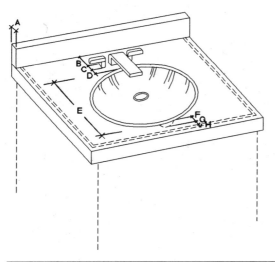

Figure 105   How to verify that the lavatory will fit in the cabinet.

Shapes of Lavatory Fixtures

The overall shape of the lavatory and the faucet installed on that lavatory dramatically affects the function of the lavatory. The bowl should be as large as possible to facilitate hand washing, face washing and brushing of teeth. For shampooing hair at a lavatory, a special oversized fixture with a separate pull-out, hand-held spray is ideal.

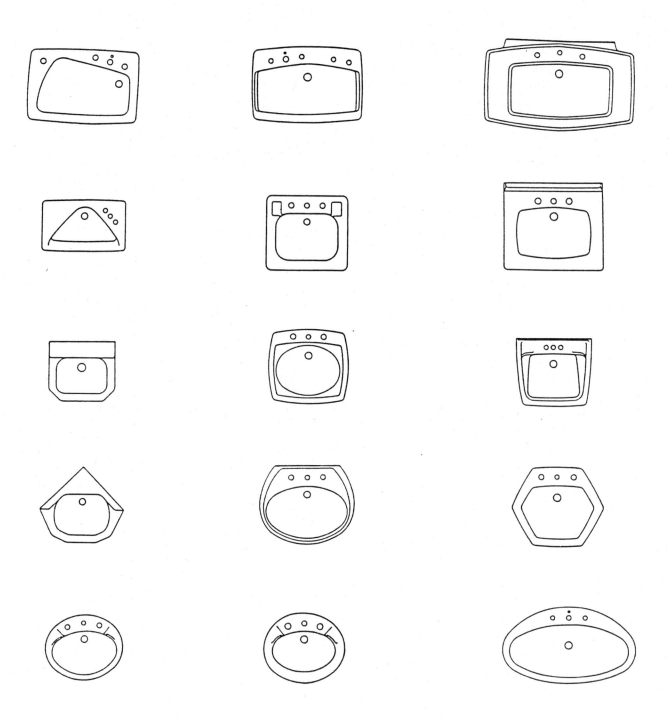

Figure 106   *Typical lavatory shapes and relative sizes.*

TOILET FIXTURES

A toilet, or water closet, is designed as the fixture used for both male and female urination and defecation in North America. The fixture holds this human waste and then flushes it out through the waste lines in the home to the city sewer system or to a septic system.

Selecting The Right Name

The term "water closet" comes from a European home design that featured the toilet and a small lavatory in one room separated from a larger room housing the bathtub - an early version of compartmentalizing the bathroom. This design allows one family member to be bathing while another uses the toilet. Therefore, the term "water closet" really refers to the room, not the fixture.

In the United States, the term "toilet" is most often used. All kinds of secondary names have been created for this fixture as well, such as the commode, or the john. You and your company will decide if you want to use the trade designation "water closet", or if you prefer to call the fixture a toilet when talking to clients so that they are not confused by unfamiliar terms.

Toilet Construction

Nearly all toilets are made of vitreous china - a hard, high-fired, non-porous, ceramic material similar to porcelain. Fused to the china's surface is a high-gloss glaze which further adds to its excellent sanitary properties.

Toilet Water Usage

For many years, conventional toilets required more than five gallons of water per flush. In the 1980s the new standard for water saving toilets was 3.5 GPF (13.25L), 1.6 GPF (6.1L) toilets were planned for the future. Today the limit by law is 1.6 GPF (6.1L) toilets.

This substantial reduction in water usage is making new demands on the designers and manufacturers of toilets and is leading to new engineering solutions in these fixtures.

Toilet Options

The chart on the following page, takes the specifier through the toilet selection process.

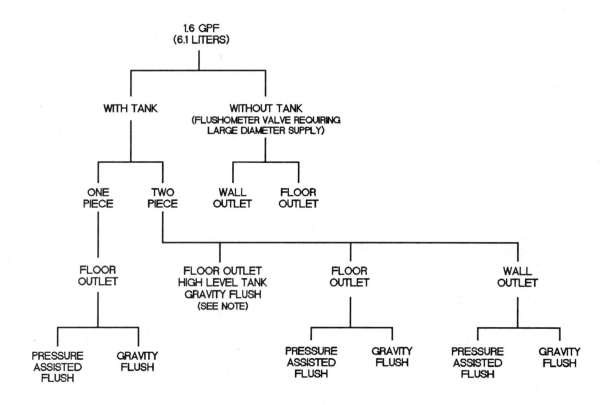

OPTIONS AVAILABLE WHEN SELECTING THE
RIGHT TOILET FOR A SPECIFIC INSTALLATION

1.6 GPF
(6.1 LITERS)

WITH TANK

WITHOUT TANK
(FLUSHOMETER VALVE REQUIRING
LARGE DIAMETER SUPPLY)

ONE
PIECE

TWO
PIECE

WALL
OUTLET

FLOOR
OUTLET

FLOOR
OUTLET

FLOOR OUTLET
HIGH LEVEL TANK
GRAVITY FLUSH
(SEE NOTE)

FLOOR
OUTLET

WALL
OUTLET

PRESSURE
ASSISTED
FLUSH

GRAVITY
FLUSH

PRESSURE
ASSISTED
FLUSH

GRAVITY
FLUSH

PRESSURE
ASSISTED
FLUSH

GRAVITY
FLUSH

FLOOR OUTLET TOILETS USUALLY HAVE A 12" (30.48 CM) ROUGH-IN (THE
DIMENSION FROM THE CENTER OF THE FLOOR OUTLET TO THE FINISHED
SURFACE OF THE WALL) IN REMODELING INSTALLATIONS (AND POSSIBLY IN
OTHERS) 10" (25.4 CM) OR 14" (35.56 CM) ROUGH-INS MAY BE REQUIRED. NOT
NOT ALL TOILET TYPES OFFER THESE OPTIONS.

Figure 107   This chart takes the specifier through the toilet selection process.

Toilet Styles and Types

FLUSHOMETER

One kind of toilet is a bowl which has no tank. It is fitted with a flushometer valve operating off the main water supply. These bowls, normally confined to commercial and institutional buildings, are available in floor outlet models and in wall outlet models which come with either top inlets or back inlets for the flushometer valves. The term "flushometer" also applies to the valve used in the newer pressure-assisted toilets, developed after 1.6GPF limit went into effect.

Figure 108   (Courtesy of American Standard Inc.) A flushometer toilet does not have a tank.

TOILETS WITH STORAGE TANKS

More widely used are toilets with tanks. These may be one-piece or two-piece toilets. Most two-piece models are close-coupled, the tank being supported by and bolted to the bowl. While most are floor standing and have a floor outlet, there are models with wall outlets and they may be either floor-standing or wall-mounted. There are also nostalgic designs with period-style high level tanks. There is a wide choice of elongated or round bowls, each accepting standard-size seats. Some luxury toilets are supplied with seats specifically designed for the toilet.

Figure 109   (Courtesy of American Standard Inc.) Toilets with storage tanks may be one-piece units or two-piece units, as seen above.

One supplier hides the tank in the wall, with only a flush plate showing. This tank has a carrier system to connect with wall-hung toilets made by others. This installs between standard 16" studs. Another model, in a housing of the designer's choice, projects 6" out from the wall. Either model conserves bathroom space.

Toilet Rough-in Dimensions

A wide variety of floor standing toilets with floor outlets have a 12" rough-in dimension (the distance from the center of the outlet to the finished surface of the wall). There are a limited selection of models with either a 10" (25.4cm) or a 14" (35.56cm) rough-in which are sometimes required for retro-fit projects.

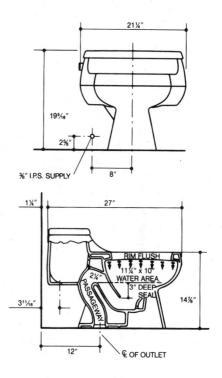

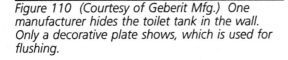

Figure 110 (Courtesy of Geberit Mfg.) One manufacturer hides the toilet tank in the wall. Only a decorative plate shows, which is used for flushing.

Figure 111 (Courtesy of Kohler Co.) The rough-in dimensions for this one-piece toilet specify where the floor outlet and where the supply lines should come in.

Flushing Methods and Devices

Toilets are flushed either from a tank or directly from the water supply, the latter mostly in commercial installations. Residential toilets are available either with a gravity flush or with a pressure-assisted flush. In a gravity flush, the force of gravity alone is employed, and the tank needs only a back-flow-protected fill valve (ball cock) and a flush valve. The second type has a pressure vessel in the tank which contains both water and air. The air is compressed by supply system pressure as the refill charges the tank. When the toilet is flushed, the air pushes the water out of the tank at high velocity. The toilet bowl, which has been specially designed to accept this water stream is quickly emptied.

A variation is a model equipped with a low-power electric pump. This requires electricity, and must be hard-wired.

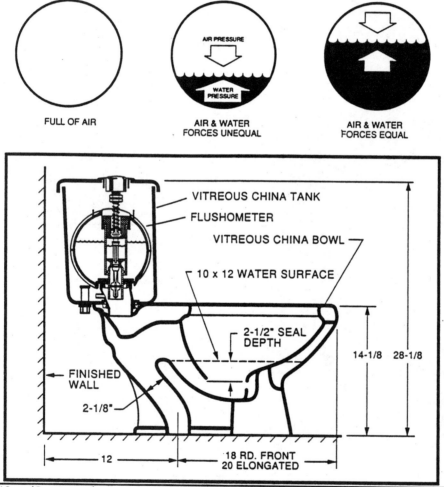

Figure 112   (Courtesy of American Standard Inc.) A generic cross-section of a pressure-assisted 1.6 GPF (6.1 L) flushing system.

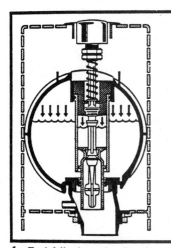
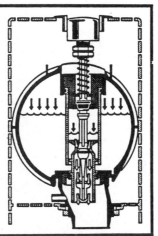
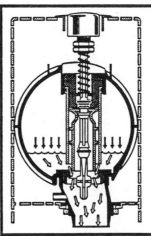
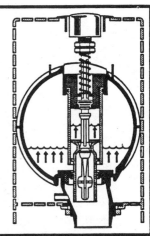

1. *Tank fully charged and ready to be flushed. Air and water pressures equal.*

2. *Water in valve cartridge discharges when flush button is pushed.*

3. *The main valve now opens. Flush water surges into the bowl.*

4. *Bowl empties within 4 seconds. Waste is carried through drainline at crest of "charged" water torrent. Flush valve closes. Tank begins refill cycle.*

Figure 113   (Courtesy of American Standard Inc.)
The four drawings above demonstrate the theory of operation for a pressure-assisted toilet.

FLUSHOMETER TOILETS

Toilets without tanks can only be used where large diameter pipes make an adequate flow rate over 25 GPM (95L) available. The flush is controlled by a flushometer valve which may be an exposed fitting, connected to the top of the toilet bowl, or a fitting concealed in the wall and connected to the back of the bowl. Flush valves are available with a hand operated lever or with a no-touch infra-red or proximity activator.

Flushing Action of Bowls

There are six basic approaches to designing the flushing action, each with its own unique performance characteristics. In addition to performance considerations, factors to consider in design include:

- Water surface area provided in the bowl;

- Depth of water seal (from the surface of the water down to the top of the trap entrance);

- Trapway size (The actual dimensional measurement of the passageway. The latter is based on standards of performance involving the passage of balls of varying diameters.);

- Boxed or open rim.

SIPHON VORTEX

This flushing action is based on diagonal rim outlets which cause a swirling or "whirlpool" action. The resulting rapid filling of the trap triggers the siphoning of the bowl contents. Vortex designs are known for their large water surface area and extremely quiet operation. New ANSI standards for low-consumption siphon vortex models require that it pass a 2" (5cm) ball and have a water spot of 10"-12" (25-30cm).

Siphon Action Reverse Trap

As the name implies, this type features a trap at the rear. It should be understood, however, that this feature is not unique to the reverse trap design - all locate the trap in the rear. However, some models are available without a jet.

Nevertheless, toilets specifically designated by this term have certain design and performance characteristics which relate to industry standards. In addition to introducing incoming water around the rim, a specific jet outlet is directed into the upward leg of the trap to enhance the siphoning action.

Siphon Wash

This system relies entirely on the incoming rush of water from the rim with rapid filling of the trap, triggering siphoning of the bowl contents. With the advent of low-consumption models, some of these may also have an added jet.

Siphon Jet

Similar in basic concept to the siphon action reverse trap design, this style is more advanced in efficiency. The jet in this case delivers flow with such a volume as to begin the siphoning action instantly, without any rise in the level of water in the bowl before the contents are drawn through the outlet. In addition to quiet operation, siphon jet

designs also provide a larger water surface area.

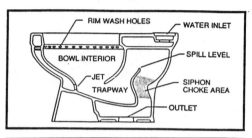

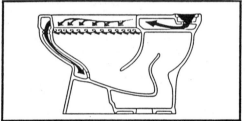

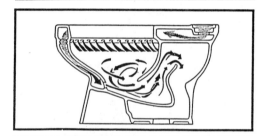

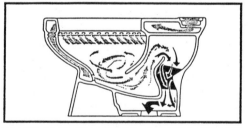

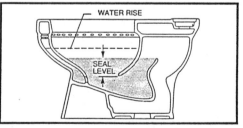

Figure 114　(Courtesy of American Standard Inc.)
Flushing action of a Siphon-Jet bowl.

BLOWOUT

This is the one design in the group that doesn't incorporate a siphoning action. Instead it relies entirely on the driving force of a jet action. Because of the water capacity required to accomplish this, blowout designs are used in tankless installations only, in combination with a flush valve. Such designs are known for their generous trapway size and large water surface area. This is what we described earlier as a flushometer toilet.

WASHDOWN

No longer much of a factor in installations, this type is unique in having its trap located in the front (which accounts for the external protrusion in the front of the bowl). While this design is really quite efficient in operation, it is characteristically more noisy than other types, and its small water surface makes it more vulnerable to soiling and staining.

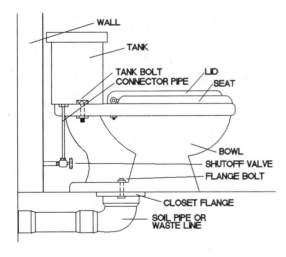

Figure 115   The anatomy of a standard toilet.

TOILET PLANNING POINTERS FROM THE PROS

- **Specify the Actuator Finish:** Always check the tank lever or push button actuator finish against other fitting finishes if you wish all to blend together. The tank lever can be a button at the top of the tank, a valve on the side of the tank, or a valve on the front of the tank. Decorative actuators are generally the most effective for toilets with the actuator on the front of the tank.

- **Verify the Floor Outlet Rough-In:** If you are working in a house that is 50 years old or older, double-check the drain outlet dimension by measuring from the finished wall surface to the center of the bolts on each side of the existing toilet. The 10" (25.4cm) and 14" (35.56cm) rough-in dimension toilets were used in many cases in the old days. You may need to order a fixture that is available in one of these older rough-ins. This approach will severely limit the models you have to choose from. Alternatively, you may select to use an offset flange to modify the old outlet center dimension to today's more standard 12" (30.48cm). The offset hurkle ring lets you offset the fixture outlet by up to 2" (5.08cm).

- **Measure from Finished Wall:** Remember, the rough-in dimension is always from the finished wall surface to the center of the drain. If you are installing a tile wainscotting around the room, and planning on a "mud" tile installation, you may need to rough-in the toilet at 13-1/2" (34.29cm) from the drywall surface so that you truly have a 12" (30.48cm) finished rough-in outlet from the finished tile surface to the center of the floor outlet.

Realize the PSI Will Vary: All toilets recommend a particular PSI (pounds per square inch of pressure available at the fixture) so that it can clean the bowl with one flush. However, remember that the time of year, the household activities, and the neighborhood activities will affect the available water pressure. This is discussed in Volume 2 under "Plumbing".

Think About Cleanability: Some toilets are easier to clean than others. If this is a major concern of your client, look for a one-piece toilet, and in particular, one with straight sides which conceal the caps that cover the bolts holding the toilet above the floor outlet.

Remember Fixture Sizes Vary: One European toilet is only 14-7/8" (37.78cm) wide. Typical North American products are from 20" (50.8cm) to 24" (60.96cm) wide. The normal seat height is 14" (35.56cm) to 15" (38.1cm) high. Seat height in universal design is designated at 18" (45.72cm).

Become Familiar with Industry Jargon: In some parts of the country a one-piece toilet will be referred to as a "low boy" or a "low profile" fixture. Make sure you understand regional terms.

Understand That Different Supply Line Sizes and Rough-ins are Specified for Different Toilets: A low-profile toilet requires 1/2" (1.27cm) rigid water supply lines - not the 3/8" (.95cm) lines typically called for with a two-piece toilet. Additionally, the height of the supply lines for a one-piece toilet is generally lower than for a two-piece toilet. Check each manufacturers' specification sheet before specifying the supply line pipe diameter/type and/or pipe. Make sure you identify this dimension before you specify the finish baseboard material. There is nothing more unsightly than a 4-1/2" (11.43cm) ceramic tile baseboard with 1/4" (.63cm) round trim that is interrupted by a supply line that is half in/half out of the baseboard dimension.

Cover Cleaning Concerns with Your Client when Discussing 1.6 GPF (6.1 L) Toilets: 1.6 GPF (6.1 L) toilets have an operational concern that your client must be aware of. Bathroom professionals always recommend that gravity flush 1.6 GPF (6.1 L) toilets be designed with a decorative toilet brush as a standard accessory next to the fixture. And, the homeowner must be forewarned to expect to use it.

This concern has to do with the water surface area commonly called the "water spot". In the past, the bigger the water surface area the better the operation of the toilet for the user. With a smaller water spot as a standard part of the 1.6 GPF (6.1 L) toilet, there may be some scouring required after using the toilet.

- **Make Sure the Client is Prepared for the Noise Associated with 1.6 (6.1 L) Pressure-Assisted Toilets:** Pressure-assisted 1.6 GPF (6.1 L) systems cost more than gravity flow units and they are noisier. Although the noise is only heard for an instant, as the pressure moves the water through the system, this may be unacceptable in a powder room adjacent to an entertaining area, or in the middle of the night in the master suite. To minimize the transmission of this noise, try to avoid placing a pressure tank toilet on a common wall separating the fixture from spaces inhabited by guests or other sleeping family members.

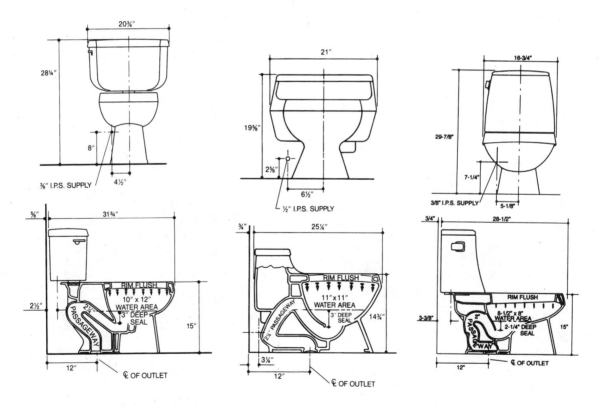

Figure 116   Typical toilet shapes and sizes.

BIDET FIXTURES

Two different types of bidets are available from manufacturers.

- Rim-filled with vertical spray

- Over-rim with horizontal spray

Rim-filled with Vertical Spray

This type of bidet provides an ascending jet spray, as well as a bowl filling mechanism through holes along the rim. A vertical spray delivers water through the outlet in the center of the bowl, allowing the user to direct the spray to the desired area simply by sliding their body forward and backward on the bidet. This type of bidet requires the following components:

- individual hot and cold valves

- a diverter valve

- a pop-up drain control

- spray fitting and connections to the water ways.

Such bidet fittings come complete from the faucet manufacturer. Specify deck-mount or wall-mount fittings according to the type of bidet chosen. To insure compatibility, some faucet manufacturers will require that you specify the bidet model chosen. Because the bowl can be filled to a height above the vertical spray, the possibility of contaminated water entering the potable water system exists. This phenomenon is called "back flow". This situation can occur if the city's water supply temporarily has negative pressure (if it sucks instead of pushes), causing a vacuum to be created that would pull contaminated water

Figure 117   (Courtesy of American Standard Inc.) The bidet on the left has an over the rim horizontal spray. The bidet on the right, a vertical jet.

standing above an inlet into the potable (fresh) water supply.

To prevent such water contamination due to a back flow, a vacuum breaker must be installed behind the bidet. This protective device breaks the back flow, or suction action, by allowing air into the piping system. Check that the vacuum breaker is supplied with the selected bidet fitting. This will insure adaptability between the systems. Alternatively, there are firms that provide "fit-all" vacuum breaker systems that adapt to most faucet lines, and may be more attractive as well.

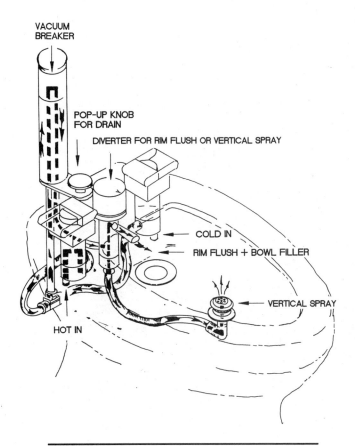

VACUUM BREAKER

POP-UP KNOB FOR DRAIN

DIVERTER FOR RIM FLUSH OR VERTICAL SPRAY

COLD IN

RIM FLUSH + BOWL FILLER

VERTICAL SPRAY

HOT IN

Figure 118   The drawing of this bidet shows how a vacuum breaker is installed behind a bidet that has a vertical spray, and how this backflow

Over-rim with Horizontal Spray

This bidet has no ascending jet spray in the center of the unit. It is filled by means of a deck-mounted faucet - rather like a lavatory faucet - that discharges water over the rim in a horizontal stream. This type of fixture is generally less expensive to purchase and install because both the bidet and the faucet are simpler to produce and a vacuum breaker is not required.

BIDET PLANNING POINTERS FROM THE PROS

- **The Drain Location:** The bidet drain is more like that of a lavatory's than that of a toilet. Therefore, there is no fixed rough-in recommendation for the drain outlet. Refer to the selected manufacturer's literature on rough-in specifications.

- **Coordinate with Toilet:** Because bidets are installed adjacent to, or across from toilets, fixture manufacturers design suites of products so that the rim height is coordinated between the toilet and bidet, as is the shape and configuration of the fixture.

- **Select the Faucets:** The faucets selected for the bidet must be compatible with the fixture. Not all china products accept valves from other manufacturers. If you order fixtures and fittings from different manufacturers, the hole configuration on the fixture or the shank on the valve and bidet fitting may not coordinate with one another.

Figure 119   (Courtesy of Absolute) This bathroom suite of fixtures includes a toilet and bidet attractively seen against a wood back wall.

Figure 120   (Courtesy of Kohler Co.) The bidet and toilet are designed en suite because they're generally installed adjacent or opposite to one another.

Figure 121   (Courtesy of Kohler Co.) The toilet and bidet are well placed in this bathroom. The toilet paper holder is in a proper location. The ledge behind the fixtures provides a spot for towels and soap used at the bidet.

Personal Hygiene System at Toilet

Some manufacturers, recognizing some reluctance in American consumers to accept bidets, are combining the functions of both toilet and bidet in one fixture. In at least one case, this dual function is designed into the toilet. In others, the bidet seat is an add-on that can go with the toilet or be purchased in the after-market.

Figure 122 (Courtesy of Toto) Personal hygiene system at toilet.

URINAL FIXTURES

Urinals are available in a wall-hung variety, a stall type that extends from the floor up, and a trough that is mounted horizontally on the wall. Wall-hung units are most widely used. They require the least amount of space, offer the most placement flexibility and typically are the most attractive. They are made of vitreous china.

Although it would make sense to install urinals in residential bathrooms, they are rarely seen because most are designed to rely on the building's water pressure and piping system to deliver the necessary water to complete the flushing action and therefore do not have a storage tank. They commonly use the flushometer valve discussed earlier under toilets. Designers also have not designed them into home plans. They would be ideal in a master suite where the gentleman has a small room with his toilet and a urinal, and the lady has a toilet and a bidet. Other ideal locations are boys' bathrooms and the entry bathroom off the deck, pool or patio area.

BATHTUB FIXTURES

There is a wide variety of bathtubs available today. Although there are many different shapes and sizes, there are four broad categories of bathtubs as defined by the installation method.

Types of Bathtub Fixtures

RECESSED

This type of bathtub comes without finished ends and with one finished side, typically called the "apron". The bathtub is designed to slip between two end walls and against a back wall. You must specify a left or right drain so that the drain is in the proper relationship to the finished front. When you are standing in front of the bathtub - about to enter - and the drain is on the left, it is a left hand bathtub. Many bathtubs feature well engineered, integral backrests and grab bars. Typical sizes are 30" (76.2cm) to 34" 86.36cm) wide, 14" (35.56cm) to 20" (50.8cm) deep, and 60" (152.4cm) long. Bathtubs are made of enameled cast iron, enameled steel and proprietary materials, as well as fiberglass and acrylics. These bathtubs generally have an integral tile flange on the two side walls and the back so that when the wet wall material is installed, water will not be able to "wick" up behind the surround material and damage drywall or wood studs. Many manufacturers also offer a tile bead kit which allows you to transform a bathtub without such a flange into a recessed unit.

CORNER

These units are available in two styles. One type is available in a configuration similar to the standard recessed bathtub. However, in addition to the front being finished, one end has a finished panel as well. Another type of fixture is designed to fill a corner and features three angled or curved finished sides. Several manufacturers have introduced sculpted bathtub shapes that offer a wider variety of configurations for corner installations. This second type of corner bathtub generally requires from 4' (121.92cm) to 5' (152.4cm) along the back two walls, and extends from 5' (152.4cm) to 6' (182.88cm) out from the back corner into the center of room. They are a space efficient way to plan a whirlpool bath if the available back wall space is limited.

FREE-STANDING

Unique, free-standing bathtubs are also available from several manufacturers. The free-standing bathtub literally stands in the middle of the room. Several manufacturers offer a recreated claw foot bathtub reminiscent of Victorian-style bathrooms. A curved, oblong shaped bathtub attractively trimmed in wood is also available. Some of these bathtubs are available with a whirlpool system. As you will see when we talk about safety and showering in Volume 4, these free-standing bathtubs should never be planned as showering facilities.

PLATFORM

The last type of bathtub is a platform bathtub. This bathtub has no finished panels. It is designed to drop into a platform made of another material. You will find the bathtubs available in enameled steel, cast iron, proprietary materials, acrylic, gel coat, fiberglass or ABS plastics. Designs are similar regardless of material, but there are some limitations on the cast iron fixture sizes. Because these bathtubs are dropped into a platform, the edge detailing of the bathtub adds to the design statement.

For this type of an installation, the designer should be very careful about the relationship of the raised bathtub ledge and any back corners of the platform if the bathtub will also serve as a shower. Water can "pool" in the corners, and cause a cleaning problem.

Alternatively, some designers prefer to extend the platform material over the bathtub to create an under-mounted installation. This latter installation may make it uncomfortable for users to rest their head on the bathtub ledge when lounging. It also will significantly increase the cost to change the bathtub if ever necessary.

If a bathtub is a separate fixture from a stall shower, a decorative protective material is installed, which extends upwards from the bathtub or deck, 4" (10.16cm) to 12" (30.48) along the walls that flank the bathtub. This material typically matches or contrasts with the deck-ing material. Where the bathtub doubles as a shower, contrasting material may be specified, the bathtub may have integral walls, or the bathtub and walls may be made out of the same material but in a four-piece configuration to facilitate moving the bathtub into position in a renovation situation. These types of surround materials will be discussed in more detail when we look at bathtub/shower combination fixtures.

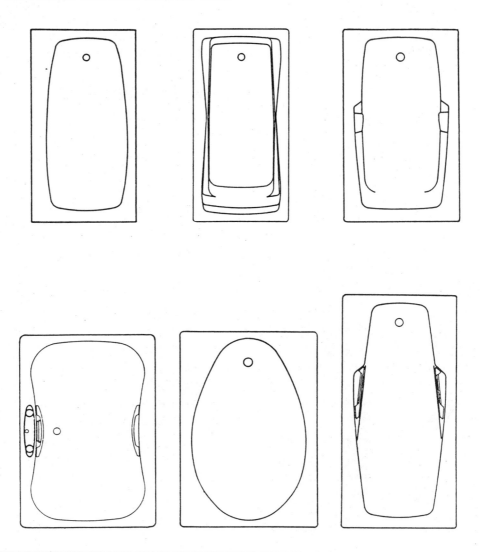

Figure 123   Typical bathtub shapes and relative sizes.

Figure 124 Courtesy of Allia Some bathtubs have a removable apron.

Figure 125   Many bathtubs are designed to be installed in a platform.

Whirlpool Bathtub

A whirlpool hydromassage system is installed as part of the bathtub in many upscale bathrooms today.

Most manufacturers provide a totally integrated whirlpool system and bathtub which has been factory tested before shipment. Although Chapter 3 discusses the ergonomic planning considerations for this type of fixture, you should also be familiar with the individual mechanical elements of a whirlpool system.

MECHANICAL ELEMENTS

- **Pump:** The pump is at the heart of the system. The size of the pump varies in horsepower rating from 1/2 HP to 1-1/2 HP. However, the horsepower rating is not the only contributing factor to the engineering of the pump and jet system. Therefore, rely on the gallons per minute of water flow pushed through the jets when evaluating the system, rather than simply focusing on the pump horsepower rating. Generally, whirlpool tubs are capable of delivering 5 to 7 gallons (19 to 27L) of water per minute, per jet. The system should have UL approved components. The major manufacturers have the entire system UL approved for additional safety assurance and for customer satisfaction.

- **Activator:** The pump may be activated by a timer switch installed on the wall. If used, locate it out of reach of the bathtub so that the chance of an electrical accident is avoided. Most codes specify a distance of 60" (152.4cm) or more.

Alternatively, an air switch installed directly on the bathtub may be available. Check the price list - this type of starter may carry an extra charge to you. When an air switch is depressed it increases the air pressure and a bubble of air travels down a length of tube to an electrical switch at the pump. For both safety and convenience the air switch is superior to an electrical switch. A third type of switch is also available on luxury bathtubs called a "capitance switch". It activates the bathtub when it senses the electrical differences which occur when a person lightly touches the control panel.

- **Wiring:** Both 120 and 240 volt pumps are available. Generally, whirlpool bathtubs with a one horsepower motor or less will operate off a 120 volt circuit. Whirlpool bathtubs that have a motor larger than one horsepower will generally require a 240 volt circuit. Regardless of the motor size, if an in-line heater is included, a 240 volt circuit may be needed.

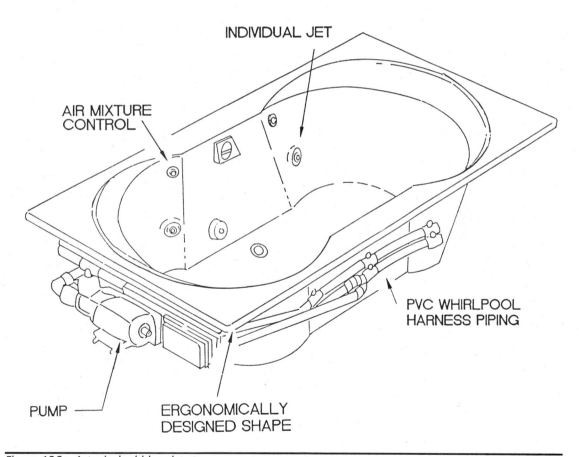

INDIVIDUAL JET

AIR MIXTURE CONTROL

PVC WHIRLPOOL HARNESS PIPING

PUMP

ERGONOMICALLY DESIGNED SHAPE

Figure 126   A typical whirlpool system.

ACCESSIBILITY

The pump must be accessible for future servicing, a requirement often overlooked by inexperienced bathroom designers. Check the manufacturer's literature or find out from your supplier where the pump is in relationship to the overall configuration of the bathtub.

For factory installed systems, the pump fits within the envelope of the tub. Some manufacturers do offer alternative pump locations of up to 60" (152.4cm) away from the bathtub. Verify such an option by reviewing the fixture literature.

If the manufacturer's specifications do allow a remote location, consider concealing the pump in a vanity cabinet adjacent to the bathtub, in a closet space near the bathtub, or behind a concealed access door along the front apron panel of the bathtub. Wherever it is placed, it must be on the same level as the base of the bathtub to provide a complete drain after each use.

NOISE

Be sure to alert your clients to the noise level of all whirlpool systems. The majority of the noise is caused as the large volume of water is pushed through the piping and into the bathtub. Therefore, you cannot design a silent system. However, you can minimize the noise by mounting the pump on a thick rubber block and enclosing it on three sides.

PLACEMENT

For proper performance and safety the pump/motor assembly must be no higher than the highest jet (which is 2"

(5.08cm) below the water level) and no lower than the suction fitting. The piping used to connect the system must also be designed to remain rigid through the fixture's years of use. At the jobsite, the installation crew must also be instructed not to pick the bathtub up by the piping.

This pump/jet placement and piping design are required so that a 100% drain-out of used bath water will occur every time the bathtub is emptied. If this placement criterion is overlooked, or if the pipe flexes during the bathtub's years of use, the first water to enter the fixture would be contaminated water from the last bath.

THE JETS

There are two different approaches to whirlpool jet design:

- **Volume/Pressure Relationship:**

  1. Fewer jets with larger outlets, that are serviced by bigger water lines. The jets operate on a high-volume, low-pressure system that provides a comfortable bathing experience for the user as softly pulsating water rolls around the body. They are generally noisier than the next option.

  2. More jets with smaller outlets serviced by small water lines. These jets operate on a low-volume, high-pressure system to bring the water to the numerous jets which can be individually adjusted for the user's comfort.

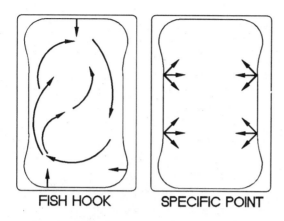

FISH HOOK   SPECIFIC POINT

Figure 127   Whirlpool bathtub water patterns.

MIXING AIR WITH WATER

Better systems inject the air into the water, thereby providing a complete mixture of air and water for a more effective massage. This mixture of air and water is called a "venturi" effect. To maximize the flexibility of the system, better bathtubs have jets that are individually controlled for spray direction, volume and air/water mixture. The jets in well-engineered bathtubs are also nearly flush to the bathtub's interior.

However, there is a drawback to mixing air with water: the room temperature, 72°F - 75°F (22°C - 24°C) air will cool the bath water. Additionally, the jet controls add another visual element to the bathtub. You should think about the overall look your clients hope to achieve as you recommend matching the whirlpool bathtub component parts to the bathtub finish (the most inconspicuous approach) or contrasting the tub finish and matching the bathtub fittings to the faucet finish specified elsewhere.

THREE WAYS TO JET A BATHTUB:

There are three ways to design a whirlpool bathtub system:

- **Integrated System Provided By Manufacturer:** Purchase a totally integrated and engineered system which includes the bathtub, the on/off activator, the water suction intake, all the jets and related trim, all the rigid self-draining piping, and the whirlpool pump. The manufacturer then takes responsibility for designing the bathtub for the user's comfort, as well as engineering the whirlpool system so that it meets all appropriate code approvals. In this case, it is possible for the manufacturer to get UL approval for the entire design.

- **Customized Bathtub with System Installed at Jobsite:** Design a totally customized, cast polymer (cultured marble), natural stone, solid surface, or ceramic tile bathtub and create a custom designed whirlpool system. Although you gain total design flexibility with this alternative, the responsibility for the success of the system and the comfort of the bathtub rests squarely on your shoulders. Make sure that you have the expertise and the available craftsmen necessary to create such a bathtub.

- **Locally Jetting a Manufactured Bathtub:** Purchase a bathtub and then have it "jetted" by a local specialty source. If your business community has stable companies that specialize in jetting bathtubs, this may be an alternative to purchasing a system designed by a manufacturer. However, here again, you take responsibility for making sure that the system fits the bathtub, that no damage occurs to the bathtub in handling, and for upholding an effective warranty. Consider also, your responsibility if the company that jetted the bathtub should go out of business. Make sure your client understands that once the bathtub is drilled, the bathtub manufacturer's warranty is void and the local jetter's warranty activates.

BATHTUB PLANNING POINTERS FROM THE PROS

Once the bathtub's equipment has been installed and the bathtub has been placed with the comfort, safety and pleasure of the user in mind, the following special construction constraints must be considered.

- **Hot Water Requirements:** The whirlpool bathtub relies on the hot water system installed in the house to fill the bathtub. Therefore, the existing hot water tank capacity and its recovery rate need to be verified before a bathtub is specified. At an initial filling, you can generally expect about 70% of the hot water tank's capacity to be delivered at the temperature set. Therefore, a 40 gallon hot water tank will deliver about 30 gallons (113.55L) of 120°F (67°C) water.

The recovery rate of gas hot water tanks is faster than electric tanks, therefore if the initial drain is not adequate to fill the tub, the recovery rate must be taken into account. The manufacturer's literature will tell you how many gallons of water the bathtub will require.

The capacity of whirlpool bathtubs ranges from 50 to 140 gallons (190 to 530 L) of water. A good rule of thumb would be to size the water heater to provide enough hot water for 2/3 the capacity of the bathtub, with the balance being cold water.
If the existing tank is not adequate, you have three options:

- increase the size of the household hot water heater or install two water heaters side-by-side;

- provide a separate water heater specifically for the whirlpool;

- specify several tankless water heaters along the supply line.

Generally, the first approach is the best one if other water needs are marginally met by the current system. If you select the third option, be forewarned that the tankless systems are not designed to heat the large volume of water required for these bathtubs. Therefore, you may be required to install a series of 240 volt tankless heaters, which becomes cost prohibitive in most cases.

Do not confuse the purpose of an "in-line heater" with that of a storage tank or a tankless water heater. As stated above, the purpose of the tank or tankless water heater is to heat water before it enters the bathtub at the start of the bath. The in-line heater simply <u>maintains</u> the water temperature in the bathtub during the hydromassage bath.

An in-line heater is a good enhancement for a whirlpool tub that will be used by family members for an extended period of time. Just as the piping and pump require service access, such a heater should be reachable by repairmen in the future. Make sure you have enough electrical power for the 240V circuit this heater will require as well.

- **Water Flow Rate:** Regardless of how much hot water is available, if the plumbing supply lines are not large enough and/or if the bathtub filler spout is not adequate, it takes so long to fill the bathtub that the water cools before the bather can begin to enjoy the hydromassage experience.

  Normally 3/4" (1.9cm) nominal (inside dimension) hot and cold supply lines service a bath with three fixtures. 1/2" (1.27cm) nominal individual branches then bring hot and cold water to the standard bathtub fittings. A 1/2" (1.27cm) spout is then used to fill the bathtub.

  To provide the increased flow of water needed to fill bigger bathtubs, a 3/4" (1.9cm) individual water supply branch line and 3/4" (1.9cm) bath spout and valve should be used to maximize the water flow to the bathtub. Remem-

ber, the entire system must be increased in size. If a 3/4" (1.9cm) valve is installed with a 1/2" (1.27cm) branch line, or the reverse, the water supply will not be adequate. Alternatively, doubling up on the bathtub fillers may help get the water into the bathtub fast enough.

- **Accessibility:** Be sure the bathtub you specify is not too large to get into the house, down the hall and around the corner into the bathroom. In new construction, the bathtub is installed during the framing stage. However, in a renovation situation, a large bathtub may be difficult to maneuver into the bathroom. Find out how much the bathtub weighs. A single tradesman may not be able to lift the bathtub without help.

- **Supporting the Fixture:** Typical North American floor systems are designed to carry 40 pounds (18 kilograms) of weight per square foot. Some large bathtubs may require additional support. Verify the weight of the bathtub when it is filled with water and people. If such information isn't available, you can compute the weight as follows: one gallon of water equals 8.33 pounds (3.8 kilograms) and 7.51gallons (3.5 kilograms) of water equals one cubic foot. Once you know how much the bathtub weighs when filled, determine if the existing floor joist construction is adequate enough to support the bathtub.

Figure 128   (Courtesy of American Standard Inc.) Whirlpool bathtubs are available in configurations similar to standard bathtubs. Ideally, they should be deeper to ensure a comfortable bath.

Figure 129   (Courtesy of Eljer Plumbingware) Oval shaped whirlpool bathtubs offer an excellent configuration for small spaces.

Figure 130 *(Courtesy of Kohler Co.) Many whirlpools have unusual shapes and special features. This has ten small jets on sloping backrest that pulsate in sequence to simulate hand massage.*

Figure 131 *(Courtesy of Jacuzzi) Many different square whirlpool bathtubs have been designed to accommodate two bathers.*

Figure 132   (Courtesy of Allia)   Some whirlpool bathtubs have reclining seats built-in to make bathing for two even more confortable.

SHOWER STALL FIXTURES

Stall showers are the ideal fixture for the daily showering ritual that is so much a part of a North American's life. Stall showers come in many sizes and configurations. Chapter 3 identifies minimum sizes accepted by the national building codes and recommended sizes based on human ergonomic studies. The materials that shower pans (the floor and front curb of the shower) and enclosures are made of is the focus of this volume.

Types of Pans

MASONRY AND STONE

Masonry and molded-stone shower pans are available. Masonry pans are of a cement construction with chips of ground stone used as a filler, much like Terrazzo. Terrazzo is a combination of white cement and marble chips. The mixture is poured into a mold and then subjected to high temperatures and pressure for curing. When removed from the mold, the pan has a smooth finish with a homogeneous wall structure.

SOLID SURFACE

Major manufacturers offer solid surface shower pans in popular sizes. Skilled fabricators can also create custom pans for you.

PLASTIC

Fiberglass reinforced gel coat, acrylic and ABS plastic shower pans are available. See *Section 1* for a detailed description of how this material is manufactured.

CAST POLYMER

Cast polymer shower pans are also available. The manufacturing process for this material appears on page 127.

These last three types of pan materials offer an added advantage. The walls in the surround can be made out of the same or similar surfacing. With plastic materials, the enclosure can actually be made in one piece with no seams. These one piece units can be attractively sculpted to include built-in grab bars, grooming recess areas and reclining seats.

SHOWER PLANNING POINTERS FROM THE PROS

- **Make Sure You Can Get It in the House:** When selecting a one-piece shower, or a one-piece bathtub/shower combination, you must remember to verify hallway widths and door openings in a remodeling project. Typically, these fixtures are put in place during the framing stage in new construction. But, in a renovation scenario, the shower must be moved through finished spaces. Therefore, units that feature a separate pan and three walls are more typically specified.

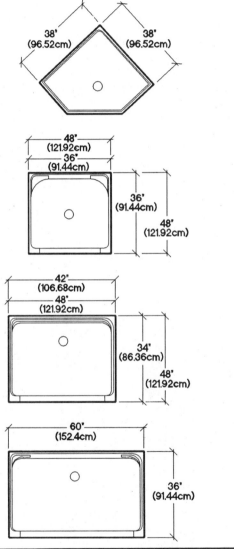

Figure 133   *Typical stall shower pan shapes and sizes.*

- **Specify the Drain Location:** The drain location of all premade

pans is determined by the manufacturer. It is typically in the center of square or round enclosures and off to one side in rectangular units. The location of the drain needs to be clearly specified on the plans to assist the plumber during the rough-in stage. Compare the existing drain in a renovation situation with the specifications for a new pan to make sure they are compatible.

- **Specify the Curb:** All of the man-made materials pans are designed with a ledge at the front, which is called a "curb" or a "threshold." Much like a recessed bathtub, the other three sides of the pan have a raised lip or tile flange so that

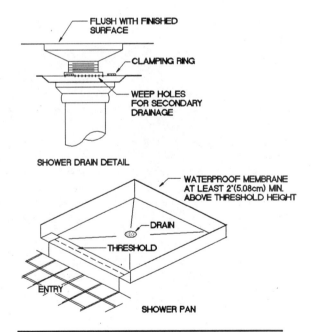

Figure 134
Shower pan and drain detail.

the waterproof drywall can sit on a ledge, rather than extending all the way down to the pan. This minimizes the problem of water wicking up behind the drywall and behind the surrounding finished wall surface material.

When you're planning a ceramic tile pan, you have complete flexibility in size and shape of the enclosure. You're also responsible for making sure the pan is watertight.

BATHTUB/SHOWER COMBINATION UNIT FIXTURES

As you will learn when you study Chapter 3, combination bathtub/shower units do not provide a comfortable bath, nor a safe showering experience. However, the reality of the real design world is that we are often limited to this sort of combination fixture because of space constraints. Bathtubs can be installed with a separate wall surface surrounding them. In this installation, it is always desirable to extend the wet wall surround material past the end of the bathtub and then down to the floor. This protects the wallboard around the bathtub from water damage over the years of use.

Alternatively, the bathtub and wall surface materials can be the same, with the walls available in a separate panel configuration. This option allows the technician to bring the material into a small, difficult-to-reach bathroom and then complete the installation on site. In room addition work or in new construction, a one-piece combination bathtub/shower can be installed. This last choice provides a fixture that is the easiest to clean, the least susceptible to water damage, and the most flexible in its overall design. Today manufacturers provide sculpted units with benches and seats in large, oversized showers, fold-down seating areas in bathtub/shower combinations, built-in grab bars, and storage shelves all seamlessly formed.

Figure 135   A stall shower at the end of a bathtub.

Figure 136 *A corner stall shower takes up little floor space.*

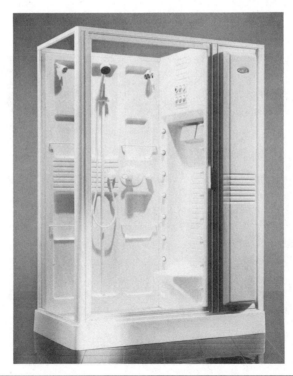

Figure 137 *(Courtesy of Jacuzzi)* *Fully programmed shower systems are available.*

Figure 138   (Courtesy of Eljer Plumbingware)   A stall shower can be designed to accommodate a physically challenged user by keeping the shower floor threshold minimal, including a wide enough enclosure for a wheelchair to enter and featuring grab bars.

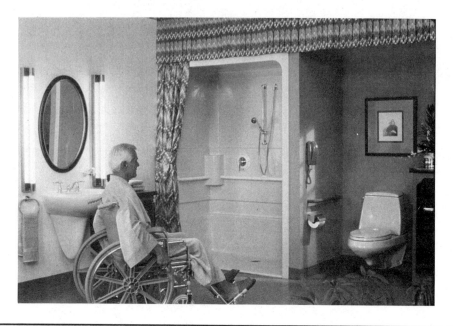

Figure 139   (Courtesy of Kohler Co.)   Another example of a barrier free shower.

Figure 140   (Courtesy of Kohler Co.) A shower can be enhanced by the addition of a shower system that features multiple water functions.

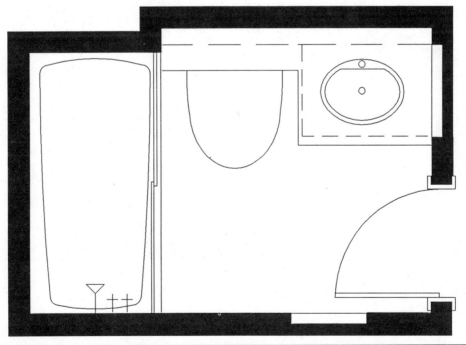

Figure 141   A typical small hall bathroom has the basic three fixtures. This small space is enhanced by the addition of a whirlpool system to the standard bathtub size, and the extension of a countertop across the back of the one-piece toilet.

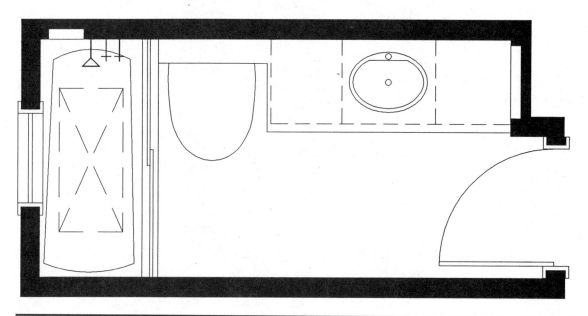

Figure 142   A slightly larger version of a typical bathroom is visually improved with the addition of a sky-light above the whirlpool bathtub, and a mirrored soffit that extends across the vanity cabinetry and the toilet area.

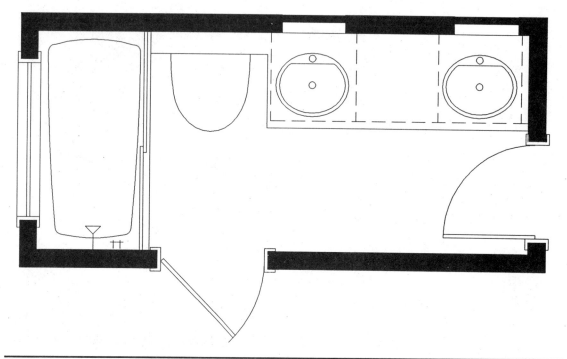

Figure 143   In a small bathroom, two lavatories can be planned as long as the client understands that there will be very little counter space on one side of each of the lavatories.

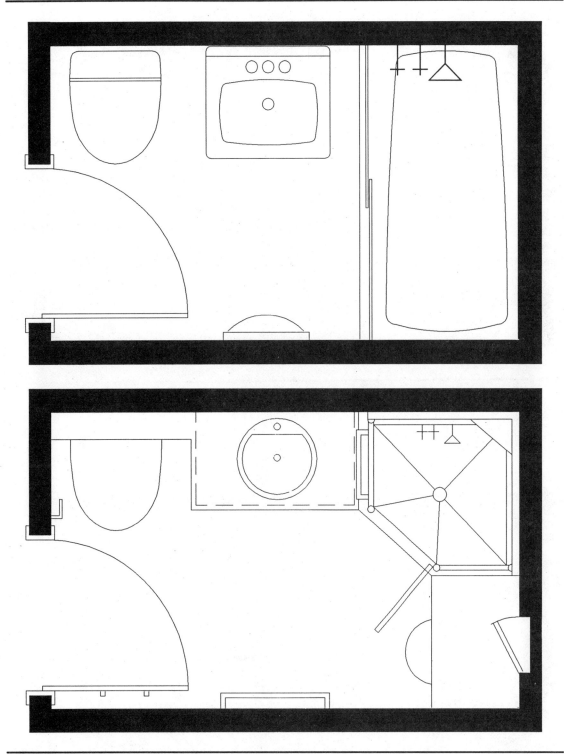

Figure 144   A typical hall bathroom was transformed into a more functional area by switching the standard bathtub to a corner shower. The rough plumbing remains in basically the same location, therefore this switch is affordable. A countertop extension across the back of the one-piece toilet extends the countertop. On the other side of the stall shower a vanity dressing counter is included.

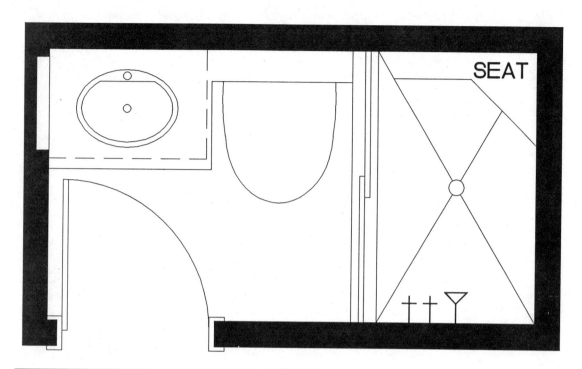

Figure 145   A stall shower can take the place of a bathtub in a small area. A sliding door to the shower works well. Consider a clear door to increase the visual size ot the space.

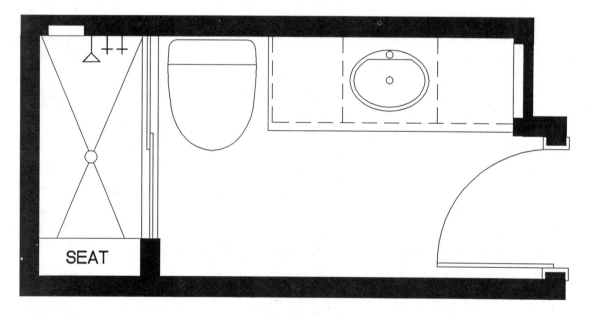

Figure 146   A slightly larger bathroom has been converted from one with a standard bathtub to one with a shower.

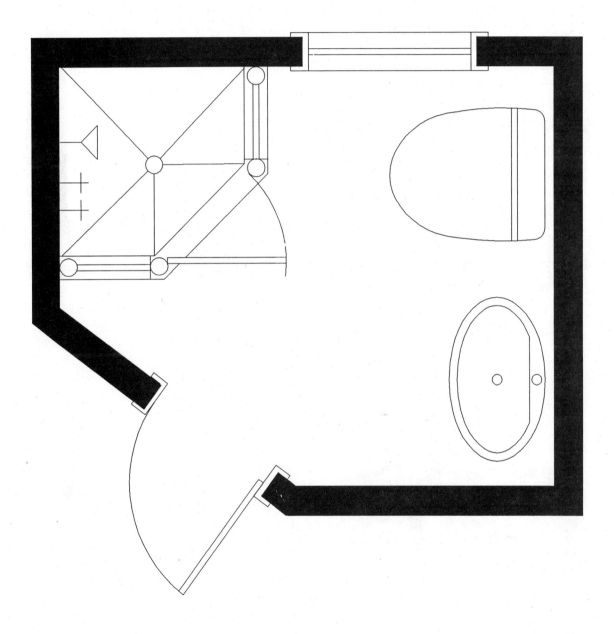

Figure 147 A corner angled shower can be used when clearance is a problem, or to repeat the angle in another wall.

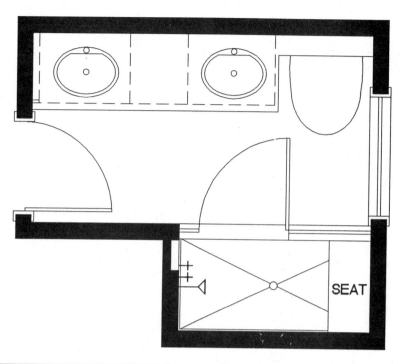

Figure 148   Many typical bathrooms place the bathtub opposite the toilet and vanity area. In this example, a shower has replaced the bathtub fixture.

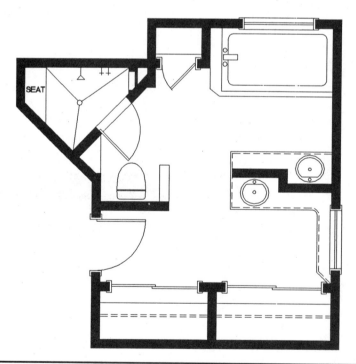

Figure 149   A custom angled shower has been designed to solve several space problems in this bathroom. Note the tight fit between the swinging shower door and the toilet. The back-to-back lavatories create two private grooming areas for adult usage.

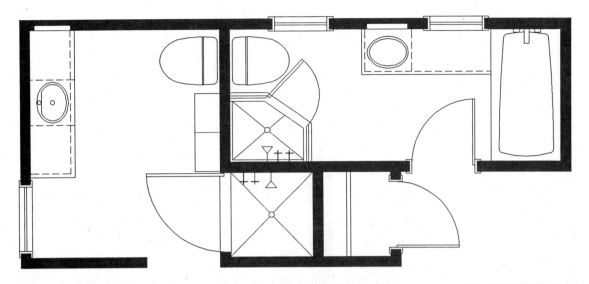

Figure 150   To minimize plumbing costs many homes have bathrooms that are back-to-back. In this example, the master bathroom is enhanced by the addition of tall cabinets along the toilet wall. In the adjacent hall bathroom a new closet has been added. Using a standard sized whirlpool bathtub and an angled shower, allowed separate fixtures to be included in this small hall bathroom space. Note how the vanity extends underneath the window and the sink is placed off-center.

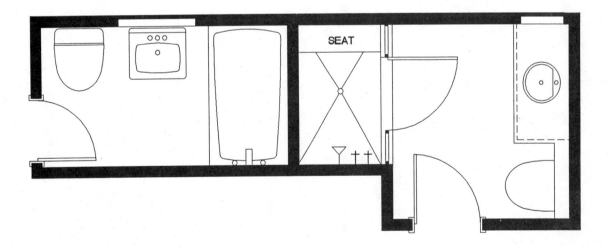

Figure 151   Another example of back-to-back bathrooms. The bathroom off the hall is a straight forward affair, a toilet, pedestal lavatory and whirlpool bathtub. This is an excellent arrangement if this bathroom will be predominantely used by guests. The master bathroom includes a large, luxurious shower and a vanity cabinet that includes a countertop stretching across the back of the toilet.

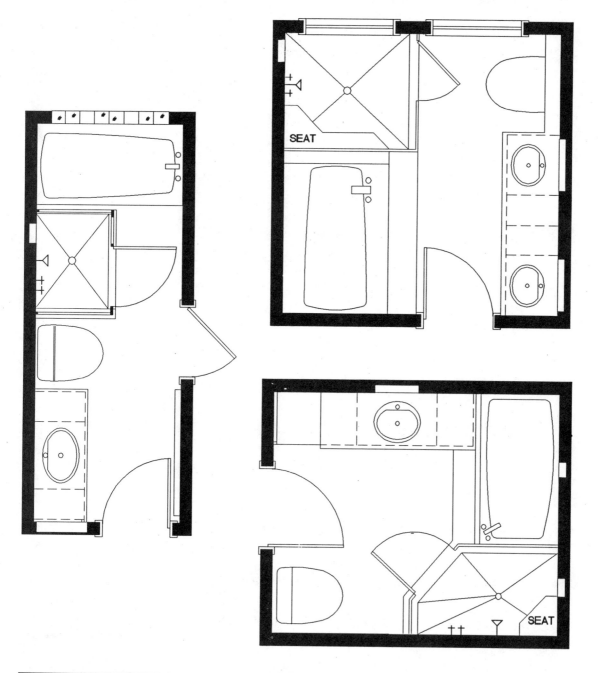

Figure 152 *These three bathrooms demonstrate three typical ways bathtubs and showers can be featured adjacent to one another in small bathroom spaces. Placing the shower at the end of a bathtub works well. Placing the two fixtures at right angles to one another would be an excellent way to squeeze both fixtures in. Creating an angled custom shower may be a good solution in an awkward space.*

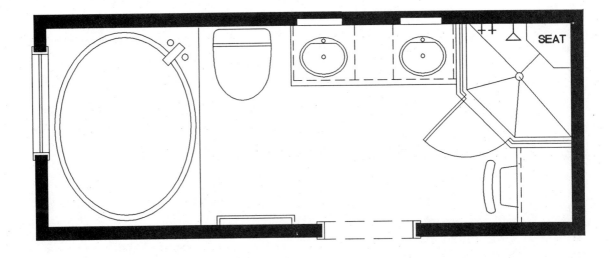

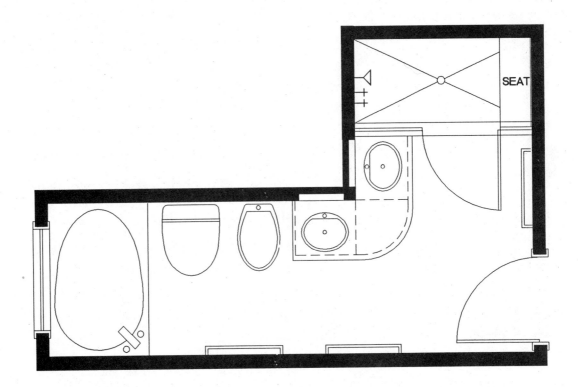

Figure 153   Awkward-sized bathrooms can feel luxurious with creative fixture placement. In the first ex-ample, a custom angled shower is sandwiched between the vanity and dressing area. This minimalist ap-proach to the shower allows a large bathtub underneath the window. In the second example, a curved, center cabinet attractively connects the double lavatory vanity area and the whirlpool bathtub section.

Section **3**

Fitting Materials

After the fixture materials have been selected, you and the client will choose the fittings. Whether they are called the "trim", the "brass" or the "faucets", these water delivering devices are available in a myriad of different materials and finishes.

CONSTRUCTION

Plastics (ABS, Acetal, CPVC and Rubber)

These are smooth, relatively soft materials commonly used in valve systems and cartridges or the gasket material under the fitting. Some extremely low cost fittings feature plastic bodies or waterways. Plastic materials are inexpensive and not prone to a lime or scale buildup. The smooth, slippery surfaces ease the passage of water and debris, as opposed to rougher surfaces that can catch or slow such material.

Plastic valves can be damaged by line debris, such as sand and silt. Unless the plastic receives special preparation, or is of "plating grade," they are not as durable nor as strong as other materials and are difficult to plate with special fin-ishes. Additionally, they can be attacked by certain petroleum based products.

Color matching plastic components to other components made from metal can be difficult due to the differences in texture, gloss and light reflection.

Zinc

Zinc is a silvery-white metal that is cast into forms and shapes. It is stronger and more durable than some plastics and smoother than brass. Therefore it re-quires less polishing and buffing for a finished product. Zinc must be fully pro-tected from contact with water by plat-ing because it quickly corrodes and disintegrates if unprotected pieces come in contact with water.

Brass

Brass is generally considered the best material for faucet construction be-cause it is a strong, durable metal virtu-ally unaffected by prolonged contact with water. Brass is an alloy of copper and zinc, with trace materials such as lead that improve machining, or silicon to improve casting. It varies in color from yellow to red and can be melted and poured into molds or machined from stock or rods.

Brass faucet bodies may be sand cast, much like a cast iron bathtub. Faucet component parts manufactured this way tend to have the lowest density and can be porous, which can cause pin holes and leaks. Because sand molds cool the brass quickly, this type of brass faucet must have the highest lead content.

Gravity die casting is another way that brass faucets are manufactured. Molten brass is manually poured or automatically injected into a machined metal form. Waterways and other hollows are either machined or formed through the use of a sand core. This method of casting provides greater density than sand casting, but still is inspected at the factory for pinhole leaks.

Forging is another method of forming faucet bodies from brass. In the forging process, a heated brass "plug" is pressed by extremely high pressure between two machined metal forms, which produces a smooth component part that requires little polishing. Water ways and other hollows are formed through machining. This process results in a fitting with few surface imperfections and a high-quality surface luster.

Lastly, brass stock, bars, rods, tubing or thin sheets can be machined or cold stamped into desired forms and shapes. Again, minimal polishing is required and low lead content brass can be used.

No matter what manufacturing process is used, brass provides a durable, long-lasting faucet material that stands up well. Even if the finish is damaged, the brass underneath holds up to heavy

use. Unfortunately, because it also is a relatively costly raw material and involves complicated manufacturing processes, brass fittings have an initial high purchase price for the client.

Copper

Copper is used for waterways of fabricated fittings and in some valve connections. Because it is softer than brass, copper can be easily shaped and bent. If uncoated, copper is prone to surface corrosion and scratching.

FITTING FINISHING OPTIONS

Over the last several years there has been a dramatic increase in the various finishing options available to the designer. However, you should not make your selection solely on appearance. There are two other factors that should be a part of your product review:

- Determining how resistant the finish on the faucet will be to abrasive cleaners and to deterioration caused by chemical properties in the water that could attack the finish.

- Identifying what the anticipated use of the fitting will be.

Because most damage to the faucet will result due to chemical attack, there is no alternative to a durable chrome finish on fittings that will be used in a home with serious water concerns, or in a bathroom that will receive constant heavy usage by family members.

If the anticipated usage and quality of water is such that alternative decorative faucets can be selected, another design dilemma faces you: how to make sure that all the fittings and accessories selected for the space blend attractively in the finished room.

Most manufacturers offer a complete line of faucet sets. These items will include towel bars, paper holders and other accessories to match their faucet offerings. Occasionally, a client will select specialized equipment that is not part of a "full line" product offering. Or, a client may like one manufacturer's decorative bathtub set and another company's accessories. Although various finishes will blend, if the client is expecting a perfect match, only one manufacturer's product should be specified.

This problem is magnified if the client wants the colored fittings to match fixtures, wet walls and counter surfaces made from other materials; *for example,* a client who expects the white epoxy coated faucets to match the white solid surface countertop and the white acrylic shower stall. Because of the fixture and surfacing material composition differences a match cannot be promised. Remember, a bathroom lavatory is china or enamel, the faucets have an epoxy coating, the wet walls/countertop solid surfacing are a blend of polyesters and acrylics, and the bathtub enclosure is an acrylic fixture. Talk to the client about colors blending with one another, not matching.

To overcome this color match dilemma, consider these solutions:

- Try to use only one surfacing material throughout the project. *For example,* solid surface materials in the shower and on the vanity top. Or, ceramic tile on all surfaces.

- In your showroom, display a bathroom setting that is all white. Make sure that the whites on the floor, fixture, counter, wall and fittings blend but don't match. This will give you a chance to explain the color variation to a client before the final project specifications are completed.

- Specify fittings that have a colored, chrome or brass escutcheon plate separating them from the counter or wall. Such a color break will help camouflage slight differences in color tones.

Chrome

POLISHED CHROME

Polished chrome is the most popular finish for bathroom fittings and hardware. It is extremely hard and does not oxidize in the air as do most other metals, thereby eliminating the need for regular polishing. Chrome is electrochemically deposited over the nickel plated base metal. The nickel provides luster, brilliance and corrosion prevention, while the chrome contributes color and tarnish resistance. It is a very bright and durable finish.

BRUSHED OR MATTED CHROME

A brushed finish is created by using a wire wheel to score the surface of the component part. This can result in a surface with sharp peaks and valleys that does not take the chrome finish quite as well during the plating process because the coating shears away from the peaks and accumulates in the valleys.

A matte finish produces similar appearance without producing noticeable brush marks or the sharp peaks that are difficult for plating. This process is similar to sand blasting the components with fine glass beads to create a soft matted surface that plates better, to produce a finish as durable as polished chrome.

Brass Fittings and Finishes

POLISHED BRASS

The fitting may be solid brass or a thin coating of brass applied over a base metal. Polishing a solid brass fitting is an expensive process where the brass components are buffed with a jeweler's rouge to a fine luster.

Alternatively, the look of polished brass can be created by applying a flash coating of brass, or gold formulated to be the color of brass, to a fitting via an electrode chemical bath. In either case, the brass must be protected.

One of two types of a protective coating may be used:

- a lacquer top coat or

- a clear epoxy coating.

The latter is considered to be the more durable choice.

The lacquer coating is sprayed on in a liquid form that quickly dries without baking. It provides protection only if the fixture is seldom, if ever, used. Lacquer is attacked by water, therefore it must be dried quickly after each use.

The epoxy coating is the second, clear finish used over brass. It is a powder or a liquid which is sprayed onto the components and then baked at approximately 375°F to 425°F (190°C to 218°C) to provide thorough, even coverage and protection. As with lacquer, the epoxy coating can be scratched, even by mild abrasives, which will result in a milky or cloudy appearance. Additionally, strong solvents will attack the coating. However, epoxy-coated brass fixtures are tested to insure durability in a constant moisture environment.

ANTIQUE BRASS

Antique brass is a popular finish for a traditional look. With higher quality products, the finish is electro-plated. With less expensive products, the finish is sprayed over the metal with tinted lacquers. Durability of an antique brass finish is fair. With its darker coloring, oxidation may not be as noticeable as on polished brass.

Polished and Satin Gold Plate

Gold plate has once again come into fashion for bathroom fittings and hardware. Gold plate provides a truly stunning, unique finish, but the consumer should be aware of vast differences in the quality and durability of gold plate available. The highly polished brass product is first nickel plated and then 24 karat gold is applied. Durability depends on the thickness of the gold layer.

According to industry standards, plating to a thickness of less than 7 millionths of an inch gold is "gold wash" or "gold flash." Between 8 and 12 millionths, is "gold plating" and from 13 to 50 millionths is "heavy gold plating."

All quality gold plated bathroom and hardware fittings should fall into the latter category. Low quality gold wash or gold flash is not durable and can wear after only 3 to 6 months of normal handling. It is very difficult for the layman to distinguish between high and low quality gold plate. It is important to always purchase fittings from reputable dealers and never hesitate to ask for data on gold plated parts.

Gold plate is available in either a polished or satin finish. Given a quality plating job, both finishes provide good durability. Quality gold will not tarnish. Maintenance of a satin gold finish is somewhat easier than polished gold because it hides marks better. The secret to long lasting gold plate is to clean it only with a soft, damp cloth. **NEVER** expose gold plate to abrasives or acids as can be found in many commercial cleaners.

Nickel

This hard, silver-white metal is used extensively in alloys and for plating because of its resistance to oxidation. It has a deep rich luster to the finish.

Pewter

This is a dull, silvery-gray alloy of tin with brass, copper or lead added during the manufacturing process. Faucets are available in polished and brushed pewter finishes.

Colored Coatings

A tinted, epoxy coating is used to create a colored finish. The powder is sprinkled on (or a liquid is sprayed on to the components) and then baked at about 375°F to 425°F (190°C to 218°C) to provide thorough, even coverage and protection. The coating can be scratched by mild abrasives, which results in an unattractive finish.

The key is to clean and dry the faucet frequently after use to avoid the need for heavy cleaning and to never use an abrasive cleaner.

Section **4**

Fitting Design and Construction

LAVATORY FITTINGS

At the turn of the century, indoor plumbing systems brought water to the "taps" - one for hot water and one for cold water. The lavatory was a bowl, with a stopper at the bottom, to allow the user to fill the bowl with hot and cold water mixed from these two separate taps. It is not uncommon to see this type of system still in use around the world.

In North America, hot and cold water is now channeled through a "mixing" faucet, or common outlet or spout. The hot and cold water is regulated by adjusting two separate handles, by turning/pulling/pushing a single handle, by walking up to a faucet that has a proximity sensor, or by touching an electronic pad.

Types of Lavatory Fittings

SINGLE-HANDLE CONTROL

Single-handle controls are located above the spout or to the side of the spout. Single-handle lavatory faucets are available with different length spouts. Therefore, be sure you specify the proper length for the planned use.

The control is turned left or right, pulled up or down, or pushed front to back. These controls are sometimes confusing to individuals not familiar with their operation.

When evaluating the function of single handle faucets - at the lavatory or any other fixture - there are two key factors: the faucet's comfort zone swing and the volume control swing or lift. The typical faucet must be adjusted for both of these factors with use. Some faucets may be turned off leaving the control in a memory position. This allows the user to leave the faucet preset at a comfortable temperature setting for the next use.

- **Comfort Zone:** Human beings are comfortable using water that ranges from 95°F - 105°F (35°C - 41°C). The distance of the fitting swing within this comfort zone determines how much adjustability is offered to the user. The total distance of travel from cold to hot should be as great as possible. A handle with a 120 degree arc from the hottest setting to the coldest, and with a 40 degree arc within the comfort zone from 95°F - 105°F (35°C - 41°C), is a functional, safe fitting design.

- **Volume Control:** Most single-handle faucets have a 15 degree lift from the off to the fully on position. Some faucets offer a 20 degree lift. This lift range starts with the valve in a closed position and at the top of the scale the valve is completely open. The ideal faucet design allows the water flow rate to be increased gradually as the faucet valve is opened with a lift/twist/turn action. The water flow should begin at one degree off the lift and continue in a gradual increase that is in proportion with the degree of movement. This type of "fine tuning" offers the user a faucet that is safe and easy to use. Unfortunately, some single- handle faucet designs do not allow the water flow to begin until the faucet reaches approximately 7 degrees of the movement. With this type of fitting, the range of control for the user is dramatically decreased.

SINGLE HOLE FAUCET/ONE OR TWO HANDLES

Faucets are available where only one hole is required in the lavatory ledge or in the vanity top. This single hole type of faucet can feature either separate hot and cold handles or a single control attached to the spout. These fittings are sometimes shipped with an escutcheon plate which can be used to cover water supply holes which are not used by this type of faucet.

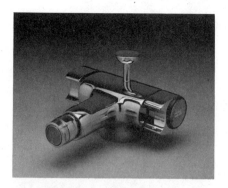

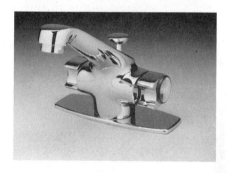

*Figure 154   (Courtesy of American Standard Inc.)
Single hole faucets.*

TWO HANDLE FAUCETS

4" (10.16cm) Center Faucet Set: Small faucets are available where the spout and two separate handles require three holes and are placed along a single escutcheon plate. The drilling is generally 4" (10.16cm) on center for this type of faucet. Although this is generally an economical faucet, because the handles are very close to the spout, it may be difficult to clean. Unless it has lever handles, some people may also find it difficult to use.

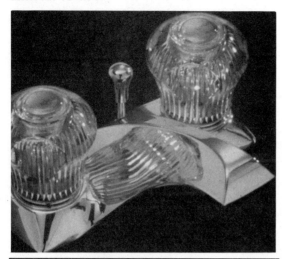

Figure 155   (Courtesy of Kohler Co.)
A 4" (10.16cm) center faucet.

Widespread Faucet Set: Some decorative faucets eliminate the escutcheon plate and separately mount the spout and two handles. The spacing is flexible and may be anywhere from 8" - 12" (20.3cm - 30.48cm).

Figure 156   (Courtesy of Eljer Plumbingware)
A mini-widespread faucet.

These faucets are usually more attractive and are easier to use and to clean. Lavatories with standard platform mounting offer an 8" (20.3cm) spread. Lavatories which are designed to be used with counter-mounted faucets can feature a spread from 6" to 12" (15.2cm to 30.48cm).

Figure 157   (Courtesy of Delta Faucet Co.)
A widespread faucet.

ELECTRONICALLY CONTROLLED

One of the newest innovations in plumbing fittings is the electronic water control. There are two versions: proximity and touch pad.

Commercial use of proximity products is widely accepted. *For example,* public restroom lavatory faucets that deliver water at a set temperature and volume which is activated when the user's hands are placed underneath the spout or as the individual approaches the lavatory. This type of operation is not as successful residentially because clients want to be able to control the on/off capability, the water temperature and the volume of the water flow. Consequently, touch pad controls are more popular residentially.

Touch pad controls contain several functions: hot and cold water variations; incremental volume increases; a digital read out; and memorizing the ideal setting of temperature and flow rate for up to five persons. These controls may be installed flush with the countertop for lavatory use or as part of a faucet.

Figure 158   (Courtesy of American Standard Inc.) A faucet which features a temperature read-out.

SPECIAL LAVATORY FAUCET ATTACHMENTS

Spray Attachments

Special purpose lavatory faucets are also available. For example, hand-held sprays are available as part of a pull-out spray faucet, or as a separate hand-held faucet.

Integral sprays offer a conventional spray device at the end of a flexible hose. A separate spray is connected to the water line underneath the sink. You must provide an acceptable backflow preventing device when using such a spray. Some municipalities require that a vacuum breaker be installed if you specify a pull-out, integrated spray faucet. Alternatively, a faucet with check valves should also satisfy the inspector. Either

of these protections is required because of the functional differences between the two types of sprays:

- **Conventional Faucet:** With a conventional separate faucet and spray you have both a basic spout and the spray spout, providing two fluid channels. Therefore, if a negative pressure condition developed while someone had left the hose submerged in a lavatory filled with contaminated water, the basic spout would still draw in air which would break the vacuum. This would prevent the contaminated water from entering the clean water supply.

- **Pull-out Spray Faucet:** With the pull-out spray you only have one hose. Therefore, if the city's water supply was reduced in pressure for any reason and a pull-out spray was submerged in a lavatory full of contaminated water, the water would be pulled into the city pipelines and would contaminate the potable (fresh) water source.

A "vacuum breaker" prevents such contamination by allowing air into the system, which will stop the flow of contaminated water back into the system.

Before the introduction of the double stop protection built into new, well-engineered faucets which feature check valves (a device which only lets water travel in one direction), the specification of a vacuum breaker as the only acceptable method available to protect the potable water supply has come under question. Testing has demonstrated that a faucet designed with a check valve mechanism prevents the backflow situation as well as the typical vacuum breaker and therefore is becoming more acceptable.

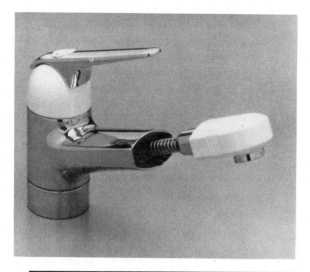

Figure 159   (Courtesy of KWC) A vanity faucet with a pull-out spray.

Drinking Fountain

Several manufacturers offer a spout that can be turned so that it is comfortable to use as a drinking fountain. This might be an ideal faucet design for a family where the bathroom users wake up during the night for a drink of water. It is also a useful feature to use when brushing one's teeth.

Also on the market today are cold water taps which are ideal for drinking water taps at secondary locations. These systems can be connected to a filtration system if your client has requested one.

Aerator

Most faucets include an aerator at the end of the spout that mixes air with water so splash-back is minimized. When a bathroom project is finished it is not uncommon for the client to complain that the water volume is not as high as it should be. Advise the client to unscrew the aerator and remove the sediment from the screen on a regular basis.

Pop-up Assembly

A "pop-up" assembly allows the user to close the drain when filling the bowl with water. Almost all assemblies are part of the faucet. However, faucets are also available without this feature, so make sure you specify the right model number.

This lavatory drain fitting consists of a brass or plastic waste outlet into which a sliding metal or plastic stopper is fitted. A lever that passes out the side of the drain fitting is connected to a lift rod on top of the lavatory faucet. This rod is lifted to lower the stopper and allow the lavatory to be filled. It is depressed to raise the stopper and drain the lavatory. The stopper should be periodically removed and cleaned to make sure that it does not become coated with soap film and/or other debris.

Shut-off Valve

Hot and cold water is supplied to the lavatory through supply lines that are either inside the vanity cabinet below the lavatory or exposed behind a pedestal or wall-hung lavatory. Individual shut-off valves should be installed at each supply line. The drain line from the lavatory connects to a waste line with a trap providing a water seal, as is common in all plumbing fixtures.

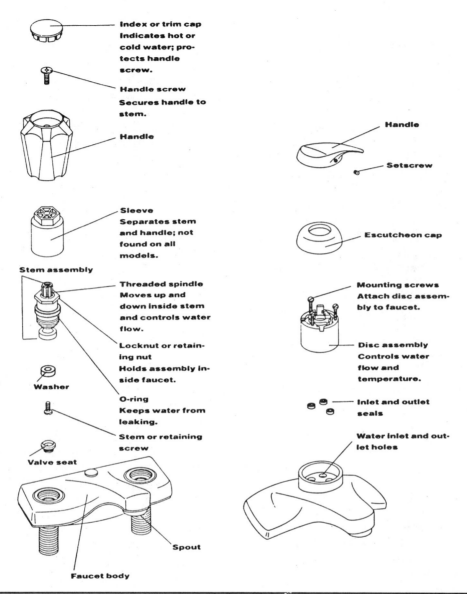

Figure 160   (Courtesy of Home Magazine)   A typical faucet anatomy.

ENGINEERING THE FAUCET

In addition to the design of the faucet, the bathroom specialist must understand how faucets operate. All faucets feature either a washer or a washerless design. Each manufacturer has detailed training material available to introduce you to your range of choices. The following description is reprinted, courtesy of **American Standard Inc.**

Washer Design

Faucets with washers feature a compression seal mechanism. Water enters the valve area through the "seat" and is controlled by a rubber washer. When the user turns the handle, the stem twists, causing the washer to raise or lower in relation to the seat. This action provides the "on/off" and volume control in the washer design faucet.

There is also a primary seal to shut the water off and a secondary seal on the stem to prevent the mechanism from leaking. If there is no limiting control over the amount of torque applied to the handle, washers can be abused and wear out. These types of faucets are called "compression" faucets and always have two handles.

COMPRESSION VALVING - TWO-HANDLE: RISING STEM COMPRESSION VALVES

Attributes: The one-piece threaded valve stem rises (along with handle) when rotated to open water flow and lowers to close. As the valve stem rises, the washer, O-ring or diaphragm fixed at the bottom of the valve stem is lifted away from the valve seat, allowing water to flow through the valve body.

Advantages: Low manufacturing cost. Easy low-cost repair by replacing washer or O-ring. Simplest valve operation; easiest repair by homeowner. Very unlikely to clog.

Disadvantages: Seat washers and O-rings wear out quickly because of the grinding action caused when rotated and squeezed between valve stem and valve seat - frequent maintenance required. If seat washer or screw loosens, "chatter" or water hammer can occur.

COMPRESSION VALVING - TWO-HANDLE: NON-RISING STEM COMPRESSION VALVES

Attributes: Multiple-piece valve assembly usually consisting of a housing with a tabbed plunger that rises and falls when handle is operated, but without rotating plunger or washer attached to it. Handle does not rise when opened.

Advantages: Longer life because washer does not rotate against seat, eliminating grinding action. Handle does not rise when valve is opened. Easy, low-cost repair by replacing washer. Simple operation, easy repair for homeowner. Less handle wobble than rising stem compression valve.

Disadvantages: Manufacturing cost higher than rising stem compression due to additional parts. Still a compression valve with washer. Lever handles become out of alignment as washer begins to wear. If seat washer or screw loosens, "chatter" or water hammer can occur. Handle must be rotated several turns to reach full open. Changes in water temperature will cause valve stem to expand or contract, causing change in amount of water flowing, as well as output temperature.

Washerless Design

Other types of faucets are collectively called "washerless". They are named after the particular mechanism they employ to control water flow: a cartridge, a ball or a disc. Although they're collectively known as washerless, they do utilize neoprene rubber seals or O-rings around various parts of the faucet assembly to prevent leaking.

SHEER ACTION VALVING - TWO-HANDLE: ROTATING PLASTIC DISC AGAINST SEPARATE SEATS

Attributes: Plastic discs with holes (usually assembled as a cartridge to the valve stem) that rotate against rubber seats (washers or O-rings) which are forced against disc by separate springs. Water flow controlled by rotating holes in disc to align with seats and hole in valve body.

Advantages: Usually quarter-turn action; handles always in alignment. Low manufacturing cost. Simple operation and repair by the client. Built-in stops prevent over-tightening. Reversing valve rotation is possible.

Disadvantages: Rubber seats wear out quickly due to grinding action of rotating disc. Soft rubber seats grip to plastic disc to maintain water-tight seal, but this gripping action also causes rapid wear of seats as disc slides across them. Not recommended for extreme hot water applications. Prone to quick failure in water with line contaminants (sand, rust, silt, solder) as they will score plastic disc or rubber seat. Problem is aggravated by small openings in disc which tends to catch rather than pass line debris.

SHEER ACTION VALVING - TWO-HANDLE: ROTATING PLASTIC DISC OR SLEEVE AGAINST SEATS WITHIN A SELF-CONTAINED CARTRIDGE

Attributes: Same as rotating plastic disc against separate seats, but seats or O-rings are in a self-contained cartridge for easy replacement.

Advantages: Quarter-and half-turn action, handles always in alignment. Low manufacturing cost. Fast and easy replacement, relatively low-cost repair. Simple operation, repair by the homeowner.

Disadvantages: Tends to wear quickly as with rotating plastic disc against separate seats, but may have slightly longer life due to cartridge design maintaining better lubrication and tighter fit between components. Prone to quick failure in water with line contaminants (sand, rust, silt, solder) as they

will score plastic disc or rubber seat. Problem is aggravated by small openings in disc which tends to catch rather than pass line debris.

SHEER ACTION VALVING - TWO-HANDLE: TWO ROTATING CERAMIC DISCS WITHIN A SELF-CONTAINED CARTRIDGE

Attributes: Current state-of-the-art in valving technologies. Ceramic is an extremely hard, durable material that is unaffected by water temperature or line debris. Valve consists of two polished ceramic discs that rotate against each other when the handle is turned and allow water to pass through as holes in each disc become aligned.

Advantages: After being "fired" the ceramic discs are nearly as hard as diamonds. The discs are completely unaffected by water temperature or debris in the line such as sand, silt or solder.

When properly polished to an almost perfect smoothness and flatness, there is no room for air or water to seep between the two discs, eliminating the possibility of leaks.

A perfectly smooth pair of ceramic discs do not rely on lubricants for easy operation. The two surfaces continue to polish each other through normal use so a lifetime of smooth, easy operation is assured.

Disadvantages: Compared to an all-plastic cartridge, a relatively high cost to produce and replace. But viewed over the life of the fitting, the best investment and lowest "life-cycle" cost.

There are some ceramic disc valves on the market that do not feature the level of polishing required for smoothness and flatness, and instead rely on extensive lubrication for smooth rotation. This lubrication quickly washes out in use (especially on the hot side) causing very stiff rotation. This continues for many thousands of on/off cycles until the discs have been ground sufficiently smooth (through the user's hard efforts). Discuss the different types of ceramic disc valves available with your plumbing fixture and fittings supplier or manufacturer.

SHEER ACTION VALVING - ONE-HANDLE: ROTATING BALL WITH SEPARATE SEATS

Attributes: A hollow plastic, brass or stainless steel ball attached to the end of the handle stem that rotates in a housing against soft rubber seats pushed towards the ball by separate springs. Ball valve held in body via screwed on bonnet with an O- ring seal. Water flow is controlled by aligning the holes in the ball against the water inlets.

Advantages: Inexpensive, simple design easily understood by installer. Requires frequent maintenance due to leaks.

Disadvantages: Grinding action of ball valve against seats and stem seal causes excessive wear and frequent failure - water will leak out between valve body and ball and deck of lavatory. Remedy is either constant replacement (difficult because of separate seats and springs) or tightening the bonnet nut. Latter results in stiffer handle operation each time bonnet is tightened to eliminate leaking.

Ball system creates awkward operation - the only off position is full-forward in the center. This means a complex

"gear shift" motion is required with every use to find both the correct temperature and water flow - a real inconvenience when used frequently. Because the ball design is not a perfect sphere, it has high and low spots which translates to stiff and soft spots in the handle movement. This is further aggravated as the bonnet is tightened to stop leaks.

SHEER ACTION VALVING - ONE-HANDLE: PLASTIC DISCS OR SLEEVES

Attributes: Either two plastic discs or rotating sleeves that control water flow through a sheering action. Usually a completely self-contained cartridge system. Rubber seals or O-rings provide the seal between plastic parts. Sleeve design requires two-step handle movement: lift to control flow, rotate to control temperature.

Advantages: Relatively inexpensive valving system to manufacture. Cartridge design provides easy replacement. Can provide long dependable life in clean water conditions. Most permit user to rotate handle to desired temperature and then activate water flow through simple lift motion.

Disadvantages: Sleeve system, because of the greater surface areas coming in contact with each other, becomes stiff through use as lubricants are washed away. This is especially difficult with knob handles that must be firmly gripped and pulled to activate - a difficult operation for small children or the elderly. Motion can be so stiff and removal so difficult that a special tool was created for this purpose.

When in use, the push/pull motion of sleeve systems expose an area beneath the handle that traditionally builds up with a residue from cleansers and water seepage that is very difficult to keep clean. Lever handles, also because of this push/pull motion, operate as a lever and fulcrum and are notorious for being loose and having excessive handle play.

As with plastic two-handle valving, these are prone to scoring and leaks when sand, scale, rust, silt or line solder pass through the valve.

SHEER ACTION VALVING - ONE-HANDLE: CERAMIC DISCS

Attributes: Current state-of-the-art in valving technologies. Ceramic is an extremely hard, durable material that is unaffected by water temperature or line debris. Valve consists of two polished ceramic discs that slide rather than rotate against each other when the handle is lifted and turned. Water passes through holes in each disc as they are aligned.

Advantages: After being "fired" the ceramic discs are nearly as hard as diamonds and are impervious to water. The discs are completely unaffected by water temperature or debris in the line such as sand, silt or solder.

When properly polished to an almost perfect smoothness and flatness, there is no room for air or water to seep between the two discs, eliminating the possibility of leaks.

Disadvantages: Compared to an all-plastic cartridge, a relatively high cost to produce and replace. But viewed over the life of the fitting, the best investment and lowest "life-cycle" cost.

BATHTUB FITTINGS

Bathtub fittings include the valve, the spout and as a separate component a waste/over-flow. A separate hand-held personal shower may also be included for the bathtub.

Delivering Water to the Bathtub: The Spout and Valves

ADEQUATE WATER FLOW RATE

Before selecting the finished bathtub fittings, you must be sure the necessary water flow rate is provided by the fittings you're considering. As covered in an earlier section of this manual on whirlpool bathtub design, typically, a 3/4" (1.9cm) nominal (inside dimension) hot and cold supply line services a bathroom with three standard fixtures. 1/2" (1.27cm) nominal individual branches then bring hot and cold water to the standard bathtub fittings. These standard bathtub fittings generally are 1/2" (1.27cm) IPS (iron pipe size) fittings which restrict the water flow to about 9.0 gallons (34 liters) per minute at the bathtub spout. For a larger bathtub, a flow rate of 10 to 20 gallons (38 to 76 liters) per minute is more desirable. Therefore, a 3/4" (1.9cm) fitting and a 3/4" (1.9cm) supply line that is not channeled through a 1/2" (1.27cm) diverter may be required.

The available water pressure and the engineering of the plumbing system affect the actual flow of water available at the fitting. Therefore, these connections will not guarantee the needed flow rate. However, a 3/4" (1.9cm) valve does deliver more water faster than a 1/2" (1.27cm) valve. Novice designers sometimes make the mistake of specifying a larger branch line to the bathtub fitting, but then fail to specify a 3/4" (1.9cm) bathtub spout and valve. If you imagine a fireman's hose being "throttled down" to a garden hose you can get an idea of how important it is to increase the size of the entire system.

Your goal is to be sure the fitting delivers water to the bathtub fast enough that the water does not cool before the bather enters.

Mounting the Fitting on the Bathtub Rim or on the Platform

In addition to making sure that the supply line, valve and spout are correctly sized to fill the bathtub in a reasonable amount of time, be sure that the spout and valves can be properly connected on the fixture rim or on the bathtub deck.

Most deck mounted fittings will require connection from underneath the finished deck. This means you must also plan access for future servicing. Some manufacturers now provide "quick connect" systems which allow you to attach the deck-mounted spout more easily than in the past.

Make sure that the overall deck ledge depth is less than the overall dimension of the spout outlet. Alternatively, the spout might actually be part of the bathtub.

A Hand-held Shower at the Bathtub

A hand-held shower is one of the most useful fittings you can suggest for a client. It makes washing hair in the tub, or rinsing off, much more pleasant. It is extremely useful when bathing children or pets. And, it makes cleaning the bathtub much easier.

There are several systems for you to choose from. The typical installation requires the use of a bathtub filler and a diverter valve to channel the water from the bathtub spout outlet to the hand-held spray. The diverter category offers two mechanical options: a rotary action valve or a spring-loaded push or lift type valve.

Figure 161   (Courtesy of American Standard Inc.)
Recommended fitting placement on a platform next to a bathtub.

Figure 162   (Courtesy of American Standard Inc.)
A hand-held shower at the bathtub.

Some codes consider the spring-loaded diverter as an acceptable back-flow prevention, therefore no vacuum breaker is required. This is because the spring-loaded push or lift type diverter opens the secondary channel, the spout, to the atmosphere in the event of negative pressure.

The second option, a rotary action valve, does not provide back-flow prevention protection. This type of installation, as well as the deck-mounted, single-lever feed, requires a vacuum breaker placed well above the bathtub along the wall. To avoid this being unsightly, install the vacuum breaker inside a closet or on the other side of the wall.

The Waste and Overflow

The last element in a bathtub is the waste and overflow. The waste is the drain in the bottom of the bathtub. Generally, the overflow fitting is along the end wall of the fixture. It limits the overall amount of water in the bathtub. Because the distance from the bottom of the bathtub to the waste overflow varies between fixture models, make sure you order the correct waste and overflow to fit the bathtub you have specified.

POP-UP AND TRIP LEVER DRAIN

The standard, North American pop-up or trip-lever type waste and overflow are economical and fit most bathtubs. The trip lever version has a stopper below the perforated drain. The pop-up version has a lift-up mechanism in the open drain. Either is activated when a lever is "tripped" or a rotary knob is turned.

CABLE DRAIN

An alternative is a cable drain which places no mechanical components in the tubular passageway of the system. Rather, a cable runs outside the system, connects the handle of the overflow to a plug-lift mechanism just below the outlet's flange. It is important to provide access to the plumbing wall behind the bathtub when specifying a cable drain because the mechanism is not accessible from inside the bathtub.

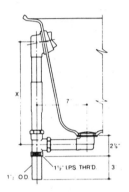

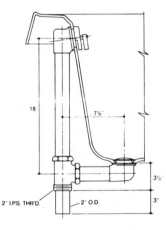

Figure 163   Bathtub waste and overflow system.

BATHTUB/SHOWER COMBINATION FITTINGS

The bathtub may also serve as a combination shower. In this installation, the fittings include the bathtub filler/spout, a diverter valve that allows the water to be directed down to the bathtub spout or up to the showerhead, and the showerhead itself. These three are typically installed on one common wall in a straight line.

Access to the Pipes

In all installations the supply lines are serviced by shut-off valves. In many installations an access panel is included so that these shut-off valves are accessible in a closet behind the bathtub, or through an access panel in the wall which is camouflaged behind a piece of furniture. Alternatively, some have shut-off valves that are accessible from underneath the escutcheon plate. This feature eliminates the need for an access panel.

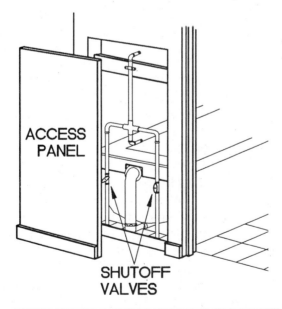

Figure 164   Provide access to bathtub/shower piping.

The Diverter

The diverter for a bathtub/shower combination can be a knob that you pull on top of the bathtub spout, it can be a handle diverter that is placed between the hot and cold valve on the wall which you either push or turn, or it can be a button diverter on a single-handle shower control.

SHOWER FITTINGS

Following is a more detailed discussion of shower fittings that are appropriate for either a separate, stand-alone stall configuration or a bathtub/shower combination.

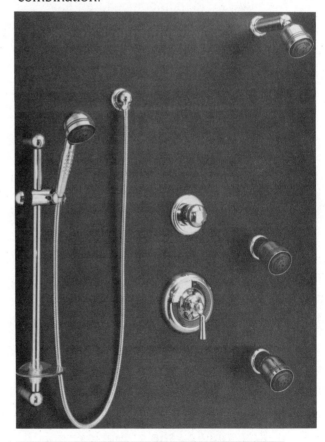

Figure 165   (Courtesy of Kohler Co.)   Shower fittings.

Safety in the Shower

Before we discuss shower valve or head placement, let's return to the issue of safety in the bathroom. The bathrooms that you design must be functionally and ergonomically correct and they must be safe.

The bathroom is one of the most dangerous rooms in the house. One source puts the number of scalding injuries alone in the United States at more than 150,000 each year. According to the **National Safe Kids Campaign** in 1988, as many as 37,000 of these victims were children and 5,000 of them were most often scalded by hot tap water in the bathtub. Remember, children have thinner skin than adults and are therefore more easily burned in less time and by lower temperature water.

In recently released statistics from the **American Association of Retired Persons**, showers and bathtubs ranked third among products associated with death among people 50 years of age or older. The main cause was falls while showering and/or bathing. In Chapter 3, we'll talk about preventing falls by the proper installation of grab bars and handrails. However, such falls can also be caused when the user is startled by a sudden change in water temperature while showering or bathing. This type of accident can be prevented with the proper shower valve. Because of the importance of safety in bathroom planning, we'll begin the discussion of shower planning by introducing you to pressure-balanced valves and temperature-limiting valves.

Just imagine the scenario: the shower is operating at the desired setting when another family member

flushes a toilet in the house, the cold water line pressure decreases while the hot water remains constant. A child may be standing under scalding hot water.

Scald Protection Devices

Scalding accidents can be eliminated. Scald protection valves are available. Currently there are four broad categories of fittings which offer such protection.

TYPES OF SCALD PROTECTION DEVICES

- **Pressure Balancing Valve:** A pressure balancing valve adjusts the mix of the hot and cold water in response to changes in relative supply inlet pressures. The valve compensates for the reduction of pressure in one supply line by increasing the flow coming from the supply and/or reducing the flow coming from the other supply. This type of valve does not compensate for changes in the temperature of hot and cold supplies. Therefore, the valve would not react to water temperature changes that occur because of a diminishing hot water supply.

- **Thermostatic Valve:** This system adjusts the mix of hot and cold water in response to changes in temperature. It automatically adjusts the flow of hot and cold water to maintain a relatively constant temperature. It can be slow to respond or it can briefly overcompensate for changes in supply pressures. This means that you may have one to two seconds of a noticeable temperature change as the water supply cuts off or as the valve adjusts. This valve will supply a constant temperature shower because it will adjust the cold water supply as a reaction to a diminishing hot water supply.

- **Combination Valve:** A combination of pressure balancing and thermostatic control. This system compensates for both temperature and pressure fluctuations of supply inlets.

- **Temperature Limiting Valve:** A high temperature limit stop that's adjustable by the installer or a family member. The high temperature limit stop prevents scalding by limiting the temperature of the water than can pass through the valve. The device is located under the lever and escutcheon of single-handle faucets and requires a simple screwdriver for access. A limit can be set for the hot water temperature delivered at the faucet, which is changeable as the family's life-stage and safety standards change.

All of these systems are designed to be used with a showerhead minimum flow rating of 2.5 gallons (9.5L) per minute. They are designed to perform under supply pressures up to 125 pounds (57 kilograms) per square inch.

Any well-designed bathroom today should include pressure balanced or thermostatically controlled valves at the shower and/or bathtub/shower combination.

PRESSURE BALANCING SYSTEMS

Pressure balanced shower valves contain a mechanism that maintains a constant hot and cold water temperature via a floating diaphragm or spool system.

- **Diaphragm:** A floating diaphragm continually equalizes or balances the hot and cold water pressure during decreases and surges caused by water demands throughout the plumbing system. It accomplishes this task by freely moving back and forth to increase or decrease the pressure as needed. Because the valve is controlled by pressure, the flow rate at the outlet may change as the change in temperature is compensated. It's not uncommon for the water pressure to drop as a temperature balance occurs. The diaphragm automatically recovers as the relative supply pressures are normalized.

- **Spool System:** This pressure balanced valve features a metal spool that slides back and forth inside the valve housing. Hot and cold supplies flow into separate hollows at both ends of the spool and out the holes in the sides of the spools to be mixed by the user. The spool slides back and forth based on the relative pressure of the hot and cold supply. Pressure changes will force the spool toward the side with the lower relative pressure. The design of the spool and housing feature fewer openings for water to flow the farther the spool is pushed into the housing. This means the supply under higher pressure has fewer outlets into the mixing valve. The side under lower pressure will have more or larger outlets. This system resists clogging by line debris and has a fast response time. It also automatically recovers as relative supply pressures are normalized. This system is more expensive than the diaphragm system and can be noisy.

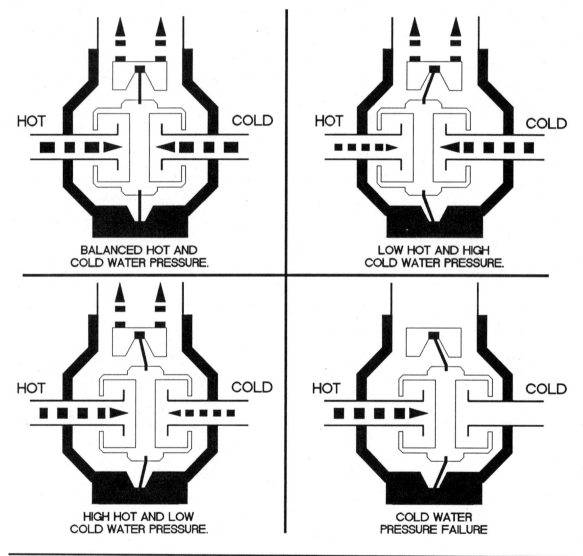

Figure 166   Pressure balanced valve for scald protection.

THERMOSTATIC SYSTEMS

- **Liquid System:** In a thermostatically controlled valve, a coil filled with a fluid or wax substance is wrapped around the hot water portion of the valve. The coil responds instantly to changes in temperature and shuts down the hot water flow into the mixing chamber if the temperature gets too high. This material, similar to an automobile thermostat, responds instantly by rapidly expanding or contracting with changes in temperature. This system compensates for both temperature and pressure changes of inlet supplies. The responsiveness of the fluid elements degrades over time and replacement may be more costly than the adjustments and/or repairs required to the pressure balance valve.

- **The Memory Metal System:** An alternative to this system uses a metal strip with two different metals, or a single metal alloy that flexes or changes shape in response to temperature changes. Again, the metal loses responsiveness over time, which can be accelerated if damaging water conditions exist.

- **The Electronically Controlled System:** A third variation is an electronically controlled system which features electronic sensors that measure the water temperature and are linked to a computer which adjusts the mix of hot and cold water. This is an excellent system, but is expensive to produce and to install, because both a plumber and an electrician are required.

Low-Flow Showerhead Concerns

A special safety note: There appears to be an increased scald hazard with low-flow showerheads. A few manufacturers of such low-flow heads have cautioned that showerheads of less than 2.0 GPM (8L) have a greater potential of scalding the user than standard 2.5 GPM (9.5L) showerheads.

The concern is based on a thermal shock research project conducted by **Delta Faucet Co.**, in which it was found that greatest water temperature increases occurred when a washing machine was turned on. Flushing a toilet often causes a significant pressure change, as hot water forces the shower's cold water back into its supply line, leaving only hot water coming out of the shower.

Consumer Reports tested showerheads using 1/2" (1.27cm) supply lines and a quick opening valve that simulated a toilet flushing. Under the specific conditions created, there was indeed a scald hazard.

The Basic Components of a Shower

THE VALVE

- **Manual Mixing Valves:** Basic mixing valve options for the shower are similar to those previously discussed for the lavatory: Two handle faucets and single-control faucets are available.

- **Electronic Mixing Valves:** The valve acts as an electronic thermostatic valve because it maintains the temperature that has been programmed in by the user. When turned on, the unit always resets and delivers at an initial 98°F (37°C). Depressing either the "up" or "down" button shifts the readout display to the "set point mode," causing the numbers to change in the direction of warmer or cooler until released. Once that button is released, the readout reverts to the actual temperature mode so the water temperature begins to move towards the selected setting and stops when it gets there. There is a hot limit device built into the valve, as well as an integral pressure balancing mode.

THE SHOWERHEAD

- **Flow Rating:** The flow of the showerhead is rated in gallons per minute (GPM). Flow in the U.S. is limited by law to not more than 2.5 GPM (9.5L). Some manufacturers also offer flow restriction mechanisms that reduce flow even lower, to 1.7 GPM (6.4L).

  These 1.7 GPM showerheads do conserve water, but the highly aerated water may not deliver an ideal shower. Because of the increased amount of air between the aerated water drops, the water temperature will cool dramatically from the time it leaves the showerhead until it reaches the bather's body. Because hu-

mans are sensitive to a drop of two degrees F, this type of showerhead may be undesirable.

TYPES OF SHOWERHEADS

Ergonomic and usage considerations for showerhead design and placement are discussed in Chapter 3. In this section, we will identify the different types of showerheads available.

There are numerous shower heads available today. Generally there are five broad categories of showering options:

- Personal Hand-held Shower
- Wall-mounted Shower
- Overhead Shower
- Body Spray Shower
- Body Mist Shower

- **Personal Hand-held Shower:** The personal hand-held shower is ideal in showers that will be used by people of varying heights, as well as near a bench in the shower that is out of the stream of water.

  Hand-held showers are also a great addition to a shower that will be used by an elderly person who may need assistance while bathing. Shower cleaning is also much easier with a hand-held shower.

- **Wall-mounted Shower:** The wall-mounted showerhead is the most typical installation.

- **Overhead Shower:** The overhead shower is placed on the ceiling and is oftentimes called a "shampoo head." It may require a great deal of water to operate - check the manufacturer's specifications.

- **Body Spray Shower:** A body spray is a group of individual showerheads, installed in a series of two or three, on opposite walls, or from the front on opposite sides of the body.

- **Body Mist Shower:** A body mist shower is a series of jets of water in a single bar designed to gently wash the body. When mounted at the right height, both body sprays and body mists are designed to allow a person to take a shower without getting his/her face and/or hair wet.

Figure 167 Examples of the types of showerheads available.

WATER PATTERNS

When considering any showerhead, some key functions to discuss with your client are:

- **Adjustment:** The basic spray adjustment from fine to coarse: Consumer Reports found that people much prefer the control that is on the side of the showerhead as opposed to in the center which forces the user to reach into the stream of water.

- **Spray Pattern:** A full spray pattern is more desirable than one that only delivers water around the perimeter of the head, leaving a hollow in the center.

- **Water Action:** Showerheads can offer a soft, gentle action or a pulsating, invigorating massage.

Designing a Multiple-Showerhead Enclosure

When specifying multiple-showerheads in an enclosure, ask a key question: *"Is this enclosure designed for one person to use with multiple heads that offer them a variety of shower experiences; or, is it a shower enclosure with multiple heads that will be used by more than one person at the same time?"*

DETERMINE HOW THE SHOWER WILL BE USED

If the shower is designed for one person, a diverter system can be designed to offer the user a choice of the various heads. For example, an overhead shampoo showerhead could be used in place of body sprays, rather than concurrently. This type of arrangement is designed with one mixing valve and a diverting device to direct the water to the various heads.

Alternatively, the shower can be designed for one user, but with water delivered from several sources so that the person is able to stay wet and warm all over while showering.

Or, several users may enjoy the shower together. When two or more heads operate at the same time, you must pay particular attention to the water pressure, the size of the piping and the flow rate of the showerheads, as well as the mixer and diverter device.

A common problem in a multiple shower head installation is the failure of the various heads to discharge water uniformly. Any manifold fed from a single branch will tend to give stronger output at the first outlet in the line, with diminishing pressure at those outlets more distant. To compensate for this problem, plumb each bank of heads with a manifold loop or a pressure equalizing loop that maintains a balanced pressure at all heads on the run.

Another typical complaint about multiple head shower enclosures plumbed on the same line is that the water temperature is different at the different heads. If the pipes are not insulated there can be anywhere from a 3 degree to a 7 degree Fahrenheit temperature difference between the head closest to the valve and the one farthest away.

The plumber or designer must know which outlet port is connected to which showering device. *For example,* typically the overhead fixed shower should be in the "default" mode (the port that is used when the water is first turned on), rather than the hand-held shower because the overhead shower is what people use most often.

DIVERTING WATER: TYPES OF DIVERTERS

You may be initially confused about operational terms used to describe a diverter. The "way" designation tells you the number of output selections possible: how many ways the water can get "out" of the valve. The "ports" refer to the total number of piping connections. Thus, a five-port, three-way diverter offers a hot and cold inlet, and three outlets or three "ways" the water can get out. For simplicity, we suggest that you define a diverter by the number of ways water exits it.

- **Two-Way Diverter:** A key element of the enclosure is how many ways the user can divert the water. A typical, two-way diverter valve has one outlet at the bottom and a second at the top, allowing the unit to be of a push/pull variety that switches water from a bathtub filler below to a showerhead above, or to one of two showerheads. The hot and cold inlets are located on either side. The diverter is an integral part of the valve which is turned, pushed or pulled to operate. This type diverter provides two output selections that cannot be used simultaneously.

- **Three-Way Diverter:** diverter can be a three-way diverter, but have five ports.

Such a diverter may be a modular type. This diverter is mounted separately on the wall. The most common types are a push/pull two-way style or a three-way rotary style. Like the integral two-way system, the modular push/pull design will not permit simultaneous use of two output modes.

The three-way rotary styles generally provide simultaneous operation and a position between the two settings. The three-way rotary will not permit the use of all three modes, but will allow two.

Make sure your client understands that this method of diversion splits the incoming available water flow and then channels the water to the two outlets. Therefore, there may be a significant reduction in the flow rate of each showerhead.

SEPARATE VALVES

An alternative to the multi-port diverter valve is to plumb the multiple-head shower enclosure with separate valves controlling each head. Separate control valves are installed for each outlet, or for each group of outlets. In this installation, each showerhead has its own volume and temperature control so that each one can be adjusted separately. If more than one person will be in the shower at once, such water temperature controls may be desirable.

SINGLE VALVE, SEPARATE VOLUME CONTROLS

When designing a multi-head shower for one person, a single, thermostatically controlled mixing valve can set the temperature for all outlets in the enclosure. Individual volume controls then feed water to each showerhead. This system allows all the heads in the shower to operate at once and at the same temperature.

MAINTAINING WATER FLOW

For installations that include multiple shower outlets intended to operate simultaneously it's extremely important to specify supply lines and valving with adequate flow capacity. As is the case with the oversized bathtub application, some manufacturers offer 3/4" (1.91cm) shower valves, which are necessary if the valve serves multiple heads.

A 1/2" (1.27cm) supply line will provide 20 to 22 gallons (76 to 83 liters) of water per minute with 45 psi. A 3/4" (1.91cm) supply line will provide 30 to 35 gallons (114 to 132 liters) of water per minute at 45 psi. Therefore, a 3/4" (1.91cm) supply line should be planned for a large, multi-head shower enclosure, along with a 3/4" (1.91cm) mixing valve so that no restrictions are placed on the water flow.

Remember however, that at the flow rates above with each outlet limited by law to 2.5 GPM, you can use up to eight heads off the 1/2" supply line if they are dedicated lines, serving only the shower.

To determine how many heads can be used on an existing supply line, divide the showerhead flow rate into the flow rating of the mixing valve fed by the supply line. If you don't calculate the water supply side of the equation for a custom shower, you can create a shower space which is impressive to look at, but frustrating to use.

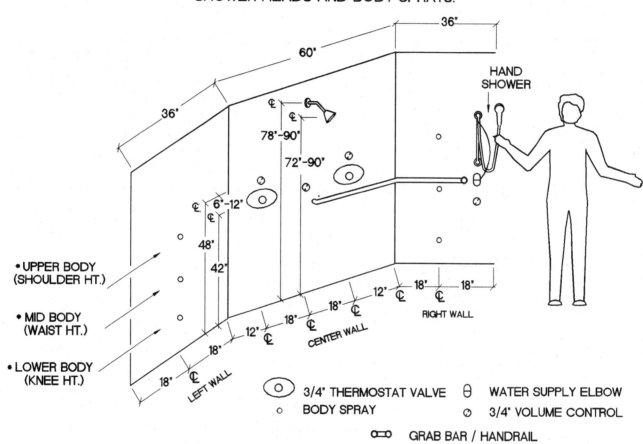

CUSTOM SHOWER WITH MULTIPLE
SHOWER HEADS AND BODY SPRAYS.

36"

60"

36"

HAND
SHOWER

78"-90"

72"-90"

6"-12"

48"

42"

• UPPER BODY
(SHOULDER HT.)

• MID BODY
(WAIST HT.)

• LOWER BODY
(KNEE HT.)

18"

18"

18"

12"

18"

18"

12"

18"

18"

18"

LEFT WALL

CENTER WALL

RIGHT WALL

⬭○ 3/4" THERMOSTAT VALVE   θ   WATER SUPPLY ELBOW

○   BODY SPRAY   ⊘   3/4" VOLUME CONTROL

○══○ GRAB BAR / HANDRAIL

❋ NOTE : CONSULT WITH CLIENT FOR SPECIFIC
VALVE AND HEAD DIMENSION LOCATIONS,
WHICH WILL VARY WITH EACH CLIENTS HEIGHT.

Figure 168 Plumbing fixture schematic for multiple-head shower enclosure showing imperial dimensions.

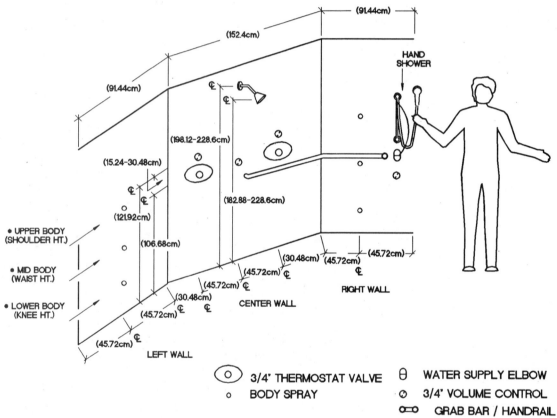

CUSTOM SHOWER WITH MULTIPLE
SHOWER HEADS AND BODY SPRAYS.

(91.44cm)

(152.4cm)

(91.44cm)

HAND
SHOWER

(198.12-228.6cm)

(15.24-30.48cm)

(182.88-228.6cm)

(121.92cm)

* UPPER BODY
(SHOULDER HT.)

(106.68cm)

* MID BODY
(WAIST HT.)

(45.72cm)

* LOWER BODY
(KNEE HT.)

(30.48cm)   (45.72cm)

(45.72cm)   RIGHT WALL

(45.72cm)

(45.72cm)

(30.48cm)   CENTER WALL

(45.72cm)

(45.72cm)   LEFT WALL

⊙ 3/4" THERMOSTAT VALVE   θ   WATER SUPPLY ELBOW

o   BODY SPRAY   ⊘   3/4" VOLUME CONTROL

                                o▭o   GRAB BAR / HANDRAIL

✳ NOTE : CONSULT WITH CLIENT FOR SPECIFIC
VALVE AND HEAD DIMENSION LOCATIONS,
WHICH WILL VARY WITH EACH CLIENTS HEIGHT.

Figure 169 Plumbing fixture schematic for multiple-head shower enclosure showing metric dimensions.

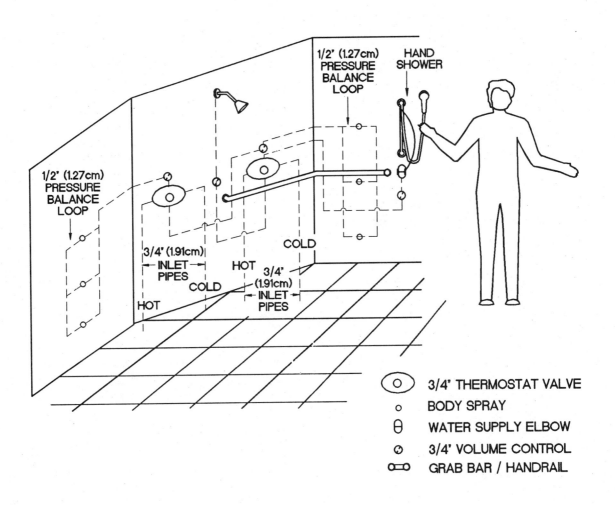

CUSTOM SHOWER WITH MULTIPLE
SHOWER HEADS AND BODY SPRAYS.

1/2" (1.27cm)
PRESSURE
BALANCE
LOOP

HAND
SHOWER

1/2" (1.27cm)
PRESSURE
BALANCE
LOOP

3/4" (1.91cm)
INLET
PIPES

HOT

COLD

3/4"
(1.91cm)
INLET
PIPES

COLD

HOT

⊙ 3/4" THERMOSTAT VALVE
o BODY SPRAY
θ WATER SUPPLY ELBOW
⊘ 3/4" VOLUME CONTROL
o═o GRAB BAR / HANDRAIL

Figure 170   Plumbing supply pipe schematic for multiple-head shower enclosure.

SECTION **5**

Fixture and Fitting Material Use and Care

Imagine this scene: Your clients have invested a substantial amount of money and have lived through the rigors of building a new home or the horrors of remodeling an existing one. They are about to enter their beautiful new bathroom (which your workmen have carefully cleaned and polished so that it sparkles) to take that first bath or shower. From this day forward, the clients will use that bathroom - and care for it. Part of your professional responsibility is to give them the information needed to protect the fine products you have specified and/or installed.

Obtain specific use and care instructions from each manufacturer and make sure your client gets a copy of the applicable information. The following is offered as general guidelines for fixture maintenance.

FIXTURES

ABS Plastics

Wipe down the fixture with a clean, dry, soft cloth after use. ABS plastic fixtures should be cleaned with a non-abrasive cleaner. Do not use scouring cleansers, scouring pads, ammonia compounds, or any other cleaners containing petroleum distillates, dry cleaning solvents, acetone (fingernail polish remover), paint thinner or benzene. A regular cleaning with a window cleaning spray is recommended. The user can apply a liquid non-grain wax to seal and protect the fixture finish.

Acrylics

Acrylics should never be cleaned with an abrasive cleaner. Again, the fixture should be wiped down with a soft cloth after each use to prevent a build-up of soap film. If the surface becomes dull, advise your client to use a nonabrasive, automotive-type rubbing compound on the unit, followed by a good application of non-grain paste wax.

Enameled Cast Iron/Steel

These finishes are extremely durable and can be cleaned with mild soap and warm water. Nonabrasive cleaners are fine to use, but avoid cleaners that contain silica or sand because abrasive materials pit the enamel surface over the life of the fixture, and make it more difficult to clean over the years.

Ceramic Tile

Wipe down tile fixtures with a soft cloth after use to eliminate hard water mineral deposit or soap film build-up. Regular maintenance with products recommended by the tile and/or grout manufacturer minimizes grout color deterioration. Use only the suggested products. Often, grout deteriorates in appearance because of a build-up of soap film caused by detergent-based cleaning products that are not properly rinsed off.

Gel Coating and Cast Polymer Surfaces

Gel-coated surfaces are easy to care for as long as you do not damage the finish by using an abrasive cleaner. Instruct the client to wipe out the bathtub or shower after each use.

Make sure the user understands that a cultured marble top can be burned by a cigarette or scratched by a sharp object. If the gel coat does become damaged, tell your client to look in the Yellow Pages under "fiberglass repair" to locate a qualified repair expert.

Solid Surfacing Material

MATTE/SATIN FINISH

Wiping the surface with a damp cloth removes water marks. For stains, wipe with soapy water or ammonia-based cleaners. On stubborn stains, use an abrasive cleanser with an abrasive (Scotch-Brite) pad. For a like new appearance, rub occasionally with pad alone.

SEMIGLOSS FINISH

Use a non-abrasive cleanser and a white Scotch-Brite pad to remove stubborn stains. Rub occasionally with pad alone to maintain original look.

HIGH GLOSS FINISH

Use only non-abrasive cleaners with a soft cloth or sponge to remove stains. Stubborn stains can be buffed away using white polishing compound and a low speed polisher equipped with a wool pad. Finish with a countertop wax.

Vitreous China

Do not use harsh abrasive cleaners because they can scratch the glass-like glaze surface. Softer abrasive cleaners can be used for daily/weekly maintenance. Do not use in-the-tank cleaners on toilets because they may affect the working parts of the flush valve. A simple, weekly cleaning of the bowl will keep the toilet sparkling and fresh. If you are specifying a gravity 1.6 gallon flushing toilet, include a toilet brush placed close to the toilet as part of the bathroom design. Because of the smaller "water spot" in some ultra-low flush toilets, the use of a brush may be required to clean the bowl after use.

Toilet bowl cleaners are good for inside the bowl only. Any cleaner that splashes on plated or plastic surfaces should be wiped off immediately. Bowl cleaners should never be used to clean any other materials.

Wood Products

Wood products should be cleaned with a mild soap and water and wiped down after each use. If, after years of use, the protective finish becomes scratched and dulled, it can be refinished by a craftsman who refinishes fine furniture.

FITTINGS

To avoid a build-up of mineral deposits in hard water areas, and to prevent excess skin oils from permanently discoloring fittings, suggest to your clients that they wipe the faucets off when they dry their hands. When cleaning any faucet, mild soap and warm water are recommended, followed by drying with a soft cloth.

Many cleaners contain chemicals, such as ammonia, which will attack the finish and should not be used on any fitting. A vinegar solution can be used to remove stubborn water stains. An application of a product such as plain spray wax is also an effective cleaner for fittings. Note the word plain! Do not use a scented wax of any kind.

MAINTENANCE

Clearing a Clogged Drain

Part of the use and care of any bathroom is the occasional need to clear a clogged drain. Recommend that the client keep one of several tools on hand:

- Plunger

- Slip Joint Pliers

- Closet or Drain Line Auger, or "Snake"

PLUNGER

The plunger can be used to clear a clog in a toilet or lavatory. The plunger is used in a fixture filled with water to create a vacuum which forces the clog through the line and clears the fixture or pipe. In place of a plunger, some products are available on the market which chemically attempt to break through grease or hair clogs in the toilet passageway or in a lavatory trap. The instructions must be followed very carefully when using these products. Generally, most plumbers suggest the use of a plunger rather than chemical products.

SLIP JOINT PLIERS

Slip joint pliers are used to disassemble a trap so that the drain can be cleared. However, before disassembling the lavatory should be filled with water and a plunger used in an attempt to create a vacuum to force the clog clear.

AUGER

A closet/drain/trap auger is a tool that is used to mechanically break-free and move a clog. It can break a toilet if improperly used, so it is best reserved as a tool for the professionals. In a bathtub application, the cover is removed from the overflow, and an auger is pushed or "snaked" through the opening to force a clog free. The closet auger is used in the same fashion to clear a blockage in a toilet, or in the clean-out on the exterior of a house for a trap blockage.

Removing Debris from the Lavatory Faucet

Periodically, the aerator in the faucet spout should be cleaned and the basin drain should be cleared of any debris attached to the plastic portion of the drain assembly in a lavatory. The areator is removed by simply unscrewing it from the spout.

Whirlpool System Treatment

In hard water areas, it may be necessary to clean fixtures more regularly or to install water softening devices to keep mineral deposits from forming. If such hard water conditions exist, a whirlpool bath system should be cleaned at least twice a month using two teaspoons of low-foaming dishwasher detergent, such as Cascade, and four ounces of household bleach, such as Clorox, in a bathtub full of warm water.

Instruct your client to run the unit for 10 to 15 minutes and then drain the bathtub. Fill with clear cold water and run for another 5 to 10 minutes. This will ensure that no hard water mineral deposits buildup in the fixtures.

SECTION **6**

Specialty Planning

We've already discussed the addition of whirlpool jets to a standard bathtub. A steam shower is a marvelous amenity in a standard shower. A sauna is a special addition to a bathroom as well.

Let's consider planning criteria for steam rooms and saunas.

STEAM SHOWERS

Explanation of Use

Steam showers are yet another way to provide a relaxing, refreshing experience. A steam bath invigorates the body systems and cleanses the skin by opening the pores and flushing the dirt out. The normal steam bath lasts from 10 to 20 minutes in an enclosed environment with high humidity and temperature levels. It is then followed by a lukewarm shower to relax, or a cold shower to stimulate the body.

In the past, steam rooms were only available at the finest private clubs and spas. Today, including a steam bath as part of a stall shower is an affordable addition to even a modest bathroom space.

The steam bath is energy efficient and doesn't require any more floor space than the stall shower you're already planning.

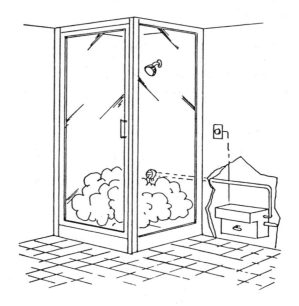

Figure 171 Typical steam bath.

Enclosure Design

The following constraints and/or planning concerns must be taken into account when considering a steam bath.

WET WALL MATERIAL

Avoid specifying any material that may be subject to decay because of prolonged exposure to steam or moisture. Verify with the specific manufacturers if their wall surfacing material is acceptable in a high heat, high humidity environment. *For example,* Du Pont currently doesn't recommend Corian as a wall surface material in any steam room. Also, use a waterproof substrate material behind the decorative surfacing material you do select.

In all applications, use waterproof adhesives or silicone sealants, as well as waterproof or epoxy paint.

GLASS

Specify a completely enclosed, vaporproof door. Fixed or operable transom panels are available as an accessory to standard shower doors to enclose the space to create a steam environment.

SEAT DESIGN

Place any permanent or portable benches well away from the steam nozzle. A person sitting in the steam room can be burned by an unexpected burst of steam.

CEILING SLANT

Slanting the steam room ceiling away from the seating area is recommended. A slanted ceiling insures that as steam condenses on the ceiling it runs down the slant, away from the seated user. The ceiling should be 7' (213.36cm) high.

SIZING THE GENERATOR

Choosing the appropriate generator for the steam room is the most important factor for a functional steam room in the home. A properly sized steam generator should produce a comfortable temperature in 5 to 10 minutes.

The cubic footage of the enclosure determines the size of generator needed. The construction and decorative surfacing materials also affect the size of generator you specify. The surround temperature must also be taken into account.

Wall Material: The porosity level of the material selected effects the cubic footage formula used to determine the generator size. Common surfacing materials and their affect in the cubic footage calculations are as follows:

- **All Glass or Glass Block:** Add 20% to 40% to the actual cubic footage of the enclosure.

- **Ceramic Tile on Waterproof Sheetrock:** Add 15% to the actual cubic footage.

- **Ceramic Tile on Cement Board:** Add 20% to the actual cubic footage.

- **Ceramic Tile on Mortar Bed (Mud) Substrate:** Add 25% to the actual cubic footage.

- **Ceramic Tile on Cinderblock or Concrete:** Add 75% to the actual cubic footage.

- **Fiberglass, Acrylic or Cultured Marble:** Decrease the actual cubic footage by 20%.

- **Natural Stone, Marble, Travertine, or Slate:** Add 100% to the actual cubic footage.

Determine Cubic Footage: When calculating the cubic footage of the enclosure, do not deduct for the bench area, since it requires nearly the same surface area. Remember, it is the surface area to which heat is lost in a steam enclosure.

Surrounding Temperature: Ambient room temperature should be between 68° and 72° Fahrenheit (20°C and 22°C).

If the steam room is installed against exterior walls, particularly in a cold climate, the walls should be insulated or the generator will need to be increased in size. Typically, it's recommended that you add 10% to the generator size for each exterior wall, whether insulated or not.

Pipe Run Length: Although the generator can be located in many different places, the closer it is to the steam enclosure, the better. Some manufacturers will tell you that it can be as far as 20 feet (6.10m) away from the enclosure, others say as much as 50 feet (15.24m). However, the farther the generator is from the enclosure, the longer it takes for steam to get there. Add an additional 15 cubic feet (4.57m) to the overall shower enclosure size for pipe runs between 15' (4.57m) and 25' (7.62m).

After you determine the cubic footage of the steam room based on these additional criteria, refer to a specification chart provided by the manufacturer to determine the proper steam generator model.

If the calculated cubic footage capacity falls between two models, always choose the larger unit.

SAUNAS

Explanation of Use

Although sauna procedures are as varied as the individual users, most enthusiasts recommend briefly showering, then entering the sauna for 5 to 15 minutes. The individual may sit or lie in the insulated wooden room. The lower bench is always cooler than the higher one. Next, a cool shower, a swim in the pool or a roll in the snow invigorates the body's system. A short 10 to 15 minute rest follows. Finally, a second visit to the sauna for about 20 minutes is enjoyed. During the second visit, a brief whisking of the skin increases circulation.

Ladling water over the hot stones can also add a refreshing burst of humidity during the final moments. A second 20 minute rest is suggested, followed by a final shower and a light snack.

Enclosure Designs

SIZING RECOMMENDATIONS

Popular family saunas range in size from 4' x 3' (121.92cm x 91.44cm) to 6' (182.88cm) squares, with other rectangle shapes also available. Regardless of the overall shape, a 7' (213.36cm) ceiling is recommended to prevent heat from rising into unused space. A 1'-8" (50.8cm) to 2'-0" (60.96cm) wide door that is 6'-8" (203.2cm) high and swings out without any type of locking device is used to minimize heat loss and to maximize safety. Because showering and resting are an integral part of the sauna experience, this specialty fixture should be located near the bathroom or swimming pool, with a dressing and resting area near by.

WALL, FLOOR AND CEILING MATERIALS

The overall sauna enclosure is generally built out of wood. Although the traditional sauna uses aspen wood, kiln-dried, clear, all-heart, A-grade redwood is an adequate substitute for the

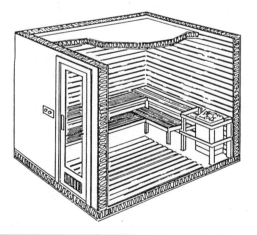

Figure 172 Typical sauna design.

modern day sauna because of its ability to withstand extreme temperature changes. Redwood acts as an insulator on walls, ceiling and floor. And it diffuses the heat so that the surfaces remain warm, but not hot, to the touch.

VENTILATION/LIGHTING

The sauna should feature soft, subdued lighting and good ventilation to prevent people from becoming dizzy. Prefabricated units offer an ideal design solution for sauna planning.

The manufacturer provides you with an easy-to-assemble, well-thought-out system that generally includes the following parts:

- **Intake Vent:** An intake vent, which is located near the floor in the wall behind the stove, or installed in the sauna door.

- **Outlet:** An outlet, for cross ventilation, at the opposite wall approximately level with, but not below, the intake vent, or a few inches from the ceiling.

- **Lighting:** A lighting system that is soft and controlled from the outside of the enclosure.

FUEL SOURCES

A stove used in the sauna may be electric or gas. The proper kilowatt (KW) rating for electric heaters, or **British Thermal Unit** (BTU) for gas heaters, is based on the size of the sauna, as well as the wall insulation, and the location of the sauna in relationship to air-conditioned or non-air-conditioned adjacent spaces.

For example, for a 5' x 7' (152.4cm x 213.36cm) sauna installed indoors with good insulation, 1 KW of electricity per 40 cubic feet of room space is adequate. 1,000 BTUs for a gas heater planned for every 15 cubic feet of space will also do the job. (Of course, the traditionalist client may select a wood burning stove with a chimney.) The sauna must also include a control, located just outside the sauna room.

A WORD OF CAUTION

As you can imagine, indoor whirlpool bath, steam rooms, or saunas do offer rest, relaxation and invigoration for your client. However, a word of caution is in order. While these certainly are socializing spaces, care must be taken in their use.

In all three systems, the extreme temperature present stimulates the cardiovascular system. Individuals with high blood pressure, respiratory or heart disease, circulatory problems, or chronic illnesses, such as diabetes or epilepsy, should check with a physician before installing any of these unique relaxation experiences.

Individuals under the influence of alcohol or other drugs, should also avoid whirlpools, saunas and steam rooms.

Whatever your client's choice - a comfortable, quiet bath, a revitalizing stall shower, a luxurious indoor whirlpool bath, a relaxing steam bath or sauna - it's up to you to carefully question them, apply thorough product knowledge and in-depth technical knowledge to create a special fixture arrangement for the new bathroom.

SECTION **7**

Surfacing Materials

In addition to the fixtures and fittings in the bathroom, other key ingredients of a successful project include the surfacing materials that you select, as well as the storage system designed for the room. Surfacing materials run the gamut from hardwood floors to natural stone slabs, to individual ceramic tiles. Decorative laminates and solid surfacing materials are also choices. However, before selecting any of these surfaces, you must first understand the importance of a proper substrate material.

CAST POLYMERS (CULTURED MARBLES AND ONYX)

Cast polymers have been discussed at length in an earlier section, however, in slab form, cast polymers can be used in bathtub and/or shower enclosures, as well as for vanity tops. They're available in marbleized patterns, granite-like textured patterns, or solid colors.

CERAMIC TILE

Ceramic tile is a favorite surface product for many bathroom designers. It is a beautiful material, which offers wide design flexibility.

However, without a solid understanding of the product, installation methods and care recommendations, the profitable job and a pleased client may elude you.

Figure 173 (Courtesy of American Olean Tile Co.) An example of a bathroom which features ceramic tile surfacing materials.

Tile is composed of clays, shales, porcelain or baked dirt. These raw products are pressed or extruded into shapes and then fired in a kiln, baked in an oven or cured in the sun.

The differences between raw materials, manufacturing methods and surface finishes make some types of tile more durable in heavy use areas than others. The firing method will also affect the moisture absorption rate of different types of tile, therefore making some more appropriate for high moisture bathroom areas.

Tile specified by bathroom designers for any surface other than decorative vertical areas should be selected after careful investigation into its appropriateness for the planned installation.

As you consider a tile for a specific installation;

- Refer to the manufacturer's literature for usage recommendations.

- Check the porosity of the tile.

- Check the availability of trim (curved shapes for smooth corners, edges and coves).

- Think through your grout selection.

- Make sure that you have specified the recommended installation method for the tile you have selected.

To help you do that, American Olean Tile Company has generously contributed the following information from their program "Start to Finish":

Types of Tile Available

GLAZED TILE

A coating of glass-forming minerals and ceramic stains is called the glaze. The glaze is sprayed onto the body of the tile (known as the bisque) before firing. The finished surface may have a shiny luster. Some glazed surfaces can be slippery to certain footwear, especially when the footwear or surface is wet. Glazed tiles are also available in a variety of finishes; some have a slip-resistant glazed texture. Various sizes, shapes and thicknesses are available.

Shiny, high-gloss glazed tiles may dull slightly with wear over a period of time with continued use. Black or dark-colored glazed tiles will show wear more rapidly than lighter colors. The type of glaze often determines the recommended end use of the tile, (i.e., walls, floors, counters).

CERAMIC MOSAICS

Ceramic mosaic tiles are distinguished from other kinds of ceramic tile by their small size, which must not exceed 6 sq. in. (2.45 x 2.45 in.)(6.2cm x 6.2cm). The most common types are natural clay and porcelain in which the color is throughout the tile rather than an applied surface such as a glaze. However, glazes may be applied as well. Porcelain ceramic mosaic tiles are always vitreous (natural clay) or impervious (porcelain). Therefore, they have a very low water absorption rate, less than 0.5%. They have a harder, denser body than non-vitreous wall tile.

Ceramic mosaics are usually sold face-mounted with paper, back-mounted with plastisol, or mesh-backed in 12" x 12" (30.48cm x 30.48cm) or 12" x 24" (30.48cm x 60.96cm) sheets. Mounted sheets facilitate installation and control the evenness of spacing.

When combined with the appropriate trim, the small-size units allow contour design applications in bathroom layouts. Porcelain mosaics are impervious, stain-resistant, dent-proof and frost- proof. They are suitable for interior and exterior walls, floors, countertops, and vanity tops. They are also used extensively in the linings of swimming pools. Creative graphics, murals and geometric designs can be planned with ceramic mosaics.

PREGROUTED SHEETS

Glazed and ceramic mosaic tile may be ordered from manufacturers in pre-grouted 2' x 2' (60.96cm x 60.96cm) sheets. They come in several size tiles, glazes and colors. The sheets save installation time and produce a uniform installation for showers, bathtubs, walls, vanities, and bathroom floors.

QUARRY TILE

Quarry tile is made from shale, clays or earth which is extruded to produce an unglazed product which has color throughout the tile body. There is a great variety of quality levels within the broad term quarry tile. The earthen clay tiles may be very soft and irregular in shape. Other types of quarry tile are so porous that they require a penetrating sealer to protect the surface.

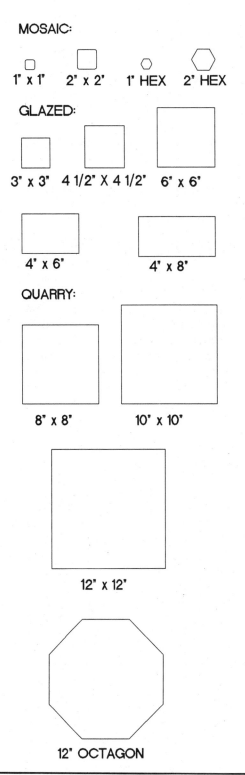

MOSAIC:

1" x 1"   2" x 2"   1" HEX   2" HEX

GLAZED:

3" x 3"   4 1/2" X 4 1/2"   6" x 6"

4" x 6"   4" x 8"

QUARRY:

8" x 8"   10" x 10"

12" x 12"

12" OCTAGON

Figure 174 Typical tile shapes and sizes.

Before such a sealer is applied, the tile and grout must be allowed to cure for at least two weeks. During this curing time, the area must be protected and, ideally, work must stop.

Other so-called quarry tiles must be stained and sealed. If such extra steps in the installation process must be completed, the designer should include the extra costs in the estimate.

Certain manufacturers' quarry tile meet the ANSI standards and are considered stain-resistant although not stain-proof. Thus, application and renewal of a sealer is optional. To achieve the subtle patina or rich glow of natural quarry clay, seasoning the tile with oil-based cleaners (e.g., Murphy's Oil Soap or Lestoil) is preferred to sealing.

Quarry tile is suitable for interior residential and commercial floors, walls and fireplace facings. Quarry tile may be used on exterior surfaces when proper installation methods are followed.

DECORATIVE TILE

Within the family of glazed ceramic tile, there is a sub-category often called "Decos". These attractive accent pieces may include a raised or recessed relief pattern or feature a painted or silk-screened design. Generally the relief designs are planned for vertical use only because the three-dimensional tiles are difficult to clean on a counter surface or floor area. Some of the hand-painted tiles may be so delicate that general countertop or floor cleaning will damage the pattern; but they are popular for walls and as inserts in a backsplash.

Figure 175   (Courtesy of American Standard Inc.) Tile patterns can match designs on the plumbing fixtures.

Some decorative tiles create a design which flows from tile to tile to give designers great flexibility for a unique, one-of-a-kind wall, border or backsplash. Others are one-of-a-kind art pieces that should be showcased within the field of plain tile.

CERAMIC TILE PLANNING POINTERS FROM THE PROS

- **Manufacturers' recommendation:** Ceramic tile specified by bathroom designers for any surface other than decorative vertical areas should be selected after careful investigation into their appropriateness for the planned installation.

  The hardness of a glaze plus tile body determines a tile's end use. Manufacturer's specification sheets or catalogs will suggest approved applications.

  As you and your client consider ceramic tile for a specific installation, first refer to the manufacturer's literature for usage recommendations. If recommendations are not available, ask if the tile meets the ANSI standards. If not, find out what is non-standard about the tile. As harmony in color is one of the parts of this standard, the tile may meet all other tests necessary for approval, but rather than a blended color, may offer a lovely variety of hues.

- **Determine porosity:** The porosity of the tile is also critical for bathroom countertops as well as for floor installations in these ar-

eas. Grooming aids can ruin a new counter surface if the wrong tile has been selected. Tiles are considered vitreous if the absorption is 3% or less and impervious if their absorption is 0.5% or less, as is the case with porcelain ceramic mosaics.

- **Select glazed or unglazed surfaces:** The glaze finish is another criterion to consider. Some tiles come two ways; high-gloss or matte. For bathrooms, a good choice is glossy finish tile for walls. The heavy use of a vanity countertop may cause a glossy surface to become dull over time.

  With a matte glaze, wear is not nearly as noticeable. Both tiles have the same degree of hardness. For floors, matte or unglazed porcelain are recommended.

  Glazed tile, smooth to the touch, can be slip-resistant due to a special manufacturing process. Textured glazes with noticeably rough surface are also slip-resistant. Varying degrees of slip resistance are needed for a variety of end uses. Safe bathroom design demands that slip resistant tiles be specified for floor applications.

Select the Correct Surface Trim

Just as important as the tile shapes is the availability of trim shapes. While the floor can be installed with nothing more than a plain or field tile edge (tile without any finished or shaped edge), the countertop, bathtub enclosure, shower stall, floor baseboard treatment or vanity top calls for specially designed pieces to complete the installation. Trim shapes are available with 3/4" (1.9cm) radius for conventional mortar installation, and 1/4" (.64cm) radius for organic adhesive installations. These trim shapes are generally more expensive than the square footage price of the field tile because of the cost of production. The color and texture match is generally good between field tile and trim shapes, but there may be a slight or pronounced texture difference in some selections.

When you're using ceramic tile for the first time, visually compare a field tile and trim shapes before the order is placed. If there is any variation, the client should approve the difference before the order is placed.

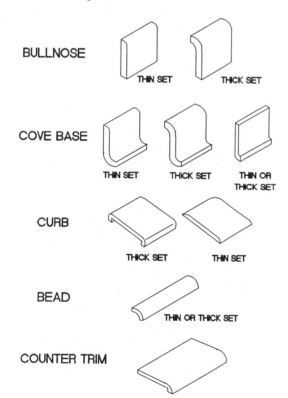

Figure 176 (Courtesy of The Ceramic Tile Council of America) Tile trim is designed for either "thin-set" organic adhesive or "thick-set" conventional mortar installations.

Grouts

Different types of grout are available, each designed for a particular kind of installation and to be used with specific tile sizes and shapes. Definitions of various grout types may be found in the **Tile Council of America Inc's** "Handbook for Ceramic Tile Installation", P.O. Box 1787, Clemson, SC 29633-1787.

Generally, four broad categories of grout will be specified by the bathroom designer:

EPOXY

Epoxy grouts, in several colors, are used when superior strength and chemical resistance are desired. New formulas produce nearly flush joints and are effective in vertical joints such as backsplashes and cove base trim. Epoxy grouts are more expensive than other types of grouts.

SILICONE RUBBER

Silicone rubber grouts, in white, are used in areas where great elasticity and moisture resistance are required. They're ideal for bathroom applications (walls, floors or vanity tops). These grouts are not recommended for kitchen countertops because of their chemical properties which make them unsuitable for food areas.

DRY-SET

Dry-set grouts (non-sanded grout), in white or colors, are suited for grout joints not exceeding 1/8" (.32cm) in width.

SANDED

Sanded grouts, in white and colors, are used for grout joints up to 3/8" (.95cm) in width. The sand is added to the grout to insure proper strength of the wider joint. Most often used for floors and ceramic mosaics.

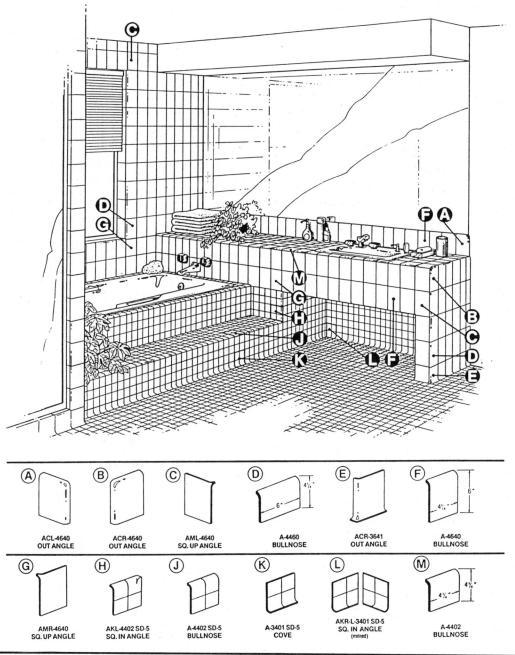

Figure 177 (Courtesy of American Olean Tile Co.) A bathroom perspective that demonstrates where you would use trim pieces.

GROUT PLANNING POINTERS FROM THE PROS

- **Coordinate the Tile and Grout Color:** A tile surface will offer a more harmonious look if the grout color and the tile color are similar. The pronounced grid pattern, which is created with contrasting grout, can enhance the design potential of large bathroom spaces. Plan a design with contrasting grout as you would one with grid wall covering. Check for proper scale.

- **Test Color First:** Follow manufacturer's installation directions precisely to avoid possible staining. If you're unsure about grout and tile relationship, try a test panel first to avoid problems.

- **Make Sure Clients Understand What They're Getting:** Talk about grout with your customers every time. Many customers expect white grout, others may have seen tile with colored grout. Find out what they want; help them select the best combination to meet their expectations.

- **Latex Additive:** Both dry-set and sanded grout are enhanced by the addition of a latex additive during the installation process. The latex additive increases the bonding strength and provides a better cure. Also, you can expect less water absorption, so use latex for wet areas (showers, bathtub surrounds or sink counters).

- **Sealing the Grout:** Sealers help preserve true grout colors. Epoxy grouts do not require sealers. For cement joints, you must wait until the joint is completely cured. Use in a test area first to be sure the effect is right. Several coats of sealer may be applied in areas of heavy use (countertops, shower stalls, etc.) as needed.

- **Show Clients Colored Grouts:** This selection is as important as the tile. Most manufacturers showrooms feature colored grout in vignettes and sample panels. Invite your customers to browse for ideas.

- **Explain Variations in Grout Color:** Help clients understand that grout color may appear darker when wet immediately after it is installed. After curing it will return to the expected shade. Make sure they understand that the grout on the shower floor may always look darker than that on the adjacent bathroom floor because it is always damp.

- **Beware of Uneven Grout Colors Caused by Jobsite Conditions:** Beware of uneven drying when grouting near a heat duct, hot air vent or air conditioner. Peculiar shade variations sometimes occur. This can be prevented by shutting off the source of air or frequently wetting the grout in that area. Uniform drying will produce more uniform color.

- **Maintenance:** Poor maintenance can discolor any grout. Colorful grout in a shower or luxury bathtub surround coated with soap film will soon be dull and discolored. Shampoo chemicals can react with the grout, making blotch spots. Floors with sanded cement grout are sometimes washed with dirty water and carelessly rinsed. The suspended dirt in wash water can be absorbed by the cement floor grout. This can be avoided by changing water frequently.

Method of Installation

Three methods of installation are used for ceramic tile projects.

MASTIC (ORGANIC ADHESIVE):

In this method, tile is directly applied to the subfloor, decking or cement with troweled on mastic. When this method is used, the floor will only be raised the thickness of the tile.

Manufacturers state that a mastic installation may use any of the following base surfaces: existing tile, fiberglass, wood, paneling, brick, masonry, concrete, plywood or vinyl. The surface must be dry, flat and free of dirt and grease. Any existing structural problems cannot be camouflaged by the tile installation. If there is a bow in the floor before the tile is installed, it will be there after the tile is installed.

CONVENTIONAL MORTAR BED (MUD):

In this method, the tile is installed on a bed of mortar 3/4" to 1-1/4"

(1.91cm to 3.2cm) thick. Two systems are popular in the United States. In one, the tile is set on a mortar bed while it is still soft. In the other, tile is set on a cured mortar bed.

THIN SET OVER BACKERBOARD:

A glass-mesh concrete backerboard may take the place of a conventional mortar bed. It is unaffected by moisture and has one of the lowest coefficients of expansion of all building panels. Additionally, the boards are only one-half the weight of conventional mortar installations. In either the second or third method of installation, the floor or vanity height will be raised the thickness of the tile and the mortar bed or glass mesh concrete backerboard.

This height difference may require special floor preparation. In new construction, the subfloor can be recessed to accommodate a tile floor. In renovation projects, a transition method between the new higher tile floor and adjoining floors must be specified. Special toe-kick heights must also be detailed so that the industrial standard of 4" (10.16cm) high kick space is maintained.

Most tile setters recommend the mortar installation be used over wood subfloors. The advantage to this type of installation is that the tile (installed with a cleavage membrane) will "float" on top of the wood.

Normal wood expansion and contraction will not cause cracks in the tile or grout. The mortar installation is also more desirable when there is a heavy wear pattern.

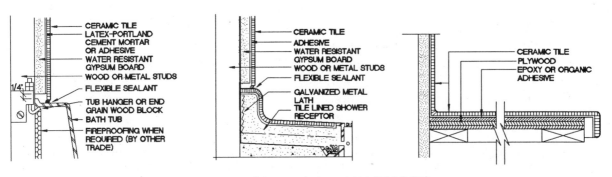

MASTIC (ORGANIC ADHESIVE)

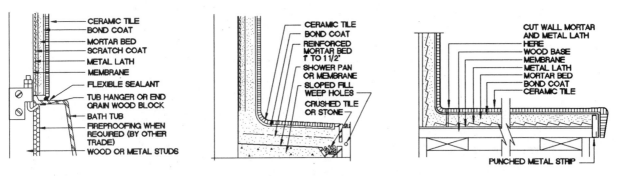

CONVENTIONAL MOTAR BED (MUD)

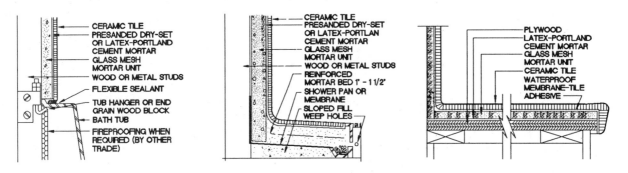

THINSET OVER BACKERBOARD

Figure 178   (Courtesy of The Ceramic Tile Council of America) The three most typical methods of installing tile on countertops, bathtub walls and shower receptors.

Cabinet Installer's Preparation

What should the cabinet installers do to prepare the bathroom vanity for the tile setter?

Tile, much like a house, is only as strong as its foundation, and the foundation is made up of what is installed below the tile surface.

The use of a 4' to 6' (121.92cm to 182.88cm) level and an 8' to 10' (243.84cm to 304.8cm) straight edge is recommended to insure a level surface. When necessary, cabinets should be shimmed underneath the toe kicks. A baseboard, floor covering or toe kick skin is then installed to conceal the shims.

If the backsplash area is to be tiled, it must be patched and solid. The tile installation requires a smooth and even surface.

The type of decking material and the decking installation varies with each type of tile setting method. Detailed methods and standards are listed in the **Handbook for Ceramic Tile Installation**.

The cabinets must be level and plumb. The maximum variations allowable are as follows:

	Walls	Floors & Counters
Dry-set Mortar	1/8" in 8' run	1/8" in 10' run
Epoxy Mortar	1/8" in 8' run	1/8" in 10' run
Organic Adhesive	1/8" in 8' run	1/16" in 3' run

TILE PLANNING POINTERS FROM THE PROS

VANITY TOPS

- The cabinets must be level and square so that backsplash grout lines will be straight. A 4' to 6' (121.92cm to 182.88cm) level should be used. For longer runs, a 4' (121.92cm) level and 8' (243.84cm) straight edge should be used.

- If the backsplash area is to be tiled, it must be patched and solid. An organic adhesive installation requires a smooth and even surface.

- In many parts of the country, plywood decking is used. In other lo-cales, traditional lumber decking is preferred. Traditional decking is often specified to provide flexibility under the tile. Generally, grade-one or grade-two kiln-dried Douglas fir, 1" x 4" (2.54cm x 10.16cm) or 1" x 6" (2.54cm x 15.24cm) spaced 1/4" (.63cm) apart, is used. It may be installed perpendicular to the backsplash (from the front of the cabinet to the back) or running parallel with the cabinet face. Tile craftspeople and carpenters differ in their opinions as to which is better. The decking should be delivered to the house several days before the installation to allow the wood to reach the relative humidity of the room.

Figure 179 An unusual tile application

- The decking should overhang the cabinets and flush out with the face of the drawers and doors.

- Fixture cutouts are made during the tile decking installation. Unbox the fixture and place it in the cutout to ensure a proper fit before the tile craftspeople arrive at the job site. Whenever possible, any cutout should be a minimum of 2" (5.08cm) away from the sheetrock or plastered backsplash.

- The elimination of stress is critical when countertop overhangs and toilet extensions are planned. The tile must have a solid base. If any movement occurs when pressure is placed on the top, the tile and/or grout will crack. The undersiding of the decking should be finished to match the cabinets or correspond with other products used in the project.

FLOORS

- In renovation jobs, removing the existing floor covering is recommended. Generally, this is necessary if vinyl tiles or cushioned vinyl floors are installed over a slab or wood foundation. In many parts of the country, tile is installed directly over old, non-cushioned sheet vinyl.

- Doors may require modification to accommodate a tile floor. With a mastic installation, the designer is only concerned with the thickness of the tile. When a conventional mortar installation is planned, the designer must allow clearance for a 3/4" to 1-1/4" (1.91cm to 3.18cm) thick mortar bed, plus the thickness of the tile. A glass-mesh concrete backerboard installation will require a clearance dimension equal to the thickness of the board, plus the tile.

- Allow enough time for the door modification. Interior hollow-core or solid-core doors are easy to cut down. Pocket doors must be the type which can be removed from the pocket.

- If the new tile floor will be higher than the finished flooring of an adjacent room, the tile selected must have trim pieces or a threshold must be planned. Thresholds are generally marble or wood. Solid surface material can also be used as a threshold.

- Make sure a tile backerboard does not interfere with the toilet supply line escutcheon plate.

Figure 180   (Courtesy of American Standard Inc.) An attractive tile pattern is introduced in the center of the floor.

WALLS

- Whenever planning a tile enclosure around a bathtub, make sure the tile extends past the bathtub and runs down to the floor. This extra tile width will protect the drywall surface underneath from moisture damage over years of use.

- When planning a tile wainscot in a bathroom, specify the height so it has some relationship with the vanity and its backsplash. You may eliminate the backsplash completely and run the trim or molding at the top of the wainscotting in place of a backsplash. Alternatively, you can step the wainscotting up so it ties in at the same elevation as the backsplash.

- When planning a 36" (91.44cm) high tiled privacy wall which shields the toilet area from view, plan to tile the entire wall if the floor in the room is also tiled. This small wall section can be quite awkward if it has a tile baseboard at the bottom of it and a tile cap at the top, but no tile in between.

- If you are going to be tiling the wall area around the toilet, make sure you take the added dimension of the installation method and tile thickness into account when you determine finished wall dimensions. *For example,* if you're going to tile three walls around a toilet with a conventional mortar installation, you need to maintain a minimum clearance between your drywall of 33" to 35" (83.82cm to 88.9cm) to make sure the job meets the code requirement of 30" (76.2cm) between the finished side walls. Another typical error occurs when a tile wainscotting finish is applied to the wall behind the toilet, which then reduces the actual finished floor distance from the wall to the toilet's floor outlet. That 12-inch (30.48cm) rough-in dimension must be from the center of the floor outlet to the finished surface on the wall, not the drywall behind the tile.

- If you are planning to tile all four walls in a room, plus the ceiling, decide where it is most important to have grout lines on the wall line up with the grout lines on the ceiling. Generally, as you stand at the doorway, the wall at the far end of the room, or the most important wall will be the focal point. Therefore, this wall should be the wall the tile setters start with: running the tile up the wall and then across the ceiling. If the room is square, the grout lines will run down the wall on the opposite side. However, in renovation situations this may not occur.

- If you are tiling a wall surface, remember to decide where you're going to install the accessories (the toilet paper holder, towel bars and robe hooks) and make sure you determine how you're going to install the accessories on the new tile surface.

Figure 181   A shaped tile is attractively combined with solid surfacing materials in this small bathroom. Note how the baseboard is made out of the solid surfacing material rather than the tile.

Figure 182   (Courtesy of Eljer Plumbingware) An attractive bathroom combines ceramic tile at the floor, wainscotting and vanity top.

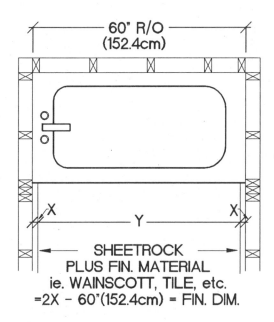

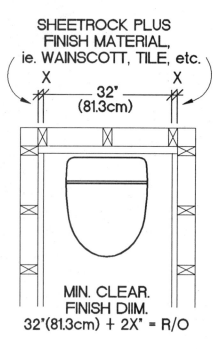

Figure 183   When planning wainscotting on the wall, make sure that you adjust rough openings to provide adequate clearance space.

Figure 184 *(Courtesy of Eljer Plumbingware) A dramatic tile wall is created in this bathroom. The tile combines beautifuly with the natural stone at the floor.*

Figure 185 *A small bathroom is enhanced by the designer's artistic combination of solid surfacing and ceramic tile.*

SHOWER PANS

Ceramic tile is not waterproof. A membrane must be installed between the backing material and the tile to insure a waterproof shower pan. Some installers prepare for the membrane installation as follows:

- **Cut the sheetrock** or plaster 9" (22.86cm) above the wood or slab floor.

- **After the drain** (designed for a tile pan) is installed, make sure the floor is solid and tight around the drain.

- **Build a standard curb** using three 2" x 4" (5.08cm x 1016cm) stacked on top of each other. The curb will be 4-1/2" (11.43cm) higher than the wood or slab floor. Generally, any barrier less than 9" (22.86cm) high is identified as a shower curb. Higher than 9" (22.86cm), it is identified as a Roman bathtub.

  Note: A shower design using universal considerations will have a 1/2" high curb or possibly none at all.

- **Installing Blocking:** The blocking must be a minimum of 4-1/2" (11.43cm) above the curb.

  Blocking Method No. 1: Install 2" x 10" (5.08cm x 25.4cm) boards between the studs all around the enclosure. The sheetrock or plaster will extend 1/2" (1.27cm) past the blocking.

Figure 186   Another example of ceramic tile, solid surfacing and laminates working well together.

Blocking Method No. 2: Install 1/4" (.64cm) plywood, face-nailed to studs, all around the enclosure. The sheetrock or plaster will extend 1/4" (.64cm) past the plywood.

- **The waterproof membrane** is then installed in the pan, over the blocking and on the curb. The membrane may be tar, lead, PVC or fiberglass. The plaster or sheetrock on the walls must be flush-out with the membrane installed over the blocking.

- **Inspect for water tightness.** First, install a temporary drain cap. Then fill the pan with water to 1" (2.54cm) below the curb. Allow the water to stand for 12 hours. To verify the seal, inspect the water level for any reduction.

Figure 187 (Courtesy of American Standard Inc.) Tile wainscotting surrounds this attic conversion bathroom. Note the stripe on the wall tiles behind the pedestal lavatories, which is repeated in the fixture.

Figure 188 Ceramic tile and a solid surface are used to create this planter box next to a stall shower.

Figure 189 (Courtesy of American Olean Tile Co.) Ceramic tile has been used to create a dramatic diagonal pattern in this attic bathroom. Variations in color are used to create the design at the walls and bathtub platform.

DECORATIVE LAMINATES

Laminate surfaces are found on bathroom wall areas, countertops, cabinet interiors, cabinet doors, and bathtub platforms.

Figure 190 (Courtesy of Wilsonart International) Laminate surfaces can be used on a bathtub deck if properly sealed.

The following information describes the different types of laminates available:

Types of Laminate

HIGH-PRESSURE DECORATIVE LAMINATES

High-pressure decorative laminate is composed of three types of paper fused under heat and pressure into a single surface. The top coat is a melamine resin-saturated overlay. The second

sheet is the decorative surface, a melamine resin-saturated paper carrying either a surface color or gravure print. Under these two levels is a core or body made up of three to nine sheets of phenolic resin-saturated kraft paper. The entire assembly is pressed at between 1,000 to 1,200 pounds (450 to 545 kilograms) per square inch for about an hour, at temperatures exceeding 280°F (138 C).

High-pressure decorative laminates are divided into forming and non-forming grades. Non-forming laminate is rigid, while forming laminate has been adjusted in the curing process to be more flexible so that it can be bent under heat. This process is called "post-forming".

The cabinet industry uses vertical-grade high-pressure decorative laminate which is .030" (.08cm) thick. Countertop fabricators use a horizontal grade of high pressure decorative laminate which is .050" (.13cm) thick. Both thicknesses are offered in forming and non- forming grades. The post forming grade is .042" (.11cm) thick.

High-pressure decorative laminates are used most frequently on countertop surfaces. They are also used by many cabinet manufacturers for cabinet door styles. The high-pressure decorative laminate is generally applied to a particle board substrate. Occasionally, codes may call for a plywood substrate for a countertop.

Of all the laminates available, high-pressure decorative laminates offer the greatest impact resistance. They are available in a wide range of colors, patterns, textures and finishes. Some manufacturers offer special fire-resistant, abrasion-resistant, chemical-resistant surfaces. Others fabricate laminate in a grooved tambour form. Generally, all high-pressure decorative laminates have excellent stain, abrasion, scuff and wear resistance. However, because the lami-nate is applied to a substrate, if a chip occurs, it is not repairable. Shiny sur-faces show scratches more easily than dull finishes. Solid colors show scratches to a greater extent than pattern surfaces.

Figure 191   (Courtesy of Kohler Co.) Laminates also combine beautifully with other materials. Here a laminate countertop is seen with ceramic tile.

In addition to the wide spectrum of colors and patterns available, several special-purpose laminates are also offered for the designer's consideration:

COLOR-THROUGH LAMINATES

Color-through laminates are similar to standard, high-pressure decorative laminates, except that the melamine color sheets are used throughout the material instead of the phenolic core or body kraft paper layer. Therefore, the laminate contains color throughout and no joint line will be visible after fabrication. These laminates are used for special edge treatments where the surface is engraved or routed to reveal other colors. Or they can be used throughout the room for the total countertop installation. The material is more costly than ordinary high-pressure, decorative laminates and the fabrication takes a bit more attention and care.

COMPOSITE PANELS

A composite panel is a layer of kraft paper impregnated with either melamine resin or polyester resin, which is thermal-set or thermal-fused (fused with heat and pressure) to a substrate of particle board, fiber board or some other material. It is sold as laminate board. This differs from high-pressure laminate, which is sold in sheets to fabricators who apply it to boards themselves. It is sometimes known as low-pressure laminate, short cycle laminate, melamine or MCP.

Composite panels generally have just one print sheet on the surface, although some suppliers offer an overlay sheet. Both front and back of the panels are laminated to avoid warping. Generally, these panels are offered in a limited range of colors and patterns.

Composite panels are used in vertical or light-use horizontal applications, such as shelving. They should not be used for countertops.

Generally, because they are thermal-set, composite panels are joined to the substrate with a stronger bond than high-pressure laminate, paper or other surfaces, which are mechanically fused. It will not delaminate because it becomes part of the substrate surface.

Composite panels have a lower weight than high-pressure laminates and offer some cost savings. However, composite panels offer less impact and abrasion resistance than high-pressure laminates. One company, Nevamar, offers a full line of matched composite boards and laminates. These are called LamMates, and they permit the designer to combine the durability of high-pressure laminates with the economy of MCP in cabinetry.

NATURAL STONE

Types of Stone

FLAGSTONE

Flagging is a process whereby stone is split into thin slabs suitable for paving. Although generally identified as "flagstone", bluestone and slate are the most common types of flagging stones used.

Bluestone is a rough sandstone paver, usually buff, blue, green or gray in color. Slate is a smooth, gray, sedimentary stone. The thicker the stones, the less likely that cracks will occur over the lifetime of the floor. The weight of the floor must be carefully computed when used over wood foundations.

Both bluestone and slate absorb heat rather than reflect it and can get quite hot. Irregularly cut stones are the least expensive pre-cut, patterned stone.

GRANITE

Polished granite countertops are a popular element of up-scale bathrooms. A natural stone countertop conveys a sense of beauty and warmth that is combined with a durable work surface that can withstand the expected high use of the new bathroom.

Granite is an igneous rock (class of rock formed by a change of the molten material to a solid state) with visible coarse grains. It consists of quartz, feldspar, mica, and other colored minerals.

Granite isn't as subject to staining as marble is because of an extremely low absorption rate. The stone is less prone than marble to scratching. Its coarse grain also makes it more slip-resistant than marble.

Coloration: When specifying color variation, include shade, clarity and movement of the granite. There will be slight variations from slab to slab because of mineral content and veining, which adds to the character of the natural stone. Granite is available in three different finishes: a highly polished surface, which is appropriate for most countertop applications, a thermal finish, which has a rough-textured touch and a honed finish which provides a matte surface ideal for a bathroom floor application.

Fabrication: Granite countertops differ from solid surfacing tops in that the fabrication is simpler and completed at the factory; therefore, installation costs are generally less for granite surfaces. Consequently, designers should only compare installed prices when attempting to identify a realistic cost difference between a solid surface top and a granite one.

Measuring the countertops for installation has evolved into a precise process that can be completed when the cabinets are ordered. Working from the bathroom design layout and using newly developed measuring techniques to calculate exact dimensions, craftsmen can prefabricate granite and deliver it to the jobsite ready for installation.

Sizing: For most countertops, the optimum thickness is 1-1/4" (3.18cm). The difference in cost over more fragile 3/4" (1.91cm) slabs is minimal and the added thickness gives more strength for water closet extensions and cutouts, while reducing the risk of breakage during transportation and installation. For example, a 1-1/4" (3.18cm) granite slab can support 12" (30.48cm) of overhang. Keep in mind the weight of these tops as you schedule the installation crews.

Granite slabs for countertops can measure up to 4-1/2' (131.16cm) wide and up to 9' (274.32cm) long. This allows greater flexibility in countertop design. Should more than one piece be necessary, the slabs can be matched for color and grain consistency and then cut to butt squarely against each other. For this type of installation, locate seams in the most inconspicuous or unobtrusive locations possible, around cutouts or back corners.

Figure 192   This luxurious bathroom uses natural stone at the floor, behind the pedestal, at the counter-top and the bathtub platform. Note how it is attractively combined with the ceramic tile.

MARBLE

Marble is recrystallized limestone. After earthen materials are crystallized into limestone, they are subjected to pressure and heat from the earth's movement. Italian marble is world renowned. Belgium, Spain, Greece and France are also known for quarry marble. Alabama and Tennessee offer U.S. marble products.

Unless the finish is etched, honed or pummeled, marble is slippery when wet. Therefore, use it as a bathroom flooring surface only if it features one of these slip-resistant finishing treatments.

Marble is brittle and must be handled like glass during installation. Once installed, edges at doorways must be protected by a sturdy threshold.

Coloration: Numerous minerals are present which account for the markings and color range associated with marble. Marble is available in white, red, green, yellow and black. Some marbles feature directional patterns; others offer a general, overall design.

The more colorful and decorative the marble, the more fragile it is. Each vein in a stone is the result of natural discoloration from water. It is like a tiny fracture which, under pressure, can lead to breakage.

Durability: Marble is rated according to an A-B-C-D classification based on the fragility of the stones. A and B marbles are solid and sound. C and D marbles are the most fragile, but also the most colorful and decorative.

The grade of marble affects pricing: the more fragile and decorative it is, the more expensive. Before specifying marble, advise the client about durability.

Slab vs. Tile: Traditionally, marble is used in large slabs. Suppliers differ on the size and thickness of countertops they stock. Many slabs are available 1-1/4" (3.18cm) thick. Other suppliers, however, stock 3/4" (1.91cm) thick countertops; some carry 1-1/2" (3.81cm) thick slabs. The appearance of a 1-1/2" (3.81cm) thick counter can be achieved by joining the 3/4" (1.9cm) counter to a 3/4" (1.91cm) edge treatment. The pieces can be glued together so that the seam is unnoticeable.

An alternative is 6" x 6" x 1/2" (15.24 x 15.24 x 1.27cm) marble tiles that are installed by a tile setter following specifications developed by the Ceramic Tile Institute.

Maintenance: Marble is soft and porous. This means it stains easily if not initially sealed with at least two coats of a penetrating sealer. And it must be frequently resealed. White marble is softer and less dense then colored marble, so it's more easily stained. Dark marble shows scratches more easily.

Finishing: Marble may be polished so that it has a shiny appearance. Although there are degrees of shine to which marble can be polished, the final polish is achieved by adding a slightly moistened acidic compound to a smooth marble surface. A heavy brush or felt pad is applied under tremendous pressure. This action produces heat which creates a chemical reaction that changes the surface of the stone itself. The compound is rinsed off and the stone is left polished.

TERRAZZO

Terrazzo is a slurry mixture of stone chips consisting of marble and cement. This marble aggregate concrete produces a hard and durable flooring surface. It is also used as a wall treatment.

It is available in field tiles of a more solid nature and decorative border tiles in various patterns and colors to match or contrast with the field tiles. Such a combination can provide a dramatic "old world" look.

Figure 193   In this bathroom, marble is used on the floor and walls. Contrasting colors create an effective border pattern.

SOLID SURFACING

General Introduction

The designer has many solid surfacing materials to choose from. Materials currently available from major manufacturers are **Avonite, Du Pont Corian, Fountainhead by Nevamar, Gibraltar by Wilsonart International** and **Surrell by Formica**. Other materials are being continually introduced onto the market.

The designer should compare these new materials against the guidelines detailed in the following review of the major products to ascertain their level of quality and durability. Although the major product offerings vary in composition and breadth of product line, there are some common features:

- All solid surfacing material is stain resistant because it is non-porous, and repairable because the color runs through the material.

- All manufacturers recommend cleaning with a damp cloth or sponge and ordinary household soap or mild cleanser.

- The color-through feature of these materials means that severe stains (including cigarette burns) can be removed with a 320 to 400 grit sandpaper, steel wool and/or a buffing pad.

- While most products have excellent resistance to household chemicals, paint removers and oven cleaners can sometimes cause damage. Further, industrial chemicals, as might be found in a commercial installation may affect various products in different ways. If exposure to industrial chemicals is a concern, check with the manufacturer.

- All of the manufacturers offer solid surfaces with a factory finish which may be sanded to a matte finish or can be buffed or polished to a high gloss. None of the manufacturers recommend high-gloss finishes on dark colors in heavy use areas, such as kitchen countertop surfaces.

- When properly fabricated, the seam between two pieces of all the solid surfacing materials is almost imperceptible. However, you should never promise an invisible seam.

- Solid surfacing is quite "fabricator sensitive" and all manufacturers stress the importance of retaining only qualified and/or certified fabricators.

- Companies offer sheet goods in 1/2" (1.27cm) and 3/4" (1.91cm) thicknesses. Other thicknesses are available and vary by company. The availability of molded lavatories also varies by company.

- Manufacturers recommend that unsupported overhangs should not exceed 12" (30.48cm) with 3/4" (1.91cm) sheets and 6" (15.24cm) with 1/2" (1.27cm) sheets.

- Manufacturers recommend that the material "float" on the substrate; most recommend perimeter frames and a web support system rather than a full substrate.

- Although solid surfacing is considered more durable than laminates, it is not impervious to heat. Because solid surface materials expand when heated, all

manufacturers recommend at least 1/8" (.32cm) clearance on wall-to-wall installation.

- Most manufacturers, recommend these materials for interior use only. Potential problems with exterior use of some of the materials include shrinkage and expansion as well as color changes with exposure to direct sunlight.

Figure 194   Solid surfacing combines beautifully with other materials. In this award winning bathroom, solid surfacing material is featured on the vanity top, while natural stone tiles are at the floor and bathtub deck.

Current Products

Although these similarities exist in the major materials, there are differences in each of the major brands that relate to composition, warranties and applications.

The makers of Avonite describe the product as follows:

AVONITE

A patented formulation composed of polyester alloys and fillers not found in standard polyesters. Because of this, it is exceptionally durable. Avonite offers a 10-year warranty to back up that claim. The replacement expense for material and labor are covered by the warranty for projects that were installed properly.

Avonite's textured granite, gemstone or crystelle look, is first created by curing a special liquid polymer into a solid, then pulverizing it into particles. These particles are then used as suspended particulates during the final casting. This process gives Avonite its depth of color and translucency. There is an extensive color pallet. A new material called **"Formstone"** has been formulated with a modified acrylic matrix which provides exceptional post-forming capabilities for creating extremes in curbed shapes.

Avonite produces a Class I fire rated material and a Class III designer material ideal for moderate post-forming and high polishing. The Class III coefficient of expansion and contraction is greater than Class I and different fabrication procedures are recommended in extreme heat conditions. Avonite also warranties that its materials will not fade. A special patch kit provides the ability to repair ac-

cidental nicks and a unique inlay kit can create stone in stone or "Intarsia" looks.

Figure 195   Solid surfacing materials allow custom fabrication in unusual shapes, as seen at this vanity.

Du Pont describes Corian as follows:

CORIAN

A solid color, veined or stone look material. Corian is available in a variety of sheets, thicknesses and in a full range of kitchen sinks and bathroom lavatories for creating custom integrated sink worktops with Du Pont's joint adhesive system. All are of homogeneous, mineral-filled methyl methacrylate polymer, a tough, rigid, high performance, transparent acrylic with a Class 1 fire rating. Corian solid surface material is 100 percent acrylic-based.

Because it is a thermoformable acrylic with a mineral filler, Corian is an excellent product for thermoforming into custom designs such as bathtub and shower surrounds, and for forming sweeping, graceful curves. Corian also is available in a liquid form so color inlay patterns in Corian can be created. Du Pont-certified or approved fabricators should fabricate and install the product. Corian is not recommended for exterior surfaces, steam room wet walls, below-grade masonry walls, direct application on cinder block or concrete, on flooring or structural applications.

Du Pont has introduced a new 10-year limited installed warranty covering the material, fabrication and installation against defects when fabricated by a Du Pont-certified or approved fabricator/installer.

Nevamar describes Fountainhead as follows:

FOUNTAINHEAD

A solid color and textured surface with a soft stone appearance. Classic color pallet for sheets, kitchen sinks and vanities. The manufacturer also supplies liquid inlay so fabricator can create solid or matrix color designs. The material is a combination of engineered polyester and acrylic with alumina trihydrate as a filler. Fountainhead is a thermal-set plastic that can be thermal-formed to accommodate most common applications.

Nevamar designates "Accredited" fabricators who have demonstrated competent fabrication in actual installations; accreditation can be verified by the fabricator's ID card, which carries his accreditation number. The product does carry a 10-year limited warranty.

Wilsonart International describes Gibraltar as follows:

GIBRALTAR

A solid color and stone look collection, the product is a polyester and acrylic blend, with fire-retardant mineral fillers. In terms of design, Gibraltar solid colors match Wilsonart International laminate colors for increased design versatility - for perfectly matching laminate cabinets and backsplashes with solid surfacing tops. In addition, Gibraltar features a unique computerized color consistency, so that problems with mismatching are eliminated. The product is warranted for 10-years against failure, based on being installed by a Certified Fabricator.

Formica describes Surrell as follows:

SURRELL

A unique, totally homogeneous, densified, mineral-filled polyester. Available in a wide variety of sheets, vanities, lavatory bowls, kitchen sinks, shower bases, bathtubs and wet wall kits. A fully densified casting process is one in which all the air is removed from the mixture before it is cast. This results in a material that is denser and stronger than traditional cast polymer materials.

WALL MATERIALS

Wallpaper

Within the bathroom industry, a perplexing dilemma continually faces the designer - how to combine style with function. Wall coverings are often the planner's salvation.

MANUFACTURING METHODS

The patterns in wall coverings are achieved by using two methods: machine prints and hand prints. In machine printing, all the wallpaper rolls are printed in a continuous "run" and are identical in color. Hand prints are printed by a process called "silk screening" and cannot be matched for color as closely as machine prints because each roll is individually handscreened with slight color or variations occurring from roll to roll.

Figure 196   (Courtesy of American Standard Inc.) Striped wallcovering enhances this small bathroom.

To protect the hand print edges, the rolls are normally manufactured with selvages (untrimmed edges). A color variation will also occur in grass cloths and similar materials. The fibers from which they are made do not respond evenly to dyes; color gradually lightens or darkens from one edge of a strip to the other and varies along the length of the roll.

DETERMINING QUANTITIES

The following procedure is suggested to determine wallpaper quantities for papers from American sources, which are based on Imperial sizes and generally have 50 to 60 square feet of product on each double roll.

- Measure the width of each wall to be papered. Round the figure up to the next full foot measurement.

- Add the wall dimensions together.

- Multiply this figure by the ceiling height plus 4". Again, round up the figure to the next full foot measurement.

- Subtract the wall space covered by windows, doors and appliances from the total square footage to be covered.

- Depending on the pattern match, divide the actual wall space to be covered as follows:

    18" Repeat = Divide by 30
    19 to 24" Repeat = Divide by 27
    25" Repeat = Divide by 24

- Always round up to the next full number of rolls.

For papers which are sized metrically, you can assume 28 to 30 square feet. Therefore, you generally need to order twice the amount of product.

WALL COVERING

TYPE	HOW SOLD	SPECIAL COMMENTS
Common Papers		
Untreated Vinyl-Coated Cloth-Backed	Single, double & triple rolls, 18" - 27" wide; length & width combine to provide 30 sq.ft. per roll after waste allowance.	Susceptible to grease stains and abrasions; pattern inks may run if washed; strippable if cloth-backed
Vinyls		
Laminated to Paper Laminated to Woven Fabric Impregnated Cloth on Paper Backing Laminated to Unwoven Fabric	Same as common papers; heaviest grades also available in widths to 54" and lengths to 30yards.	Most durable type currently available; may be scrubbed; almost always strippable.
Foils		
Metallic Aluminum Laminated to Paper Aluminum Laminated to Cloth	Same as common papers.	Fragile and hard to handle; may cause glare in sunny areas; available in striking super graphics.
Flocks		
On Paper On Vinyl On Foil	Same as common papers.	Vinyl flocks washable; all may be damaged by excessive rubbing.
Pre-Pasted Coverings		
Papers Vinyls/Foils Flocks	Same as common papers.	Ideal for the inexperienced.
Fabrics		
Untreated Laminated to Paper Self Adhesive	Bolts usually 45" wide, but also in widths of 54" & 60"; sold by the yard.	Easy to clean with dry-cleaning fluids or powders.
Felt		
Laminated to Paper	Bolts 54" wide; sold by the yard.	May be vacuumed, but stains are hard to remove; some colors fade.
Textured Coverings		
Grass Cloth Hemp Burlap Overprinted Designs	Double rolls, 36" wide and 24' long except burlap, which is also available in widths to 54"	All available in either natural or synthetic fibers.
Murals		
On Paper OnVinyl On Foil	Strips 10' to 12' long, with matching paper for surrounding areas.	Muslin or unbleached cotton may be substituted for lining paper to create strippable material.
Cork		
Laminated to Paper Laminated to Burlap	Widths up to 36" lengths in 24' or 36'.	Keep well vacuumed; all cork surfaces are washable; cork absorbs and deadens sounds within a room.
Laminated Wood Veneers		
Random Patterns	Strips 10" to 24" wide and up to 12' long; end-matched strips for taller walls available on request from manufacturer.	Fire-resistant; allowed by strictest codes where solid wood paneling is banned.
Gypsum Coated Wall Fabric	Single rolls, 4' wide and 40 yards long.	Dries to plaster-like surface; available only in pastel shades, but may be painted in other colors.
Leather	Single dressed hides; one large cowhide covers from 25 to 40 square feet.	Expensive, handsome and durable; stains are difficult, but can be removed by brushing on rubber cement and peeling it off.

Paint

Painting is one of the finishing steps in a bathroom project. Often the designer is not responsible for this activity, but is expected to understand the craft and make recommendations to the client. A basic understanding of paints will aid the designer.

PAINT COVERAGE

Paint is designed to bond itself to either a fresh, new surface or an old, uneven one. It should cover and help to protect the surface against the assaults of weather, airborne chemicals and dirt. It should remain flexible enough to stay intact for years while the walls settle, vibrate, expand and contract.

Recent fears of toxic emissions from **Volatile Organic Compounds** (VOC) in all interior materials, including paints, have led to legislation in many areas and have increased preference for latex paints, which have little or no VOC. So be sure to check local codes.

PAINT MATERIAL COMPOSITION

An astonishing variety of materials have gone into paint mixture over the years, but most commonly used paints today contain certain ingredients, each with a specific function.

Pigments are made from minute particles of earth, metals or chemical compounds and give paint its color.

Resins are binders that give paint the ability to form a thin, tough film. The binders are normally chemicals or plastics such as alkyds, acrylics, polyvinyls or urethanes.

Plasticizers are chemical agents used to keep the paint elastic after it dries.

Solvents make the mixture of pigment, resin and plasticizer thin enough to be used with a brush or roller.

PAINT GLOSS CHOICES

The two major types of finishing coats -latex and alkyd paints - come in versions labeled flat, satin semi-gloss, egg shell and high gloss.

- **High gloss paints** are the most wear- resistant and moisture-resistant because of their relatively high proportion of resin. The more resin, the heavier and tougher the film. The high resin film of the glossy paints makes them ideal for areas subject to heavy use and frequent washing.

- **Semi-gloss paints** afford moderate durability with a less obtrusive shine for most woodwork.

- **Flat paints** provide a desirable low-glare surface for walls and ceilings that do not need frequent washing.

PAINT CLASSIFICATIONS

Latex Paint: This paint provides simplified cleanup, is odor-free and quick-drying. Water is the solvent for latex paint, which is made of plastic resin and either acrylics or tough polyvinyls. Its water solvency gives latex advantages which have made it the most widely used paint for walls and ceilings in living areas, other than kitchens and bathrooms. Tools, spills and hands can be cleaned with soap and water while the latex is wet. Latex paint is almost free of odor and harmful fumes, and a coat is usually dry in little more than an hour.

Latex adheres to most surfaces painted with flat oil or latex paint; it does not adhere to some alkyds and tends to peel away from any high gloss finish. Latex can be used over unprimed wall board, bare masonry and fresh plaster patches that have set but are not quite dry. Its water solvency imposes certain limitations on latex paint. Although it can be applied directly over wallpaper, the water in the paint may soak the paper away from the wall. If latex is applied to raw wood, the water swells the fibers and roughens the surface - a disadvantage where smooth finish is desirable. Used on bare steel, it rusts the metal. Flat latex is less resistant to abrasion and washing than either oil or alkyd paint, and the high gloss latex is less shiny and less durable than comparable alkyds or oils.

Alkyd Paint: This paint has replaced oil-based paints in most cases. It is considered the best type of paint to use in rooms which will receive a great deal of use. Any painted or wallpapered surface, or bare wood, can be covered with paint made from a synthetic resin called alkyd (often combined with other resins). This type of paint will adhere to bare masonry or plaster but should not be used on bare wallboard because it will raise a nap on the wallboard's paper covering.

Alkyd is the most durable of the common finishing paints. It is practically odor-free. Most alkyds are sufficiently

dry for a second coat in four to six hours. Although some latex paints will not bond well to alkyd, most other paints can be applied over it.

Glass Block

Glass block is enjoying a rekindled interest among designers. While popular in the 1930s and 1940s, the use of glass block came to a standstill in the 1970s. These translucent hollow blocks of glass are ideal for bathroom use. They transmit light, yet provide privacy. When used in exterior wall installations, they deaden outside noise and offer insulating qualities similar to thermal-pane windows. Available in a variety of shapes, sizes, textures and colors, glass block offers great design flexibility.

However, installation is not easy and should not be attempted by anyone other than a skilled mason. The blocks are non-porous, slick and heavy. During installation, they are slippery and difficult to align.

Alternatives to glass block are decorative glass-looking products that are made out of plastic materials. These substitutes are very strong, as well as being light weight. Assembly is generally quicker with these types of acrylic and proprietary polymer blocks because they have an engineered inner locking system which fastens them together. Therefore, traditional mortar joints are not required. Some of the manufacturers have available preformed, weather-resistant sealant that looks like a mortar joint to complete the finished product.

In some municipalities, glass block may not meet building codes standards for use in bathrooms. Always check local codes.

Figure 197   (Courtesy of Eljer Plumbingware)
Glass block is used below a bathtub platform to
add drama.

Figure 198   Glass block is used to create the stall
shower at the end of the bathtub.

Figure 199   Glass block is used to create privacy
shield for toilet and to create a custom shower
enclosure. The blocks help to extend the visual
size of this small bathroom space.

FLOORING MATERIALS

Resilient Flooring

Better materials and the manufacturers' ability to improve photographic realism have improved the ability of vinyl to mimic natural materials such as wood, marble, slate, granite and ceramic tile. However, the trend today in vinyl floor patterns is towards graphic simplicity which highlights simple, geometric patterns. Vinyl remains one of the easiest floors to maintain.

VINYL SHEET

Vinyl sheet flooring is available as "inlaid" (the pattern going throughout the wear layer of vinyl) and as "rotogravure" (the pattern is printed on a sheet). Both are then covered with a layer of wearing surface. The thickness of the wear layer does not dictate the durability of the floor or the price. Thick vinyl wear layers resist scuffs and stains well, but lose their gloss more quickly than a thinner urethane wear layer which maintains a high-gloss surface better and provides a more scuff-resistant surface.

Vinyl sheet floor coverings range from having no cushion at all to a thick cushion beneath the wear layer. Although the thick cushion increases comfort, the vinyl can be dented by heavy objects.

Figure 200   This simple, white vinyl floor supports the bathroom design.

VINYL TILE

Solid or pure vinyl tiles are available. Both can be installed on suspended wood subfloors or over on-grade and be-low-grade concrete. They're durable and easily cleaned. Solid vinyl tiles don't have a wear layer top coat. Composition vinyl tiles do feature this easy mainte-nance advantage.

DECORATIVE LAMINATE

In 1996, several manufacturers intro-duced decorative laminate flooring in simulated planks and tiles **(Wilsonart, Formica, Bruce, Interprint and Arm-strong Flooring)** to name a few.

- Wilsonart products include 7 3/4" x 46 1/2" simulated hardwood "planks" or 15 1/2" square simu-lated stone, marble and ceramic tile. These are "tongue-and-grooved" and can be laid over any existing flooring.

- Formica's laminate flooring is sup-plied by Ellstrom Manufacturing, Seattle, a leading producer of lami-nated wood and high-tech com-posite panels.

- Interprint offers custom hand-painted squares or woodgrain pat-terns under the melamine.

Laminated flooring has been popular in Europe for several years, where the Swedish manufacturing giant Perstorp Flooring, Inc. has been the leading sup-plier.

Wood Floors

Throughout the house, wood floors are in great demand today. Wood is also a viable flooring material for some bath-room projects.

Wood floors are graded according to standards that measure color, grain and imperfections. Clear or Select grades are generally specified for a formal look and for lighter finishes. Select and #1 Com-mon grades are used for traditional and light-to-medium stained floors. For rustic and specialty areas specify #2 Common, which features wide color variations and character marks like knots, streaks and worm holes.

Woods used for floors are all cold weather hardwoods. The slow growth in cold temperatures provides the most du-rable wood possible.

Oak, with its beautiful grain and du-rability, is the most popular wood floor-ing in residential use. Maple is popular for commercial use because it is the hardest.

WOOD FLOOR STYLES

There are several styles of flooring currently being used.

- **Plank Flooring:** Interlocking flooring which is blind-nailed. Ran-dom lengths of 9" to 96" (23cm to 244cm) are used, as well as ran-dom widths.

- **Strip Flooring:** Tongue and groove flooring, and butt flooring, which is top-nailed. All boards are the same width 2" or 2-1/4" (5.08cm or 5.72cm) and random lengths.

- **Parquet:** Simulated 12" x 12" (30.48 x 30.48cm) tiles or actual individual pieces of wood.

SECTION **8**

Bathroom Storage

Bathroom cabinet systems are manufactured in sophisticated plants that specialize in both kitchen and bathroom cabinetry, or just in bathroom cabinetry systems.

Whether you represent a specific cabinet line or not, as a bathroom specialist you must be familiar with the production methods and sizing choices.

CABINET SIZES

Base cabinets, which are set on the floor, are 21" deep (front to back) and 28 1/2" to 34 1/2" (72 cm to 88 cm) high including a subbase, or "toe kick," that is 4" (10 cm) high. Wall cabinets, which are affixed to the wall with screws, are 6" to 12" (14 cm to 30 cm) deep. Standard height for wall cabinets for general storage is 30" (76 cm), but other common heights are 24" (61 cm), 36" (84 cm) and 42" (107 cm). Tall cabinets to be used as linen or utility cabinets are 84" (213 cm) or 96" (244 cm) high.

Cabinets can be classified by:

- **Type of manufacturer** - stock or custom;

- **Type of construction** - framed or frameless;

- **Construction material** - wood, decorative laminate or steel.

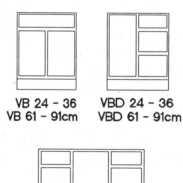

VB 24 - 36   VBD 24 - 36
VB 61 - 91cm   VBD 61 - 91cm

VBD 42 -48
VBD 107 - 122cm

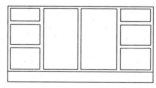

VBD 58 - 60
VBD 147 -152cm

Figure 201 Typical vanity sizes.

CABINET TYPES

Stock

Stock cabinet manufacturers offer a full range of widths made in 3" (8 cm) modules from 9" (23 cm) to 48" (122 cm). These are made in quantity, in advance, to go into a warehouse for quick delivery. Because the cabinets are produced in quantity, the line cannot be stopped to manufacture special units. Therefore, the range of products is limited to the sizes listed in the catalog.

Custom

Custom cabinet manufacturers make cabinets order-by-order, after a bathroom has been designed and sold. Generally, they are made in the same 3" (8 cm) modules as stock cabinets, but special sizes are also made for a perfect fit in the bathroom. Custom producers offer a wide range of wood species, finishes and special units.

Semi-Custom

Semi-custom cabinets are produced by both stock and custom manufacturers. These usually are produced on a stock basis, but with many more standard interior fittings and accessories than regular stock units, although not as many as are available on custom units.

CABINET CONSTRUCTION

Framed

Framed cabinets are made with face frames to which doors are attached. The face frame is composed of horizontal rails and vertical stiles. Some have complete frames to which the top, bottom, sides and back can be attached. In recent years, however, interior frames have been replaced by corner blocks, or gussets, for rigidity.

Frameless

Frameless cabinets have no frames at all. They are simply boxes, made of heavier material for rigidity. Door hinges are mortised into the sides and the doors usually fit over the entire front of the case, flush with each other and with drawer fronts. This dictates a tight reveal, usually 1/8" (.32cm) or less. With such tight tolerances, the slightest misalignment is obvious, which is why the doors usually have (and need) six-way adjustable hinges.

Frameless construction was brought to the United States from Europe where it was developed to meet the needs of quick reconstruction after World War II. The German cabinet and furniture industry led in this production development when they perfected the 32mm cabinet construction system in which proper sized holes are predrilled (by machines) in particleboard components surfaced with melamine or laminate face panels.

Frameless cabinets are not necessarily better than framed, but they can be produced more easily after a heavy investment in machinery. U.S. manufacturers now make frameless cabinets with and without the 32mm system.

CONSTRUCTION MATERIAL

More than 70% of U.S. cabinets are manufactured of wood, and 75% of them are oak. Other popular woods are cherry and maple.

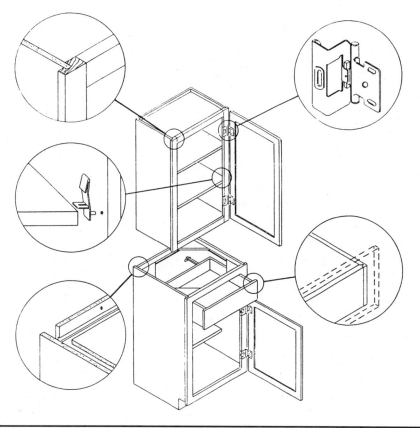

Figure 202   Framed cabinet construction overview.

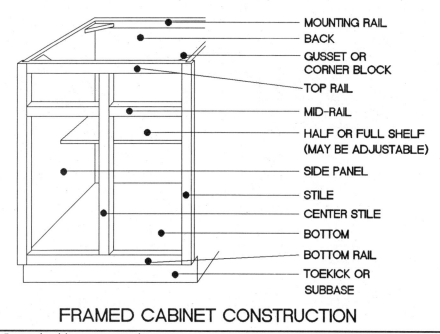

MOUNTING RAIL
BACK
GUSSET OR
CORNER BLOCK
TOP RAIL
MID-RAIL
HALF OR FULL SHELF
(MAY BE ADJUSTABLE)
SIDE PANEL
STILE
CENTER STILE
BOTTOM
BOTTOM RAIL
TOEKICK OR
SUBBASE

FRAMED CABINET CONSTRUCTION

Figure 203   Framed cabinet construction terms.

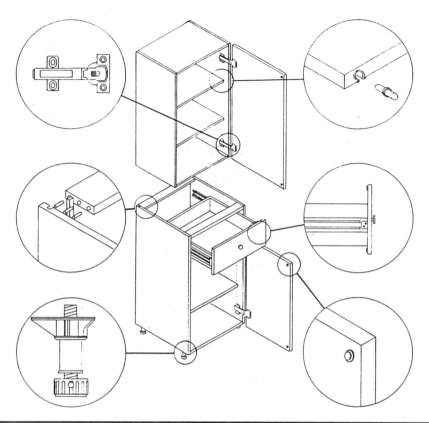

Figure 204   Frameless cabinet construction overview.

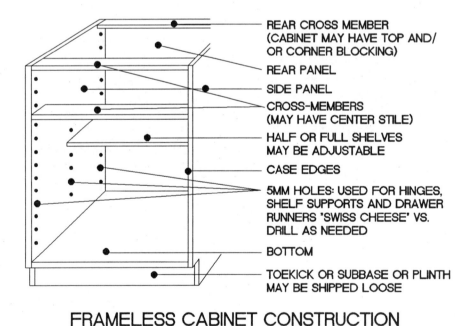

Figure 205   Frameless cabinet construction terms.

Most of the remaining cabinets are surfaced with a decorative laminate, usually on an industrial grade particleboard substrate. High-pressure laminate is the premium material.

Many manufacturers use a melamine laminated board for vanity cabinets as well. This is a low-pressure melamine that is not as resistant to impact as high-pressure laminate. However, it is much easier and less expansive to buy this stock melamine board and cut it into cabinet components than it is to lay up high-pressure laminate on a substrate and then cut it into components.

Manufacturers, of course, can use similar materials in different ways and get varying results. This means you should study the specifications and the use and care requirements for the lines you represent.

While most consumers think that they should prefer wood, it is not as stable dimensionally as industrial grade particleboard or medium density fiberboard, both widely used as cabinet core stock.

Particleboard

In broad terms, particleboards fall into three general categories: Western board, Midwest aspen board and Southern pine board. For all-around quality, western board is generally considered the best. It is easy to cut and shape and does not tend to fuzz up when machined for radius edges.

Particleboard, as its name implies, is composed of particles of wood fall-off bonded together with resin under pressure. The size of the particles in these man-made boards generally is used to identify its stability and screw holding capacity.

For example, underlayment is a form of particleboard that has a low density and low resin content. Therefore, it is not recommended for a laminate substrate because it has lower dimensional stability, structural strength and moisture resistance.

Better particleboard materials are rated as 45-pound commercial grade. This board is recommended for normal laminating. It has smaller particles of wood by-products, which then increase the surface space available for the resin to bond to. It therefore has good dimensional stability and provides a smooth surface for laminate bonding.

The finest type of substrate material is medium density fiber board, also known as MDF. This board is made of even finer fibers than normal particleboard. Its density adds superior screw holding power, a tight, clean edge and an extremely smooth surface. The MDF edge can be shaped to a profile and painted, resulting in an acceptable, finished edge for many surfaces.

Today, with the advent of new technology and improved resin and glue methods, the best interior surface for many cabinet applications is some type of man-made board that has been covered with either a laminate, solid-colored surface or a laminated, wood-grain surface.

FINISHING

Finishing is a factor in cabinet quality and price. Some fine custom producers have 12 or more steps in the finish

process and include hand-wiping between steps. You should learn all the details of the finishing process developed
by the manufacturers that you represent.

The high-gloss finishes are either
polyester or enamel. To achieve a high-
gloss polyester finish is time-consuming
and expensive. High-gloss enamel finishes are easier but less durable.

Glossy HP laminate is often considered quite acceptable at a much lower
price. In all cases, however, glossy finishes require more care than matte finishes.

DOORS SET THE STYLE

The doors and drawer fronts are the
most visible parts of cabinets, so they determine the style of the cabinets and, indeed, usually the entire bathroom.
While a single manufacturer might offer
dozens of door styles, the style types are
limited.

Flat **"slab"** doors are simple, flat
pieces of lumber or plywood. Some are
made up of several vertical pieces covered with a veneer. Sometimes they are
routed with a square or provincial
groove.

"Raised panel" doors are made
with two horizontal rails and two vertical stiles, with a thinner panel floating
between. The center panel is machined
down at the four edges so the panel is
"raised". When this look is achieved by
routing, and the door is in fact one
piece, it is a **"false raised panel"** door.
If the panel is flat, it is a **"recessed
panel"** door. These are used in "Traditional" style rooms.

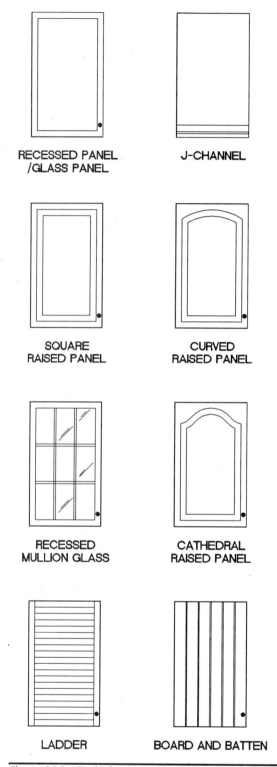

RECESSED PANEL /GLASS PANEL

J-CHANNEL

SQUARE RAISED PANEL

CURVED RAISED PANEL

RECESSED MULLION GLASS

CATHEDRAL RAISED PANEL

LADDER

BOARD AND BATTEN

Figure 206   Typical cabinet door styles.

A **"cathedral"** door usually has a raised or recessed panel, but a cathedral-type arch is formed into the upper rail.

A **"board-and-batten"** style has vertical boards with chamfered edges, held together by a horizontal batten on the back. Sometimes this look is achieved by routing vertical grooves in the front of a slab door. This is used in "Country" or "American" styling. When the boards or grooves are horizontal it is a **"lattice"** door.

Framed cabinets usually have lipped doors, with the lip fitting over the edge of the face frame. Some manufacturers produce a door that fits into the face frame. This inset door style is popular in "English Country" rooms.

Frameless cabinets have flush or flush overlay doors with square edges. This is "Contemporary" styling.

GENERIC NOMENCLATURE

Although you are required to learn the specific nomenclature system developed by the manufacturer you represent, the **National Kitchen & Bath Association** has established a generic cabinet coding system. This nomenclature provides standardized definitions for sizes and types of cabinets in this manual.

The system is based on an 11-character code which explains each cabinet category, type of cabinet, width of cabinet, and height (if variable). This system also identifies non-standard cabinet configuration details. The code includes both alpha and numeric symbols. The code is divided as follows:

- **The first character defines the general type of cabinet**.

There are six general cabinet categories, one accessory category and one molding/trim category. The six general cabinet categories are:

"W" defines all wall cabinets.

"T" defines all tall cabinets.

"B" defines all base cabinets.

"V" defines all vanity cabinets.

"D" defines all desk cabinets.

"F" defines all furniture cabinets. (For some manufacturers vanity and desk cabinets are interchangeable. Therefore, the **"V"** designation is used in both applications. A **"D"** designation is applied only if sizing between the two casework systems differs.)

Molding and trim pieces are identified by a separate code that describes each piece. There is no major category that sets them apart from the other groupings.

- **The second set of characters identifies the type of cabinet.**

For example, a **"VB"** is a vanity base blind corner cabinet.

A **"VC"** is a vanity base corner cabinet. It may have fixed, adjustable or rotary shelving, which is designated by a letter.

A **"WO"** is a wall cabinet that has no doors, therefore it is called an open cabinet.

- **The next two numeric symbols identify the width of the cabinet.**

This dimension is always listed because case widths are variable. For most manufacturers, these are 3" (7 cm) modules, from 9" (23 cm) to 48" (122 cm).

- **The next two numeric symbols identify the height of the cabinet.**
These two digits are used only if there are varying heights to choose from.

For example, in wall cabinets you can choose from heights of 12" (30 cm), 15" (38 cm), 18" (46 cm), 24" (61 cm) and 30" (76 cm). Some manufacturers also offer heights of 36" (91 cm) and 42" (107 cm).

This is not the case in base vanity cabinets where one standard height is used throughout the bathroom, so no height dimension is part of that code.

Heights assumed for the general categories are as follows (all plus 1-1/2", or 4 cm, for countertop):

A. Kitchen base cabinets, 34-1/2" (87 cm).

B. Furniture and vanities, 30" to 34-1/2" (76 cm to 79 cm).

C. Tall cabinets, 84" (213 cm), except as specified.

D. Desk cabinets, 28-1/2" to 30" (72 cm to 76 cm).

- **The last two characters in the nomenclature system identify any non-standard configurations within that specific cabinet unit.**

For example, a **"D"** would identify a diagonal corner unit; a **"GD"** would identify glass doors; **"D3"** would mean three drawers; **"TO"** would mean tilt-out drawer head.

- Accessories to be added to the cabinet are designated following the cabinet code. *For example,* **"HU"** for hamper unit.

Miscellaneous trim and finish pieces with no specific category heading have individual codes.

Thus, **"VP"** is a valance panel. **"VP-C"** is one in contemporary styling, and **"VP-T"** is traditional.

A corbel bracket is **"CB"**. **"OCM"** is outside corner molding. **"CM"** is crown molding.

Typical Vanity Sizes

Wall Cabinets

Although wall cabinets were tradionally designed for kitchen usage, creative designers can adapt these various sizes for interesting and functional bathroom applications.

Figure 207 *Wall cabinets are traditionally designed for kitchen usage. However, creative designers can adapt these various sizes for interesting and functional bathroom adaption.*

Tall Cabinets

Tall cabinets provide excellent storage in a bathroom space when counter-top requirements have been met. Tall cabinets are attractively used to separate double lavatories, or to flank lavatory or toilet areas.

Figure 208   (Courtesy of Allmilmo) Some manufacturers create total vanity systems that include special-ized wall units.

Figure 209   (Courtesy of Allia) Vanity cabinets of varying depths can help you use all the wallspace available in a small space.

Cabinet Description		Nomenclature	Tips from the Pros
VANITY CABINETS			
Single Door * full height door * 1 shelf		V12FD V15FD V18FD V21FD	• When specifying, find out if the standard shelf is included or if a second one is available. A second shelf is often usable in this cabinet.
Single Door * 1 door * 1 drawer * 1 shelf	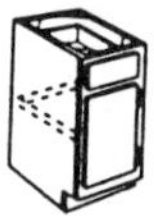	V12 V15 V18 V21	
Double Door * full height doors * 1 shelf	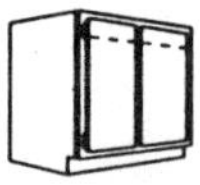	V24FD V27FD V33FD V36FD	
Double Door * 2 doors * 1 drawer * 1 shelf	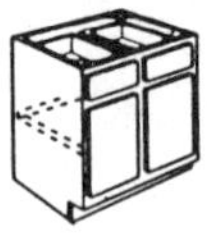	V24 V27 V33 V36 V38	
Vanity Bowl Unit * 3 full height doors	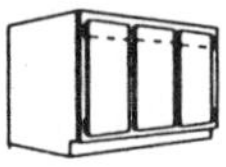	VS42FD VS48FD	
Vanity Bowl Drawer Unit * 1 full height door * 2 deep drawers L or R, top drawer false	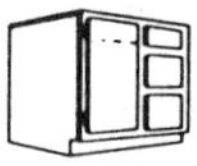	VSD24 VSD30 VSD36	
Vanity Bowl Double Drawer Unit * full height door * 6 drawers	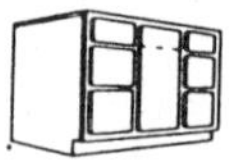	VSDD42 VSDD48	
Vanity Drawer * 3 drawers	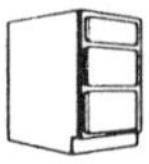	VD12D3 VD15D3 VD18D3	
Suspended Drawer * full width shallow drawer * optional desk leg recesses may be avlbl	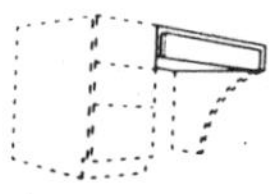	VD24SD VD30SD VD36SD	
Vanity Hamper * full height door * detachable wire basket tilts out w/door or separate	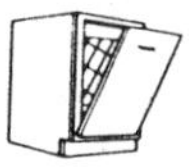	V18HA	
Vanity Storage 48" (122 cm) height * 2 adjustable shelves	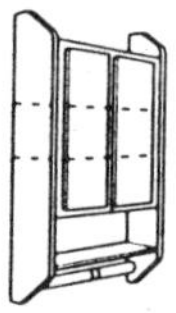	VS2648	

Figure 210   Typical vanity cabinet sizes.

About The KCMA Certification Program

The Kitchen Cabinet Manufacturers Association Certification Program assures the specifier or user of kitchen cabinets and bath vanities that the cabinet bearing the blue and white seal complies with the rigorous standards set by the American National Standards Institute (ANSI) and sponsored by the Kitchen Cabinet Manufacturers Association (KCMA). Further, the cabinet is an exact duplicate of samples that have been independently tested. The KCMA Certification Program is open to all cabinet manufacturers. Manufacturers may certify one, several, or all of their cabinet lines. Because of this option, only those lines certified are listed.

Compliance with ANSI/KCMA standards is assured by initial cabinet testing, periodic unannounced plant pick-up and testing, and additional testing resulting from complaints. All testing is performed by an experienced independent laboratory.

The kitchen and bath cabinets of certified manufacturers comply with ANSI/KCMA A 161.1-1990, "Recommended Performance and construction Standards for Kitchen Cabinets." The cabinets also comply with the provision of paragraph 611-1.1, "HUD Minimum Property Standards - Housing 4910.1," 9/8/86.

Companies not licensed with the KCMA Program may not claim or imply conformance with these standards for their products. KCMA, as the proprietary sponsor, reserves the right to question any claims of conformance and to test the products of any manufacturer making such claims. Should KCMA discover that a manufacturer is falsely representing that his products meet these standards, KCMA will take appropriate legal action.

ANSI KCMA A161.1-1995
CERTIFIED CABINET ®

Requirements Cabinets Must Meet To Earn The KCMA Certification Seal

GENERAL CONSTRUCTION REQUIREMENTS

- All cabinets must be fully enclosed with backs, bottoms, sides, and tops on wall cabinets; and backs, bottoms, and sides on base cabinets, with certain specified exceptions on kitchen sink fronts, sink bases, oven cabinets, and refrigerator cabinets.
- All cabinets designed to rest on the floor must be provided with a toe space at least two inches deep and three inches high.
- All utility cabinets must meet the same construction requirements as base and wall cabinets.
- Doors must be properly aligned, have means of closure, and close without excessive binding or looseness.
- All materials must ensure rigidity in compliance with performance standards.

- Face frames, when used, must provide rigid construction.
- For frameless cabinets, the ends, tops/bottoms, and back shall be of thickness necessary to provide rigid construction.

- Corner or lineal bracing must be provided at points where necessary to ensure rigidity and proper joining of various components.
- All wood parts must be dried to a moisture content of 10 percent or less at time of fabrication.

- All materials used in cabinets must be suitable for use in the kitchen and bath environment where they may be exposed to grease, solvents, water, detergent, steam and other substances usually found in these rooms.
- All exposed plywood and composition board edges must be filled and sanded, edge-banded, or otherwise finished to ensure compliance with the performance standards.
- All exterior exposed parts of cabinets must have nails and staples set and holes filled.
- All exposed construction joints must be fitted in a workmanlike manner consistent with specifications.
- Exposed cabinet hardware must comply with the finishing standards of ANSI/BHMA A 156.9-1988.

A 10-pound sand bag strikes a cabinet door to measure the ability of the door and connections to withstand impacts.

Figure 211   The KCMA certification program.

Requirements Cabinets Must Meet
To Earn The KCMA Certification Seal

A door is opened and closed 25,000 times to test its ability to operate under the stress of normal use.

FOUR STRUCTURAL TESTS MEASURE CABINET'S STRUCTURAL INTEGRITY, INSTALLATION

- All shelves and bottoms are loaded at 15 pounds per square foot, and loading is maintained for seven days to ensure that there is no excessive deflection and no visible sign of joint separation or failure of any part of the cabinets or the mounting system.
- Mounted wall cabinets are loaded to ensure that the cabinet will accept a net loading of 500 pounds without any visible sign of failure in the cabinet or the mounting system.
- To test the strength of base-front joints, a load of 250 pounds is applied against the inside of cabinet-front stiles for cabinets with drawer rail, or 200 pounds is applied for cabinets without drawer rail, to ensure reliable front joints that will not open during stress in service or during installation.

- To test the ability of shelves, bottoms, and drawer bottoms to withstand the dropping of cans and other items, a three-pound steel ball is dropped from six inches above the surface. After the test the drawer must not be damaged and must operate as before the test with no visible sign of joint separation or failure of any part of the cabinet or mounting system.
- To test the ability of cabinet doors and connections to withstand impacts, a 10-pound sandbag is used to strike the center of a closed cabinet door and repeated with the door opened to a 45-degree angle. The door must operate as before the test and show no damage or sign of separation or failure in the system.

TWO DOOR OPERATION TESTS MEASURE DURABILITY

- To test the ability of doors, hinges, and means of attachment to withstand loading, 65 pounds of weight is applied on the door. The weighted door is slowly operated for 10 cycles from 90 degrees open to 20 degrees open and returned to the 90 degree position. The door must remain weighted for 10 minutes, after which the door and hinges must show no visible signs of damage, and connections between cabinet-and-hinge and door-and-hinge must show no sign of looseness.
- To test the ability of doors, door-holding devices, hinges, and attachment devices to operate under the stress of normal use, doors are opened and closed through a full 90-degree swing for 25,000 cycles. At the test's conclusion the door must be operable, the door-holding device must hold the door in closed position, hinges must show no visible signs of damage, connections between

cabinet and hinge and door and hinge must show no sign of looseness, and other specifications must be met.

TWO DRAWER TESTS REQUIRED

- To test the ability of drawers and drawer mechanisms to operate with loading during normal use, drawers are loaded at 15 pounds per square foot and operated through 25,000 cycles. The drawers must then remain operable with no failure in any part of the drawer assembly or operating system, and drawer bottoms must not be deflected to interfere with drawer operation.
- To test the ability of the drawer-front assembly to withstand the impact of closing the drawer under normal use, a three-pound weight is dropped 8 inches against loading bars 10 times, after which

A cabinet door is weighted with 65 pounds, then operated 10 times to test the ability of the door and hinges to withstand loading.

Figure 211   The KCMA certification program continued.

Requirements Cabinets Must Meet
To Earn The KCMA Certification Seal

looseness or structural damage to the drawer-front assembly that impairs operation must not be evident.

FIVE FINISH TESTS CONDUCTED

These tests create, in accelerated form, the cumulative effects of years of normal kitchen conditions on pre-finished cabinets. Cabinet finishes are inspected to ensure that stringent standards of appearance are also met.

- To test the ability of the finish to withstand high heat, a cabinet door is placed in a hotbox at 120 degrees Fahrenheit (plus or minus 2 degrees) and 70 percent relative humidity (plus or minus 2 percent) for 24 hours. After this test the finish must show no appreciable discoloration and no evidence of blistering, checks, or other film failures.
- To test the ability of the finish to withstand hot and cold cycles for prolonged periods, a cabinet door is placed in a hotbox at 120 degrees Fahrenheit (plus or minus 2 degrees) for 1 hour, removed for 1/2 hour, and allowed to return to room temperature and humidity conditions, and then placed in a coldbox for 1 hour at -5 degrees Fahrenheit (plus or minus 2 degrees). The cycle is repeated five times. The finish must then show no appreciable discoloration and no evidence of blistering, cold checking, or other film failure.
- To test the ability of the finish to withstand substances typically found in the kitchen and bath, exterior exposed surfaces of doors, front frames, and drawer fronts are subjected to vinegar, lemon, orange and grape juices, tomato catsup, coffee, olive oil, and 100-proof alcohol for 24 hours and to mustard for 1 hour. After this test, the finish must show no appreciable discoloration, stain, or whitening that will not disperse with ordinary polishing and no indication of blistering, checks, or other film failure.
- To test the ability of the finish to withstand long periods of exposure to a detergent and water solution, a cabinet door edge is subjected to exposure to a standardized detergent formula for 24 hours. The door edge must then show no delamination or swelling and no appreciable discoloration or evidence of blistering, checking, whitening, or other film failure.

A steel ball drop tests the ability of drawers and shelves to withstand the dropping of cans or other items.

A 24-hour detergent and water solution test checks the door's finish.

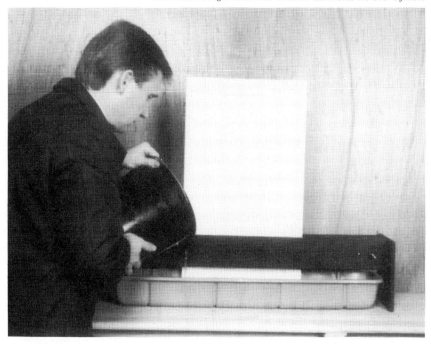

Figure 211   The KCMA certification program continued.

CHAPTER 3

Bathroom Planning Standards and Safety Criteria

*F*or much too long the bathroom has been a miserable space accommodated in the smallest area with the least amount of money. In the past, bathroom design focused solely on the space required for the three basic fixtures. Little regard was given to the human anatomy of the user and his/her safe, comfortable movement in the space. In the years ahead, successful bathroom designers will plan rooms that are designed around the people that will use them, rather than the fixtures that will be installed in them.

THE CHANGING AMERICAN FAMILY

Emergence of lifestyle changes and new bathroom fixtures and equipment lead to the need for new bathroom planning guidelines. Some of the major changes considered were:

Families are Shrinking and Changing

We will see multi-generational families living together in the future, as well as more individuals living in non-traditional groupings. The "All-American" family will have fewer children - but more parents in need of elder-care. Therefore, safety within the bathroom and a space that presents no barriers is a critical part of planning for today and tomorrow.

Time is our most precious commodity. Busy North Americans have more money than they have time. Therefore, the advantage of a more convenient space remains at the heart of a well-planned bathroom. Time-saving equipment and surfaces that are easy to maintain are critical elements of a well-planned bathroom.

Quality Is No Longer a Luxury, It Is Expected

The consumer of today demands quality: in service, profession skills and product. This emphasis on quality has increased the importance of your services as a comparative shopper and a true design expert.

The Master Suite Concept

The shift of importance of the bathroom within the home dramatically changes the look, feel and integration of all materials, equipment and systems within a combination of personal hygiene and relaxation space - often referred to as a master suite. For example, such a master bathroom suite requires more emphasis on adjustable lighting systems, equipment that minimizes noise and maximizes ventilation, and cabinetry that blends attractively with furnishings in the adjacent bedroom space.

Bathrooms are Often Shared

In addition to the changes in the way we use the bathroom, another trend affecting our industry is who uses the bathroom. The idea of the bathroom as a private sanctuary for one is gone. Today, adults often use showers and bathtubs together, and either share or require separate lavatories. This is a result of the fact that most households consist of dual career couples who must both rise and prepare for their busy day simultaneously.

Research

In 1992, NKBA published the first set of Bathroom Planning Guidelines ever. They evolved through years of research by leading Certified Bathroom Designers in conjunction with industry advisors from major bathroom product manufacturers. Soon after, a new committee was formed to study the impact that Universal Design Criteria would have on the guidelines.

Well known and published experts such as Ron Mace, FAIA from The Center For Accessible Design, Raleigh, North Carolina, Abir Mullick from the Department of Architecture at the State University of New York, Buffalo and Margaret Wylde from the Institute of Technical Development in Oxford, Mississippi, were teamed with leading CBD's. The committee re-examined the basic assumptions of design for the idealized, able-bodied, non-elderly adult. The result was increased appreciation for diversity, flexibility and adaptability in design and the basis for the new NKBA 41 Bathroom Planning Guidelines.

A Note about these Guidelines

These standards have been established to provide a yardstick by which you can judge the efficiency of a bathroom plan you've created. They should not be interpreted as hard and fast rules that you must never deviate from. The true bathroom planning professional knows that meeting each clients specific requests within the space constraints before you and the budget limitations are set is the true standard of excellence.

Never break a building or safety code to accommodate a client's request! However, modifying these guidelines is certainly acceptable as long as both you and the client know that you are deviating from an industry standard. Always remember how hard it is for your client to visualize what a new bathroom space will look like. Don't be too quick to make the floorspace smaller or to limit the size of a doorway. Once you've demonstrated before the client in your showroom display, or in another manner, space constraints, accept the challenge of defining the space to satisfy their preferences, using these guidelines for information and inspiration.

UNIVERSAL DESIGN

Before we can begin our study of human ergonomic standards, you should become familar with the concept of Universal Design.

A DEFINITION OF UNIVERSAL DESIGN

There has been much written about the aging of America. A full one-third of the North American population today is currently between the ages of 35 and 54. Our life expectancy has been extended far beyond that of our parents or grandparents. People's attitude toward aging has also dramatically changed - they're looking forward to healthy years at home. You, as a conscientious bathroom designer can make those years at home both convenient and safe. This concept of accessible design for all users, no matter what their age or ability, is the definition of Universal Design.

Planning for Aging in Place

The vast majority of older Americans age in place, ie. remain in their single family homes for at least the first 10 years of retirement. Most older people inevitably face age-related changes that can affect mobility, reach, hand grip, strength, stamina, vision, hearing, sense of smell and tactile and thermal touch. The ability to function independently may be a major factor in determining whether a person is able to remain at home in spite of temporary or permanent disabiliites.

The bathroom space is an important consideration when designing for the life span of a client because of its role in independent living. The ability to perform basic hygiene rituals in private is an instrumental activity of daily living that may help an older person remain independent. Older Americans want, need and are willing to pay for products and services that afford them convenience, dignity and independence.

Bathroom design that facilitates aging in place involves new ideas, as well as long-standing, but under-utilized practices and products. Bathroom designers can play a key role as change agents in diffusing those new and old ideas because of their mediator role between (a) developers of innovative features and products and (b) the consumer.

In planning new homes and remodeled bathrooms for mature clients, designers can incorporate and encourage the inclusion of features that respond to the user's decreasing physical capabilities. The resulting environments will therefore compensate for age-related changes and optimize independence and safety.

What are the typical physical limitations faced by aging persons? An aging person's surroundings become progressively more important as they become less able to tolerate demands from their environment. Age-related changes that create special needs relevant to bathroom design include normal declines in strength, reaction time, sense of balance and sensory perception. Furthermore, the debilitating affects of specific diseases or chronic conditions affect the functional ability of a large percentage of older people.

Specific conditions that directly affect the use of the bathroom and that are most common among the elderly are arthritis, sensory impairments, heart conditions and orthopedic impairments. The overall objective in bathroom planning for aging in place includes anthropometrically designed washing and rest areas, reduced safety hazard and increases environmental cues. Bathroom design features can provide a prosthetic or an accommodating environment for mature adults and their potential, perhaps multiple, physical impairments.

RECOMMENDATIONS

Design recommendations for mature clients' bathrooms:

Equipment/Fixtures

- Adjustable height lavatories or two lavatories, one to accommo-

date seated user and another to accommodate standing user.

- Bathtubs should have built-in grab bars and space for seated transfer.

- Showers that are open allow for roll-in entry.

- Provide single handle lever controls for lavatory, bathtub and showers, they are easier to manipulate and keep clean.

- Hand-held showers offer flexibility from a seated to a standing position.

Bathroom Layout

NKBA recommends clear floor space for wheelchair access at all three centers in the bathroom; lavatory/grooming, toilet/bidet and bathing/showering. While these clearances are liberal for an able-bodied adult, they provide space for use of mobility aids in the future.

Storage Arrangement

- Wall cabinet depth storage low on walls is easy for all users to access.

- C-shaped door and handle pulls recommended on cabinets to maximize flexibility.

- Interior storage systems, such as divider drawers, roll-out shelves and tray dividers are oftentimes suggested for maturing clients to provide clear accessibility and easy retrieval of items stored in cabinets.

- A seated working area at a sink and at a make-up area is also highly recommended for an aging consumer.

Visibility Restrictions

Our eyes begin to change in our mid-40s. The lenses start to thicken and become yellow. The surface becomes less even. The pupil becomes smaller, and the muscles that control its opening and closing become increasingly slow to respond. In addition, the yellow film that forms over the eye with age tends to cahnge color perception - for instance, light blue, pink and salmon, seen as very distinct shades through the eyes of a young client, may be hard to differentiate by the middle-aged and older consumer, just as black, gray, dark blue and brown begin to seem increasingly similar.

- Constrasting colors for countertop edges, electrical outlets and sinks were suggested to compensate for low vision aging traits.

- Include higher general lighting levels.

- Increase task lighting above the work surfaces.

- Matte finishes on surfaces, rather than shiny.

Flooring

- Non-slip surfaces are vital throughout the bathroom in wet

and dry areas. Smaller tiles, increase the number of grout lines, thereby providing a more slip resistant surface.

- Loose area rugs are never recommended on a floor surface where a mature client might accidently stumble.

THE CONCEPT OF UNIVERSAL DESIGN

Although design to meet the special needs of older people may be an appropriate step, the best goal ultimately is universal or adaptable design. Instead of labeling people as "special" or incorporating non-standard features, universal or life-span design addresses the needs of persons of all ages and functional levels. Thus, no group is stigmatized and the products appeal to a wider market.

Barrier-free or universal design is a planning concept where safety is of paramount importance and no technological or physical barriers are placed in front of the user as they attempt to use the space. In bathroom planning, this means the room must be safe for children as well as mature adults. The planning considerations suggested by the CBDs make sense for all of us.

Controls that are easy to operate, bathtubs with built-in grab bars, a place to be seated when one showers - these are important considerations for the 6-year-old, a busy adult, as well as a mature adult.

Further Reading Suggestions

For an indepth examination of universal bathroom planning, refer to NKBA's **Universal Bathroom Plan-**

ning, **Design That Adapts To People**, written by Mary Jo Peterson, CKD, CBD, CHE and **Enabling Products Sourcebook 2**, written by ProMature Group and published by NKBA. Contact **NKBA**, 687 Willow Grove Street, Hackettstown, NJ 07840.

Other authors quoted are as follows:

- **B. S. Guetzko**
  Charleston School of Art & Design
  University of Charleston
  Charleston, West Virginia 25304

- **Betty Jo White**
  Department of Clothing, Textiles
  and Interior Design
  Kansas State University
  Manhattan, Kansas 66506

SECTION 2

TYPICAL PLANNING CONSIDERATIONS

BATHROOM FIXTURES AND EQUIPMENT

Through history, bathroom fixtures and equipment have evolved from a pure function of basic human need into one which involves luxury and aesthetic preference. While the product choices available today are vast, the functional requirements remain unchanged. A review of fixture and equipment functional considerations follow.

Lavatory and Faucet Design

To accommodate face, hand and hair washing, the bowl should be as large and as deep as possible. The faucet spout should extend over the bowl and project water towards the user, rather than projecting vertically towards the drain in the bowl. The faucet handles should also be carefully selected. Smooth, round knobs are harder to operate than lever or grooved handles.

Faucet handles that are widely spread apart are easier to grasp than those that are close to the spout and single levers are easier yet. Large, high-arched spouts are easier for the user to get his/her hands under than straight, short, stubby spouts.

Electronically controlled valves may be specified to eliminate the need for the user to physically turn, twist or pull a faucet handle.

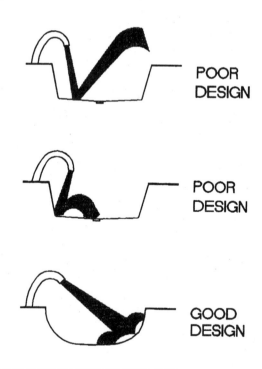

POOR DESIGN

POOR DESIGN

GOOD DESIGN

Figure 212 Typical lavatory shapes and water trajectory pattern comparison.

The Toilet

An individual's personal habits regarding the use of the toilet is generally not something that a person is comfortable discussing with a stranger. Therefore, it is important for you to understand human anatomy as it relates to the design of a toilet so that you can guide your client through the fixture selection process professionally and competently.

In Dr. Alexander Kira's book, *The Bathroom*, he discusses at length how important proper posture is for human defecation. Dr. Kira feels that typical toilet design is not adequate for this human activity. He recommends that toilet bowls and seats should be lower to encourage a modified squat position for human defecation, or higher to accommodate a lean-on posture. He notes that the squat position is medically sound and is the norm throughout much of the world.

FULL FREE SQUAT

SUPPORTED
SEMI-SQUAT

LEAN-ON
WATER CLOSET

MODIFIED
CONVENTIONAL
WATER CLOSET

MODIFIED CONVENTIONAL
WATER CLOSET WITH
FOOT REST

MODIFIED
CONVENTIONAL
SEAT

Figure 213   (Courtesy of Dr. Alexander Kira) Comparing standard and elevated toilet designs.

In addition to the height of the toilet, the overall depth of the fixture and the design of the seat are important considerations. Let's tackle these two issues separately.

- The bowl shape of a standard toilet is round. The overall fixture depth from front to back is between 25" (63.5cm) and 28"(71.12cm). In addition to the standard round toilet, there are elongated toilets which are an extra 2" (5.08cm) long. Unfortunately, many designers simply see this as a more expensive fixture. It is a far superior design when

compared to the round shape. The extra 2" (5.08cm) long in overall fixture depth provides a much more comfortable arrangement for both men and women. The elongated front bowl and seat should be specified for all bathroom projects.

- The actual design of the seat is equally important. Ideally, a contoured shape, which distributes the weight more comfortably, is preferable to one single large round opening. The seat should be contoured ato the buttocks rather than being perfectly flat.

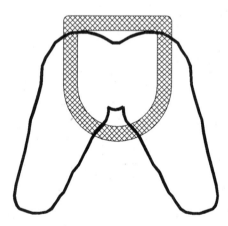

CONVENTIONAL
BOWL SHAPE

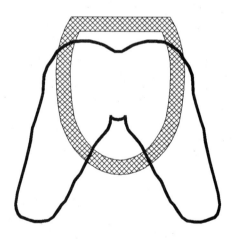

PERFERRED
ELONGATED
BOWL SHAPE

Figure 214 Comparing toilet seat designs.

Toilet Accessory Placement

- A horizontal handrail should be placed adjacent to the toilet seat. More information about handrail/grab bar design and installation appear in the 41 Planning Guidelines found in Section 8.

- The toilet paper holder should be installed slightly in front of the edge of the toilet bowl. When specifying a recessed toilet paper holder, verify that the wall or cabinet space is clear from any obstructions such as cabinet drawers, pocket doors, plumbing pipes, vent pipes, heating or air conditioning chaseways. When-

ever you're working within the absolute minimum 30" (76.2cm) toilet wall space width avoid surface-mounted paper holders if at all possible. NKBA recommends a 32" (81.28cm) toilet wall space whenever possible.

- If a countertop will extend across the tank, a one-piece, low-profile toilet should be specified so that the tank is accessible for servicing. Alternatively, the extended top may be hinged so that it can be moved out of the way for access to a two-piece toilet tank. The extension should only be 3" (7.62cm) to 5" (12.7cm) deep so that the fixture seat and cover can remain in a stable upright position.

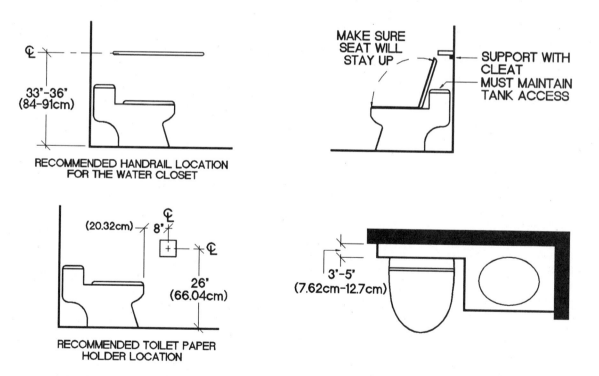

Figure 215 Toilet accessory placement.

The Bidet

Although common in Europe, the bidet is still a largely misunderstood and unused fixture in the American bathroom.

Pronounced *bee-day,* the fixture is thought to have originated with Napoleon's cavalrymen. The horsemen straddled a small basin of water on a portable wooden bench, as if riding a small horse, and washed the part of the body in contact with the saddle. Users felt cleaner, refreshed and were able to avoid irritation and rashes. Bidet means "*small horse*" in French. Brought home by the cavalrymen, the bidet became a convenient way for the entire family to cleanse the pelvic part of the body.

How the Bidet is Used

Kohler Co. produced an excellent piece of literature that explains how to use the bidet. With Kohler's permission, we quote:

"*Why a bidet?* With all the emphasis on personal cleanliness, it is ironic that the bidet has been virtually ignored and its purpose misunderstood.

Essentially, the bidet is a sit down wash basin. Men as well as women use it for convenient cleansing of the urinary and anal areas of the body, or simply for quick partial bathing.

There is nothing complicated about using a bidet. The user sits astride the bidet facing the hot and cold water controls. These faucets control both temperature and volume. Fresh water enters the fixture through a vertical spray in the center of the bowl, through a flushing rim or integral filler, or through a special bidet faucet spout that delivers a horizontal stream of water. *(* See Note)*

Flowing water from the horizontal or vertical spray, and the soap and water bathing offered by the bidet are excellent means of personal cleanliness. After all, if dry tissue isn't sufficient to clean your hands, it is only logical that soap and water should be used to cleanse other parts of the body as well.

You don't have to be totally undressed to use a bidet; in fact, there is no need to remove much more clothing than you do when using the toilet.

Bidets have been used in Europe, Latin America and South America for decades. Women find the fixture an incomparable aid to personal cleanliness, for douching and especially for use during the menstrual period. But it can also be as important a hygienic aid for men and for young people of both sexes.

Many doctors recommend regular use of the bidet, not only for hygienic reasons but also to help prevent infections, soothe an irritation or heal a rash.

The bidet also serves admirably as a foot bath, since it is roomy, has both hot and cold water adjustments and is low enough to use comfortably while seated on a chair or adjacent toilet."

*Note: *There is some concern about a vertical ascending jet spray in a bidet allowing contaminated water back into the fresh water supply. Codes generally require a vacuum breaker with a vertical spray bidet. This is not necessary for a horizontal spray bidet, one reason why the horizontal spray unit is generally less expensive to purchase and install. Frequent users oftentimes prefer a vertical spray for ease of use and comfort. With either design, a stopper retains water in the bowl.*

The typical bidet is a separate fixture from the toilet. However, there are special toilet seats which convert to a bidet and bidet attachments which can be installed adjacent to the toilet.

The Shape of the Bidet

When considering a bidet design, pay close attention to the shape of the opening. To use the bidet effectively, users must have comfortable reaching room in front and back of the body. Many bidets have only a 14" (35.56cm) to 16" (40.64cm) opening, which will force the user to shift back and forth for both front and rear body access. Be sure that the controls are easily accessible to the user as they sit facing the wall, straddling the fixture. Also important is locating the accessories close to the bidet, and planning accessible storage for towels, soaps, other aids and a robe hook for garments.

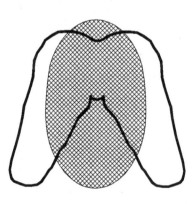

**CONVENTIONAL
BIDET SHAPE**

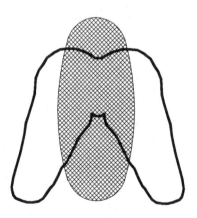

**PREFERRED
ELONGATED
BIDET SHAPE**

Figure 216 Comparing bidet shapes.

The Urinal

In North America the toilet serves as a receptacle for both male and female urine. The acceptable Western practice of female urination while in a seated position is suited to a well-designed toilet. However, inherent problems exist for men who use the toilet for urination. Inevitably, stained walls and damaged floors will result from the backsplash of the urine stream as it hits the hard surface of a conventional toilet. This problem increases among young, elderly or ill household male members because the individual's control over the urine stream's initial point of contact decreases.

Whenever possible, a separate urinal specifically designed for residential use should be suggested, with waterproof material installed around the fixture. If you are unable to plan a separate urinal, then specify a one-piece toilet for ease of cleaning and sanitizing.

Placement locations are recommended as follows:

Urinal Height Placement

- In a residential installation the front extended lip of the urinal should be 19 1/2" (49.53cm) for children and 24" (60.96cm) for adults off the floor. For custom placement for an adult user, the extended lip of the urinal should be placed approximately 3" (7.62cm) below the user's inseam dimension.

Urinal Wall Space

- A minimum of 15" (38.1cm) of space from the fixture centerline to any side obstacle should be planned. Always allow 3" (7.62cm) from the edge of the fixture to a side wall. 30" (76.2cm) from the centerline of the urinal to the centerline of an adjacent toilet is the minimum dimension when two fixtures are placed side-by-side.

- 18" (45.72.cm) of space from the fixture centerline to a side obstacle, or 36" (91.44cm) of space from the centerline of a urinal and water closet installed side-by-side is a more comfortable spacing recommendation.

Urinal Walkway Space

- To provide adequate standing room, allow a minimum of 21" (53.34cm) of floor area from the front edge of the urinal to any obstacle opposite it. 30" (76.2cm) of floor space in front of the urinal is recommended if at all possible.

Urinal Surfacing Protection

- 12" (30.48cm) of wall space on each side of the urinal, 48" (121.92cm) high should be covered in a durable wall surfacing material. Similarly, the floor surface 12" (30.48cm) in front of the fixture should be stain resistant as well.

Figure 217   A residential urinal installation.

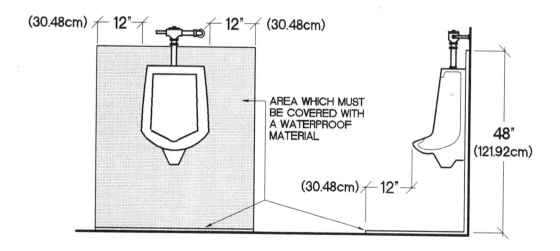

Figure 218   Protecting walls around urinal.

Typical Bathroom Fixtures

Following is a review of typical fixtures.

*Figure 219   (Courtesy of American Standard Inc.) The jetted bathtub, toilet and pedestal lavatory all re-
peat curvilinear design details.*

Figure 220   (Courtesy of Kohler Company) The relationship between the low-profile water closet and matching bidet to the baseboard should be carefully detailed.

Figure 221   (Courtesy of Kohler Company) The toilet in this bathroom is located in a semi-private compartment.

STANDARD BATHTUB

A bathtub is ideally suited for a relaxing rest in warm, soothing water. It is not an ideal shower receptor because of the fixture's high sides, curved bottom and narrow width.

Even a bathtub that is solely reserved for bathing is a dangerous fixture for users because of the likelihood of falling or slipping while entering or exiting the bathtub, or while changing from a seated to a standing position. Therefore, carefully consider how users are going to get in and out of the bathtub and how they are going to change from a standing to a seated position.

Stepping into the Bathtub

Standard bathtubs are 14" (35.56cm) high, special fixtures range up to 24" (60.96cm). Most have a relatively narrow front edge that can be comfortably and safely stepped over by an adult.

In a situation where the user is expected to step from the finished floor into the bathtub, without assuming a seated position, Professor Kira recommends the optimum width of the rim to be about 2 1/2" (6.35cm). Children and elderly adults may need to sit on the edge of the bathtub and swing their legs into it.

Sunken Bathtubs

Some new construction plans call for a sunken bathtub. These bathtubs are very dangerous and should be avoided. In addition to entering and exiting accidents, an unsuspecting guest or child can easily fall into the bathtub. Cleaning is also very difficult.

Platform Bathtubs

Bathtubs are oftentimes placed in a decorative platform. The platform may be surrounded by a step. Steps of any kind are dangerous and should be eliminated. If the bathtub design does not feature an interesting outer edge, the fixture may be undermounted in the deck.

Whether surface or undermounted, it should be held close to the front edge of the platform to facilitate entry and exit. This criteria is recommended because the ideal way to enter and exit a deeper bathtub is for the user to lean against the rim and gradually shift to a seating position on the rim, and then to a seating position at the bottom of the bathtub.

This entry approach is considered the safest since the person is moving from one seated position to another. Because of the posture assumed in this method of entry, the front edge of the bathtub must be free from any obstructions such as bars, controls, faucets or the varying heights associated with the top-mounted, self-rimming bathtub fixture. Proper support provided by grab bars or handrails must also be included in the design.

Bathtub Sizes and Shapes

Once you've thought through the safety factors and made sure that people can get in and out of the bathtub comfortably, it's time to turn your attention to selecting a bathtub. It's a big mistake to specify a bathtub that isn't large enough for the bather to stretch out and enjoy the water experience.

Figure 222   Entering the bathtub - poor design.

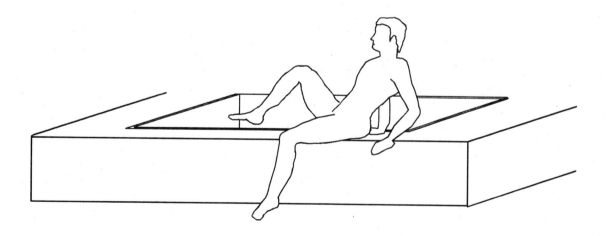

Figure 223   Entering the bathtub - good design.

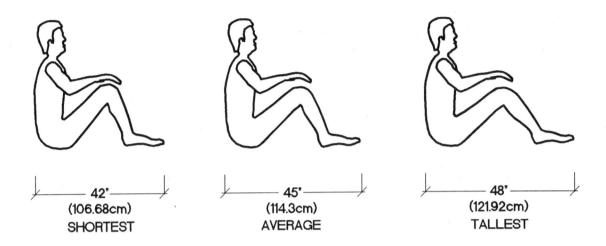

42"
(106.68cm)
SHORTEST

45"
(114.3cm)
AVERAGE

48"
(121.92cm)
TALLEST

Figure 224   Bathtub sitting space requirements.

To select the right bathtub for the family members using it, first consider how tall they are. If the plan includes a 72" (182.88cm) long bathtub for a petite 5' (152.4cm) tall user, she may tend to *"float away"* from the backrest. Similarly, a 6'-2" (187.96cm) bather will not be

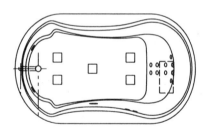

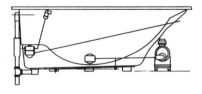

Figure 225   A manufactured bathtub has a sculpted shape to fit the human body.

comfortable scrunched into a 14" (35.56cm) high, 60" (152.4cm) long standard bathtub. When faced with two bathers of different heights, look for a bathtub that has been designed to accommodate both a short and tall user.

It's another mistake to assume that creating a custom, ceramic tile bathtub is easy. Major manufacturers spend a great deal of time sculpting the interiors of their bathtubs to suit the human shape. Attempting to duplicate such engineering is difficult in job-built, custom, ceramic tile bathtubs. Another disadvantage of tile bathtubs is that the tiles and grout joints may be uncomfortable to sit on, as well as difficult to clean.

And don't ignore the necessary extra space two people will need to enjoy the bathtub together. If the bathtub will be used by two people, plan at least a 42" (106.68cm) wide clear interior if they'll be sitting adjacent to one another while bathing. A 36" (91.44cm) wide interior space is adequate for two individuals who sit opposite one another in the bathtub.

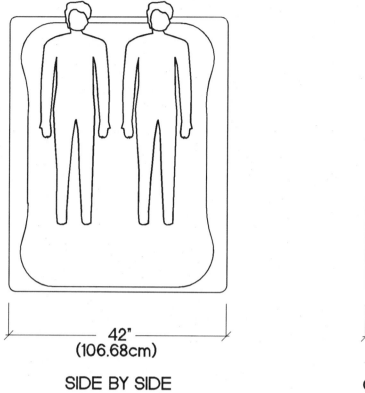

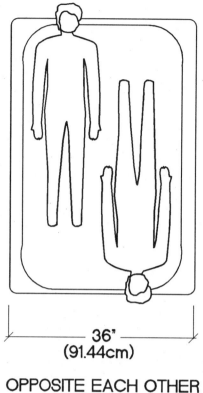

42"
(106.68cm)

36"
(91.44cm)

SIDE BY SIDE

OPPOSITE EACH OTHER

Figure 226   Space required for two people in a bathtub together.

Jetted Bathtubs

Estimates are that about 20% of all bathtubs sold today feature a hydromassage, or jetted system. New home builders report that jetted bathtubs are an expected part of a well-planned master bathroom.

Introduced in 1968, the bathtubs have changed the way bathers enjoy a warm bath. The system was originally designed for therapeutic use in hospitals. The whirling motion of thousands of bubbles bouncing and bursting against the skin increases blood circulation along the surface of the skin. This acts as a massage on tired or painful muscles and joints. It is important to realize that a jetted bathtub does not replace the traditional American bath or shower. Wash-

ing and rinsing must be done before and after this rejuvenating experience.

A variety of manufacturers offer jetted baths in a wide array of sizes, shapes and colors. Standard 5' (152.4cm) long units that look just like a conventional bathtub, other than the jets, are available. Larger, more luxurious models are contoured to fit the body with built-in seats, arm and headrests. These internal contours are critical for comfort because the user is going to relax in the water for quite some time. The only way your clients are going to know which shape is right for them is to sit in the bathtub. Therefore, your showroom should have models in various sizes and shapes. Alternatively, you may want to visit a distributor's showroom or that of a decorative plumbing and hardware firm to afford your client the opportunity to sit in the actual bathtub they are considering purchasing.

The heart of this type of bathtub is the pump, the jets and the tubing. The engineering of this system has a lot to do with the quality, performance and cost of the pump. The mechanics of the system are covered in detail in Chapter 1.

Following are key issues you need to discuss with your client regarding the design of the bathtub to ensure a comfortable bathing experience for the user.

- *What will the bather look at?* Generally, the person will stay in the bathtub for about twenty minutes, in water temperatures that range from 95°F (52.8°C) for children and elderly adults to 103/104°F (57.2/57.8°C) for others. Think about the view that surrounds the bathtub.

- *What type of Hydromassage does the client prefer?* Some systems provide many small pinpoint jets of water. Another approach is a system with just a few large jets which create a vigorous overall swirling water pattern. Other systems have bubbles entering the bottom of the bathtub. Study all systems available from the manufacturers that you represent so that you can suggest a well thought-out recommendation to each client.

- *How will you maintain a comfortable bathing area?* Include a flexible lighting system above the bathtub and make sure ventilation in the area is adequate.

- *Does the client understand how to safely enjoy the jetted bathtub?* A word of caution, while these certainly are social spaces, care must

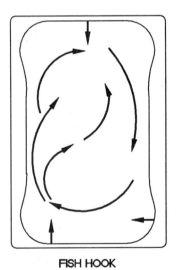

FISH HOOK

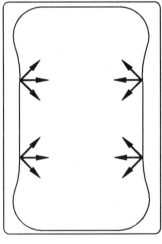

SPECIFIC POINT

Figure 227   Comparison of jetted bathtub water patterns.

be taken in their use. The extreme temperatures present stimulate a person's cardiovascular system. Individuals with high blood pressure, respiratory or heart disease, circulatory problems or chronic illness such as diabetes or epilepsy should check with their physician before plunging into one of these unique bathing experiences. Individuals under the influence of drugs which speed up metabolism or persons under the influence of alcohol which impairs judgement, should also avoid such bathtubs.

Following are a series of photos and drawings depicting bathroom plans which feature luxurious bathing areas.

Figure 228 (Courtesy of American Standard Inc.) This bathing pool incorporates built-in grab bars, an easy to reach deck-mounted filler and convenient entry ledge.

Figure 229 *This bathroom features limestone surfacing, decorative border tiles and a recessed plant niche.*

Figure 230 *This bathroom features a platform bathtub with wainscott panel, fluted columns and an etched glass shower enclosure.*

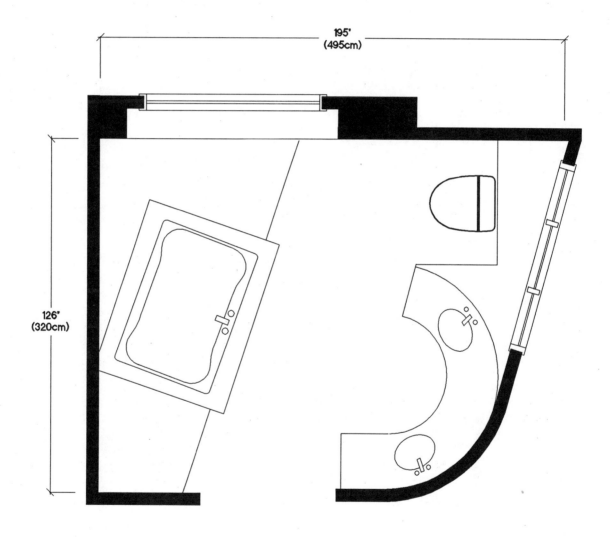

Figure 231   Luxury bathing area directs view toward window.

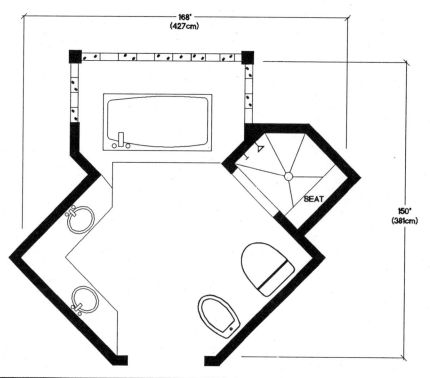

Figure 232   Luxury bathing area is drenched in diffused light.

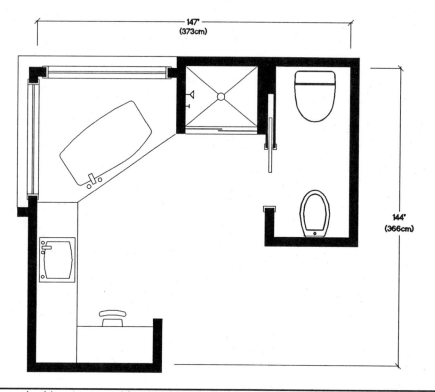

Figure 233   Luxury bathing area provides exterior view and natural light.

Stall Showers

Showering in a stall shower is a quick, efficient method of cleaning the body. If properly planned, it can also be safe and comfortable. And with a little creativity, it can be a fun spot to rest and relax in as well.

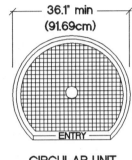

CIRCULAR UNIT

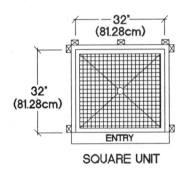

SQUARE UNIT

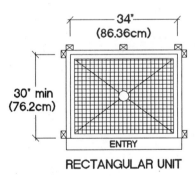

RECTANGULAR UNIT

MIN. 1,024 SQ.INCHES
MIN. 6,606.44 SQ.CENTIMETERS

Figure 234 Minimum shower sizes allowed by building codes.

The minimum size of a stall shower is established by building codes. The minimum shower enclosure must be at least 1,024 square inches (6,606.44 square cm). Therefore, a 32" x 32" square (81.28cm x 81.28cm) is the smallest shape that can be specified under any circumstance. However, NKBA recommends an interior minimum of 34" x 34" (86.36cm x 86.36cm) be specified whenever possible.

THE WELL-PLANNED SHOWER

A well-planned shower will be larger than this type of small cube so that the user's activities in the shower can be comfortable and safely carried out.

Following is a list of design criteria for such a shower:

- The overall size of the enclosure must be large enough to provide maneuvering room for the user.

- The height of a showerhead must be placed so that the user's head and hair can stay dry while showering, and the user can comfortably lean under the stream of water.

- A foot rest or a bench, as well as grab bars, must be included.

- The shower valves must be placed so that the user can turn the water on without getting wet and can step out of the stream when adjusting the water temperature.

- The valves must be engineered to prevent the user from being frightened or injured by an unexpected water temperature or pressure change.

- The shower door must be designed properly and swing out of the enclosure.

- A ventilation and heating system must be adequate to provide a comfortable environment for the user.

- A towel bar must be placed outside of the enclosure. A robe hook should be close by.

Let's take a look at each one of those areas individually.

Figure 235 demonstrates how much maneuvering room is needed when a typical user is standing and washing his/her hair.

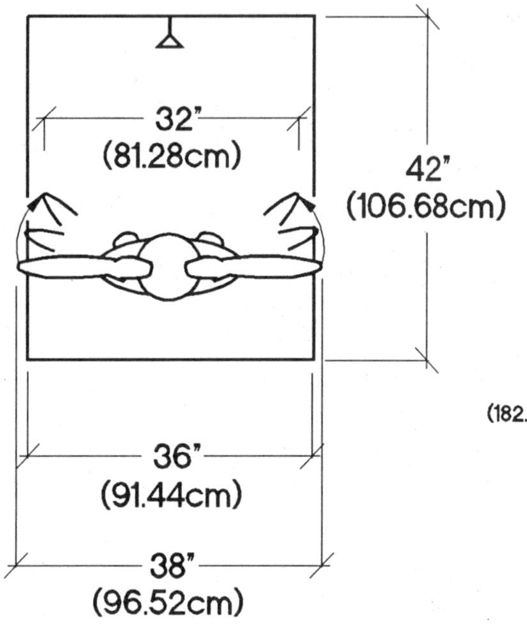

Figure 236 shows a diagram of an individual reaching down to the shower floor. A well-planned enclosure allows enough space to comfortably carry out this type of activity.

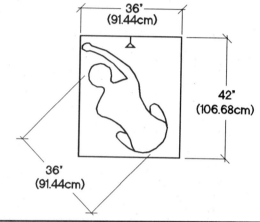

Figure 236 *Picking up an object in the shower.*

In *Figure 237* and *238* you see an average North American male at 5' 10" (177.8cm) and an average North American female at 5' 4" (162.56cm) standing under a showerhead that is installed with the supply line centered at 72" - 78" (182.88cm - 198.12cm) off the floor.

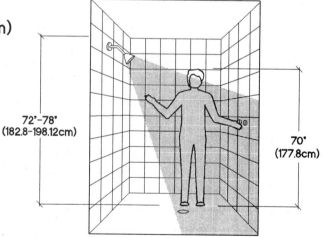

Figure 235 *Washing hair in the shower.*

Figure 237 *Average male standing under recommended showerhead height.*

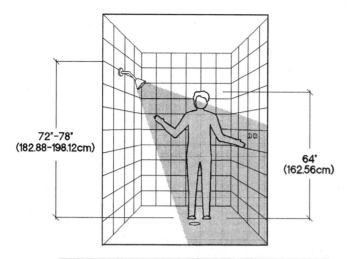

Figure 238   Average female standing under recommended showerhead height.

To determine the actual showerhead dimension, assume the supply pipe terminates 3" (7.62cm) below the rough-in height and the showerhead finishes 3" (7.62cm) below the pipe. Therefore the water spray begins 6" (15.24cm) below the rough-in dimension.

Typically, plumbers center the rough-in at 66" (167.64cm) off the floor. As you can see, this is inadequate. A properly placed showerhead should allow users to stand under the showerhead and lean forward to wet the hair or stand back and wash the body without contorting themselves. Washing hair in the shower,

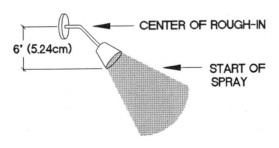

Figure 239   Showerhead dimensioning.

shaving legs or washing feet may be unsafe if the space is not planned properly.

Figure 240 demonstrates how difficult it is to maintain balance while standing on one foot trying to wash the other foot. The same diagram demonstrates the desirable alternative: providing a seat or a foot rest.

DIFFICULT TO WASH FEET

MORE DESIRABLE

Figure 240   Washing feet in the shower while standing and when seated.

Figure 241 reminds us how difficult it is to adjust shower controls in a typical installation that features the controls centered below the showerhead. A more convenient alternative is demonstrated with the controls on the wall opposite the showerhead.

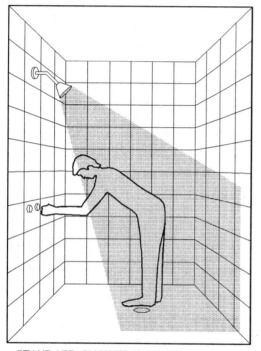

STANDARD SHOWER VALVE PLACEMENT

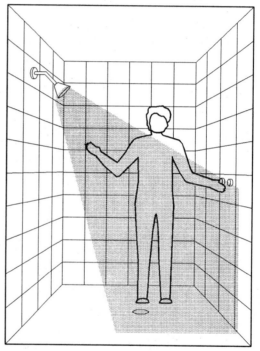

RECOMMENDED SHOWER VALVE PLACEMENT

Figure 241   Standard valve location for shower. Recommended valve location for shower.

Shower Planning Checklist

Use the following checklist to design a well-planned shower:

- The showerhead should be located so it directs the spray towards the body, away from the face and hair.

  If a fixed showerhead is installed, the water supply should be roughed in at 72" (182.88cm) to 78" (198.12cm) from the floor.

  In a shower used by people of different heights, the head can be mounted on a bar that offers flexibility in angle and in height.

  A hand-held personal shower on a hose is necessary for seated use and convenient for rinsing hair and legs, as well as rinsing soap, shampoo and conditioner off the walls or glass door.

- Controls should be located so that access is provided without requiring the user to lean into or under the stream of water. Therefore, controls should not be placed directly below the showerhead.

  The ideal location is at the side of entrance to the shower, closest to the stream of water or close to the entrance opposite the showerhead.

The shower valves should be placed from 38" - 48" (96cm - 122cm) off the floor of the shower.

- Regardless of the minimum code size, the enclosure should be large enough to allow the user to step out of the stream of water to adjust the temperature or flow of water.

  For a typical adult, an enclosure that is 42" x 36" (106.68cm x 91.44cm) in size is necessary to provide this flexibility.

- A seat or foot rest should be provided in the space. A simple 6" x 6" x 6" (15.24cm x 15.24cm x 15.24cm) triangle corner protrusion can serve as a foot rest. A 17" - 19" (43cm - 48cm) high by a minimum of 15" (38cm) deep built-in seat is ideal.

  Any bench design should be planned so that the water trajectory pattern does not continually hit the seated bather. He/she should be able to move in and out of the stream of water while seated on the bench.

  One alternative is to place the bench out of the fixed showerhead path of water and include a second, hand-held showerhead for use in the bench area.

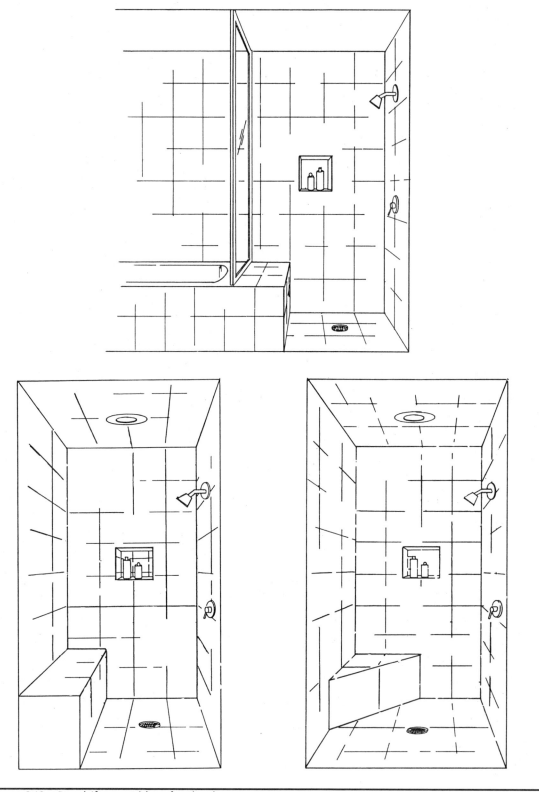

Figure 242   Bench/footrest ideas for the shower.

- Support devices should be provided for entering and leaving the enclosure, when changing position from a standing to a seated one, and when moving about under a steady stream of water with eyes closed.

Depending upon the stall shower design, a grab bar can be a continuous one that serves all functions, or several bars may be necessary.

In his book *The Bathroom*, Dr. Kira suggests that for entering or leaving, and for operating the controls, a vertical bar at the entrance is most desirable. In addition, horizontal grab bars should be provided on each surrounding wall, optional where a bench is located.

For the average North American adult, the bar should be between 33" - 36" (84cm - 91cm) above the floor.

More information about grab bar design and installation considerations can be found in the 41 Bathroom Planning Guidelines in Section 8.

- An accessible, protected storage area that does not protrude into the space should be provided for all showering equipment. It should be located along the service, side or back wall where items stored on the shelves will stay dry. A suggested finished size is 12" (30.48cm) wide, 12" (30.48cm) high and 4" (10.16cm) deep, anywhere from 15" - 48" (38cm - 122cm) off the floor.

In the past, surface-mounted, metal or porcelain soap dish/bar accessories, called "*Soap 'N Grabs*", have been installed. This accessory item is not acceptable as a grab bar because of the way it's anchored to the wall. It is also dangerous because of the way it protrudes into the space.

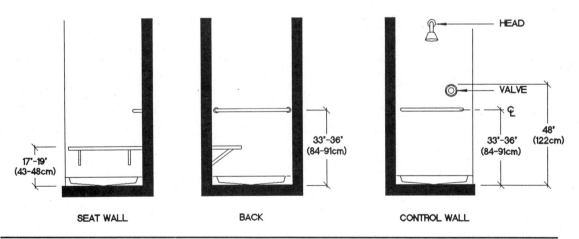

Figure 243   Shower grab bar recommendations.

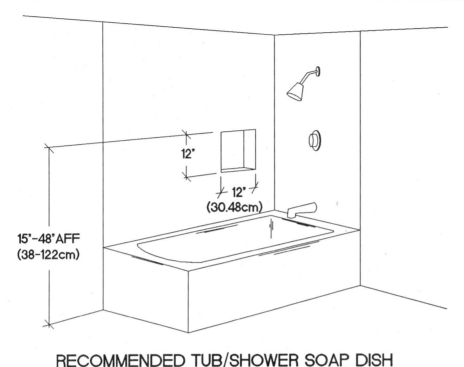

RECOMMENDED TUB/SHOWER SOAP DISH

Figure 244   Shower grooming recess within easy reach of user.

Special Showers

You may be asked to design a shower that is much more than a simple, unobtrusive, well-organized space for one to bathe in. The shower may function as an architectural statement, or be an oversized enclosure that two people can enjoy at the same time.

Planning a dramatic architectural statement requires an experienced design professional who has access to specialized materials and sophisticated tradespeople.

Showers Designed for Two

A shower designed to be used by two people is simply a larger enclosure with multiple showerheads. Before you can begin to plan such an enclosure you need to find out when the people use the shower.

If a two person shower is designed so that both can use it in the morning to accommodate similar time schedules, then two valves with two showerheads and two storage areas should be placed adjacent to one another, or opposite one another, in an enclosure with plenty of room for both people to move around.

Alternatively, if the people plan on relaxing and starting or ending the day together in the shower, pay special attention to the seating arrangement as well as the arrangement of the showerheads within the space.

Whenever planning a shower which will be used by two people at the same time, specify separate valves for the different showerheads so that each bather can adjust the water temperature.

In addition to the typical shower-head, suggest body sprays or rainbars, as well as a hand-held shower to enhance the showering experience for the users.

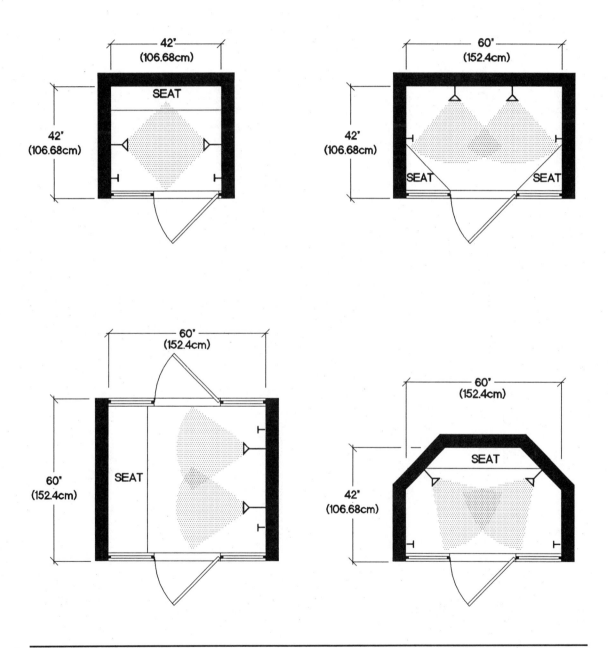

Figure 245   Two person shower ideas.

Showers Without Doors

Bathroom designers are also often asked to design a space with no door or shower curtain separating it from the adjoining areas. Generally, space that is at least 60" (152.4cm) deep, will be adequate enough to handle the water spray. Ideally, a shower with no door should include wall, floor and cabinet surfaces outside the shower enclosure that feature the same attention to waterproofing as the wet walls inside.

Forewarn the client that such an open floor plan will result in water vapor in the form of steam spreading throughout the adjacent bathroom space. In fact, just the opposite approach may be ideal for a real shower lover, or in a space where one family member plans on grooming at the vanity while another showers.

Installing a shower door system which extends to the ceiling will contain all the steam in the enclosure. When the door is opened, the colder air will rush into the enclosure causing the steam to condense on the shower walls before it escapes into the general bathroom area.

Following are examples of typical shower sizes and design ideas for bathrooms which feature stall showers.

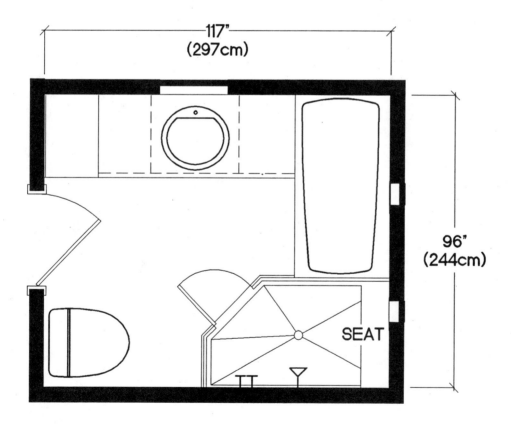

Figure 246   Small bathroom which features a stall shower.

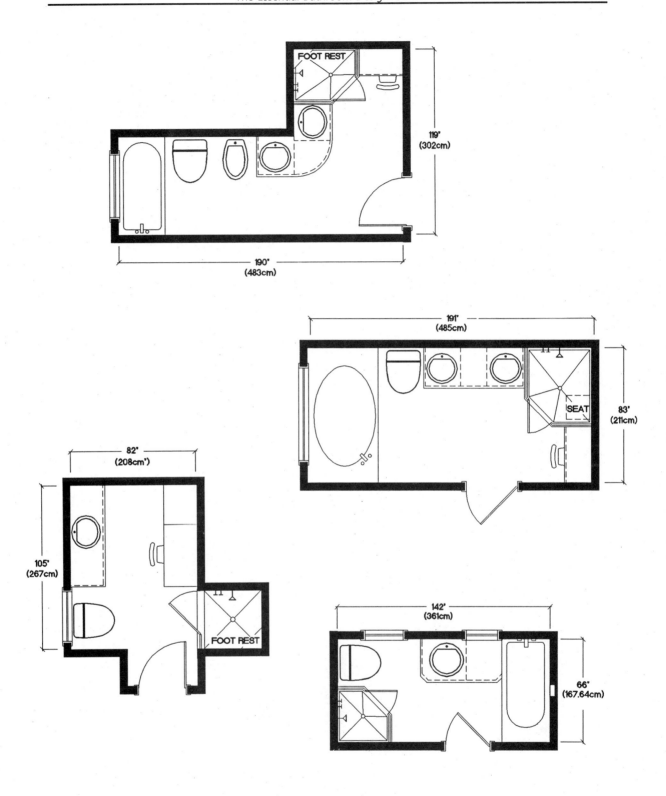

Figure 247   More small bathrooms which feature stall showers.

Combination Bathtub/Showers

A bathtub that also doubles as a shower is inherently a dangerous fixture to use and offers limited comfort to the consumer.

All of the planning concerns discussed for individual bathtubs and stall showers apply to the combination fixture. A typical installation will rarely be able to meet all planning criteria for individual bathtubs and showers.

To improve the safety and function of this type of enclosure, offset or relocate the valves so that the user is not forced to lean over the edge of the bathtub to reach controls placed directly under the showerhead.

Four piece and one piece bathtub/shower combination fixtures can also be specified which have built-in strategically placed grab bars and flip-down removable seats. These product enhancements improve the users safety as well as comfort.

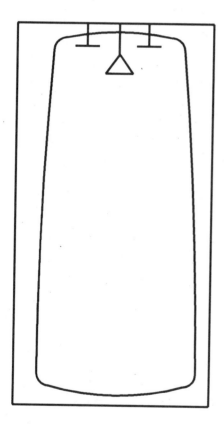

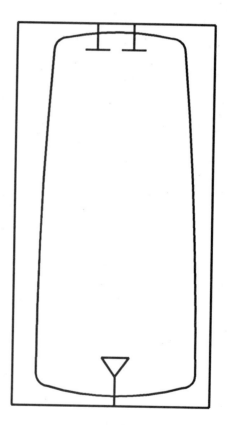

Figure 248
Typical valve placement.   *Recommended valve placement.*

Although there has been a great deal of interest in jetted bathtubs in the well-planned bathroom, an effective alternative is a steam shower.

Steam Showers

For centuries, people from other cultures have used steam to cleanse the body and relax the mind. But, North Americans have, until now, associated steam rooms with health clubs. The new generation of smaller, lighter and more economical steam generators makes it easy for homeowners and designers to add this relaxing center to a normal bathroom. A steam room can be added to a standard stall shower. And, steam baths are energy and water efficient. A standard 15 minute steam bath consumes only about 1-1/2 quarts (1.42 liters) of water and 1.8 kilowatts of electricity.

A normal steam bath lasts about 10 to 20 minutes in an enclosed environment where the humidity level reaches nearly 100%. The steam bath is then followed by a lukewarm shower to aid in relaxation, or a cold shower to stimulate the body.

Ergonomic concerns for a safe and comfortable steam room are the same as those detailed for stall showers.

Specific mechanical concerns for the bathroom designer when planning a steam room are detailed in Chapter 2.

BATHTUB/SHOWER CURTAINS AND DOORS

Earlier we discussed stall showers that don't require any sort of an enclosing door. Typically, showers do require either a door or some type of drape.

Definitions of Common Terms

Sometimes terms used in the bathroom design field can be confusing. For the purpose of this discussion, we will use the following descriptive words:

- **Shower Door/Shower Enclosure:** A sliding, folding or swinging door/panel system.

- **Surround:** The material used to finish the wet wall surface surrounding the fixture.

- **Trackless Doors:** A door that hangs or rolls along an L-shaped track.

- **Frameless Doors:** A door that is not totally encased in a metal frame.

- **Headerless Doors:** A door that does not have a horizontal header support piece mounted above the enclosure.

- **Textured or Frosted Glass:** Glass that takes on an opaque look because of its rough "hammered texture". The inside of the glass is smooth to repel soap buildup. The texture provides a decorative style as well as affording the bather a degree of privacy.

- **Tempered/Safety Glass:** Glass that is heated and cooled quickly during production. As a result, if the glass breaks it will shatter into tiny pieces rather than large, jagged chunks.

- **Plastic Doors:** A material used instead of glass. It's lightweight and able to withstand the impact of a 10 lb. (4.54kg) ball dropped 7 feet (213.36cm).

- **Anodized Aluminum:** Aluminum that has been sealed/coated by an electro-chemical process to provide corrosion resistance and color.

Shower Curtains

A shower rod and curtain can add an attractive color accent to a stall shower or a bathtub/shower combination. However, such drapery treatments are not the safest type of enclosure. They can unexpectedly wrap around a bather as they move during the shower. They can make it more difficult for the user to enter and exit the shower as well.

This approach may feature a decorative valance across the top to conceal the bar and a tie-back decorative fabric that conceals a clear or frosted utilitarian curtain behind. This application requires double bars and hooks to facilitate the installation of both the decorative drape and the plastic one.

Ideally, this type of installation should feature the decorative drape installed up to the ceiling to eliminate the unattractive space between the top of a normal shower enclosure and the ceiling above.

Shower rods are held in place with brackets that are secured to studs or by tension rods. They are available finished in a chrome or brass, or covered with a colored sleeve to match other accesso-

ries. The hooks may be clear or colored plastic, or wire.

A curved shower rod is available for corner bathtubs. These units may require a support bracket to the ceiling. This type of treatment requires two shower curtains to completely enclose the space.

Totally circular shower rods are also available, but should be avoided. Interior space is dramatically reduced and there is no clear access to the valves from within the enclosure. There is also no wall space available within the enclosure for grab bars.

Bathtub/Shower Enclosures

Glass or plastic enclosures are less decorative but are more water tight and generally easier to clean. Shower enclosures may feature bypass, swinging, pivot or accordion folding doors.

A panel can be installed above a shower door so that the area can be completely enclosed for a steam unit or for a shower in a room used by more than one person at the same time. This panel is referred to as a transom panel. It may be operable or fixed. The advantage to such an enclosed space is that steam can be contained in the shower.

Bypass Doors: Two doors that hang and roll on parallel tracks. Sliding doors are typically seen in stall showers and on bathtub/shower combinations that have at least a 42" (106.68cm) width so that a 21" (53.34cm), or preferably a 24" (60.96cm) door can be specified. Their advantage is that the sliding operation keeps the door from protruding into the space. The disadvantage is that the door typically slides on a track that can be hard to clean.

Additionally, in a bathtub/shower installation, the sliding door blocks one-half of the bathtub. Therefore, it is not an attractive bathing enclosure, nor is it easy for a parent to assist a child while bathing.

Swinging Doors: Also called a bathtub or shower screen. A door which swings open on a hinge.

In North America, swinging doors are traditionally reserved for stall showers with or without fixed side panels completing the enclosure. Make sure to check the track along the bottom of any swinging door. Some poorly designed units drip water on the floor when opened.

Recently, doors that extend only about one-half of the length of a bathtub/shower combination have been introduced in North America. These units deflect the water from a bathtub/shower in an acceptable spray pattern, yet offer a door that does not completely block the bathtub during bathing. Typically, the style is a frameless, glass door with a heavy-duty hinge that attaches it to the service wall of the enclosure. Because of their weight extra blocking is usually required at the point the door is secured to the wall.

Make sure that the door can comfortably swing without interfering with other fixtures and that it does not block access to the valves inside the shower enclosure. You should also verify that the water spray from the showerhead is not directed towards the door.

Pivot Doors: A door which pivots on a pin to open and close. They protect the room from being splattered with water, but do not imprison the bather in an unattractive enclosure.

However, some of these doors pivot into the enclosure and therefore do not meet the safety standards recommended by NKBA because an injured or ill bather could be trapped in an enclosure with the door blocking assistance from the rescue team. They may also require special wall preparation to carry their weight.

Accordion Folding Doors: A series of panels which fold against one another in an open position. Accordion folding doors are also available for both shower and bathtub/shower combinations. Extra care regarding the track maintenance and mildew prevention are concerns in this enclosure. These doors are not as waterproof as other types of enclosures.

Door Details

Doors can be framed in anodized aluminum or brass trim to match other surfaces, or they may be frameless. Epoxy-coated, colored enclosure frames are also available today. Because colors/finishes may not perfectly match between manufacturers, make sure your customer sees actual samples of all finishes you're specifying for fittings and accessories.

Tempered safety glass or plastic is always used rather than normal glass. Tempered glass cannot be drilled or altered after the tempering process because it will break. Clear, translucent, mirrored panels are available.

Your client must understand that a clear enclosure will require wiping down the doors after each use, treating the glass with a water-sheeting product, or using a squeegee to prevent water mineral deposits from gathering on the surface and discoloring the clear glass over years of use.

These special types of doors are generally ordered after all the finishing surfaces have been installed so that perfect sizing can be guaranteed. The fabrication process may add time to the project's installation schedule.

Remember, a simple, clear, frameless door allows the bathtub or shower area to be part of the bathroom space. As soon as a pattern is introduced on the shower enclosure, the overall visual space is reduced. Therefore, you should think about the effect your enclosure choice will have on the overall design before specifying a heavily detailed door design.

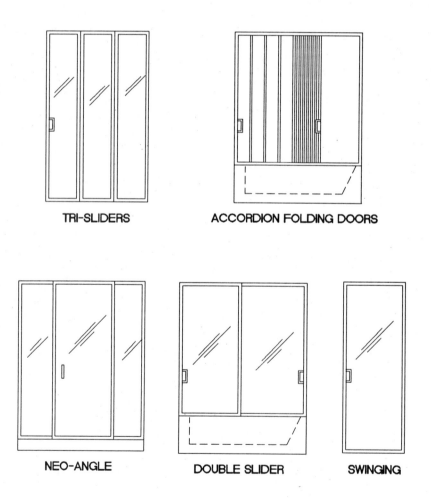

TRI-SLIDERS   ACCORDION FOLDING DOORS

NEO-ANGLE   DOUBLE SLIDER   SWINGING

Figure 249   Typical shower doors.

The last bathroom fixture we will consider is a sauna which features high heat in a low humidity environment.

SAUNAS

The sauna has a long a history as the steam bath. It's a 2,000 year-old custom that has been enjoyed by the ancient Greeks and North American Indians, along with the Finnish version (a country where there are more saunas than automobiles).

Before you can attempt to design a well-arranged sauna area, you need to understand the steps that a user goes through when enjoying a sauna.

Although sauna procedures are as varied as the individual users, most enthusiasts recommend briefly showering, then entering the sauna for five to fifteen minutes. A shower with body sprays or rainbars will be particularly appreciated by the sauna enthusiast because they will provide an all-over stimulating shower experience.

The individual may sit or lie in the insulated wooden room. The lower bench is always cooler than the higher one. Next, a cool shower, a swim in a pool, or a roll in the snow invigorates the body's system. A short ten to fifteen minute rest follows. Finally, a second visit to the sauna for about twenty minutes is enjoyed. A second twenty minute rest is suggested, followed by a final shower and light snack.

Because of the variety of activities that surround a sauna experience, the area immediately outside of the room, as well as its relationship to the showering facility, must be carefully planned. Sizing the sauna and the equipment required for this fixture are discussed in Chapter 2.

Following is a diagram detailing the space required for a comfortable bench arrangement.

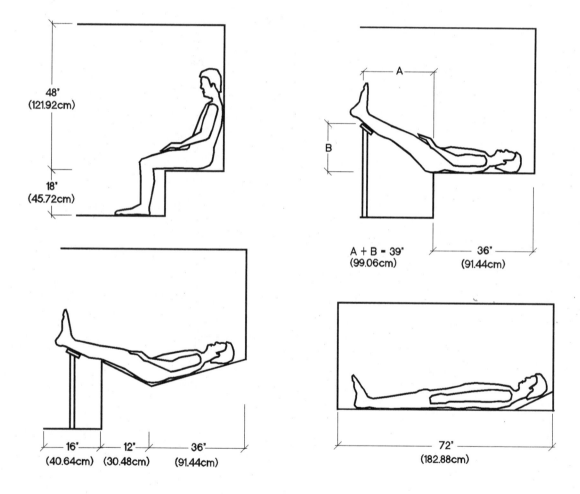

Figure 250   Types of sauna benches available.

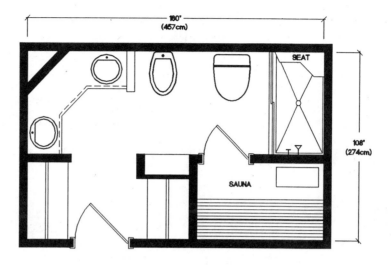

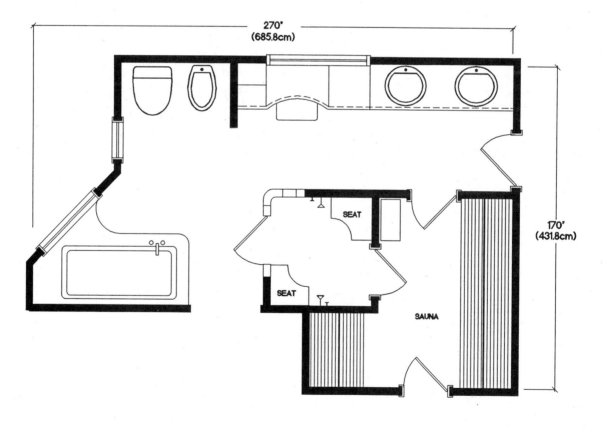

Figure 251   Sauna bathroom ideas.

SECTION **3**

HUMAN ANATOMY CONSIDERATIONS

THE HUMAN FIGURE

You will need to consider human anatomy standards as you begin the bathroom planning process. Many bathrooms are designed solely around the space required for the three basic fixtures: the lavatory, toilet, and bathing/showering fixture. Little attention is paid to the human anatomy of the user and his/her safe, comfortable movement about the space.

This focus needs to change. Bathrooms must be designed for the people who use them. The <u>people</u>, not the fixtures, should be the dominant theme. To help you understand how people move throughout a bathroom space, we'll study human ergonomic considerations in each center of activity, as well as safety criteria for these areas.

The following graphics detail typical human anatomy dimensions that can guide your planning. The average height of both males and females is listed, as well as a chart that reflects the average height of children through their growing years. An average person's eye level when seated or standing is detailed for you as well.

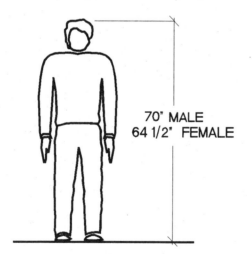
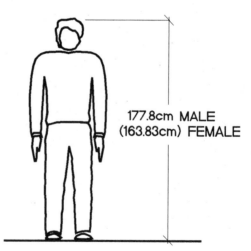

70" MALE
64 1/2" FEMALE

177.8cm MALE
(163.83cm) FEMALE

Figure 252   Average female and male height.

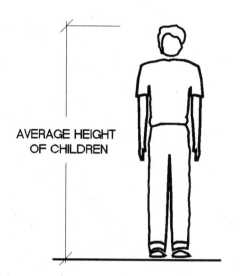

AVERAGE HEIGHT
OF CHILDREN

HEIGHT OF CHILDREN IN INCHES AND CENTIMETERS
BY AGE, SEX AND THE 95 PERCENTILE

AGE	BOYS INCHES (CM)	GIRLS INCHES (CM)
6 YEARS	50.4(128.0)	49.9(126.7)
7 YEARS	52.9(134.4)	52.2(132.7)
8 YEARS	54.8(139.3)	54.8(139.3)
9 YEARS	57.2(145.4)	58.0(147.4)
10 YEARS	59.6(151.3)	60.4(153.4)
11 YEARS	61.8(157.0)	62.9(159.7)

Figure 253   Average height of children.

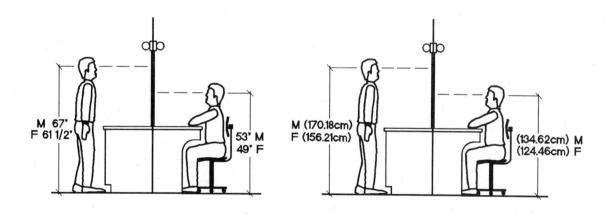

Figure 254   Average eye level of person seated and person standing. Typically, eye level is 3" below the persons overall height.

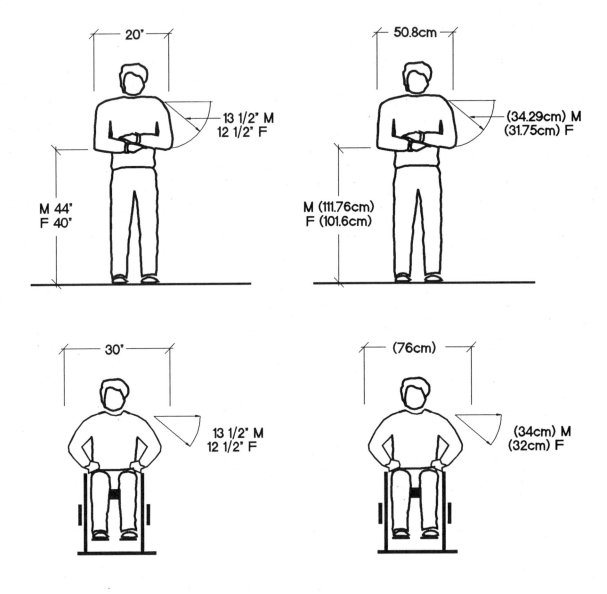

Figure 255   Typical shoulder width and elbow dimensions.

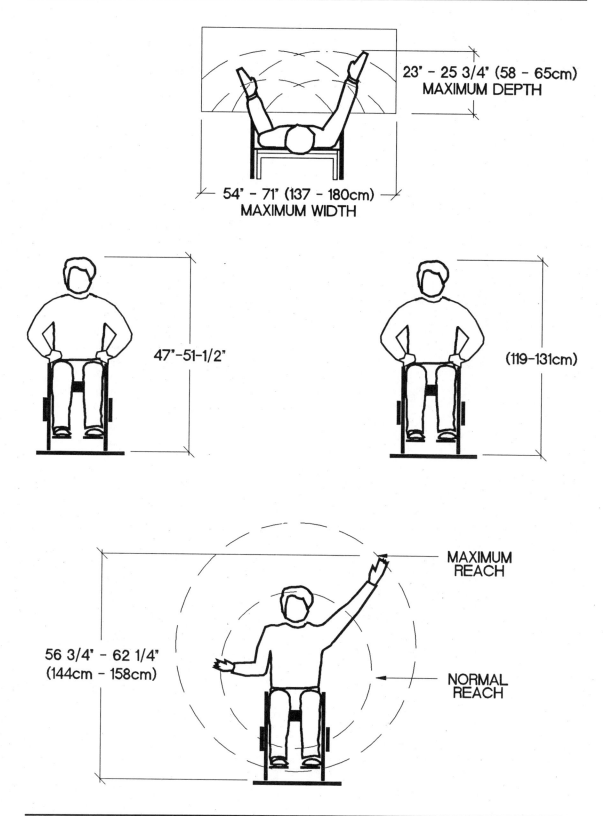

23" – 25 3/4" (58 – 65cm)
MAXIMUM DEPTH

54" – 71" (137 – 180cm)
MAXIMUM WIDTH

47"–51-1/2"

(119–131cm)

MAXIMUM
REACH

56 3/4" – 62 1/4"
(144cm – 158cm)

NORMAL
REACH

Figure 256   Typical reaching capabiliites for a seated person.

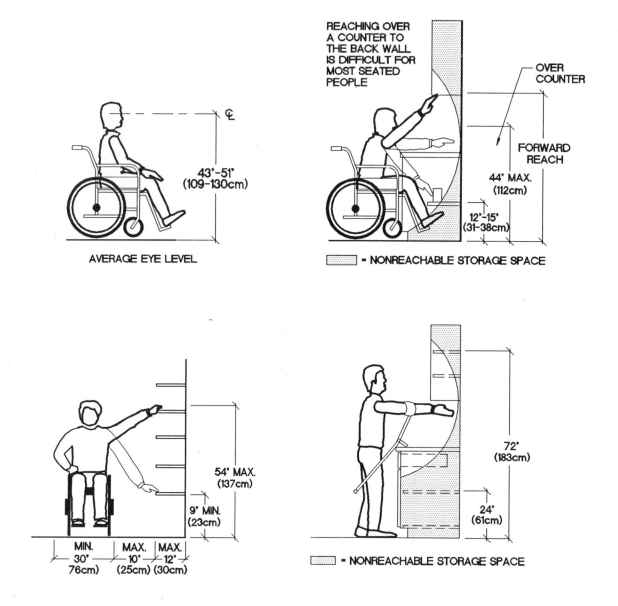

Figure 257 *Typical reaching capabiliites for mobility-impaired individual.*

The space required for one person to walk through a room, to bend over a lavatory, and to towel-dry after bathing are important dimensions for you to know. Finally, the space required for two people to pass one another with bodies parallel, with bodies parallel and one person using a wheelchair, and with bodies perpendicular and one person using a wheelchair is demonstrated.

These human figure dimensions are used to determine minimum, recommended and liberal clearance dimensions for all walkways around fixtures and grooming/storage centers in residential bathroom planning.

Figure 258   Average bending room.

Figure 259   Average stretching room.

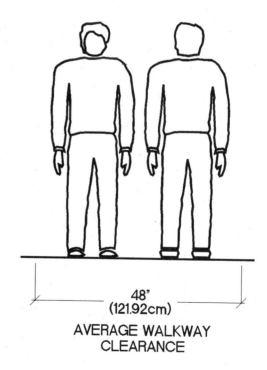

AVERAGE WALKWAY
CLEARANCE

Figure 260   Two people passing - parallel - average walkway clearance.

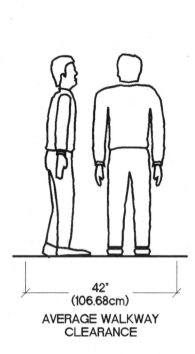

42"
(106.68cm)
AVERAGE WALKWAY
CLEARANCE

Figure 261   Two people passing - perpendicular - average walkway clearance.

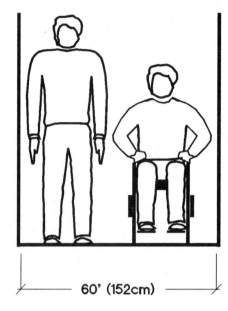

60" (152cm)

AVERAGE AISLE CLEARANCE
FOR A STANDING PERSON
TO PASS A SEATED PERSON
PARALLEL

Figure 263   Two people passing - parallel, one person using a wheelchair.

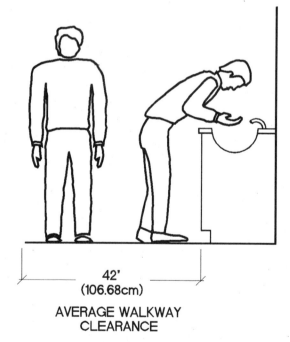

42"
(106.68cm)
AVERAGE WALKWAY
CLEARANCE

Figure 262   Two people passing - one leaning over lavatory - average walkway clearance.

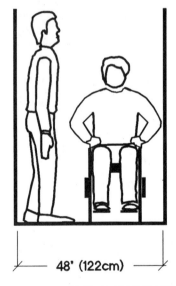

48" (122cm)

AVERAGE AISLE CLEARANCE
FOR A STANDING PERSON
TO PASS A SEATED PERSON
PERPENDICULAR

Figure 264   Two people passing - perpendicular, one person using a wheelchair.

BATHROOM CENTERS OF ACTIVITY

Once you are familiar with these basic human ergonomic dimensions, you then need to divide the bathroom into three areas of activity and become familiar with dimensions that are specific to each area. Much like a residential kitchen, the bathroom is logically divided into three broad areas of activity:

- Lavatory/Grooming Center

- Toilet/Bidet Center

- Bathing/Showering Center

Arranging the Centers for Adults

The relationship of these three centers to one another and to adjacent spaces oftentimes depends on the function of the bathroom. *For example,* in a luxurious master suite the lavatory/grooming center may actually be a part of the bedroom, or in a space adjacent to the bedroom, rather than part of a separate traditional bathroom. Or, a gracious large bathtub may be part of a bedroom, rather than a section of a functional bathroom.

The shower and the toilet are most often in a separate space because these two fixtures get the most use, and therefore need to be planned with the most durable materials. The relationship of the centers of activity is generally determined in the initial layout phase of the planning process. You must be familiar with the dimensional standards of each area in order to creatively arrange these spaces.

THE LAVATORY/GROOMING CENTER

Double Lavatory Locations

The bowl in a bathroom is called a *"lavatory"*. Many bathrooms which are designed to be used by two individuals feature separate lavatories. This is a standard approach in master suite planning in new home construction. If you are designing a bathroom with two lavatories, find out from the family if they would like the two lavatories adjacent to one another in a long, expansive countertop, or if they would prefer to locate the two lavatories in two separate centers of activity. *For example,* a long counter can be divided by a cabinet that extends down to the countertop and adds a sense of separation. Two separate vanity areas can flank each side of the bathtub or shower quite gracefully.

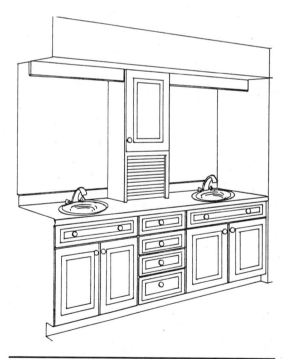

Figure 265   Double lavatory placement idea.

Lavatory Heights

Although 30" (76.2cm) to 32" (81.28cm) off the floor is the typical pedestal lavatory and vanity cabinet height placement in North America, usage considerations suggest a higher installation might be more desirable.

In the book *The Bathroom,* Professor Alexander Kira identified that the typical able-bodied adult user was more comfortable washing his/her face at a lavatory that was 34" (86.36cm) to 36" (91.44cm) off the floor and washing their hands at a lavatory that was from 36" (91.44cm) to 38" (96.52cm) off the floor. Whenever possible, NKBA recommends two lavatory heights; one 30" - 34" (76cm - 86cm) and another 34" - 42" (86cm - 107cm) be included in the bathroom.

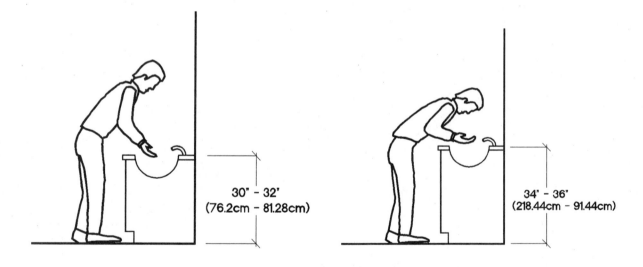

Figure 266   Standard pedestal lavatory and vanity cabinet heights.

Figure 267   Preferred lavatory heights when washing hands and face.

In Professor Kira's study, the height of the source of water was dependent on two aspects: the minimum degree of trunk flexation which was physically comfortable for the user and at which the clothing remained dry, and the desired distance (and direction) that water is brought from the stream to the face or to the hands. The standard 30" (76.2cm) to 32" (81.28cm) precludes such a comfortable posture.

Your showroom or portfolio should include vanities set at varying heights to help a client consider alternatives to the typical 30" (76.2cm) to 32" (81.28cm) height.

Elevating the Lavatory Height

When planning a bathroom, there are many ways to increase the standard fixture or vanity cabinet height so that it is more comfortable for adult use.

For example, build a platform under a pedestal lavatory. Finish this platform in the same material as the floor and maintain a height that is consistent with the baseboard. The ledge visually disappears into the floor surface.

Use a wall-hung lavatory with a trap cover or install the cabinets several inches off the floor, omitting the toe kick and *"floating"* them between two walls. Both are excellent ways to gain lavatory height flexibility. The idea of *"floating"* a cabinet is also an effective way to increase the visual perception of space in a room. By extending the flooring surface underneath the cabinet, the overall room appears larger. Lighting may be added to the open toe kick area to add a touch of drama and replace the traditional night light.

Figure 268   Elevating a pedestal lavatory on a platform.

Figure 269   *Elevating the lavatory by using a wall hung lavatory.*

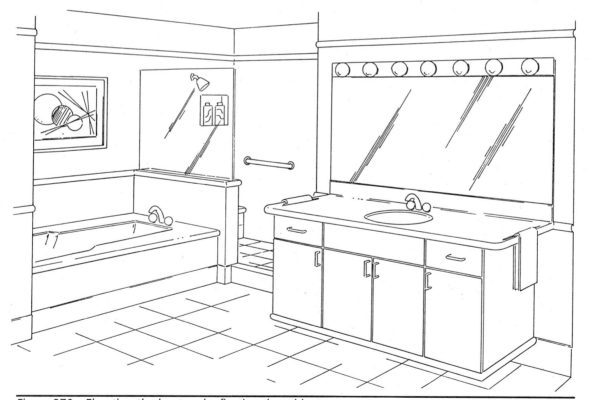

Figure 270   *Elevating the lavatory by floating the cabinets.*

Alternatively, you can increase either the overall vanity cabinet toe kick dimension or increase the overall countertop material thickness. If you increase the toe kick dimension, you should consider increasing the adjacent baseboard height as well. This check is also important if you're specifying imported cabinets which typically have a higher toe kick than domestically fabricated cabinets.

Remember the importance of consistency in all the horizontal lines that run through the space.

Increasing the countertop thickness works well if the countertop material is a focal point within the design. Watch out though - a thicker countertop can look heavy and cumbersome if you don't pay attention to the proportions of the other adjacent surfaces.

You can also increase the cabinet height to meet the raised vanity request. If this is your solution, do not simply substitute a standard 24" (60.96cm) deep kitchen cabinet for the traditional 21" (53.34cm) deep vanity. This extended depth may look out of proportion in the room. A 24" (60.96cm) deep cabinet will not seem as massive if it floats off the floor, or if the perception of depth is reduced by including a ledge along the back of the cabinet. In a showroom space, try to demonstrate these different approaches in typical bathroom settings so that clients can visualize how the lavatory area will look.

Familiarization with typical ergonomic data will help you to better meet the needs of your individual clients. Whether remodeling or a new construction project, human dimension knowledge is a very important consideration in bathroom planning.

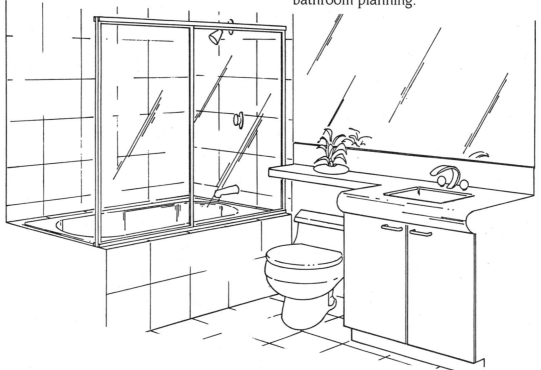

Figure 271   Elevating the lavatory by increasing the countertop thickness.

As a designer, you are obligated to pay careful attention to critical ergonomic recommendations such as NKBA 41 Bathroom Planning Guidelines found in Section 8.

Figure 272   Elevating the lavatory by increasing the toe kick height.

Figure 273   Elevating the lavatory by increasing the height of the cabinets.

SECTION **4**

BATHROOM SAFETY & WATER CONSERVATION

Home safety is an evolving concern in North America. It goes hand-in-hand with our clients' involvement in conservation efforts, waste management and their search for a better quality of life.

In the past, bathroom designers have associated safety planning concerns with spaces designed for individuals who use wheelchairs or who have other physical disabilities.

When you learn how many accidents occur in the bathroom, causing injury to otherwise healthy people, you will be more aware of how important it is to design a safe bathroom environment within the parameters of every project you work on.

For example, did you know that:

- 200,000 people are injured (400 fatally) in the bathroom every year in the United States. The most common injuries are slips/falls and scalding. **(Source: National Safety Council)**

- Preventable injury is the number one killer of children 14 and under. Each year, more than 8,000 children are killed and at least 50,000 children are disabled by preventable injury. Burns are the second leading cause of death among children in the United States. 5,000 children are scalded in the bathtub every year. **(Source: National SAFE KIDS Campaign)**

- 7 million Americans are over 55. Everyday nearly 500 people in the United States turn 65. The over 75 age group is the fastest growing senior age bracket. Over 50% of the over 55 population is physically challenged in some way. This includes eyesight and arthritic conditions. **(Source: National Center of Health Statistics)**

In general, bathroom accidents occur from any one or a combination of the following factors:

- Scalding hot water

- Slippery surfaces

- Protruding accessories

- Failure or lack of grab bars

- Poorly located water controls

- Dangerously located electrical receptacles and switches

- Shattering non-safety glass in the bathtub and/or shower area

The materials stored in the bathroom add to the danger of the space. Improper storage or use of medicines, cleaning supplies, aerosol containers and razors are all potential causes for injury.

Design improvements and proper construction methods can effectively eliminate or minimize many of the causes of bathroom accidents. Safety recommendations are as follows:

BATHTUB/SHOWER AREAS

Flooring

- Bathtubs should have a nearly flat bottom.

- Bathtubs and shower floors should have an integral, slip-resistant surface.

Enclosures

- Safety glazing to be used in all glass bathtub and shower enclosures. (See Guideline 41)

- A friction locking mechanism to be used on bathtub and shower doors. No locking latches to be specified.

- Swinging doors to be hinged on the side opposite the control valves. The doors to swing out into the bathroom and away from the source of the hot water. (See Guideline 19)

- Sliding doors are not to be used when child bathing is anticipated in the space.

Accessories

- A towel bar or ring to be placed in close proximity to the entrance to the bathtub or shower.

- Soap dishes or storage areas in the bathtub or shower to be recessed into the wall, within easy reach of the bather. (See Guideline 29)

- Surface-mounted soap dish items with a grab area, formerly called "Soap 'N Grab", are never to be referred to as grab bars. They are a surface-mounted soap dish.

Grab Bars/Handrails

For the purpose of this discussion, *"grab bars, handrails, and grip rails"* are considered to have the same safety purpose. Therefore, they may never be used as towel bars. They must meet the following safety criteria:

- **Stall Shower:** Grab bars to be installed on each wall of a shower to facilitate movement within the enclosure and entry/exit. *(See Guideline 26 - clarification 4)*

- **Bathtub/Shower:** Grab bars to be installed on each wall of the bathtub/shower to facilitate movement within the unit and entry/exit. *(See Guideline 26 - Clarification 3)*

- **Bathtub:** One grab bar on the back wall or as part of the fixture to assist the bather in rising from a seated position, and a vertical grab bar mounted on the platform or end wall to facilitate entry and exit to and from the bathing fixture.

- **Grab bar construction should be as follows:**

Note: *Towel bars are not a substitute for grab bars. Their lightweight construction and fasteners will give way if pulled or leaned on. Towels should never be hung on horizontal grab bars.*

1. Bar diameter to be 1 1/4" - 1 1/2" (3.2cm - 3.81cm) for easy gripping.

2. Bar finish to be slip-resistant. For grab bars that are part of the fixture, or for horizontal grab bars, a smooth finish is acceptable.

3. Bars to be installed at least 1 1/2" (3.81cm) from the wall to allow for knuckle clearance.

4. Bars to be rated to withstand a 300 pound (136.2kg - 1lb = .454kg) static load. They must be installed according to the manufacturer's recommendations.

In conventional framing construction, grab bars are generally attached to the studs, therefore, placement of the grab bars must be determined before the finished wall surface is applied so that proper support can be installed.

5. Bars to be free from any sharp edges, pinch points and painted ends. They must be constructed of materials which will not break or shatter in use. *(See Guideline 26 - Clarifications 1 and 2)*

Seats/Footrests

- All shower stalls and bathtubs/shower combinations to have a seat or footrest. *(See Guideline 17 - Clarifications 1 and 2)*

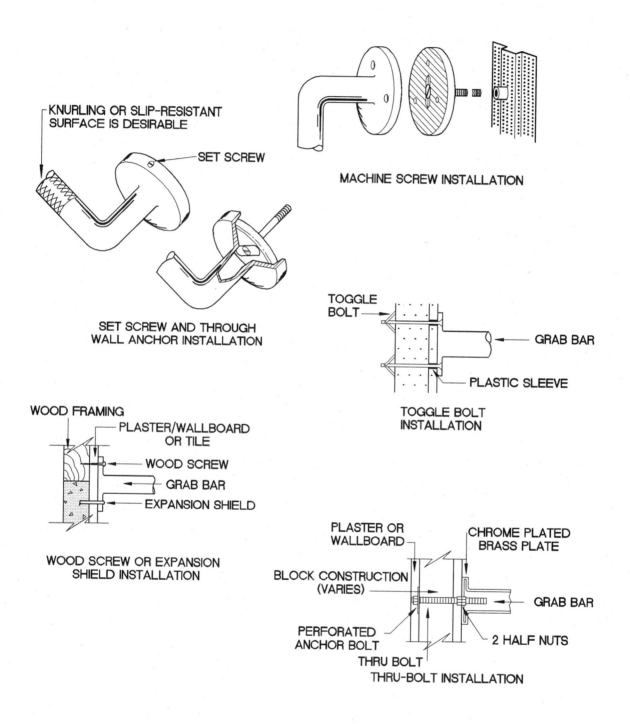

KNURLING OR SLIP-RESISTANT
SURFACE IS DESIRABLE

SET SCREW

SET SCREW AND THROUGH
WALL ANCHOR INSTALLATION

MACHINE SCREW INSTALLATION

TOGGLE
BOLT

GRAB BAR

PLASTIC SLEEVE

TOGGLE BOLT
INSTALLATION

WOOD FRAMING

PLASTER/WALLBOARD
OR TILE

WOOD SCREW

GRAB BAR

EXPANSION SHIELD

WOOD SCREW OR EXPANSION
SHIELD INSTALLATION

PLASTER OR
WALLBOARD

CHROME PLATED
BRASS PLATE

BLOCK CONSTRUCTION
(VARIES)

GRAB BAR

PERFORATED
ANCHOR BOLT

2 HALF NUTS

THRU BOLT

THRU-BOLT INSTALLATION

Figure 274   Grab bar installation recommendations.

Bathtub and Shower Valves

- **Bathtub Valves:** Located between the rim and 33" (84cm) above the floor. Bathtub controls to be accessible from inside and outside the bathtub. The hot control should always be on the left side. *(See Guideline 22b)*

- **Shower Valves:** Located from 38" - 48" (96cm - 122cm) above the bottom inside surface of the floor.

  Shower controls should be placed close to the edge of the enclosure, **not** directly below the showerhead.

  The shower controls must be safely accessible while the user is in the shower both **under** the stream of water and **outside** the stream of water, as well as from outside the shower. *(See Guideline 22a)*

- **Bathtub/Shower Combination:** If a single water valve will serve a bathtub/shower combination, it should be located 34" (86.36cm) above the bottom inside surface of the bathtub.

  Alternatively, separate valves may be specified to serve the bathtub and shower.

- All valves to be manufactured of shatter-resistant material and free from burrs and sharp edges.

- All valves to be clearly marked to indicate motion patterns. Cold water is always on the right and hot water is always on the left.

- All shower valves to be equipped with a temperature and/or pressure-balancing mixing device to eliminate the possibility of sudden temperature changes. *(See Guideline 21)*

- In bathrooms used by children or the elderly, shower valves or faucets to be equipped with a temperature limiting control valve that can be set to deliver a maximum water temperature of 100° - 110° Fahrenheit. (55° - 61°Celsius)

TOILET AREA

- Toilet paper holder to be installed slightly in front of the edge of the toilet bowl, on a side wall.

- Recessed toilet paper holders to be used in narrow areas.

- Horizontal grab bar to be placed adjacent to the toilet seat. *(See Guideline 26 - Clarifications 5a and 5b)*

ELECTRICAL

- Connect all circuits to a ground fault circuit interrupter **(GFCI)**. *(See Guideline 35)*

- Electrical receptacles along the vanity to be installed as far away from the water source as possible.

- Only permanently installed wall or ceiling heaters to be used in the bathroom.

- All light fixtures above bathtub/showers to be moisture-proof special purpose fixtures. *(See Guideline 35)*

- Any switches, timers, or other electric controlling devices to be placed so that they are not readily accessible from inside any water fixtures.

- Wall-mounted light fixtures to be hung or mounted no lower than 68" (172.72cm) above the finished floor except when they are installed above a permanent structure that will prevent users from walking under the fixture.

- A night light to be included in bathrooms used during night time sleeping hours.

STORAGE CABINETRY

- Drawers to feature hardware or catches that prevent them from being accidentally pulled completely out.

- All base cabinets to have a toe tick recess which is at least 3" x 3" (7.62cm x 7.62cm).

- Medicine storage areas and cleaning equipment storage areas to be lockable or be out of reach of children.

- Door sizing to be carefully planned so that large single doors do not swing into narrow walkways separating the cabinetry and opposite walls or fixtures.

- Cabinets placed above the toilet to be 4" (10.16cm) to 8" (20.32cm) in depth. This reduced depth eliminates the possibility of a seated individual hitting his or her head when rising from the toilet.

- Countertop space extending across the toilet tank to be 3" (7.62cm) to 5" (12.7cm) so that the toilet seat and lid can remain in a stable, upright position.

WINDOWS AND DOORS

- Safety glazing to be specified for all large window areas or fixed glass panels in the bathtub/shower area.

- Windows are not to be used for ventilation over the bathtub or other fixtures that would require the user to assume an awkward or unbalanced position to operate the window.

- Opaque glass to be installed for privacy whenever the exterior area is of a public nature.

- Windows to be installed at least 48" (121.92cm) off the floor to assist in privacy screening.

- In multiple door bathrooms, no door contact to occur when any, or all, are in use. To verify correct door placement and swing, consider drawing doors open on the floor plan.

- In bathrooms used by more than one person, the entry door opening is not to interrupt another person's use of the lavatory or toilet. To avoid any disruption of bathroom space, bifold or pocket doors may be used.

- Smooth glass, ceramic or plastic door knobs are not to be used in bathrooms.

- Door knobs to be positioned 2 3/4" (6.98cm) in from the edge of the door.

- Clothes hooks to be placed above adult eye level height. The average person's eye level is a 3" (7.62cm) below his/her overall height.

- Closet door knobs to be passage latch hardware that can be opened from both inside and outside the closet.

- Privacy latches to be unlockable on bathroom entry doors from the outside of the bathroom.

- Clear floor space of 32" (81cm) at all doorways and not more than 24" (61cm) deep in the direction of travel. *(See Guidelines 1a, 1b, and 1c)*

FLOORING

- Carpeting not to be specified in bathrooms except infrequently used guest or powder rooms. The possibility of contamination in the form of fungi and bacteria overshadows any aesthetic and maintenance advantages.

- Area carpets (even those with non-slip backing) are not to be specified in bathrooms.

- All hard surface floors to be a slip-resistant type. *(See Guideline 30)*

- The transition slope between bathroom doorways and adjoining room floorcovering to be gradual to avoid tripping.

CONSERVATION

As the family reviews the exciting plans for their new bathroom, they should also be encouraged to alter their living habits in the interest of water energy conservation. They may be surprised to know that bathing uses 30% of the total household water.

The savings in water is only one benefit. Energy costs to heat water can also be reduced. The savings earned by a family that installs water saving fixtures and fittings and practices water-saving living habits could pay for the extra cabinetry planned for the new bathroom.

To reduce water consumption, the following recommendations are made:

- Don't use hot water needlessly or let it run unnecessarily long when shaving, washing hands, brushing teeth or showering.

- Repair all dripping water faucets. One drop per second from a leaking faucet adds up to 60 gallons (227.1 liters) a week down the drain. Less than a dollar's worth of faucet washers can solve this problem.

- When washing clothes, do not use higher than necessary water levels or temperatures.

- Reduce the amount of water for bathtub baths and the length of time for showers. Remember, it's not necessary to fill the bathtub to the overflow or over the jets because the user's body will displace approximately 15 gallons of water.

- Install reduced-flow showerheads and faucets. Conventional showerheads use 6 to 8 gallons (22.7 to 30.28 liters) of water per minute. Reduced-flow showerheads dramatically limit the flow.

Many manufacturers limit the flow of water to a maximum 3 gallons (11.36 liters) per minute (2 - 2.75 GPM at normal water pressure of 30 to 80 PSI). Such water use reduction can save the average family of four as much as 36,500 gallons (138152.5 liters) of water annually, based on one daily, five minute shower per person.

1.7 gallon shower heads are also available. Adequate water pressure is critical for the proper operation of reduced-flow showerheads. Moreover, such showerheads may be counter-productive in extreme soft water areas.

SECTION **5**

BATHROOM STORAGE SYSTEMS

PLANNING FOR STORAGE

A well-organized storage system is as important in the bathroom as it is in the kitchen.

Your first responsibility is to plan a bathroom storage system that provides clear visibility and easy access to all cabinet interiors.

Second, you must plan a storage system that requires minimal time and energy on the user's part to locate, retrieve and replace items stored within the vanity cabinets.

In a previous discussion about vanity heights and anatomy considerations, we illustrated the preferred vanity height of 34" - 36" (86.36cm - 91.44cm) over the standard 30" - 32" (76.2cm - 81.28cm).

In this section, we'll study how ergonomic data is applied to arrive at functional storage areas, functional reaching limits and typical work curves of the bathroom user which guide us in arranging bathroom cabinetry.

REACHING LIMITS

The functional limits of able-bodied adults was studied at Cornell University some time ago. To determine the functional limits of storage areas, work curves were drawn for 300 women ranging in height from 4' 10" (147.32cm) to 6' 0" (182.88cm) tall.

The maximum, composite, shoulder to grasping fingertip reach of the individuals in the middle group, 5' 3" (160.02cm) to 5' 7" (170.18cm), established 76" (193.04cm) as the highest comfortable overhead reach for the user when standing immediately in front of a storage system.

When the user was required to reach over a 25" (63.5cm) deep counter space, the comfortable reach to a top shelf height was lowered to 66" (167.64cm).

In the same manner, 48" (121.92cm) was set as the side-to-side reach and 24" (60.96cm) off the floor as the lowest point of fingertip level from the floor. Use these dimensions to assist you in planning counter space for female bathroom users.

To adapt the information for the average American male at 5'-10" (177.80cm), the **National Kitchen & Bath Association** recommends that the fingertip reach height be extended to 82" (208.28) off the floor and the over counter reach to 78" (198.12). All other dimensions would remain constant for both men and women.

Human Energy Consumption

The same study determined that the normal work curve, or elbow circle, had a maximum depth of 16" (40.64cm) for the middle group of people studied.

Another study identified the amount of energy it took to reach up to shelves or bend down to shelves in a typical kitchen. Again, this information is easily transferable to bathroom planning. The study, entitled *Oxygen Consumed for Household Tasks,* was made to determine how much energy was required for various household activities. The study included:

- Reaching up with the arms to three heights above the floor: 46" (116.84cm), 56" (142.24cm) and 72" (182.88cm).

- Reaching down by trunk bend to two heights above the floor: 24" (60.96cm) and 3" (7.62cm).

- Reaching down by knee bend to 3" (7.62cm) above the floor.

- Stepping up 7" (17.78cm) above the floor.

- Pivoting the body with arms extended at a height of 36" (91.44cm) above the floor.

The study measured the physiological energy expended for the different tasks. Oxygen intake was used as a yardstick because it is part of the body's energy cycle. The conclusions of the study were as follows:

- Reaching up with the arms required less energy than bending the body.

- Energy consumed is in proportion to the height of the reach.

- Reaching down to 3" (7.62cm) above the floor by trunk bend required less energy than reaching by knee bend. However, reaching by knee bend is favored by specialists in body mechanics because it involves less body strain.

WORK CURVES

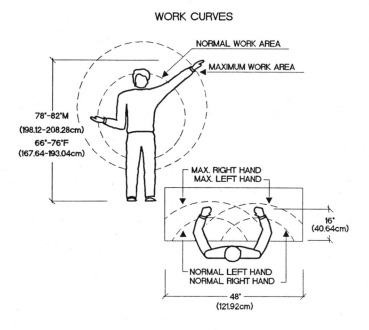

Figure 275   Work curves, reaching limits.

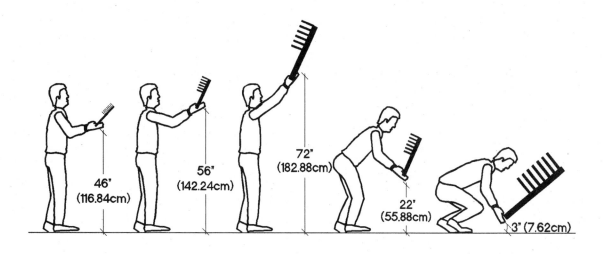

Figure 276   Human energy consumed in bathroom activities.

COUNTERTOP HEIGHTS

Ideal countertop heights have also been studied by kitchen and bathroom designers. Professor Alexander Kira studied the ideal height for a lavatory when the user was washing hands or face. Countertop heights designed for grooming areas can be planned with kitchen standards in mind.

The kitchen industry standard of 36" 991.44cm) off the floor as a countertop height is based on research that again revolved around women ranging in height from approximately 5' 3" to 5' 6" (160cm to 168cm). The concept was to provide a work surface that allowed the user to maintain good posture when standing at a countertop.

Good posture is defined as one in which the head, neck, chest and abdomen are balanced vertically, one upon the other, so that the weight is carried mainly by the bony framework of the skeleton, thereby placing a minimum of effort and strain on the muscles and ligaments of the body. Good posture and good lighting are critical in any work environment to avoid strain, to limit fatigue and to minimize the user's energy expenditure.

To determine the proper surface height for men, as well as bathroom users of different height, ask the clients to stand erect with elbows flexed. Normal usage counter heights are placed 2" (5.08cm) to 3" (7.62cm) below the floor-to-elbow dimension of the user. This countertop height allows the person to stand at the counter and easily pick-up and replace grooming items or equipment in use.

STORAGE GUIDELINES

Once you understand how much energy and time it takes to bend down to the floor or reach up to a top shelf, you can turn your attention to designing an efficient storage system.

When planning a bathroom storage system, follow three guiding principles:

- Store all bathroom equipment where it is used.

- Make sure that all supplies are clearly visible.

- Make sure that all items are easily accessible without first moving other items.

These general tips have led household management specialists to develop storage principles.

Store items at first or last place of use. *For example,* this is the general principle behind the requirement that washcloths and hand towels be placed near the vanity and bath towels near the bathing/showering area. The user should have ready access to these bathroom linens during the grooming or showering process.

Store items in multiple locations if used for different tasks. *For example,* plan hanging space for two bath towels for an individual with long hair so that one towel can be used for hair drying, the other for body drying.

Items used together should be stored together. Plan cosmetic storage so that all like items are grouped together. This allows the user to select among all the available choices: *For example,* all hair equipment, i.e., conditioners, gels, styling mists, blow dryers, curling irons, brushes, combs, picks, mirrors, etc. should be together so that this equipment is easily categorized and cataloged by the user.

Stored items should be easy to locate at a glance. Compartmentalized drawers within the bathroom storage system, stacked roll-out shelves within the cabinetry, multi-tiered shelving systems, shallow shelf storage, and door-shelving systems are all examples of how bathroom storage systems should be divided so this rule can be followed.

Realize that items stored in a bathroom are smaller than those items stored in kitchens. Therefore, the bathroom storage system is not simply a miniature version of a kitchen storage system. It requires many more divisions within the cabinetry to separate stored items to insure clear visibility and easy accessibility.

Frequently used items should be stored within easy reach. Based on the Cornell research quoted earlier, frequently used items should be stored from approximately 22" (55.88cm) to 56" (142.24cm) off the floor. Less frequently used items can be placed below or above that dimension. Most items used most frequently should be stored in front of less frequently used items. The NKBA Guidelines suggest storage be placed between 15" (38cm) and 48" (122cm) above the floor.

Based on these principles, it's easy to see how critical it is to plan the interior of the vanity cabinets carefully.

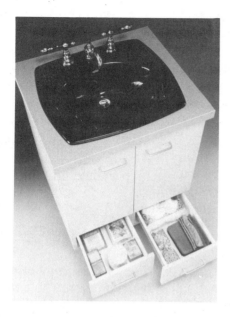

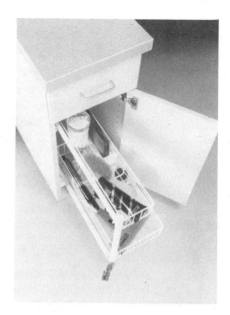

Figure 277   (Courtesy of St. Charles Company)
A storage system under the lavatory.

Figure 279   (Courtesy of St. Charles Company)
A pull-out bathroom storage rack.

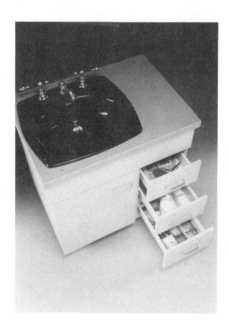

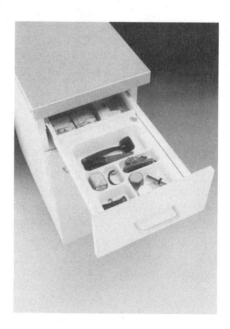

Figure 278   (Courtesy of St. Charles Company)
A drawer area under the lavatory.

Figure 280   (Courtesy of St. Charles Company)
An organized bathroom drawer.

Figure 281   (Courtesy of St. Charles Company)
A removable bathroom hamper.

Figure 283   (Courtesy of St. Charles Company)
A built-in waste paper basket.

Figure 282   (Courtesy of St. Charles Company)
A tall bathroom storage cabinet.

Figure 284   (Courtesy of St. Charles Company)
A tall bathroom storage cabinet above the toilet.

BATHROOM ACCESSORIES

ESSENTIAL EXTRAS

A successful bathroom designer is familiar with all accessory options. These elements are small, but important parts of any bathroom space. Carefully selecting them and correctly placing them according to the client's needs and wants will result in a bathroom that's convenient and easy to use as well as safe for all.

A general category of bathroom products is grouped together under the broad heading of "*accessories*". These items fall into the following general categories:

- Towel Storage

- Vanity Grooming Items

- Toilet/Bidet Storage Areas

- Specialized Accessories

- Bathroom Appliances

- Shower/bathtub Grooming Item Storage

- Medicine/Storage Cabinets

- Mirrors

Towel Storage

Towels are an important part of any bathroom plan. They need to be stored close to the bathroom, as well as hung within the bathroom space.

A general guideline is to allow between 24" and 36" (61cm and 91cm) of towel bar space for each family member using the bathroom. This assumes one bath towel, one hand towel and one washcloth per person, each folded in half and hung side by side. However, this recommendation needs to be personalized, some clients may stack the towels or use oversized bath sheets.

In many bathrooms, a washcloth for each user should be located in the bathtub and/or shower area, as well as a second cloth adjacent to the individual's lavatory. Additionally, for women, plan a towel rod that will accommodate two bath towels: one to dry the body off and one to dry the hair with.

Bathroom linens should be stored close to the point of use. Therefore, the washcloths and hand towels should be adjacent to the vanity area and bath towels close to the shower and/or bathtub facility.

Bathroom linens can be placed on towel bars, towel shelves, towel pins, towel rings, or kept in a towel basket. Towel bars are the most typical item used to store towels. You can create your own special towel storage area using some of the following ideas.

- A solid surface, wood or laminate countertop can be extended beyond the overall width dimension of the vanity, and can then feature a routed-out section to create a customized towel bar at the end of the vanity. This works very well if a free-standing vanity is specified that has both ends open.

- The 14 1/2" (36.83cm) wide space between studs can provide an interesting location for a recessed towel bar arrangement. Tension bars or custom bars can be installed in a sheetrock enclosure created by recessing into the space between the two studs.

  Make sure that there are no obstructions in this wall space: heat vents, vent pipes, pocket doors, etc. Remember, you will increase the noise transference from the bathroom to the adjacent room with this recessed approach - so make sure that the other side of the wall is a closet or that bathroom noises will not annoy people in the adjacent room.

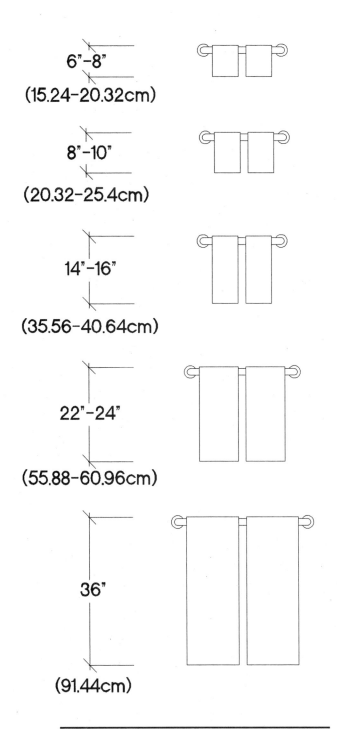

6"-8"
(15.24-20.32cm)

8"-10"
(20.32-25.4cm)

14"-16"
(35.56-40.64cm)

22"-24"
(55.88-60.96cm)

36"
(91.44cm)

Figure 285   Hanging towel space requirements.

- Consider creating a custom towel bar that also becomes a sculpture in the bathroom, perhaps a "step ladder" configuration made out of a custom acrylic, metal or wood bar.
Whenever considering a custom design, be sure to find out how far an unsupported rod can span without sagging. *For example,* a brass rod can be longer than an acrylic one.

- Install pegs along an apron panel for another interesting way to create towel storage in the bathroom. This may be an ideal solution for a children's bath: the pegs can be periodically moved up when the bathroom is repainted or wallcovering is replaced.

- Towel bars can be stacked one above the other. Consider the user's maximum grasping reach and plan each bar carefully according to the dimensions listed above. NKBA guidelines recommend that towel bars be located no more than 48" (122cm) and no less than 15" (39cm) above the floor.

Make sure that the towel bar location does not result in a folded towel covering up a duplex outlet or toggle switch that operates the electrical system in the bathroom. Do not hang towels immediately adjacent to the toilet or residential urinal.

- Towel bars can be installed adjacent to one another along a horizontal wall. This is a typical solution in a 5' x 7' (152.4cm x 213.36) or a 5' x 10' (152.4cm x 304.8cm) bath with a common plumbing wall: the towel bars are installed on the wall opposite the vanity and toilet.

Whenever installing towel bars on a wall, make sure that the plan reflects the overall depth of the towel bars. This dimension is particularly important to note if the towel bars are installed perpendicular to any cabinetry because a filler will be needed so that the cabinet door will open against the towel bar, rather than binding on the end of the towel bar.

- Towel rings are also used in some applications. Hooks are another alternative. In both cases, a common problem may develop: the towels will not dry as quickly as they would if they are spread out along a bar.

- Towel bars may also be wall- or floor-mounted, heated units. In one variety, the towel bar is heated with recirculating hot water and is called a *"hydronic heated towel bar".* Alternatively, a 120v electrical circuit can be used to electrically heat a towel bar.

The former method of heating a towel bar is common in Europe. The latter is more appropriate for a floor-mounted, movable towel bar.

Electric towel bars can be installed with a timer switch so that towels are only heated as needed. Electrically heated towel bars do not heat as quickly, or as thoroughly, as hydronic heated towel bars. The client needs to understand that they must weave the towel through the bars of the heated towel bar in order to properly heat the towel.

Pay particular attention to the overall size of an electric towel bar and the distance it protrudes from the wall when laying out adjacent spaces.

A very important note: *A heated towel bar is not a good idea in a bathroom that will be used by small children.*

Keeping all these ideas in mind, review *Figure 286* which suggests several different towel storage solutions.

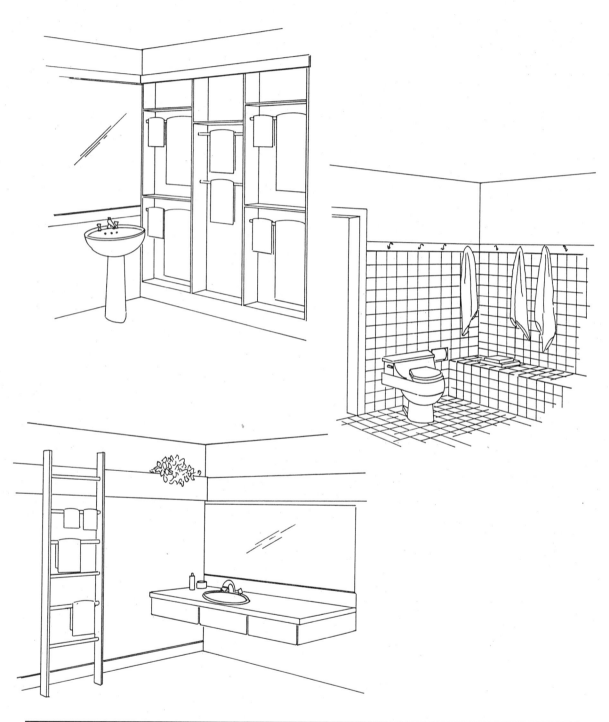

Figure 286   Towel storage ideas.

Vanity Grooming Items

Many manufacturers today offer attractive, wall-mounted accessories that augment the storage surrounding the lavatory. The accessories are very important to use with a pedestal lavatory.

Generally, a pedestal lavatory should have a ledge or shelf directly above it to facilitate storage. To keep the soap, glass, toothbrush and toothpaste off the counter or this ledge, special, attractive, wall-mounted receptacles can be installed.

Figure 287   Wall-mounted accessories.

Toilet/Bidet Storage Areas

Refer to *Guideline 28 in Section 8* for more detailed information about dimensional requirements for storage at the toilet/bidet area.

From a planning standpoint, the centerlines of all of these accessories need to be called out on the elevation plans so that the installer can include the proper blocking behind the drywall to provide a secure installation.

Figure 288   (Courtesy of Wilsonart International)   The accessories around the bidet and toilet are an important part of the plan.

Specialized Accessories

Built-in, special purpose accessories are also available to the bathroom specialist. These include the following:

- A scale that is recessed into the wall. The unit folds down to use and then retracts into the wall when stored.

- A magazine rack/toilet paper holder: This unit again recesses into the wall and provides a small shelf, bar for the toilet paper holder and rack for magazines. The unit can be custom fabricated out of solid surfacing, decorative laminate or wood, as well as purchased from manufacturers.

- Pull-out mirrors: These mirrors often feature a circular, fluorescent lighting system. The mirrors mount on the wall and then pull out for close viewing in either a normal or magnified mirror. They are a marvelous addition to a bathroom planned for a client who has sight limitations. Be sure your client understands the difference in magnification: 3x magnification is typically used. 5x is available as well.

- Electrical accessories: Which include, but are not limited to: built-in hairdryers, rechargeable razors, curling irons, contact lens cleaners, and toothbrushes

All of these items need storage areas planned to include an electrical outlet close-by.

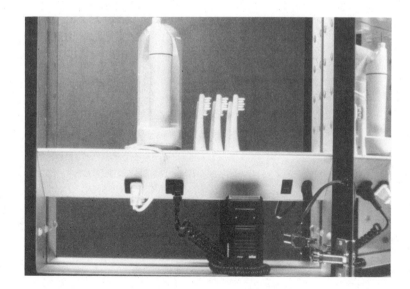

Figure 289   (Courtesy of Robern)   A medicine cabinet may provide an electrical outlet for bathroom grooming items.

Bathroom Appliances

Although not generally considered accessories, a comment should be made about appliances that may be included in a bathroom.

An instant hot water heater might be ideal for a client who enjoys a cup of tea in the morning. Space for a coffeemaker might be an excellent addition to a master suite. A small microwave, undercounter refrigerator and service lavatory are not unheard of in large master suites. Such a center invites the adults to enjoy a snack without having to go to the main kitchen.

Many bathrooms today feature a television and/or a radio, as well as a telephone. Make sure your clients understand they can receive an electrical shock from all of these items. A kitchen built-in warming drawer or laundry room clothes dryer may be installed as an alternative to a heated towel bar.

All of these appliances need to be selected before the final plans are completed so that their dimensions can be considered during the final design phase. Don't neglect to note all plumbing, electrical and mechanical requirements in the specifications.

Shower/Bathtub Grooming Item Storage

A bathing area, stall shower or combination bathtub/shower should include an area to store grooming items such as soap, shampoo and conditioner. This area should not interfere with the user, recessing the unit is recommended whenever possible. For some clients a storage spot for the toothbrush/tooth-paste/mouthwash may also be requested

If a jetted bathtub is planned, the storage ledge might be neatly concealed within the overall platform configuration. A soap dish, washcloth hook and ledge for bathroom accessories can then be out of sight so that the user can enjoy their view of a collection of shells or plants rather than these necessities of bathing.

In a bathtub/shower combination or stall shower, consider a grooming shelf along the service wall or side wall. Ideally, this shelf should not protrude because such an installation may result in an injury if someone falls against it. A corner shelf unit, one that is part of the service wall, or a recessed enclosure, are better solutions than surface mounted shelves.

Recessed grooming areas are totally custom installations, therefore the designer should measure what the client plans on using in the shower or bathtub/shower area and plan the recessed area accordingly. If ceramic tile is used, the placement of this recess should be carefully calculated to minimize any cuts in the tile.

Additionally, the finish method used around the perimeter of this enclosure must be carefully calculated and the proper trim tiles ordered.

Medicine/Storage Cabinets

The term "*medicine cabinet*" has long been associated with a shallow cabinet that is either recessed between the studs or is surface-mounted on the wall behind the lavatory. These cabinets can also be installed in many other areas as well. This type of shelf space is imminently practical. The following chart indicates various items stored and the recommended shelf depth for each.

ITEMS TO BE STORED	DEPTH					
	4"	8"	12"	16"	20"	24"
BATHROOM SUPPLIES & EQUIP.				■		
BED, FOLDING						■
BEDDING					■	
BEVERAGES, FOOD IN CASES			■			
BOOKS		■				
BUSINESS PAPERS			■			
CHRISTMAS DECORATIONS			■			
CLEANING SUPPLIES	■					
CLOTHING IN DRAWERS						■
CLOTHING ON HANGERS					■	
CLOTHING ON HOOKS				■		
DINNERWARE			■			
DRAWER FILES				■		
ELECTRIC FANS			■			
GLASSWARE	■					
INFANTS' EQUIPMENT						■
LUGGAGE						■
MAGAZINES		■				
RADIOS			■			
RECORD PLAYER, RECORDS				■		
SEWING EQUIPMENT						■
TOILET SUPPLIES	■					
TOOLS (HAND-HELD)			■			
TRAYS, PLATTERS, BOWLS				■		
UTENSILS				■		

Figure 290   Typical shelf space requirements.

Figure 291   *(Courtesy of Robern)*   *A well designed medicine cabinet system.*

RECESSED INSTALLATIONS

A recessed medicine cabinet is designed to fit between the 2" x 4" (5.08cm x 10.16cm) studs of a typical framing system in North America, which features studs spaced 16" (40.64cm) on center. Because the nominal (actual) dimension of a 2" x 4" (5.08cm x 10.16cm) stud is 1 1/2" x 3 1/2" (3.81cm x 8.89cm), the actual space between studs measures 14 1/2" (36.83cm).

Medicine cabinets generally have a rough opening size of 14 1/2" (36.83cm) wide x 3 1/2" (8.89cm) deep. The actual finished door size may be larger. When placing such a cabinet behind a lavatory, before you select a specific cabinet, consider the height of the family members who will use the bathroom. In a bathroom where both adults and children share the space, a long narrow medicine cabinet may be more desirable than a horizontal unit.

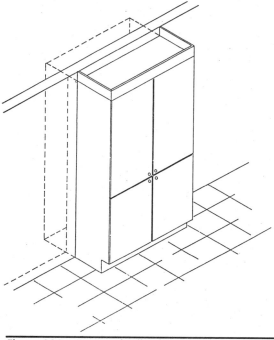

Figure 292   Recessed tall cabinet ideas.

Elaborate on the concept of a shallow recessed storage to create a floor-to-ceiling unit. Recess the unit 3" (7.62cm) into the wall, and then extend it 3" (7.62cm) to 6" (15.24cm) into the room's floor space to provide the appearance of shallow cabinet storage.

CREATING A CUSTOM CABINET

In addition to ready-made medicine/storage cabinets, custom units can also be fabricated. Recess metal cans into the wall between studs, then add custom-made, surface-mounted doors or mirrors (frame or frameless) over them. This allows total design flexibility. *For example,* you may opt to install three framed mirrors along the large vanity, with two perimeter mirrors concealing recessed storage.

Alternatively, you may install a plate glass mirror behind a vanity and feature two recessed cabinets behind large, frameless mirror sections on the side walls.

When presenting any type of recessed installation, always draw the mirrors to scale on the floor plan and locate the seams between the fixed and operable mirror sections.

Be sure to position the cabinets carefully so that these seams do not fall at the middle of a lavatory.

Make sure there are no vent pipes, pocket doors, heat registers, or other mechanical system elements concealed within the wall.

Do not try to install two recessed medicine cabinets back-to-back in adjoining bathrooms that share a common plumbing wall.

If you're designing a recessed medicine cabinet that's larger than the rough-in opening of 14-1/2" (36.83cm) between studs, the recessed area needs to be prepared with a header and rough sill to receive the recessed can. The manufacturer supplies rough-in sizes with the product.

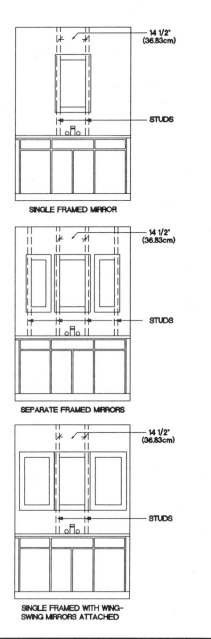

SINGLE FRAMED MIRROR

SEPARATE FRAMED MIRRORS

SINGLE FRAMED WITH WING-SWING MIRRORS ATTACHED

Figure 293   Locate mirror seams away from lavatory center line.

SURFACE-MOUNTED INSTALLATIONS

Surface-mounted medicine cabinets are hung on the wall so that their full depth protrudes into the room. Therefore, they can be placed anywhere within the space. However, this type of cabinet can appear cumbersome and may obstruct surface-mounted light fixtures or towel bars on an adjacent wall.

Alternatively, you can furr out a wall section to accommodate a recessed cabinet in a space where recessing the unit is impossible and you wish to avoid the look of a surface-mounted unit.

MEDICINE CABINET DOORS

All of these units are available with hinged or sliding doors. Remember that sliding doors always block at least one-half of the opening. Make sure a swinging door does not collide with towel bars or other wall-mounted accessories installed at a right angle to the swing door.

Both types are available with decorative frames to complement any styling. Elegant, beveled, frameless mirrors are also available.

Many recessed and surface-mounted systems are also available with an integral lighting system or matching side or canopy lights; consequently, the cabinet will require special electrical wiring.

Mirrors

Mirrors are a functional requirement of the bathroom that also allow you to dramatically expand the visual perception of space. They are practical for a grooming station and add a sense of movement and life to any room.

MIRROR THICKNESS

In the past, 1/4" (.63cm) plate glass mirror was always recommended to insure a distortion-free reflection. Today, both 3/16" (.47cm) and 1/4" (.63cm) glass are manufactured following a "*float*" procedure, so either thickness is acceptable. Limiting the design to 4 x 8 (121.92cm x 243.84cm) sheet sizes in a 3/16" (.47cm) thickness will provide the most affordable installation.

When specifying a large section of plate glass mirror, double check access into the room to be sure large sections can be maneuvered through the house and into the bathroom.

DESIGN CONSIDERATIONS

When specifying large, expansive mirror walls, you may face warranty limitations. When you draw mirrors in a perspective, don't show them as one sheet if there will be seams. And, don't install mirrors behind a pedestal lavatory because they'll reflect the pipes. You should also avoid installing accessories along a mirrored wall as well.

Make sure your clients know what the mirrored surfaces will reflect - clients may be shocked at a full-length front or side view of themselves as they use the toilet.

Dramatic grid and tambour mirror-like plastic substitutes may be used on cabinets, walls, ceilings and columns. These products are not designed for heavy use areas or grooming stations; rather, drama and beauty should dictate their placement.

MIRROR SAFETY

For optimum safety, tempered glass or mirror-like plastic should be considered for wall surfaces in a bathroom. Be prepared - in many installations the dramatic increase in cost for this type of mirror surface may eliminate the option. Regardless of the cost differential, plastic type mirrors are always recommended for ceiling installations.

DESIGNING THE MIRROR

Mirrors can change the perception of space in the following ways:

- Mirror one or both long walls to widen a narrow room.

- Install floor to ceiling mirrors to add overall height to the space.

- Mirror a wall to reflect a private garden beyond and bring the outdoors in.

- Combine mirrors with wood, marble, or solid surfacing and horizontal, diagonal or vertical alternating sections to add a unique touch to the overall space.

SECTION **7**

BATHROOM CLOSET PLANNING

CLOSET CONSIDERATIONS

Many bathrooms include a clothes closet or a linen closet adjacent to the bathroom or as an important part of the space. The items to be stored in the closet need to be identified at the time of the survey. *For example,* a closet designed to store men's clothing for an individual who is 5' 10" (177.8cm) tall allows the designer to install double, parallel poles throughout the majority of the space. However, a closet designed for a women who predominantly wears dresses to work cannot be double poled. And pole placement for a child's closet is different from that of an adult.

Specialized Closet Requests

In addition to hanging space, you need to find out what other type of organized compartments are requested for items such as shoes, sweaters, hats, purses.

Would the client use organized hanging storage for belts, ties, scarves or costume jewelry? A seating area for putting on shoes and socks? Does the client wish *to have some sort of an ironing or steam pressing option in the closet for last minute clothing touch-ups? Would the client use a counter, shelf or rod system to facilitate packing if they are frequent travelers? Is drawer or counter space needed for other jewelry or purse/pocket items? Would the family like to have a hamper in the space?*

All of these questions need to be answered before the closet is planned.

Closet Sizing

Once the questions are answered, the available space should be surveyed so that you can determine the type of closet. There are three broad categories of closets:

- Reach-in Spaces

- Edge-in Spaces

- Walk-in Spaces

Reach-in Closet: The minimum front to back depth of a space for hanging clothes is 24" (60.96cm). The accessible rod length is equal to the width of the door opening plus 6" (15.24cm) on each side.

Edge-in Closet: By providing an edge-in space of at least 18" (45.72cm) in front of the standard 24" (60.96cm) deep closet space, the accessible rod length can be much longer than the door width.

Walk-in Closet: This type provides rods on one or both sides, with an access path in the middle of at least 24" (60.96cm) wide. A wider access space within the closet should be planned whenever possible. The perimeter of the space can be surrounded by poles, with the center space left as a dressing/maneuvering area, or with additional closet furniture in the center.

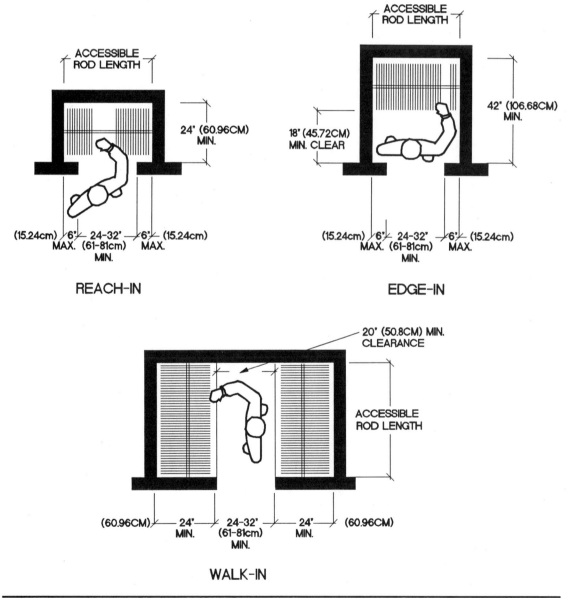

Figure 294   Reach-in, Edge-in and Walk-in closet space.

Rod Placement

Recommended rod placement is as follows:

- **Floor Length Gowns and Robes:** Pole centered 68" (172.72cm) to 72" (182.88cm) off the floor.

- **Adult Street Length Dresses and Coats:** Pole centered 54" (137.16cm) to 63" (160.02cm) off the floor.

- **Adult Shirts, Folded Pants, Skirts and Jackets:** Pole centered 48" (121.92cm) off the floor.

- **Children's Clothing:** Pole centered 32" (81.28cm) to 45" (114.3cm) off the floor.

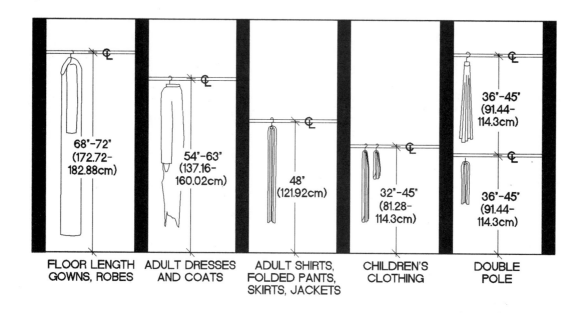

FLOOR LENGTH GOWNS, ROBES — 68"-72" (172.72-182.88cm)

ADULT DRESSES AND COATS — 54"-63" (137.16-160.02cm)

ADULT SHIRTS, FOLDED PANTS, SKIRTS, JACKETS — 48" (121.92cm)

CHILDREN'S CLOTHING — 32"-45" (81.28-114.3cm)

DOUBLE POLE — 36"-45" (91.44-114.3cm)

Figure 295   Rod placement recommendations.

Double Poles

Space double poles from 36"
(91.44cm) to 45" (114.3cm) apart. Generally, allow 2" (5.08cm) from the pole to
the bottom of the next layer of hanging
garments. Double poling often eliminates the standard shelf found above a
pole in a typical closet. If the rod is installed underneath a shelf, it should be
placed 2" (5.08cm) to 3" (7.62cm) below
the shelf to allow space to lift the hanger
off the rod.

New Closet Ideas

Many intriguing options are available
today in place of standard shelves and
poles. Additionally, complete closet systems are available through several manufacturers so that a storage system is
easy to specify.

Be sure to include adequate, color-
corrected lighting, a full-length mirror
and good ventilation to insure proper air
circulation throughout all closet spaces
you design.

Following are several examples of
well-planned closet spaces.

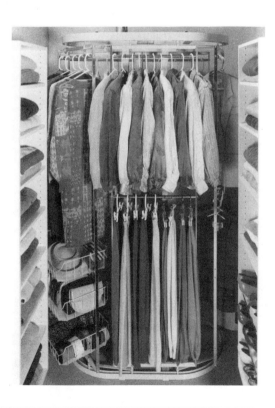

Figure 296 (Courtesy of White Industries)
Closet carousel.

Figure 297   (Courtesy of White Industries)   Closet storage system features folding storage which glides on track to reveal hanging storage in back.

Figure 298   *(Courtesy of Tru-Space)   Closet storage system offers a wide variety of special storage.*

Figure 299   *(Courtesy of Tru-Space)*   *Closet storage system for child's clothes and toys.*

Figure 300   *(Courtesy of Closet Maid)*   *Closet storage system with shallow and deep shelving.*

Figure 301 *(Courtesy of Closet Maid)* *Closet storage system is adjustable.*

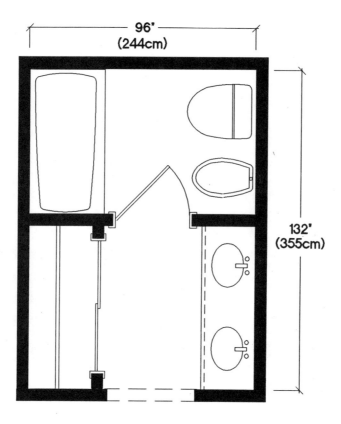

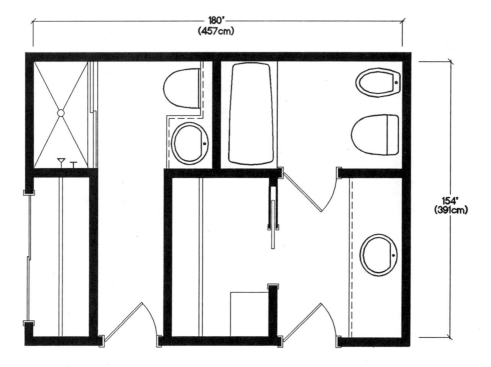

Figure 302   Large bathrooms with closets.

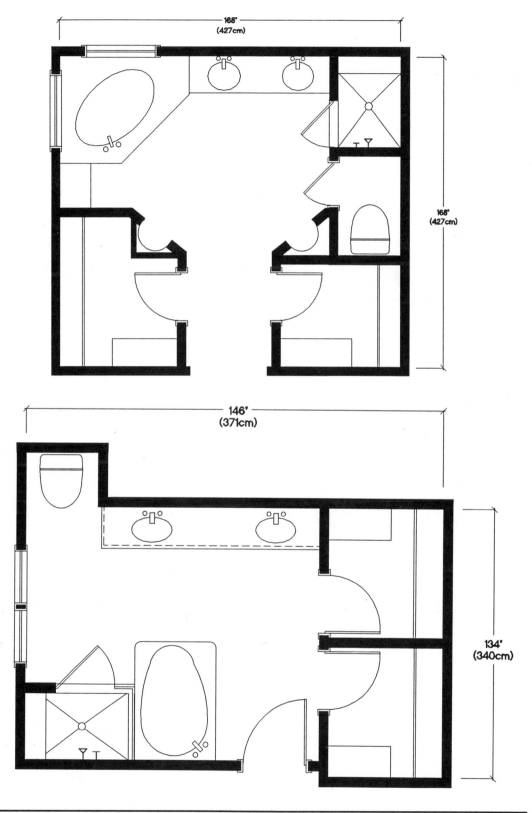

Figure 303   Large bathrooms with walk-in closets.

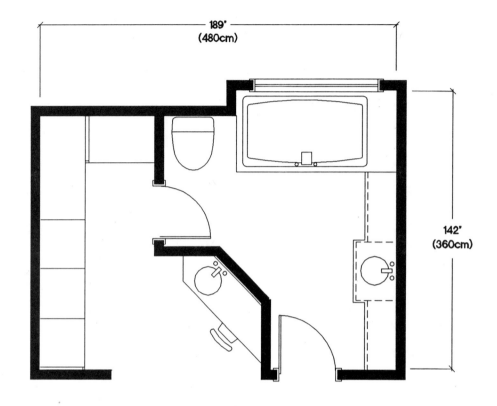

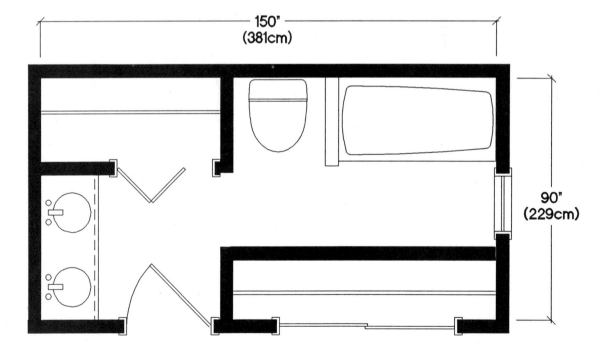

Figure 304   Medium bathrooms with edge-in closets.

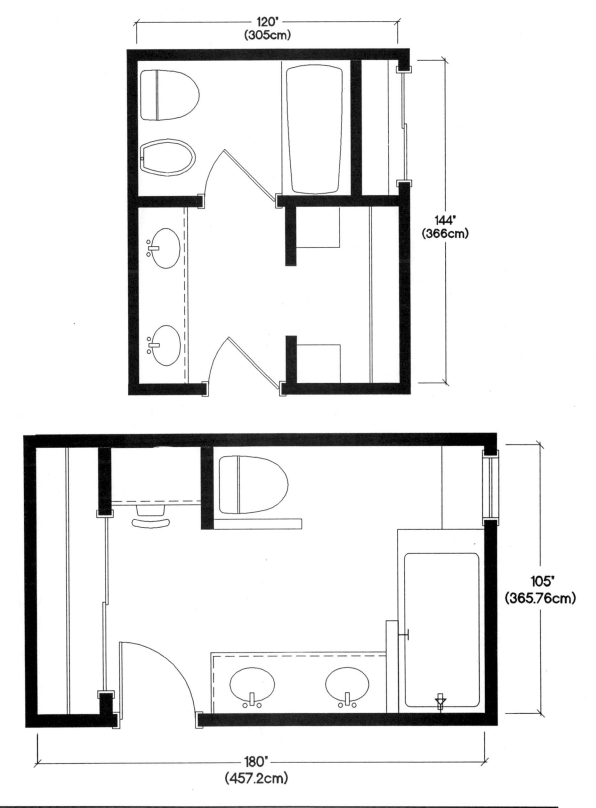

Figure 305   Medium bathrooms with closets.

SECTION **8**

41 GUIDELINES OF BATHROOM PLANNING

The ideal bathroom design for any home will depend on a number of factors, particularly on lifestyle habits and individual users. Therefore, a design considered excellent for one family may be unsuitable for another. Nevertheless, you need a set of guidelines as a basis to start the planning process.

The guidelines which follow have been developed by the **National Kitchen & Bath Association** to serve as a basis for bathroom planning. It is intended that a bathroom which follows these recommendations will be functional, safe and universal. NKBA readily acknowledges that not every guideline will fit every design situation. There are 40 million pre-existing homes in the United States alone and most do not meet accessibility standards. As the bathroom designer, you will be required to make frequent judgement calls and compromises in order to achieve the best solution for your client.

The 41 Guidelines of Bathroom Planning are segmented into six sections for easy referencing during the planning process.

I.   Clear Floor Spaces and Door Openings

II. Lavatories

III. Showers and Bathtubs

IV. Toilets and Bidets

V.   Grab Bars, Storage and Flooring

VI. Controls and Mechanical Systems

Use these guidelines as the basis for determining the design solution. Remember that meeting client requests, construction constraints and the budget are your primary goals. While you must never deviate from local safety or building codes, the NKBA planning guidelines are intended to be modified as necessary for specific project requirements. The important thing is for you to know the guidelines first, and then make intelligent design decisions to follow or modify the guideline as you customize the bathroom space for each client.

NKBA's 41 Guidelines of Bathroom Planning

SECTION I: Clear Floor Spaces and Door Openings

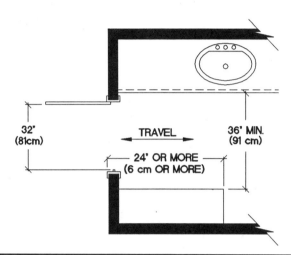

Figure 306
Guideline 1a - *The clear space at doorways should be at least 32" (81cm) wide and not more than 24" (61cm) deep in the direction of travel.*

Guideline 1a Clarification - *While a designer should always try to meet this goal, physical constraints of a job site may require deviation from the guideline. Be aware that a lesser clearance may not allow for full use by all people.*

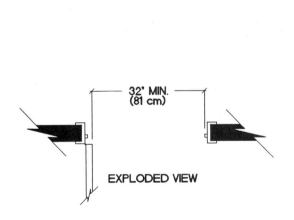

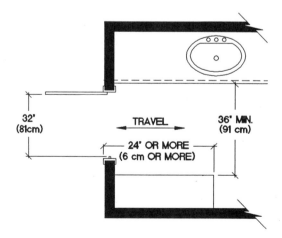

Figure 307 **Guideline 1b -** *The clear space at a doorway must be measured at the narrowest point.*

Figure 308 **Guideline 1c -** *Walkways (passages between vertical objects greater than 24" (61cm) deep in the direction of travel), should be a minimum of 36" (91cm) wide.*

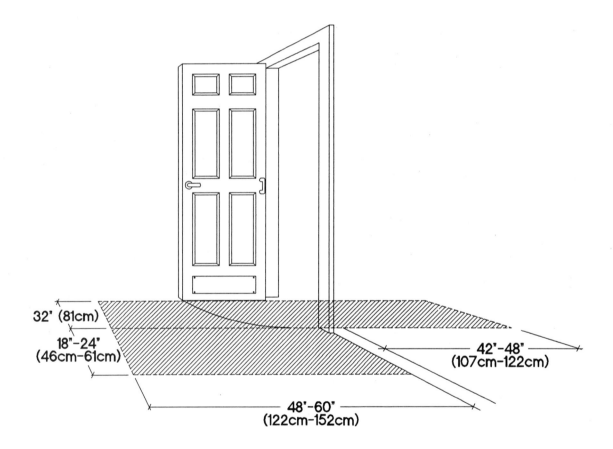

32" (81cm)

18"-24"
(46cm-61cm)

42"-48"
(107cm-122cm)

48"-60"
(122cm-152cm)

Figure 309 **Guideline 2 -** *A clear floor space at least the width of the door on the push side and a larger clear floor space on the pull side should be planned at doors for maneuvering to open, close, and pass through the doorway. The exact amount needed will depend on the type of door and the approach.*

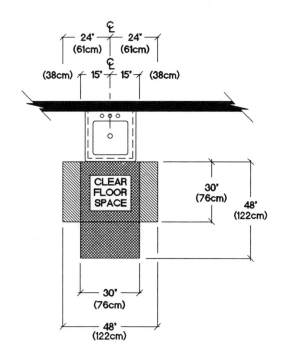

Figure 310 **Guideline 3 -** *A minimum clear floor space of 30" x 48" (76cm x 122cm) either parallel or perpendicular should be provided at the lavatory.*

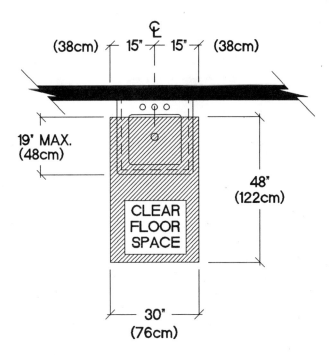

Figure 311 **Guideline 3 Clarification -** *Up to 19" (48cm) of the 48" (122cm) clear floor space dimension can extend under the lavatory when a knee space is provided.*

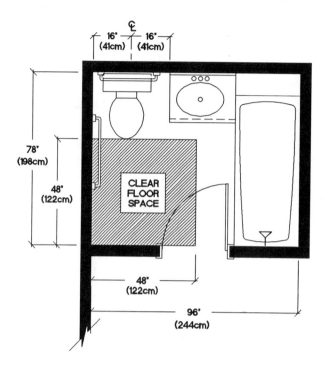

Figure 312 **Guideline 4a -** *A minimum clear floor space of 48" x 48" (122cm x 122cm) should be provided in front of the toilet. A minimum of 16" (41cm) of that clear floor space must extend to each side of the centerline of the fixture.*

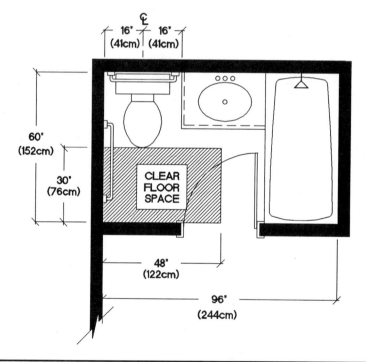

Figure 313 **Guideline 4a Clarification -** *While a designer should always try to meet this goal, physical constraints of a job site may require deviation from the guideline. If a 48" x 48" (122cm x 122cm) clear floor space is unavailable, this space may be reduced to 30" x 48" (76cm x 122cm). This compromise may not allow for full use by all people.*

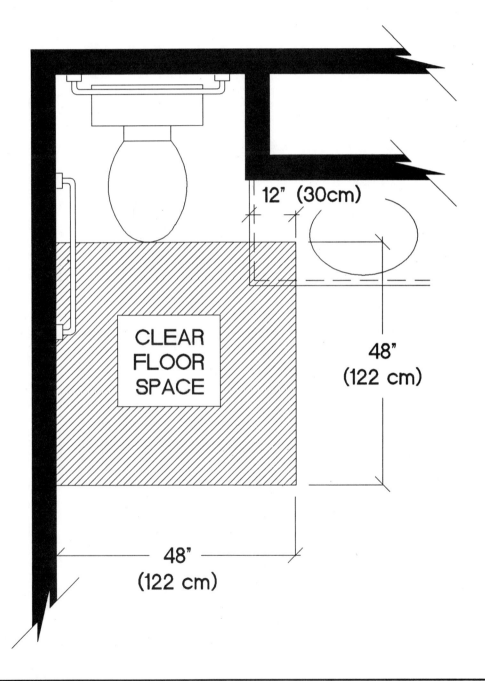

CLEAR
FLOOR
SPACE

12" (30cm)

48"
(122 cm)

48"
(122 cm)

Figure 314 **Guideline 4b -** *Up to 12" (30cm) of the 48" x 48" (122cm x 122cm) clear floor space can extend under the lavatory when total access to a knee space is provided.*

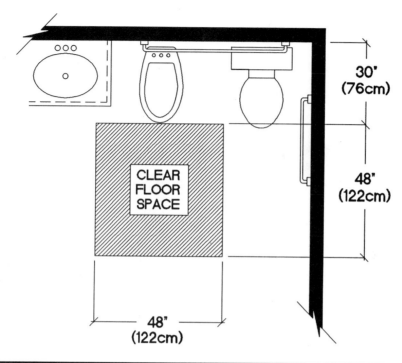

Figure 315 **Guideline 5 -** *A minimum clear floor space of 48" x 48" (122cm x 122cm) from the front of the bidet should be provided.*

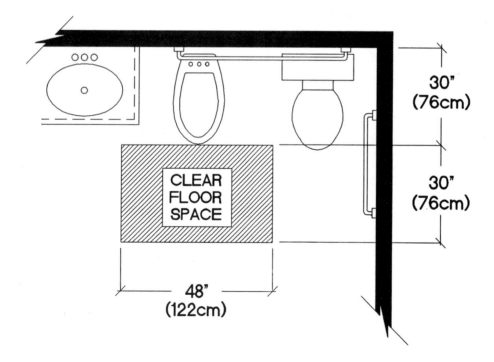

Figure 316 **Guideline 5 Clarification 1 -** *While a designer should always try to meet this goal, physical constraints of a job site may require deviation from the guideline. If a 48" x 48" (122cm x 122cm) clear floor space is not available, this space may be reduced to 30" x 48" (76cm x 122cm). This compromise may not allow for full use by all people.*

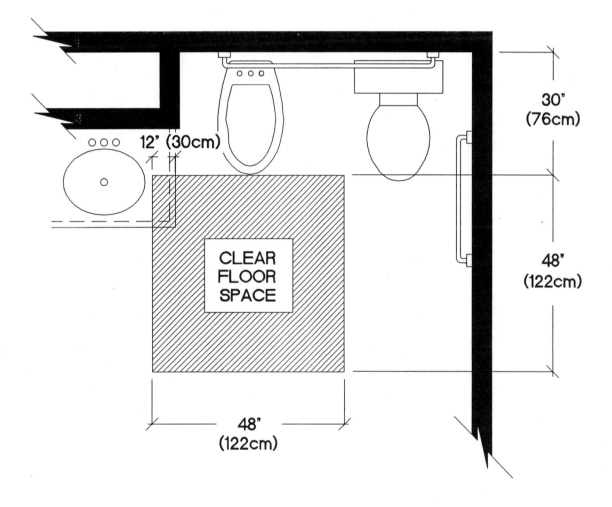

12" (30cm)

30"
(76cm)

CLEAR
FLOOR
SPACE

48"
(122cm)

48"
(122cm)

Figure 317 **Guideline 5 Clarification 2 -** *Up to 12" (30cm) of the 48" x 48" (122cm x 122cm) of the clear floor space can extend under the lavatory when total access to a knee space is provided.*

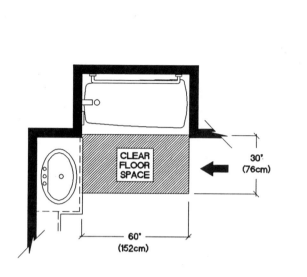

PARALLEL APPROACH

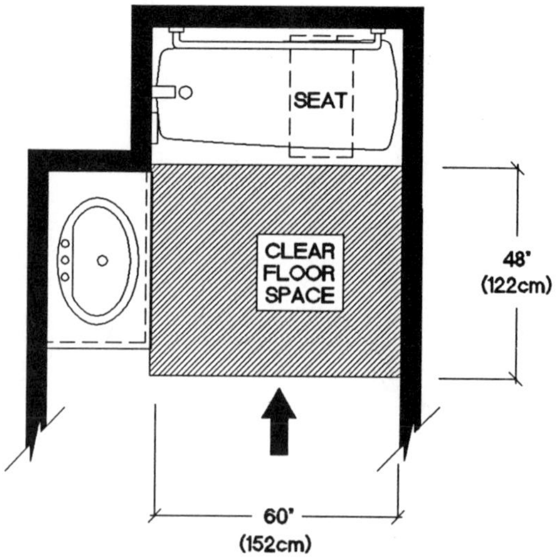

Figure 318 **Guideline 6a -** *The minimum clear floor space at a bathtub is 60" (152cm) wide by 30" (76cm) deep for a parallel approach, even with the length of the bathtub.*

PERPENDICULAR APPROACH

Figure 319 **Guideline 6b -** *The minimum clear floor space at a bathtub is 60" (152cm) wide x 48" (122cm) deep for a perpendicular approach.*

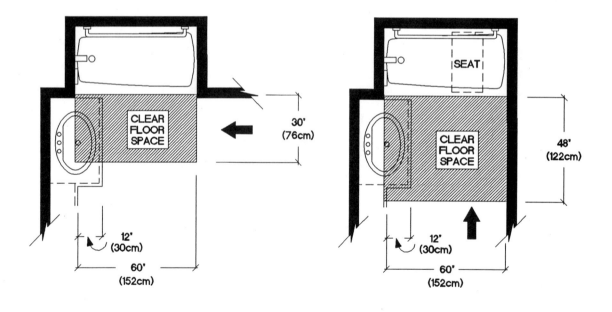

PERPENDICULAR APPROACH

PARALLEL APPROACH

Figure 320 **Guideline 6a, 6b Clarification 1 -** *Up to 12" (30cm) of the 60" (152cm) clear floor space required for parallel or perpendicular approach can extend under the lavatory when total access to a kneespace is provided.*

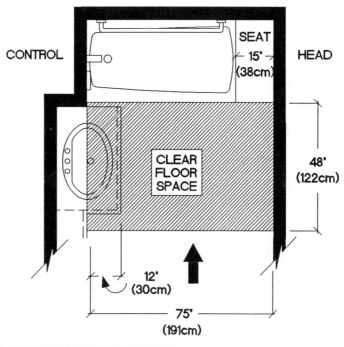

Figure 321 **Guideline 6a, 6b Clarification 2 -** *If a built-in seat is planned, increase the width of the clear floor space by the depth of the seat, a minimum 15" (38cm).*

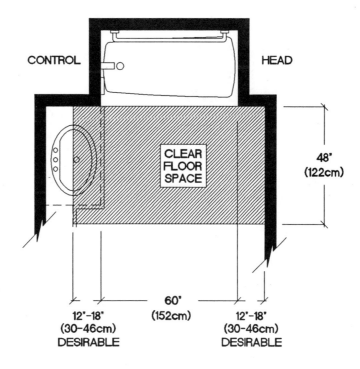

Figure 322 **Guideline 6a, 6b Clarification 3 -** *An additional 12"-18" (30cm-46cm) of clear floor space beyond the control wall is desirable to ease access to controls. The same 12"-18" (30cm-46cm) of clear floor space is desirable beyond the head of the bathtub for maneuvering mobility aids for transfer.*

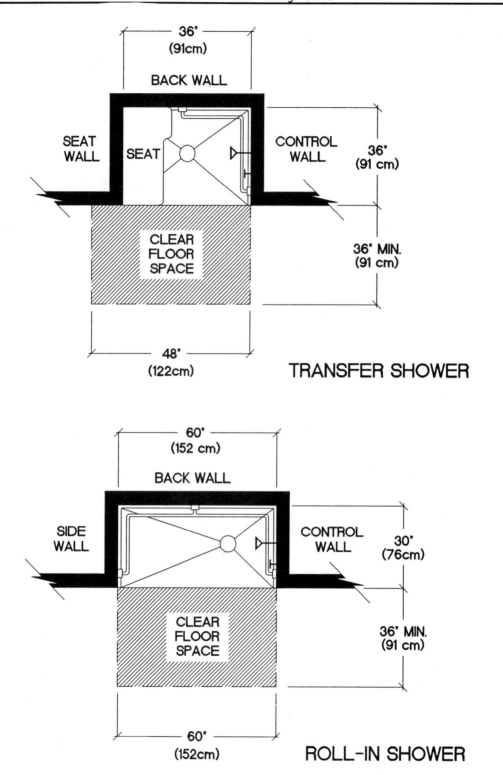

Figure 323 **Guideline 7** - *The minimum clear floor space at showers less than 60" (152cm) wide should be 36" (91cm) deep by the width of the shower plus 12" (30cm). The 12" (30cm) should extend beyond the seat wall. At a shower that is 60" (152cm) wide or greater, clear floor space should be 36" (91cm) deep by the width of the shower.*

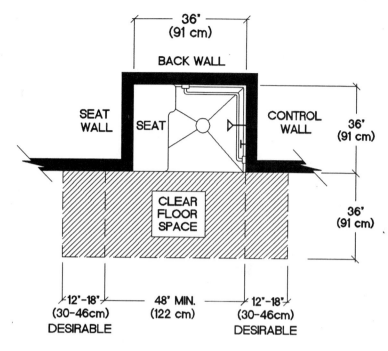

TRANSFER SHOWER

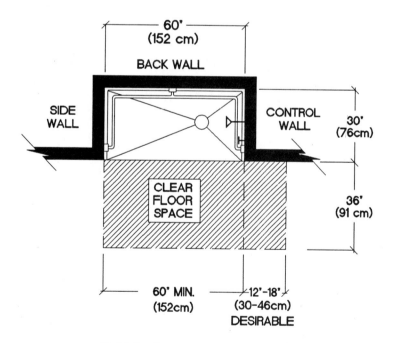

ROLL-IN SHOWER

Figure 324 **Guideline 7 Clarification** - *An additional 12"-18" (30cm-46cm) of clear floor space beyond the control wall is desirable to ease access to controls. The same 12"-18" (30cm-46cm) of clear floor space is desirable beyond the side wall opposite the control wall for maneuvering aids for transfer.*

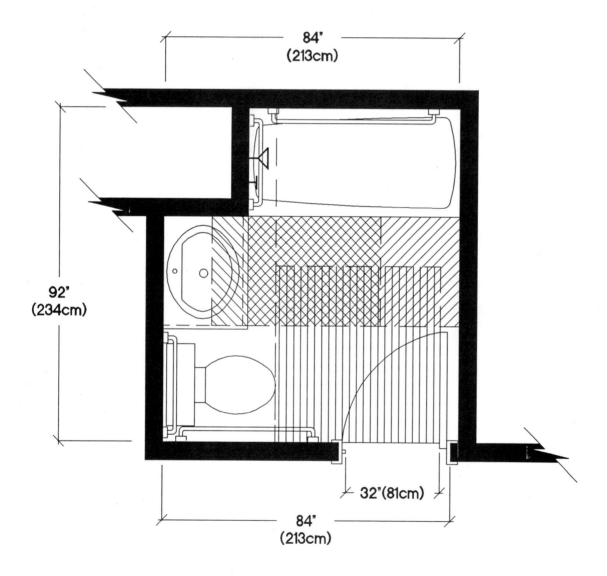

Figure 325 **Guideline 8 -** *Clear floor spaces required at each fixture may overlap.*

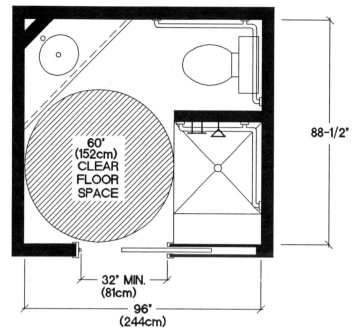

MINIMUM 60" (152cm) DIAMETER FOR 360. TURNS

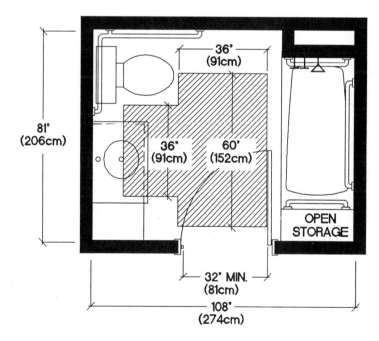

MINIMUM 36" x 36" x 60" (91cm x 91cm x 152cm)
SPACE FOR T-TURNS

Figure 326 **Guideline 9 -** *Space for turning (mobility aids) 180° should be planned in the bathroom. A minimum diameter of 60" (152cm) for 360° turns and/or a minimum T-turn space of 36" (91cm) x 36" (91cm) x 60" (152cm).*

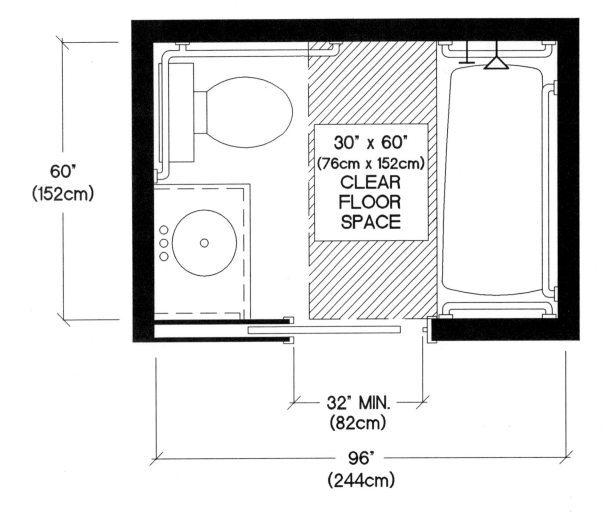

60"
(152cm)

30" x 60"
(76cm x 152cm)
CLEAR
FLOOR
SPACE

— 32" MIN. —
(82cm)

96"
(244cm)

ALTERNATIVE TO TURNING SPACE
30" x 60" (76cm x 152cm) CLEAR FLOOR SPACE

Figure 327 **Guideline 9 Clarification** - *While a designer should always try to meet this goal, physical constraints of a job site may require deviation from the guideline. When space for a 360° diameter or T-turn is unavailable, a 30" x 60" (76cm x 152cm) clear floor space can be substituted, but this compromise will not allow full access by all users.*

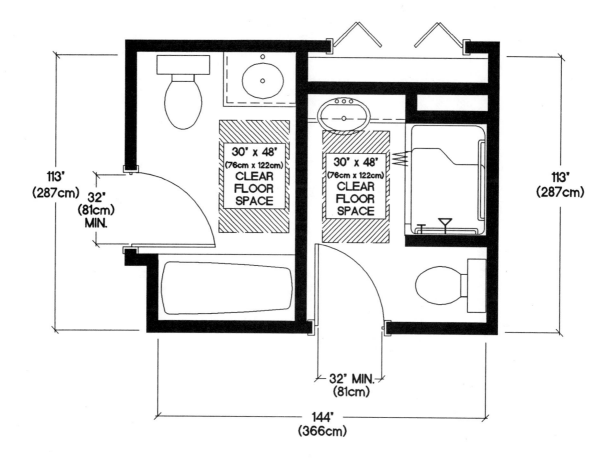

113'
(287cm)

32"
(81cm)
MIN.

30" x 48"
(76cm x 122cm)
CLEAR
FLOOR
SPACE

30" x 48"
(76cm x 122cm)
CLEAR
FLOOR
SPACE

113'
(287cm)

32" MIN.
(81cm)

144'
(366cm)

Figure 328 **Guideline 10 -** *A minimum clear floor space of 30" x 48" (76cm-122cm) is* **required** *beyond the door swing in a bathroom.*

SECTION II: Lavatories

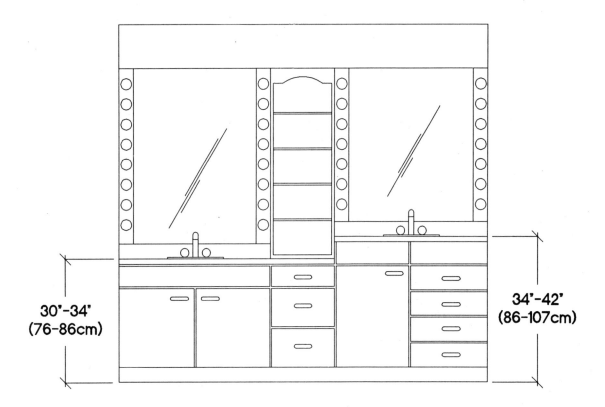

30"-34"
(76-86cm)

34"-42"
(86-107cm)

VARIED VANITY COUNTER HEIGHTS ARE DESIRABLE

Figure 329   **Guideline 11 -** *When more than one vanity is included, one may be 30"-34" (76cm-86cm) high and another at 34"-42" (86cm-107cm) high. Vanity height should fit the user(s).*

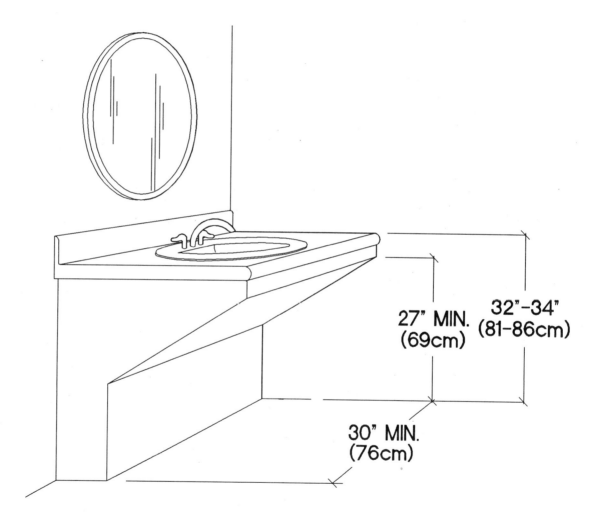

27" MIN.
(69cm)

32"-34"
(81-86cm)

30" MIN.
(76cm)

Figure 330 **Guideline 12** - *Kneespace (which may be open or adaptable) should be provided at a lavatory. The kneespace should be a minimum of 27" (69cm) above the floor at the front edge, decreasing progressively as the depth increases, and the recommended width is a minimum of 30" (76cm) wide.*

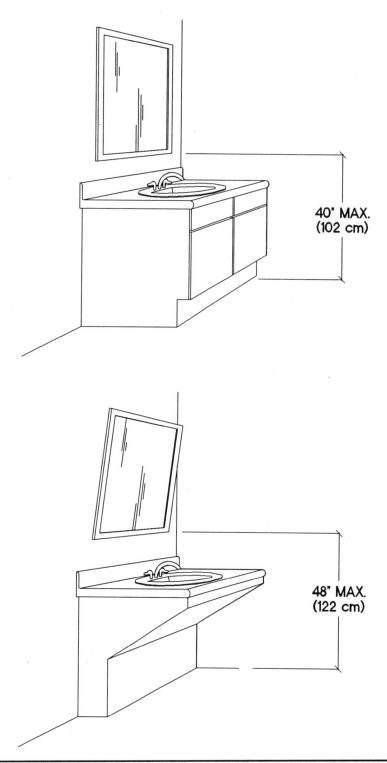

Figure 331 **Guideline 13 -** *The bottom edge of the mirror over the lavatory should be a maximum of 40" (102cm) above the floor or a maximum of 48" (122cm) above the floor if it is tilted.*

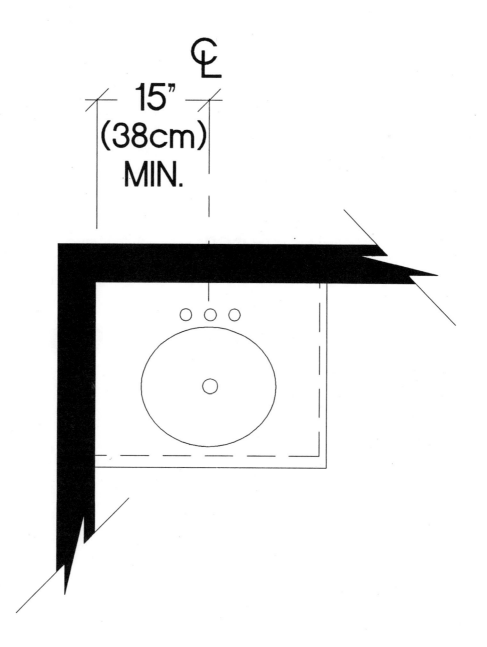

Figure 332 **Guideline 14 -** *The minimum clearance from the centerline of the lavatory to any side wall is 15" (38cm).*

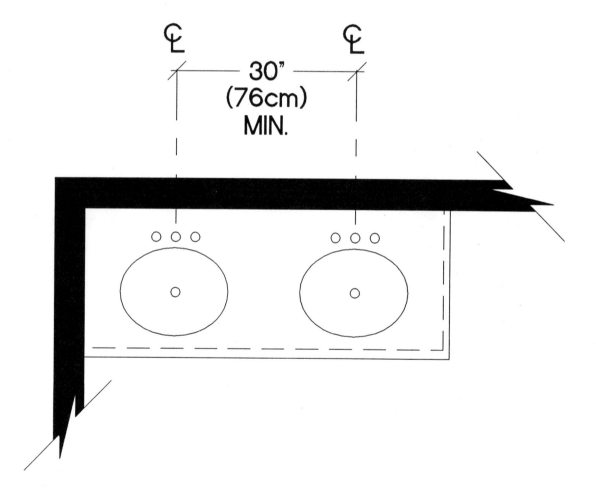

Figure 333 **Guideline 15 -** *The minimum clearance between two bowls in the lavatory center is 30"*
(76cm), centerline to centerline.

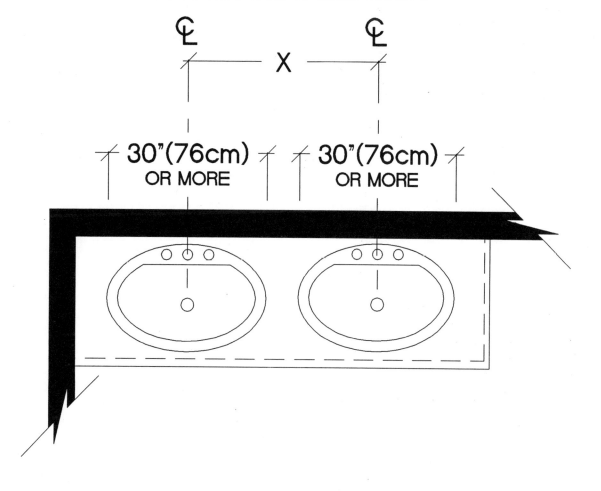

Figure 334 **Guideline 15 Clarification -** *When using lavatories that are 30" (76cm) wide or greater, the minimum distance of 30" (76cm) between centerlines of the two bowls must be increased to allow proper installation of each lavatory.*

SECTION III: Showers and Bathtubs

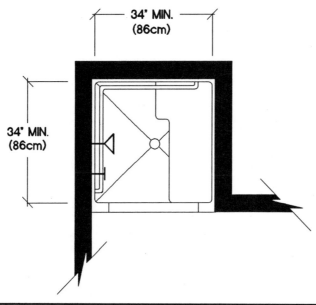

Figure 335 **Guideline 16 -** *In an enclosed shower, the minimum usable interior dimensions are 34" (86cm) x 34" (86cm). These dimensions are measured from wall to wall. Grab bars, controls, movable and folding seats do not diminish the measurement.*

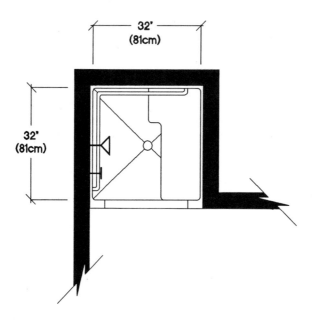

Figure 336 **Guideline 16 Clarification -** *While a designer should always try to meet this goal, physical constraints of a job site may require deviation from the guideline. If a 34" x 34" (86cm x 86cm) interior dimension is unavailable, these dimensions may be reduced to 32" x 32"(81cm x 81cm). Be aware that this compromise may not allow for full use by all people.*

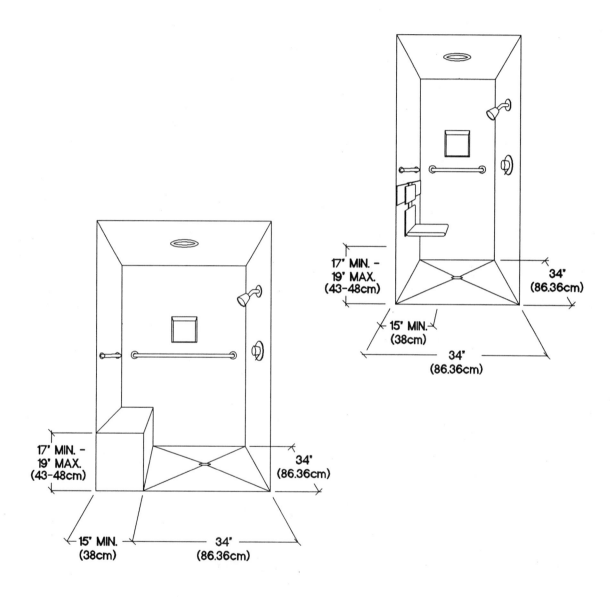

Figure 337
Guideline 17 - *Showers should include a bench or seat that is 17-19" (43cm-48cm) above the floor and a minimum of 15" (38cm) deep.*

Guideline 17 Clarification 1 - *Built-in permanent seats should not encroach upon the minimum 34" x 34" (86cm x 86cm) interior clear floor space of the shower.*

Guideline 17 Clarification 2 - *Reinforced wall supports for future placement of hanging and folding seat hardware should be planned at the time of shower installation.*

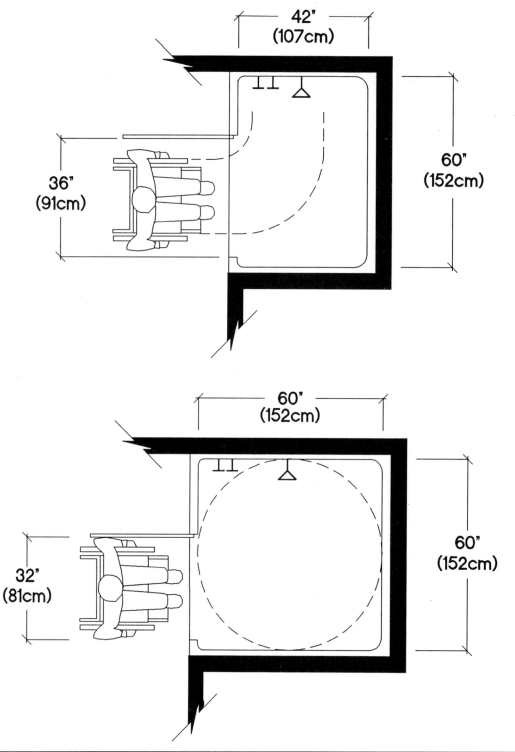

Figure 338 **Guideline 18 -** *The width of the door opening must take into consideration the interior space in the shower for entry and maneuvering. When the shower is 60" (152cm) deep, a person can enter straight into the shower and turn after entry, therefore 32" (81cm) is adequate. If the shower is 42" (107cm) deep, the entry must be increased to 36" (91cm) in order to allow for turning space.*

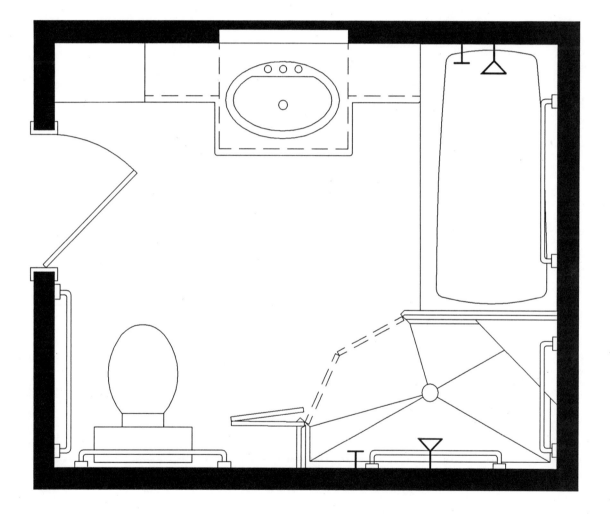

Figure 339 **Guideline 19 -** *Shower doors must open **into** the bathroom.*

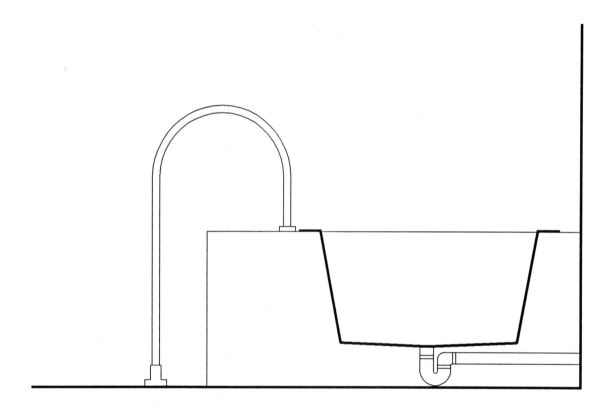

Figure 340 **Guideline 20 -** Steps should **not** be planned at the bathtub or shower area. Safety rails should be installed to facilitate transfer to and from the fixture.

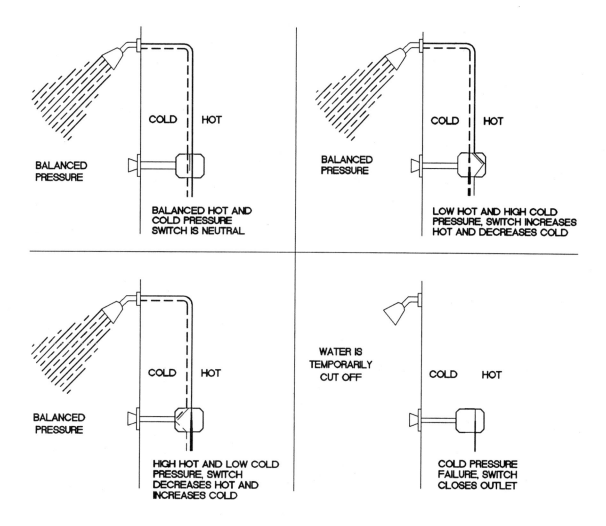

Figure 341 **Guideline 21 -** *All showerheads should be equipped with pressure balance/temperature regulator or temperature limiting device.*

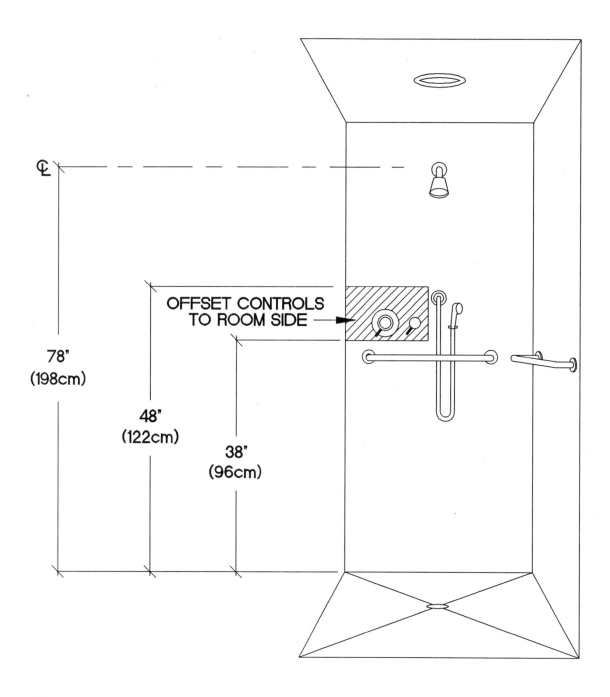

C̶L̶

78"
(198cm)

OFFSET CONTROLS
TO ROOM SIDE ◄—

48"
(122cm)

38"
(96cm)

Figure 342

Guideline 22a - *Shower controls should be accessible from inside and outside the fixture. Shower controls should be located between 38"-48" (96cm - 122cm) above the floor (placed above the grab bar) and offset toward the room.*

Guideline 22a Clarification - *A handheld showerhead may be used in place of or in addition to a fixed showerhead. When mounted, a handheld showerhead should be no higher than 48" (122cm) in its lowest position.*

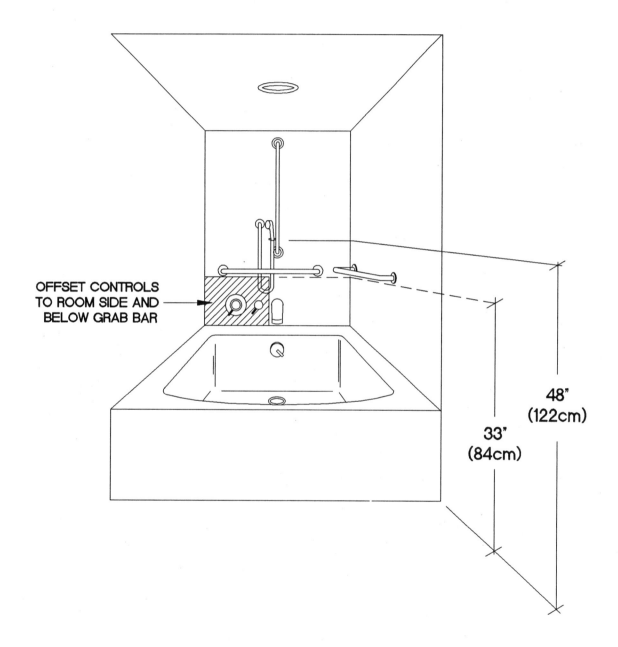

OFFSET CONTROLS
TO ROOM SIDE AND
BELOW GRAB BAR

48"
(122cm)

33"
(84cm)

Figure 343 **Guideline 22b** - *Bathtub controls should be accessible from inside and outside the fixture. Bathtub controls should be located between the rim of the bathtub and 33" (84cm) above the floor, placed below the grab bar and offset toward the room.*

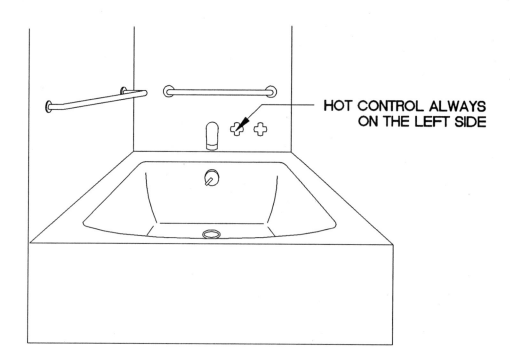

HOT CONTROL ALWAYS
ON THE LEFT SIDE

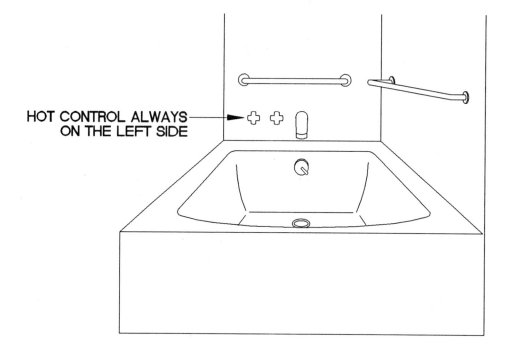

HOT CONTROL ALWAYS
ON THE LEFT SIDE

*Figure 344   **Guideline 22b Clarification -** If separate hot and cold controls are used in a bathtub (not permissible in a shower), for safe use the hot control is always on the left as viewed from inside the fixture.*

SECTION IV: Toilets and Bidets

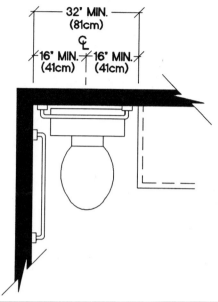

Figure 345 **Guideline 23a -** *A minimum 16" (41cm) clearance should be allowed from the centerline of the toilet or bidet to any obstruction, fixture or equipment (except grab bars) on either side.*

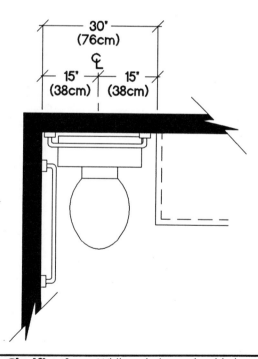

Figure 346 **Guideline 23a Clarification -** *While a designer should always try to meet this goal, physical constraints of a job site may require deviation from the guideline. If a 32" (81cm) clearance is unavailable, this space may be reduced to 30" (76cm). Be aware that this compromise may not allow for full use by all people.*

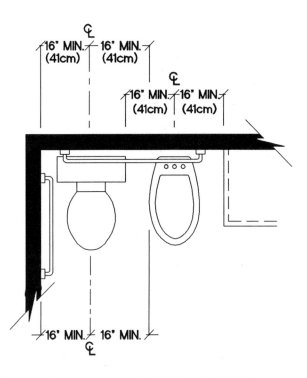

Figure 347 **Guideline 23b** *- When the toilet and bidet are planned adjacent to one another, the 16" minimum (41cm) centerline clearance to all obstructions should be maintained.*

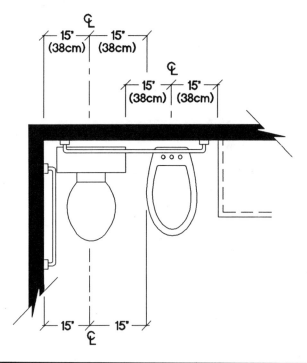

Figure 348 **Guideline 23b Clarification** *- While a designer should always try to meet this goal, physical constraints of a job site may require deviation from the guideline. If a 16" (41cm) centerline clearance to an obstruction is unavailable, this centerline clearance may be reduced to 15" (38cm). Be aware that this compromise may not allow for full use by all people.*

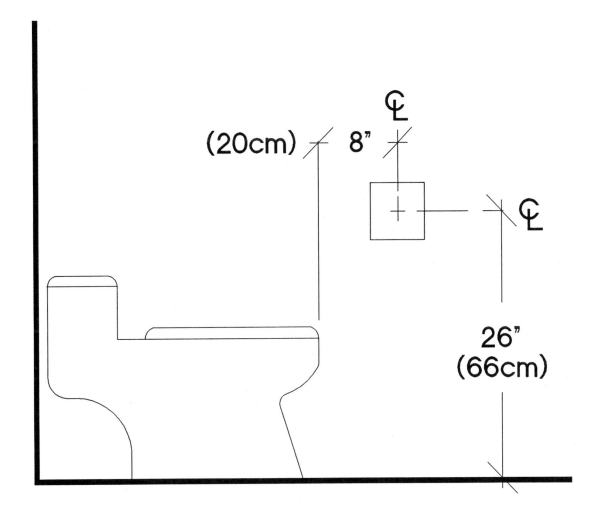

RECOMMENDED TOILET PAPER
HOLDER LOCATION

Figure 349 **Guideline 24 -** *The toilet paper holder should be installed within reach of a person seated on the toilet. Ideal location is slightly in front of the edge of the toilet bowl, centered at 26" (66cm) above the floor.*

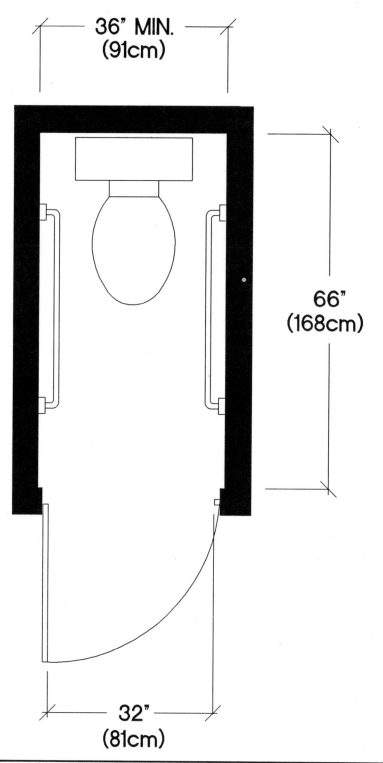

Figure 350 **Guideline 25** - *Compartmental toilet areas should be a minimum 36" (91cm) x 66" (168cm) with a swing-out door or a pocket door.*

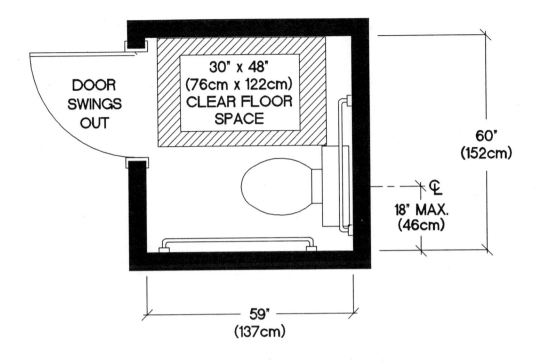

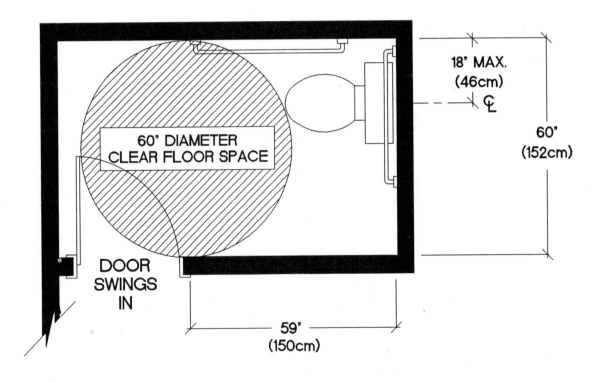

Figure 351 **Guideline 25 Clarification -** *The amount of space needed for a private toilet area will be affected by the mobility of the person using it.*

SECTION V: Grab bars, Storage and Flooring

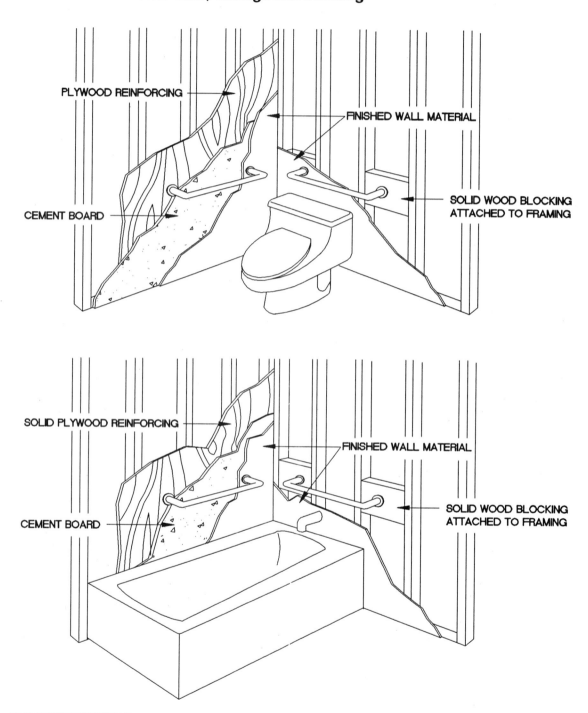

PLYWOOD REINFORCING

FINISHED WALL MATERIAL

CEMENT BOARD

SOLID WOOD BLOCKING ATTACHED TO FRAMING

SOLID PLYWOOD REINFORCING

FINISHED WALL MATERIAL

CEMENT BOARD

SOLID WOOD BLOCKING ATTACHED TO FRAMING

Figure 352 **Guideline 26** - *Walls should be prepared (reinforced) at the time of construction to allow for installation of grab bars. Grab bars should also be installed in the bathtub, shower and toilet areas at the time of construction.*

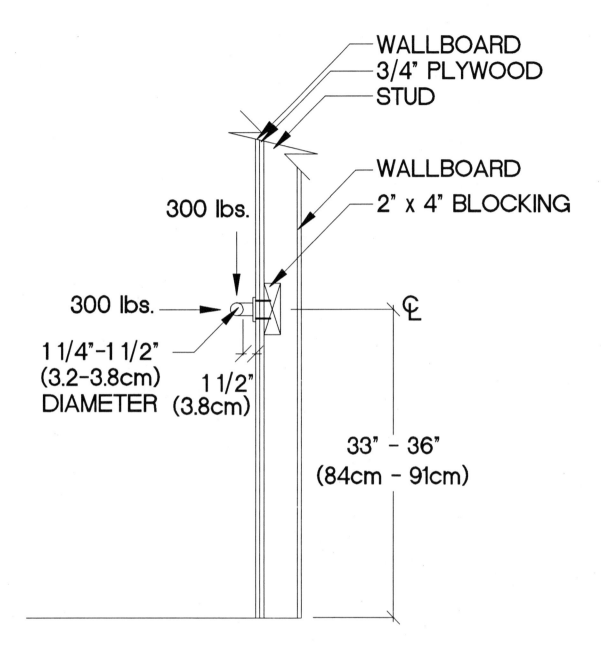

WALLBOARD
3/4" PLYWOOD
STUD

WALLBOARD
2" x 4" BLOCKING

300 lbs.

300 lbs.

1 1/4"-1 1/2"
(3.2-3.8cm)
DIAMETER

1 1/2"
(3.8cm)

℄

33" - 36"
(84cm - 91cm)

GRAB BAR SPECIFICATIONS

Figure 353
Guideline 26 Clarification 1 - *Reinforced areas must bear a static load of 300 lbs. (136kg). The use of cement board does not negate the need for blocking or plywood reinforcing.*

Guideline 26 Clarification 2 - *Grab bars should be installed 33" - 36" (84cm - 91cm) above the floor, should be 1 1/4"-1 1/2" (3.2cm-3.8cm) diameter, extend 1 1/2 (3.8cm) from the wall, support a 300 lbs. (136 kg) load, and they should have a slip-resistant surface. When shapes other than round are used for grab bars, the width of the largest point should not exceed 2" (5.1cm). Towel bars must not be substituted as grab bars.*

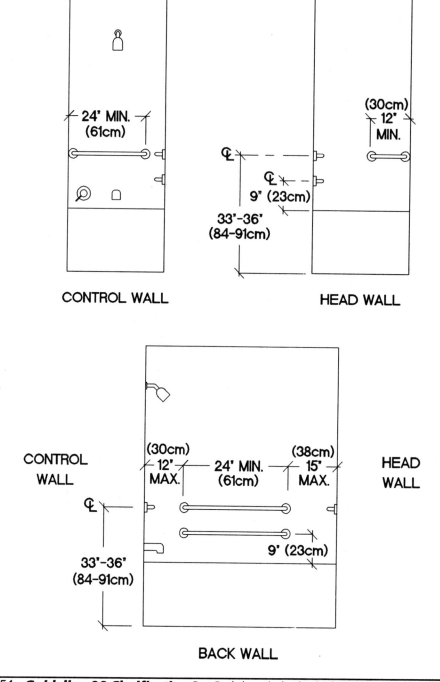

CONTROL WALL

HEAD WALL

BACK WALL

Figure 354 **Guideline 26 Clarification 3 -** *Grab bars in bathtub/shower areas should be at least 24" (61cm) wide on the control wall, at least 12" (30cm) wide on the head wall and at least 24" (61cm) wide on the back wall, beginning no more than 12" (30cm) from the control wall and no more than 15" (38cm) from the head wall. If a second grab bar is desired on the back wall, it should be located 9" (23cm) above the bathtub deck, the same width as the grab bar above it.*

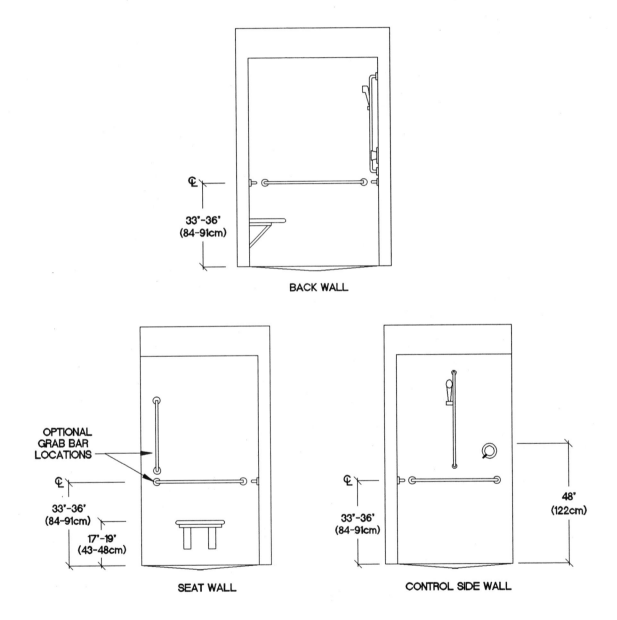

Figure 355 **Guideline 26 Clarification 4 -** *Grab bars in shower stalls should be included on each surrounding wall (optional on wall where bench is located) and should be no more than 9" (23cm) shorter than the width of the wall to which they are attached.*

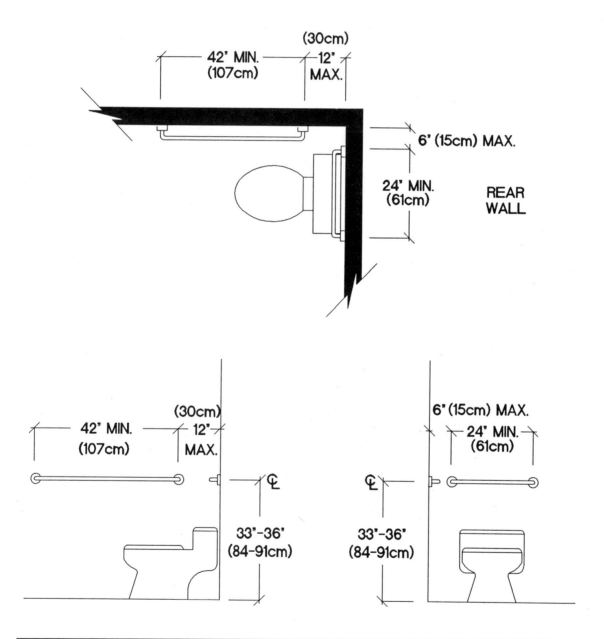

Figure 356 **Guideline 26 Clarification 5a -** *The first grab bar in the toilet area should be located on the side wall closest to the toilet, a maximum 12" (30cm) from the rear wall. It should be at least 42" (107cm) wide. An optional secondary grab bar in the toilet area may be located on the rear wall, a maximum 6" (15cm) from the side wall. It should be at least 24" (61cm) wide.*

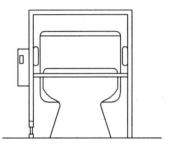

SIDE GRAB BARS ATTACHED
BELOW TOILET SEAT

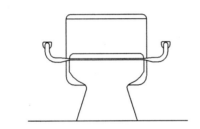

ELECTRONIC SEAT
ELEVATOR

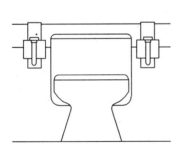

RAIL SYSTEM WITH
SUPPORT ARMS

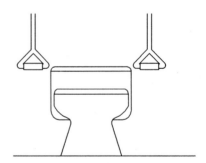

HAND RAILS SUSPENDED
FROM CEILING

Figure 357 **Guideline 26 Clarification 5b** - *Alternatives for grab bars in the toilet area include, but are not limited to, side grab bars attached below the toilet seat, a rail system mounted to the back wall with perpendicular support arms at sides of the toilet seat, an electronic seat elevator or hand rails suspended from the ceiling.*

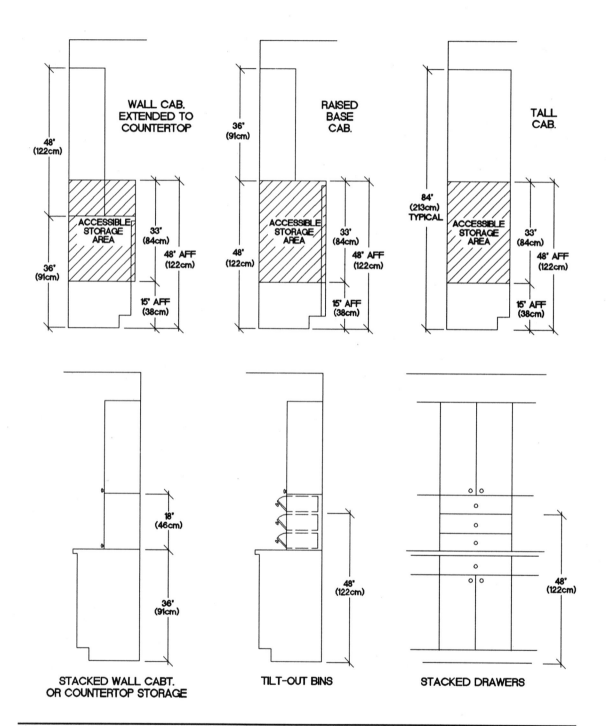

Figure 358 **Guideline 27 -** *Storage for toiletries, linens, grooming and general bathroom supplies should be provided within 15" - 48" (38cm - 122cm) above the floor.*

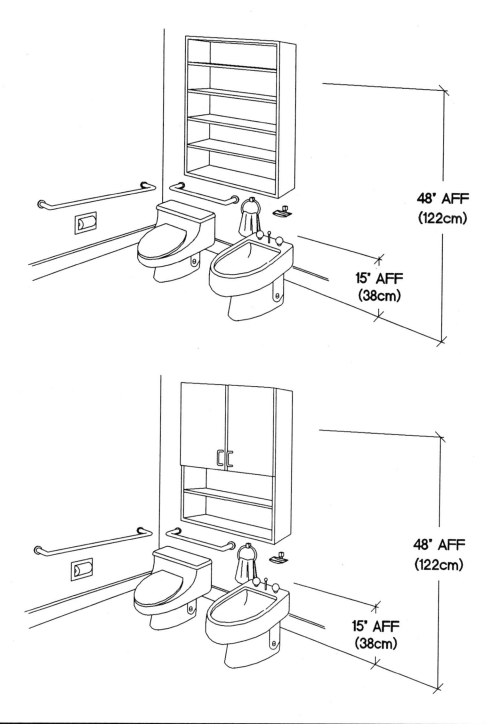

Figure 359 **Guideline 28 -** *Storage for soap, towels and other personal hygiene items should be installed within reach of a person seated on the bidet or toilet and within 15" - 48" (38cm - 122cm) above the floor. Storage areas should not interfere with the use of the fixture.*

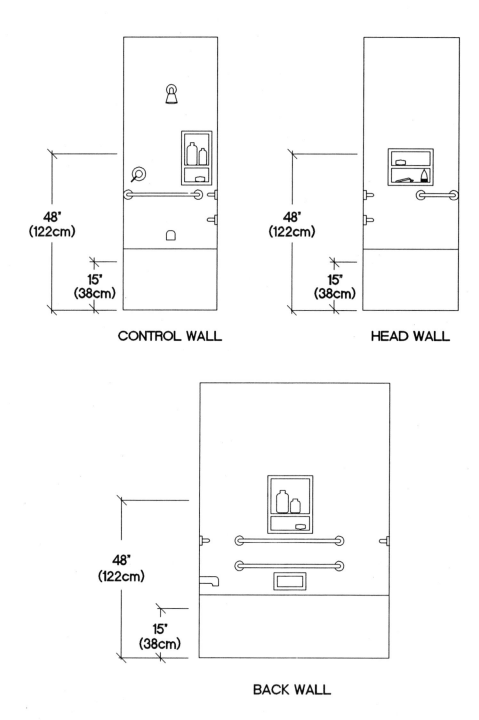

Figure 360   **Guideline 29 -** *In the bathtub/shower area, storage for soap, and other personal hygiene items should be provided within the 15" - 48" (38cm - 122cm) above the floor within the universal reach range.*

Figure 361   ***Guideline 30*** - *All flooring should be slip resistant.*

SECTION VI: Controls and Mechanical Systems

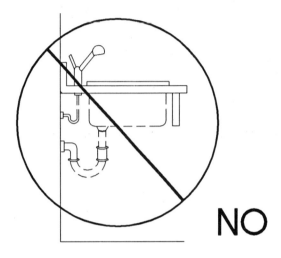

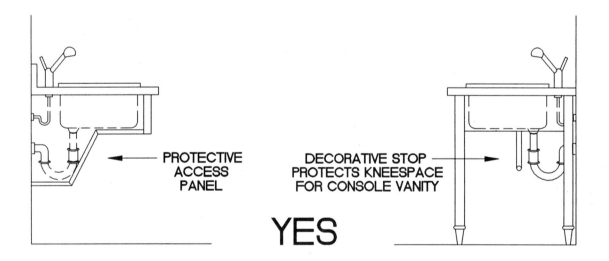

Figure 362 **Guideline 31** - *Exposed pipes and mechanicals should be covered by a protective panel or shroud. When using a console table, care must be given to keep plumbing attractive and out of contact with a seated user.*

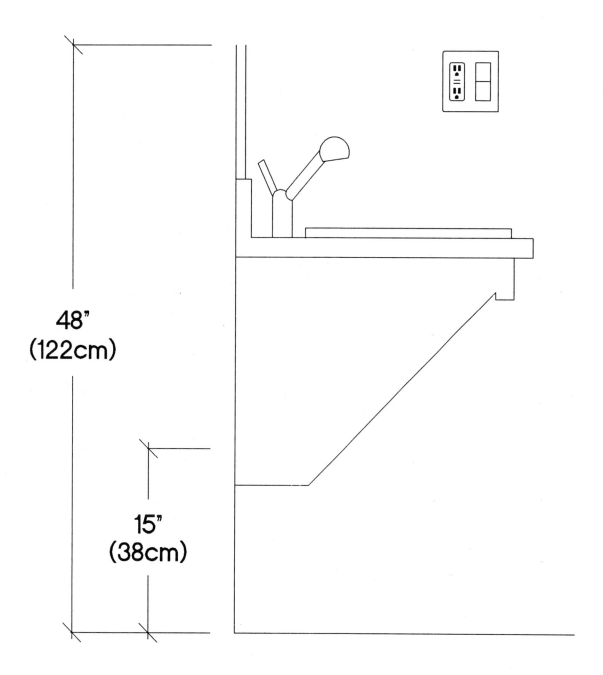

Figure 363 **Guideline 32 -** *Controls, dispensers, outlets and operating mechanisms should be 15" - 48" (38cm -122cm) above the floor and should be operable with a closed fist.*

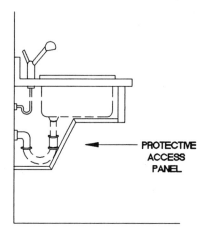

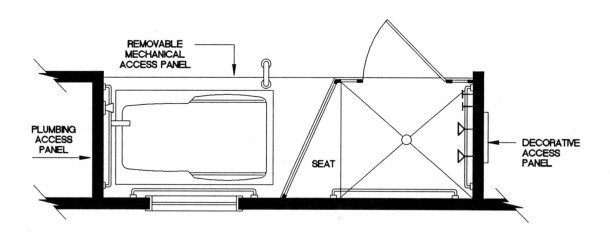

Figure 364 **Guideline 33** - *All mechanical, electrical and plumbing systems should have access panels.*

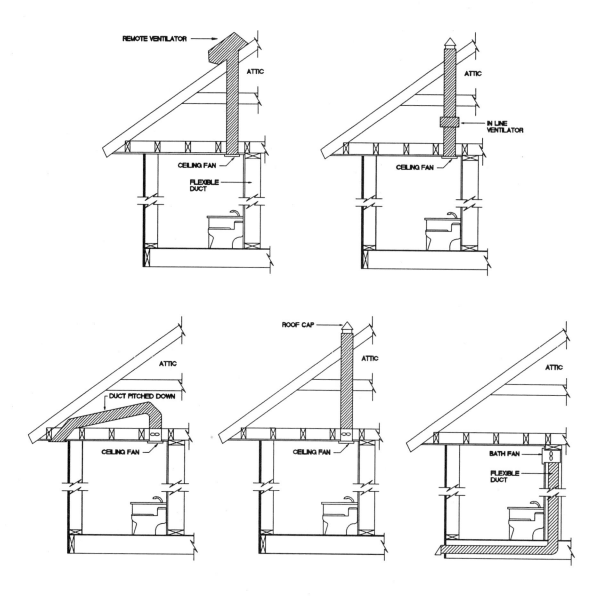

Figure 365 **Guideline 34 -** *Mechanical ventilation systems to the outside should be included in the plan to vent the entire room. The minimum size of the system can be calculated as follows:*

$$\frac{Cubic\ Space\ (LxWxH)\ x\ 8\ (changes\ of\ air\ per\ hour)}{60\ minutes} = minimum\ cubic\ feet\ per\ minute\ (CFM)$$

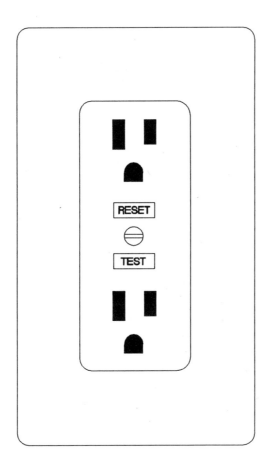

*Figure 366 **Guideline 35** - Ground fault circuit interrupters must be specified on all receptacles, lights and switches in the bathroom. All light fixtures above the bathtub/shower units must be moisture-proof special-purpose fixtures.*

HEAT LAMP   HEAT/FAN/LIGHT

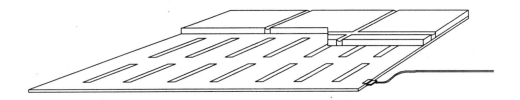

RADIANT FLOOR SYSTEM

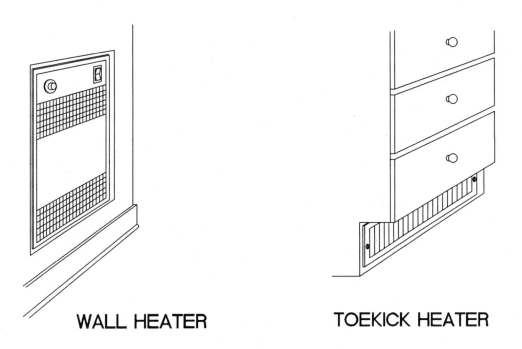

WALL HEATER   TOEKICK HEATER

Figure 367 **Guideline 36 -** *In addition to a primary heat source, auxiliary heating may be planned in the bathroom.*

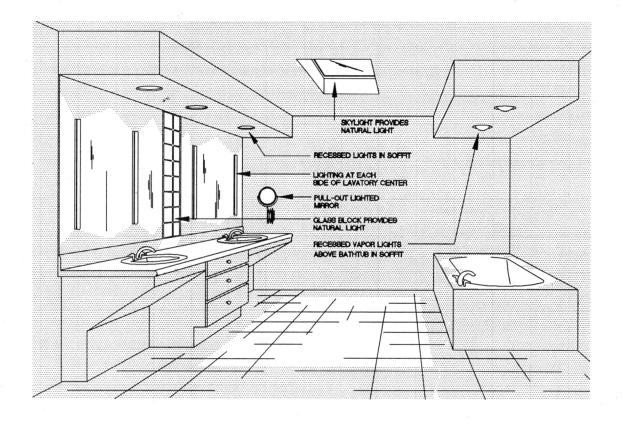

SKYLIGHT PROVIDES
NATURAL LIGHT

RECESSED LIGHTS IN SOFFIT

LIGHTING AT EACH
SIDE OF LAVATORY CENTER

PULL-OUT LIGHTED
MIRROR

GLASS BLOCK PROVIDES
NATURAL LIGHT

RECESSED VAPOR LIGHTS
ABOVE BATHTUB IN SOFFIT

Figure 368 **Guideline 37 -** *Every functional area in the bathroom should be well illuminated by appropriate task lighting, night lights and/or general lighting. No lighting fixture, including hanging fixtures, should be within reach of a person seated or standing in the bathtub/shower area.*

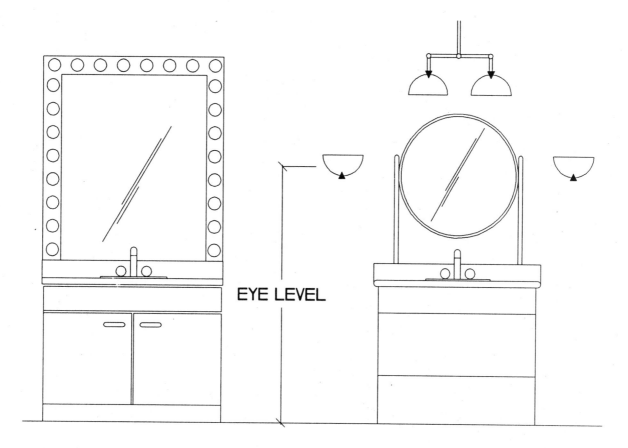

EYE LEVEL

Figure 369 **Guideline 37 Clarification -** *The vanity area should include both overhead and side lighting locations. Side lighting may be planned at eye level which will be approximately 3" (8cm) below a users overall height.*

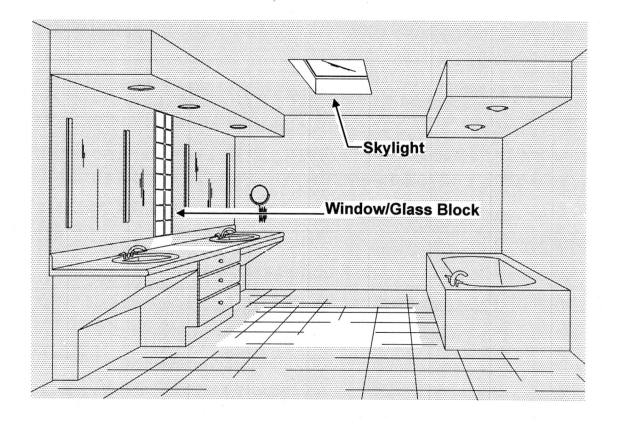

Figure 370 **Guideline 38 -** *When possible, bathroom lighting should include a window/skylight area equal to a minimum of 10% of the square footage of the bathroom.*

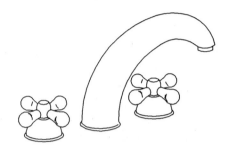

**EASY GRIP
TWO HANDLE
TUB FILLER/CONTROLS**

**SINGLE LEVER
SHOWER CONTROL**

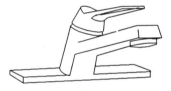

**SINGLE LEVER
LAVATORY FAUCET**

**INFRARED/MOTION SENSOR
LAVATORY FAUCET**

**TOUCH
SENSITIVE**

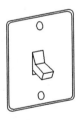

TOGGLE

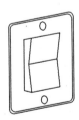

ROCKER

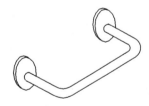

DEEP PULL

Figure 371 **Guideline 39** - *Controls, handles and door/drawer pulls should be operable with one hand, require only a minimal amount of strength for operation, and should not require tight grasping, pinching or twisting of the wrist. (Includes handles knobs/pulls on entry and exit doors, cabinets, drawers and plumbing fixtures, as well as light and thermostat controls/switches, intercoms, and other room controls.)*

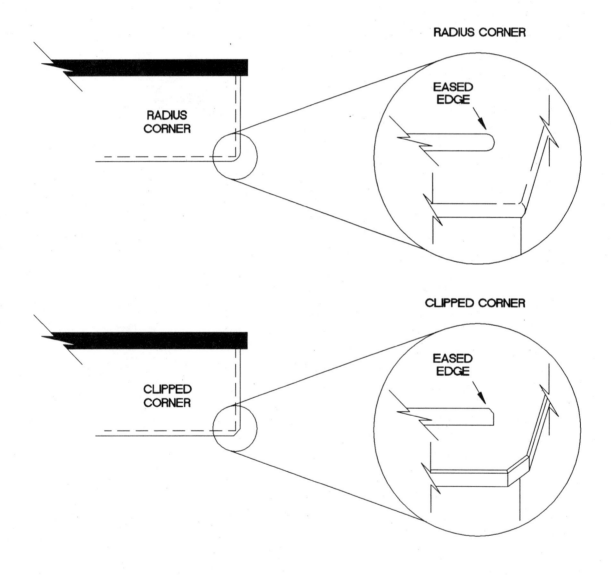

Figure 372 **Guideline 40 -** Use clipped or radius corners for open countertops; countertop edges
should be eased to eliminate sharp edges.

Figure 373 **Guideline 41** - *Any glass used as a bathtub/shower enclosure, partition, or other glass application within 18" (46cm) of the floor should be one of three kinds of safety glazing; laminated glass with a plastic interlayer, tempered glass or approved plastics such as those found in the model safety glazing code.*

SECTION **9**

INTERVIEWING THE CLIENT - FINDING OUT WHAT THE FAMILY WANTS

GATHERING YOUR INFORMATION

Before you apply any of the bathroom planning principles, you must interview the client and inspect the jobsite in order to identify the family's wants and needs, the jobsite limitations and the funds available for the project. Even the smallest bathroom can fulfill the client's dreams if you, as the designer, take the time to find out what those dreams are.

Depending on your type of business, you'll either complete this interview in the client's home or in your showroom. In either situation, an organized list helps you to ask all the important questions. The National Kitchen and Bath Association offers an interview form to help you gather all pertinent information.

The form covers the following areas:

- General Client Information

- Specific Bathroom Questions

- Design Information

- A Storage Checklist

- Product/Project Specifications

- Existing Construction Details

- Jobsite Dimensions

At first glance, this form might seem too long. Don't be intimidated by its length. Look at the individual segments and identify which are appropriate for your business. Only NKBA members can use this copyrighted form or modify it as they see fit.

REVIEWING THE SURVEY FORM

Cover Sheet

The cover sheet is designed to record all of the specific client information. The residence and the jobsite address (if different) are noted. Space for all appropriate telephone numbers is included. If the family is working with an allied professional, jot the necessary information in the bottom right-hand corner. Presentation dates are highlighted in the lower left-hand corner. These remind you to schedule an appointment to present your ideas during your first meeting, or indicate that you'll call them for an appointment when the design is ready. Use this form to jot down the times that are most convenient for your clients. This will help you schedule your time more efficiently.

BATH DESIGN SURVEY FORM

Name: _____

Residence Address: _____

_____

Jobsite Address: _____

_____

Phone: _____

Work: _____

Work: _____

Date: _____

Designer: _____

Appointment:

Scheduled: _____

Call When Ready: _____

Times Available: _____

Directions: _____

Allied Professionals:

Name: _____

Firm: _____

Address: _____

Phone: _____

General Client Information

If the clients are planning to re-model, start by asking how long they've lived at their present address and when the house was built. This information is important when you begin to consider construction constraints.

Next ask: "*How did you learn about our firm?*" By obtaining this information from each client you'll be able to track where most of your business comes from; referrals, the Yellow Pages, show-room location or another source.

Ask when the homeowners would like to start and to finish the project. The dates could affect the materials you specify. It is also helpful to know if the prospective clients have worked with any other designers in the past. If so, ask what they were dissatisfied with and why they're still looking for the expert they wish to do business with.

The form also helps you find out if an allied professional or a specific builder will be part of the design and/or construction team. You can use the questions to determine if the clients plan to handle any portion of the project on their own.

Next ask: "*What budget range have you established for your bathroom project?*" If your clients hesitate to reveal the budget, impress on them that unless you have an established budget figure from them, you cannot begin the planning process. *Why?* Because the budget will affect the extensiveness of the construction changes and the number and quality of products specified.

Many designers waste a great deal of time designing rooms that don't fall within the budget for the project - because they neglected to find out the financial parameters during the information gathering stage.

Pricing a bathroom is easy if there's little or no design involved. Add up the prices of the products, include set charges for any other services and complete the estimate. Completely redesigning a room requires a different approach.

To prepare yourself to lead the budget discussion you need to understand how the cost of different portions of the project affects the overall price.

The brands, style and quality of the products specified affect the item price. You might specify a two-piece, standard white, toilet that retails for $159.00 or a $1,200.00 low-profile, one-piece toilet in a designer color. Such cost differences greatly affect the selling price of the bathroom. To easily explain this to your client try to separate the products that you represent into good, better, best and ultra categories.

The amount of equipment needed will have a major impact on the price of the project. *For example,* a 120" (304.8cm) wall of vanity cabinetry is more costly than a single 36" (91.44cm) wide vanity cabinet.

Specifying major structural changes to accommodate the new plan can boost the labor cost so that it equals or exceeds the total cost of all the materials combined.

Next, determine the reasons for remodeling. If the home is being remodeled for long-term investment, the owners may be willing to invest more money than if they're simply "fixing up" the house to sell it.

Determine exactly who is going to make the final buying decision. *"How do you do that?"* Ask survey question 13.

Once you've gathered the business and family information, it's time to find out about the room itself. *What do the clients dislike about their present bathroom? What do they like about the room?*

General Client Information

1. How long have you lived at, or how much time do you spend at the jobsite residence?_____

2. When was the house built?_____ How old is the present bathroom? _____

3. How did you learn about our firm?_____

4. When would you like to start the project?_____

5. When would you like the project to be completed?_____
   _____

6. Has anyone assisted you in preparing a design for the bathroom? _____
   _____

7. Do you plan on retaining an interior designer or architect to assist in the bathroom planning?_____
   _____

8. Do you have a specific builder/contractor or other subcontractor/specialist with whom you would like to work? _____
   _____

9. What portion of the project, if any, will be your responsibility? _____
   _____

10. What budget range have you established for your bathroom project? _____

11. How long do you intend to own the jobsite residence?_____

12. What are your plans regarding this home? _____
    a. Is it a long or short-term investment? _____
    b. Is return on investment a primary concern? _____
    c. Do you plan on renting the jobsite residence in the future? _____

13. What family members will share in the final decision-making process?_____
    _____

14. Would you like our firm to assist you in securing project financing? _____Yes _____ No

15. What do you dislike most about your present bathroom? _____
    _____
    _____

16. What do you like about your present bathroom? _____
    _____
    _____

BMF7

Specific Bathroom Questions

After you know a bit about the family and the reasons for the project, it's time to concentrate on the specifics of the bathroom under discussion.

The next section of the interview form reminds you to find out what type of bathroom it is, who uses it, when they use it and if they use it alone or with other people. Specific activities that take place in the bathroom and specific equipment needs are also identified in this section of the survey.

This information will help personalize the space. *For example,* ask about their habits when washing their own hair or that of children so that the appropriate lavatory height can be specified.

The *"Family Member Characteristics"* chart gives you a spot to jot down any minor physical limitations or special requests the users of the space might have. Special attention should be paid to a room designed for an older client or someone who is physically limited. Be sure to take limited sight, balance problems or grasping difficulties into consideration. Regardless of age, many people suffer from these limitations.

The ability to incorporate solutions to these physical limitations in the bathroom is an important part of successful design. *For example,* include a make-up area with a pull-out mirror for a client who has poor sight. If any major physical disabilities need to be considered, use the supplement form found in Section 11, Barrier-Free Planning.

Specific Bathroom Questions

1. Is this a master _____ , children _____ , or guest _____ bath project?

2. How many bathrooms are in the home?_____
_____

3. Who will use the bathroom?_____

4. What is the primary time of day that the bathroom is used? _____

5. On an average, how long does each user stay in the bathroom?_____
_____

6. How many family members will use the bathroom at one time?_____

7. Have you considered privacy zoning to allow several users to occupy the space at one time? _____

8. Do you prefer separate showering and bathing areas?_____

9. Would you like to consider either a tub or shower that will accommodate more than one person?_____

10. Do you prefer that the water closet and/or bidet be separated from the other fixtures, and placed in its own compartment? _____

11. What activities will take place in the bathroom?

Applying Make-up/	Dressing _____	Reading/Lounging_____	Water Relaxation:
Hair Care _____	Exercising _____	Showering _____	1. Sauna _____
Bathing _____	Laundering _____	Sunning _____	2. Steam _____
			3. Whirlpool _____

12. What appliances do you plan on using in the bathroom?_____

Bar Sink _____	Curling Iron _____	Microwave _____	Towel Warmer:
Blowdryer:	Electrical	Radio _____	Hydronic _____
Hand-Held _____	Toothbrush_____	Refrigerator _____	Electric _____
Wallmount _____	Hot Plate _____	Television _____	
Coffeemaker _____	Hot Rollers_____	Other_____	

13. Other: _____

14. Family Member Characteristics:

Name	Age	Handed (left or right)	Height	Physical Limitations

BMF7

Design Information

The *"Design Information"* questions
help you create a bathroom that looks
as good as it functions.

Design Information

1. What type of feeling would you like your new bathroom space to have?

   Sleek/Contemporary _____ Welcoming/Country _____ Traditional _____

   Strictly Functional _____ An Adult Retreat Feeling _____ Other _____

2. What colors are you considering for your new bathroom? _____

3. What colors do you like _____ and dislike _____ ?

4. What are color preferences of other family members? _____

5. How important is it to you that the bathroom flow to adjacent spaces, from a design similarity standpoint? _____

   _____

6. Can the bathroom make its own individual design statement? _____

7. Have you made a sketch or collected pictures of ideas for your new bathroom? _____

8. Design Notes:

   _____

   _____

   _____

   _____

   _____

   _____

   _____

   _____

   _____

   _____

   _____

Storage Checklist

Even the smallest 5' x 7' (152.4cm x 213.36cm) bathroom can be more than a room filled with three primary fixtures. You should be a storage specialist as well as a bathroom planner. Therefore, the survey includes a list of specific types of storage needs the client might request in the bathroom.

Take a few moments to find out if any of these specific items are important to the client and you'll do a better job customizing the room for the needs of the user.

Storage Checklist

1. Clothing Closets   Yes_____ No _____   Shelf Length: His_____ Hers _____
   Double Pole _____ Single Pole _____

2. Laundry Facilities   Yes_____ No_____   Equipment Size _____

3. Plant Area, Sunning Space   Yes_____ No_____   Size _____

4. Medicine Storage   Yes_____ No_____   Shelf Length _____

5. Bath Linen Storage   Yes_____ No_____   Shelf Length _____

6. Bathroom Paper Product Storage   Yes_____ No_____   Shelf Length _____

7. Shoe Polishing Paraphernalia Storage   Yes_____ No_____   Shelf Length _____

8. Cleaning Supply Storage   Yes_____ No_____   Shelf Length _____

9. Hair Grooming Equipment Storage   Yes_____ No_____   For Whom _____

   What type or equipment _____

   _____

   _____ Shelf Length _____

10. Hand and Foot Grooming Storage   Yes_____ No _____   For Whom _____

    What type of equipment _____

    _____

    _____ Shelf Length _____

11. Personal Hygiene Equipment Storage   Yes_____ No_____   For Whom _____

12. Make-up and Shaving Equipment Storage   Yes_____ No_____   For Whom _____

    What type of equipment _____

    _____

13. Personal Pampering Item Storage   Yes_____ No _____   For Whom _____

    What type of equipment _____

    _____

    _____ Shelf Length _____

14. Other _____

_____

_____

_____

_____

_____

_____

_____

_____

Project Specifications

The interview form then identifies each major product category and gives you an excellent chart to record pertinent information about these key elements of the bathroom.

Part of the chart allows you to note whether you, the bathroom specialist, or the owner, is going to furnish the item and install it. Typical choices, finishes and materials are listed. In many cases, most of this information will be based on the designer's recommendations. In other cases, the client will have specific requests or might have identified preferences when you toured the showroom with them.

Some designers rely heavily on this section of the survey, others rarely use it. It is particularly useful if you work in partnership with other employees of the firm who prepare your drawings or detailed specifications. If you fill this part of the form out at the jobsite or while you're visiting with the client in the office, you'll do a better job gathering all the information you need to share with your design colleague.

Project Specifications

Category	Source					Description
		Furn By		Install By		
	Use Exist	BS	O/OA	BS	O/OA	Check Appropriate Space(s)
Cabinetry						_____Wood Species _____ Decorative Lam. _____ Steel _____ Other Accessories _____
Countertops						_____ Wood _____ Decorative Lam. _____ Marble _____ Cultured Marble _____ Granite _____ Solid Surface _____ Tile _____Size _____Grout _____ Countertop Ext. over Water Closet Backsplash: Height _____ Edge Treatment _____ End Splash Sides _____ _____
Fascia/Soffit						_____ Open _____Flush _____ Extended _____ Recessed _____ Wallpaper _____ Paint _____ Wood _____ Lighted _____ Gallery Rail Other _____
Bath Fixtures Fittings & Finishes Water Closet						_____ 1 Piece _____2 Piece _____ Wall Hung _____ High Flush Tank _____ Elongated _____ Round _____ Handicapped Color _____ Trip Lever Finish _____ Stop & Supply Finish _____
Bidet						_____ Vert. Spray _____ Horiz. Spray Color _____ Faucet Finish _____ Vacuum Breaker _____
Tub						_____Cast Iron _____Steel _____Fiberglass _____Acrylic _____Ceramic Tile _____Whirlpool _____Cult. Marble _____Skirted _____Platform _____Platform w/steps _____Left Drain _____Right Drain _____Other Color _____ Whirlpool Access _____ Waste & Overflow Finish _____ Fitting Type _____ Finish _____ Fitting Location _____

KEY   BS = Bathroom Specialist   O = Owner   OA = Owner's Agent

BMF7

Category	Source					Description
	Furn By		**Install By**			
	Use Exist	BS	O/OA	BS	O/OA	Check Appropriate Space(s)
Bath Fixtures (Continued) Shower						_____ 1 Piece _____ Multiple Piece Shower Wall Material _____ Shower Floor Material _____ Shower Valve #1 Type _____ Shower Valve #2 Type _____ Shower Head #1 Type _____ Shower Head #2 Type _____ Body Sprays _____ Hand-Held Showers _____ Diverter _____ Shower Drain _____ Finish _____ Grooming Recess_____ Size _____ Bench _____ Size _____ Other _____
Lavatory						_____ Pedestal/ _____ Wall-Hung Trap Cover _____ Rimmed _____ Self-Rimmed _____ Under-Counter _____ Integral _____ 4" Centers _____ 8" Centers _____ Single Hole No. of Bowls _____ Size _____ Adjacent to one another? _____ Separate from one another?_____ Both in bathroom?_____ One located outside of bathroom? _____ Color _____ Fitting Type_____ Finish _____ Drilling Spread_____
Ventilation						_____ Fan _____ Fan, Light (Combo) _____ Fan, Light, Heat (Combo) _____ Switch _____ Timer CFM Capacity_____ Duct Work Space _____
Heat Lamp						_____ Switch _____ Timer Placement_____
Enclosures (Steam Door/s, Shower Doors, Drapes, Etc.)						_____ Tub _____ Shower _____ Steam_____ Finish _____ Size _____ Type _____ Material _____ Curtain Rod Finish_____ Size _____ Curtain(s) Color _____ Size _____
Light Fixtures						_____ Incandescent _____ Fluorescent _____ Vapor Proof _____ Halogen

Category	Source					Description
		Furn. By		Install By		
	Use Exist	BS	O/OA	BS	O/OA	Check appropriate space(s)
Accessories Glass Shelves Medicine Cabinet, Mirror						_____ Surface Mt. _____ Recessed Size _____ Color _____ Mirror Size _____ Shelf Size _____ Edge Treatment _____
Towel Bars						Finish _____ Size _____ No. _____
Towel Rings						Finish _____ Size _____ No. _____
Robe Hooks						Finish _____ Size _____ No. _____
Tub Soap Dish						_____ Surface Mt. _____ Recessed Finish _____ Placement _____
Shower Soap Dish						_____ Surface Mt. _____ Recessed Finish _____ Placement _____
Bidet Soap Dish						_____ Surface Mt. _____ Recessed Finish _____ Placement _____
Lavatory Soap Dish						_____ Surface Mt. _____ Recessed Finish _____ Placement _____
Tub/Shower Grab Bars						Finish _____ Placement _____
Paper Holder						_____ Surface Mt. _____ Recessed Finish _____ Placement _____
Magazine Rack						_____ Surface Mt. _____ Recessed Finish _____ Placement _____
Soap/Lotion Dispenser						Finish _____ Placement _____
Tumbler						Finish _____ Placement _____
Tissue Holder						Finish _____ Placement _____
Scale						Finish _____ Placement _____
Toothbrush Holder						Finish _____ Placement _____
Hamper						Finish _____ Placement _____
Windows and Doors Windows						Casing: _____ Match Existing _____ Finish _____ Replace All _____ Finish _____ Size _____ Profile Size _____ Finish _____ _____ Slider _____ Bow _____ Casement _____ Bay _____ Double-Hung _____ Support _____ Skylight _____ Roof Other _____ Exterior Wall Patch _____ Sink Vent Relocation _____ Pass-Thru Surfacing _____ New Window Sizes: _____ #1 _____ Screen _____ #2 _____ Screen _____ #3 _____ Screen _____ #4 _____ Screen _____

Category	Source					Description
		Furn By		Install By		
	Use Exist	BS	O/OA	BS	O/OA	Check Appropriate Space(s)
Doors						Casing _____ Match Existing _____ Finish _____ Replace All _____ Finish _____ Size _____ Profile New Doors: _____ Solid Core Size _____ Hinge _____ Screen _____ _____ Steel Size _____ Hinge _____ Screen _____ _____ Hollow Core Size _____ Hinge _____ _____ Bifold Size _____ Hinge _____ _____ Pocket Size _____ Hinge _____ _____ Accordian Size _____ Hinge _____ Other _____ Ext. Wall/Floor Patch _____ Hardware: Finish _____ _____ Passage _____ Knob _____ Privacy _____ Lever
Flooring						_____ Carpet _____ Vinyl _____ Marble _____ Wood _____ Tile _____ Size _____ Grout _____ Other _____ _____ Underlayment _____ Sub Floor _____ Water Damage _____ Baseboards _____ Threshholds _____
Decorative Surfaces Wall Covering						Wall Material _____ Ceiling Material _____ Tub Walls & Ceiling _____ Shower Walls & Ceiling _____ Water Damage _____
Window Treatment						_____ Horiz. Blind _____ Vert. Blind _____ Woven Wood _____ Draperies _____ Shade _____ Roman Shade _____ Shutters _____ Greenhouse _____ Other _____
Sauna						Capacity _____ Interior _____ Style _____ Heater _____ Timer Location _____ Wall Material _____ Floor Material _____
Steam Bath						_____ Tub _____ Shower Steam Generator Location _____ Timer Location _____ Wall Material _____ Floor Material _____

Category	Source					Description
		Furn By		Install By		
	Use Exist	BS	O/OA	BS	O/OA	Check Appropriate Space(s)
Exercise Equipment						Types
Construction Electrical						
Plumbing						
General Carpentry Demolition						
Trash Removal						
Structural Changes						
Installation						
Other						

Miscellaneous Information _____

_____

_____

_____

_____

_____

Existing Construction Details

If your business methods include a jobsite inspection for remodeling work, the information that you'll gather under the "*Existing Construction Details*" section is critical.

Creative bathroom plans are firmly grounded in the designer's technical expertise in the mechanical elements of the plan and the designer's knowledge of the construction constraints that exist on the individual jobsites. You learned about typical North American building systems in Volumes 1 and 2 of this series.

The survey form provides you with an organized way to survey the existing conditons on the jobsite. To begin, walk through the house, inspect the basement or attic, and make sure you understand the orientation of the bathroom to the balance of the floor plan.

Next, identify construction limitations: *Where are the water supply pipes located? Are there rooms above and below the bathroom? What kind of condition are the walls, floors and ceilings in? What type of flooring exists and what direction do the floor joists run in? What is the exterior finish of the dwelling?*

Find out what type of windows are used, and if they can be moved. The same two questions need to be answered about doors. These are two very important questions. Oftentimes the overall plan can be dramatically enhanced by a relatively minor interior door change. Or, there may be a spectacular view that the client would like to include in the bathroom. If you don't ask the right questions, you won't gather this information.

Existing Construction Details

Construction:

Construction of House:　☐ Single Story　☐ Multi Story　Style of house _____

Room above or below bathroom: _____

Condition and covering of walls: _____

floors: _____

ceilings: _____

soffit/fascia: _____

Squareness of corners _____ Parallel walls to within 3/4" _____

Construction of Floor:　☐ Slab　☐ Frame

Direction of floor joist:　☐ Parallel to longest wall　☐ Perpendicular to longest wall　Joist Height _____

Exterior:　☐ Brick　☐ Aluminum　☐ Stucco　☐ Wood　☐ Other

Interior:　☐ Drywall　☐ Lath & Plaster　☐ Wood　☐ Stone/Brick

Windows can be changed:　☐ Yes　☐ No

Windows:　☐ Sliders　☐ Double-Hung　☐ Skylights　☐ Casement　☐ Greenhouse

Doors can be relocated:　☐ Yes　☐ No

Location of walls can be changed:　☐ Yes　☐ No　Direction of load bearing partition _____

Sewage System:　☐ City Service　☐ Septic System　☐ Other

Type of roof material _____ Age of roof _____

Household heating/cooling system _____ Age of home _____

Access:

Can equipment fit into room? _____

Basement _____ Crawlspace _____ Attic _____

Material Storage _____ Trash Collection Area _____

Plumbing:

Location of existing vent stack _____ _ Type of trap _____

Electrical:

GFCI existing:　☐ Yes　☐ No

New wiring access:　☐ Hard　☐ Average　☐ Easy

Existing electrical service capacity _____ The following # of 120V circuits available: _____

The following # of 240V circuits available: _____

Can the location of the fixtures be changed?

Water Closet　☐ Yes　☐ No　　　Bidet　　　☐ Yes　☐ No

Lavatory #1　☐ Yes　☐ No　　　Lavatory #2　☐ Yes　☐ No

Bathtub　　☐ Yes　☐ No　　　Shower　　☐ Yes　☐ No

Miscellaneous Information: _____ _____

_____

_____

The next set of questions will help the installation experts: *Can you get material in the house? Where will you store it? What electrical service is available? What needs to be added?*

The form concludes with charts you can use to note the placement of windows, heating/cooling outlets, medicine cabinets, and other mechanical elements. Any fixtures you are retaining or relocating are also dimensioned on the final page. Add a piece of graph paper to the survey to use to take preliminary dimensions.

Existing Wall Elevation Dimensioning

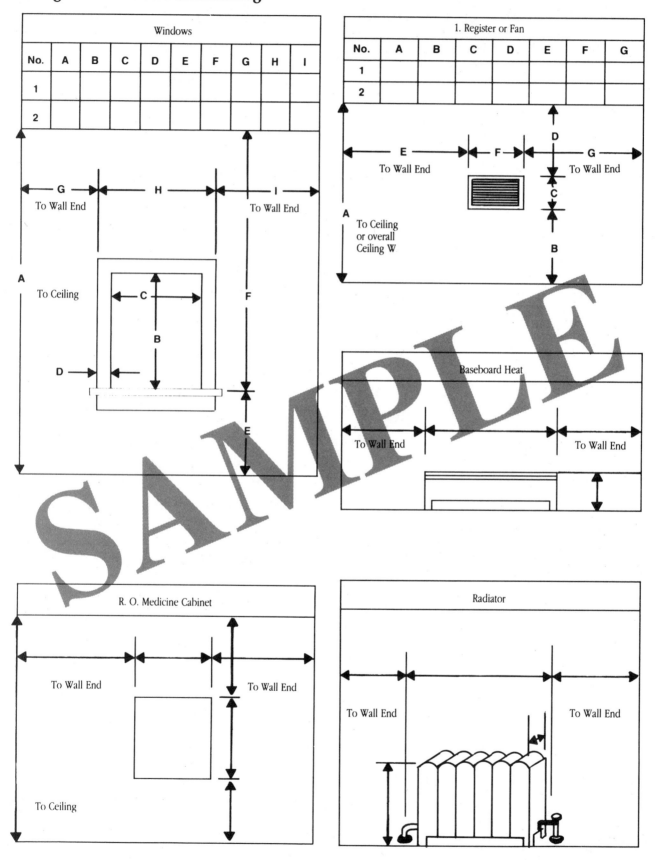

Windows									
No.	A	B	C	D	E	F	G	H	I
1									
2									

1. Register or Fan							
No.	A	B	C	D	E	F	G
1							
2							

Baseboard Heat

R. O. Medicine Cabinet

Radiator

SAMPLE

Existing Fixture Dimensioning

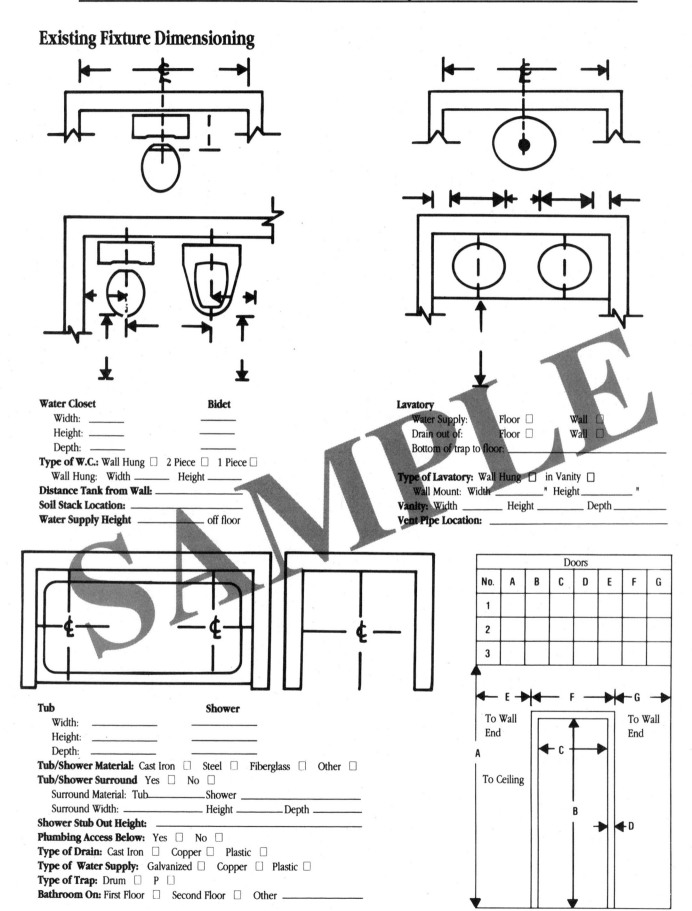

Water Closet   **Bidet**

Width: _____   _____

Height: _____   _____

Depth: _____   _____

Type of W.C.: Wall Hung ☐   2 Piece ☐   1 Piece ☐

Wall Hung: Width _____ Height _____

Distance Tank from Wall: _____

Soil Stack Location: _____

Water Supply Height _____ off floor

Lavatory

Water Supply: Floor ☐   Wall ☐

Drain out of: Floor ☐   Wall ☐

Bottom of trap to floor: _____

Type of Lavatory: Wall Hung ☐   in Vanity ☐

Wall Mount: Width _____ " Height _____ "

Vanity: Width _____ Height _____ Depth _____

Vent Pipe Location: _____

Tub   **Shower**

Width: _____   _____

Height: _____   _____

Depth: _____   _____

Tub/Shower Material: Cast Iron ☐   Steel ☐   Fiberglass ☐   Other ☐

Tub/Shower Surround   Yes ☐   No ☐

Surround Material: Tub _____ Shower _____

Surround Width: _____ Height _____ Depth _____

Shower Stub Out Height: _____

Plumbing Access Below: Yes ☐   No ☐

Type of Drain: Cast Iron ☐   Copper ☐   Plastic ☐

Type of Water Supply: Galvanized ☐   Copper ☐   Plastic ☐

Type of Trap: Drum ☐   P ☐

Bathroom On: First Floor ☐   Second Floor ☐   Other _____

Doors							
No.	A	B	C	D	E	F	G
1							
2							
3							

E — To Wall End   F   G — To Wall End

A — To Ceiling

B   C   D

Final Considerations

Regardless of the size of the bathroom, planning the room so that it reflects the client's lifestyle, fits within budget, and can be constructed within the construction constraints of the project requires careful questioning and sensitive listening by the designer.

Many novice bathroom specialists make the mistake of thinking everyone uses their bathroom just as the designer does. Another misconception is that small spaces are impossible design challenges. Really successful bathroom specialists don't fall into either one of these traps. They begin the planning process with a careful information gathering program. Whether you are sitting down with a client in your showroom reviewing the information necessary to specify products for a new home under construction, or gather around the dining room table on the jobsite as the clients begin to plan a remodeling program, you need to carefully gather this information.

PUTTING IT ALL TOGETHER - CREATING THE BEST PLAN

Although the three bathroom fixtures are somewhat standard, the way the room will be used dictates how the space will be arranged.

After you have learned the planning and safety criteria standards for each center of activity in the bathroom, you must begin the design process by identifying what type of bathroom your clients need. To assist you in this review, the following material is reprinted from the NKBA textbook *Beyond The Basic Bathroom.*

In this section we will study specific solutions to special types of bathrooms. We will consider the following typical client requests:

- Dividing the room into zones - The Family Bathroom

- Planning the area for youngsters - The Children's Bathroom.

- Designing guest space - The Powder Room

- Creating a total environment - The Adult Bathroom

THE FAMILY BATHROOM

The traditional approach to bathroom design is to place all three fixtures in one room. When the bathroom must be shared by several family members, the designer should consider dividing the space into compartments.

By separating the fixtures into individual specialized zones, several family members can use the bathroom together - while retaining some privacy. This is often a critical element in the successful design for a bathroom shared by children. Territorial battles may be eliminated with such careful planning.

Bathrooms are traditionally small. When compartment partitions are added, they become even smaller. Careful thought must be given to expected usage, lighting, ventilation, access and storage.

Zoning Ideas

Several successful ways to divide a bathroom are:

- Place the bathtub/shower and toilet in one space, with a single or double lavatory in a second area. A combination heat/light and ventilation fan unit should be included in the bathtub/shower/toilet area. A pocket entry door is much better than a swinging unit. Include bath towel bars within the compartment. To expand the room, a window or skylight is a great addition. A shower curtain or clear glass door is a much better idea than a frosted sliding door in these small spaces. Storage should be provided for extra toilet tissue, bathing, grooming and reading material.

- Consider placing the toilet in its own compartment. Ideally, a small hand washing lavatory should be placed in the cubicle. If possible, plan two doors leading into the cubicle: one from the hallway (pocket door) and one from the bathroom (pocket or swinging door). This keeps the toilet available to all family members. Natural or artificial ventilation must be included in this small place.

- A second or third grooming station, either in a bedroom or the utility room, may also solve the morning congestion problem.

A vanity with lavatory may be placed in a bedroom. If it can be located against the bathroom plumbing wall, expenses will be minimized. Side-wall medicine cabinets, a duplex outlet and good lighting will increase the storage and create a total grooming center.

The utility room is another good spot for a grooming station. Deep utility sinks are available that can double as a lavatory. A medicine cabinet above and proper mirror lighting can turn the laundry area into a muti-use center!

- A double bathroom which shares one fixture is an excellent way to compartmentalize the spaces. The bathtub/shower or toilet may serve two separate vanity areas. This is a great way to provide the feeling of two bathrooms, yet conserve on floor space.

- Dividing a single space into three separate areas may be the best approach. One long vanity with the toilet and bathtub/shower in their own nooks will allow three people to use the space concurrently. Keep the walking space in the vanity areas as large as possible.

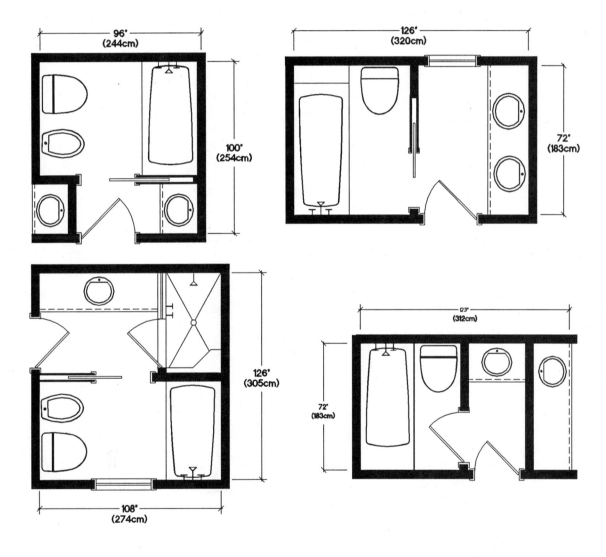

Figure 374   Zoning ideas that place the bathtub/shower and toilet in an area separated from the lavatories.

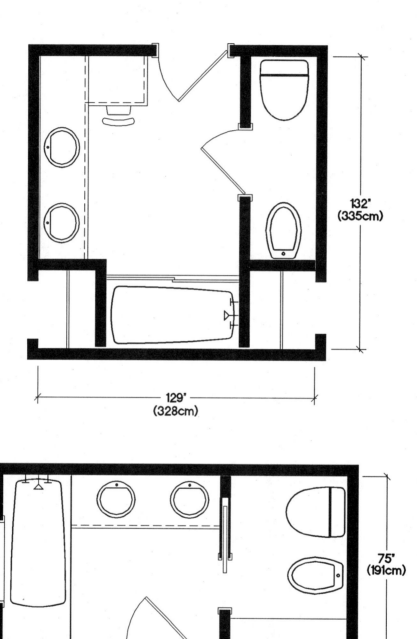

Figure 375   *Zoning ideas that place the toilet/bidet area in its own compartment.*

THE CHILDREN'S BATHROOM

When the space is being planned for the family youngsters, safety and accessibility are major concerns of the planner.

Children have a fascination with anything new: medicine, faucets, electrical outlets! Children also face accessibility limitations because of their shorter height and less firm grasp.

All of these concerns make planning a child's bathroom a challenge for the bathroom specialist.

Safety

Safety is a major concern. During the planning stage, the following safety recommendations should be considered.

- Plan medicine storage cabinets out of reach of little ones. Ideally, the cabinet should have a lock on it.

- Include an above floor level area for cleaning supplies.

- Safety latches should be included on any drawers or cabinet doors which will store adult grooming aids. This will prevent any young artists from painting a lipstick masterpiece on the wallpaper or tasting sweet smelling perfume.

- Specify door locks which can be opened from the outside in an emergency.

- Order specially designed shower valves which balance the water pressure inside the valve. For an extra safety measure, the valve can also have a thermostatic control device which limits the water temperature to a predetermined setting.

- Recommend single handle water controls. They are easier for children to operate.

- Plan on non-skid floor surfaces and avoid carpeting until the children are past the water fascination stage. Carpet is never appropriate for toilet areas predominately used by boys.

- Use timer switches on ventilation fans or heaters so that the units will shut off automatically if someone forgets to flip the switch.

- Always include a night light in the bathroom so late night users will not stumble as they enter the room.

Accessibility

After safety has been carefully considered, the question of special height installations should be addressed. Generally, standard fixtures and installations are recommended because the children will outgrow their needs.

Adjustability is a unique design approach. Designers may include the following "changeable" ideas in their plans.

- Install a pull-out step under the lavatory for smaller children. When they no longer need the helpmate, simply remove the roll-out.

- Install hand-held or pole-mounted showerheads, which can be raised as the children grow.

- Use mirror squares secured with tape on the wall for the small children. The mirror can be moved up the wall until the standard vanity mirror becomes visible to the child.

- Place the children's grooming aids in a drawer, decorative vanity top holder, or mounted on the inside of a door. Normal back wall recessed cabinet placement is just too far away.

- Order a few extra rolls of wallpaper so that towel bars can be installed lower than normal. When they are raised to a normal position, the surface can be repaired or replaced.

Child-Proofing

Easy care, durable and repairable surfaces are a key to a successful child-proof bathroom. Surfaces which withstand spilling, splashing, spotting, dripping, bumping and scratching should be specified.

As children grow, as they explore, as they learn about life and themselves, the bathroom plays an important part in their development. A room that protects them from accidents, encourages the development of good life-long grooming and hygiene habits and is warm and inviting is the goal of the professional bathroom specialist.

Arranging Centers for Children

When planning a childrens bathroom arrangement, zoning considerations are often of primary importance since the space is usually shared by more than one child. Refer back to the floorplans in *Figures 374 and 375* which illustrate bathroom arrangements that would serve children well.

Alternatively, you might have two separate bathrooms that back up to one another, but serve each child individually. Refer to *Figures 376 and 377* for examples of back-to-back bathroom arrangements.

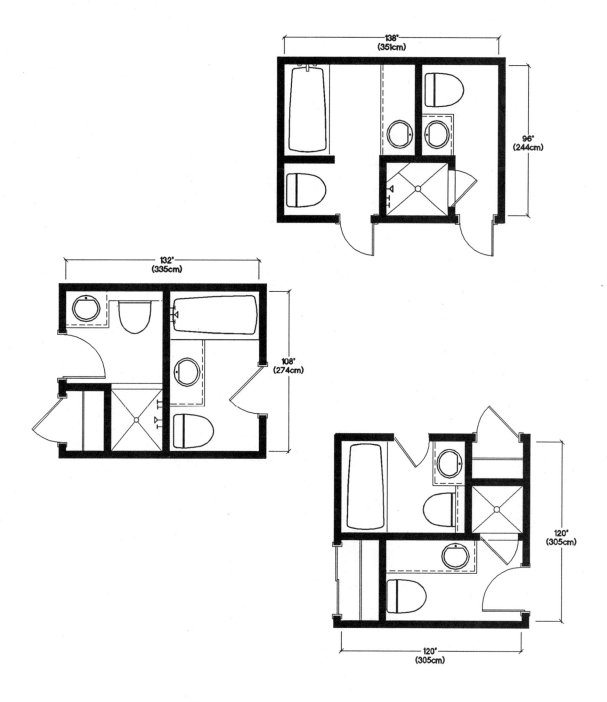

Figure 376   Dual bathroom arrangements suitable for children.

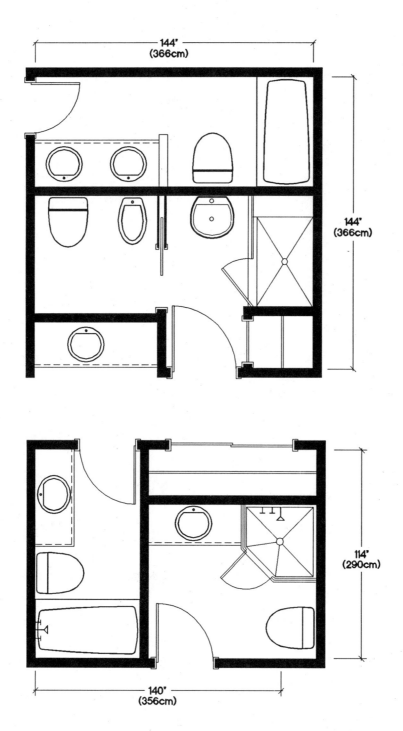

Figure 377   Dual bathroom arrangements suitable for children.

THE POWDER ROOM

The half-bath is so named because the bathing and/or showering fixture is eliminated. This small space is often planned as a guest bathroom so that the family bathrooms are not on display.

Although it obviously requires less space than a fully equipped bathroom, care should be taken to ensure that the space remains comfortable for guests when they are using either one of the two primary fixtures, as well as when they enter or exit the room. Many designers erroneously assume that because smaller fixtures are used, they can be placed closer together. This is incorrect. The size of the user does not change just because the fixtures are smaller!

Although storage requirements are minimal for a half-bath reserved exclusively for guest use, provision should be made for hand towels, an accessible toilet-tissue dispenser, space for an extra roll of toilet tissue, facial tissue, decorative soap and a small waste paper basket. Functional lighting at the mirror is also important in this small space.

Powder rooms are often located near the living areas of the house so that they are easily accessible to guests. Screening the entry door, providing effective sound control and planning an efficient odor removal system are also key elements of a successful powder room design.

Entry

The door leading to the powder room should not open into the living, dining or family room. It should be off the entry hall, utility area or bedroom hallway. The comings and goings of this room should be gracefully separated from the general gathering areas.

Soundproofing

Soundproofing the bathroom walls is important in any bathroom space, but becomes extremely critical for a gracious powder room design.

Ventilation

Similarly, good ventilation is a major concern in the design of a powder room. More than an operable window for ventilation is required. A quiet, efficient, mechanical ventilation system (which can be activated by the light switch) will whisk offensive odors out of the small space before their lingering presence confronts the next user, or worse yet, drifts into nearby guest-occupied areas.

Drama is a key element in the success of a powder room design. Guests will be in the area for only a few moments so unusual surfaces, extensive mirrors and elegant fixtures which create a *"wow"* environment are all very effective design ideas.

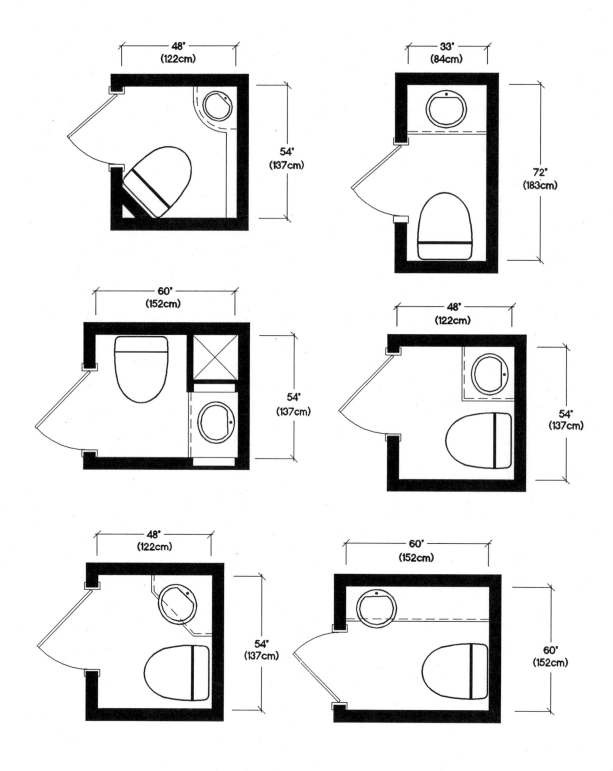

Figure 378   Typical powder room floor plans.

AN ADULT BATHROOM

The combination of a family room, kitchen and dining area, often called *"The Great Room,"* has an exciting counterpart for the 90s - *"The Superbath."*

The superbath joins the master bathroom, wardrobe areas and bedroom into one enlarged adult retreat. At one extreme, room additions are required to expand the available square footage. When new space is not possible, clients search for ways to squeeze every inch of convenience and every drop of beauty out of the existing area.

To ensure a successful sale, the professional bathroom specialist must understand why the clients are interested in a superbath. Just as we must understand what creativity is before we apply it, designers must learn why people are attracted to this type of room before they begin to plan it.

A specialist who prematurely jumps into the design process without a firm foundation of knowledge may mistakenly present a bathroom which features a beautiful bathtub for two - when the reason for the project was to separate a husband and wife who were tired of sharing the same tiny space!

There seem to be three major reasons for the new interest in a space which was initially designed to simply serve physical needs and personal hygiene:

- The emotional desire for privacy.

- The physical need for relaxation.

- The mental search for efficiency.

Privacy Planning

People have always relished privacy. Even in the most open of families, the bathroom is the one room where it is socially acceptable to enter the room, close the door and, if one chooses, lock it. An enlarged space, which provides an attractive and comfortable place to fix hair, or a spot to peruse the daily newspaper, is a natural extension of the private nature of the bathroom.

When space is limited and the clients dream of a large bathroom, one approach is to join the bedroom and master bathroom. The vanity and bathtub area become part of the bedroom. The toilet is housed in a separate compartment. This type of plan incorporates both bedroom and bathroom into a private adult retreat where the boundry begins at the bedroom door, rather than at the bathroom door.

Privacy might also mean no bumping into your partner for the first time in years! "His" and "Her" rooms with separate vanity and closet spaces offer another very desirable plan.

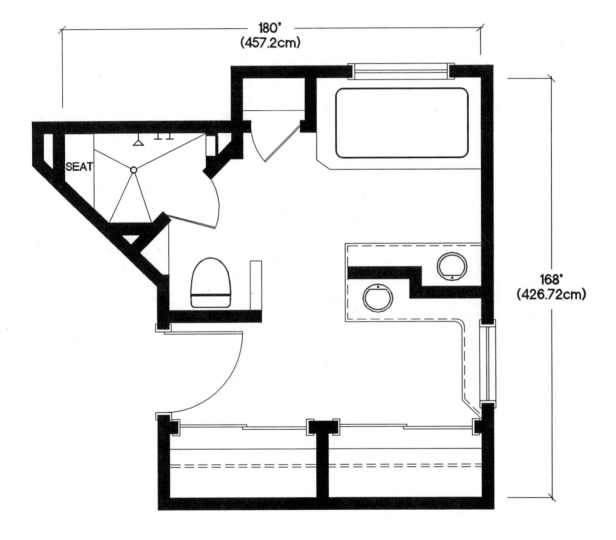

Figure 379   The bathtub and vanity area are open to the bedroom in this master suite.

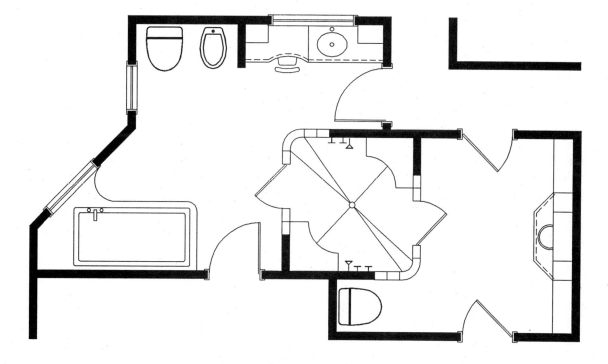

Figure 380   Two completely separate bathrooms are created in this solution.

Relaxation Planning

Relaxation is a major part of coping with today's world. Regardless of how much our clients love their families, the peace and solitude of a few moments alone in a steeping hot bathtub is seen as absolute heaven! The whirlpools, saunas and hot tubs which clients are clamoring for today provide this floating relaxation for one-or for several. When the clients dream of relaxing in this manner, a cramped, dull, utilitarian room is far from the ideal setting. A greenhouse window over the bathtub or a private screened garden outside the window will help set the stage. An aesthetically pleasing room will help enhance the restful atmosphere. A small TV, phone or bookcase close by will make the bathing experience very special.

Efficiency Planning

Efficiency is often a goal for the bathroom project. When one considers the equipment needed to get dressed and ready to go, it is easy to see why improved storage is often requested. Logically, one should be able to enter a well-planned bathroom and emerge dressed and groomed. Clothing storage (both clean and soiled) should be part of the bathroom. Adequate cabinets with interior storage aids are a "must." You may be able to improve the storage system with one of these ideas.

- Divided shallow drawers for make-up.

- Deeper drawers for hair equipment.

- Shallow adjustable shelves for medical supplies.

- Angled racks for shoes.

- Hooks for belts, ties, scarves and purses.

- Drawers for underwear and sweaters.

- Double-pole storage for slacks and shirts.

- A built-in ironing board for last minute touch-ups.

- A mini sewing kit for repairs.

- A special spot for shoe polish and paraphernalia.

These items will make a room work as well as a properly planned kitchen does for the cook, and it will be very special to the owner.

A thoughtfully designed Superbath can provide a treasured space in which the client enjoys privacy, find a quiet moment of relaxation or organize personal belongings.

Finding the Space

When all of these commodities are requested, such a complete superbath needs lots of space! Many of our existing homes just don't have the needed floor area readily available. A bathroom specialist may be able to suggest possible ways to carve out a place for the bath. Here are a few ideas that have been tried before:

- In a master suite, make the bedroom smaller and the bath larger.

- Turn the closets into the bathroom area.

- Eliminate dresser-type furniture in the bedroom and replace it with built-in cabinetry in the bathroom/closet area.

- Turn an unused bedroom next to an existing bathroom into one large superbath.

- Combine two small bathrooms into a single large one. By using compartments to separate the bathtub and toilet from the vanity area, two people can still use the new space.

- Add space to the existing house to provide a spot for this special room with the addition of a bumpout cantilevered addition tucked below the existing roof overhang.

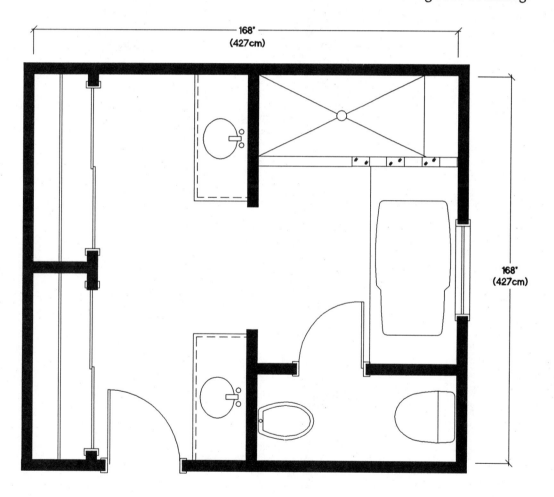

Figure 381   Master bathroom suite with separate toilet/bidet area, bathtub/shower area, two lavatories and two closets.

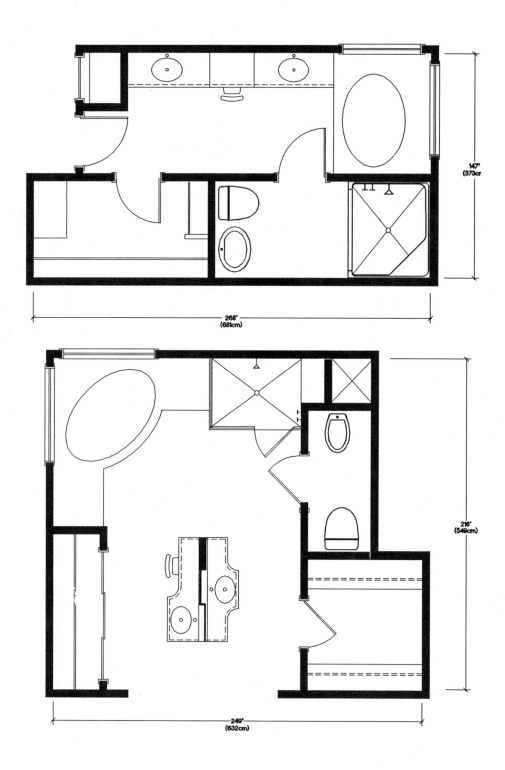

Figure 382   Suggested master bathroom arrangements.

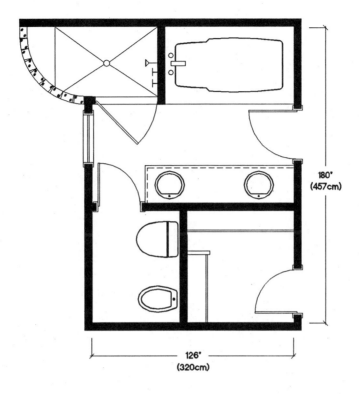

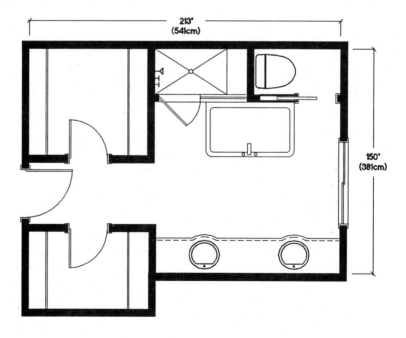

Figure 383   More suggested master bathroom arrangements.

SECTION **11**

BARRIER-FREE PLANNING

SPECIAL CONCERNS

On occasion, you may be called upon to plan a bathroom space for a client who uses a wheelchair. This request is not as uncommon as it was once thought to be. Medical advances, a healthier lifestyle and the aging of the "baby boomers" all contribute to more requests for barrier-free planning.

The most basic concern when designing the bathroom for a person who uses a wheelchair is to provide access to the space and to the fixtures. Access will insure that the user can master the responsibilities of personal hygiene and grooming rather than being victimized by these chores.

The constraints imposed by the wheelchair should be considered one by one:

- Eye level and reach are lower and static. This reduction affects windowsill heights, grab bar placement and the location of switches and duplex outlets.

- Wheelchairs consume space. The turning radius, footrest room requirements and maneuverability must be carefully planned.

- Wheelchairs cannot step up, step over or step down. Ground or floor level changes are one of the major stumbling blocks for the individual who uses a wheelchair.

- Moving in and out of the chair is a consideration. Transfer methods must be planned to facilitate the use of the shower, bathtub and toilet.

- The use of foot and arm rests limit access to standard lavatory vanity areas.

NKBA has developed an auxillary client survey that will help you determine the questions to ask and the information to gather. From time to time, this survey may need to be customized to fit the special requirements of your project.

A sample of this survey form follows and may be obtained by contacting NKBA and requesting Form #4025.

Form #4025

UNIVERSAL BATHROOM PLANNING CLIENT SURVEY

Name: _____ Date: _____

Address: _____

City, State, Zip: _____

Phone: _____ Work: _____

Jobsite Address: _____

City, State, Zip: _____

Directions: _____

_____

Appointment: _____

Date: _____ Address: _____

Time: _____ City/State/Zip: _____

Phone: _____ Comment: _____

_____

Allied Professional: _____

_____

_____

Pertinent Information: _____

I. THE CLIENT - PHYSICAL PROFILE

Sight:

Do you wear glasses for reading? _____ for distance? _____

Any visual impairments that influence the type/amount of lighting needed? _____

Are you taking any medications that affect your sight? _____

Hearing:

What issues regarding your ability to hear will affect the design process?_____

Tactile/Touch:

Can you feel hot and cold?_____ texture?_____

Taste/Smell:

Do you know of any change in your sense of taste? _____ smell? _____

Strength & Function:

What can you lift? _____ carry? _____

Do you have more strength on one side than the other? _____

Do you use both hands fully?_____ palms only?_____

How is your grip?_____Left Side? _____ Right Side? _____

How is your balance? _____Standing? _____ Bending?_____

Areas of Physical Limitation:

Does your mobility or balance vary by time of day? _____

Is there an assistant who helps sometimes? _____ All the time? _____

What adaptive equipment do you use?_____

Weight?_____Height?_____

Prognosis: (Is condition stable? Is further deterioration anticipated? Is improvement anticipated?)

Consultants:

Physician _____ telephone:_____

Occupational Therapist _____ telephone:_____

Comments from Physician and Occupational Therapist:

_____

Transfer Information: (Prefer right, left, or forward?)

_____

Special Safety Concerns:

_____

Reach and Grasp Profile:

Have your client position themselves as shown where applicable, fill in the appropriate reach/grasp measurements.

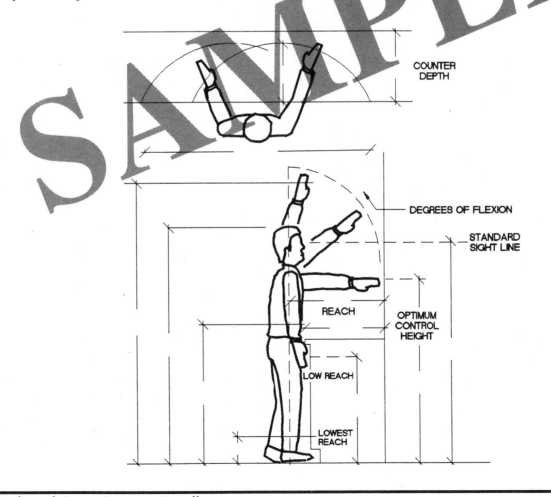

Reach and Grasp Range - Standing

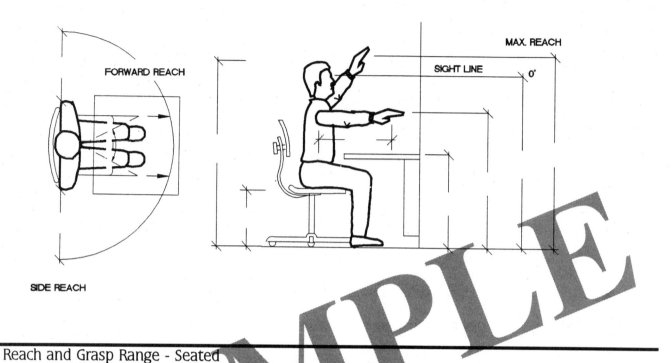

FORWARD REACH

SIDE REACH

MAX. REACH

SIGHT LINE

0°

Reach and Grasp Range - Seated

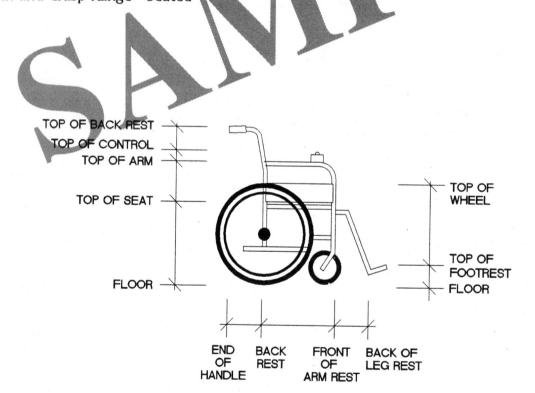

TOP OF BACK REST

TOP OF CONTROL

TOP OF ARM

TOP OF SEAT

FLOOR

TOP OF WHEEL

TOP OF FOOTREST

FLOOR

END OF HANDLE

BACK REST

FRONT OF ARM REST

BACK OF LEG REST

Wheelchair Profile

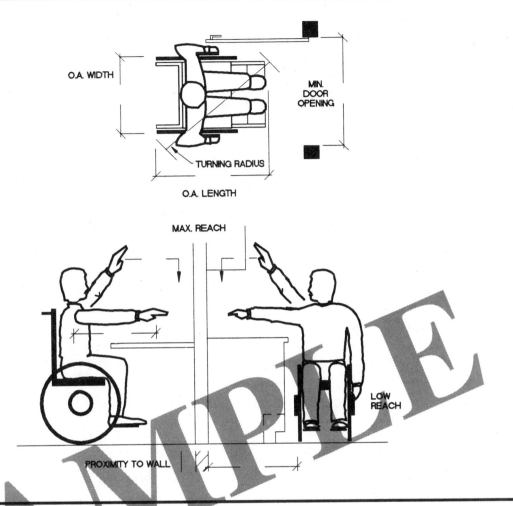

Wheelchair Profile - Reach Range

What activities in the bathroom would you like to do that you are not able to do now?

_____

_____

_____

Bathroom

1. Sink/Lavatory Area

Are there any access concerns? _____sink?_____

Is the present height/depth of the sink/lav comfortable for you? _____

present height _____ preferred height_____

What height range is best for storage?_____

Is there a need for open space below the sink and vanity? _____

_____

Does the present faucet operate easily for you?_____

      preferred location & style _____

Do you wish a knee space at the sink/lav area? _____

Comments/Concerns _____

_____

2. Bathtub/Shower Area

Do you prefer a bath? _____ or shower? _____

Is your bathtub easy and safe to get into and use? _____

Is there a bathtub/shower seat? ____ should one be included in the plan_____

Is there a hand-held spray? _____ should one be included in the plan_____

Can the controls be reached from both a sitting and standing position? _____

Are the controls easy to use? _____

      present style and location _____

      preferred style and location_____

Is the bathtub/shower floor non-slip? _____

How will you approach/transfer to the bathtub/shower? _____

_____

_____

Comments/Concerns_____

_____

3. Toilet Area

Is the present toilet at a height that is safe and comfortable for your approach/transfer?

_____

Do you prefer a standard height toilet or a raised height toilet?_____

Will you use an elevated seat? _____

What height must the seat be? _____

Present clearances

    left _____

    right_____

    front_____

Preferred clearances

    left _____

    right_____

    front_____

TOILET			
#	A	B	C	D
1				
2				
3				
4				

Is the toilet paper dispenser within your reach? _____

    present location_____

    preferred location_____

Is the flush lever easily and safely used? _____

    present location _____

    preferred location_____

4. Support System

Where do you need grab bars in the toilet area?_____

_____

Where do you need grab bars at the bathtub/shower? _____

5. Storage

Is there adequate storage within your reach?_____

_____

Are the medicine cabinet and shelves within your reach? _____

_____

Are the storage areas safely and easily opened? _____

_____

For what items do you need storage? _____

_____

Any unusual sized items? _____

_____

Do you have any supportive or hygiene equipment that requires storage? (list items and dimensions) _____

_____

6. Counter Heights

current height_____ preferred height _____

Is there enough work space? _____ knee space?_____

7. Accessories and Controls

Are towel racks easily and safely used? _____

_____

Are towel racks likely to be used as grab bars? _____

_____

Are the light/fan switches easy to use? _____

present height and style_____

Are outlet locations safe and easy to use? _____

      present height _____

      preferred height _____

8. Moving Around

What problems exist in entering and moving around in the bathroom? _____

_____

What style door do you prefer? pocket _____ hinge_____ other_____

What is your door swing preference? (check clear floor space outside door) _____

Where would you like the door handle located? _____

9. Lighting and Ventilation

Is there enough lighting

    for bathing_____

    in the lav/mirror area _____

    in the toilet area _____

    for general illumination _____

Is the bathroom well ventilated? _____

10. Other Concerns/Comments

Is there a safe and easy exit in case of fire? _____

Are the windows operable? _____

Comments _____

Wheelchair Measurements

Each wheelchair must be measured carefully, especially front-to-back measurements, which determine the turning radius. The following dimensions are based on an average adult-sized wheelchair:

- Usual height at top of arm rests is 30" (76.2cm). This is important for moving under countertops.

- Space for knees is a minimum of 27" (68.58cm) above the floor and 18" (45.72cm) wide.

- With foot rests in use, the average toe height is 8" (20.32cm) above the floor.

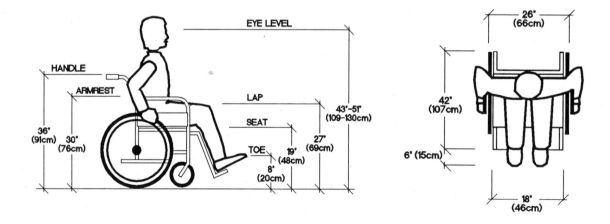

Figure 384   Average adult-sized wheelchair dimensions.

As you begin planning the bathroom, the wheelchair's turning radius will require at least 60" (152.4cm) of floorspace. At 9" - 12" (22.86cm - 30.48cm) above the floor, this dimensional requirement of 60" (152.4cm) will decrease.

Up to 6" (15.24cm) of the required 60" (152.4cm) can be provided by a toekick that is a minimum 6" (15.24cm) deep and 9" (22.86cm) high. Up to 19" (48.26cm) of the required 60" (152.4cm) can be provided by the clear floor of a kneespace if the kneespace is a minimum of 48" (121.92cm) wide.

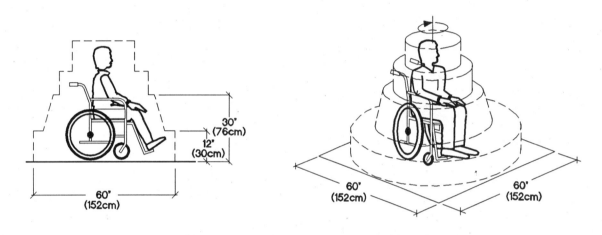

Figure 385   Space requirements decrease as height above the floor increases.

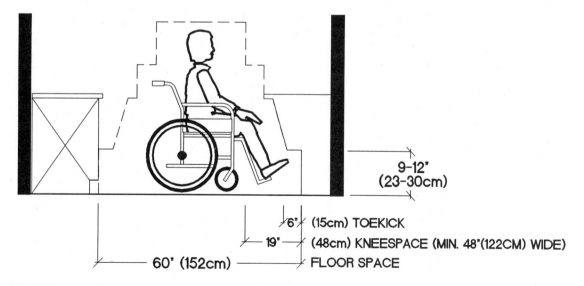

Figure 386   Clear floorspace may include toekick and kneespace if minimum dimensions are met.

When a full radius turn can not be accommodated, provide floor space for a T-turn. A T-turn requires a 36" x 60" (91.44cm x 152.4cm) aisle with a 36" x 36" (91.44cm x 91.44cm) leg at its center.

Beyond turning floor space requirements, you will also need to consider floor space needs at fixtures and equipment. Based on the average wheelchair dimensions provided, a minimum floor space of 30" x 48" (76.2cm x 121.92cm) should be planned in front of every fixture. The orientation of the floor space provided will determine whether a parallel approach or perpendicular approach will be used. Whenever possible, space for both approaches should be planned 48" x 48" (121.92cm x 121.92cm).

Just as with the turning circle, up to 19" (48.26cm) of this clear floor space may extend into a knee space (under a lavatory or adjacent to a toilet).

The countertop height most practical for the wheelchair user is 31" (78.74cm), with a 29" (73.66cm) distance from the floor to the bottom surface of the top. The standard countertop depth of 21" (53.34cm) is impractical for the person using a wheelchair. They will use only the front 16" (40.64cm) of the countertop's depth. The extra 5" (12.7cm) of depth should be used for storage, as their reach to above-counter storage will be limited.

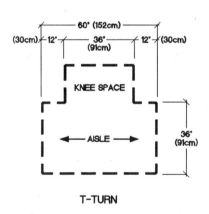

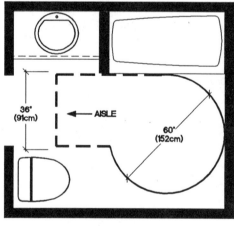

Figure 387   Wheelchair turning options with limited floor space.

Cabinetry Considerations

- Frameless construction offers easier access to interior contents.

- Raising toekicks to 9" - 12" (23cm - 30cm) high provides clearance for wheelchair foot rests.

- Doors should be hinged so that they swing 180 degrees.

- Tambour doors that roll up or sliding doors on cabinets, eliminate the door as an obstruction to move around.

- Use easy to grasp pulls or touch latches on doors.

Lavatory Center

- Provide kneespace under the lavatory.

- Consider floor clearance space required to face and use the lavatory.

- Specify a single lever faucet or touchless electronic control.

- Plan storage for towels, supplies and accessories within easy reach of lavatory.

- Provide protective covering for drain and water pipes.

Bathtub/Shower Center

- Determine whether the bathtub/shower will be a transfer type or roll-in type.

- Provide adequate clear floor space required for entry into the bathtub/shower (will vary with fixture selection).

- Specify a hand-held shower head.

- Plan adequate grab bars.

- Specify control location within easy reach while in and out of the bathtub/shower.

- Specify single lever controls for bathtub fillers, showerheads and diverters.

- Plan seats inside bathtub/shower.

Toilet/Bidet Considerations

- Provide adequate clear floor space for transfer, 48" x 48" (122cm x 122cm) is recommended.

- Specify adequate grab bars.

- Wall-mounted toilet with a concealed tank is recommended.

- An 18" high seat is considered optimum.

Conclusion

A properly planned bathroom can improve the physical and emotional well being of the person who uses a wheelchair. A well-designed space will minimize their weakness and compensate for their disabilities. As professionals, we should be prepared to expand the special design services as necessary to plan and install a bathroom that is just right for the client's individual needs.

For more detailed information on planning a barrier-free and universal bathroom, consult NKBA's **"Universal Bathroom Planning - Design that Adapts to People"** book written by Mary Jo Peterson, CKD, CBD, CHE.

SECTION **12**

THE SUBTRACTION METHOD OF BATHROOM DESIGN

USING YOUR INFORMATION

At this point you have learned the bathroom equipment/fixtures/fittings and surfaces you will specify as well as the planning guidelines you must follow.

We have also reviewed planning considerations appropriate for childrens bathrooms, powder rooms and adult retreats. You now have all the information you need to design a bathroom.

Successful planners take a systematic approach to the art of bathroom design. They use an approach called *"The Subtraction Method"* of planning. Before starting, you should have any dimensions and information provided by the client and your own sketch and measurements, plus the fixture, equipment and cabinet line you will use. Be sure you are thoroughly familiar with the client survey form.

Step No. 1 - Draw Room Outline

Draw the overall outline of the room. The perimeter of the space will provide a framework in which you can move activity templates around.

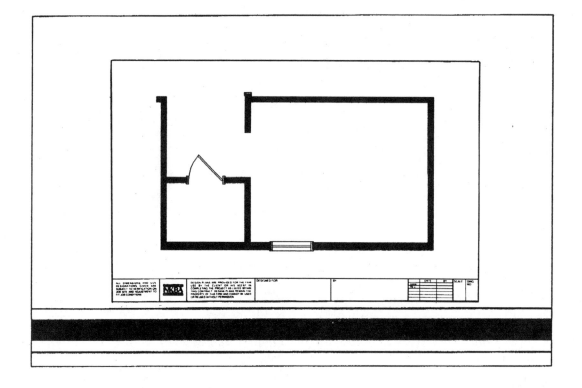

Figure 388   Subtraction Method Step #1 - Outline the room.

Step No. 2 - Template Centers of Activity

Identify the general centers of activity required for the bathroom under consideration. Make a list of these areas, noting the approximate equipment to be located in each. In our example these areas would be as follows:

- **Vanity Area with Two Side-by-Side Lavatories:** Approximate Size = 96" (243.84cm) long x 64" (162.56cm) deep. It includes a 22" (55.88cm) deep countertop, plus 30" x 48" (76cm x 121.92cm) of clear floor space.

- **Toilet/Bidet Center:** Approximate Size = 72" (182.88cm) long x 75" (190.5cm) deep. It includes a 27" (68.58cm) deep toilet and 24" (60.96cm) deep bidet, plus 48" x 48" (122cm x 122cm) clear floor space in front of the fixtures.

- **Soaking Bathtub:** Approximate Size = 48" (121.92cm) wide x 72" (182.88cm) long space required for bathtub selected by client.

- **Stall Shower:** Approximate Size = 60" (152.4cm) wide x 48" (121.92cm) deep requested by client.

- **Walk-in Closet:** Approximate Size = 48" (121.92cm) wide x 60" (152.4cm) long is existing.

- **Walkway from Master Bedroom to Bath:** Approximate Size = 36" (91.44cm) wide is existing.

- **Tall Storage:** Approximate Size = 60" (152.4cm) wide x 18" (45.72cm) deep.

Once you have identified these requested centers of activity and their overall sizes, you can draw templates of the proposed areas to assist in the conceptual design process.

Alternatively, some designers take the room outline and photocopy six or so plans. They then use templates from the manufacturers to do quick sketches as they explore possible locations.

Talented designers maintain a second list of the client's priorities. It's rare that all the client's requests can be met within the available space. Therefore, you need to know if the client would settle for a single lavatory if they could then have a bigger shower. Or, if the bidet would be eliminated in favor of tall linen storage, or a bigger closet.

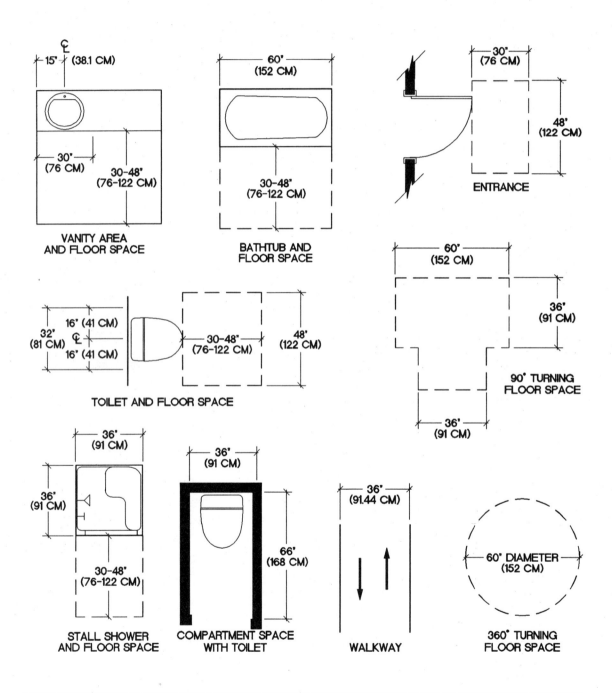

Figure 389   Subtraction Method Step #2 - Template the centers of activity.

Step No. 3 - Note Construction and or Project Limitations

On the floor plan, locate any mechanical systems that require specific fixture placement. *For example,* if you do not have the option of moving the toilet drain or the bathtub drain, draw the fixture on the plan first so that all other proposed center locations revolve around this fixed element. This same approach should be used with any window, door or other element in the space that cannot be changed.

In this example, the walkway from the master bedroom is not movable. Therefore, the bathroom entrance and the probable closet location become part of the established parameters for the pro-

ject. Similarly, the window cannot be relocated, therefore, it becomes a given. Other than these limitations, the fixtures can be located anywhere within the space in our example.

Once you've measured the available space you can mix your practical technical knowledge with your creative ability. As you study any plan, challenge yourself to be more than a fixture supplier or cabinet salesperson.

Become a creative space planner who looks at each room with an eye for finding the best solution. Use your creative approach to problem solving to transform a difficult space into a bathroom filled with solutions.

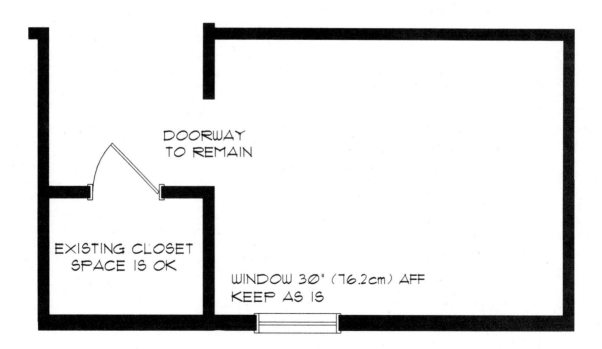

Figure 390   Subtraction Method Step #3 - Identify construction constraints.

Step No. 4 - Consider Several Creative Solutions

JUST WHAT IS "CREATIVITY"?

Creativity is the emergence of something new which is relative, useful or important.

Remember that new doesn't necessarily mean something that's never existed before. Rather, new generally means an accumulation of knowledge coming together in a unique manner to supply an answer not reached before or a solution not tried in the past.

It means rearranging existing knowledge to create new knowledge. It means taking the same tools and the same concepts and using them in a slightly different way. *For example,* taking an idea that you have seen in a magazine and adapting it to fit a specific bathroom problem.

Creativity is not something that only a few people have. We can be trained to increase our level of creativity through diligence, perseverance and dedication. As Thomas Edison once said: *"Creativity is 99% perspiration and 1% inspiration."*

To increase your ability to think creatively, you need to understand the steps your mind goes through during the creative problem solving process.

There are five stages:

- Preparation

- Incubation

- Illumination

- Elaboration

- Verification

Preparation: To be truly creative, you need to learn everything about your subject matter - bathroom design. That's what you've been doing as you've studied the various aspects of this publication. Mechanical systems outlined in Chapter 1, all of the equipment and fixtures detailed for you in Chapter 2, and all of the human ergonomic considerations discussed in this chapter give you the necessary preparation to develop a creative solution for each bathroom project that you work on.

Once you have attained your accreditation as a **Certified Bathroom Designer** you should continue to study trade journals and consumer magazines, attend trade conferences and other seminars to refine and increase your level of expertise. Dedicate yourself to life-long education: to a continual effort to *"remaster"* all of the details and dimensions of bathroom design.

Incubation: The second plateau in the creative process is the incubation stage. As you sketch possible solutions in concept form, you're entering this stage.

Allow your conscious, rational self to relax, to stop thinking in a logical fashion so that you can start exploring possibilities outside of a normal approach.

To make sure that you don't block your creative self be aware of the following:

- **Don't fear failure.** If you are afraid of failure, you won't explore all of the possibilities.

- **Don't be afraid of unusual ideas.** As you look at a possibility, think of a solution that is exactly the opposite of your current consideration.

- **Don't be too occupied with order and tradition.** Think about the non-traditional and the unusual. To help you in this process keep an "*idea file*" close to your drawing board.

Save magazine pictures or sketches that include good bathroom ideas. Categorize them by toilet area, stall shower, vanity, etc. Then, as you sit at your desk and ponder a problem, flip through these pictures; they'll help you to generate a solution.

The use of templates or patterns as suggested in Step 2 encourages you to employ free-hand sketching at the drawing board as you think though alternative approaches.

If you seem to hit a block, leave the project for a while and think about the room in a more relaxed manner, for example, as you drive home tonight, or in the shower tomorrow morning. Or, sit at your desk and close your eyes for a moment and imagine different solutions. This type of free association often results in a solution not thought of before.

Illumination: The third part in the creative process is called illumination. That's the moment when you do think of the solution. In our example, after moving our templates representing the centers throughout the space, a "*corridor*" layout has been selected.

Placing the vanity and toilet/bidet area adjacent to one another along one long wall allows a continuation of the storage system and will provide design continuity. By locating the bathing pool directly opposite the vanity area, the seated bather will be able to enjoy the window. The square shower has been enhanced with the introduction of an angled glass section that also allows the inclusion of a seat within the enclosure.

As mentioned earlier, the closet, tall storage and walkway were dictated by the shape of the room.

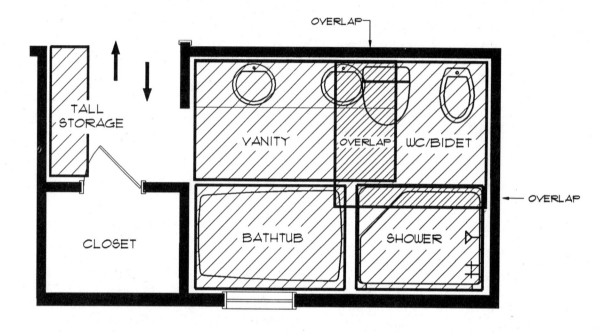

Figure 391   Subtraction Method Step #4 - Proposed solution by template positioning.

Elaboration: The fourth stage of the creative process is elaboration. It's now time for you to return to reality and carefully analyze your solution by laying out each element of the space and checking the dimensional feasibility of the solution. Now is the time to work out the plan in all its details using your judgement in determining what compromises to make. Additionally, now is the time to prepare the specifications.

During the elaboration stage, you will once again use the *"subtraction method"* of planning because it is a mathematical way to layout the space and verify each element in the planning process.

Verification: The last stage is verification. Your detailed plan now needs to be tested, refined and evaluated for future use. You will check the plan on paper and visit the jobsite when the project is completed. Ask yourself: *"How installable was the solution? Did the solution justify the expense? Is there any easier way I could create a similar solution in the future but with less jobsite labor or less product cost? Is the client really enjoying the solution?"*

Let's look at the vanity wall in our solution to demonstrate the details of the subtraction layout method.

Step No. 5 - Select Priority Area

Now you will actually place the most important element of the plan. Note the overall wall dimension of 144" (365.76cm). The toilet and bidet should be placed first, because of the importance of maintaining adequate clearance around these two fixtures and because of the variety of cabinets sizes available to you. As you begin the subtraction method, concentrate on the elements that are not movable, demand the most space, or are most important to the client.

In this example, we are going to allow more than the absolute minimum of 15" (38.1cm) from a wall to the center line of each fixture, and increase it to 16-1/2" (41.91cm) as recommended by NKBA. Therefore, starting from the right-hand wall measure over 16-1/2" (41.91cm) to the centerline of the bidet, 33" (83.82cm) to the centerline of the toilet and then 16-1/2" (41.91cm) to the edge of the area reserved for the vanity. When you add the centerlines together, you'll find that 66" (167.64cm) is required for this placement of the toilet and bidet. Subtract 66" (167.64cm) from 144" (365.76cm). There are 78" (198.12cm) remaining for the vanity, which must house the two lavatories.

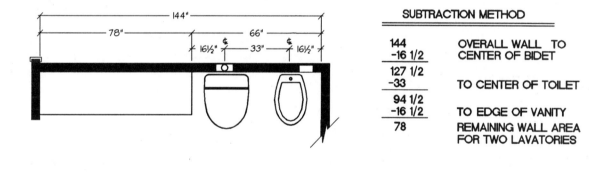

SUBTRACTION METHOD

144	OVERALL WALL TO
-16 1/2	CENTER OF BIDET
127 1/2	
-33	TO CENTER OF TOILET
94 1/2	
-16 1/2	TO EDGE OF VANITY
78	REMAINING WALL AREA FOR TWO LAVATORIES

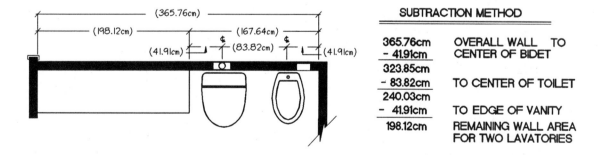

SUBTRACTION METHOD

365.76cm	OVERALL WALL TO
- 41.91cm	CENTER OF BIDET
323.85cm	
- 83.82cm	TO CENTER OF TOILET
240.03cm	
- 41.91cm	TO EDGE OF VANITY
198.12cm	REMAINING WALL AREA FOR TWO LAVATORIES

Figure 392   Subtraction Method Step #5 - Select priority area.

Step No. 6 - Consider Alternatives

You will now think through alternative approaches to the next area of activity. This example will consider various approaches to the vanity area.

OPTION A

- You could place the lavatories close together, with a small cabinet on each side, as well as one in the middle. Let's assume that the lavatory you've selected fits in a 24" (60.96cm) wide cabinet. Therefore, your first approach may be to attempt to place two 24" (60.96cm) vanity cabinets, separated by a 12" (30.48cm) unit in the center, and finished with a 12" (30.48cm) unit on each side. But, when you add these dimensions up, you'll find that the total is 84" (213.36cm). That's 6" (15.24cm) more than you have available. You could minimize the toilet and bidet area by 6" (15.24cm) and gain the space for the vanity area. But, in the solution under consideration we've opted not to minimize the clearance space around the fixtures. Therefore, this approach to the vanity is not possible.

OPTION B

- You could suggest to your clients that a single bowl centered in the large vanity, may be a wiser choice than two lavatories. Assume that the client really wants two lavatories, therefore this is not an option.

OPTION C

- You could place the two lavatories close together in the middle, with space on either side. This might be particularly desirable if a couple shares the bathroom and one of them is left-handed and the other is right-handed. They would then stand close together in the center of the vanity, moving to opposite counters for their own grooming areas. The disadvantage to this is that there would not be enough elbow room for tasks requiring both hands when they were both standing immediately adjacent to one another.

To ascertain whether this solution would work or not, take the overall 78" (198.12cm) and subtract 48" (121.92cm) from it, which represents the two smallest cabinets the lavatories can fit in. The balance of 30" (76.2cm) is then divided in half to provide the proposed vanity arrangement of a 15" (38.1cm) base on one end, two 24" (60.96cm) lavatory bases in the center, and a 15" (38.1cm) base cabinet on the other end.

OPTION D

- Or place the two lavatories, allowing for the minimum elbow room, at each end and locate the remainder of the counter space in the center.

This might be the ideal solution for a family that does not normally use the lavatories concurrently. The larger, center counter

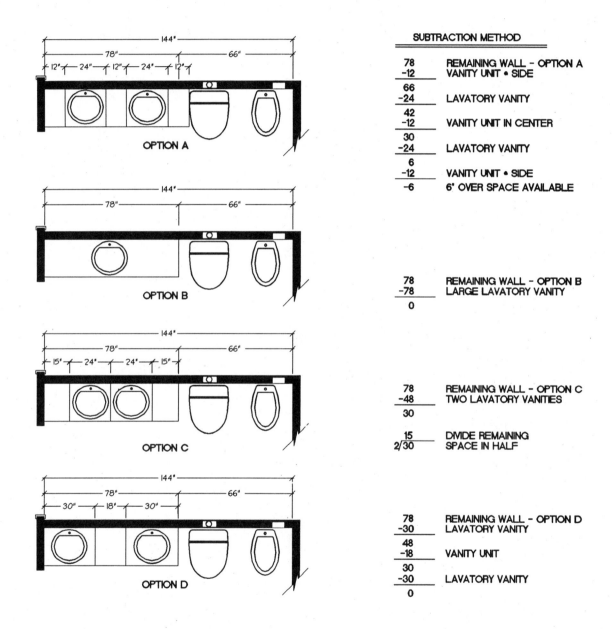

SUBTRACTION METHOD

78 −12	REMAINING WALL – OPTION A VANITY UNIT • SIDE
66 −24	LAVATORY VANITY
42 −12	VANITY UNIT IN CENTER
30 −24	LAVATORY VANITY
6 −12	VANITY UNIT • SIDE
−6	6" OVER SPACE AVAILABLE

78 −78	REMAINING WALL – OPTION B LARGE LAVATORY VANITY
0	

78 −48	REMAINING WALL – OPTION C TWO LAVATORY VANITIES
30	
15 2/30	DIVIDE REMAINING SPACE IN HALF

78 −30	REMAINING WALL – OPTION D LAVATORY VANITY
48 −18	VANITY UNIT
30 −30	LAVATORY VANITY
0	

Figure 393   Subtraction Method Step #6 - Consider alternatives.

could be used by each single adult, rather than a smaller counter on one side. The 78" (198.12cm) of space is now divided differently, because a minimum cabinet size does not meet the 15" (38cm) minimum clearance from the centerline of the lavatory to the side wall. Therefore, select a 30" (76.2cm) wide vanity cabinet.

The 30" (76.2cm) vanity allows adequate clearance from the edge of the bowl to the wall opposite it and from the edge of the bowl to the edge of the counter to the right. The 30"/18"/30" (76.2cm/45.72cm/76.2cm) configuration also provides cabinet door size continuity.

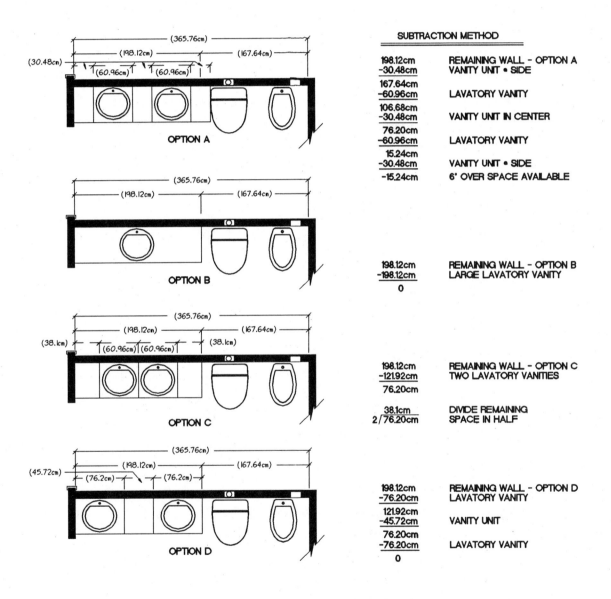

Figure 394   Subtraction Method Step #6 - Consider alternatives.

Door sizing consistency and convenience are both important parts of any bathroom plan. Follow these helpful hints from experienced bathroom specialists:

- Avoid 24" (60.96cm) wide cabinets with large single doors in narrow bathrooms or order this size with split doors. Opt for a 27" (68.58cm) or 30" (76.2cm) so that the two smaller doors will not block the walkway. Specify these base vanity sizes with "*butt-doors*" so that the user will not be forced to reach around a large center stile.

- 9" (22.86cm) or 12" (30.48cm) vanity cabinets or drawer banks in frame type construction provide small, narrow, awkward openings. They should be avoided if at all possible.

- Try to keep all door sizes within a 3" (7.62cm) incremental spacing. Therefore, combining 15" (38.1cm), 18" (45.72cm), 30" (76.2cm), 33" (83.82cm) and 36" (91.44cm) wide vanities provides excellent door size continuity.

- Don't simply divide an available space in half when planning cabinetry. A cabinet with fewer doors and larger openings is preferable to one with more doors with smaller openings. This is particularly critical if the bathroom vanity cabinet system has a center stile separating doors. *For example*, in 54" (137.16cm) of space don't divide it into two 27" (68.58cm) units, opt for one 18"

(45.72cm) unit adjacent to a 36" (91.44cm).

- If possible, maintain horizontal continuity throughout the cabinet elevation. Yet, don't hesitate to combine full height doors, drawer banks and standard vanities in the lavatory area. *For example,* full height doors on both of the lavatories in our example could be quite attractive in a contemporary setting. The three-drawer bank in the center creates a vertical break, which nicely balances the countertop to soffit molding trim above.

Other cabinet layout hints from the pros are:

- If you are raising the overall vanity height above the 30" (76.2cm) to 32" (81.28cm) standard, realize that any seating areas will need to be mounted at the lower height.

- When installing an 18" (45.72cm) deep vanity in a shallow area, make sure to check the overall lavatory dimension, including the overflow at the front of the bowl. Some lavatories won't fit in reduced depth cabinets. An attractive alternative is to step back the cabinets on each side of the lavatory to provide the necessary walkway access, and allow the lavatory cabinet to jut into the space by employing an angled or curved arrangement.

- Hold the cabinets off the floor and continue the floor surface under the vanity arrangement to increase the perceived size of the space.

Let's select Option "D" and install a 30" (76.2cm) vanity cabinet to the left, an 18" (45.72cm) three-drawer unit in the center, and a 30" (76.2cm) vanity cabinet to the right. Specify a finished side on the right because the end of this cabinet is exposed. Because the lavatory cabinet to the left does not have any operable drawers, a filler or scribe strip is not necessary between the cabinet and the wall. If this were a standard cabinet, especially frameless, with an operable drawer, a filler would be needed to keep

the drawer away from the door casing on the perpendicular wall. Otherwise the door casing would impede the drawer's movement and accessibility.

Step No. 7 - Draw the Solution

Draw in the water closet, the bidet, the base vanity cabinet depth (remember to use a dash line). Then use a solid line to indicate the countertop overhang. The dimensions listed will relate to the cabinets, rather than the 3/4" (1.9cm) to 1" (2.54cm) expected overhang on the countertop surface. Note the centerline dimensions of all the fixtures as well.

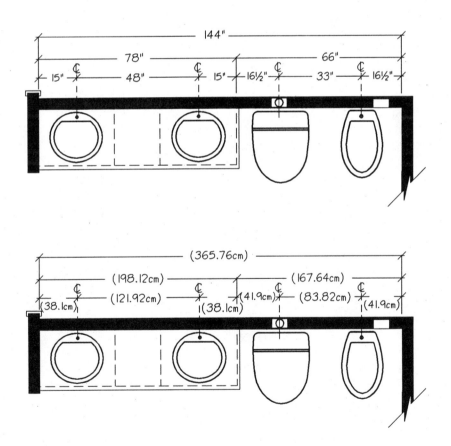

Figure 395 Subtraction Method Step #7 - Draw the solution.

Step No. 8 - Determine Vertical Relationship

The subtraction method is used in determining vertical as well as horizontal relationships within a bathroom plan. Specifying the horizontal and vertical relationship of the elements in the bathroom is an important part of the process because many small items are placed according to the individual needs of each client. These individual products are installed adjacent to, above or below one another.

Some designers prefer to establish the entire floor plan and then return to each wall to lay out the elevations. Other designers like to work on one wall at a time: laying out the floor plan, then sketching a rough elevation to determine vertical height relationships so that all of the cabinet call-outs can be prepared in one stage. You should determine which system you are most comfortable with - and then stick to it. The key is to be consistent in your use of your own personalized subtraction method.

THE TOILET/BIDET AREA

Once the horizontal space has been arranged, you must determine the overall vertical relationship of the storage elements planned on the wall behind the toilet and above the vanity. First sketch a quick elevation as you decide the overall design approach that you'll take in this area. In our solution, the toilet/bidet area will have hanging rod space for towels above the two fixtures. A horizontal band will be created by narrow cabinets that are installed at a different level than the mirror and cabinet combination behind the vanities.

You will now dimension the wall space required for the fixtures and the hanging linens. A decision is also made at this time regarding the overall height of the mirror and trim behind the vanity.

The designer elects to hang the towel bars at 47" (119.38cm) above the floor, following the NKBA storage recommendation. Supplemental storage for cleaning supplies and other less frequently needed items is placed above at 74" (187.96cm) to the top of the cabinet. The cabinets specified are 15" (38cm) high, which will leave 12" (30.48cm) between the cabinet bottom and towel bar centerline, and 6" (15.24cm) between the bottom of a 16" (40.64cm) towel and toilet tank cover.

- 74" - 15" = 59" - 47" = 12" between cabinets and towel bar 187.96cm - 38.1cm = 149.86cm - 119.38cm = 30.48cm)

- 47" - 25" = 22" - 16 = 6" between towel and toilet (119.38cm - 63.5cm = 55.88cm - 40.64cm = 15.24cm)

Then the overall 66" (167.64cm) space is divided into two equal cabinet widths of 33" (83.82cm). This simplifies the overall layout of the space.

Figure 396   Subtraction Method Step #8 - Determine vertical relationship.

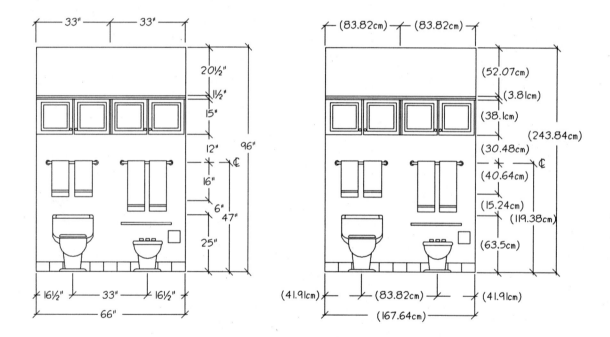

Figure 397   Subtraction Method Step #8 - Determine vertical relationship.

THE LAVATORY AREA

The wall layout continues above the vanity arrangement. Our sample design calls for a tall countertop-to-molding cabinet separating the two vanities. To maintain design continuity, an 18" (45.72cm) wide unit, which echoes the drawer bank width below, has been selected. This then leaves 30" (76.2cm) of space on each side. We will now center individual, framed, recessed medicine/storage cabinets above each lavatory.

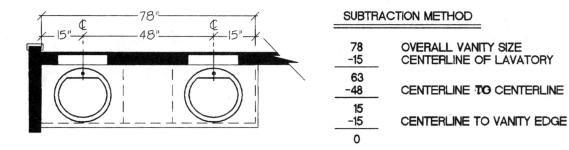

SUBTRACTION METHOD

78	OVERALL VANITY SIZE
-15	CENTERLINE OF LAVATORY
63	
-48	CENTERLINE TO CENTERLINE
15	
-15	CENTERLINE TO VANITY EDGE
0	

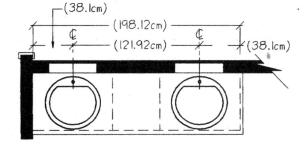

SUBTRACTION METHOD

198.12cm	OVERALL VANITY SIZE
- 38.1cm	CENTERLINE OF LAVATORY
160.02cm	
-121.92cm	CENTERLINE TO CENTERLINE
38.1cm	
- 38.1cm	CENTERLINE TO VANITY EDGE
0	

Figure 398   Subtraction Method Step #8 - Determine vertical relationship.

- Starting at the left-hand wall, to the center of the lavatory/medicine cabinet equals 15" (38.1cm). The overall medicine cabinet framed width is 18" (45.72cm). Therefore, subtract 9" (22.86cm) from the 15" (38.1cm) which leaves a 6" (15.24cm) reveal from the edge of the wall to the medicine cabinet.

We then complete the dimensioning by scaling off the same 18" (45.72cm) width centered on the second lavatory plumbing line to the right.

Returning to the overall vanity size of 78" (198.12cm), we subtract the following dimensions:

- 78" (198.12cm) Overall Vanity Size

- - 6" (15.24cm) For Left Hand Reveal

- - 18" (45.72cm) For First Medicine Cabinet

- - 18" (45.72cm) For Second Medicine Cabinet

- - 6" (15.24cm) For Anticipated Reveal Space to the Far Right

- = 30" (76.2cm) Balance

The 30" in the middle is then our centerline spacing from medicine cabinet frame one to medicine cabinet frame two.

To complete this dimension line, subtract another set of dimensions from the overall of 144" (365.76cm):

- 144" (365.76cm) Overall Dimension

- - 6" (15.24cm) Reveal

- - 18" (45.72cm) Medicine Cabinet

- - 30" (76.2cm) Space

- - 18" (45.72cm) Second Medicine Cabinet

- = 72" (182.88cm) Balance

The remaining 72" (182.88cm) gives us our dimension from the edge of medicine cabinet frame number two to the far right hand wall.

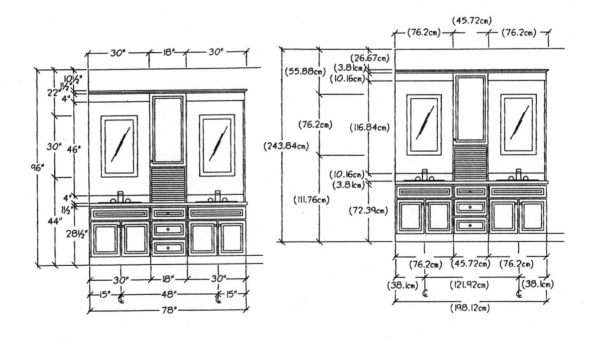

Figure 399   Subtraction Method Step #8 - Determine vertical relationships.

In Step No. 5 you called out the centerlines for the lavatory plumbing. Use
these same measurements as the center

for the recessed medicine cabinet. This
allows you to finish dimensioning the
wall as follows:

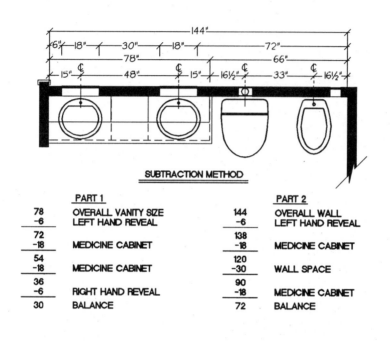

SUBTRACTION METHOD

	PART 1			PART 2	
78	OVERALL VANITY SIZE		144	OVERALL WALL	
-6	LEFT HAND REVEAL		-6	LEFT HAND REVEAL	
72			138		
-18	MEDICINE CABINET		-18	MEDICINE CABINET	
54			120		
-18	MEDICINE CABINET		-30	WALL SPACE	
36			90		
-6	RIGHT HAND REVEAL		-18	MEDICINE CABINET	
30	BALANCE		72	BALANCE	

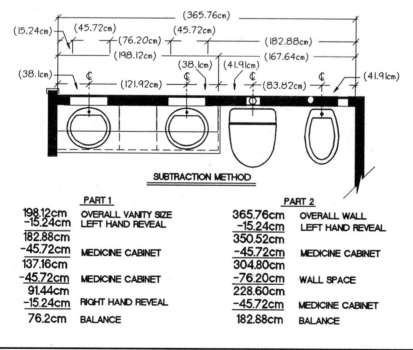

SUBTRACTION METHOD

	PART 1			PART 2	
198.12cm	OVERALL VANITY SIZE		365.76cm	OVERALL WALL	
-15.24cm	LEFT HAND REVEAL		-15.24cm	LEFT HAND REVEAL	
182.88cm			350.52cm		
-45.72cm	MEDICINE CABINET		-45.72cm	MEDICINE CABINET	
137.16cm			304.80cm		
-45.72cm	MEDICINE CABINET		-76.20cm	WALL SPACE	
91.44cm			228.60cm		
-15.24cm	RIGHT HAND REVEAL		-45.72cm	MEDICINE CABINET	
76.2cm	BALANCE		182.88cm	BALANCE	

Figure 400   Subtraction Method Step #8 - Determine vertical relationships.

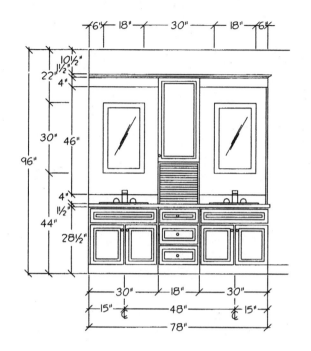

SUBTRACTION METHOD

78	VANITY WALL AREA
-6	LEFT HAND REVEAL
72	
-18	FIRST MEDICINE CABINET
54	
-30	CENTER WALL SECTION
24	
-18	SECOND MEDICINE CABINET
6	
-6	RIGHT HAND REVEAL
0	BALANCE

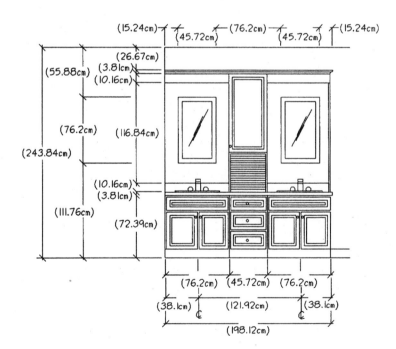

SUBTRACTION METHOD

198.12cm	VANITY WALL AREA
- 15.24cm	LEFT HAND REVEAL
182.88cm	
- 45.72cm	FIRST MEDICINE CABINET
137.16cm	
- 76.20cm	CENTER WALL SECTION
60.96cm	
- 45.72cm	SECOND MEDICINE CABINET
15.24cm	
- 15.24cm	RIGHT HAND REVEAL
0	BALANCE

Figure 401   Subtraction Method Step #8 - Determine vertical relationships.

Step No. 9 - Verify All Dimensions

Once you have completed the layout process for each wall, or after the entire room is laid out, you will go back and *"double check"* all of your floor plan dimensions. It is not uncommon for a bathroom project to come to a grinding halt during the installation phase because of a dimensional mistake on the plan or an incorrect product on the jobsite. Therefore the order check system really involves two steps; double checking all dimensions and double checking all equipment. First, verify that your original field dimensions are accurate. You may wish to return to the jobsite for another check. This small time investment can be reasonable compared to the time, money and frustration caused by errors discovered after the project begins. Next, each wall is systematically checked against the overall dimensions to verify fixture sizes, reveal dimensions, center lines and cabinet sizes.

Once the specifications are prepared, all item dimensions and mechanical requirements should be double checked against the manufacturer's literature.

Steps involved in order check system:

Part #1: Verify the overall wall dimension. We'll assume that you have verified that you do indeed have 144" (365.76cm) of finished wall space with no windows or doors to develop.

Part #2: Verify construction constraints. Additionally, verify that there are no hidden vents or mechanical system elements which will preclude recessing two medicine cabinets, or including the plumbing necessary for the two vanities as well as the toilet and bidet.

Part #3: Verify fixture center lines. Complete each one of these steps by always starting and moving in the same direction. In our example, we'll move from the left hand corner of the vanity wall to the right. Therefore, our 144" (365.76cm) will have the following items subtracted from it:

- 144" (Overall Dimension

- - 15" (38.1cm) To the Center of the First Lavatory

- - 48" (121.94cm) To the Center of the Second Lavatory

- - 15" (38.1cm) To the Edge of the Cabinet

- = 66" (167.64cm) Balance

The remaining dimension should be 66".

We'll continue our check by subtracting the following:

- 66" (167.64cm)

- - 16 1/2" (41.91cm) To the Center of The Bidet

- - 33" (83.82cm) To the Center of the Toilet

- - 16-1/2" (41.91cm) To the wall.

- = 0" Balance

The remaining dimension should now be 0". With this step, we've verified the centerlines and the overall cabinet size.

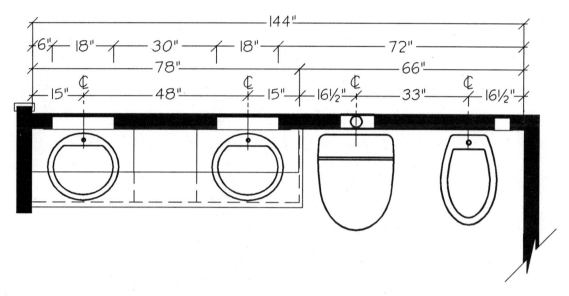

SUBTRACTION METHOD

PART 3

144	OVERALL WALL
−15	LEFT WALL TO CENTER OF LAVATORY
129	
−48	TO CENTER OF 2ND LAVATORY
81	
−15	TO RIGHT EDGE OF VANITY
66	REMAINING WALL
−16 1/2	EDGE OF VANITY TO CENTER OF BIDET
49 1/2	
−33	TO CENTER OF TOILET
16 1/2	
−16 1/2	TO RIGHT WALL
0	BALANCE

Figure 402   Subtraction Method Step #9 - Verify centerlines.

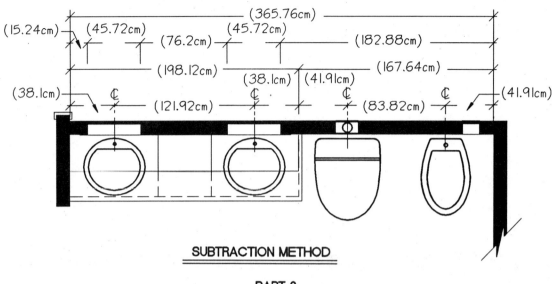

SUBTRACTION METHOD

PART 3

365.76cm	OVERALL WALL
− 38.10cm	LEFT WALL TO CENTER OF LAVATORY
327.66cm	
−121.92cm	TO CENTER OF 2ND LAVATORY
205.74cm	
− 38.10cm	TO RIGHT EDGE OF VANITY
167.64cm	REMAINING WALL
− 41.91cm	EDGE OF VANITY TO CENTER OF BIDET
125.73cm	
− 83.82cm	TO CENTER OF TOILET
41.91cm	
− 41.91cm	TO RIGHT WALL
0	BALANCE

Figure 403   Subtraction Method Step #9 - Verify centerlines.

Part #4: Verify cabinet sizes. From our overall vanity size of 78" (198.12cm):

- 78" (198.12cm)

- − 30" (76.2cm) For the First Lavatory Cabinet

- − 18" (45.72cm) For the Middle Vanity Cabinet

- − 30" (76.2cm) For the Second Lavatory

- = 0" Balance

The resulting 0" indicates that the cabinet layout does equal the overall dimension available.

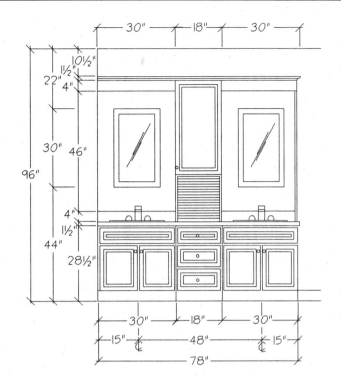

SUBTRACTION METHOD

78	VANITY WALL AREA
-30	FIRST SINK CABINET
48	
-18	MIDDLE VANITY CABINET
30	
-30	SECOND SINK CABINET
0	BALANCE

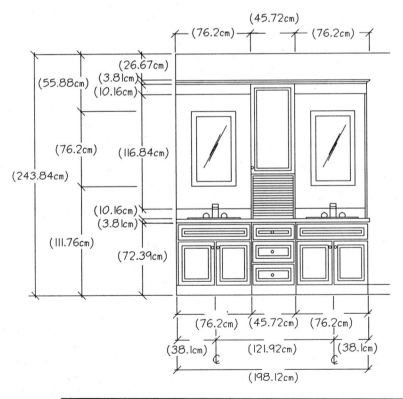

SUBTRACTION METHOD

198.12cm	VANITY WALL AREA
- 76.20cm	FIRST SINK CABINET
121.92cm	
- 45.72cm	MIDDLE VANITY CABINET
76.20cm	
- 76.20cm	SECOND SINK CABINET
0	BALANCE

Figure 404   Subtraction Method Step #9 - Verify cabinet sizes.

Part 5: Verify accessory centerlines. Our overall 78" (198.12cm) has the following dimensions subtracted:

- 78" (198.12cm)

- - 6" (15.24cm) For the Left-hand Reveal

- - 18" (45.72cm) For the First Medicine Cabinet

- - 30" (76.2cm) For the Center Wall Section

- - 18" For the Second Medicine Cabinet

- - 6" (15.24cm) For the Left Hand Reveal

- = 0" Balance

The resulting 0" tells us that the medicine cabinets are perfectly centered above the lavatories. *(See Figure 405)*

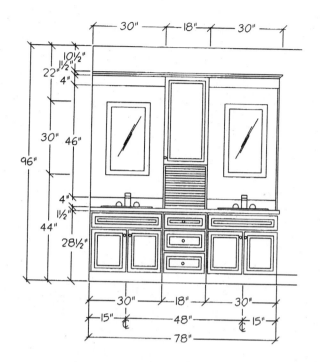

SUBTRACTION METHOD

78	VANITY WALL AREA
−6	LEFT HAND REVEAL
72	
−18	FIRST MEDICINE CABINET
54	
−30	CENTER WALL SECTION
24	
−18	SECOND MEDICINE CABINET
6	
−6	RIGHT HAND REVEAL
0	BALANCE

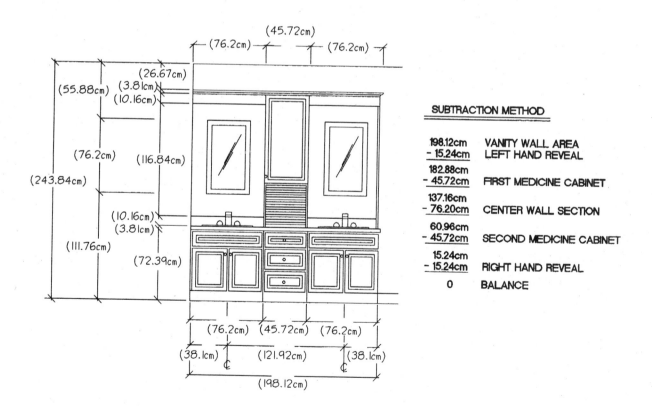

SUBTRACTION METHOD

198.12cm	VANITY WALL AREA
− 15.24cm	LEFT HAND REVEAL
182.88cm	
− 45.72cm	FIRST MEDICINE CABINET
137.16cm	
− 76.20cm	CENTER WALL SECTION
60.96cm	
− 45.72cm	SECOND MEDICINE CABINET
15.24cm	
− 15.24cm	RIGHT HAND REVEAL
0	BALANCE

Figure 405   Subtraction Method Step #9 - Verify accessory placement.

A second check will verify the relationship of the recessed medicine cabinets to the center cabinet. *(See Figure 406)*

The overall 78" (198.12cm) has the following dimensions subtracted:

- 78" (198.12cm)

- - 6" (15.24cm) For the Left Hand Reveal

- - 18" (45.72cm) For the Medicine Cabinet

- - 6" (15.24cm) For the Reveal

- - 18" (45.72cm) For the Wall Cabinet

- - 6" (15.24cm) For the Reveal

- - 18" ((45.72) For the Wall Cabinet

- - 6" (15.24cm) For the Reveal

- = 0" Balance

We have now verified that the wall elements line-up symmetrically.

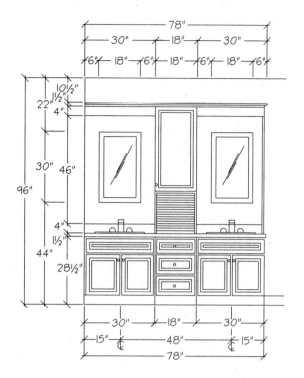

SUBTRACTION METHOD

78	VANITY WALL AREA
-6	LEFT HAND REVEAL
72	
-18	FIRST MEDICINE CABINET
54	
-6	REVEAL
48	
-18	MIDDLE WALL CABINET
30	
-6	REVEAL
24	
-18	SECOND MEDICINE CABINET
6	
-6	REVEAL
0	BALANCE

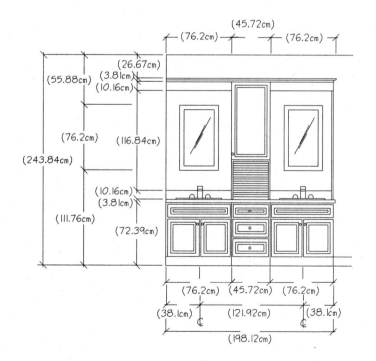

SUBTRACTION METHOD

198.12cm	VANITY WALL AREA
- 15.24cm	LEFT HAND REVEAL
182.88cm	
- 45.72cm	FIRST MEDICINE CABINET
137.16cm	
- 15.24cm	REVEAL
121.92cm	
- 45.72cm	MIDDLE WALL CABINET
76.20cm	
- 15.24cm	REVEAL
60.96cm	
- 45.72cm	SECOND MEDICINE CABINET
15.24cm	
- 15.24cm	REVEAL
0	BALANCE

Figure 406   Subtraction Method Step #9 - Verify recessed medicine cabinet to center cabinet.

Verify all Vertical Relationships.

The same step is used to verify the height relationship to all elements in the elevations.

Medicine Cabinet Elevation

- 96" (243.84cm) Ceiling Height

- - 10 1/2" (26.67cm) Area Above Cabinet

- - 1 1/2" (3.81cm) Molding Dimension

- - 14" (35.56cm) Reveal Above Medicine Cabinet

- - 30" (76.2cm) Medicine Cabinet Overall Height

- - 6" (15.24cm) Reveal Below Medicine Cabinet and Backsplash Top

- - 4" (10.16cm) Countertop Backsplash

- - 1 1/2" (3.81cm) Countertop Thickness

- - 28 1/2" (72.39cm) Vanity Cabinet Height

- = 0" Balance

Center Cabinet Elevation

- 96" (243.84cm) Ceiling Height

- - 10 1/2" (26.67cm) Area Above Cabinet

- - 1 1/2" (3.81cm) Molding Dimension

- - 54" (137.16cm) Wall Cabinet Height

- - 1 1/2" (3.81cm) Countertop Thickness

- - 28 1/2" (72.39cm) Vanity Cabinet Height

- = 0" Balance

Toilet/Bidet Elevation

- 96" (243.84cm) Ceiling Height

- - 20 1/2" (52.07cm) Area Above Cabinet

- - 1 1/2" (3.81cm) Molding Thickness

- - 15" (38.1cm) Cabinet Height

- - 12" (30.48cm) Reveal

- - 16" (40.64cm) Towels

- - 6" (15.24cm) Reveal

- - 25" (63.5cm) Fixture (toilet)

- = 0" Balance

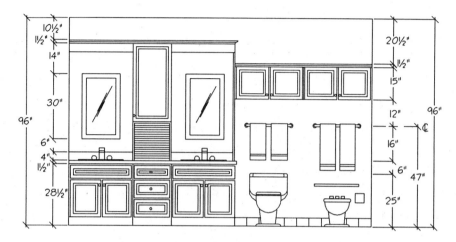

SUBTRACTION METHOD

CENTER CABINET ELEVATION

96	CEILING HEIGHT
-10 1/2	AREA ABOVE CABINETS
85 1/2	
-1 1/2	MOLDING
84	
-54	WALL CABINET HEIGHT
30	
-1 1/2"	COUNTERTOP THICKNESS
28 1/2	
-28 1/2	VANITY HEIGHT
0	BALANCE

MEDICINE CABINET ELEVATION

96	CEILING HEIGHT
-10 1/2	AREA ABOVE CABINETS
85 1/2	
-1 1/2	MOLDING
84	
-14	REVEAL ABOVE MEDICINE CABINET
70	
-30	MEDICINE CABINET
40	
-6	REVEAL BELOW MEDICINE CABINET AND TOP OF BACKSPLASH
34	
-4	BACKSPLASH
30	
-1 1/2	COUNTERTOP THICKNESS
28 1/2	
-28 1/2	VANITY HEIGHT
0	BALANCE

WATER CLOSET ELEVATION

96	CEILING HEIGHT
-20 1/2	AREA ABOVE CABINETS
75 1/2	
-1 1/2	MOLDING
74	
-15	WALL CABINET HEIGHT
59	
-12	REVEAL
47	
-16	TOWEL AND TOP OF BACKSPLASH
31	
-6	REVEAL
25	
-25	TOILET HEIGHT
0	BALANCE

Figure 407   Subtraction Method Step #9 - Verify all vertical relationships.

SUBTRACTION METHOD

CENTER CABINET ELEVATION

243.84cm	CEILING HEIGHT
- 26.67cm	AREA ABOVE CABINETS
217.17cm	
- 3.81cm	MOLDING
213.36cm	
-137.16cm	WALL CABINET HEIGHT
76.20cm	
- 3.81cm	COUNTERTOP THICKNESS
72.39cm	
- 72.39cm	VANITY HEIGHT
0	BALANCE

MEDICINE CABINET ELEVATION

243.84cm	CEILING HEIGHT
- 26.67cm	AREA ABOVE CABINETS
217.17cm	
- 3.81cm	MOLDING
213.36cm	
- 35.56cm	REVEAL ABOVE MEDICINE CABINET
177.80cm	
- 76.20cm	MEDICINE CABINET
101.60cm	
- 15.24cm	REVEAL BELOW MEDICINE CABINET
86.36cm	AND TOP OF BACKSPLASH
- 10.16cm	BACKSPLASH
76.20cm	
- 3.81cm	COUNTERTOP THICKNESS
72.39cm	
- 72.39cm	VANITY HEIGHT
0	BALANCE

WATER CLOSET ELEVATION

243.84cm	CEILING HEIGHT
- 52.07cm	AREA ABOVE CABINETS
191.77cm	
- 3.81cm	MOLDING
187.96cm	
- 38.10cm	WALL CABINET HEIGHT
149.86cm	
- 30.48cm	REVEAL
119.38cm	
- 78.74cm	TOWEL
86.36cm	AND TOP OF BACKSPLASH
- 15.24cm	REVEAL
63.50cm	
- 63.50cm	TOILET HEIGHT
0	BALANCE

Figure 408   Subtraction Method Step #9 - Verify all vertical relationships.

Step No. 10 - Verify All Equipment Sizes

Lastly, but quite important, check all assumed dimensions and installation requirements against the manufacturer's literature.

This is the final step in a successful subtration method operation. It is important that you follow each of these steps carefully and complete them in order. This will result in a correct and competent solution.

Figure 409   The completed job.

CHAPTER **4**

Drawing and Presentation Standards for the Bathroom Professional

THE PROFESSIONAL PRESENTATION

Successful bathroom designs rely on a complete and professional set of project documents. A complete drawing presentation includes a floor plan, mechanical plan, construction plan (if job requires) and interpretive sketches.

Such a presentation provides a clear and concise description of the project's

scope for everyone involved. Errors caused by misinterpreting information are minimized. And you, as the bathroom design specialist, present a professional image to the client and other tradespeople.

Examples of complete sets of project documents can be found in Appendix B - NKBA Graphic & Presentation Standards.

For your convenience you will find metric equivalent representations within this chapter.

Inspecting and Measuring the Design Space

PREPARING TO MEASURE

Before the project documents can be started, you must carefully measure and inspect the physical space. The measuring steps you take depend on whether the project involves remodeling or new construction.

To assist you, bathroom layout sheets and client survey forms are available from the **National Kitchen & Bath Association**. These forms include a 1/2" scale (1:20cm) layout grid and specifications list.

Other tools you'll need are:

- 25 ft. metal tape measure

- Pencils, pens of different colors

- Note pad or clipboard

MEASURING THE REMODELING JOB

When preparing for a remodeling job, it's wise to follow a few simple steps to insure concise and accurate planning.

- **1. Visually inspect the space** and draw a proportionally correct room outline. Include all windows and doors: indicate north/south orientation and adjacent room or view information.

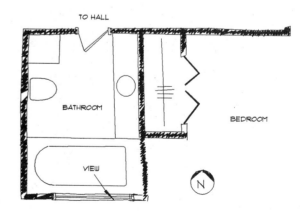

Figure 410   Draw the room with accurate proportions.

2. Measure the ceiling height.
Measuring floor to ceiling is difficult. Many designers prefer to mark a midpoint on the wall, measuring from the ceiling down to the mark and then from the mark to the floor. Others measure from the ceiling down, pushing the tape down with their knee while holding it flat against the wall, while still others prefer to push the tape up from the floor to the ceiling. The measurement should be repeated at several locations to determine levelness. Record the height in a circle at the center of the floor plan.

3. Select a corner as a starting point. If possible, clear a path approximately 3' (91.44cm) above the floor and measure the full length of the wall. Record the total dimension on the plan.

Check corners for squareness.
The corner squareness is determined by marking a point 3' (91.44cm) out from the corner on one wall and 4' (121.92cm) out from the corner on the adjacent wall and measuring the distance between the two points. If the distance is 5' (152.4cm), the corner is square, but any other measurement indicates the corner is out of

Figure 411   Measuring the ceiling.

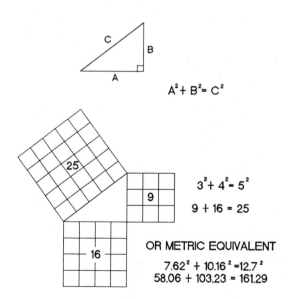

$$A^2 + B^2 = C^2$$

$$3^2 + 4^2 = 5^2$$
$$9 + 16 = 25$$

OR METRIC EQUIVALENT
$$7.62^2 + 10.16^2 = 12.7^2$$
$$58.06 + 103.23 = 161.29$$

Figure 412   Functions of a Right Triangle.

square. If this is the case, make a note on your plan.

This formula is known as:
The Pythagorean Theorum

$$(A^2 + B^2 = C^2)$$

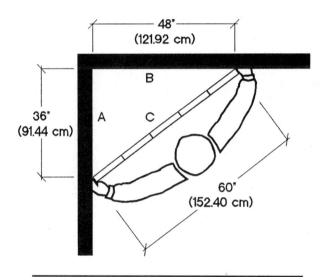

Figure 413   Determining corner squareness.

- 4. **Return to the starting point** and measure from the corner to the nearest obstacle (door, window, pipe chase, etc.) and record results. Measure the obstacle from outside edge to outside edge and record the dimension. Continue the process until the opposite corner is reached.

- 5. **Stop and confirm the accuracy** of your measurements by comparing the sum of all individual dimensions to the total wall measurement.

- 6. **Repeat steps 3, 4 and 5 for each wall.**

- 7. **Complete the National Kitchen & Bath Association survey form** noting any important height dimensions; such as window heights from floor and ceiling, door heights, heating, ventilation and air conditioning units.

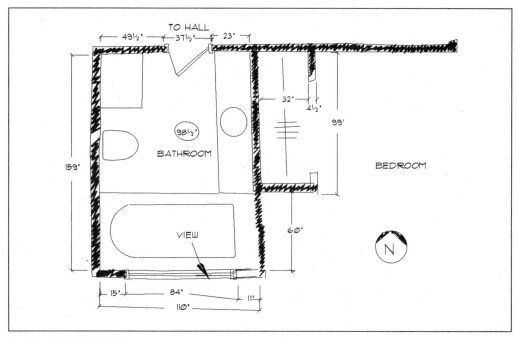

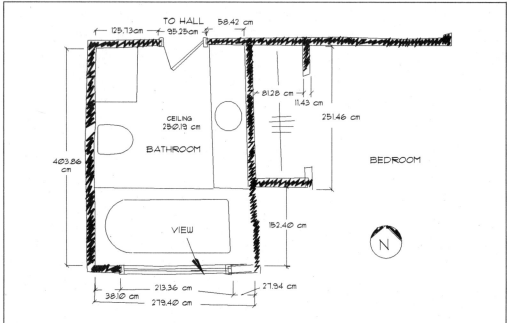

Figure 414   Jobsite floor plans with dimensions noted.

- **8. Identify plumbing and electrical/lighting centerlines** by returning to the starting point and measuring from corner to center of outlets, switches, fixtures, lighting, venting, and plumbing locations. Record center location with standard symbols found in the *NKBA Graphics and Presentations Standards* within this manual.

- **9. Make your final inspection.** Measure any free-standing furniture pieces, check electrical service panel conditions and check any areas such as basement or attic, which may be affected during the remodeling process. Take photos or videos of existing space to jog your memory during the design process.

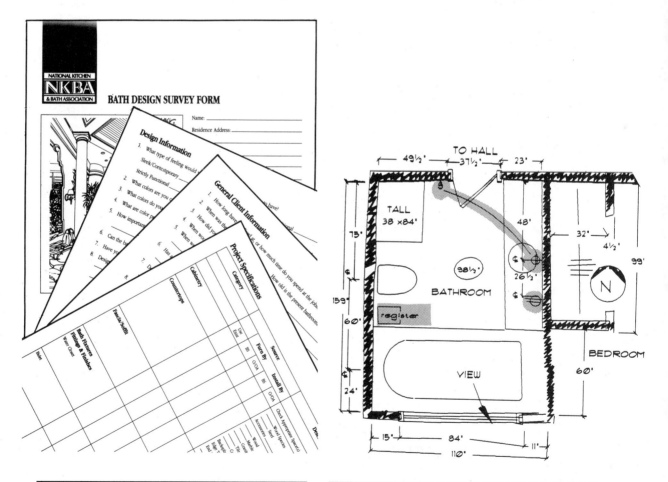

Figure 415   National Kitchen & Bath Association Survey Forms.

Figure 416   Indicate mechanical elements to clarify and eliminate possible errors later.

MEASURING NEW CONSTRUCTION

When measuring a new construction site during the framing stages the process is the same, however, it must be noted that all dimensions will be made from stud wall to stud wall during the jobsite visit.

Architectural elements will be located from stud wall to rough opening. Compare the measurements to the architects blueprints. If there is any discrepancy, discuss the difference and any ramifications to the plan with the builder or homeowner.

Verify where doors and windows lead, their size, direction and trim size. Verify the type and thickness of the material for finishing the walls, ceilings, and floors.

After the jobsite has been measured, the draftsperson will adjust the rough dimensions; subtracting material and finish depths for each wall surface so that the plan reflects finished wall dimensions. Be sure to confirm what finished materials are to be used before placing any product orders. These finished dimensions can make a big difference in product specifications. Substituting 1/16" (.15cm) vinyl with a 1/2" (1.27cm) thick marble floor alters the finished floor to ceiling dimension, which in turn affects tall cabinet and soffit dimensions.

MEASURING UNUSUAL WALLS

Measuring unusual walls, such as angles and/or curves, requires more time and a different technique. The most accurate approach to measuring an unusual angle is to first lay out a (90°) right triangle on the floor in the corner.

Trigonometric Formulas

Once the triangle is located on the floor, measure at least two of its legs and apply the appropriate trigonometric formula.

Begin by determining what angle needs to be found. Then identify the opposite, adjacent and hypotenuse sides of the triangle. The opposite side is the side which is directly opposite the angle. The hypotenuse is the longest side of the triangle and the remaining leg is termed the adjacent side. Use one of the following trigonometric formulas to determine the angle:

- **Sine (SIN)** equals the opposite side divided by the hypotenuse.

- **Cosine (COS)** equals the adjacent side divided by the hypotenuse.

- **Tangent (TAN)** equals the opposite side divided by the adjacent side.

In our example, the opposite side and hypotenuse are known, therefore the Sine Formula is appropriately selected. Your answer is a decimal number which should be rounded to the nearest ten thousandth. Then use The Table of Trigonometric functions to find the correct angle.

To use the table, look under the appropriate column (SIN, COS or TAN) and find the closest decimal number. Then find the corresponding angle which is shown at the far left of that row.

Table of Trigonometric Functions

Angle	Sin	Cos	Tan	Angle	Sin	Cos	Tan
1°	.0175	.9998	.0175	46°	.7193	.6947	1.0355
2°	.0349	.9994	.0349	47°	.7314	.6820	1.0724
3°	.0523	.9986	.0524	48°	.7431	.6691	1.1106
4°	.0698	.9976	.0699	49°	.7547	.6561	1.1504
5°	.0872	.9962	.0875	50°	.7660	.6428	1.1918
6°	.1045	.9945	.1051	51°	.7771	.6293	1.2349
7°	.1219	.9925	.1228	52°	.7880	.6157	1.2799
8°	.1392	.9903	.1405	53°	.7986	.6018	1.3279
9°	.1564	.9877	.1584	54°	.8090	.5878	1.3764
10°	.1736	.9848	.1763	55°	.8192	.5736	1.4281
11°	.1908	.9816	.1944	56°	.8290	.5592	1.4826
12°	.2079	.9781	.2126	57°	.8387	.5446	1.5399
13°	.2250	.9744	.2309	58°	.8480	.5299	1.6003
14°	.2419	.9703	.2493	59°	.8572	.5150	1.6643
15°	.2588	.9659	.2679	60°	.8660	.5000	1.7321
16°	.2756	.9613	.2867	61°	.8746	.4848	1.8040
17°	.2924	.9563	.3057	62°	.8829	.4695	1.8807
18°	.3090	.9511	.3249	63°	.8910	.4540	1.9626
19°	.3256	.9455	.3443	64°	.8988	.4384	2.0503
20°	.3420	.9397	.3640	65°	.9063	.4226	2.1445
21°	.3584	.9336	.3839	66°	.9135	.4067	2.2460
22°	.3746	.9272	.4040	67°	.9205	.3907	2.3559
23°	.3907	.9205	.4245	68°	.9272	.3746	2.4751
24°	.4067	.9135	.4452	69°	.9336	.3584	2.6051
25°	.4226	.9063	.4663	70°	.9397	.3420	2.7475
26°	.4384	.8988	.4877	71°	.9455	.3256	2.9042
27°	.4540	.8910	.5095	72°	.9511	.3090	3.0777
28°	.4695	.8829	.5317	73°	.9563	.2924	3.2709
29°	.4848	.8746	.5543	74°	.9613	.2756	3.4874
30°	.5000	.8660	.5774	75°	.9659	.2588	3.7321
31°	.5150	.8572	.6009	76°	.9703	.2419	4.0108
32°	.5299	.8480	.6249	77°	.9744	.2250	4.3315
33°	.5446	.8387	.6494	78°	.9781	.2079	4.7046
34°	.5592	.8290	.6745	79°	.9816	.1908	5.1446
35°	.5736	.8192	.7002	80°	.9848	.1736	5.6713
36°	.5878	.8090	.7265	81°	.9877	.1564	6.3138
37°	.6018	.7986	.7536	82°	.9903	.1392	7.1154
38°	.6157	.7880	.7813	83°	.9925	.1219	8.1443
39°	.6293	.7771	.8098	84°	.9945	.1045	9.5144
40°	.6428	.7660	.8391	85°	.9962	.0872	11.4301
41°	.6561	.7547	.8693	86°	.9976	.0698	14.3007
42°	.6691	.7431	.9004	87°	.9986	.0523	19.0811
43°	.6820	.7314	.9325	88°	.9994	.0349	28.6363
44°	.6947	.7193	.9657	89°	.9998	.0175	57.2900
45°	.7071	.7071	1.0000	90°	1.0000	.0000	

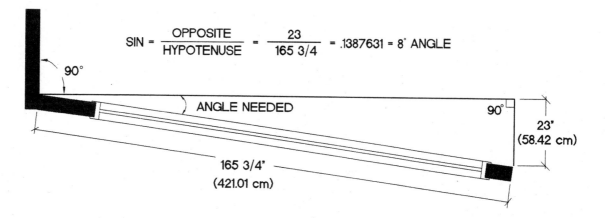

$$SIN = \frac{OPPOSITE}{HYPOTENUSE} = \frac{23}{165\ 3/4} = .1387631 = 8°\ ANGLE$$

90°

ANGLE NEEDED   90°

23"
(58.42 cm)

165 3/4"
(421.01 cm)

Figure 417   Table of Trigonometric Functions - Measuring an angled wall and determining its angle.

MEASURING A CURVED WALL

Measuring a curved wall requires that the radius of the curve be established. The radius is found by first locating a straight line which terminates at any two points along the curve. This line is referred to as a *Chord.* By determining the exact center of the chord and measuring the perpendicular length from this point to the wall, the *Rise* is established.

Use the following formulas to determine the radius:

- $$\frac{(1/2 \text{ Chord})^2 + \text{Rise}^2}{\text{Rise}} = \text{Diameter}$$

- $$\frac{\text{Diameter}}{2} = \text{Radius}$$

For bathroom planning purposes, a 36" (91.44cm) chord dimension is recommended because this measurement represents the widest cabinet you should place against a curved wall.

For example, if you were to use a yardstick (36") (91.44cm) as a chord and found the rise to be 3" (7.62cm), the formula would be calculated as follows:

Imperial Formulation

- $$\frac{(1/2\ (36))^2 + 3^2}{3} =$$

- $$\frac{18^2 + 3^2}{3} =$$

- $$\frac{324 + 9}{3} =$$

- $$\frac{333}{3} =$$

- $111 = \text{Diameter}$

- $$\frac{111}{2} =$$

- $55\ 1/2" = \text{Radius}$

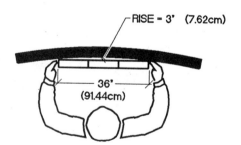

Figure 418   Measuring a curved wall.

Metric Equivalent in Centimeters

- $$\frac{1/2\ (91.44))^2 + 7.62^2}{7.62} =$$

- $$\frac{45.72^2 + 7.62^2}{7.62} =$$

- $$\frac{2090.3184 + 58.0644}{7.62} =$$

- $$\frac{2148.3828}{7.62} =$$

- 281.94 = Diameter

- $$\frac{281.94}{2}$$

- 140.97 = Radius

Now that the radius is established, the length of the curve (referred to as the arc below) can be determined with the following formula:

Formula: $A = \dfrac{\pi \times R \times <}{180}$

Legend: A = length of arc or curve
π = "pi" = 3.14
R = Radius
< = Angle
x = Multiply

Figure 419 A bathroom which utilizes curves.

SECTION 2

Preparation of the Plans

UNDERSTANDING BLUEPRINTS

Many bathroom specialists who are affiliated with decorative plumbing and hardware firms do not visit and measure the jobsite themselves. Much of their clientele consists of tradespeople or homeowners who are building a new home or planning a major renovation for which architectural plans have been prepared. Therefore, the bathroom specialist must have a clear understanding of how to read and understand blueprints.

CLARIFICATION OF TERMS

To begin our discussion, let's clarify some of the more common terms associated with plans preparation:

- **Blueprint:** This word is a holdover from early methods of reproducing builder's plans. In order to produce quantities of large sheets of paper, without using an expensive plate printing process, the "blueprinting" process was created and became the standard of the building industry.

  To make a real "blueprint", an original black and white drawing was reversed onto an ink negative, which made the black lines white on a blue background. This process is not frequently used today. Black line or blue line drawings are much more typical. However, while we still call these drawings "a set of blueprints", a better term would be "plans".

- **Plans:** This term represents a standardized set of drawings and diagrams which communicate the exact construction of a building. Plans may be on microfilm for bidding purposes or may be full-sized and stored rolled up in a tube or laid flat in shallow drawers.

The industry has specified a standard language of symbols to represent construction materials in building plans. Additionally, *Architectural Graphics and Standards,* published by John Wiley & Sons, sets other drawing standards.

A conscientious bathroom designer needs to learn this language of symbols and must be as proficient in understanding its meanings as in communicating in English.

Sometimes communicating with symbols is complicated because of local dialects and accents that develop when a particular architect or company within one area develops specialized symbols for their own use. When this happens, a *"dictionary"* of these symbols is shown on the title sheet of the plans as a *"Key to Materials"*. **Always check the key before attempting to read a set of plans.**

- **Take-off:** This refers to a bidding firm reviewing the plans and developing an estimate for the specific part of the project they are responsible for. The bathroom specialist will *"take-off"* all of the bathroom fixtures and fittings, and perhaps the cabinetry and surfaces for his/her estimate. If the firm specializes in decorative hardware, the designer will do a *"take-off"* from the door schedule as well.

- **Specifications (Specs):** There are written documents accompanying the architect's plans, namely *"Specifications"* and *"Schedules"*. The specifications are descriptions, in words, of the materials to be used and the quality expected. *For example,* the *"specs"* would state the grade of wood that is to be installed in the flooring. Including specifications in plans would complicate the drawing beyond readability. There-

fore, the specifications are generally a separate document.

Smaller projects might use a short form of specification based on a form developed by the **Federal Housing Administration** called *"Description of Materials"*. In the mid 1960s, the **Construction Specification Institute** issued a standard designated, *"Format for Construction Specification"*, which is arranged as nearly as possible in the same order as the work will be performed. This form of specification is used on many projects in the industry.

The specifications are generally written by the architect or by a specification writer. In either case, the individual is expected to apply a knowledge of materials, building codes, and customer expectations to develop a detailed list. However, as a bathroom professional, it is highly recommended that you have your subcontractors verify that the specs and designs of the architect have met all codes, prior to bidding the job.

Because specifications give more detailed expectations of quality and quantity of materials than would be possible in illustrated plans, they need to be carefully reviewed during the *"take-off"*.

- **Schedule:** Within the plans there may be additional pages inserted which have lists of like items specified for the home. There will be a reference number circled on the plan which corresponds to a number on the schedule. *For example,* a schedule may list the exact size and construction of each door in the project.

Because the schedule is a tabulated list of materials needed for the job, it can be considered a short form of specifications for materials. Schedules are useful because they provide quick on-the-job information. *For example,* all the doors will be listed on the door schedule. Therefore, during the *"take-off"*, the schedule can be referenced, rather than painstakingly noting every single door on the plan.

A GUIDE TO PLANS

A complete set of plans contains:

- Title Page

- Site Plan

- Floor Plan

- Elevations

- Construction Details and Sections

- Footing and Foundation Details

- Structural Framing

- Mechanical Plans (Plumbing, Electrical, Ventilation, Air Conditioning, Heating, Etc.)

The plans may also include specific millwork drawings, interior design drawings and landscape plans.

Following this discussion you will find a series of graphics depicting the contents of a complete set of Architectural plans.

Title Page

This is the first page in a set of building plans. It may include any or all of the following:

- The name of the building or project

- The location

- The owner's name

- The architect and/or architectural firm's name

- The names of consulting engineers and/or Interior Designers.

- The set number (of the number of sets distributed)

- A key to the symbols for materials

- An index to the drawings

The title page may also contain a site plan if it is not on a separate sheet.

Site Plan

This is an overhead view of the property around the building. On most projects, it includes the entire property, showing the lot lines and the grades or layout of the land before construction begins. It is sometimes called a *"Plot Plan"*. When reviewing a site plan, make sure that you establish the property lines. Envision the property, as it will look upon completion. Pay particular attention to the orientation of the building on the site, and the affect of this orientation on any of the bathrooms you will be working on.

Floor Plan

The floor plan becomes the central reference point for all other construction drawings because it is the easiest to understand. Because it's an overhead *cutaway view* of the overall project, most people can imagine walking through the home by looking at a floor plan. Generally, the floor plan shows the entire building. Building plans include separate sheets of floor plans for each story of the building, including the basement. It's possible to see the arrangement of the walls and partitions, stairs, doors and windows from these drawings.

On the floor plan there are numbers. These refer to detail drawings that follow or to a schedule of materials. Therefore, you can use the floor plan as a visual index to locate the specifics of each area shown. Sometimes numbers on the plan may also refer to exact sections of the specifications. If in doubt, go over the numbering code with the architect or client before beginning your *"take-off"*.

The dimensions given on the plans are exact, whereas the drawings may not be perfectly to scale. Look for the note *"NTS" (Not to Scale)*. Look for areas on the plan that are shaded or somehow differentiated from the balance of the plan. This plan notation generally indicates changes have been made. **Always use the dimensions listed. Never scale a blueprint during the "take-off" stage.**

Most architectural plans indicate dimensions from the center of partitions and support columns rather than from the finished wall surface. Architects follow this dimensioning process because building materials (such as lumber) may vary in thickness, whereas the center point will always remain standard.

It is the standard of the bathroom industry to dimension finished walls only. This standard has been established because of the critical fit of the products specified for the bathroom. You will need to verify the finished wall dimensions of the project under consideration before you complete your *"take-off"*.

Elevations

The elevation is a flat projection of one side of a building or space. In architectural plans, the elevations show the exterior views of the building and the sections show an interior cut view of the entire building.

It is the standard in the bathroom industry to show interior wall views as individual elevations.

Construction Details and Sections

A section is a "*sliced*" open part of a building, showing inner construction. Sections can be implanted in other plans as a detail, or may be collected on pages of their own. Technically, there are several ways of representing the unseen details in a section. A good source of reference for you to further understand blueprint reading is, *Blueprint Reading for the Building Trades* by John Traister.

Standard sections of a bathroom plan will show a cut view of a wall illustrating cabinetry, molding, soffit and backsplash relationships.

A detail is a large scale blow-up of an important part of the building. *For example,* the installation of doors or bathroom framing might be shown in detail. Such details are small, but reveal important relationships of materials which cannot be communicated by a simple floor plan or elevation.

Several details may be located on their own detail sheet or they may be included on other drawing sheets.

Footings and Foundations

The foundation serves as an anchor for the building. The foundation plans show how the building is affixed to the concrete walls below.

Structural Framing

The structural framing is an illustration of what holds the building up. Before considering any design alternatives, find out if the walls surrounding the bathroom are load bearing walls or non-structural partitions.

Mechanicals

The mechanicals are a set of drawings, usually found at the back of the plans, which show the arrangement of the heating, ventilating, air conditioning, plumbing, electrical installation and specialized machinery.

Because many of these trades are specialized in themselves, it is not surprising that the mechanicals can be difficult to understand. Each trade has developed a sub-set of symbols and a specialized language to show the details.

It's critical for you to understand all of these mechanicals. You should ask: "*Is there any flexibility in the plumbing supply line, drain or vent locations?*"

You need to look for proper heating and air conditioning vents or ducts in the bathroom plans as well.

Miscellaneous Plans

You may find some additional drawings such as millwork drawings, which are provided by a supplier of equipment and materials, rather than by the architect. They are much more detailed drawings of a specific part of the project. Typically, locally-fabricated cabinet companies provide shop drawings.

There may also be a set of interior design plans showing the location of furniture, specifying the finish of walls and ceilings. Lastly, detail of final landscaping may be shown pictorially.

HINTS FROM THE SPECIALISTS

The showroom specialist, or any bathroom designer who is involved in new construction planning, needs to thoroughly understand a set of blueprints before the "*take-off*" begins.

Seasoned experts in the decorative plumbing and hardware industry share the following hints with you regarding how to read a blueprint:

- Make sure that you and your clients understand that rooms always look bigger in 1/2" (1.27cm) scale than in 1/4" (.63cm) or 1/8" (.31cm) scales. The same also applys for metric ratios.

- Don't ever plan a room that has furniture in it without knowing what size the furniture is and where it's going to be placed.

- When you're doing a hardware "*take-off*", be methodical in your review. *For example,* when you are doing a "*take-off*" for doors, start by counting the number of doors in the entire plan or refer to the door schedule. Make sure you end up with that number of doors and corresponding hardware when you finish your "*take-off*". Consider dividing the doors by groups: key lock, passage and privacy. You can then count the cabinet hardware by areas and total to check quantity.

Missing any item during the "*take-off*" is very costly: in terms of reordering, delay time, and customer frustration. **Check and double check!**

- If your clients add any items that are not on the schedule, consider whether they will change the plans. *For example,* if a client requests that you add grab bars in a shower or bathtub, you have now changed the framing plans. You need to add blocking in the walls during the framing stage so that the grab bars can support 300lbs. (136.2kg) of static weight. Any changes in framing, electrical, plumbing or construction that products require must be clearly communicated to the builder or architect so that the appropriate notes can be incorporated into the plans.

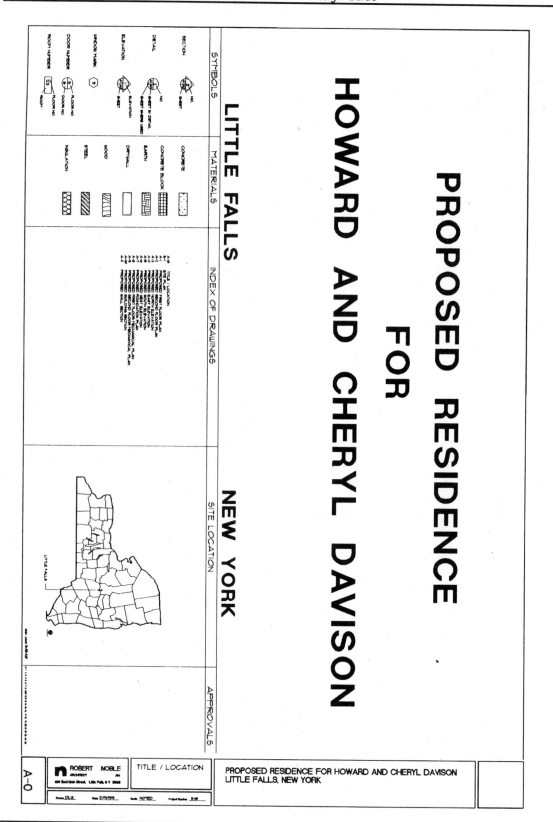

Figure 420   Typical blueprint Title Page.

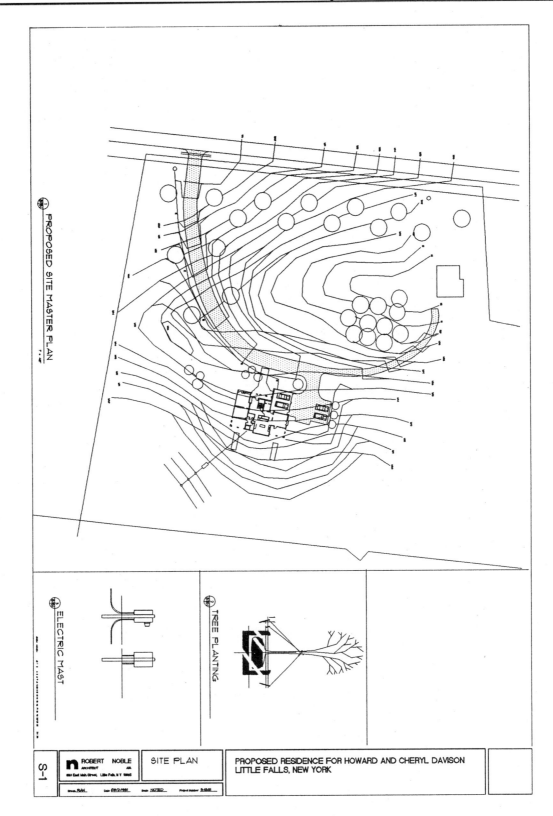

Figure 421   Typical blueprint Site Plan.

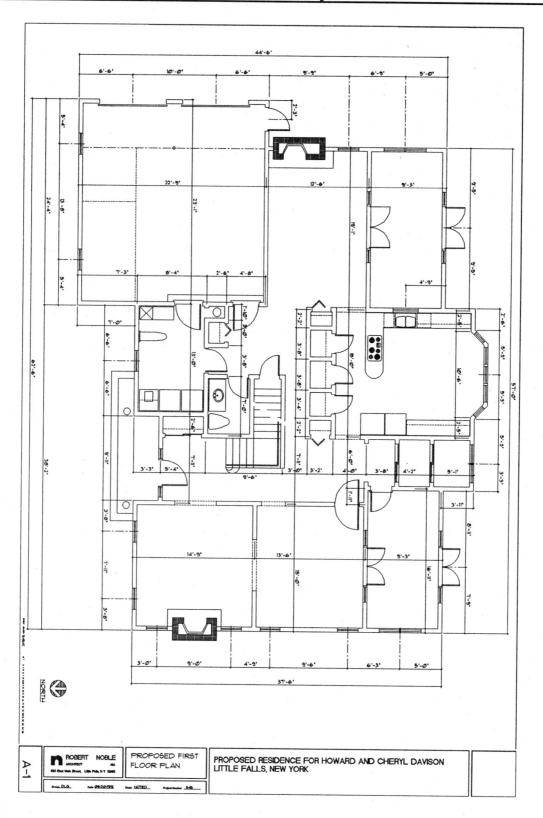

Figure 422   Typical blueprint Floor Plan.

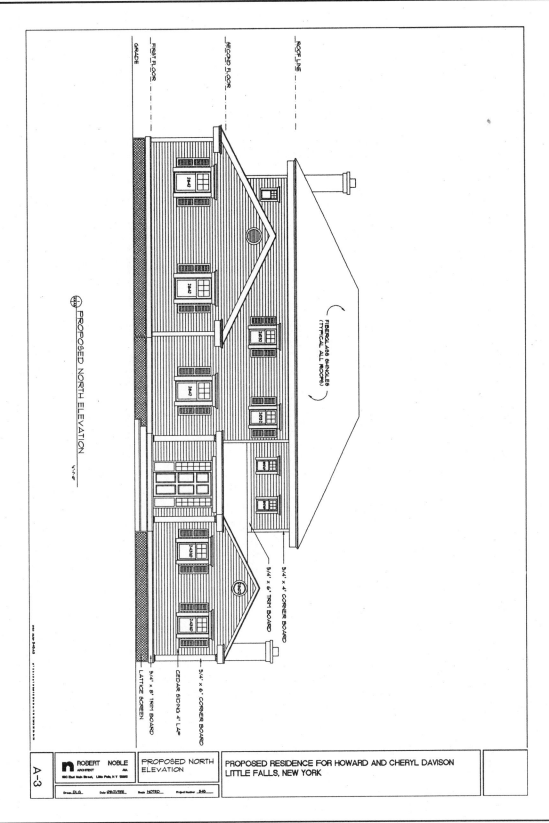

Figure 423   Typical blueprint Elevation.

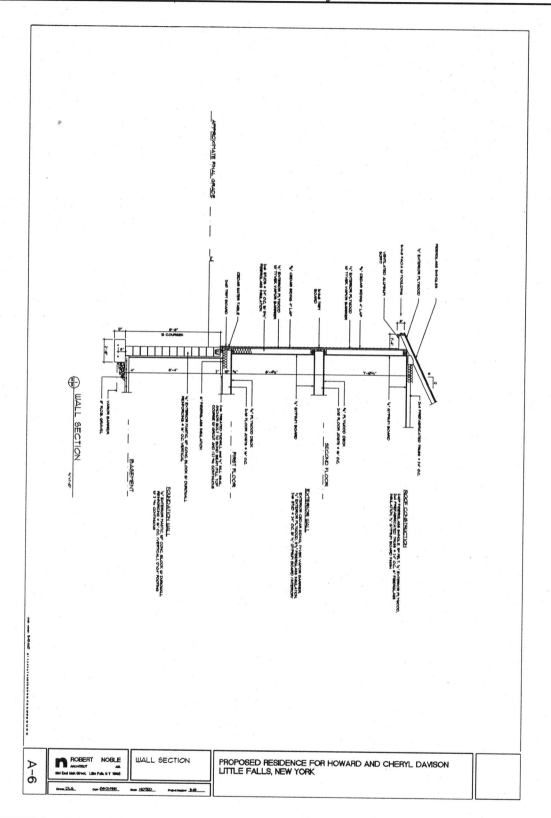

Figure 424   Typical blueprint Section.

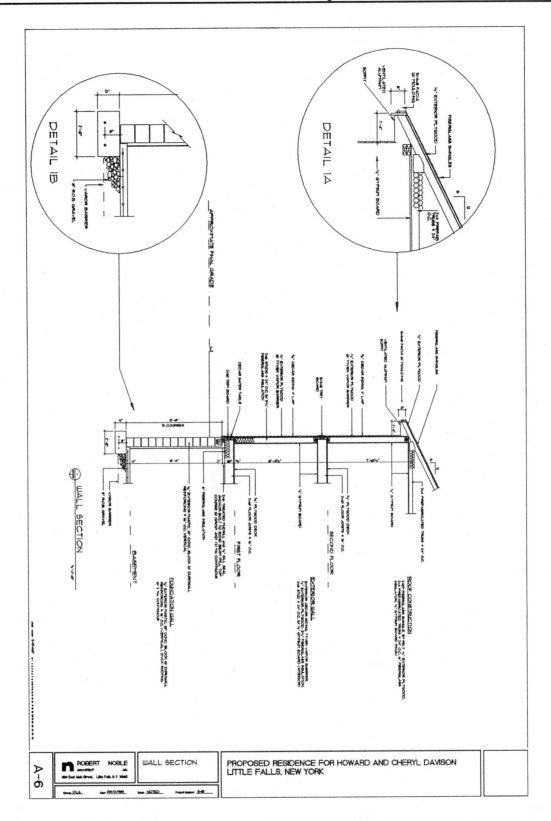

Figure 425   Typical blueprint Construction Details.

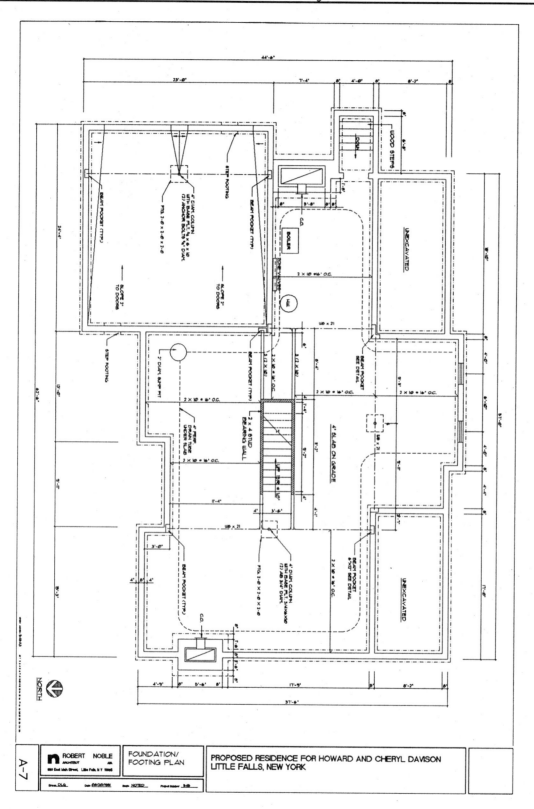

Figure 426   Typical blueprint Foundation Plan.

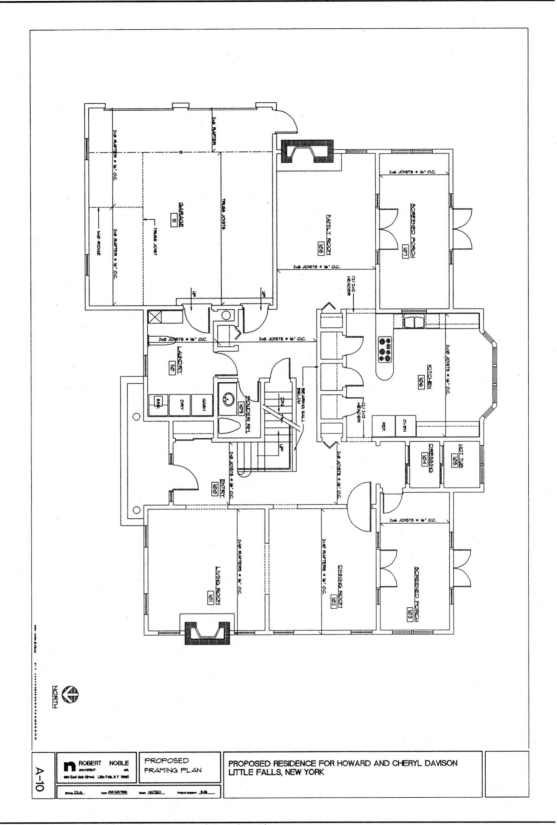

Figure 427 *Typical blueprint Structural Framing Plan.*

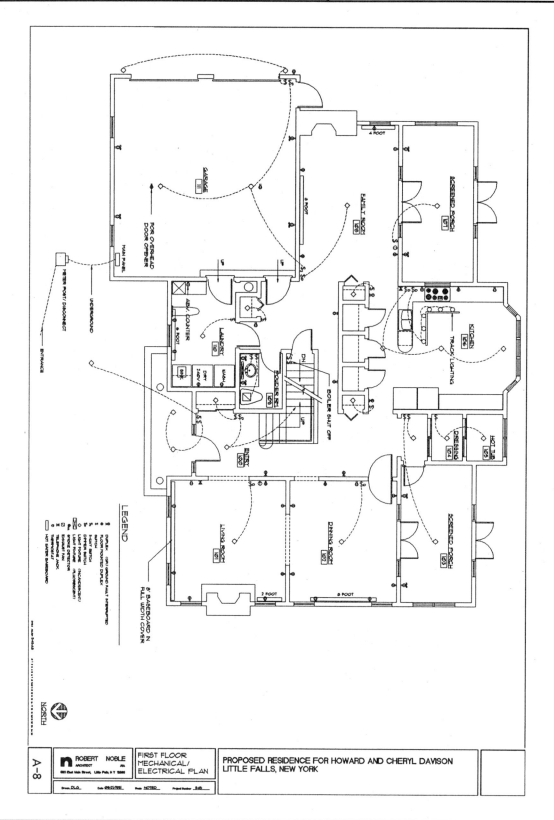

Figure 428   Typical blueprint Mechanical Plan.

SECTION **3**

Drafting Basics

EQUIPMENT CONSIDERATIONS

Well-drafted plans start with the right equipment. Purchase the best quality equipment you can afford. Drafting tools should be used for their intended purpose only and should always be kept clean.

The following list of equipment is recommended:

- drafting paper (vellum)

- drafting board or portable draft-pak

- T-Square, parallel bar or drafting machine

- pencils and leads

- pencil pointer (mechanical lead sharpener)

- architect's scale

- triangles

- erasers

- drafting tape

- templates

- compass

- curves

- dusting brush

- erasing shield

The following list of additional equipment may be useful, but is not required:

- plan enhancements (ie. stick-on ready artwork)

- pens and inks

- electric eraser

- lettering guide

- markers and colored pencils

- computer system with plotter and/or printer

Drafting Equipment

Drafting Paper: Special drafting paper is required for production of professional drawing presentations. The paper most often used is called *"Vellum 1000x"*. This is translucent paper with high strength. Preprinted vellum paper is available for NKBA members through the **National Kitchen & Bath Association** in two sizes, 11" x 17" (27.94cm x 43.18cm) and 17" x 22" (43.18cm x 55.88cm).

to be used, the working edge (left or right-handedness) of the board must be straight and true. A 10° to 15° slope will provide a comfortable drawing surface, as well as a clear view of your work in progress. A portable draftpak includes the tilt option, storage and built-in parallel bar.

For used or worn surfaces, or to protect new surfaces, a vinyl covering can be mounted on the board surface. The common brand names for this material are **"Vyco"** and **"Borco"**.

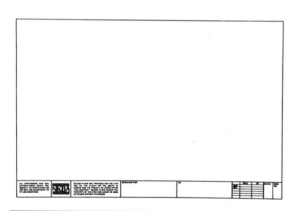

Figure 429   NKBA Vellum paper

Figure 430   Portable draftpak station can be set up anywhere.

Drafting Board: The drafting board should accommodate the largest size drawing paper you normally use.

The board's surface should be perfectly smooth and constructed so as not to warp or bend. If a T-Square is going

T-Square/Parallel Bar: The T-Square is the most economical form of drafting straightedge equipment. It is used to draw horizontal lines and to keep the drawing square. To use a T-Square, hold it firmly against one edge of the board and then slide it vertically along that edge to position your triangle or draw horizontal lines.

Use only the top edge of the T-Square for drawing lines. The bottom edge may not be parallel with the top edge which would result in an out-of-square drawing if both edges were used. To check the T-Square for straightness, draw a line from the T-Squares left edge to its right edge. Turn the T-Square over and draw another line beginning at the same location. If there is a difference of more than 1/16 of an inch (.15cm) at any location, the T-Square should not be used. For vertical lines, a triangle is required. A T-square is not recommended for production of high quality drawing documents because it relys mostly on the users skill.

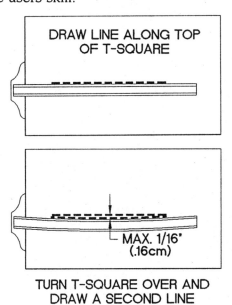

DRAW LINE ALONG TOP OF T-SQUARE

TURN T-SQUARE OVER AND DRAW A SECOND LINE

MAX. 1/16" (.16cm)

Figure 431   Determine whether the T-Square is square.

Most bathroom designers prefer to use a parallel bar drafting system. The parallel bar works similarly to the T-Square, but is permanently attached to the drafting board. The parallel bar attaches to the board's corners with wires

which glide on pulleys. Errors are limited with the use of a parallel bar because it is not hand-held and therefore, is less likely to slip out of squareness. *Refer to Figure 430* for an example of a parallel bar on the draftpak.

Drafting Machine: For the best quality drafting, a drafting machine or *"arm"* is recommended. These are expensive mechanical straight edges which enable the user to draw horizontal, vertical and any other angled line without additional equipment. There are various models available ranging from the compact, clip-on to larger V-track types.

A drafting machine offers the highest level of linear accuracy possible. The straight edges are interchangable allowing flexibility in working in different scales or changing from the imperial to the metric system.

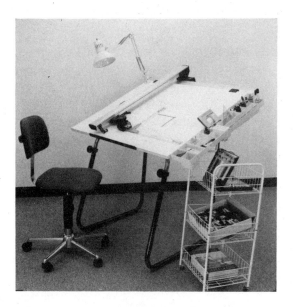

Figure 432   Drafting machine station.

Computers are fast becoming a replacement to standard drafting methods. Drawings are done with the aid of a computer system and then stored in hard drive directories or on floppy disks for easy and organized retrieval. Presentation drawings are either printed or stored by mechanical means. A more detailed discussion on computers and computer aided design follows later in this publication.

Figure 433 Computer aided drafting station.

Pencils and Leads: The selection of pencils and drawing leads is next in importance.

Most draftspeople avoid wooden cased drawing pencils, preferring a drafting lead holder. The holder acts as a shell for the lead and enables you to easily push the lead out for convenient sharpening. There are also mechanical pencils that hold very thin leads, which when pushed out do not require any sharpening. These save time and eliminates the extra tool, however, the line quality is limited to the thickness of the

lead and the thin leads break often until the user becomes accustomed to applying just the right amount of pressure.

There are 17 varieties of leads. They are classified by degrees of hardness and identified by a letter and/or number. The neutrals, such as B, HB, F and H are mid-range hardness. From B,2B to 6B the lead is consecutively softer. From 2H through 9H, the leads become consecutively harder. For most drafting purposes, the 3H, 2H, H and F are sufficient. You should experiment to discover which lead hardness works best for you. The softer leads, such as 2B and 3B, are recommended for pencil renderings with shades and shadows.The softer the lead is, the easier it flows and the more it will smear. The harder lead such as a 2H will produce a crisp line which will not smear as readily.

Practice is required to develop consistent pencil line work. As a line is drawn the pencil should be rotated between your fingers and the pressure exerted should remain constant. This insures consistent line width. **Do not press too hard because your paper may tear or have permanent indents.**

Pencil Pointer: A pencil pointer is used to sharpen the lead in a mechanical pencil. **Keeping a sharp point on the lead is one of the key elements in developing good line-work.** Leads can be sharpened on sandpaper, but to achieve the most efficient point, use a mechanical pencil pointer. These are available in many different brands and models ranging from portable and clip-on models to heavy, paper-weight types.

Architect's Scale: An architect's scale is used to measure and scale a drawing. The most common architect's scale is triangular in shape and offers eleven different scales in feet and inches:

```
┌─────────────────────────────────┐
│          IMPERIAL SCALE         │
│                                 │
│   FULL SCALE      1/16" Gradations │
│                                 │
│        1/8" = 1'0"              │
│                                 │
│        1/4" = 1'0"              │
│                                 │
│        3/8" = 1'0"              │
│                                 │
│        3/4" = 1'0"              │
│                                 │
│        1/2" = 1'0"              │
│                                 │
│          1" = 1'0"              │
│                                 │
│      1 1/2" = 1'0"              │
│                                 │
│          3" = 1'0"              │
│                                 │
│        3/32" = 1'0"            │
│                                 │
│        3/16" = 1'0"            │
└─────────────────────────────────┘
```

The most common metric scale offers six different scales (ratios):

```
┌─────────────────────────────────┐
│          METRIC SCALE           │
│                                 │
│  1cm = 10cm ............ (1:10 ratio) │
│                                 │
│  1cm = 20cm ............ (1:20 ratio) │
│                                 │
│  1cm = 30cm ............ (1:30 ratio) │
│                                 │
│  1cm = 40cm ............ (1:40 ratio) │
│                                 │
│  1cm = 50cm ............ (1:50 ratio) │
│                                 │
│  1cm = 60cm ............ (1:60 ratio) │
└─────────────────────────────────┘
```

For your bathroom plans, all drawings will be prepared at the scale 1/2" =1'0", 1cm = 24cm or 1cm = 20cm. Flat scales are also available with four scales. These are sometimes preferred because they eliminate time spent hunting for the right scale.

MEASURING WITH A SCALE

To accurately measure with a scale, first select the proper edge and place it on the drawing parallel with the line to be measured. Start from the zero and count the number of full feet in the measurement and mark the exact point with a very sharp pencil. Then, start from the zero and going in the opposite direction, mark the number of inches.

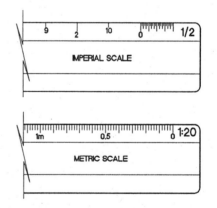

Figure 434   1/2" = 1' 0" or a 1:20cm ratio are the industry standards. (1:24 is used as a metric conversion.)

Triangles: A handy drafting tool is a three-sided plastic piece called a triangle. It may list a different scale on each side and may also have bathroom fixture template outlines within the center spaces. The **National Kitchen & Bath Association** offers one of these to its members.

Triangles are used with both T-Squares and parallel bars to draw vertical and angular lines. The triangle rests on the horizontal straight edge to insure that vertical lines will be perpendicular to the horizontal lines. Two triangles are required; one with 45° angles and another with 30° and 60° angles. Both triangles should be made of clear or tinted plastic and have eased or beveled edges. The tinted plastic is easier to see and reduces shadows caused by overhead lighting. The beveled or eased edge makes the triangle easier to pick up and is absolutely necessary if any inking is to be done.

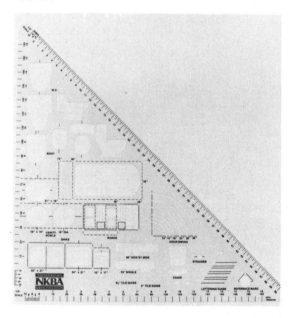

Figure 435   The triangle.

Either triangle may be used to draw vertical lines. Begin by holding the T-Square or parallel bar firmly and placing the triangle horizontally along the upper edge. Slide the triangle into position and hold it with your left hand, pull the pen-

cil upward along the vertical edge. If you are left-handed, reverse these instructions.

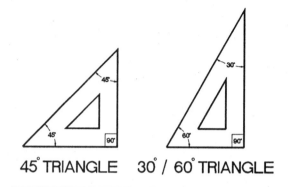

45° TRIANGLE   30°/60° TRIANGLE

Figure 436   Two triangles are generally used for drafting.

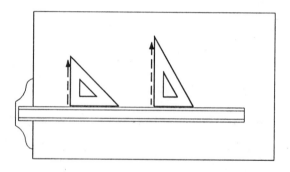

Figure 437   Draw vertical lines from the bottom of triangle upwards.

The same process is used to draw lines at angles. Locate the triangle and pull the pencil from the left to right always gradually rotating the pencil between your fingers. This will insure the most accurate and consistent line work. The most common angles, 75°, 60°, 45°, 30° and 15° can be easily drawn with the two triangles mentioned.

If odd angles are required, an adjustable triangle, which can be set at any desired angle, is available.

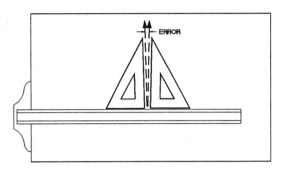

Figure 439
Determining whether the triangles are square.

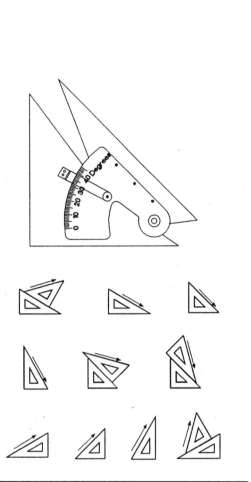

Figure 438   *Triangles can be combined to achieve various other angles or an adjustable triangle may be used.*

CHECKING FOR ACCURACY

To check the accuracy of a 90° angle of a triangle, draw a vertical line from its bottom to its top point. Turn the triangle over and draw another line beginning at the same location as the first line. If there is a difference of more than 1/32" (.07cm) at the top of an eight inch line, the triangle should not be used.

Eraser: Erasing is a major part of the design and planning process. **Choosing the appropriate eraser and proper technique is as important as drawing a line properly.** The wrong eraser may stain or even tear the paper. Look for a soft eraser, such as the *"pink-pearl"* or *"white vinyl-lite"* brands which are most popular. These are available in convenient holders which can be refilled much like the lead holder. When erasing, be sure to hold the paper tightly in place and apply only as much pressure as is necessary. For hard to remove lines, place a smooth, hard surface under the area to be erased (a plastic triangle works well).

Drafting Tape: Drafting tape is necessary to hold your drawing in place throughout the drawing process. To easily remove the tape after completion of the drawing, drafting tape, not masking or scotch tape, should be used. Drafting tape can be purchased in a variety of widths and in packages with easy *"tear-off"* cutting edges. Also available are drafting tape *"dots"*, these are round pieces of tape which peel off a roll of paper. The dots are convenient to use and are less likely to roll up after the T-Square or parallel bar has passed over them a few times.

Templates: Templates for plan and elevational views are available for almost everything; bathroom fixtures and equipment, door swings, circles and ellipses. Lettering templates are also available.

Many of the templates for bathroom fixtures and equipment available in drafting supply stores are designed for architects in 1/8"-1/4" scales. As a bathroom specialist you will require 1/2" or 1:20cm scaled templates. 1/2" scaled templates are available through the **National Kitchen & Bath Association** and the **American Society of Interior Designers**, as well as many manufacturers of bathroom fixtures and equipment.

Using templates saves time and produces a consistent, professional-looking portfolio.

Compass: A compass is used to draw circles or arcs which are not on your templates. Most compasses will produce circles with diameters ranging from 3/16" (.47cm) to 13" (33.02cm). The compass features one end with an adjustable needle point and another end with lead point. To keep the circle radius consistent, the pencil lead end must be sharpened in a beveled fashion with the beveled edge facing out. To sharpen the pencil lead point, rub the bevel side back and forth along sandpaper. The bevel point should be between 1/64"-1/32" shorter than the needle point.

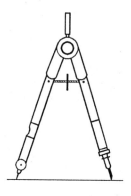

Figure 441   When templates are not available a compass can be used to draw any size circle.

Drawing a Compass Curve

While drawing the curve, hold the compass perpendicular to the paper with a light touch to avoid making a hole in the paper. Special attachments are also

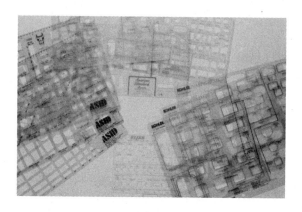

Figure 440   Examples of available templates.

available for replacing the lead with an ink pen-point.

Curves: Irregular curves, commonly referred to as "*french*" curves, are used to draw curved lines other than circles or arcs. A clear or tinted plastic curve with several small curves and a few long slightly curved edges is recommended. To draw an irregular curve, plot several points through which the curve must pass, then select the curved edge which most closely matches.

For complex curved lines more points will be necessary and the curve may have to be drawn in sections, rotating and moving the irregular curve until the desired curvilinear line is completed. Flexible curves are also available. These are wires covered in a rubber-like material which can be manipulated to fit almost any large, curved shape.

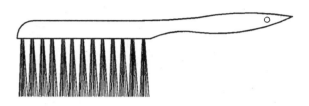

Figure 443   *Use the dusting brush to keep drawings clear of debris.*

Erasing Shield: An erasing shield is a thin, metal instrument with various shaped holes. This tool is used to isolate a specific area of the drawing to be erased, eliminating over erasing and redrawing.

Figure 442   *The french curve can be used to draft accurate irregular curves.*

Dusting Brush: A dusting brush typically has a handle with long, soft bristles made of nylon or horsehair. The brush is used for removing eraser shavings and graphite particles from the drawing without smudging. A brush is necessary to keep your drawing clean and clear of debris.

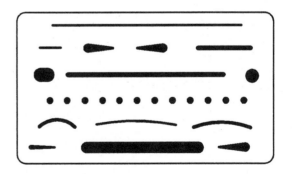

Figure 444   *Use an erasing shield to protect your drawing while erasing.*

Additional Equipment

Plan Enhancements: Sheets of press or stick-on lettering, symbols and shading are an easy way to graphically enhance drawings. Lettering machines also enhance the plan by enabling you to type out letters or numbers onto clear sticky-back tape which is then applied to the drawing. These machines have become smaller and more economical in recent years.

The press-on lettering takes more time and precision to mount, although it looks more natural on the original drawing. However, if blueprints or photocopies are going to be used, the difference between the two isn't noticeable. Symbols such as electrical symbols, arrows, plants, trees and dot shading are also available in sheets of sticky-back or press-on format.

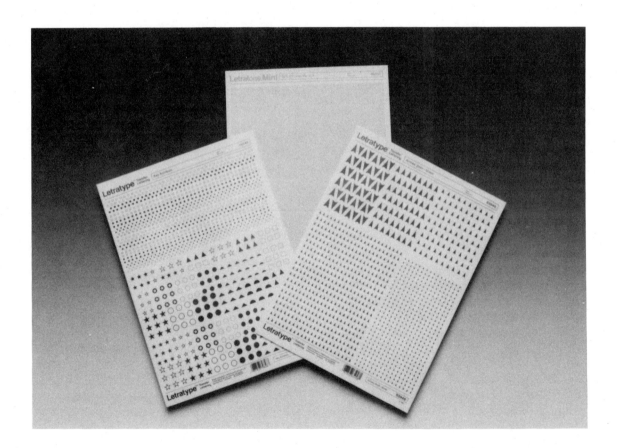

Figure 445   Various accessories and underlays can be used to enhance plans.

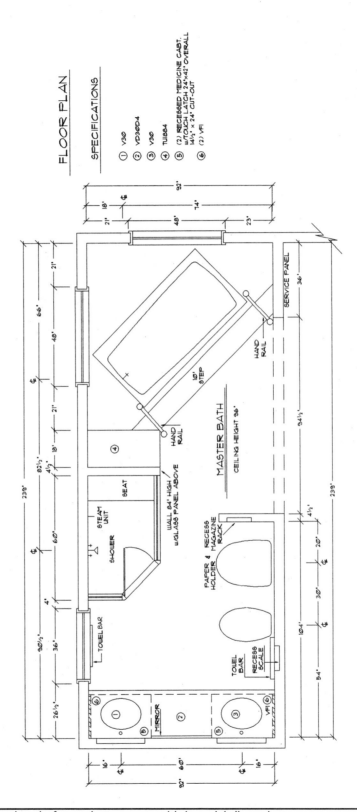

Figure 446   Floor plans before enhancements with imperial dimensions.

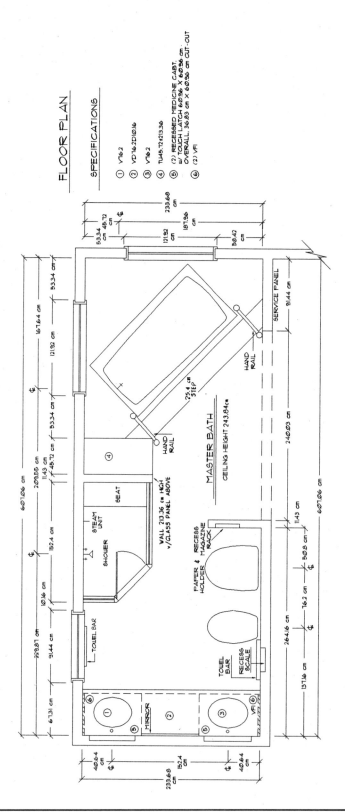

Figure 447   Floor plans before enhancements with metric dimensions.

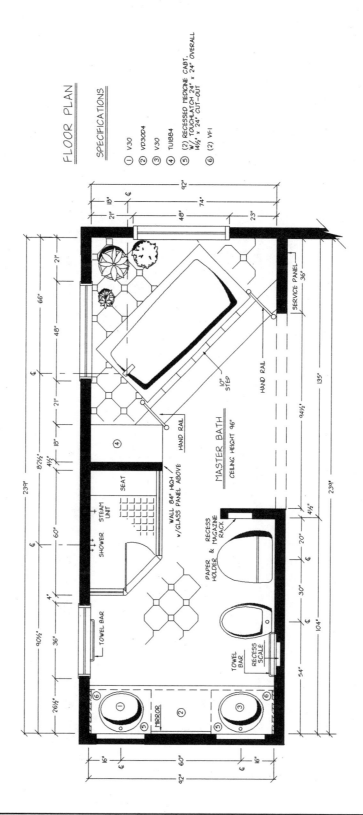

Figure 448   Floor plans after enhancements with imperial dimensions.

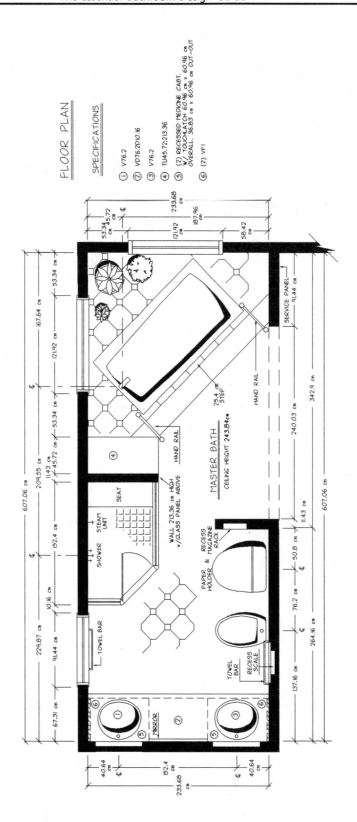

Figure 449   Floor plans after enhancements with metric dimensions.

Pens and Inks: An inking pen is one of the easiest and most economical ways to improve the quality of your drawings. In the past, inking a drawing was time-consuming and required skill because the only tool available was a ruling pen, which works like a fountain pen. They were hard to control because the ink was easily smeared and could unexpectedly drip onto the drawing. The technical pens available today eliminate these worries.

Although it still takes a bit of practice and the ink will smear if rubbed too soon, with a little patience, inking is easily learned. The technical pen is engineered to allow ink to flow out only when it is needed. Some pens are available with snap-on ink cartridge refills, virtually eliminating any handling of messy ink.

THE FIRST RULE OF INKING

The first rule of inking is to use a straight edge with a slightly raised or beveled edge to eliminate ink bleeding. You will find proper cleaning and maintenance of your pen vital. If the pen is not going to be used every few days, it should be emptied and cleaned after each use. There are cleaning solutions and machines available which are specially formulated to remove clogged ink.

Electric Eraser: An electric eraser will become one of your most used tools. It will save you time and improve the quality of your presentations. Today's electric erasers are light-weight and cordless. **Over erasing can wear a hole through the paper, so use this tool carefully.**

Lettering Guide: A lettering guide is used to draw guide lines for lettering. By

placing the pencil lead in the appropriate hole, the draftsperson can quickly layout consistently even guide lines without measuring. This is recommended for areas such as the specifications on a floor plan.

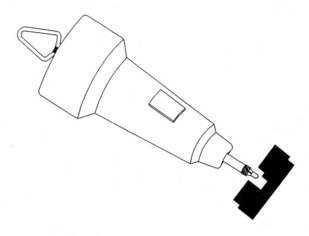

Figure 450   Electric eraser.

Markers and Colored Pencils: To make your renderings beautiful, add color to your interpretive drawings. The mastering of color marker and pencil renderings is an art form all its own. Hinting at the color of cabinets and fixtures makes a presentation come to life.

There are a wide variety of colored pencils and markers from which to choose. When selecting colored pencils look for soft, heavily-pigmented leads which will give even tones and make blending easy. Markers should always be tested on the paper on which they are to be used to determine whether they will bleed or cause the line art ink to bleed.

The type of paper used with marker and pencil renderings will greatly affect the finished appearance. Transparent marker papers soften the colors; opaque white plotter or marker papers reveal the true brilliance of colors and blueprints or sepia prints mute colors. All of these papers are acceptable for marker and pencil renderings. **Drafting vellum is not acceptable.** The color will not adhere to vellum, it will puddle on top of the paper and run.

Computer Aided Drafting

Computer-Aided Drafting and Design programs are a part of the design industry. Because of their speed and accuracy, computers are a powerful asset. If you currently own a computer, the investment in specialized design software is minimal. However, if you have nothing to build upon, expect to invest between $8,000 and $15,000 in combined software and hardware for a single drafting station.

There has recently been an influx of computer software packages for the kitchen and bathroom industry. The many software programs available can be categorized in one of two groups:

- The first category and most familiar to the industry is the pre-customized software program. The pre-customized program utilizes predetermined criteria to perform automatic placement of elements and fill-in of materials. *For example,* you type in dimensions of the room, select window and door placement, equipment placement and the computer completes the design, placing cabinets, fillers, tile, etc. These programs are easy to use, fast and offer three dimensional viewing in minutes. Some programs are available with a color and/or pricing option. These programs however are limited to kitchens and bathrooms only.

- Traditional drafting software programs act as a drafting tool, known as computer aided drafting (CAD). Using various commands, you draw the design on the computer screen with a mouse, digitizer or stylus, instead of on paper. A CAD program can be individually customized by the user and is limited only by the designer's imagination. These programs are broad in scope and are not limited to just kitchens and bathrooms. Complete homes and other building structures can be created.

Automated drafting encourages creative planning because it's easy to try a number of design options on the screen. Changes made by clients can also be made in the same manner. No more hours spent re-drawing and no more messy presentations caused by extensive erasing and white-outs!

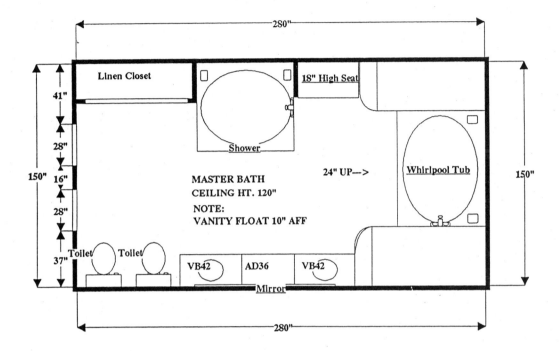

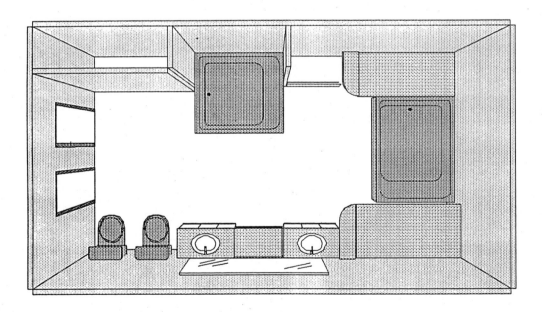

Figure 451 (Courtesy of Auto-Graph Designing Systems, Inc.) Drawing presentation completed by a computer.

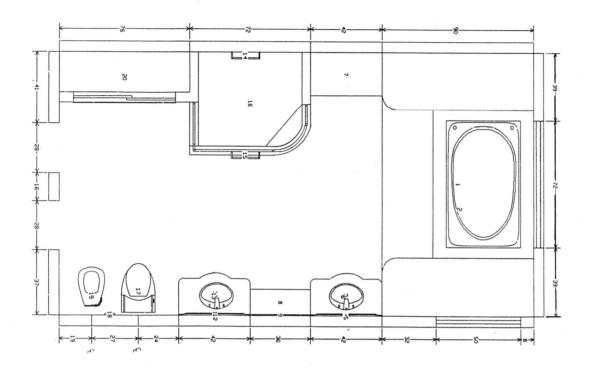

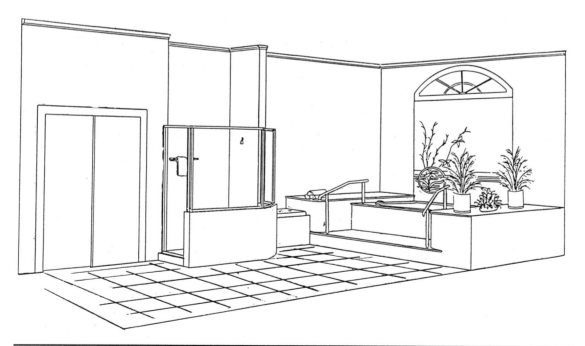

Figure 452   (Courtesy of Eljer Plumbingware)   Drawing presentation completed by a computer.

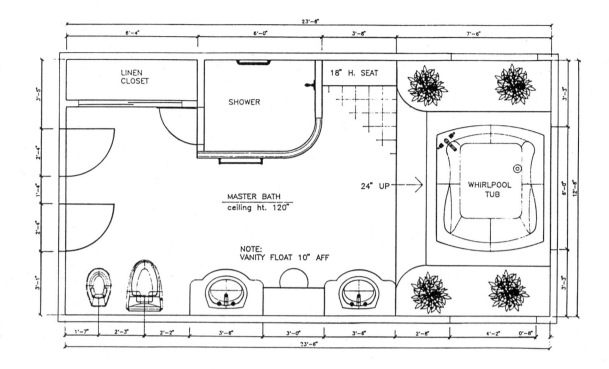

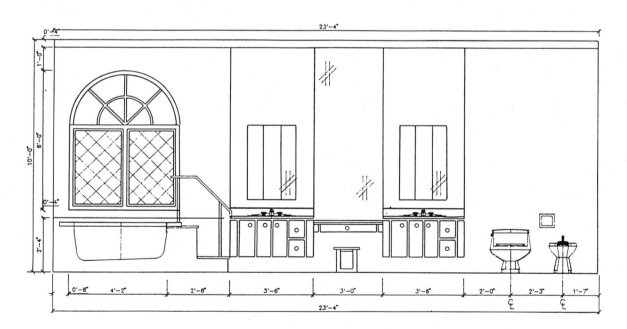

Figure 453   (Courtesy of American Standard Inc.)   Drawing presentation completed by a computer.

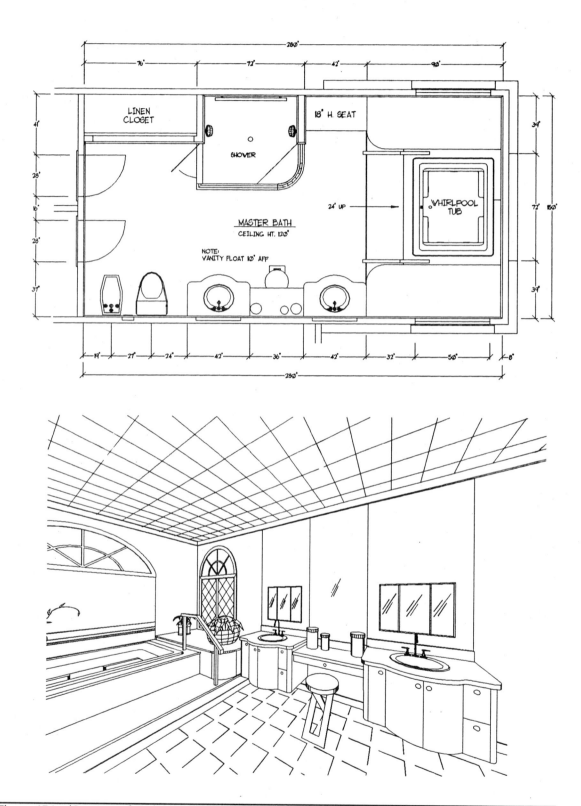

LINEN
CLOSET

18" H. SEAT

SHOWER

24" UP

WHIRLPOOL
TUB

MASTER BATH
CEILING HT. 120"

NOTE:
VANITY FLOAT 12" AFF

Figure 454   (Courtesy of CadKit)   Drawing presentation completed by a computer.

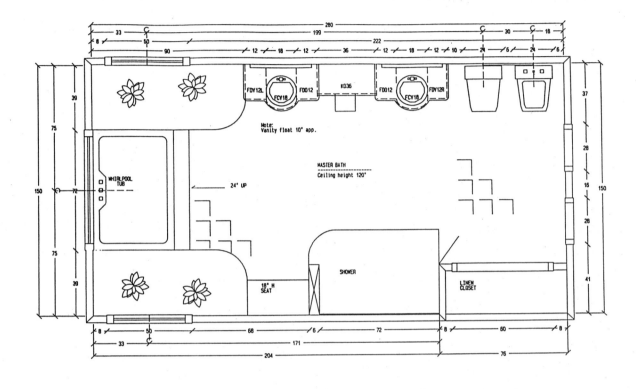

Figure 455 *(Courtesy of Twenty-Twenty)* *Drawing presentation completed by a computer.*

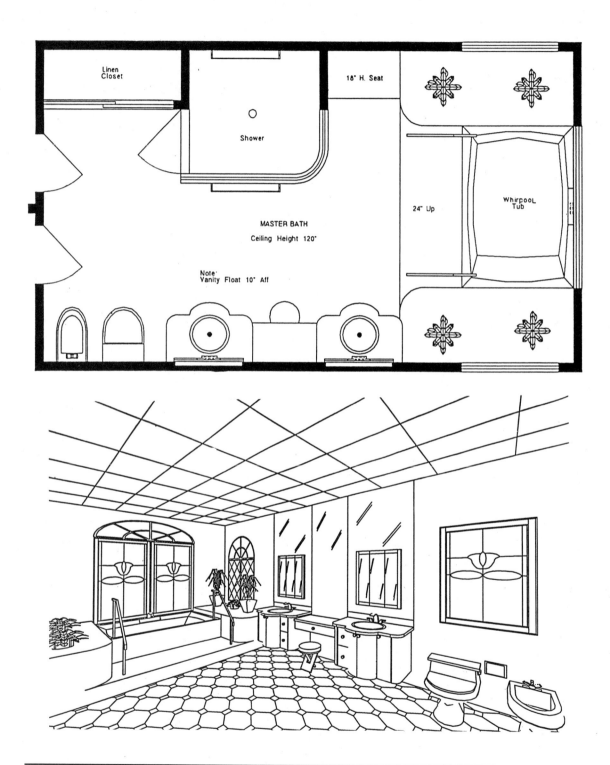

Figure 456 *(Courtesy of Planit, USA)   Drawing presentation completed by a computer.*

SECTION **4**

The Importance of Lettering

ENHANCING DRAWING APPEARANCE

A drawing relies on lettering to convey information that is not graphically obvious. Skillful lettering enhances the appearance and more importantly, the clarity, of the drawing. By contrast, poor lettering is difficult to read and detracts from the drawing. **Consistency is the most important element in performing skillful lettering.**

Lettering Techniques

There are various techniques for lettering a drawing. Freehand lettering is generally preferred on design drawings. Freehand lettering is an acquired skill. After considerable experience, a draftsperson's freehand lettering takes on an individual style that frequently enhances the presentation. However, the beginning draftsperson should first master the single stroke gothic alphabet utilizing all capital letters. This technique has acquired universal acceptance from the architectural community because it is easy to read and easily executed. Refer to *Figure 460* as a guide to develop your lettering skills.

Lettering Types

Mechanical sources may be used until you develop more skillful lettering. Notes can be typed on clear adhesive-backed film, then cut and applied directly to the drawing. Or use a lettering template. Templates (similar to stencils) are available for various lettering sizes and come with interchangeable scriber points. The template controls consistency in letter size and shape, but you are responsible for even spacing. The use of press or stick-on lettering, which was described previously under plan enhancements, is another option.

CAD Lettering

With a CAD program, lettering is typed on the computer keyboard and printed in the standard Roman style typeface. Customizable drafting programs with additional software can produce an architectural styled lettering to replace the standard type.

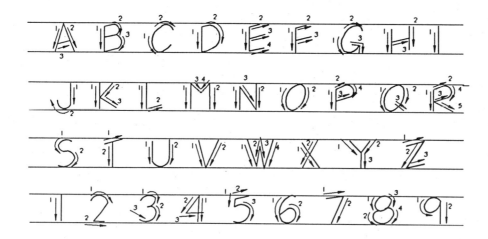

Figure 457 Follow this technique to develop skillful lettering.

STANDARD ROMAN LETTERING

ARCHITECTURAL ROMAN LETTERING

Figure 458 Computers offer various lettering options.

Examples of Lettering Uses

Lettering completes a drawing by providing information such as identification, titles, dimensions, nomenclature, specifications or legends and notes. The most general information is shown in the largest lettering and the most detailed and specific information appears in the smallest size letters.

Each sheet in a set of drawings must be identified with a title block.

Lettering Sizes

The title block pertains to the entire set of drawings and links each individual drawing sheet together as part of a total presentation.

The title block should be the largest lettering on a drawing and will demand the most skill in composition and spacing. This can be automatically achieved by using preprinted vellum, such as the **National Kitchen & Bath Association** drafting sheets.

Titles within the drawing itself rank second in size hierarchy. *For example,* on a floor plan drawing, the title might be "*Master Bath*". On an elevation drawing, the title might be "*Elevation View A1*". If the drawing includes a list of specifications or legend symbols, then the title for the list would also appear in the second size category or approximately 1/4" (.63cm) high.

The third size of lettering is approximately 1/8" (.31cm) - 3/16" (.47cm) high and will include the list of specifications, symbol descriptions, nomenclature and dimensions.

The last and smallest lettering on a drawing is used for specific notes to explain drawing details. *For example,* on a floor plan, special areas of construction may be obscure without the addition of notes explaining the detailed design process. On an elevation, a note may be needed to indicate that a particular drawerhead is, "*not operable*". **Notes should be used only when needed to eliminate possible confusion.** For clarity, hand lettering should never be any smaller than 1/8" (.31cm). Therefore, the

third lettering hierarchy will also include notes.

It's important to remain consistent in each lettering size category to ensure a professional, standardized drawing presentation.

Hand Lettering Training

Consistency is the key element in developing a skillful lettering technique.

There are five basic elements which aid in lettering consistency:

- height

- form

- direction

- weight

- spacing

Height: For consistent height of lettering and spacing between rows of lettering, guide lines are needed. It is nearly impossible to maintain straight horizontal lettering without the use of guide lines. On inked drawings, guide lines will be erased. On pencil drawings they will remain, therefore, **guide lines should be drawn with a sharp point and a light touch.**

A lettering guide helps to maintain consistency. Two guide lines should be used when all lettering will be upper case, which is the suggested standard. When upper and lower case lettering is used, three guide lines are required. The

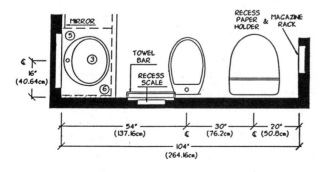

Figure 459   Typical lettering used on a bathroom plan.

spacing of guide lines will vary according to the size of lettering required.

Typically, lettering ranges from 1/8" (.32cm) in height to 1/2" (1.27cm) in height. To determine the amount of space required between rows of lettering the size of the lettering and the number of rows of lettering must be considered. Generally, the space is slightly smaller than the letter size. However, for small, lengthy notes, the space should be equal to the letter size to insure legibility.

Remember, consistency is the key, therefore make sure each letter terminates at the exact top and/or bottom of each guide line.

Lettering is used to communicate, therefore a simple and consistent form is vital. The gothic alphabet is the base from which the standard *single stroke* lettering technique has evolved. Slanted lettering should be avoided because it is directional and suggests movement which will detract from your plans.

Lettering should be kept vertical and maintain an oblong proportion. Master the vertical, single stroke lettering technique illustrated before attempting to develop an individual style.

Form: Form consistency refers to the vertical, horizontal, and curvilinear lines of each letter and how they relate to each other. Each straight line or curve should appear the same.

Direction: Directional consistency refers to the direction each stroke follows during the construction of each letter. Whenever possible, the strokes should be made by pulling, not pushing the pencil/pen across the paper. Gener-

ally a right-handed draftsperson will pull down and to the right. Practice develops consistency. If needed, a small triangle can be used as a quick and efficient way to maintain consistent vertical strokes.

Weight: Consistent line weight is also developed with practice. On pencil drawings, a *"2H"* or *"3H"* lead is recommended depending on the pressure you exert on the pencil. Rotate the pencil to keep a consistent point width and even line widths. Emphasize the start and end of each stroke by applying slightly more pressure.

When using a technical ink pen achieve the same effect by making slow and deliberate strokes and holding the pen point on the paper slightly longer at the start and end of each stroke. Keep in mind that the same technique for lettering should be used throughout the drawing presentation. **Do not mix styles or types of lettering.**

Spacing: The legibility of your lettering also depends on consistent spacing. Consistent letter spacing is not based on *"actual"* equal spaces, but rather *"perceived"* equal spaces. Each letter of the alphabet has a different profile, therefore, the letters must be visually spaced rather than measured. Letters with two vertical adjacent edges require more visual space than do angled or curved letters.

A helpful hint is to squint, if the letters appear as an even grey tone, then the spaces are even. However, if you squint and see gaps or varying gray tones, then the letters are perceived as unevenly spaced.

The space between words should be larger than the space between individual letters. For an attractive plan, try to leave twice as much space between words than between letters and leave slightly more space between sentences than between words.

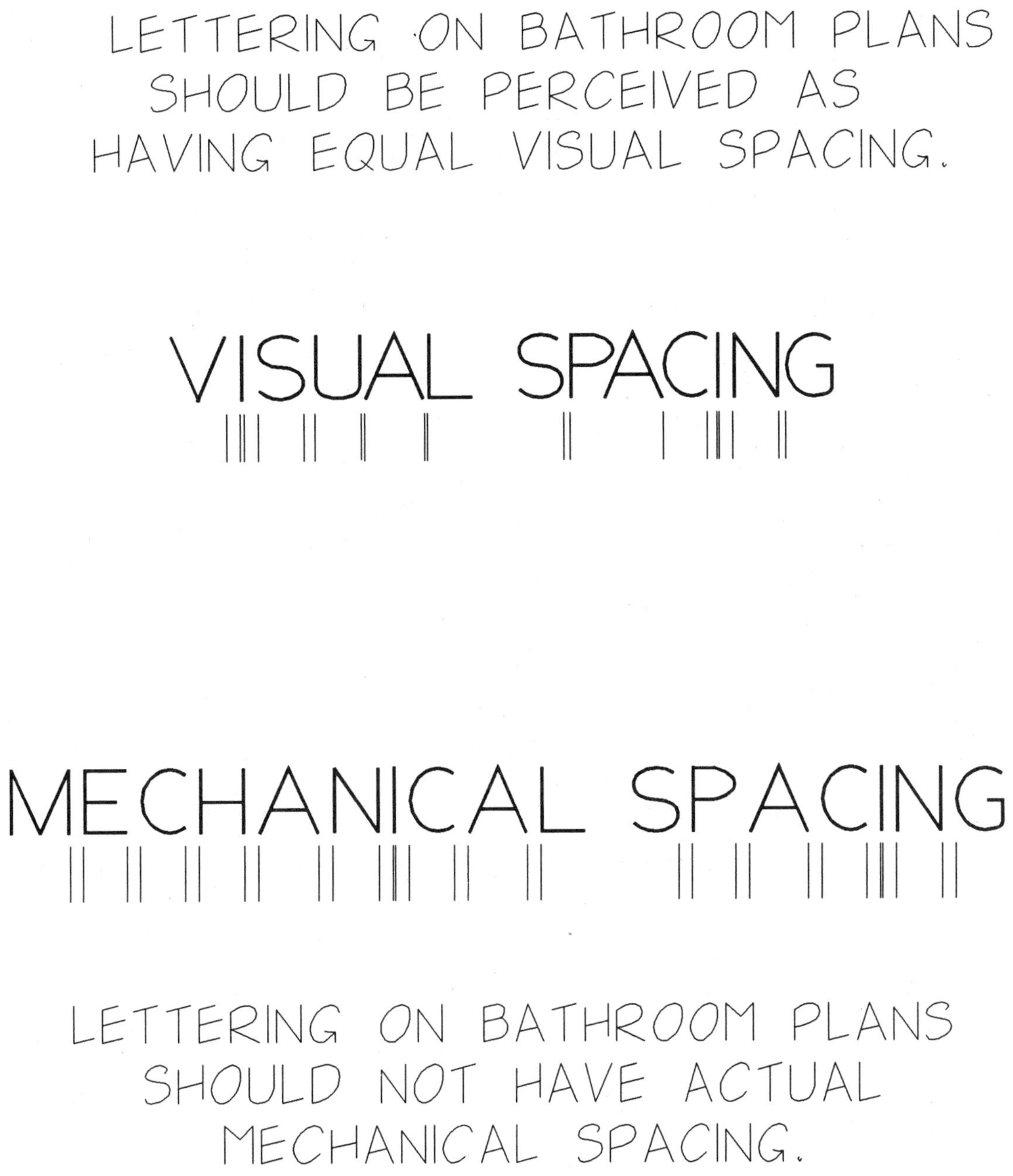

LETTERING ON BATHROOM PLANS SHOULD BE PERCEIVED AS HAVING EQUAL VISUAL SPACING.

VISUAL SPACING

MECHANICAL SPACING

LETTERING ON BATHROOM PLANS SHOULD NOT HAVE ACTUAL MECHANICAL SPACING.

Figure 460   Consistent spacing is based on appearance.

Lines and Techniques

LINE WORK

The major portion of a drawing consists of lines. Therefore, good line work is critical to the development of a professional drawing presentation. Just as skillful lettering develops through practice, so does good line work.

Layout Lines

To begin a drawing, layout lines should be kept as light as possible, similar to guide lines for lettering. We'll call these first lines "*layout lines*". Whether the final drawing is to be ink or pencil, the initial layout lines should be drawn in a hard lead, such as a 3H or 4H. The pencil should be sharp at all times to insure accuracy.

The purpose of layout lines is to verify the drawing's limits and accuracy before any finished lines are drawn. If changes are required, layout lines can be easily erased, leaving no evidence of the change. As you acquire more experience, you'll spend less time drawing layout lines and move directly to drawing final lines.

Achieving Good Line Work

"*Crisp*", "*uniform*" and "*precise*" are words that characterize good line work. To achieve pencil lines with these qualities, remember to rotate the pencil between your fingers while drawing a line.

Whenever possible, a line should be drawn in a strong, single stroke. To maintain consistent line weight, apply equal pressure throughout the length of the line. Lines which fade or do not meet at corners will be exaggerated when reproduced and may result in misinterpretation.

The final goal of the drafting process is to produce an easily interpreted graphic presentation.

Types of Lines

Lines are used to indicate a variety of objects. **Visible object lines are represented by a solid line.** These include all edges which are in front of the cut-plane and in clear view. In a floor plan visible object lines are used to show wall cabinets, tall cabinets and countertop surfaces.

Hidden object lines are represented by a series of short dashes. Any object edge which is under a visible object edge is indicated by the hidden object line. *For example,* base cabinets are under the countertop so they are drawn with a short dashed line. **Remember how important consistency is;** keep the dash length and the spacing between each dash the same. Using a 1/2" architect's scale, alternate your dashes in 3" increments to provide a well proportioned hidden line.

Witness or extension lines are drawn as a solid line which is slightly lighter or thinner than visible object lines. These lines are used to terminate dimension lines. Witness lines begin approximately 1/16" (.16cm) to 1/8" (.32cm) outside of the object being dimensioned and extend approximately 1/16" (.16cm) to 1/8" (.32cm) beyond the dimension line.

Centerlines are drawn with alternating long and short dashes. Similar to witness lines, centerlines should appear slightly lighter and thinner than object lines. However, unlike witness lines, centerlines may extend into the object being located and begin with the proper centerline symbol.

Dimension lines are also thin lines, which terminate with arrows, dots or slashes. For our purposes, dimension lines are broken in the middle and the numerical dimension is centered in the opening. This technique used by mechanical draftspersons allows for all numbers to remain vertical and reduces errors caused by misreading the dimension. Equally acceptable is to maintain a solid dimension line and list the numerical dimension above the line. All dimensions and lettering should then be

readable from the bottom edge and the right side of the plans. This is typically how architectural blueprints are dimensioned.

Cutting plane lines are represented by alternating one long dash with two short dashes. Such lines are used to indicate the origin of a section drawing when it is not obvious.

The cutting plane line is typically darker and thicker than object lines and terminates with arrows indicating the direction of the section cut. Identification is required in both the plan and elevation views. Typical identification is by letters, such as A-A, B-B, etc.

More often bathroom design plans indicate elevations with a letter and an arrow pointing to the wall without the use of a cutting plane line.

Break lines are indicated by a continuous line interrupted by the break symbol. The line weight is the same as object lines. Break lines are used when the entire plan will not fit on the sheet of drafting paper. If the drawing is detailed on both sides of the break line, then two break symbols are required with blank space between the two symbols. This usage of break lines and symbols indicates a portion of the drawing has been cut out of the middle.

When the drawing is only detailed at one side of the line the indication is that the drawing continues and only one line is necessary. This will be common in bathrooms that are part of a master bedroom.

Overhead lines are indicated by a series of long dashes. Their line weight remains the same as object lines, they are used to indicate any object edges which are above the tall cabinets such as skylights, soffits, extensive molding, etc. Using a 1/2" architect's scale, alternate your dashes in 6" increments to provide a well proportioned overhead line.

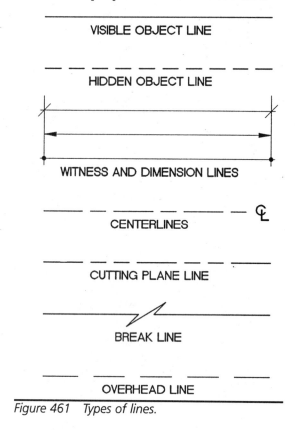

Figure 461   Types of lines.

GEOMETRIC CONSTRUCTION

Geometric construction may be divided into two categories, **simple and complex:**

- the simple elements include points, lines and planes.

- the complex elements encompass the various solids.

All geometric construction begins with a point.

Simple Construction

Conceptually, a point is without shape, form or dimension. It simply represents a position in space. A point may serve to begin or end a line, mark the intersection of two or more lines, mark a corner when two lines or planes meet, or indicate the center of a field. When a point is extended, a line is formed.

A line may be:
- straight
- curved
- angular

A line expresses:
- direction
- movement and growth
- dimensional length

As a construction element a line can:
- join
- support
- surround
- describe an edge
- articulate a surface

A straight line may be:
- vertical
- horizontal

- diagonal

An Angle: When a line is manipulated by geometric construction it may bend, becoming an angle.

A Circle: When a line is formed that connects all the points that are an equal distance from one given point, a circle is formed.

An Arc: A section of a circle is called an arc.

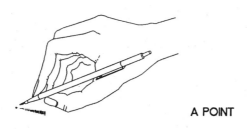

A POINT

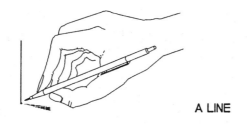

A LINE

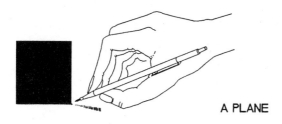

A PLANE

Figure 462   The primary elements of drawing.

Utilizing more complex mathematical formulas, lines can form an:

- ellipse

- parabola

- hyperbola

- various irregular curves

A Plane: When a line is given width, a plane is created. Conceptually, a plane has dimensional length and width, but no thickness. It may be visualized by comparing it to a piece of rigid paper. The shape of the plane is determined by its linear outline. The plane may take on any curved or angular shape the outline forms.

Complex Construction

The various solid forms which make up the complex elements consists of the:

- cube

- cylinder

- cone

- pyramid

- paraboloid

- sphere

A solid form possesses length, width and depth, and occupies space in the environment. Solids are mostly comprised of various planes. It is important to understand how solids occupy space so that you can accurately depict them in your drawing.

The most common solids found in design are rectangular. The most simplistic rectangular form is the cube, which is comprised of six square planes of equal size enclosing space. A vanity cabinet is a rectangular form.

A cylinder is formed by two circular planes which are parallel and are connected creating an enclosed space. A cylindrical form might be a column or support leg for a countertop overhang.

A cone is generated by rotating a triangle about an axis and enclosing it with a circular plane at the bottom. This form may be found in a hanging pendant light fixture.

A pyramid is similar to a cone, except it is made entirely of triangular planes. The number of planes are dependent upon the shape of the base which is angular rather than circular. Many of todays bathroom faucets have pyramidal forms as hot and cold control handles.

A paraboloid is generated by rotating a parabola about an axis and enclosing it with an ellipse. The curvilinear space which a contemporary tub/whirlpool encloses would be similar to the paraboloid form.

A sphere retains a circular shape from whatever angle it is viewed. A sphere is defined as an infinite number of points all equi-distance from one common point and radiating out in every direction. Perfect spheres are unusual in interiors, but portions of spheres are more commonly seen in faucet handles, lighting fixtures and bathroom fixtures and equipment.

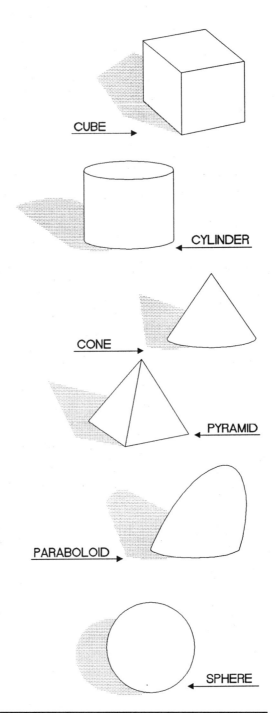

Figure 463   Types of solid forms.

DRAWING TECHNIQUES

Drawing Parallel Lines

In instances when the floor plan contains an odd angled wall, you may want to repeat the angle elsewhere within the space. To draw this, place any side of your triangle along the given angled line. Move the straight edge in position along the bottom edge of your triangle. Holding the straight edge in place, slide the triangle into the new desired position being sure to keep the bottom edge against the straight edge. Draw your line.

Drawing Perpendicular Lines

Now that you've constructed the parallel line, you'll probably need to draw a perpendicular line through it. Place your straight edge in position with the 45° triangle (short side) aligned with the line. Hold the straight edge in place and slide the triangle until its at the desired place of intersection. Draw a line through the point.

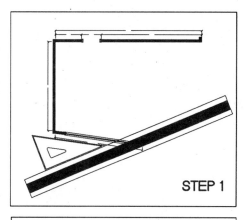

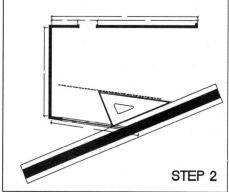

Figure 464   Constructing parallel lines.

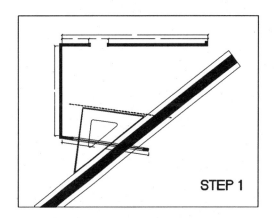

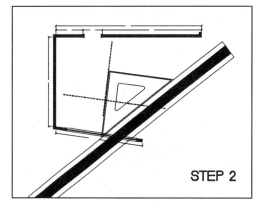

Figure 465   Constructing perpendicular lines.

Bisecting a Line

To produce symmetrical design drawings you will need to know how to bisect a line. For instance, given a length of wall on which you need to center a vanity sink cabinet, you will first need to bisect the wall line in order to determine its midpoint.

One option is to bisect a line with a compass. Set the compass larger than half the length of the line and draw an arc from each end of the line so that the two arcs intersect each other. The line which passes through the two intersecting points of the arcs will bisect the line.

Another option is to use a straight edge and triangle to bisect a line. Hold the straight edge parallel to the line and draw an equal angle from each end with your triangle toward the center of the line. Then draw a vertical line through the intersection and bisect the line.

Dividing a Line into Equal Parts

Bathroom drawings often involve decorative tile patterns which need to be illustrated in both floor plan and elevation views. A common illustration might include a 3" x 3" (7.62cm x 7.62cm) tile accent stripe between two rows of 12" x 12" (30.48cm x 30.48cm) tiles. After the 12" (30.48cm) tile is drawn, the 3" (7.62cm) tile lines can be found by dividing the 12" (30.48cm) length into four equal parts. An easier method for dividing a line equally follows.

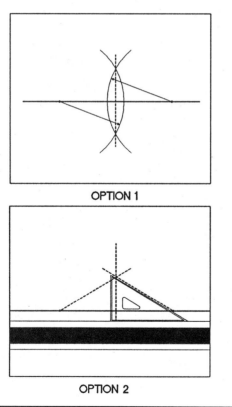

OPTION 1

OPTION 2

Figure 466   Bisecting a line.

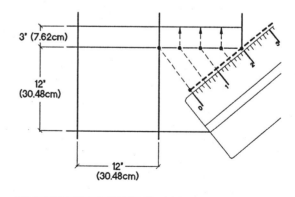

Figure 467   Dividing a line equally.

Draw a line from one end of the line to be divided at any angle. This line does not have to be the same length as the line to be divided, but rather should be of a length that can be easily divided by the required number of equal parts on the scale being used.

Mark the angled line into equal divisions using your scale. Draw a line from the last mark to the opposite end of the line to be divided. Parallel to that line, draw lines through the remaining marks and through the line to be divided.

Dividing a Space into Equal Sections

A similar method is used when the space to be divided is between two parallel lines. Find the beginning and end of the number of sections required on your scale. Pivot the scale until it spans the space equally and mark the intermediate points. Draw parallel lines through the points.

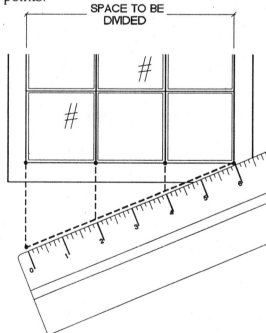

Figure 468   Dividing a space equally.

This method can be used to draw windows with mullions, glass door cabinetry with mullions or locating light fixtures evenly within a given amount of space.

Definition of Angles

As a designer, you'll find yourself confronted with unusual angles. An angle is formed by the meeting of two lines. How the two lines meet will define the type of angle.

The three types of angles are:

- acute
- right
- obtuse

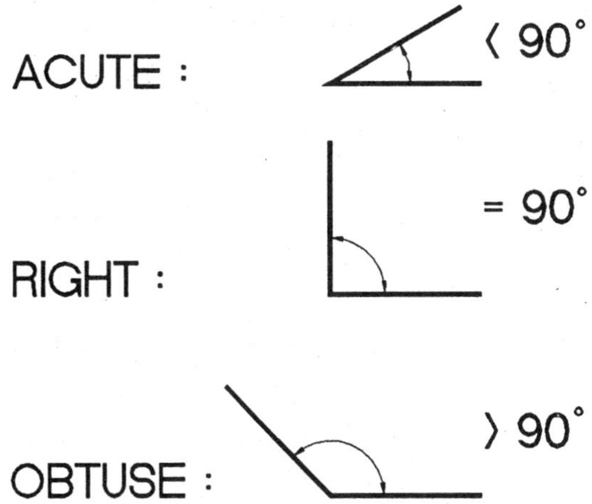

ACUTE :   〈 90°

RIGHT :   = 90°

OBTUSE :   〉 90°

Figure 469   Types of angles.

An *acute angle* is one that is less than 90°. An angle equal to 90° or with two perpendicular legs is a *right angle.* Any other angle more than 90° is called an *obtuse angle.*

Definition of Triangles

Angles are also used to define the types of triangles they create. An *acute triangle* has three angles each less than 90°. The *right triangle* has one angle equal to 90° and the *obtuse triangle* has one angle more than 90°.

You will encounter the right triangle in most angular design situations. To determine the dimensions of cabinetry to be installed on an angle, you'll need to identify the triangles it forms and their side dimensions.

First list the known geometric factors; one angle is 90°, one leg of the triangle is equal to the cabinet depth and the two other angles become known based on your choice for placement. The interior angles will add up to 180°. Therefore, if you are placing a cabinet at a 45° angle, the remaining angle will also be 45°. If you're placing a cabinet at a 30° angle, the remaining angle will be 60°.

ACUTE : ⟨ 90°

RIGHT : = 90°

OBTUSE : ⟩ 90°

Figure 470   *Types of triangles.*

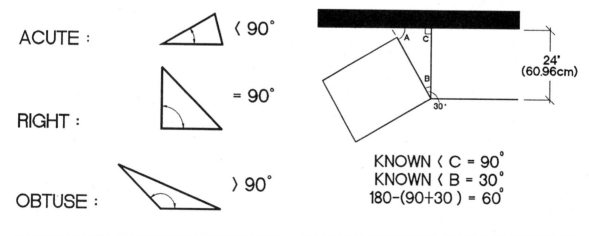

24' (60.96cm)

KNOWN ⟨ C = 90°
KNOWN ⟨ B = 30°
180−(90+30) = 60°

Figure 471   *Identifying geometric known factors.*

To compute the wall space required to place a 24" (60.96cm) wide vanity drawer at a 45° angle in the corner, use the following formula.

> Cw = Cabinet Width
> Cd = Cabinet Depth
> WSa = Wall space "a"
> TW = Total Wall space
> .7071 = Formula constant
>
> Cw x .7071 = WSa
> WSa + Cd = TW

For more information see Table of Trigonometric Functions on page 527.

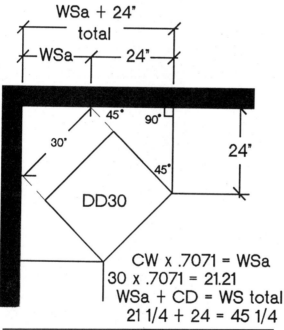

$$CW \times .7071 = WSa$$
$$30 \times .7071 = 21.21$$
$$WSa + CD = WS\ total$$
$$21\ 1/4 + 24 = 45\ 1/4$$

Figure 472   Determining the wall space required for an angled cabinet installation.

Constructing an Angle Equal to a Given Angle

In new construction, your drawings will often have to be taken from an architect's blueprint. To transfer an odd angle from a blueprint to your own drawing, follow these steps:

- Draw an arc of any radius from the intersection of the angle on the blueprint.

- Then draw an arc with the same radius on your drawing.

- Return to the blueprint. Determine the distance from intersection "x" to intersection "y" with your compass. Draw an arc from intersection "y", through intersection "x". *(Figure 473, drawing #1).*

- Repeat this process on your own working drawing. Draw the arc through the previous arc you just drew. *(Figure 473, drawing #2)*

- The point of intersection of the two arcs will also intersect the angle's second leg. *(Figure 473, drawing #2)*

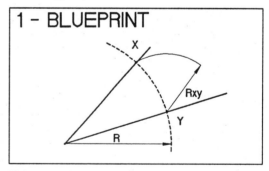

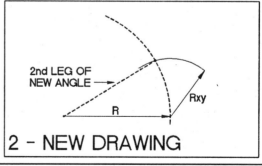

Figure 473   Constructing equal angles in plan view.

Constructing Curved Lines with Arcs

Drawing custom countertop plans will require constructing various curved lines.

- When the arc is tangent to a right angle, draw an arc with the given radius from the right angle inter- section through the two legs.

- Where the arc intersects the legs, draw another arc inside the right angle from each point so they in- tersect.

- From their point of intersection, draw another arc, which will be tangent to the right angle legs.

When the arc is tangent to two lines that are not perpendicular, the arc radius must be equal distance from each line.

Determine the radius center by con- structing parallel lines equal distance from each line. Extend these lines until they cross. The point of intersection is the radius location.

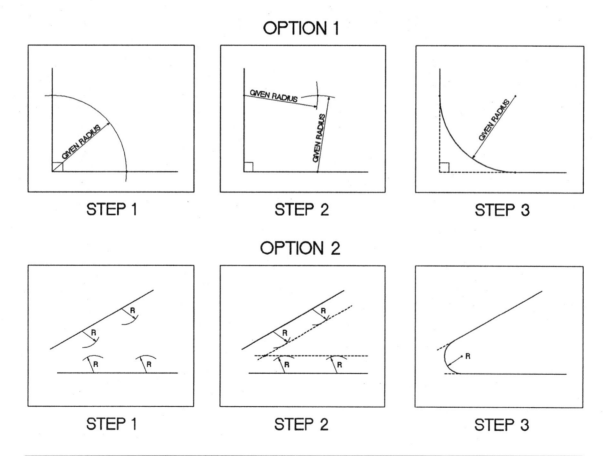

Figure 474   Constructing curved lines with arcs.

Constructing an Ellipse

You will need to construct an ellipse whenever you draw a perspective that has a circular element in it.

- First, determine where the widest point or *major axis* will fall and then where the thinnest point, called the *minor axis* will fall.

- On an edge of a sheet of paper, mark three points A, B and C so that AC equals half the major axis and BC equals half the minor axis.

- Slide point A up and down along the minor axis while pivoting from the same point and keeping point B on the major axis.

- Mark several points at C throughout the process and draw a smooth curve connecting these points.

An alternative is to sketch a rectangle which will contain the ellipse.

- Locate the major and minor axis.

- Then divide the rectangle by bisecting the line segments as illustrated in *Figure 476*, bisecting a line.

- Sketch the ellipse to align with the designated points.

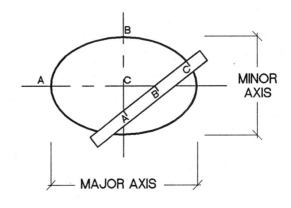

Figure 475   Constructing an ellipse in plan view.

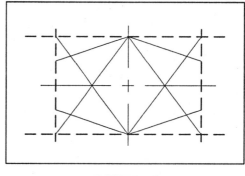

STEP 1

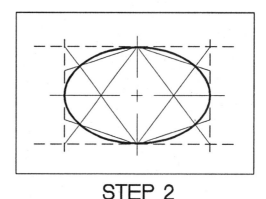

STEP 2

Figure 476   A second option for constructing an ellipse in plan view.

SECTION **6**

Drawing Symbols

FOLLOWING INDUSTRY STANDARDS

The use of graphic and presentation standards is necessary for universal industry communication. The following legends of symbols are those most frequently used in bathroom working drawings.

Wall and Partition Symbols

Typically, existing walls are shown as solid lines, approximately 1/4" (.64cm) thick with half walls shown as hollow lines. However, because drawing solid lines by hand is very time consuming, hollow lines are accepted in our industry. Be sure to note any walls that are not full height if you choose this method. Walls to be removed are shown with broken dashed lines. Existing openings that are to be enclosed are hatched with several parallel lines. Newly constructed walls should indicate the type of material used in construction, or use a symbol that is identified in the legend to distinguish them from existing partitions.

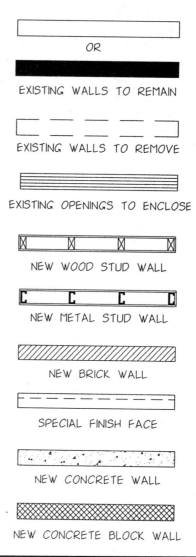

OR

EXISTING WALLS TO REMAIN

EXISTING WALLS TO REMOVE

EXISTING OPENINGS TO ENCLOSE

NEW WOOD STUD WALL

NEW METAL STUD WALL

NEW BRICK WALL

SPECIAL FINISH FACE

NEW CONCRETE WALL

NEW CONCRETE BLOCK WALL

Figure 477   Wall and partition symbols.

Door Symbols

Doors should always indicate open or cased framing and the direction of swing. In most instances, a 45° swing is acceptable. If there are any questions as to clearance, a 90° swing should be shown. A door schedule reference is only required with new doors and is indicated by placing a letter within a circle inside each door opening. If there is only one new door, the schedule information can be indicated directly within the floor plan in note form.

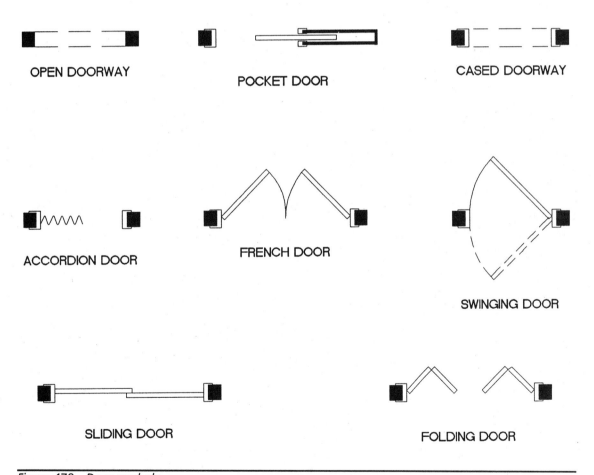

OPEN DOORWAY   POCKET DOOR   CASED DOORWAY

ACCORDION DOOR   FRENCH DOOR   SWINGING DOOR

SLIDING DOOR   FOLDING DOOR

Figure 478   Door symbols.

Window and Skylight Symbols

Open or cased framing should always be indicated on window symbols. Window sills are typically not shown unless a particular interior treatment is to be used. The indication of glass swings is optional and if shown, should be dotted lines. Skylights are shown in long dashed lines and are labeled inside. Pertinent information is referenced at the side.

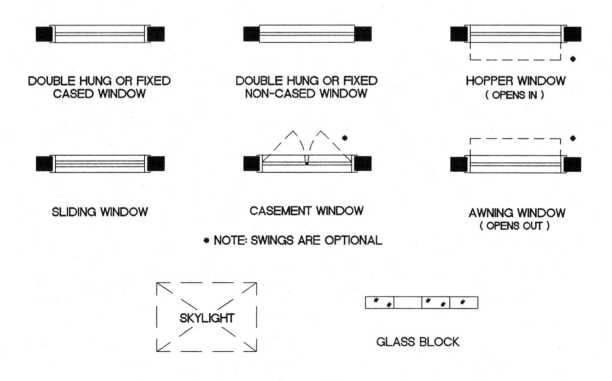

DOUBLE HUNG OR FIXED
CASED WINDOW

DOUBLE HUNG OR FIXED
NON-CASED WINDOW

HOPPER WINDOW
(OPENS IN)

SLIDING WINDOW

CASEMENT WINDOW

AWNING WINDOW
(OPENS OUT)

* NOTE: SWINGS ARE OPTIONAL

SKYLIGHT

GLASS BLOCK

Figure 479   Window, skylight and glass block symbols.

Staircase Symbols

Stairs should be indicated with a directional arrow. The risers can be broken midway, unless the design incorporates the other floor, in which case the total number of risers should be indicated. Ramps are also shown with directional arrows and should always be shown full length. The slope should be indicated in new construction drawings. Be sure to indicate up or down with an arrow. The arrow should lead from the main floor area to the secondary area.

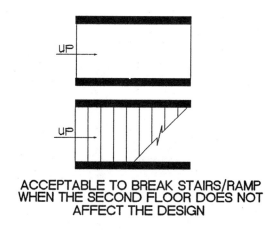

ACCEPTABLE TO BREAK STAIRS/RAMP
WHEN THE SECOND FLOOR DOES NOT
AFFECT THE DESIGN

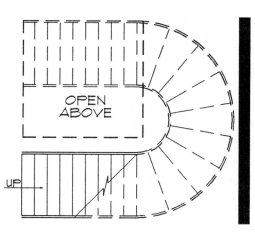

INDICATE THE ENTIRE STAIRWAY/RAMP
WHEN IT DOES AFFECT THE DESIGN

Figure 480   Staircase and ramp symbols.

Elevator Symbols

Elevators and hydraulic lifts are indicated with an outline of the interior size and an "x". The "x" *is* used to indicate that the unit runs through the entire space beyond floor and/or ceiling. Be sure to add appropriate door symbols to the elevator opening.

ADD APPROPRIATE
DOOR SYMBOL TO
ELEVATORS AND LIFTS

Figure 481   Elevator symbol.

Handrail/Grab Bar Symbols

Interior or exterior handrails, fencing, grab bars and towel bars are all shown with double solid lines. They may be labeled within the floor plan. Many designers prefer to number them with an adjacent schedule to eliminate a cluttered drawing.

HANDRAIL, TOWEL BAR,
GRAB BAR OR FENCING

Figure 482   Handrails and grab bar symbol.

Finishing Materials Symbols

It is preferred to indicate decking and flooring materials in a blank area of the drawing. However, if the drawing does not allow for a clear indication, it is better not to show any. Be sure to include the flooring in the specifications.

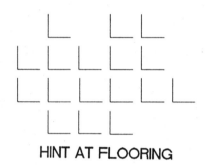

HINT AT FLOORING

Figure 483   Finishing materials symbol.

Cabinetry Symbols

Cabinetry in plan view should be indicated by an outline only. Do not indicate hidden features such as toekick or shelving. The tall cabinets and wall cabinets will have a solid outline, previously described as a visible object line. The base cabinets will be indicated with a dotted line of the hidden line type. When cabinets are stacked one above the other, the unit on top takes precedence. Use a note and arrow to indicate the cabinet at the bottom.

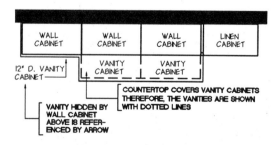

Figure 484   Cabinetry symbols.

Mechanical Symbols

For the purpose of bathroom plans, mechanical symbols include lighting, electrical, plumbing as well as heating and ventilating. The accuracy of illustrating these particular symbols is very important because the professional tradesperson must be able to interpret your drawing. These symbols are universal and will also be found on an architects blueprint. Although they are universal, your mechanical plan should always include a legend to eliminate any questions.

Figure 485   Mechanical symbols

Typical Bathroom Fixture Symbols

For the purpose of working drawings, bathroom fixture symbols should remain consistent throughout the set of drawings. The shapes of fixtures such as bathtubs and showers may differ, but the illustrative details should remain consistent. Faucet and bathtub filler locations should always be indicated on the floor plan and mechanical plan.

TYPICAL BATHROOM FIXTURE SYMBOLS

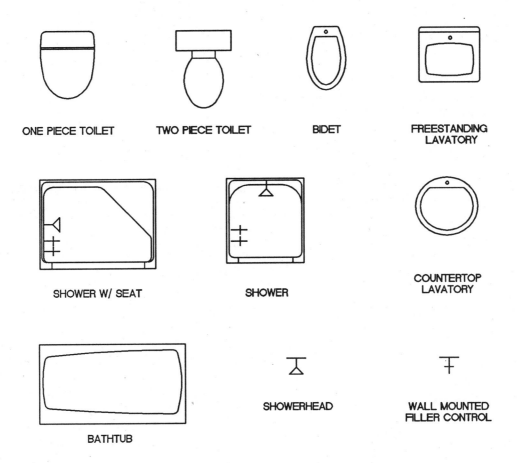

ONE PIECE TOILET   TWO PIECE TOILET   BIDET   FREESTANDING LAVATORY

SHOWER W/ SEAT   SHOWER   COUNTERTOP LAVATORY

BATHTUB   SHOWERHEAD   WALL MOUNTED FILLER CONTROL

Figure 486   Bathroom fixture symbols

SECTION **7**

Drawing a Floor Plan

10 STEPS IN DRAWING A FLOOR PLAN

To begin the drafting process, assemble your equipment within reach around your drawing board. Set your board at a comfortable incline (approximately 10° to 15°). The incline helps to insure accuracy by enabling you to see above the equipment, as well as reduces back strain caused by bending over your work.

Now you are ready to begin drawing your floor plan.

STEP 1

Tape your paper down to the board. It is important to line it up with your straight edge to make sure the drawing will be square on the sheet of paper. If the paper has a preprinted border, align the border with your straight edge and then tape the paper in place. If there is no border, then the edge of the paper can be used to align with the straight edge.

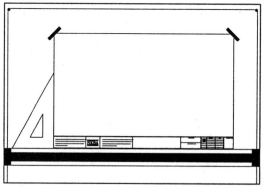

LINE PAPER EDGE OR BORDER LINE WITH STRAIGHT EDGES.

Figure 487   It is important to tape the paper down carefully.

STEP 2

Before you put pencil to paper, visualize the finished drawing. *Will you list specifications at the right side or at the bottom? Will there be a title?* Determine how much space your drawing will take up on the paper and don't forget to include space for the dimension lines. Use this information to determine where to locate the drawing on the paper. If more than one drawing will appear on the same sheet of paper, block out the spaces with light pencil outlines.

STEP 3

Begin your drawing by lightly penciling in all of the walls. By drawing all of the walls in first, any mistakes caused by incorrect scaling or measuring will be caught before too much time is spent drawing in details.

STEP 4

When the walls are complete, locate the doors and windows. The openings should be located from at least two different reference points to insure accuracy. Make sure that you show the door or window casings so that the overall dimensions listed for these openings are clearly different from the actual pass-through opening.

Step 5

At this point, if there are any mistakes they should be apparent and easily altered because all your lines have been light layout lines so far. When all the measurements have been double checked, you can darken in the final wall, window and door lines.

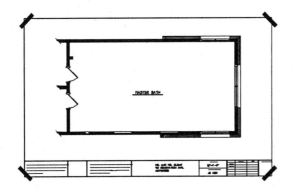

Figure 488 After the drawing is verified, darken in the walls.

STEP 6

Once the plan is on paper, draw in all your dimension lines, following a systematic method. Draw the line closest to the wall first, then the second and third set of lines. Locate the center lines of all appliances, then locate the individual openings and sections of walls, and lastly the total (overall) dimensions for each wall. Don't forget your ceiling height in the center of the drawing.

STEP 7

The remaining major interior elements of the drawing should be drawn next (such as cabinets, fixtures and furniture). These should be drawn in lightly at first and then darkened when everything is confirmed in final locations. Use the *"subtraction method"* described in Volume 4 to place all of the elements of the plan in the available space.

After the design has been finalized, darken all the solid object lines such as tall cabinets, wall cabinets and countertops. Then draw the final base cabinet lines with hidden lines (short dashes). Use a straight edge which has divided markings, such as those found on a drafting machine or triangle/template to keep the dashes consistent.

Make sure you lift your tools, as you move them across the paper to avoid smearing the pencil lead. **Remember to erase carefully so that you don't tear the paper and use your drafting brush, not your hand to remove eraser shavings and graphite.**

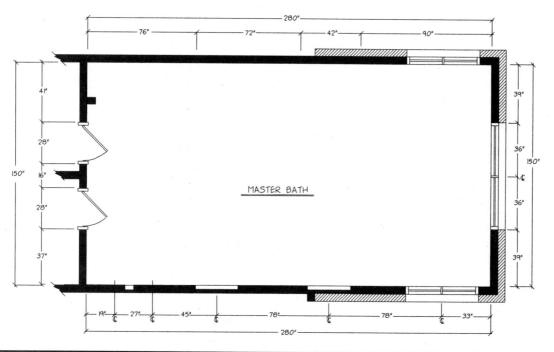

Figure 489   Indicate all required dimensions (imperial example).

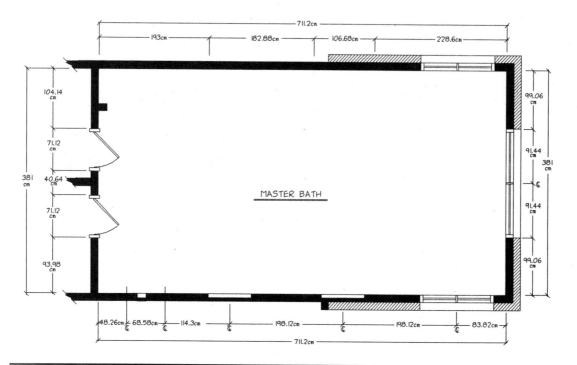

Figure 490   Indicate all required dimensions (metric example).

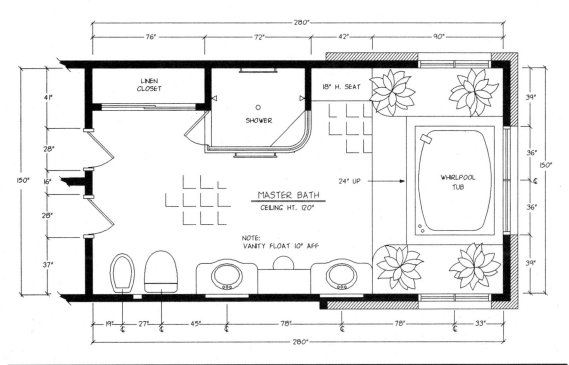

Figure 491   The interior details and notes are added to complete the floor plans (imperial example).

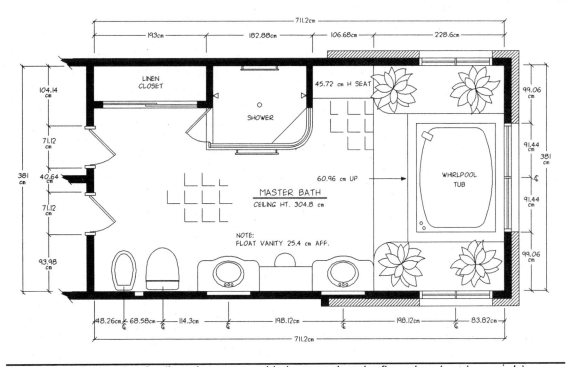

Figure 492   The interior details and notes are added to complete the floor plans (metric example).

STEP 8

Now you're ready to put in the details. Add any nomenclature, notes, accessories (such as plants, chairs and flooring) that are necessary.

STEP 9

Complete the list of specification details by corresponding numbers in the plan. (Refer to Appendix I, Graphic and Presentation Standards for more information).

STEP 10

Complete the title block. You should identify firm name, client information, job identification, drawing number, designer and draftsperson identification, drawing date and drawing scale. The title block may include additional information if desired.

Construction Plan

The next drawing that may be required in a set of complete drawings for a bathroom design presentation is the construction plan. This drawing is only required if walls or openings need to be altered from their original locations. A construction plan will show both the existing conditions of the structure or the Architect's blueprint and the changes required to the building in order to accomplish your design.

NOTE: Changes to the structure in any way must be approved by the builder/architect or licensed remodeler before proceeding with the project. Special symbols are used to clearly illustrate the construction alterations necessary. *For example*, a wall is shown solid or hollow if it is to remain unchanged, new walls to be constructed are shown with the appropriate material symbol and existing openings to be closed are hatched with parallel lines.

Universally accepted wall and partition symbols are indicated in *Figure 477*, however, whether you use these or other symbols, your construction plan should always include a legend with a sample of the symbol and its description. The construction plan should include only the walls, their dimensions and the legend. The dimensions should be indicated to the interior finished surfaces and new windows and doors should be located by a centerline as well as from outside of casing to outside of casing. Additionally, new windows and doors should be noted by manufacturer brand and model numbers whenever possible.

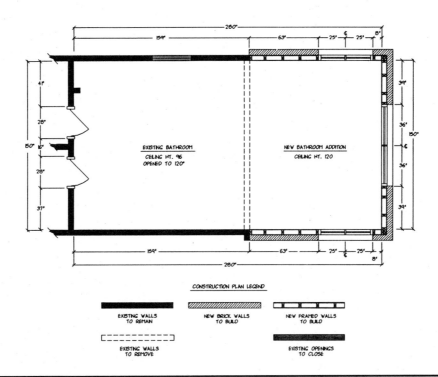

Figure 493   Construction plans illustrate existing and new construction (imperial example).

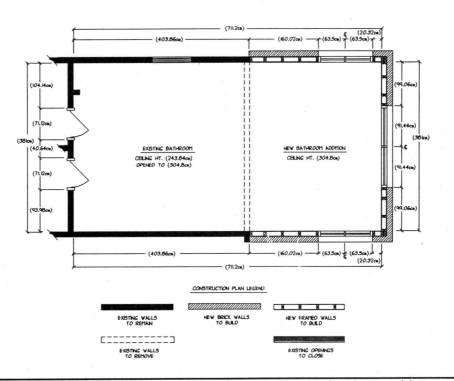

Figure 494   Construction plans illustrate existing and new construction (metric example).

Mechanical Plan

For the purpose of bathroom design, a mechanical plan communicates to the allied trades the exact location and specification of all plumbing, electrical, heating and ventilating fixtures and equipment and how they relate with the cabinetry. A mechanical plan is required with every bathroom plan and will follow the construction plan, or the floor plan if no construction plan is required.

A mechanical plan should repeat the dimensions and cabinet layout of the floor plan, but will not include the nomenclature or specifications. Rather the mechanical plan will show the appropriate mechanical symbols, as indicated in Figure 485 and repeat the symbols in a legend with their description.

For example, all electrical appliances that require 120 volt electrical service will show a special purpose outlet symbol with initials corresponding to the appliance such as "w" for whirlpool. Equipment requiring 240 volt service will use the circle with three parallel lines through it such as shown for a steam generator.

Ceiling fixtures such as lights, fans and vents are shown as if reflected in a mirror floor. This technique is commonly referred to as a reflected ceiling plan.

All ceiling or floor mounted fixtures must be dimensioned with centerlines within the walls of the mechanical plan, additionally heights of switches, outlets, etc. should be indicated.

Countertop Plan

A separate countertop plan is not required with your presentation to the client, since the outline is indicated in the floor plan. However, you may find a countertop plan helpful in illustrating the installation or fabrication to the allied tradesperson particularly in complex projects, such as those that combine various counter materials or built-up edge treatments. If you select to include a countertop plan it should show only the walls of the space and the outline of the cabinets, fixtures and equipment, applicable notes, details and dimensions. There may be up to three dimension lines for each counter section. The first dimension line should show the center of any cut-outs, such as those for sinks or cooktops. The second dimension line should indicate the overall available wall length. Notes about cut-outs, corner treatments, depth changes, and such will need to be included with arrows pointing to the specific area. A detailed profile of the counter edge treatment is often provided at a blown-up scale to clearly illustrate the counter design and its overhang relative to the face of the cabinet. Counters typically overhang the face of the door by 3/4" - 1". Therefore, it will be critical to know the exact thickness of the door. This level of detail will not only eliminate error by clearly communicating your ideas, but it will also help to establish you as the expert in the eyes of the consumer.

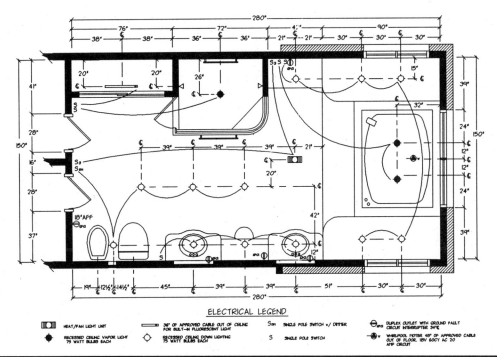

ELECTRICAL LEGEND

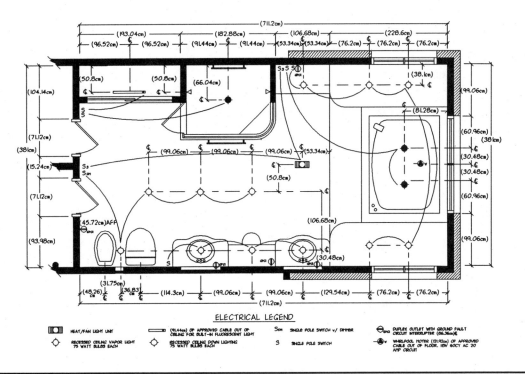

Figure 495 Mechanical plans indicate plumbing, electrical, heating and ventilation (imperial example).

Figure 496 Mechanical plans indicate plumbing, electrical, heating and ventilation (metric example).

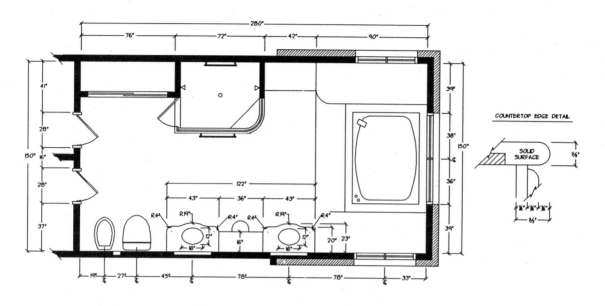

Figure 497   *Countertop plans will help to convey details such as custom edge treatments (imperial example).*

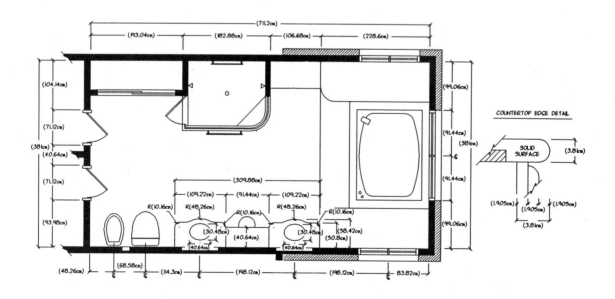

Figure 498   *Countertop plans will help to convey details such as custom edge treatments (metric example).*

Soffit Plan

A separate soffit plan is also not a requirement with your presentation to your client, but again, it may be helpful in conveying your design. Follow the same guidelines as provided for drawing a countertop plan. However, if the soffit is a complex design such as one with multiple levels or steps, it is recommended to eliminate the outline of the cabinets. If you do not draw the cabinets on the soffit plan you must be careful to compare the soffit and cabinet dimensions in order to ensure consistent reveals. Remember to include the thickness of doors when using full overlay styles and use the overhead line type to draw the soffit outline. Remember the over head line type is a long dashed line.

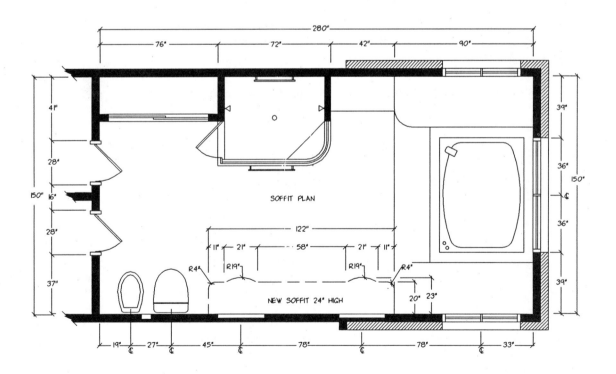

Figure 499   Soffit plans utilize the overhead line type (imperial example).

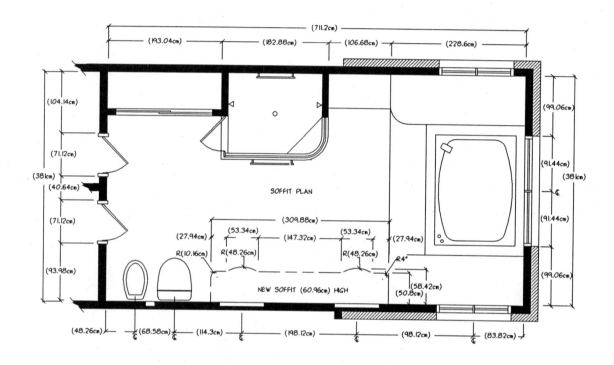

Figure 500   Soffit plans utilize the overhead line type (metric example).

INTERPRETIVE DRAWINGS

Elevations, paraline drawings and perspectives illustrate the vertical elements in a design that are not shown in a floor plan.

Elevations

An elevation is an orthographic drawing just like the floor plan, but drawn from another viewpoint. Elevations are true, scaled drawings in both height and width, however, elevations have no depth. If you choose to use elevations, several views will be required to illustrate the space. The various views should correspond with an elevation view symbol pointing to the view inside the floor plan.

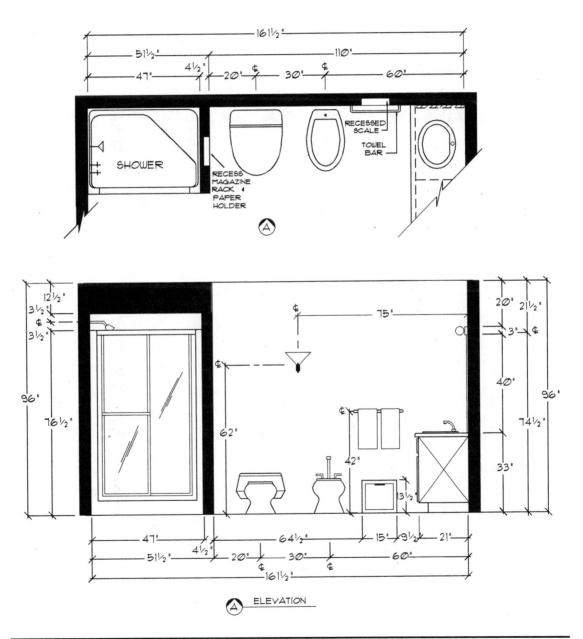

Figure 501   *The elevations correspond directly to the plans (imperial example).*

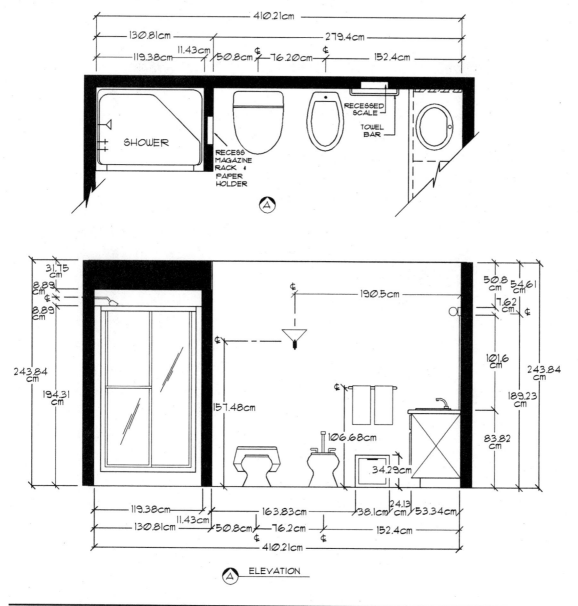

Paraline Drawings

Paraline drawings are similar to orthographic drawings and remain in a true scale format, yet offer a three dimensional view of the space.

All paraline drawings including oblique, diametric, isometric and trimetric, have three characteristics which separates them from other drawing types:

- all vertical lines remain parallel

- all horizontal lines remain parallel

- all lines indicating depth are parallel

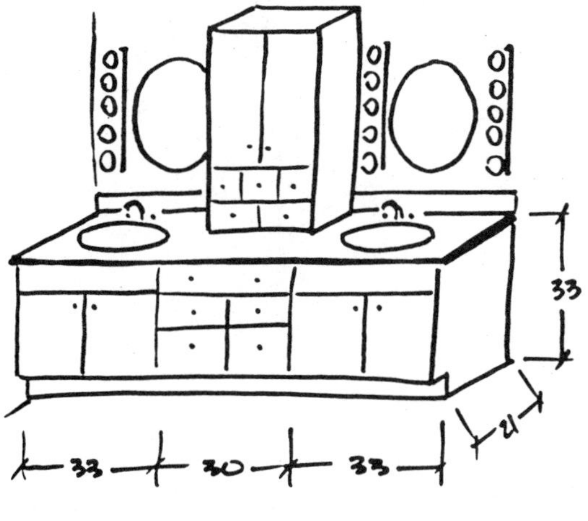

The use of paraline drawings is not recommended for client presentations because the drawings tend to appear distorted. They are however, ideal for quick pictorial representation during the design idea process.

Perspective Sketch

The realistic appearance of a perspective sketch makes it the ideal type of interpretive drawing. The perspective relies on the appearance of the space, rather than on the true scale of the space.

There are three qualities inherent to perspectives that separate them from other drawing types:

- a diminishing size in relation to distance

- a vanishing or meeting of parallel lines as they recede

- a foreshortening of horizontal elements as they move away from the horizon line

There are various techniques used to develop perspective drawing presentations. Following are several examples which demonstrate both hand drawn and computer generated presentation techniques. As you view these drawings, notice how each different method of preparation takes on individual personality. In time, you too will develop your own personal style depending on your needs and preferences.

Figure 503 Paraline sketching can help the design idea process.

Figure 504   Paralline sketching can also be used to help the designer visualize how the surfaces selected will relate to one another.

Figure 505   (Courtesy of Theodore E. Lutjen, CKD)   The thumbnail sketch provides a quick illustration.

Figure 506   (Courtesy of AMD Designs)   The traditional grid assisted drawing is popular.

Figure 507 (Courtesy of Sara Reep, CKD, ASID) Perspectives take on individual style with the addition of shading and accessories.

Figure 508   (Courtesy of AMD Designs)   Perspectives take on individual style with the addition of shading and accessories.

Figure 509   (Courtesy of Gail Drury, CKD)   Perspectives take on individual style with the addition of shading and accessories.

THE CONSTRUCTION METHOD

The original method used to construct perspectives involved complicated and time-consuming identification of points. Various points were plotted into position by locating the plan on your drawing and drawing lines from every corner to a picture plane, transferring the newly located points to yet another location by connecting them with the vanishing point.

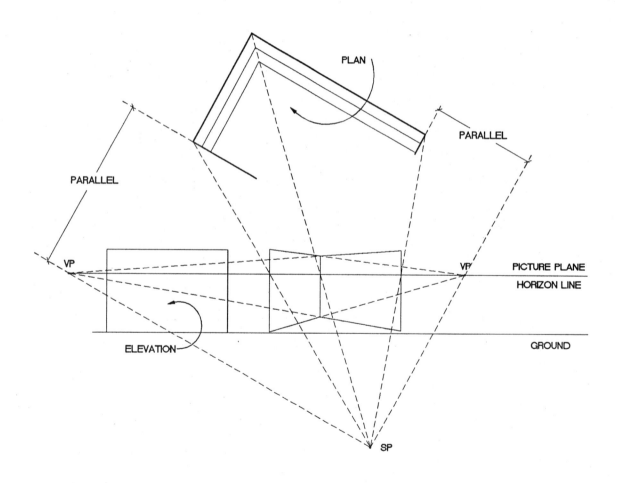

Figure 510   The construction method of perspective drawing.

THE GRID BASED METHOD

The grid method more commonly used today is based on the original construction method, but the confusing transformation of points has already been completed. The grids available from the **National Kitchen & Bath Association** have located points in one-foot increments, with additional, commonly used points, such as toekick and backsplash heights, also indicated. These are available in both one-point and two-point versions.

Refer to *Appendix A* for complete grid instructions as reprinted from the **National Kitchen & Bath Association Grid Instruction Manual.**

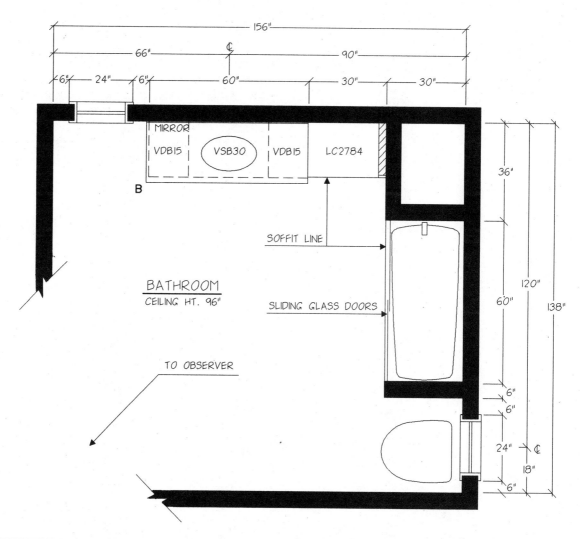

Figure 511   *A typical bathroom to be used to demonstrate the NKBA grid method of perspective drawing.*

Choosing Perspective Types

Once you are familiar with the method used to construct a one and two-point perspective, your selection will be based on the type of project. Choosing the correct type of perspective (one-point or two-point) is important.

For detailed information on one and two point perspectives, refer to *Appendix A*.

TWO-POINT

The two-point view is usually preferred because it is the most realistic. However, only two walls can be shown in a single view. Two views will be required to illustrate a complete space using two-point perspectives.

ONE-POINT

A one-point perspective illustrates three walls within a single view, eliminating the need for a second view. However, in very small and very large spaces, a one-point perspective view "crowds" the side walls and obscures details.

BIRDS-EYE

To illustrate small spaces without breaking them up or obscuring details, the one-point *"birds-eye"* perspective is recommended. A *"birds-eye view"* is taken from above the ceiling, looking down onto the floor. It encompasses all four walls. A *"birds-eye view"* is similar to looking down into a scale model. The *"birds-eye view"* is obviously not realistic. However, it does give a clear picture of the spatial relationship between the various elements of the room.

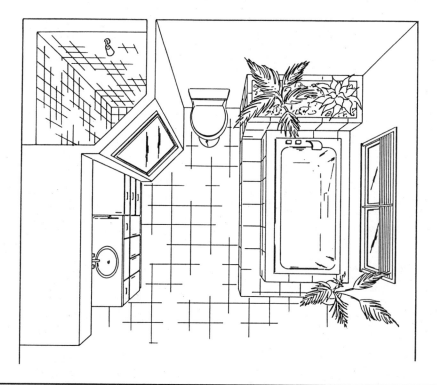

Figure 512   The birds-eye view perspective illustrates spacial relationships.

Enhancing the Perspective

Including shading, highlights, color, people and accessories to a perspective adds to the effect of realism. The lines of a drawing in perspective define the limits, but the drawing derives meaning through its figure-ground relationship. By thickening the profile line or lines of edges against space, a drawing becomes easier to interpret.

ADDING SHADING

Shading conveys even more information by defining dimension and direction. An otherwise flat object becomes three-dimensional by adding shadows. A light source is introduced which adds the degree of realism.

Because there are several light sources in an interior rather than one

(the sun) in architectural drawings, it's difficult to calculate exact shadow delineation. Therefore, the standard practice is

Figure 513   Lines define limits of objects.

to consider two light sources coming from both upper left and upper right locations.

Figure 514   Darkening profile lines emphasize the 3D quality of a perspective drawing.

Figure 515   Shadows define depth.

As you draw, think of the light shining over your left and right shoulders onto your drawing. The top and front surfaces of objects are in the most light and receive little or no shading. The sides of objects not in direct view, such as cabinet sides and the ceiling are in a light shade. The darkest shades are reserved for areas below overhangs. The principles behind these types of shadows are;

• parallel surfaces create parallel shadow edges

• perpendicular surfaces create sloping shadow edges.

By varying tonal values of shades, the perception of depth is enhanced. Two objects that appear equal in tone appear to be in the same spatial plane. If you vary the shade tones of each object, depth will be emphasized. There are several principles which may be applied to produce this effect. In black line artwork as illustrated here, the background is shaded and the foreground is left in pure, crisp line form. This technique will make two closer elements jump off the page at the viewer. If color is being used, the foreground will be bright, pure colors with dark outlines and the background should be lighter colors. When shading with pencil, the background can be blended by smudging the graphite and lightening it at the same time.

These shading techniques can be performed with pencil, pen or marker. Each medium has its own special look. The final presentation will vary depending, on your choice of medium and personal style. (See Figures 514, 515 and 516 for examples of different styles.)

Figure 516   Varying tone emphasizes depth.

ADDING PEOPLE AND ACCESSORIES

To add realism to a drawing, add people and accessories. There are several source books available with people and accessories that can be traced into your own drawing. Another good source is your local newspaper advertisement sections and department store catalogues. These sources will give you models that are up-to-date.

If the size is not exactly right, reduce or enlarge it on a copy machine and then trace it into your drawing. Or incorporate it into your software package, making it available for use at a later time.

On the following page, you'll find some of our favorite bathroom accessories to begin your tracing file.

ENHANCING WITH COLOR

Color is the ultimate enhancement. Color evokes emotion and has a far reaching effect on the viewer's perception of the design. To ignore color is to ignore one of the elements of design.

When selecting a coloring medium, be sure to also purchase black and several shades of cool grey. Begin your color collection with subtle, muted, neutral tones rather than the bright primary colors. The primary colors may look pretty, but will quickly overwhelm your drawing.

"Less is more," when applying color. Hint at color in different areas of the drawing. Use the markers and pencils together to enhance each other.

Markers give a smooth, solid appearance, ideal for base coats of solid color. They can stand on their own for such items as matte laminates and painted woods.

Use the colored pencils alone to add texture and highlights. Or go over the marker base with them.

With a little practice, your drawings will come to life.

Figure 517   Trace people and accessories to add realism to drawings.

STORING PROJECT DOCUMENTS

After you've completed your presentation drawings, you'll need a place to safely store them. The type of storage you choose depends on the type of presentation used. Use tubes or roll files for large, rolled drawings. Roll files may be vertical, horizontal or stepped. They may be made of cardboard, wood or wire.

Most professionals prefer to store drawings flat. For flat storage, there are vertical files where drawings hang on a pivoting clip that allows easy access. You may also choose flat files, which are stacks of shallow drawers sized to accommodate standard drawings. These are available in a variety of materials. Some feature drawers that can be pulled out and carried for transporting drawings.

Plan Presentation

Traditional leather portfolios may also be used for transporting and presenting drawings. Zippered portfolios with open interiors for matted drawings or ring binders with acetate folders for loose drawings are available. Some smaller portfolios can be folded to resemble a table easel for convenient viewing. Portfolios no larger than 18" x 24" (45.72cm x 60.96cm) are recommended so they can be easily viewed by clients.

Alternatively, selected drawings can be matted, framed and displayed on an easel. These can be in your showroom and then taken to trade shows or spec homes for marketing your services.

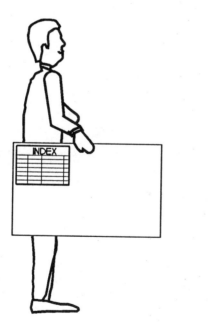

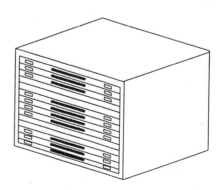

Figure 518   Stacking horizontal storage converts to portfolio case.

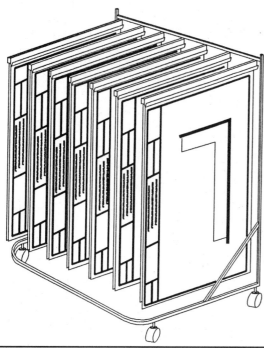

Figure 519
Vertical hanging files are easily accessed.

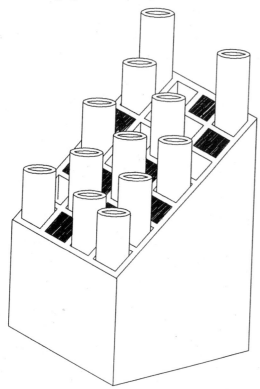

Figure 520
Rolled drawings can be stored in a tiered storage unit for easy access.

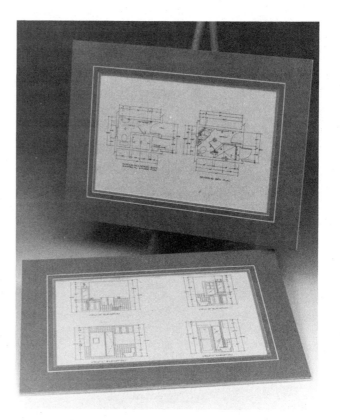

Figure 521   Table easels provide showroom display of drawings.

Figure 522   A portfolio case will allow presentation flexibility by traveling anywhere

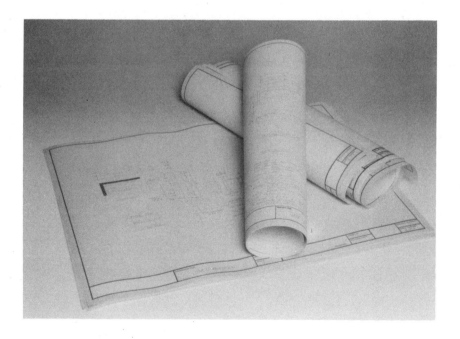

Figure 523   Rolled drawings are difficult to present.

Appendix A

How to Draw 1 & 2 Point Bathroom Perspective Renderings

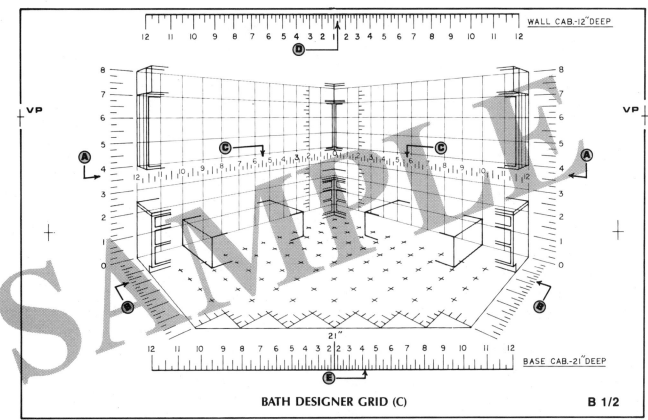

Fig. 12

HELPFUL TWO POINT PERSPECTIVE TIPS

The eye level (or horizon line) of the observer looking at the grid chart picture is 72″, the same height as the vanishing points (VP).

The height of all equipment can be determined by using the vertical scale " Ⓐ " shown on the left and right of the grid in Fig. 12.

Depth of equipment can be determined by using the " Ⓑ " scale shown on the floor.

Use scale " Ⓒ " to determine the width of equipment placed against the wall.

Use scale " Ⓓ " to determine the width of wall cabinets 12″ deep.

Use scale " Ⓔ " to determine the width of base cabinets 21″ deep.

The NKBA bathroom grid method of perspective drawing.

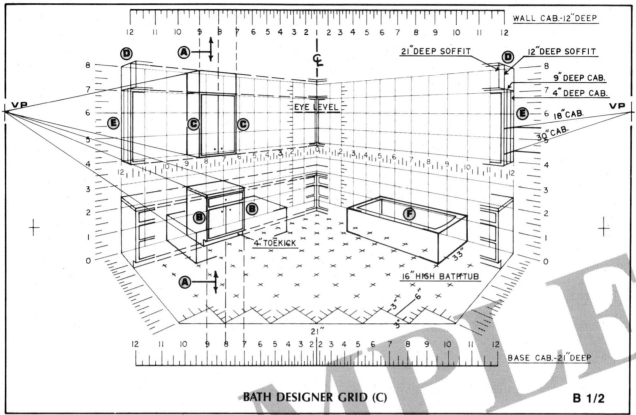

BATH DESIGNER GRID (C)   B 1/2

Fig. 13

An outline of base and wall cabinets are shown on each side of the grid. On each side of center, the outline is repeated. To draw a continuous run of cabinetry, align your triangle with the outside cabinet outline and the center outline. Now, draw a continuous line to the desired length. Also note that if you continued the line through center, it would terminate at the VP.

When you need to draw a base and wall cabinet in the middle of the grid, use the top and bottom scales (figure 13 Ⓐ). In figure 13, the base and wall cabinets begin at 7′ from the inside corner and end at 9′. To draw the base cabinet, vertically align your triangle with the 7 and 9 on the bottom scale. Project the right and left sides of the base cabinet into its proper position on the grid (figure 13 Ⓑ). To draw the wall cabinet, follow the same procedure but use the top scale (figure 13 Ⓒ).

The soffit shown in figure 13 Ⓓ is 21″ deep. To complete the entire soffit, align your triange at the preferred depth and with the same depth line in the center of the grid. Be sure that an imaginary line continuing through center goes to VP. If not, your alignment is incorrect.

Wall cabinet depths 4″ and 9″ are used for surface mounted medicine cabinets and wall cabinets over water closets (figure 13 Ⓔ).

The bathtub shown was completed by connecting the top and bottom tub guidelines on the grid (figure 13 Ⓕ). The result is a 16″ H × 33″ D × 60″ L tub. To set the tub at any desired location, use the vertical scale along the back wall to determine your start and stop points. Then, extend the tub guidelines to achieve the proper depth, height and width.

The NKBA bathroom grid method of perspective drawing.

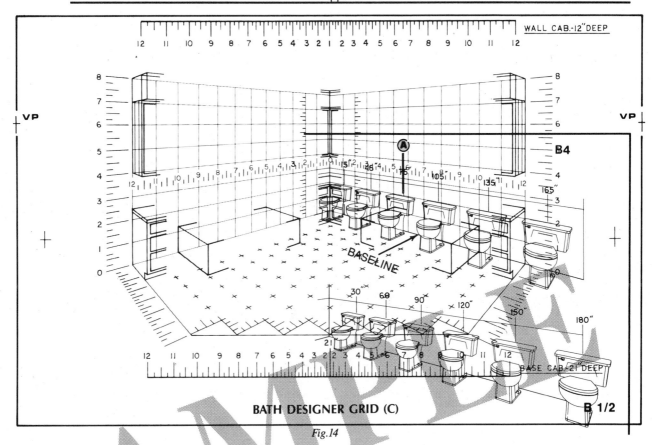

BATH DESIGNER GRID (C)

Fig.14

BATH FIXTURE OVERLAYS GRID (C)

Included with Bath Grid B1/2 are four bath fixture overlays:

1. (B3) One piece toilet and bidet
2. (B4) Two piece toilet
3. (B5) Rectangular pedestal sink
4. (B6) Oval pedestal sink

The bath fixtures on each overlay are positioned in two rows (except for the large pedestal sinks) with each fixture spaced 15″ on center from the inside corner of grid chart B1/2. By turning the overlay over, the fixtures will be in the reversed location on the opposite wall.

The decision as to when to draw the bath fixture in the drawing is up to the designer. If the bath fixture will block or partially hide the view of another object, you should draw the bath fixture first.

When tracing over the curves of the bath fixtures, try not to draw the entire curve in one stroke with your pencil. To produce a smoother curve in your drawing, use a series of short overlapping strokes. An elipse template is a very useful tool to use when drawing curves.

To place any fixture, find its centerline along the back wall of the grid by using the scale. At centerline, draw a **light** vertical guideline between the 2′ and 4′ height (figure 14 Ⓐ). This vertical guideline will help center the fixture properly.

The NKBA bathroom grid method of perspective drawing.

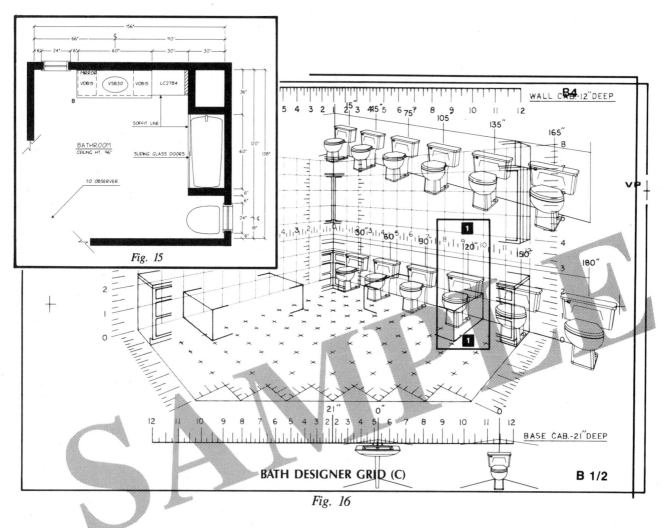

Fig. 15

Fig. 16

TWO POINT PERSPECTIVE DRAWING SEQUENCE

1 Slide grid chart B4 under your tracing paper and trace the water closet at 120" centered from the left (figure 16). Follow the step-by-step guide previously covered if more information is needed.

Select the proper grid chart for the fixture to be drawn. In our example, we will use B4 and a water centerline of 120". Slide the grid chart B4 under your tracing paper and on top of grid chart B1/2. Align the light vertical line at 120" with the vertical centerline on grid B4, (figure 16). Make **certain** that you also align the base lines of both grids. When aligned, trace the fixture.

The NKBA bathroom grid method of perspective drawing.

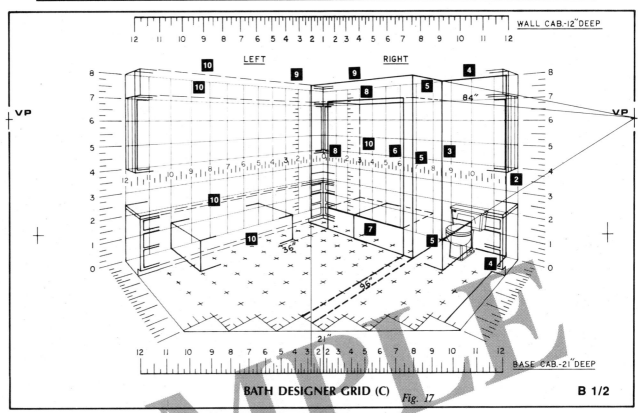

WALL CAB.-12″DEEP

BATH DESIGNER GRID (C) *Fig. 17*   B 1/2

DRAWING SEQUENCE

2 Starting on the right wall, draw a vertical line at 138″ (11′6″) from floor to 96″ (8′) ceiling (figure 17).

3 Draw a vertical line at 102″ (8′6″) from floor to ceiling (figure 17).

4 Draw the ceiling and floor lines above and behind the water closet (figure 17).

5 Draw the right side of the partition enclosing the tub (figure 17). Note that the depth of the partition is 33″. It lines up with the front of the tub as shown on the grid.

6 The partition thickness is 6″. Starting at the front of the partition, use the floor scale to make a line 6″ long. Next, at the end of the 6″ line, bring up a vertical line 84″H. (figure 17).

7 Draw top and bottom of tub by using tub guideline on grid (figure 17). Note: do not show depth now as enclosure will hide most of tub.

8 Complete the enclosure around the tub (figure 17).

9 The wall around the tub cannot be completed until the right side of the 30″ linen cabinet is drawn. The linen cabinet filler begins 30″ from the corner of the grid. Find 30″ on the base cabinet scale (found at the bottom of the grid) and make a vertical line from the **top** of the **toe space** to the 21″ deep soffit line (figure 17). Now complete the wall around the tub.

10 Lightly pencil in (shown as dotted lines) the 21″ deep soffit lines, countertop lines and toe space on the left wall. Do the same thing for the inside of the tub. Complete the inside ceiling of the tub with dark lines (figure 17).

The NKBA bathroom grid method of perspective drawing.

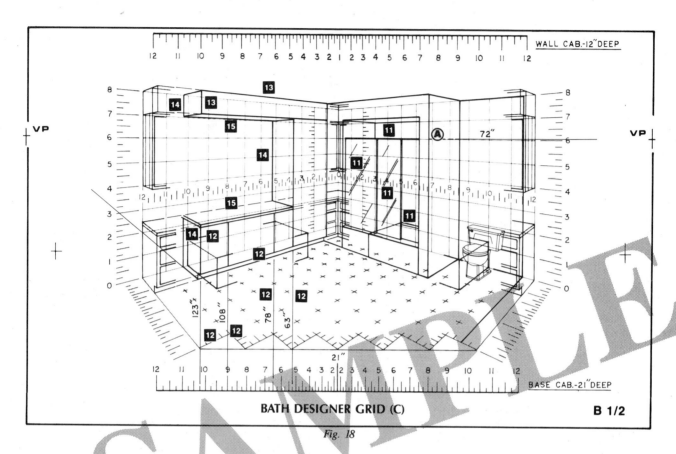

BATH DESIGNER GRID (C)   **B 1/2**

Fig. 18

DRAWING SEQUENCE *(Continued)*

11 The top of the tub enclosure is 72" (6'). At 72" along the right back wall, project a light line forward, 30" deep (figure 18Ⓐ). Now you can draw the sliding doors. If a frosted glass door is specified, leave the right door slightly ajar so a portion of the interior tub wall can be seen. Then, darken in the visible lines of the tub not covered by the doors (figure 18).

12 Using the base cabinet scale at the bottom of grid B1/2, draw the vertical left side of the 27" linen with filler, VDB15, VSB 30 and VDB15. Draw the front countertop edge and the toe space (figure 18).

13 Use the base cabinet scale to draw the front left edge of the soffit, which is also 21"D. Then, complete the remaining front of the soffit (figure 18).

14 Complete left side of 30" linen (84"H), VDB15, countertop and soffit (figure 6).

15 Complete bottom of soffit and darken back edge of countertop (figure 18).

The NKBA bathroom grid method of perspective drawing.

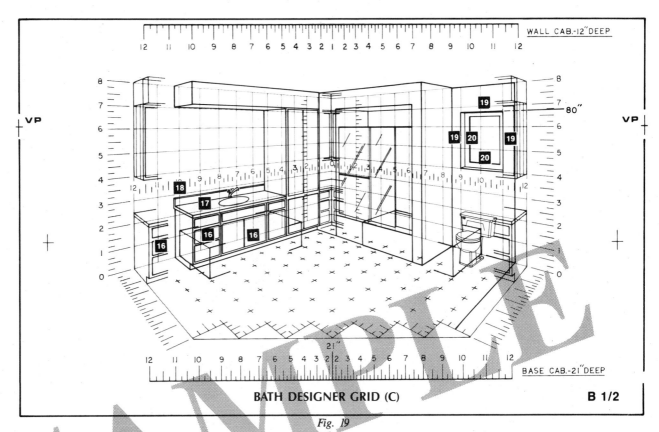

WALL CAB.-12"DEEP

VP

VP

80"

2 1"

BASE CAB.-21"DEEP

BATH DESIGNER GRID (C)   **B 1/2**

Fig. 19

DRAWING SEQUENCE *(Continued)*

16 Complete the drawers and doors on all cabinetry by using the drawer and door guide on grid B1/2 (figure 19).

17 Draw the lavatory by using grid B6 to trace the oval shape or use an elipse template to accomplish the same shape. You may also trace the faucet configurations on grid B6 or improvise by drawing a single lever faucet (figure 19).

18 After the lavatory and faucet are drawn, complete the countertop backsplash (figure 19).

19 There is a window above the water closet and to the left of the vanity. The windows are 24″W x 32″H. The height is 80″ above the floor and the openings begin 6″ from the right and left wall. Using the back wall scale, draw the perimeter of the windows (figure 19).

20 The window has depth and recesses into the wall. To show this depth, you must "guesstimate" or "fudge" what you consider to be approximately 3″. You are better off showing less depth than too much. Be sure to show the window stool in the drawing because it is below your eye level (figure 19).

The NKBA bathroom grid method of perspective drawing.

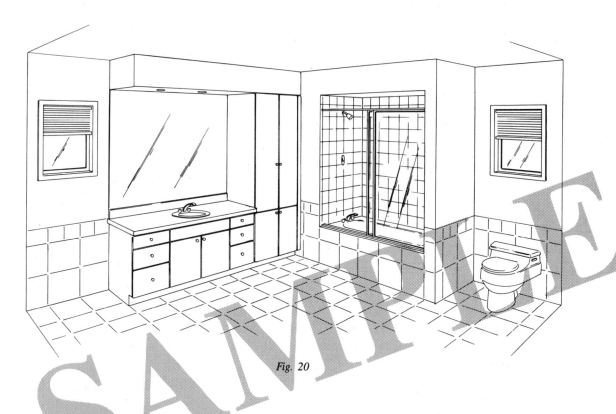

Fig. 20

All that remains are the embellishments. The mirror goes from backsplash to soffit. Use a double line on the left edge for depth. Add a few diagonal lines to show reflection (figure 20).

Tile can be easily drawn by using the back wall scale.

The blinds covering the windows are nothing more than closely spaced parallel lines.

The 12" x 12" floor is drawn by using the floor scale.

The NKBA bathroom grid method of perspective drawing.

HELPFUL ONE POINT PERSPECTIVE TIPS
BATH DESIGNER GRID (D) (ADJUSTABLE 8'-16')

The Adjustable Bath Grid has been designed so that you can complete a perspective drawing of a bathroom from 8' to 16'.

There are two parts to the adjustable grid system, B7 and B8. To use the system, first determine the room width according to your floor plan. Then, place the register mark (⊕) on B8 over the B7 scale (8'-16' at bottom of grid) at the desired room width. Align the black horizontal lines (above the register mark and scale) to assure the grids are plumb and level. Tape down the grid.

The grid chart is designed to move from 12' (one vanishing point) down to 8' and from 12' up to 16'. Only the right wall (overlay B8) will adjust; the left wall and the back wall (Grid B8) remain stationary.

If you were using a **fixed grid chart** and your room size did not coincide with the **back wall** dimensions of the grid chart, you would have to remove the tracing paper at some point during the drawing and reposition it over the grid chart in order to complete the picture. In essence, the Adjustable Bath Grid chart **repositions** (room size less than or greater than 12') the tracing paper for you before you start to draw.

The eye level of the observer in the grid chart is approximately 78" (6'6"), the same height as the vanishing point.

The **window and door** measurement (point W- 6'8") can be transferred to the back wall by using the VP. The red scale represents measurements along the back wall. The red scale is particularly useful for wall openings (doors, etc.), proper fixture placement (water closets, etc.) and determining where cabinet countertop and soffit depths terminate.

When using the Adjustable Bath Grid (D), draw the standard 21" deep base cabinets at the 24" depth shown on the grid. The 24" depth simplifies the grid chart, also adding additional depth to the back wall countertop. If needed, you can easily **fudge** the 3" difference in your drawing!

Use the base cabinet measurements for tall cabinets 21" deep. Then, carry the vertical lines up to the 24" deep soffit. Use the wall cabinet measurements for tall cabinets 12" deep. Then, carry the vertical lines down to the floor (construct toekick if necessary).

For diagonal corner base and wall cabinets and tall corner cabinets, connect corresponding points on each wall.

Heights of the wall cabinets have been shown in six common sizes. To find other sizes, simply "guesstimate" between the existing lines of the sizes shown. Do the same for any height from the floor to the ceiling.

The **broken red line on the floor** is the outside edge of a 30" deep bathtub. Use the sidewall measurements to find the desired height.

The NKBA bathroom grid method of perspective drawing.

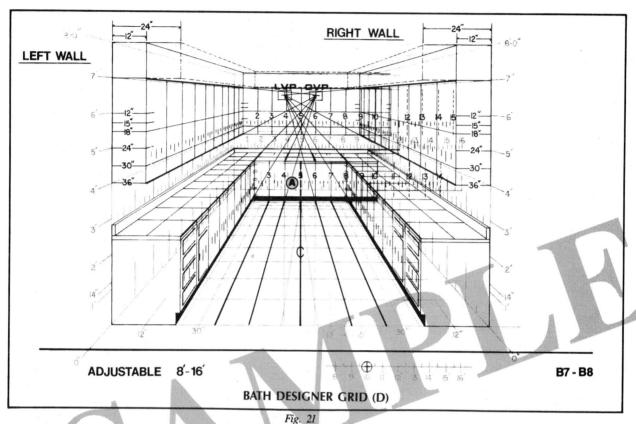

BATH DESIGNER GRID (D)

Fig. 21

UNDER 12'-0"

The grid chart at the top of the page is set at 10'. The **original vanishing point** for the 12' room is on the right (OVP), and the vanishing point that **moved with the right wall** is on the left (LVP).

At first glance, the floor lines in the center of the grid chart may look confusing (figure 21). To untangle the floor grid lines, first, tape down grids B7 and B8 to the desired size (8'-16'). Tape down the tracing paper. Divide the room width in half by making a light vertical line from countertop to floor (figure 21 Ⓐ).

Example: For room width of 10' (120") as shown by the register mark on the scale, a dotted vertical line is drawn at 5' (Ⓐ) to illustrate the guideline dividing the room in half.

Use the **OVP** for all converging lines on the **left side** of the vertical line you have just drawn and the **LVP** for the converging lines on the **right side.**

Another solution for drawing **floor grid lines** is to establish a **third vanishing point directly between** the OVP and the LVP. Use it to space the lines on the floor. Either method will work, it's what will appear aesthetically pleasing **to you** that counts.

The NKBA bathroom grid method of perspective drawing.

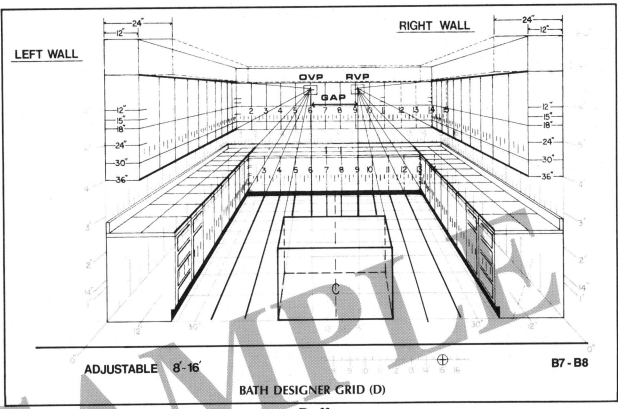

Fig. 22

OVER 12'-0"

The grid chart is set at 15'. The **original** vanishing point for the 12' room is on the left (OVP) and the vanishing point that **moved with the right wall** is on the right (RVP). The space between vanishing points is the **GAP**.

Use the OVP for converging lines on the **left side** of the **GAP** and the RVP for converging lines on the **right side.** All lines inside the **GAP** will either be **vertical or horizontal**.

The NKBA bathroom grid method of perspective drawing.

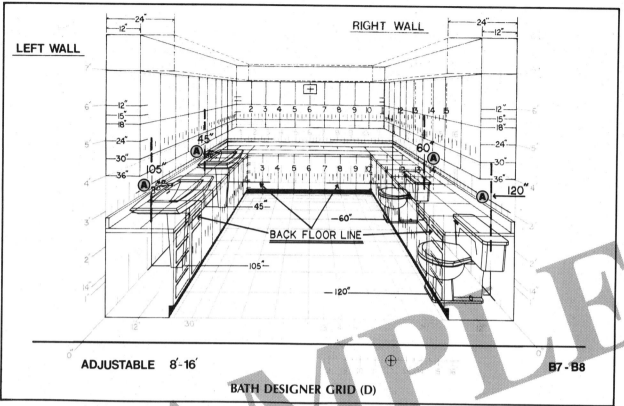

Fig. 23

FIXTURE OVERLAYS

Included with Bath Grids B7 and B8 are four bath fixture overlays:

1. (B9) Two piece toilet and rectangular pedestal sink
2. (B10) One piece toilet and oval pedestal sink
3. (B11) Bidet and diagonal corner bath fixtures
4. (B12) Back wall bath fixtures

Overlays B9, B10 and B11 are spaced 15″ on center. By turning the overlay over, the fixtures can be used on the opposite wall.

To draw any fixture, find its centerline along the back wall of the grid (red scale). At centerline, draw a light vertical line between 2′ and 4′ high (figure 23A). This vertical guideline will help center the fixture.

Select the proper grid chart for the fixture to be drawn. In figure 23, grid chart B9 is being used to draw two water closets on the right side and two pedestal lavatories on the left side. The fixture centerline(s) on B9 is aligned vertically with the guideline(s). The baseline on B9 is aligned with the red back floor line. Now the desired fixture can be drawn plumb and level. If the actual fixture centerline falls between sizes available on the grid, draw the next largest size.

The NKBA bathroom grid method of perspective drawing.

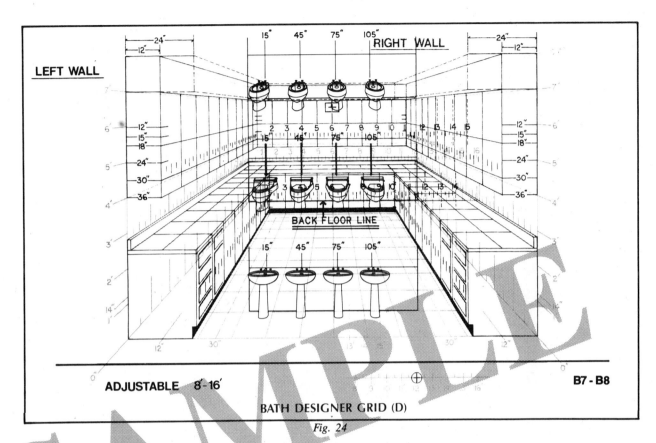

ADJUSTABLE 8´-16´   B7 - B8

BATH DESIGNER GRID (D)

Fig. 24

FIXTURE OVERLAYS *(Continued)*

When drawing head-on views, use grid B12 (figure 24). However, always draw the light vertical guidelines first. This ensures proper alignment.

The decision as to when to draw the bath fixture in the drawing is up to the designer. If the bath fixture will block or partially hide the view of another object, you should draw the bath fixture first.

When tracing over the curves of the bath fixtures, try not to draw an entire curve in one stroke with your pencil. To produce a smoother curve in your drawing, use a series of overlapping strokes. An elipse template is a very useful tool to use when drawing curves.

The NKBA bathroom grid method of perspective drawing.

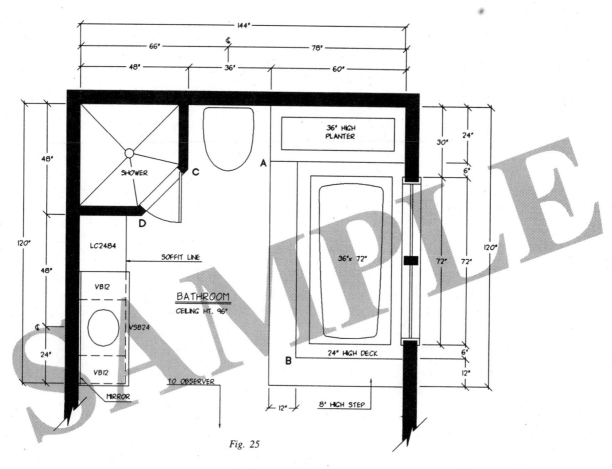

Fig. 25

ONE POINT PERSPECTIVE DRAWING SEQUENCE

The NKBA bathroom grid method of perspective drawing.

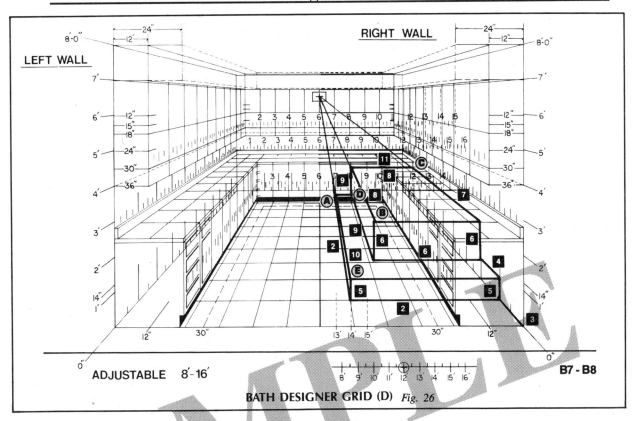

LEFT WALL

RIGHT WALL

ADJUSTABLE 8'-16'

BATH DESIGNER GRID (D) *Fig. 26*

B7 - B8

DRAWING SEQUENCE

1 Set Adjustable Bath Grid (D) at 12'-0".

2 Draw the **floor line** encompassing the planter and the step 60" from the right wall (figure 26,), Point **Ⓐ**.

3 Estimate 8" high on the right wall (figure 26).

4 Using the VP, draw the 8" high step between 10' and 9' on the right wall (figure 26).

5 Draw the face of the 8" high step **towards the observer** (figure 26), Point **Ⓔ**.

6 At the 8" x 9' point, make a vertical line that stops at the 2' high wall scale. Then, complete the face of the tub deck, stopping at point **Ⓑ** , 48" from the right wall (figure 26).

7 Align your triangle with the top right side of the tub platform and the VP. Draw a line 6' (72"), using the right wall scale and stopping at point **Ⓒ** (figure 26).

8 To draw the platform top, start at **Ⓒ** with a horizontal line 4' (48") wide. Using the VP, connect the top left of the platform (figure 26).

9 To draw the platform left side, align your triangle with point **Ⓑ** and the VP. Draw a line 6' (72"). Then, connect the back left of the platform with a vertical line, stopping at point **Ⓓ** (figure 26).

10 At point **Ⓓ** , draw a horizontal line 1' (12") to the left. Using the VP, connect this point to the step top (figure 26).

11 To draw the planter, start at **Ⓒ** by drawing a vertical line 1' (12") high using the wall scale. Using the VP at the vertical line top, draw a line that stops at the inside right corner of the room (figure 27).

The NKBA bathroom grid method of perspective drawing.

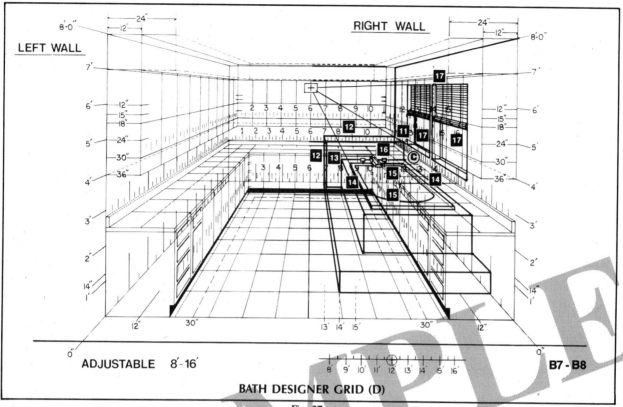

Fig. 27

DRAWING SEQUENCE *(Continued)*

12 At the top inside right corner, draw a horizontal line 5′ (60″). At 5′ (60″), bring a vertical line to the floor (figure 27).

13 Complete the planter top by using the VP and the end of the 5′ (60″) point. Make a line 24″ deep. Finish the front edge with a horizontal line going to the right wall. Finish the planter with a vertical line from the top left edge, ending at the floor (figure 27).

14 In figure 27, set the tub in the deck by making a rectangle 36″ x 72″ and keeping it 6″ from the left and right edges. Once the rectangle is drawn, double the left edge and front edge to show thickness (figure 27).

15 The inside tub edge is also a rectangle. The inside curvature is done with a French curve or elipse template. Trial and error will help to familiarize you with a radius acceptable to the eye. The right interior is visible to the eye and the right corner is drawn 16″ deep with a vertical line. The right side uses the VP. The back interior is a horizontal line. Small elipses are used to show the drain and overflow (figure 27).

16 The tub spout is drawn using the VP and is approximately 8″ long. The handles are drawn with horizontal and vertical lines, approximately 3″ high by 3″ wide (figure 27).

17 The window is 72″ W x 44″ H. It begins at 80″ and ends at the 36″H right wall scale. It's also centered above the tub. Outline the window rectangle using the right wall scale. Place the center mullion, approximately 2½″ wide. Approximate the depth of the window, remembering it's best to show less depth than more. Bring up the interior vertical lines of the window, but stop them approximately half the window height. Use the VP to show the window stool. Use the VP to draw closely spaced lines for the window shades (figure 27).

The NKBA bathroom grid method of perspective drawing.

25 Draw the cabinet doors and drawers. Shade the **near** vertical sides and the tops of the vanity base doors and drawers (figure 28).

26 Draw the vanity sink and faucet on the countertop (you can trace an oval shape on B10) (figure 28).

27 Draw **vertical lines** from floor to ceiling at points Ⓕ and Ⓖ for shower (48″ from back corner and 30″ deep) (figure 28).

28 Connect both lines at the top and bottom. Draw shower opening (figure 28).

29 Complete the right and left side of shower (figure 28).

30 Draw ceiling and all floor lines (figure 28).

Add the details: For example, draw the plants in the planter behind the tub.

Draw cabinet hardware on doors and drawers.

Draw 12″ ceramic tiles on floor and tub platform for added depth in drawing.

The NKBA bathroom grid method of perspective drawing.

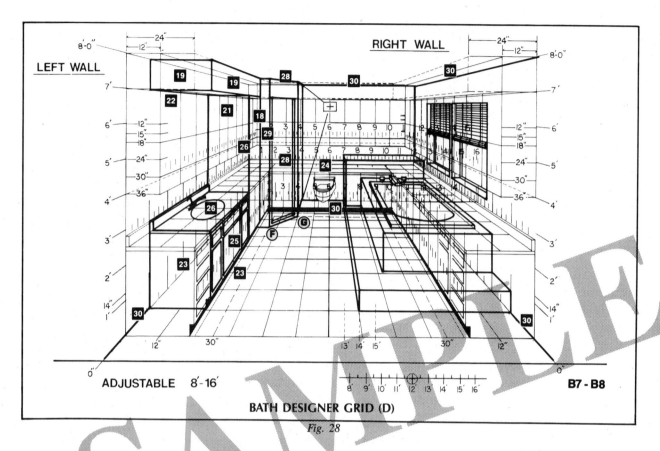

Fig. 28

DRAWING SEQUENCE *(Continued)*

You should now be familiar with using the VP and all grid scales. Therefore, further instructions will not be as explicit. This allows you to interpret more and better understand grid use by doing it. If you get stuck, follow the reference numbers found in figures 26, 27 and 28.

18 Draw the **right front vertical line** of the linen cabinet, from the top of the toekick to the top of the 24″ deep soffit (figure 28).

19 Complete the face and the end of the soffit (figure 28).

20 Draw the left front vertical line of the linen cabinet (figure 28).

21 Complete **exposed** left side of the linen cabinet (figure 28).

22 Draw the exposed soffit line against the wall (figure 28).

23 Draw the base cabinets, countertop and toekick to the left of the linen cabinet (figure 28).

24 Make light vertical line at 5′6″ (66″) on back wall. Slide overlay B12 under tracing paper. Align the vertical line behind the one piece toilet in the 60″ position with the 5′-6″ mark on the back wall. Trace toilet and remove overlay (figure 28).

The NKBA bathroom grid method of perspective drawing.

Appendix B

NKBA
Graphics and Presentation Standards

The following pages are reprinted from the National Kitchen & Bath Association Graphics and Presentation Standards for Bathroom Design. They have been included so that you might gain a better and more clear insight into the concepts and requirements for good presentation techniques.

- This book is intended for professional use by residential bathroom designers. The procedures and advice herein have been shown to be appropriate for the applications described; however, no warranty (expressed or implied) is intended or given. Moreover, the user of this book is cautioned to be familiar with and to adhere to all manufacturers' planning, installation and use/care instructions. In addition, the user is urged to become familiar with and adhere to all applicable local, state and federal building codes, licensing and legislation requirements governing the user's ability to perform all tasks associated with design and installation standards, and to collaborate with licensed practitioners who offer professional services in the technical areas of mechanical, electrical and load bearing design as required for regulatory approval, as well as health and safety regulations.

- Information about this book and Certified Bathroom Designer programs may be obtained from the National Kitchen & Bath Association, 687 Willow Grove Street, Hackettstown, New Jersey 07840, Phone (908) 852-0033, e-mail educate@nkba.org, Fax (908) 852-1695.

Table of Contents

Purpose

By standardizing floor plans and presentation drawings, Bathroom Designers will:

- Limit errors caused by misinterpreting the floor plans.

- Avoid misreading dimensions, which can result in costly errors.

- Prevent cluttering floor plans and drawings with secondary information, which often make the documents difficult to interpret.

- Create a clear understanding of the scope of the project for all persons involved in the job.

- Present a professional image to the client.

- Permit faster processing of orders.

- Simplify estimating and specification preparation.

- Help in the standardization of uniform nomenclature and symbols.

General Provisions Using Imperial Dimensions

I. Use of Standards

The use of these *National Kitchen & Bath Association Graphics and Presentation Standards* is strongly recommended. They contain a specific set of criteria which when applied by the Bathroom Specialist produce a series of project documents that include the following:

- The Floor Plan

- The Construction Plan

- The Mechanical Plan

- The Interpretive Drawings
  1) Elevations
  2) Perspective Drawings
  3) Oblique, Dimetric, Isometric and Trimetric
  4) Sketches

- Specifications

- Design Statement

- Contracts

Two sample sets of project documents for your review can be found in this publication, one uses imperial dimensions and the other is a metric conversion.

Paper: The acceptable paper for the original drawings of the floor plan, construction plan, mechanical plan, and interpretive drawings is set at a **minimum size of 11" x 17".** Translucent vellum tracing paper, imprinted with a black border and appropriate space available for the insertion of pertinent information is strongly recommended. Copies of original drawings should appear in blue or black ink only on white paper. Ozalid or photocopy prints are acceptable.

The use of lined yellow note paper, typing paper, scored graph paper or scored quadrille paper **is not acceptable.**

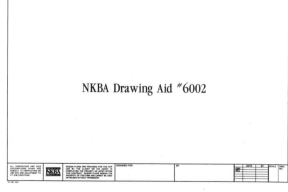

NKBA Drawing Aid #6002

II. The Floor Plan

1) **Size and Scope of Floor Plan Drawings:** Bathroom floor plans should be drawn to a scale of 1/2 inch equals 1 foot (1/2" = 1'0"). *** For metric dimensioning, see Use of Standards beginning on page 674.**

- All base cabinetry should be depicted using a dashed line (– — –) while countertops are depicted using a solid line.

- The floor plan should depict the entire room when possible. When the entire room cannot be depicted, it must show the area where cabinetry and appliances are permanently installed.

- Floor plans must show all major structural elements such as walls, door swings, door openings, partitions, windows, archways and equipment.

- When the entire room cannot be depicted, the room must be divided by *"break lines"* (–⟋⟍–) and must show all major structural elements with adjoining areas indicated and labeled.

- Finished interior dimensions are used on all project documents to denote available space for cabinetry and/or other types of equipment. If the bathroom specialist is responsible for specifying the exact method of wall construction, finish and/or partition placement, the specialist should include partition center lines on the construction plan, as well as the finished interior dimensions.

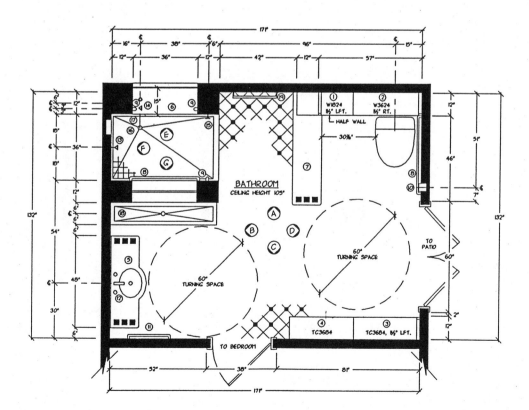

2) **Centerline (℄) dimensions:** must be given for equipment in two directions when possible.

- Mechanicals requiring centerlines include: lavatories, bathtubs/showers, toilets/bidets, fan units, light fixtures, heating and air conditioning ducts and radiators.

- Dimensions should be pulled from return walls or from the face of cabinets/fixtures/equipment opposite the mechanical element.

- Centerlines on the mechanical plan will be indicated by the symbol (℄) followed by a **long-short-long broken line** that extends into the floor area.

- When the centerline dimension line is outside the floor area, it is typically shown as the second (and, if required, the third) line following the dimension line which identifies the individual wall segments.

3) **Dimensioning of Floor Plan:** All drawing dimensions used on bathroom floor plans must be given in **Inches and Fractions of Inches ONLY**, (ie. 124 1/4").

- Combining dimensions listed in feet and inches or the exclusive use of dimensions listed in feet and inches, **10′ 4 1/4" is not acceptable** and should not be used under any circumstances. Again, this would also apply to the metric equivalent, do not combine meters and centimeters.

NOTE:

- Each set of dimensions should be at least 3/16" apart on separate dimension lines which are to intersect with witness lines. These intersecting points should be indicated by dimension arrows, dots, or slashes.

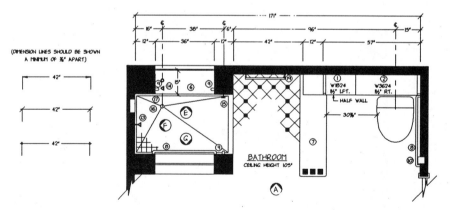

- All dimensions, whenever possible, should be shown **OUTSIDE** the wall lines.

- All lettering should be listed parallel to the title block at the bottom of the vellum paper and break the dimension line near its mid-point. This mechanical drafting technique eliminates errors in reading dimensions.

- An acceptable alternative is to draw all dimensions and lettering so that it is readable from the bottom edge or the right side of the plans with lettering on top of each dimension line.

The following dimensions **MUST** be shown on every floor plan as minimum requirements.

- Overall length of wall areas to receive cabinets, countertops, fixtures, or any equipment occupying floor and/or wall space. This dimension should always be the outside line.

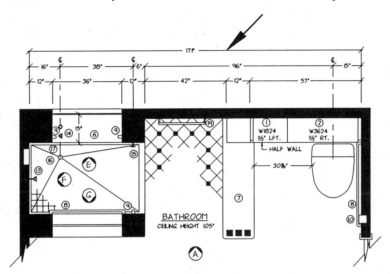

- Each wall opening, (windows, arches, doors and major appliances) and fixed structures (chimneys, wall protrusions and partitions) must be individually dimensioned. Dimensions are shown from outside trim. Trim size must be noted in the specification list. Fixtures such as radiators remaining in place must be outlined on the floor plan. These critical dimensions should be the first dimension line.

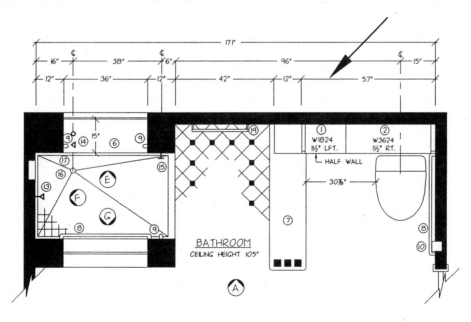

- Ceiling heights should appear on the floor plan. A separate plan for soffits is required when the soffit is a different depth than the wall or tall cabinet below. A separate soffit plan is recommended when the soffit is to be installed **PRIOR** to the wall or tall cabinet installation.

- Additional notes must be included for any deviation from standard height, width and depth. (cabinets, countertops, etc.)

- The exact opening must be given in height, width and depth for areas to be left open to receive equipment, cabinets and fixtures at a future date.

- Items such as island/peninsula vanities and bathtub platforms, must be shown with the overall dimensions given from countertop edge to opposite countertop edge, tall cabinet or wall. The exact location of the structure must be identified by dimensions which position it from two directions; from return walls or from the face of cabinets/equipment opposite the structure.

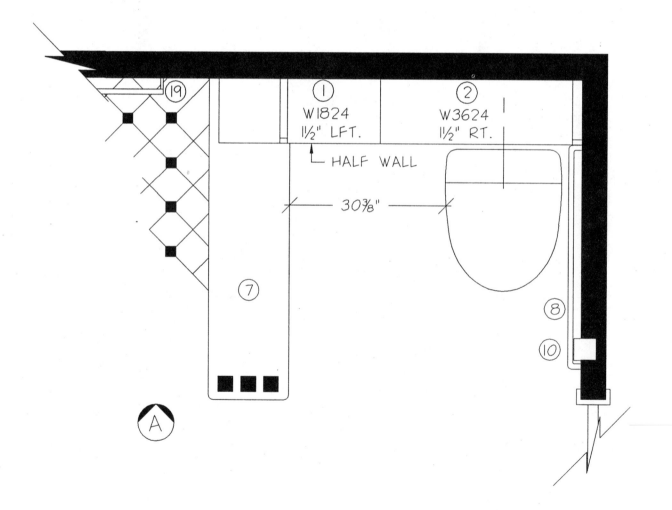

4) Cabinets/Fixtures and Equipment Nomenclature and Designation on Floor Plans:

- Cabinets should be designated and identified by manufacturer nomenclature inside the area indicating their position. Cabinet system trim and finish items are designated outside their area, with an arrow clarifying exactly where the trim piece is located.

- To insure clarity, some design firms prefer to number and call out all the cabinet nomenclature in the Floor Plan specification listing.

- Equally acceptable is the use of a circled reference number to designate each cabinet on the Floor Plan and Elevations with the cabinet code listed within the individual unit width on the elevations or in a separate cross-reference list on the elevations.

- **Regardless of which cabinet designation system is selected from above, additional information for supplementary fixtures/equipment and special provisions pertaining to the cabinets must be indicated within the cabinet or equipment area by a reference number in a circle. This additional information should then be registered in a cross-referenced specifications listing on the same sheet.**

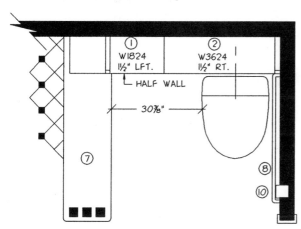

FLOOR PLAN

SPECIFICATIONS

① W1824, 1½" EXT. LEFT, UNDER CABINET LIGHT, DOOR 1½" LONGER THAN CASE TO CONCEAL LTS.

② W3624, 1½" EXT. RIGHT, UNDER CABINET LIGHTS, DOORS 1½" LONGER THAN CASE TO CONCEAL LTS.

- Special order materials or custom design features, angled cabinets, unusual tops, molding, trim details, etc., should be shown in a section view, (sometimes referred to as a *"cut view"*), a plan view in a scale larger than (1/2" = 1') (a metric equivalent is acceptable), or in elevation view.

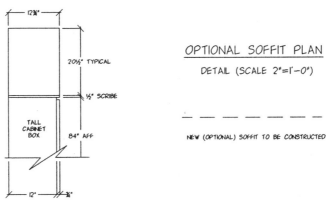

OPTIONAL SOFFIT PLAN

DETAIL (SCALE 2"=1'-0")

NEW (OPTIONAL) SOFFIT TO BE CONSTRUCTED

III. The Construction Plan

1) The purpose of the construction plan is to show the relationship of the existing space with that of the new design. The construction plan is detailed separately so that it does not clutter the floor plan. However, if construction changes are minimal it is acceptable to combine the construction plan with either the floor plan or mechanical plan.

2) Construction Plan Symbols:

- Existing walls are shown with solid lines or hollowed out lines at their full thickness.

- Wall sections to be removed are shown with an outline of broken lines.

- New walls show the material symbols applicable to the type of construction or use a symbol which is identified in the legend in order to distinguish them from existing partitions.

EXISTING WALL TO REMOVED

OR

EXISTING WALLS TO REMAIN

EXISTING OPENINGS TO ENCLOSE

WOOD STUD   METAL STUD

CONCRETE   BRICK

CONCRETE BLOCK   BRICK

NEW WALLS TO BE CONSTRUCTED

* Symbols adapted from Architectural Graphic Standards, 9th Edition

An Example of a Construction Plan:

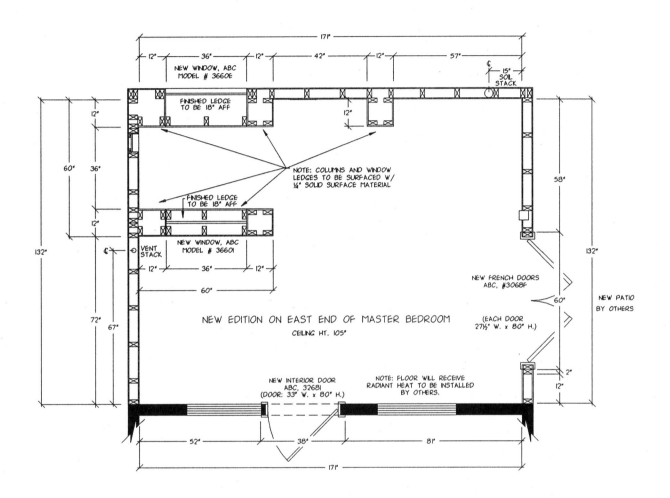

CONSTRUCTION PLAN

LEGEND

IV. The Mechanical Plan

- By detailing separate plans for the mechanicals and/or construction, it will help to clearly identify such work without cluttering the bathroom floor plan.

- The mechanical plan should show an outline of the cabinets, countertops and fixtures without nomenclature.

- The mechanicals should be placed in the proper location with the proper symbols.

- All overall room dimensions should be listed.

1) The mechanical plan will consist of the Electrical/Lighting, Plumbing, Heating, Air Conditioning and Ventilation systems. If any minor wall/door construction changes are part of the plan, they should also be detailed on the mechanical plan.

2) A mechanical legend should be prepared on the plan. This legend will be used to describe what each symbol for special purpose outlets, fixtures or equipment means.

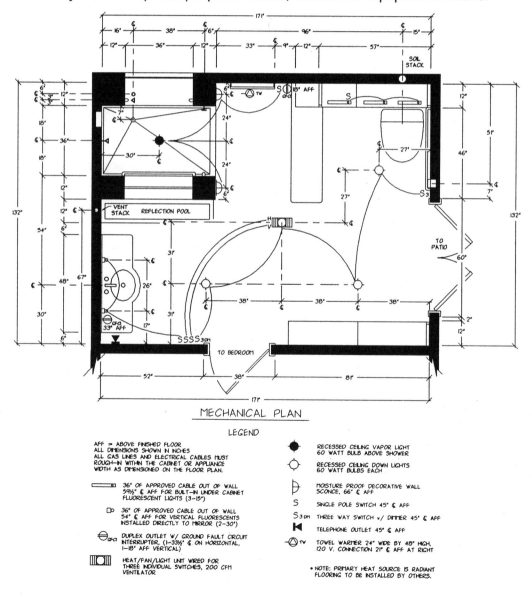

MECHANICAL PLAN

LEGEND

AFF = ABOVE FINISHED FLOOR
ALL DIMENSIONS SHOWN IN INCHES
ALL GAS LINES AND ELECTRICAL CABLES MUST
ROUGH-IN WITHIN THE CABINET OR APPLIANCE
WIDTH AS DIMENSIONED ON THE FLOOR PLAN.

36" OF APPROVED CABLE OUT OF WALL
59½" ℄ AFF FOR BUILT-IN UNDER CABINET
FLUORESCENT LIGHTS (3-15")

36" OF APPROVED CABLE OUT OF WALL
54" ℄ AFF FOR VERTICAL FLUORESCENTS
INSTALLED DIRECTLY TO MIRROR (2-30")

DUPLEX OUTLET W/ GROUND FAULT CIRCUIT
INTERRUPTER, (1-33½" ℄ ON HORIZONTAL,
1-18" AFF VERTICAL)

HEAT/FAN/LIGHT UNIT WIRED FOR
THREE INDIVIDUAL SWITCHES, 200 CFM
VENTILATOR

RECESSED CEILING VAPOR LIGHT
60 WATT BULB ABOVE SHOWER

RECESSED CEILING DOWN LIGHTS
60 WATT BULBS EACH

MOISTURE PROOF DECORATIVE WALL
SCONCE, 66" ℄ AFF

S   SINGLE POLE SWITCH 45" ℄ AFF

S₃ₒₘ THREE WAY SWITCH w/ DIMMER 45" ℄ AFF

TELEPHONE OUTLET 45" ℄ AFF

TOWEL WARMER 24" WIDE BY 48" HIGH,
120 V. CONNECTION 21" ℄ AFF AT RIGHT

• NOTE: PRIMARY HEAT SOURCE IS RADIANT
FLOORING TO BE INSTALLED BY OTHERS.

3)   Centerline (₵) dimensions must be given for all equipment in two directions when possible.

- Mechanicals requiring centerlines include: lavatories, bathtubs/showers, toilets/bidets, fan units, light fixtures, heating and air conditioning ducts and radiators.

- Centerline dimensions should be pulled from return walls or from the face of cabinets/equipment opposite the mechanical element.

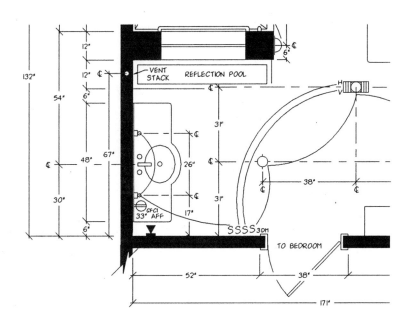

Centerlines on the mechanical plan will be indicated by the symbol (₵) followed by a **long-short-long broken line** that extends into the floor area.

₵ ————— — ——— — ——— — ——— — ——— — ———

4)   Mechanical Plan Symbols:

S	SINGLE POLE SWITCH
S_2	DOUBLE POLE SWITCH
S_3	THREE WAY SWITCH
S_4	FOUR WAY SWITCH
S_{DM}	SINGLE POLE SWITCH w/ DIMMER
S_{3DM}	THREE WAY SWITCH w/ DIMMER
S_{LM}	MASTER SWITCH FOR LOW VOLTAGE SWITCHING SYSTEM
S_L	SWITCH FOR LOW VOLTAGE SWITCHING SYSTEM
S_{WP}	WEATHERPROOF SWITCH
S_{RC}	REMOTE CONTROL SWITCH
S_D	AUTOMATIC DOOR SWITCH
S_P	SWITCH AND PILOT LAMP
S_K	KEY OPERATED SWITCH
S_F	FUSED SWITCH
S_T	TIME SWITCH
(S)	CEILING PULL SWITCH
	DUPLEX OUTLET
GFCI	DUPLEX OUTLET WITH GROUND FAULT CIRCUIT INTERRUPTER
s	SWITCH AND SINGLE RECEPTACLE OUTLET
s	SWITCH AND DUPLEX OUTLET
(B)	BLANKED OUTLET
(J)	JUNCTION BOX
(L)	OUTLET CONTROLLED BY LOW VOLTAGE SWITCHING WHEN RELAY IS INSTALLED IN OUTLET BOX
	SINGLE RECEPTACLE OULET
	TRIPLEX RECEPTACLE OULET
	QUADRUPLEX RECEPTACLE OULET
	DUPLEX RECEPTACLE OUTLET—SPLIT WIRED
	TRIPLEX RECEPTACLE OUTLET—SPLIT WIRED
(C)	CLOCK HANGER RECEPTACLE
(F)	FAN HANGER RECEPTACLE
	INTERCOM
	TELEPHONE OUTLET
(T)	THERMOSTAT
	SMOKE DETECTOR

TV	TELEVISION OUTLET
C	CABLE OUTLET
T_L	LOW VOLTAGE TRANSFORMER
	HANGING CEILING FIXTURE
	HEAT LAMP
	HEAT/LIGHT UNIT
	HEAT/FAN LIGHT W/ OOO CFM VENT.
	RECESSED CEILING DOWN LIGHTING
	RECESSED CEILING VAPOR LIGHT
	BUILT—IN LOW VOLTAGE TASK LIGHT
	BUILT—IN FLUORESCENT LIGHT
	CONTINUOUS ROW FLUORESCENT LIGHTS
	SURFACE MOUNTED FLUORESCENT LIGHT
	WALL SCONCE
DW	DISHWASHER
GD	FOOD WASTE DISPOSAL
TC	TRASH COMPACTOR
R	REFRIGERATOR OUTLET
H	HOOD W/ OOO CFM VENTILATOR
M	MICROWAVE OVEN
R	ELECTRIC RANGE/COOKTOP
WO	ELECTRIC SINGLE/DOUBLE OVEN
G	GAS SUPPLY
CT	GAS COOKTOP
WO	GAS SINGLE/DOUBLE OVEN
CW	CLOTHES WASHER
CD	CLOTHES DRYER
SA	SAUNA
ST	STEAM
WP	WHIRLPOOL
TW	TOWEL WARMER
	HEAT REGISTER

ANY STANDARD SYMBOL GIVEN ABOVE W/ THE ADDITION OF LOWERCASE SUBSCRIPT LETTERING MAY BE USED TO DESIGNATE A VARIATION OF STANDARD EQUIPMENT.

WHEN USED THEY MUST BE LISTED IN THE LEGEND OF THE MECHANICAL PLAN.

Symbols adapted from Architectural Graphic Standards, 9th Edition

V. Interpretive Drawings

Elevations and perspective renderings are considered interpretive drawings and are used as an explanatory means of understanding the floor plans.

- Under no circumstances should the interpretive drawings be used as a substitute for floor plans.

- In cases of dispute, the floor plans are the legally binding document.

- Because perspective drawings are not dimensioned to scale, many Bathroom Specialists include a disclaimer on their rendering such as this:

This drawing is an artistic interpretation of the general appearance of the floor plan. It is not meant to be an exact rendition.

---

1) **Elevation:** Elevations must show a front view of all wall areas receiving cabinets and equipment as shown on the floor plan.

Elevations should dimension all cabinets, counters, fixtures and equipment in the elevation as follows:

- Cabinets with toekick and finished height.

- A portion of the cabinet doors and drawer front should indicate style and, when applicable, placement of handles/pulls.

- Countertops indicate thickness and show backsplash

- All doors, windows or other openings in walls which will receive equipment. The window/door casing or trim will be listed within the overall opening dimensions.

- All permanent fixtures such as radiators, etc.

- All main structural elements and protrusions such as chimneys, partitions, etc.

- Centerlines for all mechanical equipment.

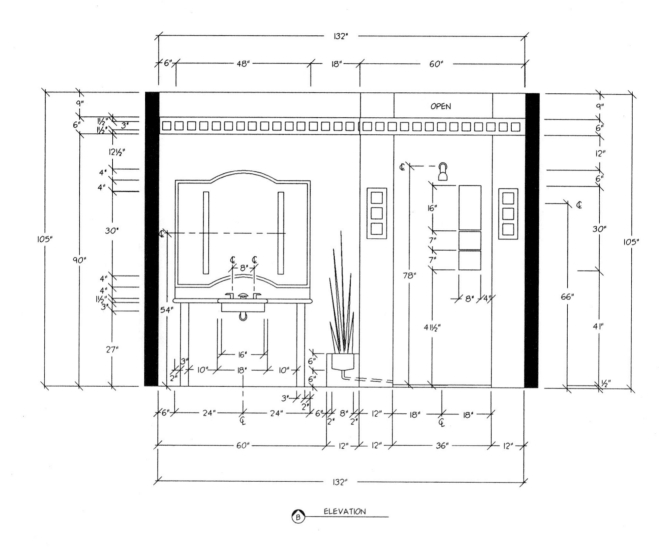

ELEVATION

B

NOTE:
DIMENSIONS MUST ACCURATELY
REPRESENT PRODUCTS USED.

2) **Perspective Drawings:** Perspectives are **not drawn to scale.** Grids, which are available through the **National Kitchen & Bath Association**, can be used as an underlay for tracing paper to accurately portray a perspective rendering. Two such grids are displayed on pages 656 and 657 for your reference.

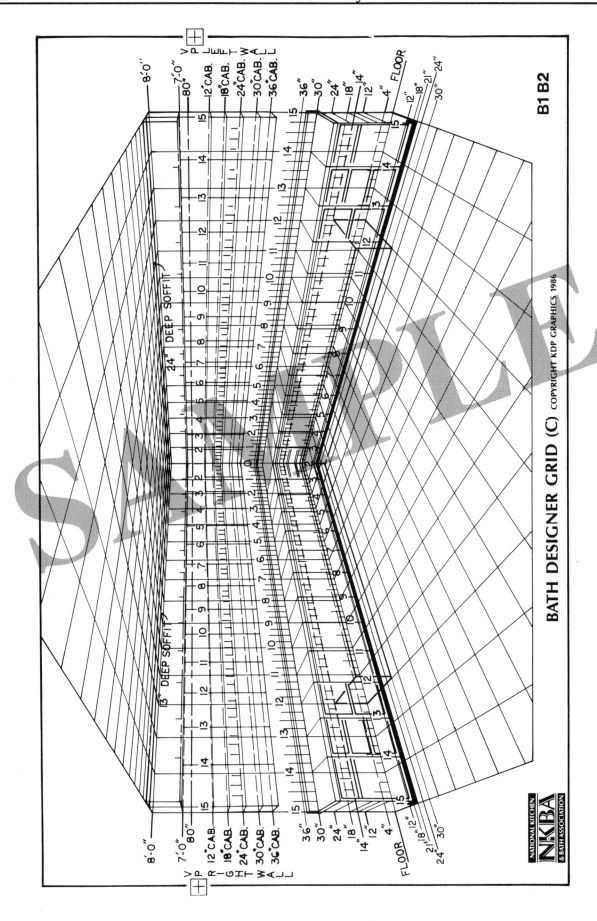

BATH DESIGNER GRID (C) COPYRIGHT KDP GRAPHICS 1986

B1 B2

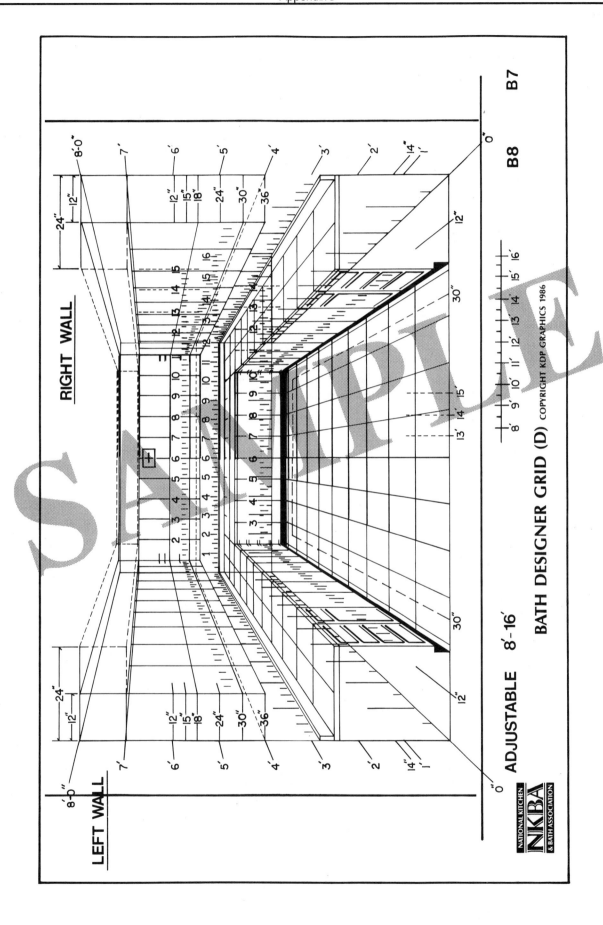

RIGHT WALL

LEFT WALL

ADJUSTABLE 8'-16'   BATH DESIGNER GRID (D) COPYRIGHT KDP GRAPHICS 1986

B7
B8

NATIONAL KITCHEN NKBA & BATH ASSOCIATION

Designers have the option of preparing a one-point or two-point perspective, with or without the use of a grid.

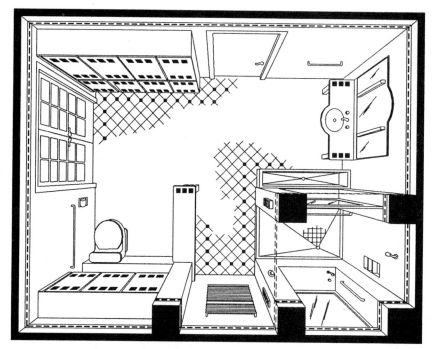

"Birds-Eye View" One Point Perspective

One Point Perspective

- The minimum requirement for perspectives shall be the reasonably correct representation of the longest cabinet or fixture run, or the most important area in terms of usage.

- Perspectives need not show the complete bathroom.

- Separate sectional views of significant areas or features are considered acceptable.

Two Point Perspective

3) Oblique, Dimetric, Isometric and Trimetric: Several types of interpretive drawings can be used to illustrate special cabinets and equipment, such as countertops or special order cabinets, where mechanical representation and dimensions are important. These drawings give a simple way to illustrate an object in three-dimensional views.

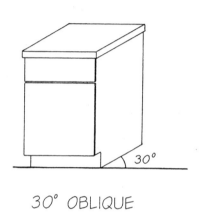

30° OBLIQUE

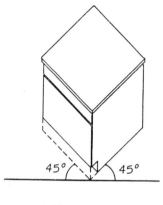

45° DIMETRIC

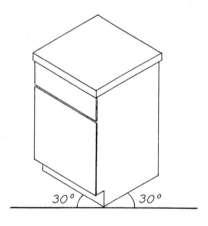

30° ISOMETRIC

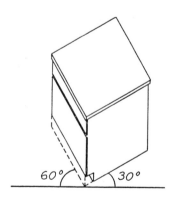

TRIMETRIC

4) **Sketches:** The use of sketches is a quick way to achieve a total picture of the bathroom without exact details in scaled dimensions. This quick freehand sketch can be studied, adjusted and sketched over, as the designer and client attempt to arrive at the most satisfactory layout for the bathroom. The quick sketch then can serve as a guide for drawing an exact plan of the bathroom.

Perspective Sketch

VI. Sample Bathroom Project Drawings

The following set of sample project drawings have been prepared by a Certified Bathroom Designer under the direction of the **National Kitchen & Bath Association.** These sample drawings include:

- Floor Plan

- Construction Plan

- Mechanical Plan

- Countertop Plan *

- Soffit Plan *

- Elevations

- Perspectives

* It is recommended to prepare countertop and soffit plan drawings to further clarify project requirements.

REDUCED SAMPLE

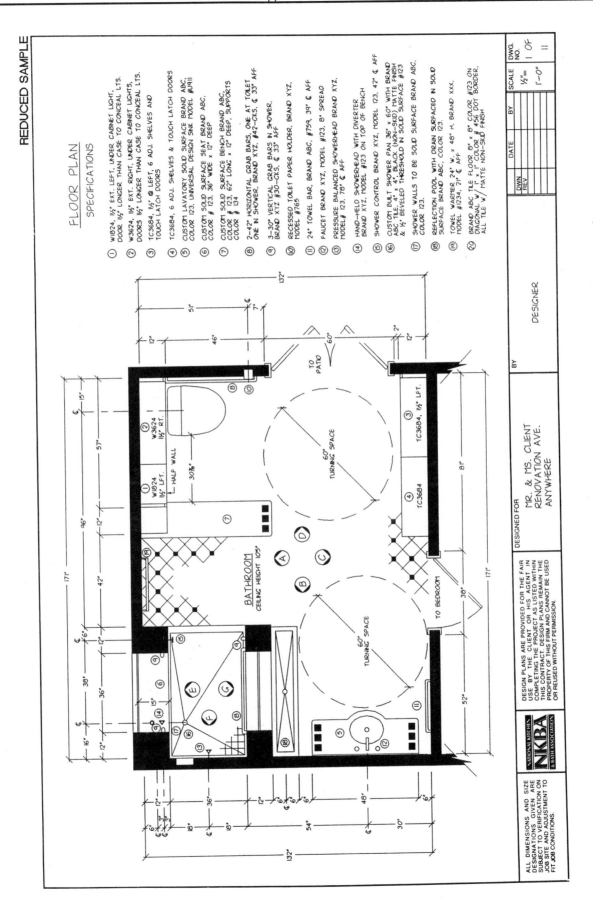

FLOOR PLAN

SPECIFICATIONS

1. W1824, 1½" EXT. LEFT, UNDER CABINET LIGHT, DOOR 1½" LONGER THAN CASE TO CONCEAL LTS.
2. W3624, 1½" EXT. RIGHT, UNDER CABINET LIGHTS, DOORS 1½" LONGER THAN CASE TO CONCEAL LTS.
3. TC3684, 1½" @ LEFT, 6 ADJ. SHELVES AND TOUCH LATCH DOORS
4. TC3684, 6 ADJ. SHELVES & TOUCH LATCH DOORS
5. CUSTOM LAVATORY SOLID SURFACE BRAND ABC, COLOR 123, UNIVERSAL DESIGN SINK, MODEL #U911
6. CUSTOM SOLID SURFACE SEAT BRAND ABC, COLOR 123, 36" WIDE x 12" DEEP
7. CUSTOM SOLID SURFACE BENCH BRAND ABC, COLOR # 123, 62" LONG x 12" DEEP, SUPPORTS COLOR # 134
8. 2-42" HORIZONTAL GRAB BARS, ONE AT TOILET ONE IN SHOWER, BRAND XYZ, #42-CKS, @ 33" AFF
9. 3-30" VERTICAL GRAB BARS IN SHOWER, BRAND XYZ #30-CKS, @ 33" AFF
10. RECESSED TOILET PAPER HOLDER, BRAND XYZ, MODEL #765
11. 24" TOWEL BAR, BRAND ABC, #759, 39" @ AFF
12. FAUCET BRAND XYZ, MODEL #123, 8" SPREAD
13. PRESSURE BALANCED SHOWERHEAD BRAND XYZ, MODEL #123, 78" @ AFF
14. HAND-HELD SHOWERHEAD WITH DIVERTER BRAND XYZ, MODEL #123 ON TOP OF BENCH
15. SHOWER CONTROL BRAND XYZ, MODEL 123, 42" @ AFF
16. CUSTOM BUILT SHOWER PAN 36" x 60" WITH BRAND ABC TILE, 4" x 4" BLACK (NON-SKID) MATTE FINISH & ½" BEVELED THRESHOLD IN SOLID SURFACE #123
17. SHOWER WALLS TO BE SOLID SURFACE BRAND ABC, COLOR 123.
18. REFLECTION POOL WITH DRAIN SURFACED IN SOLID SURFACE BRAND ABC, COLOR 123.
19. TOWEL WARMER, 24" W. x 48" H. BRAND XXX, MODEL #1234, 21" @ AFF
20. BRAND ABC TILE FLOOR 8" x 8" COLOR #123 ON DIAGONAL W/ 1" x 1" COLOR # 456 DOT BORDER, ALL TILE W/ MATTE NON-SKID FINISH

BATHROOM
CEILING HEIGHT 105"

DESIGNED FOR
MR. & MS. CLIENT
RENOVATION AVE.
ANYWHERE

BY

DESIGNER

	DATE	BY	SCALE	DWG. NO.
DWN			½"=	I OF
REV			I'-0"	II

REDUCED SAMPLE

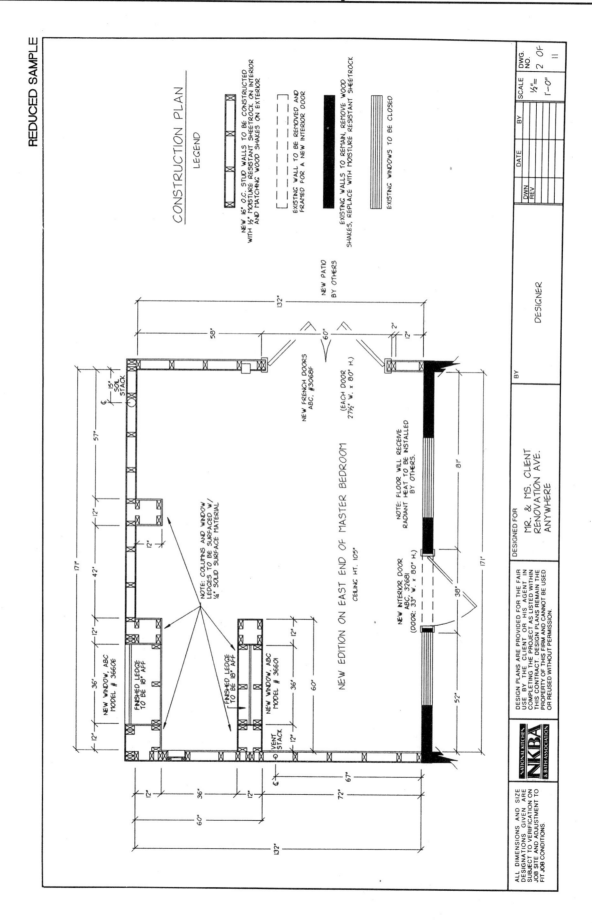

CONSTRUCTION PLAN
LEGEND

NEW 16" O.C. STUD WALLS TO BE CONSTRUCTED WITH ½" MOISTURE RESISTANT SHEETROCK ON INTERIOR AND MATCHING WOOD SHAKES ON EXTERIOR

EXISTING WALL TO BE REMOVED AND FRAMED FOR A NEW INTERIOR DOOR

EXISTING WALLS TO REMAIN, REMOVE WOOD SHAKES, REPLACE WITH MOISTURE RESISTANT SHEETROCK

EXISTING WINDOWS TO BE CLOSED

NEW PATIO BY OTHERS

NEW FRENCH DOORS ABC. #3068F
(EACH DOOR 27½" W. x 80" H.)

NEW EDITION ON EAST END OF MASTER BEDROOM
CEILING HT. 105"

NOTE: COLUMNS AND WINDOW LEDGES TO BE SURFACED W/ ¼" SOLID SURFACE MATERIAL

NOTE: FLOOR WILL RECEIVE RADIANT HEAT TO BE INSTALLED BY OTHERS.

NEW INTERIOR DOOR ABC. 3268I
(DOOR: 33" W. x 80" H.)

NEW WINDOW, ABC MODEL # 3660E

FINISHED LEDGE TO BE 18" AFF

FINISHED LEDGE TO BE 18" AFF

NEW WINDOW, ABC MODEL # 3660I

VENT STACK

SOIL STACK

132" 58" 60" 2" 12"
15" 57" 12" 12" 81" 171"
17" 42" 36" 60" 52"
12" 12" 12" 12" 105"
12" 36" 12" 72" 67"
60" 132" 38"

DESIGNER

BY

DATE	BY	SCALE	DWG. NO.
DWN REV		½"= 1'—0"	2 OF 11

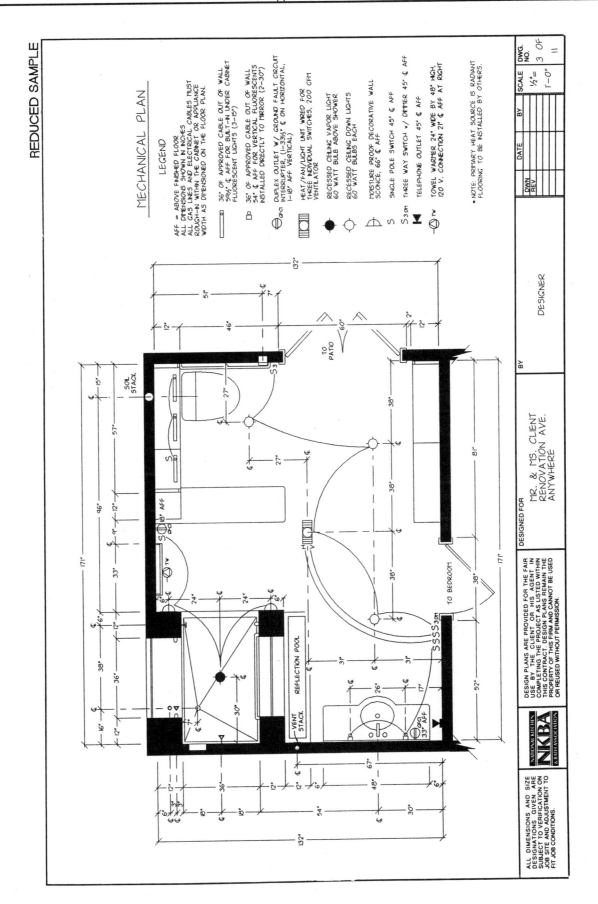

REDUCED SAMPLE

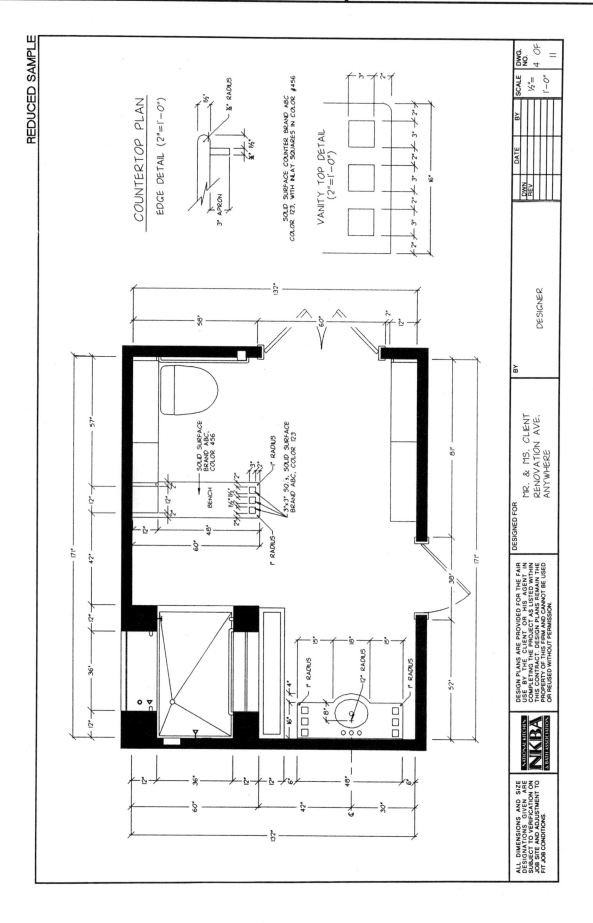

REDUCED SAMPLE

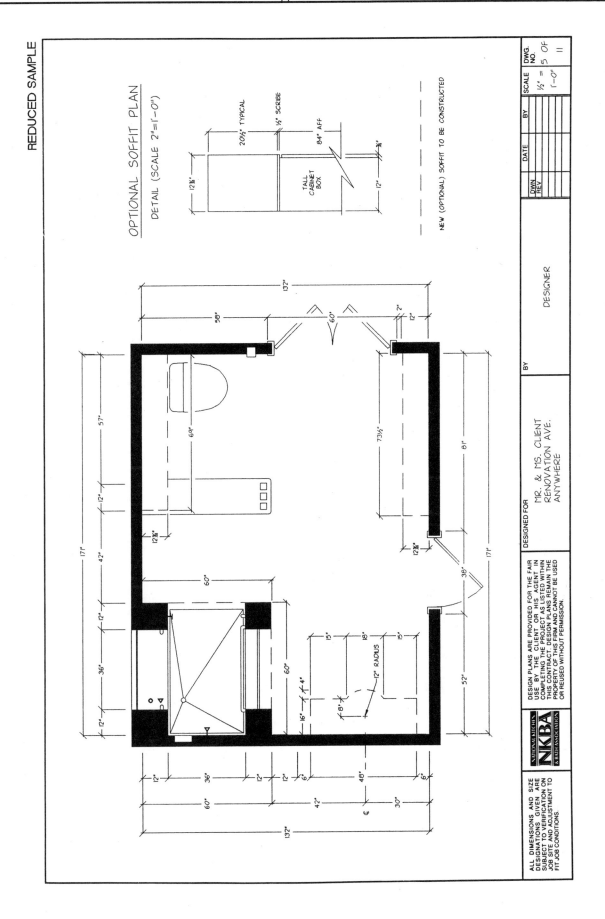

OPTIONAL SOFFIT PLAN
DETAIL (SCALE 2"=1'-0")

20½" TYPICAL

½" SCRIBE

84" AFF

TALL
CABINET
BOX

12⅛"

¾"

12"

NEW (OPTIONAL) SOFFIT TO BE CONSTRUCTED

NATIONAL KITCHEN
NKBA
& BATH ASSOCIATION

DESIGNED FOR

MR. & MS. CLIENT
RENOVATION AVE.
ANYWHERE

BY

DESIGNER

DWN
REV

DATE

BY

SCALE
½" =
1'-0"

DWG.
NO.
5 OF
11

REDUCED SAMPLE

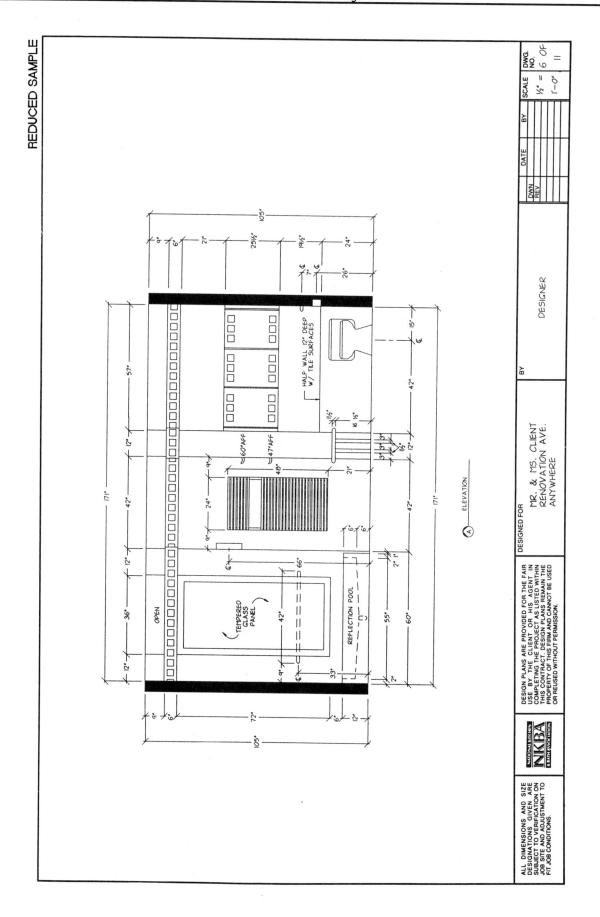

DESIGNED FOR
MR. & MS. CLIENT
RENOVATION AVE.
ANYWHERE

BY

DESIGNER

DWN	DATE	BY	SCALE	DWG. NO.
REV			½" = 1'-0"	6 OF 11

ELEVATION A

OPEN

TEMPERED GLASS PANEL

REFLECTION POOL

HALF WALL 12" DEEP W/ TILE SURFACES

60"AFF

47"AFF

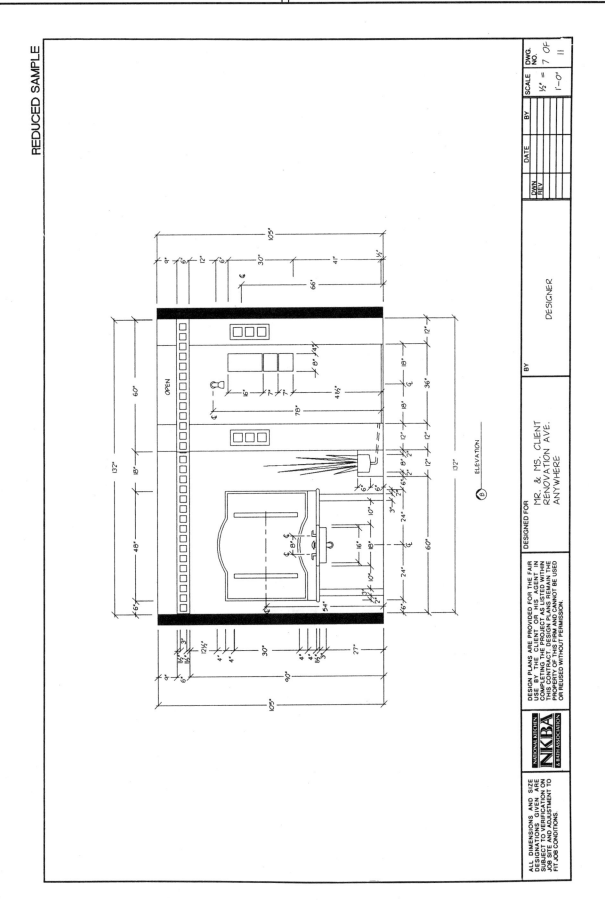

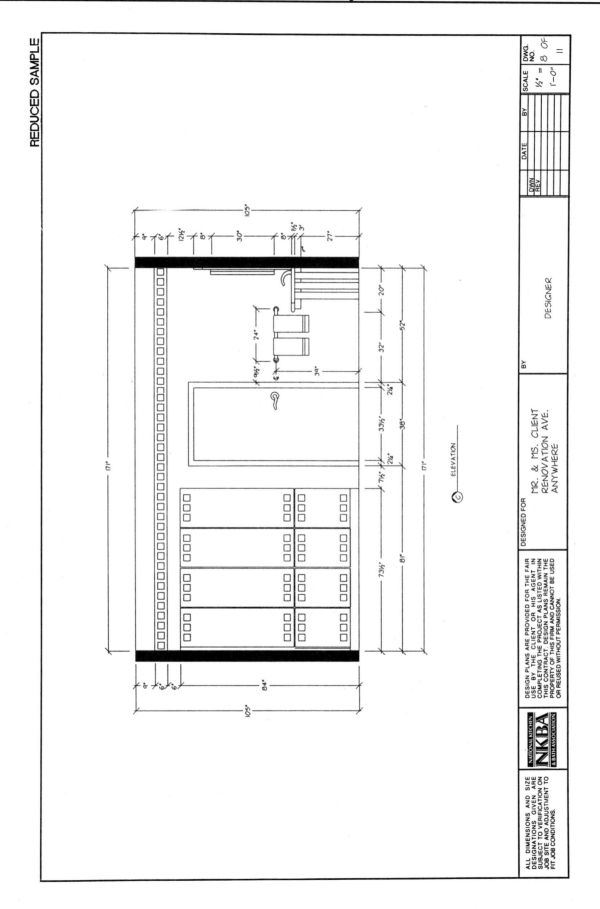

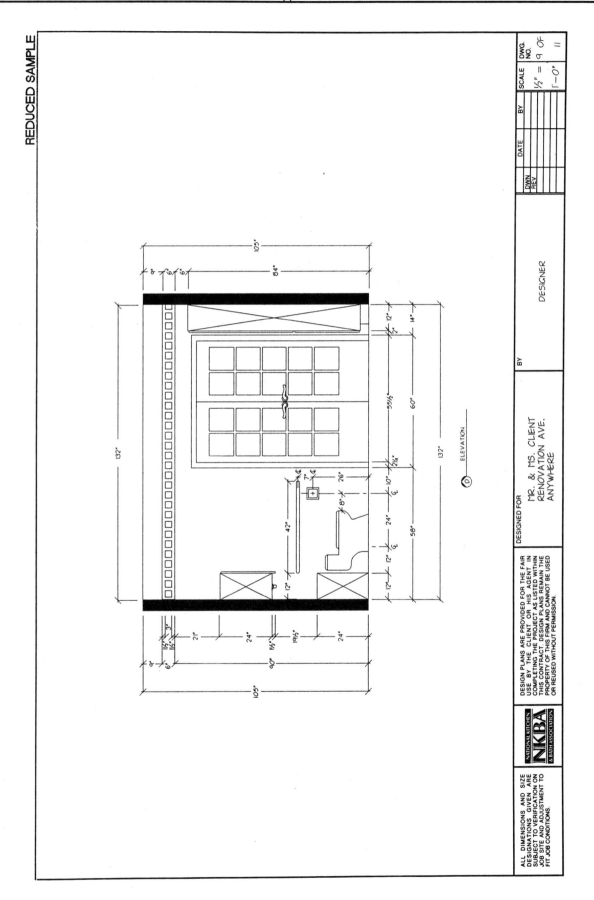

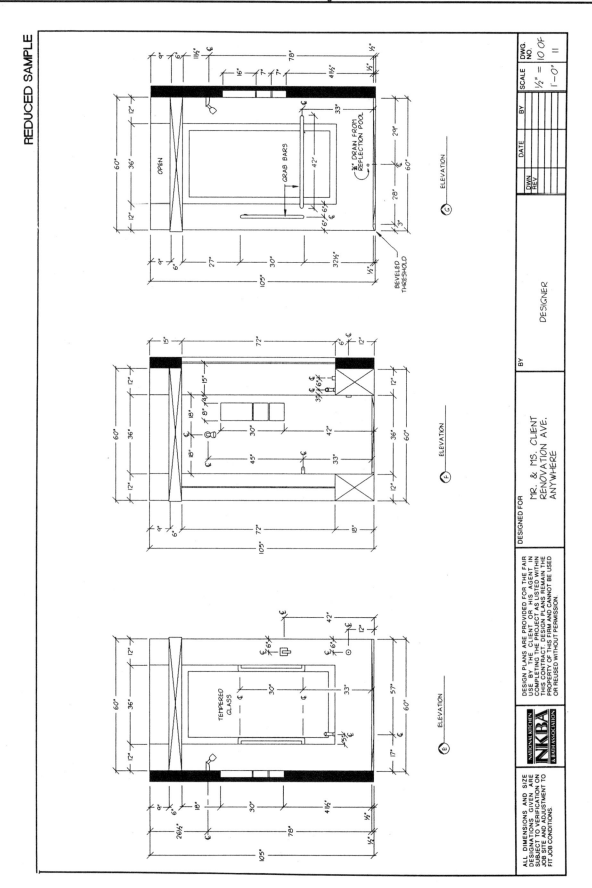

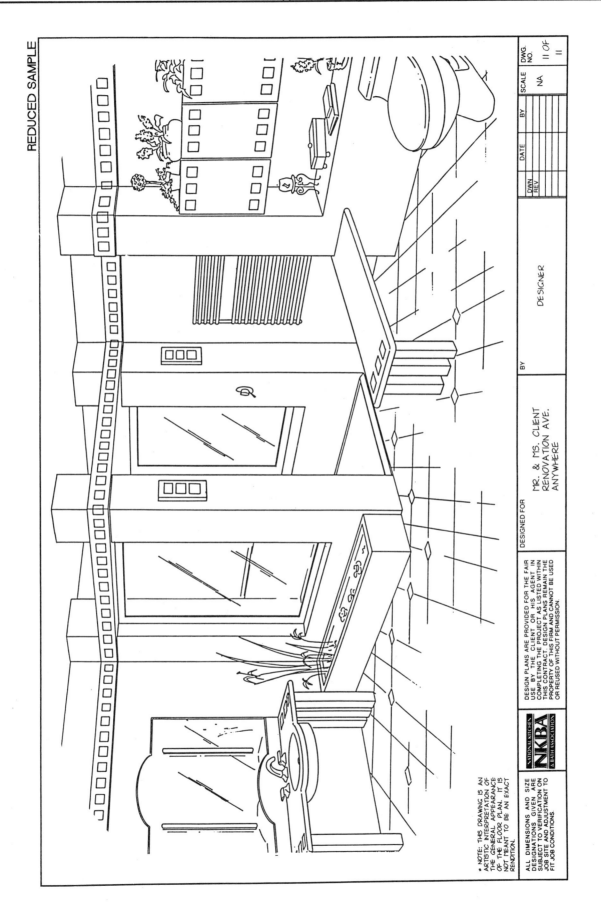

General Provisions Using Metric Dimensions

I. Use of Standards

The use of these *National Kitchen & Bath Association Graphics and Presentation Standards* is strongly recommended. They contain a specific set of criteria which when applied by the Bathroom Specialist produce a series of project documents that include the following:

- The Floor Plan

- The Construction Plan

- The Mechanical Plan

- The Interpretive Drawings

    1) Elevations
    2) Perspective Drawings
    3) Oblique, Dimetric, Isometric and Trimetric
    4) Sketches

- Specifications

- Design Statement

- Contracts

Two sample sets of project documents for your review can be found in this publication, one uses imperial dimensions and the other is a metric conversion.

Paper: The acceptable paper for the original drawings of the floor plan, construction plan, mechanical plan, and interpretive drawings is set at a **minimum size of 28cm x 43cm.** Translucent vellum tracing paper, imprinted with a black border and appropriate space available for the insertion of pertinent information is strongly recommended. Copies of original drawings should appear in blue or black ink only on white paper. Ozalid or photocopy prints are acceptable.

The use of lined yellow note paper, typing paper, scored graph paper or scored quadrille paper **is not acceptable.**

NKBA Drawing Aid #6002

II. The Floor Plan

1)   **Size and Scope of Floor Plan Drawings:** Bathroom floor plans should be drawn to a scale of 1 to 20 (ie. 1cm = 20cm). When the designer has a room dimensioned in imperial inches and wants to use a metric based cabinet brand, the industry norm is to use a 1:24 metric ratio as equal to a 1/2 inch scale. ***For imperial dimensions, see Use of Standards beginning on page 642.***

- All base cabinetry should be depicted using a dashed line (----) while countertops are depicted using a solid line.

- The floor plan should depict the entire room when possible. When the entire room cannot be depicted, it must show the area where cabinetry and appliances are permanently installed.

- Floor plans must show all major structural elements such as walls, door swings, door openings, partitions, windows, archways and equipment.

- When the entire room cannot be depicted, the room must be divided by *"break lines"* (><) and must show all major structural elements with adjoining areas indicated and labeled.

Finished interior dimensions are used on all project documents to denote available space for cabinetry and/or other types of equipment. If the bathroom specialist is responsible for specifying the exact method of wall construction, finish and/or partition placement, the specialist should include partition center lines on the construction plan, as well as the finished interior dimensions.

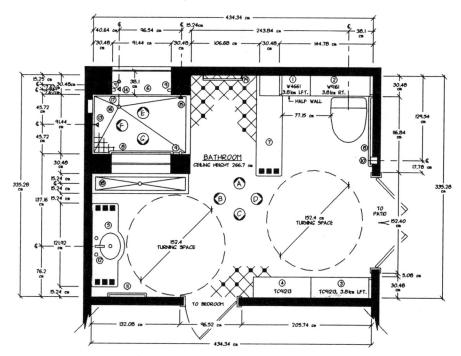

2)   **Centerline (₵) dimensions:** must be given for equipment in two directions when possible.

- Mechanicals requiring centerlines include: lavatories, bathtubs/showers, toilets/bidets, fan units, light fixtures, heating and air conditioning ducts and radiators.

- Dimensions should be pulled from return walls or from the face of cabinets/fixtures/equipment opposite the mechanical element.

- Centerlines on the mechanical plan will be indicated by the symbol (₵) followed by a **long-short-long broken line** that extends into the floor area.

- When the centerline dimension line is outside the floor area, it is typically shown as the second (and, if required, the third) line following the dimension line which identifies the individual wall segments.

3)   **Dimensioning of Floor Plan:** When using metric dimensions, some designers also list all wall dimensions in inches. This double sizing helps all parties involved clearly understand the plans.

An example of Time Saving Formulas to convert between metrics would be as follows:

Inches to Centimeters, multiply the total number of inches by 2.54
Centimeters to Inches, multiply the total number of centimeters by .3937

NOTE:
- Each set of dimensions should be at least .5cm apart on separate dimension lines which are to intersect with witness lines. These intersecting points should be indicated by dimension arrows, dots, or slashes.

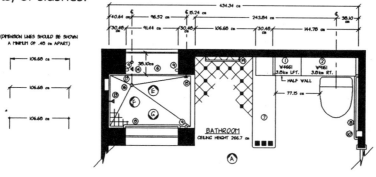

- All dimensions, whenever possible, should be shown **<u>OUTSIDE</u>** the wall lines.

- All lettering should be listed parallel to the title block at the bottom of the vellum paper and break the dimension line near its mid-point. This mechanical drafting technique eliminates errors in reading dimensions.

- An acceptable alternative is to draw all dimensions and lettering so that it is readable from the bottom edge or the right side of the plans with lettering on top of each dimension line.

The following dimensions **MUST** be shown on every floor plan as minimum requirements.

- Overall length of wall areas to receive cabinets, countertops, fixtures, or any equipment occupying floor and/or wall space. This dimension should always be the outside line.

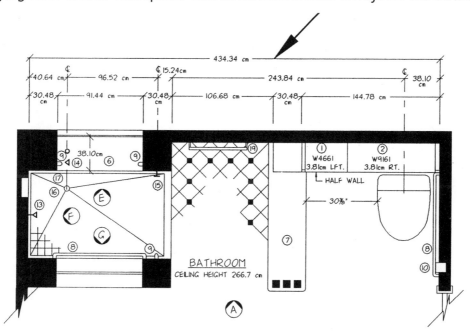

- Each wall opening, (windows, arches, doors and major appliances) and fixed structures (chimneys, wall protrusions and partitions) must be individually dimensioned. Dimensions are shown from outside trim. Trim size must be noted in the specification list. Fixtures such as radiators remaining in place must be outlined on the floor plan. These critical dimensions should be the first dimension line.

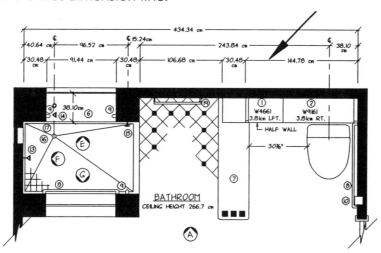

- Ceiling heights should appear on the floor plan. A separate plan for soffits is required when the soffit is a different depth than the wall or tall cabinet below. A separate soffit plan is recommended when the soffit is to be installed **PRIOR** to the wall or tall cabinet installation.

- Additional notes must be included for any deviation from standard height, width and depth. (cabinets, countertops, etc.)

- The exact opening must be given in height, width and depth for areas to be left open to receive cabinets and appliances at a future date.

- Items such as island/peninsula vanities and bathtub platforms, must be shown with the overall dimensions given from countertop edge to opposite countertop edge, tall cabinet or wall. The exact location of the structure must be identified by dimensions which position it from two directions; from return walls or from the face of cabinets/equipment opposite the structure.

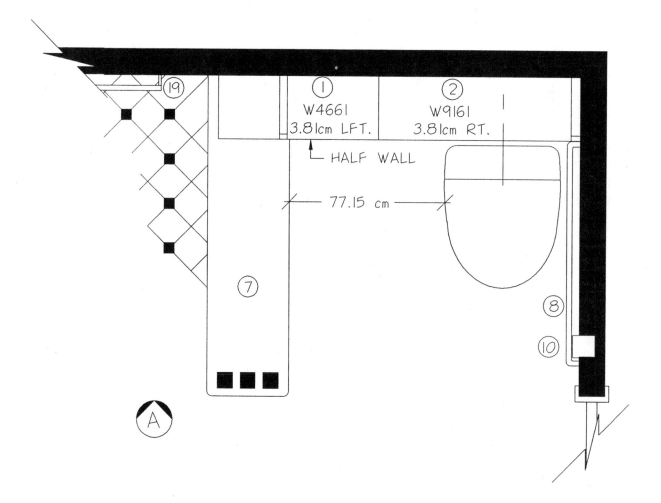

4) Cabinets/Fixtures and Equipment Nomenclature and Designation on Floor Plans:

- Cabinets should be designated and identified by manufacturer nomenclature inside the area indicating their position. Cabinet system trim and finish items are designated outside their area, with an arrow clarifying exactly where the trim piece is located.

- To insure clarity, some design firms prefer to number and call out all the cabinet nomenclature in the Floor Plan specification listing.

- Equally acceptable is the use of a circled reference number to designate each cabinet on the Floor Plan and Elevations with the cabinet code listed within the individual unit width on the elevations or in a separate cross-reference list on the elevations.

- **Regardless of which cabinet designation system is selected from above, additional information for supplementary fixtures/equipment and special provisions pertaining to the cabinets must be indicated within the cabinet or equipment area by a reference number in a circle. This additional information should then be registered in a cross-referenced specifications listing on the same sheet.**

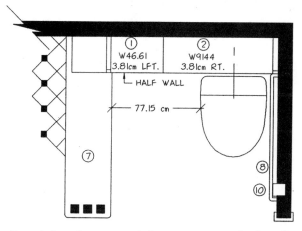

FLOOR PLAN

SPECIFICATIONS

① W4661, 3.81 cm EXT. LEFT, UNDER CABINET LIGHT, DOOR 3.81 cm LONGER THAN CASE TO CONCEAL LTS.

② W9161, 3.81cm EXT. RIGHT, UNDER CABINET LIGHTS, DOORS 3.81cm LONGER THAN CASE TO CONCEAL LTS.

- Special order materials or custom design features, angled cabinets, unusual tops, molding, trim details, etc., should be shown in a section view, (sometimes referred to as a "cut view"), a plan view in a scale larger than (1cm = 20cm), or in elevation view.

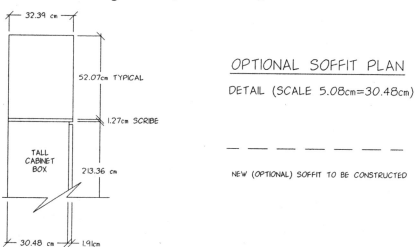

OPTIONAL SOFFIT PLAN

DETAIL (SCALE 5.08cm=30.48cm)

— — — — — — — —

NEW (OPTIONAL) SOFFIT TO BE CONSTRUCTED

III. The Construction Plan

1)   The purpose of the construction plan is to show the relationship of the existing space with that of the new design. The construction plan is detailed separately so that it does not clutter the floor plan. However, if construction changes are minimal it is acceptable to combine the construction plan with either the floor plan or mechanical plan.

2)   Construction Plan Symbols:

- Existing walls are shown with solid lines or hollowed out lines at their full thickness.

- Wall sections to be removed are shown with an outline of broken lines.

- New walls show the material symbols applicable to the type of construction or use a symbol which is identified in the legend in order to distinguish them from existing partitions.

EXISTING WALL TO REMOVED

OR

EXISTING WALLS TO REMAIN

EXISTING OPENINGS TO ENCLOSE

WOOD STUD   METAL STUD

CONCRETE   BRICK

CONCRETE BLOCK   BRICK

NEW WALLS TO BE CONSTRUCTED

* Symbols adapted from Architectural Graphic Standards, 9th Edition

An Example of a Construction Plan:

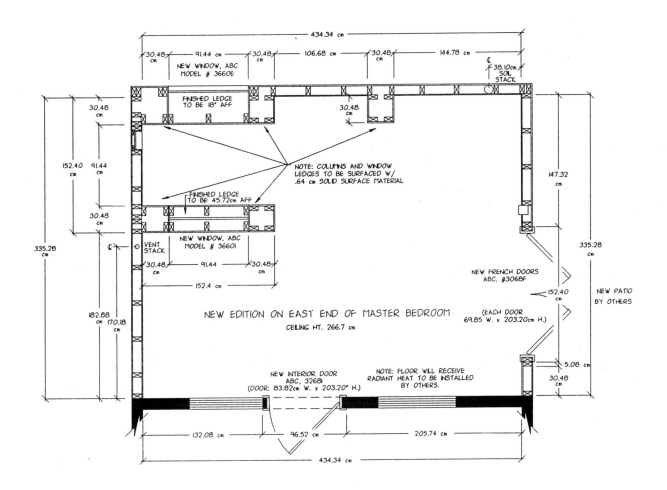

CONSTRUCTION PLAN

LEGEND

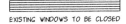

IV. The Mechanical Plan

- By detailing separate plans for the mechanicals and/or construction, it will help to clearly identify such work without cluttering the bathroom floor plan.

- The mechanical plan should show an outline of the cabinets, countertops and fixtures without nomenclature.

- The mechanicals should be placed in the proper location with the proper symbols.

- All overall room dimensions should be listed.

1) The mechanical plan will consist of the Electrical/Lighting, Plumbing, Heating, Air Conditioning and Ventilation systems. If any minor wall/door construction changes are part of the plan, they should also be detailed on the mechanical plan.

2) A mechanical legend should be prepared on the plan. This legend will be used to describe what each symbol for special purpose outlets, fixtures or equipment means.

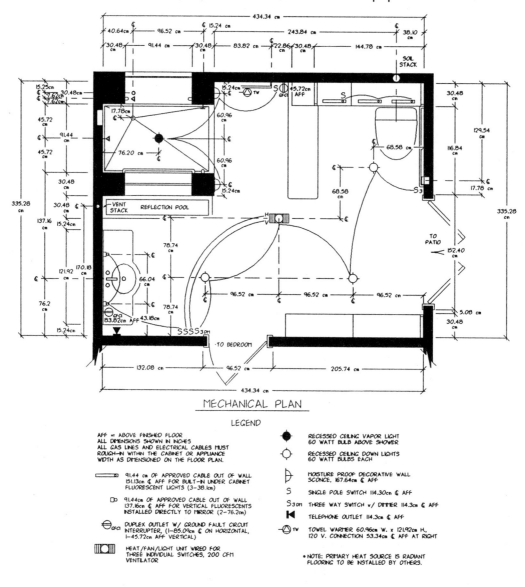

MECHANICAL PLAN

LEGEND

AFF = ABOVE FINISHED FLOOR
ALL DIMENSIONS SHOWN IN INCHES
ALL GAS LINES AND ELECTRICAL CABLES MUST ROUGH-IN WITHIN THE CABINET OR APPLIANCE WIDTH AS DIMENSIONED ON THE FLOOR PLAN.

⊐⊐ 91.44 cm OF APPROVED CABLE OUT OF WALL 151.13cm ℄ AFF FOR BUILT-IN UNDER CABINET FLUORESCENT LIGHTS (3-38.1cm)

⊏▷ 91.44cm OF APPROVED CABLE OUT OF WALL 137.16cm ℄ AFF FOR VERTICAL FLUORESCENTS INSTALLED DIRECTLY TO MIRROR (2-76.2cm)

⊖GFCI DUPLEX OUTLET W/ GROUND FAULT CIRCUIT INTERRUPTER, (1-85.09cm ℄ ON HORIZONTAL, 1-45.72cm AFF VERTICAL)

▥▥ HEAT/FAN/LIGHT UNIT WIRED FOR THREE INDIVIDUAL SWITCHES, 200 CFM VENTILATOR

● RECESSED CEILING VAPOR LIGHT 60 WATT BULB ABOVE SHOWER

○ RECESSED CEILING DOWN LIGHTS 60 WATT BULBS EACH

Ɗ MOISTURE PROOF DECORATIVE WALL SCONCE, 167.64cm ℄ AFF

S SINGLE POLE SWITCH 114.30cm ℄ AFF

S₃DM THREE WAY SWITCH w/ DIMMER 114.3cm ℄ AFF

◀ TELEPHONE OUTLET 114.3cm ℄ AFF

◁ TW TOWEL WARMER 60.96cm W. x 121.92cm H., 120 V. CONNECTION 53.34cm ℄ AFF AT RIGHT

* NOTE: PRIMARY HEAT SOURCE IS RADIANT FLOORING TO BE INSTALLED BY OTHERS.

3) Centerline (₵) dimensions must be given for all equipment in two directions when possible.

- Mechanicals requiring centerlines include: lavatories, bathtubs/showers, toilets/bidets, fan units, light fixtures, heating and air conditioning ducts and radiators.

- Centerline dimensions should be pulled from return walls or from the face of cabinets/equipment opposite the mechanical element.

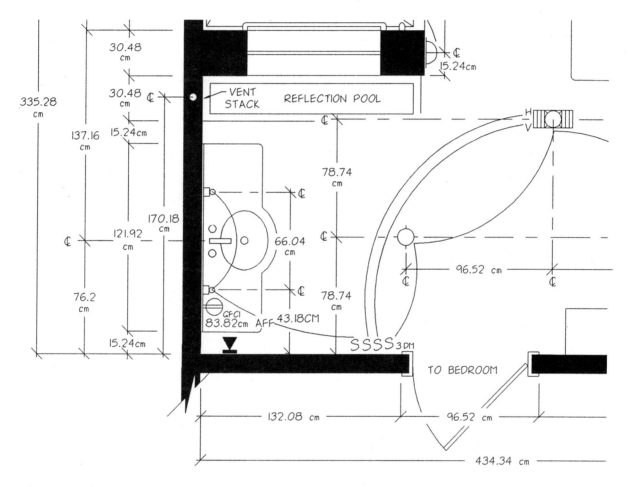

Centerlines on the mechanical plan will be indicated by the symbol (₵) followed by a **long-short-long broken line** that extends into the floor area.

₵ —— — — — — — — — — — —

4)   Mechanical Plan Symbols:

Symbol	Description	Symbol	Description
S	SINGLE POLE SWITCH	TV	TELEVISION OUTLET
S_2	DOUBLE POLE SWITCH	C	CABLE OUTLET
S_3	THREE WAY SWITCH	T_L	LOW VOLTAGE TRANSFORMER
S_4	FOUR WAY SWITCH		HANGING CEILING FIXTURE
S_{DM}	SINGLE POLE SWITCH w/ DIMMER		HEAT LAMP
S_{3DM}	THREE WAY SWITCH w/ DIMMER		HEAT/LIGHT UNIT
S_{LM}	MASTER SWITCH FOR LOW VOLTAGE SWITCHING SYSTEM		HEAT/FAN LIGHT W/ OOO CFM VENT
S_L	SWITCH FOR LOW VOLTAGE SWITCHING SYSTEM		RECESSED CEILING DOWN LIGHTING
S_{WP}	WEATHERPROOF SWITCH		RECESSED CEILING VAPOR LIGHT
S_{RC}	REMOTE CONTROL SWITCH		BUILT-IN LOW VOLTAGE TASK LIGHT
S_D	AUTOMATIC DOOR SWITCH		BUILT-IN FLUORESCENT LIGHT
S_P	SWITCH AND PILOT LAMP		CONTINUOUS ROW FLUORESCENT LIGHTS
S_K	KEY OPERATED SWITCH		SURFACE MOUNTED FLUORESCENT LIGHT
S_F	FUSED SWITCH		WALL SCONCE
S_T	TIME SWITCH	DW	DISHWASHER
S	CEILING PULL SWITCH	GD	FOOD WASTE DISPOSAL
	DUPLEX OUTLET	TC	TRASH COMPACTOR
GFCI	DUPLEX OUTLET WITH GROUND FAULT CIRCUIT INTERRUPTER	R	REFRIGERATOR OUTLET
S	SWITCH AND SINGLE RECEPTACLE OUTLET	H	HOOD W/ OOO CFM VENTILATOR
S	SWITCH AND DUPLEX OUTLET	M	MICROWAVE OVEN
B	BLANKED OUTLET	R	ELECTRIC RANGE/COOKTOP
J	JUNCTION BOX	WO	ELECTRIC SINGLE/DOUBLE OVEN
L	OUTLET CONTROLLED BY LOW VOLTAGE SWITCHING WHEN RELAY IS INSTALLED IN OUTLET BOX	G	GAS SUPPLY
	SINGLE RECEPTACLE OULET	CT	GAS COOKTOP
	TRIPLEX RECEPTACLE OULET	WO	GAS SINGLE/DOUBLE OVEN
	QUADRUPLEX RECEPTACLE OULET	CW	CLOTHES WASHER
	DUPLEX RECEPTACLE OUTLET-SPLIT WIRED	CD	CLOTHES DRYER
	TRIPLEX RECEPTACLE OUTLET-SPLIT WIRED	SA	SAUNA
C	CLOCK HANGER RECEPTACLE	ST	STEAM
F	FAN HANGER RECEPTACLE	WP	WHIRLPOOL
	INTERCOM	TW	TOWEL WARMER
	TELEPHONE OUTLET		HEAT REGISTER
T	THERMOSTAT		
	SMOKE DETECTOR		

ANY STANDARD SYMBOL GIVEN ABOVE W/ THE ADDITION OF LOWERCASE SUBSCRIPT LETTERING MAY BE USED TO DESIGNATE A VARIATION OF STANDARD EQUIPMENT.

WHEN USED THEY MUST BE LISTED IN THE LEGEND OF THE MECHANICAL PLAN.

Symbols adapted from Architectural Graphic Standards, 9th Edition

V. Interpretive Drawings

Elevations and perspective renderings are considered interpretive drawings and are used as an explanatory means of understanding the floor plans.

- Under no circumstances should the interpretive drawings be used as a substitute for floor plans.

- In cases of dispute, the floor plans are the legally binding document.

- Because perspective drawings are not dimensioned to scale, many Bathroom Specialists include a disclaimer on their rendering such as this:

> This drawing is an artistic interpretation of the general appearance of the floor plan. It is not meant to be an exact rendition.

1)   Elevation: Elevations must show a front view of all wall areas receiving cabinets/equipment as shown on the floor plan.

Elevations should dimension all cabinets, counters, fixtures and equipment in the elevation as follows:

- Cabinets with toekick and finished height.

- A portion of the cabinet doors and drawer front should indicate style and, when applicable, placement of handles/pulls.

- Countertops indicate thickness and show backsplash.

- All doors, windows or other openings in walls which will receive equipment. The window/door casing or trim will be listed within the overall opening dimensions.

- All permanent fixtures such as radiators, etc.

- All main structural elements and protrusions such as chimneys, partitions, etc.

- Centerlines for all mechanical equipment.

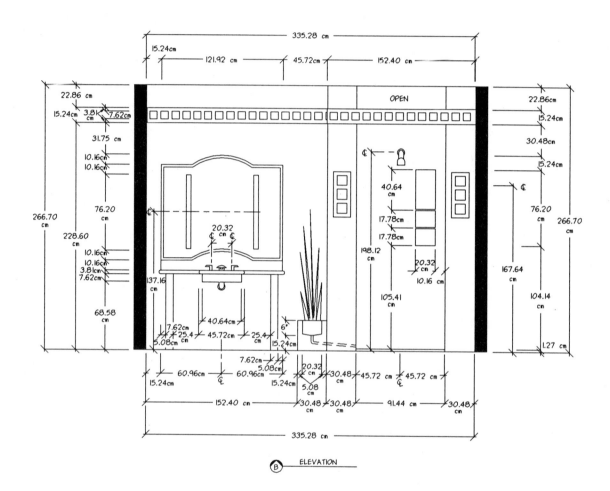

ELEVATION

NOTE:
DIMENSIONS MUST ACCURATELY
REPRESENT PRODUCTS USED.

2) **Perspective Drawings:** Perspectives are **not drawn to scale.** Grids, which are available through the **National Kitchen & Bath Association**, can be used as an underlay for tracing paper to accurately portray a perspective rendering. Two such grids are displayed on pages 688 and 689 for your reference.

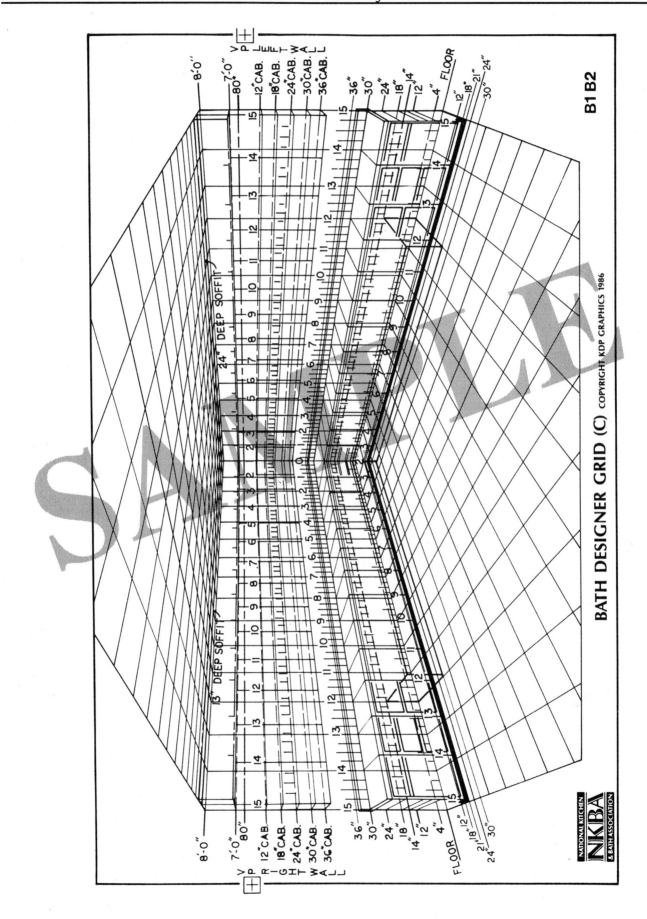

BATH DESIGNER GRID (C) COPYRIGHT KDP GRAPHICS 1986

B1 B2

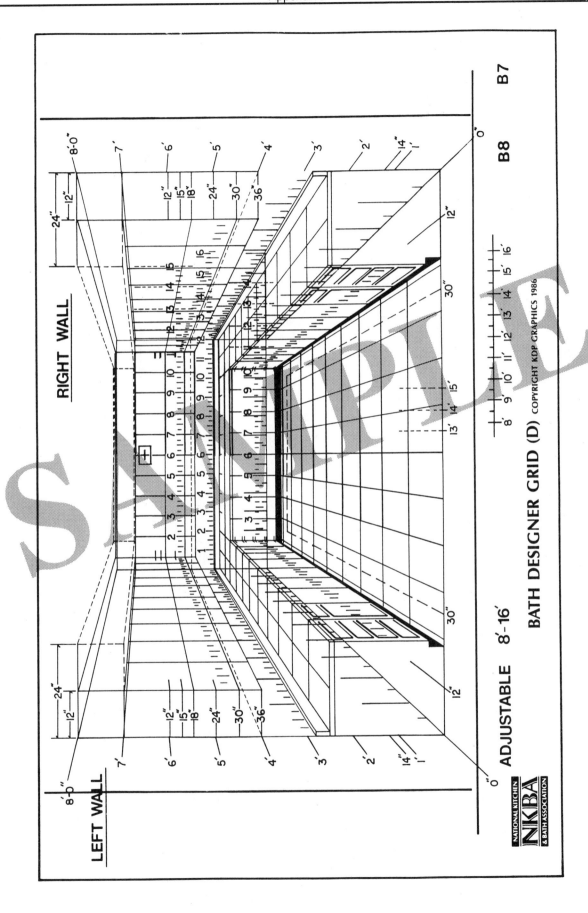

Designers have the option of preparing a one-point or two-point perspective, with or without the use of a grid.

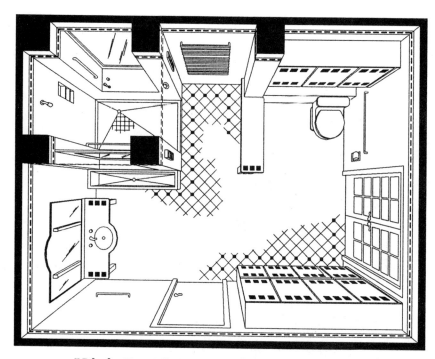

"Birds-Eye View" One Point Perspective

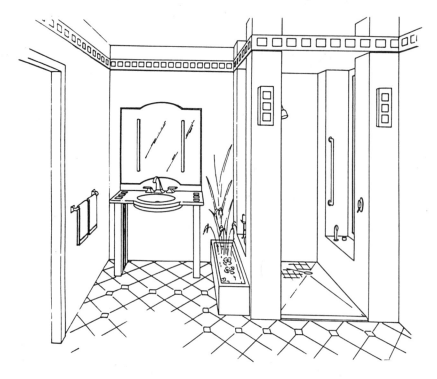

One Point Perspective

- The minimum requirement for perspectives shall be the reasonably correct representation of the longest cabinet or fixture run, or the most important area in terms of usage.

- Perspectives need not show the complete bathroom.

- Separate sectional views of significant areas or features are considered acceptable.

Two Point Perspective

3) **Oblique, Dimetric, Isometric and Trimetric:** Several types of interpretive drawings can be used to illustrate special cabinets and equipment, such as countertops or special order cabinets, where mechanical representation and dimensions are important. These drawings give a simple way to illustrate an object in three-dimensional views.

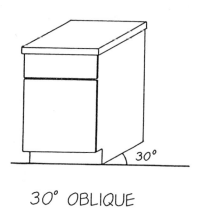

30° OBLIQUE

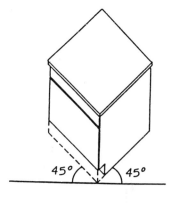

45° DIMETRIC

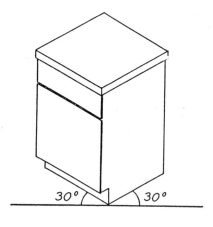

30° ISOMETRIC

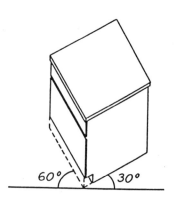

TRIMETRIC

4) **Sketches:** The use of sketches is a quick way to achieve a total picture of the bathroom without exact details in scaled dimensions. This quick freehand sketch can be studied, adjusted and sketched over, as the designer and client attempt to arrive at the most satisfactory layout for the bathroom. The quick sketch then can serve as a guide for drawing an exact plan of the bathroom.

Perspective Sketch

VI. Sample Bathroom Project Drawings

The following set of sample project drawings have been prepared by a Certified Bathroom Designer under the direction of the **National Kitchen & Bath Association.** These sample drawings include:

- Floor Plan

- Construction Plan

- Mechanical Plan

- Countertop Plan *

- Soffit Plan *

- Elevations

- Perspectives

* It is recommended to prepare countertop and soffit plan drawings to further clarify project requirements.

REDUCED SAMPLE

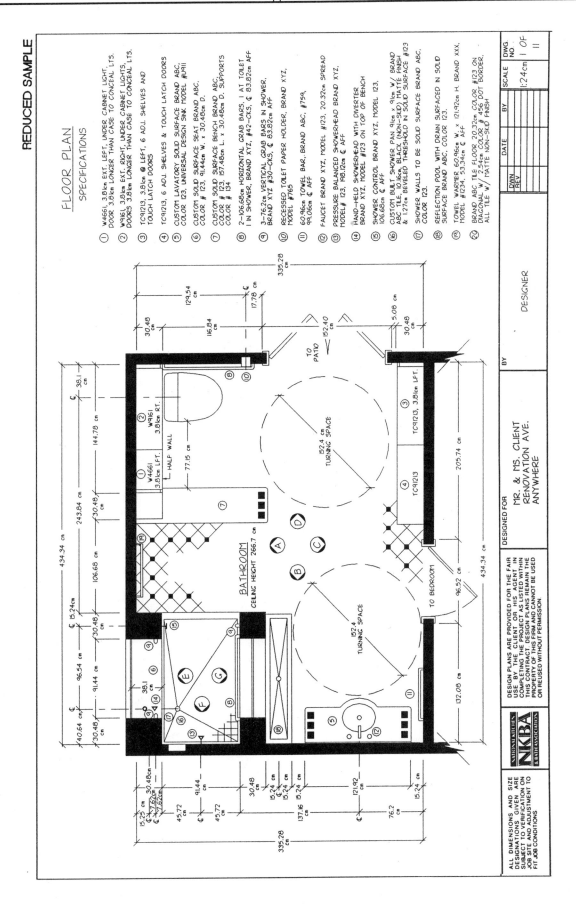

FLOOR PLAN
SPECIFICATIONS

1. W4661, 3.81cm EXT. LEFT, UNDER CABNET LIGHT, DOOR 3.81cm LONGER THAN CASE TO CONCEAL LTS.
2. W9161, 3.81cm EXT. RIGHT, UNDER CABINET LIGHTS, DOORS 3.81cm LONGER THAN CASE TO CONCEAL LTS.
3. TC91213, 3.81cm @ LEFT, 6 ADJ. SHELVES AND TOUCH LATCH DOORS
4. TC91213, 6 ADJ. SHELVES & TOUCH LATCH DOORS
5. CUSTOM LAVATORY SOLID SURFACE BRAND ABC, COLOR 123, UNIVERSAL DESIGN SINK, MODEL #URII
6. CUSTOM SOLID SURFACE SEAT BRAND ABC, COLOR 123, 91.44cm W. x 30.48cm D.
7. CUSTOM SOLID SURFACE BENCH BRAND ABC, COLOR # 123, 157.48cm L. x 30.48cm D. SUPPORTS COLOR # 134
8. 2-106.68cm HORIZONTAL GRAB BARS, I AT TOILET I IN SHOWER, BRAND XYZ, #42-CK5, @ 83.82cm AFF
9. 3-76.2cm VERTICAL GRAB BARS IN SHOWER, BRAND XYZ #30-CK5, @ 83.82cm AFF
10. RECESSED TOILET PAPER HOLDER, BRAND XYZ, MODEL #765
11. 60.96cm TOWEL BAR, BRAND ABC, #759, 99.06cm @ AFF
12. FAUCET BRAND XYZ, MODEL #123, 20.32cm SPREAD
13. PRESSURE BALANCED SHOWERHEAD BRAND XYZ, MODEL# 123, 198.12cm @ AFF
14. HAND-HELD SHOWERHEAD WITH DIVERTER BRAND XYZ, MODEL #123 ON TOP OF BENCH 106.68cm @ AFF
15. SHOWER CONTROL BRAND XYZ, MODEL 123, 106.68cm @ AFF
16. CUSTOM BUILT SHOWER PAN 9lcm x 9lcm W/ BRAND ABC TILE, 10.16cm, BLACK (NON-SKID) MATTE FINISH & 1.27cm BEVELED THRESHOLD IN SOLID SURFACE #123
17. SHOWER WALLS TO BE SOLID SURFACE BRAND ABC, COLOR 123.
18. REFLECTION POOL WITH DRAIN SURFACED IN SOLID SURFACE BRAND ABC, COLOR 123.
19. TOWEL WARMER 60.96cm W. x 121.92cm H. BRAND XXX, MODEL #1234, 53.34cm @ AFF
20. BRAND ABC TILE FLOOR 20.32cm, COLOR #123 ON DIAGONAL W/ 2.54cm COLOR #456 DOT BORDER. ALL TILE W/ MATTE NON-SKID FINISH

ALL DIMENSIONS AND SIZE DESIGNATIONS GIVEN ARE SUBJECT TO VERIFICATION ON JOB SITE AND ADJUSTMENT TO FIT JOB CONDITIONS

DESIGNED FOR
MR. & MS. CLIENT
RENOVATION AVE.
ANYWHERE

DESIGNER

BATHROOM
CEILING HEIGHT 266.7 cm

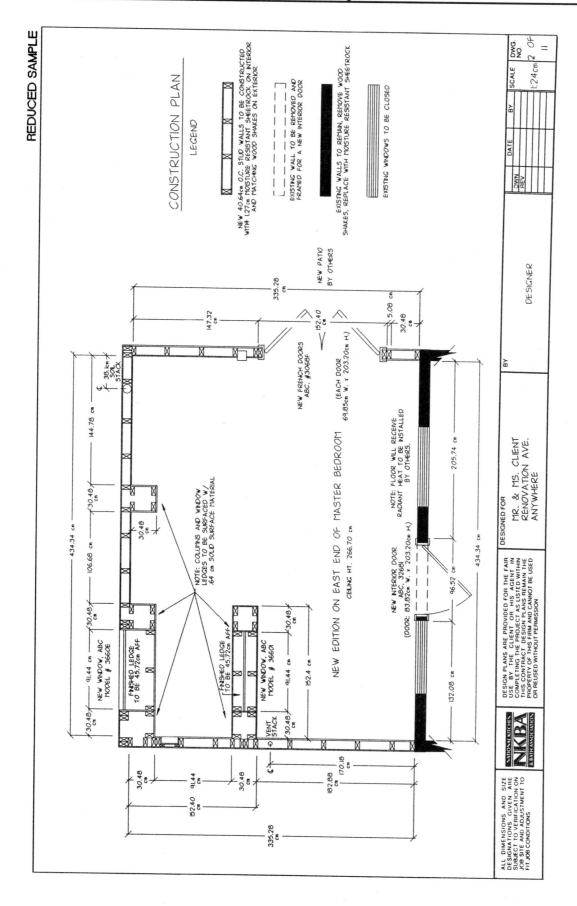

REDUCED SAMPLE

CONSTRUCTION PLAN

LEGEND

NEW 40.64cm O.C. STUD WALLS TO BE CONSTRUCTED WITH 1.27cm MOISTURE RESISTANT SHEETROCK ON INTERIOR AND MATCHING WOOD SHAKES ON EXTERIOR

EXISTING WALL TO BE REMOVED AND FRAMED FOR A NEW INTERIOR DOOR

EXISTING WALLS TO REMAIN, REMOVE WOOD SHAKES, REPLACE WITH MOISTURE RESISTANT SHEETROCK

EXISTING WINDOWS TO BE CLOSED

NEW PATIO BY OTHERS

NEW FRENCH DOORS ABC #3068F
(EACH DOOR)
69.85cm W. x 203.20cm H.)

NEW EDITION ON EAST END OF MASTER BEDROOM
CEILING HT. 266.70 cm

NOTE: COLUMNS AND WINDOW LEDGES TO BE SURFACED W/ .64 cm SOLID SURFACE MATERIAL

FINISHED LEDGE TO BE 45.72cm AFF

FINISHED LEDGE TO BE 45.72cm AFF

NEW WINDOW, ABC MODEL # 3660E

NEW WINDOW, ABC MODEL # 3660I

VENT STACK

NOTE: FLOOR WILL RECEIVE RADIANT HEAT TO BE INSTALLED BY OTHERS.

NEW INTERIOR DOOR ABC, 3268I
(DOOR: 83.52cm W. x 203.20cm H.)

335.28 cm
147.32 cm
152.40 cm
5.08 cm
30.48 cm
205.74 cm
434.34 cm
96.52 cm
132.08 cm

434.34 cm
144.78 cm
30.48 cm
30.48 cm
106.68 cm
91.44 cm
30.48 cm
91.44 cm
152.4 cm
30.48 cm
30.48 cm
30.48 cm

38.1cm SOIL STACK

30.48 cm
91.44 cm
30.48 cm
152.40 cm
182.88 cm
170.18 cm
335.28 cm

DESIGNED FOR
MR. & MS. CLIENT
RENOVATION AVE.
ANYWHERE

DESIGNER

BY

DATE   BY   SCALE   DWG. NO.
1:24cm   2 OF
DWN   REV   II

NATIONAL KITCHEN NKBA & BATH ASSOCIATION

REDUCED SAMPLE

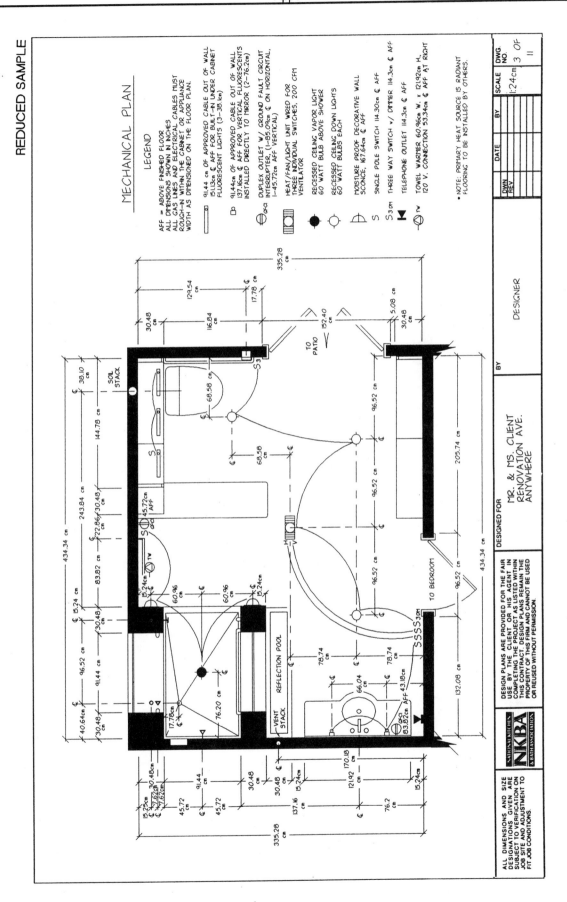

MECHANICAL PLAN

LEGEND

AFF = ABOVE FINISHED FLOOR
ALL DIMENSIONS SHOWN IN INCHES
ALL GAS LINES AND ELECTRICAL CABLES MUST
ROUGH-IN WITHIN THE CABINET OR APPLIANCE
WIDTH AS DIMENSIONED ON THE FLOOR PLAN.

91.44 cm OF APPROVED CABLE OUT OF WALL
151.13cm ℄ AFF FOR BUILT-IN UNDER CABINET
FLUORESCENT LIGHTS (3-38.1cm)

91.44cm OF APPROVED CABLE OUT OF WALL
137.16cm ℄ AFF FOR VERTICAL FLUORESCENTS
INSTALLED DIRECTLY TO MIRROR (2-76.2cm)

DUPLEX OUTLET W/ GROUND FAULT CIRCUIT
INTERRUPTER, (1-55.09cm ℄ ON HORIZONTAL,
1-45.72cm AFF VERTICAL)

HEAT/FAN/LIGHT UNIT WIRED FOR
THREE INDIVIDUAL SWITCHES, 200 CFM
VENTILATOR

RECESSED CEILING VAPOR LIGHT
60 WATT BULB ABOVE SHOWER

RECESSED CEILING DOWN LIGHTS
60 WATT BULBS EACH

MOISTURE PROOF DECORATIVE WALL
SCONCE, 167.64cm ℄ AFF

SINGLE POLE SWITCH 114.30cm ℄ AFF

THREE WAY SWITCH w/ DIMMER 114.3cm ℄ AFF

TELEPHONE OUTLET 114.3cm ℄ AFF AT RIGHT

TOWEL WARMER 60.96cm W. x 121.92cm H.,
120 V. CONNECTION 53.34cm ℄ AFF AT RIGHT

• NOTE: PRIMARY HEAT SOURCE IS RADIANT
FLOORING TO BE INSTALLED BY OTHERS.

DESIGNER

DESIGNED FOR
MR. & MS. CLIENT
RENOVATION AVE.
ANYWHERE

DWN				DATE	BY	SCALE	DWG. NO.
REV						1:24cm	3 OF
							11

DESIGN PLANS ARE PROVIDED FOR THE FAIR
USE BY THE CLIENT OR HIS AGENT IN
COMPLETING THE PROJECT AS LISTED WITHIN
THIS CONTRACT. DESIGN PLANS REMAIN THE
PROPERTY OF THIS FIRM AND CANNOT BE USED
OR REUSED WITHOUT PERMISSION.

ALL DIMENSIONS AND SIZE
DESIGNATIONS GIVEN ARE
SUBJECT TO VERIFICATION ON
JOB SITE AND ADJUSTMENT TO
FIT JOB CONDITIONS.

NKBA
NATIONAL KITCHEN & BATH ASSOCIATION

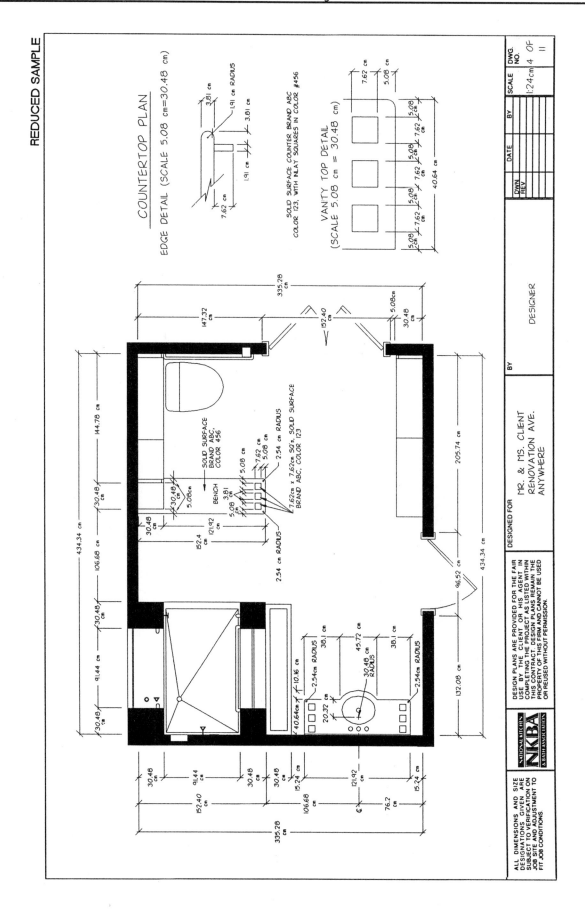

REDUCED SAMPLE

COUNTERTOP PLAN

EDGE DETAIL (SCALE 5.08 cm=30.48 cm)

3.81 cm
1.91 cm RADIUS
3.81 cm
1.91 cm
7.62 cm

SOLID SURFACE COUNTER BRAND ABC
COLOR 123, WITH INLAY SQUARES IN COLOR #456

VANITY TOP DETAIL
(SCALE 5.08 cm = 30.48 cm)

7.62 cm
5.08 cm
5.08
7.62 cm
5.08 cm
7.62 cm
40.64 cm
5.08 cm
7.62 cm
5.08 cm
7.62 cm

335.28 cm
147.32 cm
152.40 cm
5.08cm
30.48 cm

434.34 cm
144.78 cm
30.48 cm
106.68 cm
30.48 cm
91.44 cm
30.48 cm

SOLID SURFACE BRAND ABC, COLOR 456
30.48 cm
5.08cm
BENCH
30.48 cm
3.81 cm
5.08 cm
152.4 cm
121.92 cm
30.48 cm

7.62 cm
5.08 cm
2.54 cm RADIUS
2.54 cm RADIUS
7.62cm x 7.62cm SQ's, SOLID SURFACE BRAND ABC, COLOR 123

205.74 cm
434.34 cm
96.52 cm
132.08 cm

38.1 cm
2.54 cm RADIUS
45.72 cm
30.48 cm RADIUS
38.1 cm
2.54cm RADIUS
10.16 cm
40.64cm
20.32 cm

30.48 cm
91.44 cm
30.48 cm
30.48 cm
15.24 cm
152.40 cm
106.68 cm
15.24 cm
121.92 cm
76.2 cm
15.24 cm
335.28 cm

DESIGNED FOR
MR. & MS. CLIENT
RENOVATION AVE.
ANYWHERE

BY
DESIGNER

DWN
REV
DATE
BY
SCALE
1:24 cm
DWG. NO.
4 OF 11

REDUCED SAMPLE

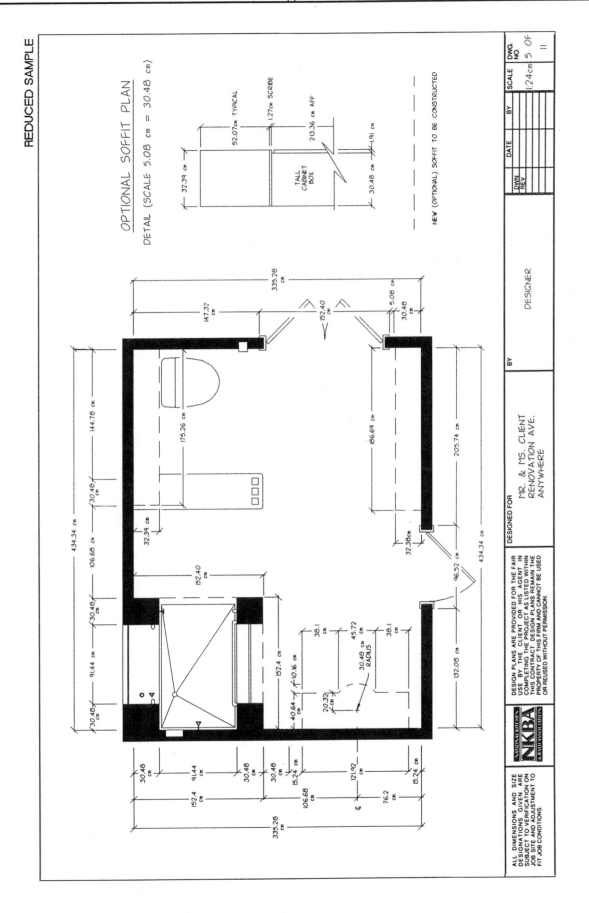

OPTIONAL SOFFIT PLAN

DETAIL (SCALE 5.08 cm = 30.48 cm)

NEW (OPTIONAL) SOFFIT TO BE CONSTRUCTED

52.07cm TYPICAL

1.27cm SCRIBE

213.36 cm AFF

1.91 cm

32.39 cm

TALL CABINET BOX

30.48 cm

DESIGNED FOR

MR. & MS. CLIENT
RENOVATION AVE.
ANYWHERE

BY

DESIGNER

DWN
REV

DATE

BY

SCALE

1:24cm

DWG. NO.

5 OF 11

REDUCED SAMPLE

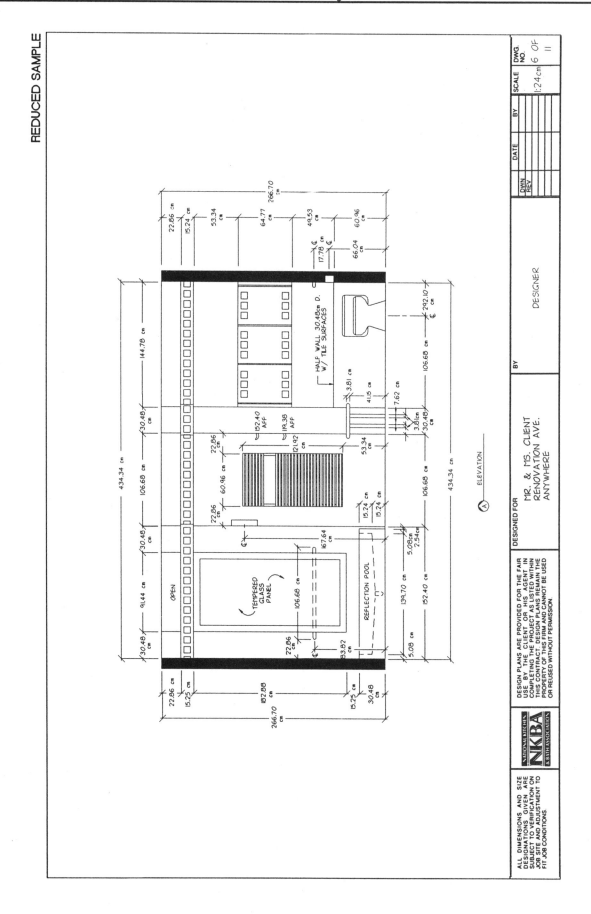

DESIGNED FOR

MR. & MS. CLIENT
RENOVATION AVE.
ANYWHERE

DESIGNER

DWN
REV

DATE

BY

SCALE 1:24 cm

DWG. NO. 6 OF 11

REDUCED SAMPLE

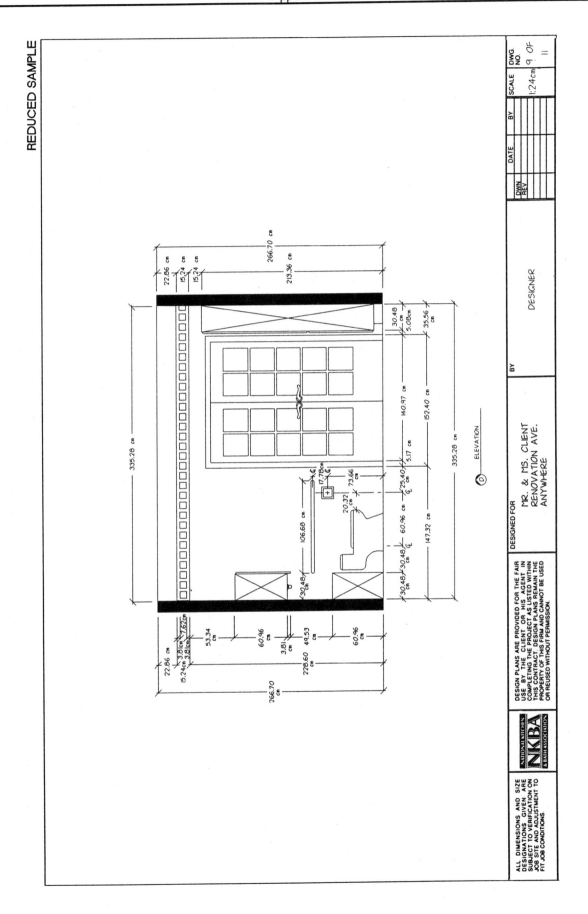

ELEVATION

NKBA
NATIONAL KITCHEN & BATH ASSOCIATION

DESIGNED FOR
MR. & MS. CLIENT
RENOVATION AVE.
ANYWHERE

BY

DESIGNER

DATE | BY | SCALE | DWG. NO.
DWN
REV

1:24cm   9. OF
11

REDUCED SAMPLE

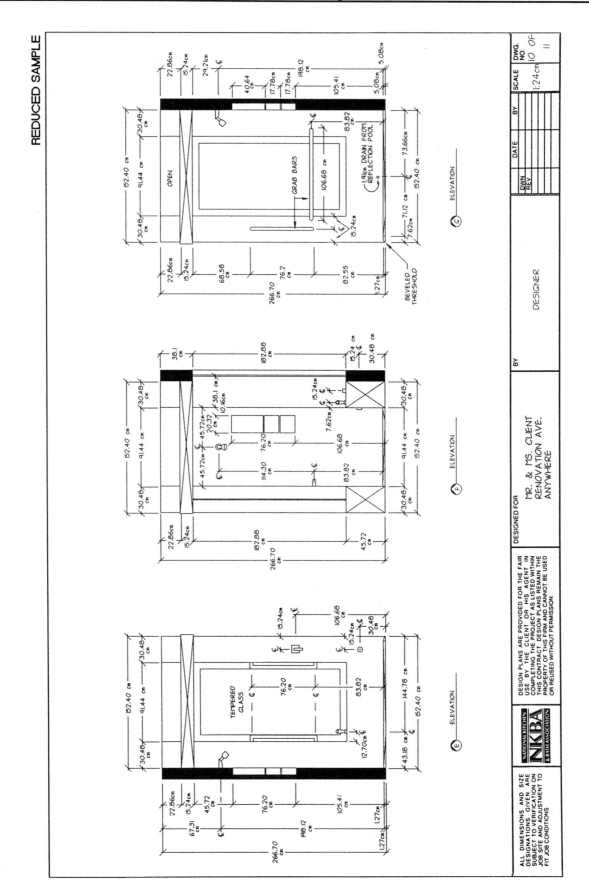

DESIGNED FOR

MR. & MS. CLIENT
RENOVATION AVE.
ANYWHERE

DESIGNER

| DWN | DATE | BY | SCALE | DWG. NO. |
| REV | | | 1:24cm | 10 OF 11 |

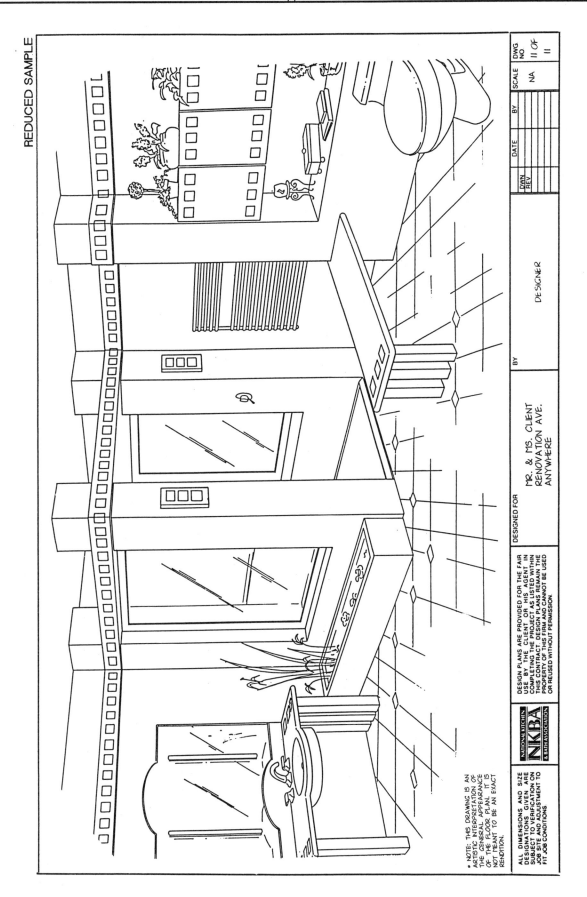

REDUCED SAMPLE

* NOTE: THIS DRAWING IS AN ARTISTIC INTERPRETATION OF THE GENERAL APPEARANCE OF THE FLOOR PLAN. IT IS NOT MEANT TO BE AN EXACT RENDITION.

ALL DIMENSIONS AND SIZE DESIGNATIONS GIVEN ARE SUBJECT TO VERIFICATION ON JOB SITE AND ADJUSTMENT TO FIT JOB CONDITIONS

DESIGN PLANS ARE PROVIDED FOR THE FAIR USE BY THE CLIENT OR HIS AGENT IN COMPLETING THE PROJECT AS LISTED WITHIN THIS CONTRACT. DESIGN PLANS REMAIN THE PROPERTY OF THIS FIRM AND CANNOT BE USED OR REUSED WITHOUT PERMISSION

DESIGNED FOR

MR. & MS. CLIENT
RENOVATION AVE.
ANYWHERE

BY

DESIGNER

DWN	DATE	BY	SCALE	DWG
REV			NA	NO
				11 OF
				11

Specifications

The purpose of the project specifications is to clearly define the details of the products listed and the scope and limits of the job. Specifications may be listed on a separate form, may be part of the working drawings or a combination of both.

- Project specifications define the area of responsibility between the Bathroom Specialist and the purchaser.

- They should clearly define all material and work affected by the job, either directly or indirectly.

- They must clearly indicate which individual has the ultimate responsibility for all or part of the above.

The following Delegation of Responsibilities shall apply: Bathroom Specialists are responsible for the accuracy of the dimensioned floor plans and the selections and designations of all cabinets/fixtures and equipment, if made or approved by them.

- Any equipment directly purchased by the Bathroom Specialist for resale, should be the responsibility of the Bathroom Specialist. Further, they must be responsible for supplying product installation instructions to the owner or the owner's agent.

- Any labor furnished by the Bathroom Specialist, whether by their own employees or through sub-contractors paid directly by them and working under their direction, should be the Bathroom Specialist's responsibility. **There should not be a Delegation of Total Responsibility to the Sub-Contractor Working Under these Conditions.**

- Any fixture/equipment purchased directly by the owner or the owner's agent from an outside source should be the responsibility of the owner or the owner's agent. The same applies to any sub-contractor, building contractor, or other labor directly hired and/or paid by the owner or the owner's agent.

- Specifications should contain descriptive references to all areas of work.

- All specification categories must be completed. If the job does not cover any given area, the words *"Not Applicable"*, *"N/A"*, or *"None"* should be inserted.

- In each area, the responsibility of either the Bathroom Specialist or the owner or the owner's agent must be assigned.

In all cases, the owner and the owner's agent must receive a completed copy of the project documents <u>PRIOR</u> to the commencement of any work.

STANDARD SPECIFICATIONS FOR BATHROOM DESIGN AND INSTALLATION

Name: _CLIENT NAME_

Home Address: _CLIENT ADDRESS_

City: _____ State _____ Phone (Home) _(123) 456-7890_

(Office) _(123) 444-4567_

(Office) _(123) 455-6789_

(Jobsite) _(Same as HOME)_

Jobsite Address _(Same as above)_

By

Hereafter called "Bathroom Specialist."

Bathroom Specialist will supply and deliver only such equipment and material as described in these specifications. Labor connected with this bathroom installation will be supplied by the Bathroom Specialist only as herein specified.

Any equipment, material and labor designated here as "Owner's responsibility" must be furnished and completed by the Owner, or the Owner's Agent in accordance with the work schedule established by the Bathroom Specialist.

Equipment, material and labor not included in these specifications can be supplied by the Bathroom Specialist at an additional cost for which authorization must be given in writing by the Owner, or the Owner's Agent.

All dimensions and cabinet designations shown on the floor plan, which are part of these specifications, are subject to adjustments dictated by job conditions.

All surfaces of walls, ceilings, windows and woodwork, except those of factory-made equipment, will be left unpainted or unfinished unless otherwise specified.

If specifications call for re-use of existing equipment, no responsibility on the part of the Bathroom Specialist for appearance, functioning or service shall be implied.

For factory-made equipment, the manufacturer's specifications for quality, design, dimensions, function and installation shall in any case take precedence over any others.

Cabinetry (as per approved drawing)

Manufacturer ABC

Cabinet Exterior   ☐ Wood   ☐ Steel   ☒ Decorative Laminate   ☐ Other

Cabinet Exterior Finish BRAND ABC, COLOR 123   Cabinet Interior Material MELAMINE   Finish WHITE

Door Style FULL OVERLAY, CUSTOM INLAY   Hardware HINGE # F0123

Special Cabinet Notes CUSTOM INLAY PATTERN @ TOP & BOTTOM OF ALL DOORS, COLOR 4566

Furnished By   ☒ Bathroom Specialist   ☐ Owner   ☐ Owner's Agent

Installation By   ☒ Bathroom Specialist   ☐ Owner   ☐ Owner's Agent

Countertops (as per approved drawing)

Manufacturer ABC   Material SOLID SURFACE

Design Details Deck Thickness 3/4" Color # 123   Edging Thickness 1 1/2" Color 123

Backsplash Thickness 1/4" Height 4"-8" Color #123   End Splash Thickness — Height — Color —

Special Countertop Notes PATTERN INLAY #4566 @ RT. & LEFT ENDS OF VANITY AND ON END OF BENCH

Furnished By   ☒ Bathroom Specialist   ☐ Owner   ☐ Owner's Agent

Installation By   ☒ Bathroom Specialist   ☐ Owner   ☐ Owner's Agent

Fascia & Soffit (as per approved drawing) OPTIONAL

Construction   ☒ Flush   ☐ Extended   ☐ Recessed   ☐ N/A (Open)

Finish Material DRYWALL - PAINTED

Special Fascia/Soffit Notes 20 1/2" HIGH, 12 3/4" DEEP, 1/2" SCRIBE SPACE ABOVE CABINETS

Furnished By   ☒ Bathroom Specialist   ☐ Owner   ☐ Owner's Agent

Installation By   ☒ Bathroom Specialist   ☐ Owner   ☐ Owner's Agent

Lighting System

Description	Qty.	Model Number	Finish	Lamp Req.	Furnished By B.S.	Furnished By O/OA	Installed By B.S.	Installed By O/OA
RECESSED DOWN LTS.	3	R123A	WHITE	60W	X		X	
DEC. WALL SCONCE	2	S 876	BLACK	2-25W	X		X	
RECESSED VAPOR LT.	1	V5678	WHITE	60W	X		X	
UNDER CAB. FLUORES.	3	F15	ALMOND	13	X		X	
VERTICAL FLUORES.	2	F30C	CHROME	13	X		X	
HEAT/LT./VENT UNIT	1	XY987	CHROME	60W	X		X	
Special Lighting System Notes								

VERTICAL FLUORESCENT MOUNTED TO VANITY MIRROR 54" TO ℄.
SCONCE @ 66" ℄ AND UNDER CAB. LTS 59 1/2" TO ℄.

Bath Fixtures, Fittings and Finishes

Item	Brand Name	Model	Finish	Furnished By B.S.	Furnished By O/OA	Installed By B.S.	Installed By O/OA	Hook Up By B.S.	Hook Up By O/OA
Water Closet	ABC	123	BLACK	X		X		X	
Seat	ABC	91	BLACK	X		X			
Fittings	ABC	L431	CHROME	X		X			
Stop and Supply	XYZ	987	"	X		X		X	
Miscellaneous									
Bidet	– NA –								
Fittings									
Stop and Supply									
Miscellaneous									
Urinal	–NA–								
Fittings									
Stop and Supply									
Miscellaneous									
Bathtub	–NA–								
Fittings									
Waste and Overflow									
Stop and Supply									
Enclosure									
Wall Surround									
Drapery Rod									
Whirlpool System	–NA–								
Fittings									
Miscellaneous									
Shower	CUSTOM: ↴								
Fittings									
Drain	ABC	D3C	CHROME	X		X			
Showerhead 1	ABC pressure balanced	123A	CHROME	X		X		X	
Showerhead 2	ABC "	479	"	X		X		X	
Stop and Supply	XYZ	987	"	X		X		X	
Enclosure	–NA–								
Wall Surround	SOLID SURFACE	ABC	123	X		X			
Shower Floor	ABC TILE (NON-SKID)	—	4567	X		X			
Drapery Rod									
Shower Drapery									
Miscellaneous	BUILT-IN SHAMPOO HOLDER		SS 123	X		X			
	" " SEAT		SS123	X		X			
	TEMPERED GL.	—	—	X		X			

Bath Fixtures, Fittings and Finishes *(Continued)*

Item	Brand Name	Model	Finish	Furnished By B.S.	O/OA	Installed By B.S.	O/OA	Hook Up By B.S.	O/OA
Lavatory 1	INTEGRAL SS	I-431	SS123	X		X			
Fittings	ABC	1234	CHROME	X		X		X	
Drilling Spread	8"								
Stop and Supply	XYZ	981	CHROME	X		X		X	
Pedestal Trap Cover									
Miscellaneous									
Lavatory 2	—NA—								
Fittings									
Drilling Spread									
Stop and Supply									
Pedestal Trap Cover									
Miscellaneous									
Steam Bath	—NA—								
Steam Enclosure									
Steam Generator									
Timer									
Miscellaneous									
Sauna	—NA—								
Interior									
Heater									
Timer									
Miscellaneous									
Spa/Hot Tub	—NA—								
Fittings									
Timer									
Heater									
Cover									
Skimmer									
Miscellaneous									
Exercise Equipment	—NA—								
Miscellaneous									
REFLECTION POOL	SOLID SURFACE	—	SS123	X		X			
· DRAIN	ABC	123	CHROME	X		X			
BENCH	SOLID SURFACE	—	SS123	X		X			
-SUPPORTS	"	—	SS456	X		X			
GRAB BARS (2)	XYZ 42"	42CKS	CHROME	X		X			
" (3)	XYZ 30"	30CKS	"	X		X			

Accessories (as per approved drawing)

Item	Brand Name	Model	Size	Finish	Furnished By B.S.	Furnished By O/OA	Installed By B.S.	Installed By O/OA	Hook Up By B.S.	Hook Up By O/OA
Mirror	CUSTOM (ELEV. B)	see dec. surfaces	48w×38H	MIRROR	X		X			
Medicine Cabinet	—NA—									
Glass Shelves	—NA—									
Towel Bar(s)	ABC	759	24"	CHROME	X		X			
Hydronic (Electric)	XXX	1234	24"w×48"H	"	X		X			
Towel Ring(s)	—NA—									
Robe Hook(s)	ABC	476H	LARGE	*SS123	X		X			
Tub Soap Dish(es)	—NA—									
Shower Soap Dish(es)	BUILT-IN SHOWER	ABC SOLID SUR.	8"w×30"H	*SS123	X		X			
Bidet Soap Dish	—NA—									
Lavatory Soap Dish(es)	—NA—									
Grab Bars	XYZ (see misc. p4)	42/30CKS	42"/30"	CHROME	X		X			
Paper Holder	XYZ	765	—	"	X		X			
Magazine Rack	—NA—									
Soap/Lotion Dispenser	—NA—									
Tumbler	—NA—									
Tissue Holder	—NA—									
Scale	—NA—									
Toothbrush Holder	—NA—									
Hamper	—NA—									
Other										

Closet Specifications —NA—

Item	Brand Name	Model	Size	Finish	Furnished By B.S.	Furnished By O/OA	Installed By B.S.	Installed By O/OA	Hook Up By B.S.	Hook Up By O/OA
Poles										
Shelf(ves)										
Drawers										
Shoe Racks										
Belt/Tie/Scarf Rack(s)										
Safe										
Ironing Board										
Miscellaneous										
Other Storage										

Windows and Doors

Item	Brand Name	Model	Finish	Hardware	Furnished By B.S.	Furnished By O/OA	Installed By B.S.	Installed By O/OA
FIXED SHOWER WINDOW	ABC	3060E	—	—	X		X	
– SOLID SURFACE CASING	ABC		SS123		X		X	
FRENCH DOORS	ABC	3068F	UNFINISHED WOOD	1234	X		X	
INTERIOR DOOR	ABC	3268I	"	123	X		X	

Special Window and Door Notes:

ALL WINDOW & DOOR GLASS TEMPERED; ALL DOORS &
THEIR CASEINGS PAINTED IVORY

Flooring

		Furnished By B.S.	Furnished By O/OA	Installed By B.S.	Installed By O/OA
Removal of Existing Floor Covering	—NA—				
Preparation of Floor for New Surface	BY OTHERS		X		X
Installation of Subfloor/Underlayment	5/8" PLYWOOD	X		X	
New Floor Covering Material Description:	CERAMIC TILE	X			X
Manufacturer ABC Pattern Name	IVORY MATTE (NON-SKID)				
Pattern Number 1234 Pattern Repeat	—				
Floor Covering Installation	SEE NOTE BELOW		X		X
Baseboard Material	SOLID SURFACE 1/4" ABC, 123	X		X	
Transition Treatment	THRESHOLD S.S. ABC, 123	X		X	
Remove and Repair Water Damaged Area	—NA—				
Remove and Reset Usable Closet	—NA—				

Special Flooring Notes: RADIANT FLOORING INSTALLED BY OTHERS; TILE
INSTALLED ON DIAGONAL WITH BORDER & 123 BLACK DOTS
2" X 2"

Decorative Surfaces (wall, ceiling, window materials)

Removal Work: Wall __X__ Ceiling __X__ Window —NA—   Preparation Work: Wall __X__ Ceiling __X__ Window _____

Description	Brand Name	Model	Finish	Material Quantity	Furnished By B.S.	Furnished By O/OA	Installed By B.S.	Installed By O/OA
DECORATIVE LAMINATE	ABC	BACKGR.→123			X		X	
INLAY BORDER		INLAY→456			X		X	
WALL PAINT (IVORY)	DEF	—	EGGSHELL	2 GAL.	X		X	
CEILING PAINT (WHITE)	DEF	—	FLAT	1 GAL.	X		X	
CASINGS & DOORS (IVORY)	DEF	—	SEMI GLOSS	2 PT.	X		X	
PRIME ALL SURFACES	DEF	—	PRIMER	2 GAL.	X		X	

Special Decorative Surface Notes:

CUSTOM MIRROR W/ BLACK FRAME (SEE ELEV. B, PG 7 OF 11)

Electrical Work (except as described above in specific equipment sections)

	Furnished By		Installed By	
	B.S.	O/OA	B.S.	O/OA
Heating System Alteration NEW RADIANT FLOOR BY OTHRS		X		X
New Service Panel				
Code Update ALL OUTLETS GFCI	X		X	
Details				
TOWEL WARMER, 120V, 21" AFF	X		X	
ALL SWITCHES 45" TO ₵ AFF	X		X	
SEE MECHANICAL PLAN FOR DETAILS				
PG. 3 OF 11.				

Plumbing (except as described above in specific equipment sections)

	Furnished By		Installed By	
	B.S.	O/OA	B.S.	O/OA
Heating System Alterations —NA—				
New Rough-in Requirements ALL NEW (SEE MECH. PLAN)	X		X	
Modifications to Existing Lines —NA—				
Details				
SEE MECH. PLAN 3 OF 11 FOR DETAILS	X		X	
NEW VENT & SOIL STACK REQUIRED	X		X	

General Carpentry (except as described above in specific equipment sections)

	Furnished By		Installed By	
	B.S.	O/OA	B.S.	O/OA
Demolition Work REMOVE WOOD SHAKES FROM EAST WALL	X		X	
Existing Fixture and Equipment Removal —NA—				
Trash Removal ARRANGE FOR DUMPSTER	X			
Reconstruction Work (Except as Previously Stated)				
Windows FRAME PER CONST. PLAN (PG 2 OF 11)		X		X
Doors FRAME PER CONST. PLAN (PG 2 OF 11)		X		X
Interior Walls DRYWALL, 1/2" MOISTURE RESISTANT	X		X	
Exterior Walls MATCH EXISTING WOOD SHAKES & FINISH	X		X	
Details NEW ADDITION PER CONSTRUCTION PLAN				
BY LICENSED REMODELING FIRM.		X		X

Miscellaneous Work

		Responsibility	
		B.S.	O/OA
Trash Removal	PILE IN DUMPSTER, EMPTY AS REQUIRED	X	
Jobsite/Room Cleanup	DAILY PICK-UP, SPECIAL POST PROJECT CLEAN-UP	X	
Building Permit(s)	AS REQUIRED	X	
Structural Engineering/Architectural Fees	AS REQUIRED BY OTHERS		X
Inspection Fees	AS REQUIRED	X	
Jobsite Delivery	STORAGE IN GARAGE AVAILABLE	X	
Other			
	SUPERVISE INSTALLATION WORK & SCHEDULE	X	

I have read these specifications and approve:

Accepted: _Client-1 Signature_

Accepted: _Client-2 Signature_

Date: 0/00/00

Authorized Company Representative

By: _Designer's Signature, CBD_

By: _____

Date: 0/00/00

Design Statement

The purpose of the design statement is to interpret the design problem and solution in order to substantiate the project to the client. Design statements may be verbal or written. Written statements maybe a separate document, may be part of the working drawings or a combination of both.

Design statements should clearly outline:

- design considerations and challenges of the project including, but not limited to: construction budget requirements, client needs and wants, special requests and lifestyle factors.

- how the designer arrived at their solution and addressed the design considerations and challenges for the project.

- aesthetic considerations such as use of principles and elements of design (ie. pattern repetition, finish/color/surface selections and other details).

It is important that a design statement be clear, concise and interesting to the reader. Written statements may be in either paragraph or bulleted/outline format. As a guideline, a design statement can be written in 250-500 words. Sample design statements follow, showing both acceptable formats.

Sample Design Statement - Paragraph Format

The primary design challenge in the bathroom design for Mr. and Ms. Client was to create a space that was functional for both Mr. Consumer who uses a wheelchair and Mrs. Consumer who stands 5' 3" tall. Additionally the consumers requested an environment that would feel like a sophisticated spa retreat and flow naturally with their bedroom decor, which is of contemporary Japanese influence. The space to be utilized was an addition which was added to the east end of the existing Master Bedroom.

The construction constraints required direct access to the bedroom somewhere along the east wall, as well as access to an exterior patio that would be built on the north wall. Other design requirements included an open roll-in shower with large seat, stool or bench area adjacent to shower, toilet with space for side transfer, lavatory with kneespace, storage closet and 60" wheelchair turning space.

The solution was derived methodically, first locating doors and then by dividing the remaining space into quarters by function. With the doors on the east and north walls, we placed the 60" diameter of floorspace required for turning in that corner. That left the other two walls for the plumbing fixtures. A custom 31 1/2" high pedestal sink was designed to accommodate both standing and sitting use and provide kneespace.

The shower was designated with four columns that framed the 36" wide seat and window areas. Controls were placed at the entrance and a hand-held showerhead was installed on the seat deck for easy access. All glass used was tempered for safety. The 1/2" curb height is easy to roll-over with a wheelchair. The 42" by 36" floorspace at the shower entrance provides the 90 degree turning space required for a wheelchair. The vertical towel warmer specified allows towels to be hung at a wide range of heights above the floor. A solid surface bench was designed opposite the shower for towel drying and aiding in transfer. Then, the remaining floorspace was utilized for the toilet and side transfer space. All corners were eased to eliminate any sharp edges and surfaces are of tile and solid surface for easy maintenance.

In order to provide the spa retreat feeling requested, a special reflecting pool for floating candles and potpourri was designed between the shower and lavatory. The semi-circular protrusion of the lavatory front was mirrored in the backsplash and mirror top. The square motif was picked-up from a shoji screen in the bedroom and used throughout the bathroom to create a unified theme. Squares are found in the molding, cabinet door style, lighting, floor and bench/lavatory supports. The neutral with black accent colors help to create a feeling of understated sophistication.

Sample Design Statement - Outline Format

The primary design challenge:

- Functional for Mr. Consumer who uses a wheelchair
- Functional for Mrs. Consumer who stands 5'3" tall
- Create an environment that would feel like a sophisticated spa retreat
- Flow naturally with their bedroom decor of Japanese influence

The construction constraints:

- Addition to east end of the existing Master Bedroom
- Direct access to the bedroom somewhere along the east wall
- Access to an exterior patio that would be built on the north wall

Other design requirements:

- Open roll-in shower with large seat
- Stool or bench area adjacent to shower
- Toilet with space for side transfer
- Lavatory with kneespace
- Storage closet
- 60" wheelchair turning space

The solution:

- Located 60" diameter floorspace directly adjacent to doors
- Custom 31 1/2" high pedestal sink accommodates seated and standing users
- Shower with 1/2" curb for roll-in access
- 36" wide shower seat with hand-held showerhead
- Controls placed at shower entrance for easy access
- All glass tempered for safety
- 42" by 36" floorspace at shower entrance for 90 degree turning
- Vertical towel warmer holds towels at multiple heights
- Solid surface bench opposite shower for towel drying and transfer
- Floorspace adjacent to toilet for side transfer
- All corners eased to eliminate any sharp edges
- Surfaces treatments of tile and solid surface for easy maintenance

Aesthetics:

- Special reflecting pool for floating candles and potpourri
- Curved protrusion of lavatory is mirrored in the backsplash and mirror top
- Square motif was picked-up from shoji screen in the bedroom
- Motif used in molding, cabinet door, lights, floor and bench/lavatory
- Neutral with black accent colors create understated sophistication

Contracts

All contract forms used **must** be in strict compliance with Federal, State and Municipal Laws and Ordinances. Reference local codes for compliance standards. Laws do vary, therefore, you should be sure your contracts meet all local requirements.

STANDARD FORM OF AGREEMENT
FOR DESIGN AND INSTALLATION

Approved by the

® **National Kitchen & Bath Association**

Between ....Purchaser

Home Address...

City ....State...........................Zip...................................

Phone Number...

Delivery Address...

And Seller

1. The Seller agrees to furnish the materials and services set forth in the drawings (numbered................................
and dated ....) and specifications annexed hereto.
The Purchaser agrees to make payment therefore in accordance with the schedule of payment.

    Contract Price... $ ....

    Sales Tax (if applicable) .... $ ....

    .... $ ....

    Total Purchase Price.. $ ....

Schedule of Payment:

    Upon signing of this agreement .... $ ....

    Upon delivery of cabinets from manufacturer .... $ ....

    Upon delivery of .... $ ....

    Upon substantial installation of .... $ ....

This contract includes the terms and provisions as set forth herein. Please read and sign where indicated.

2. The standard form of warranty shall apply to the service and equipment furnished (except where other warranties of purchased products apply). The warranty shall become effective when signed by the Seller and delivered to the Purchaser. The warranty is for one year materials and labor.

3. The delivery date, when given, shall be deemed approximate and performance is subject to delays caused by strikes, fires, acts of God or other reasons not under the control of the Seller, as well as the availability of the product at the time of delivery.

4. The Purchaser agrees to accept delivery of the product or products when ready. The risk of loss, as to damage or destruction, shall be upon the Purchaser upon the delivery and receipt of the product.

5. The Purchaser understands that the products described are specially designed and custom built and that the Seller takes immediate steps upon execution of this Agreement to design, order and construct those items set forth herein; therefore, this Agreement is not subject to cancellation by the Purchaser for any reason.

6. No installation, plumbing, electrical, flooring, decorating or other construction work is to be provided unless specifically set forth herein. In the event the Seller is to perform the installation, it is understood that the price agreed upon herein does not include possible expense entailed in coping with hidden or unknown contingencies found at the job site. In the event such contingencies arise and the Seller is required to furnish labor or materials or otherwise perform work not provided for or contemplated by the Seller, the actual costs plus (   )% thereof will be paid for by the Purchaser. Contingencies include but are not limited to: inability to reuse existing water, vent, and waste pipes; air shafts, ducts, grilles, louvres and registers; the relocation of concealed pipes, risers, wiring or conduits, the presence of which cannot be determined until the work has started; or imperfections, rotting or decay in the structure or parts thereof necessitating replacement.

7. Title to the item sold pursuant to this Agreement shall not pass to the Purchaser until the full price as set forth in this Agreement is paid to the Seller.

8. Delays in payment shall be subject to interest charges of (   )% per annum, and in no event higher than the interest rate provided by law. If the Seller is required to engage the services of a collection agency or an attorney, the Purchaser agrees to reimburse the Seller for any reasonable amounts expended in order to collect the unpaid balance.

9. If any provision of this Agreement is declared invalid by any tribunal, the remaining provisions of the Agreement shall not be affected thereby.

10. This Agreement sets forth the entire transaction between the parties; any and all prior Agreements, warranties or representations made by either party are superseded by this Agreement. All changes in this Agreement shall be made by a separate document and executed with the same formalities. No agent of the Seller, unless authorized in writing by the Seller, has any authority to waive, alter, or enlarge this contract, or to make any new or substituted or different contracts, representations, or warranties.

11. The Seller retains the right upon breach of this Agreement by the Purchaser to sell those items in the Seller's possession. In effecting any resale on breach of this Agreement by the Purchaser, the Seller shall be deemed to act in the capacity of agent for the Purchaser. The purchaser shall be liable for any net deficiency on resale.

12. The Seller agrees that it will perform this contract in conformity with customary industry practices. The Purchaser agrees that any claim for adjustment shall not be reason or cause for failure to make payment of the purchase price in full. Any unresolved controversy or claim arising from or under this contract shall be settled by arbitration and judgment upon the award rendered may be entered in any court of competent jurisdiction. The arbitration shall be held under the rules of the American Arbitration Association.

Accepted: ....
                                          Purchaser

Accepted: ....   Accepted: ....
                                                                                                         Purchaser

Date: ....   Date: ....

Titling Project Documents

Protecting Yourself

When you design a project for a client, you must protect yourself from liability when referring to the plans and drawings, and you must protect the plans themselves from being copied by your competitors.

When presenting the plans for a bathroom, **NKBA** recommends that you refer to the drawings as *"Bathroom Design Plans"* or *"Cabinet Plans"*. The design plans should have the following statement included on them in an obvious location in large or block letters.

DESIGN PLANS ARE NOT PROVIDED FOR ARCHITECTURAL OR ENGINEERING USE

The individual drawings incorporated in the overall bathroom design presentation must also be carefully labeled. It is suggested that you refer to these other drawings as *"Floor Plans"*, *"Elevations"*, *"Artist Renderings"*, and *"Mechanical Plans"*.

With respect to the *"Artist Rendering"* , **NKBA** suggests that you include a notation on the drawings which reads:

THIS RENDERING IS AN ARTIST'S INTERPRETATION OF THE GENERAL APPEARANCE OF THE ROOM, IT IS NOT INTENDED TO BE A PRECISE DEPICTION

The entire set of paperwork, which includes your design plans, specifications and contract, can be referred to as the **"Project Documents"**.

You should never refer to the design plan as an *"Architectural Drawing"*, or even as an "architectural-type drawing". **DO NOT USE THE WORDS** *"Architecture"*, *"Architectural Design"*, *"Architectural Phase"*, *"Architectural Background"*, or any other use of the word *"Architectural"* in any of the project documents that you prepare, or in any of your business stationary, promotional information or any presentation materials. Any such reference to the work that you do or documents that you prepare may result in a violation of various state laws. A court may determine that your use of the word *"Architecture/Architectural"*, could reasonably lead a client to believe that you possess a level of expertise that you do not. Worse yet, a court may find you liable for fraud and/or misrepresentation.

Laws do vary per state, therefore, it is important that you consult with your own legal counsel to be sure that you are acting within the applicable statutes in your area. You must clearly understand what drawings you are legally allowed to prepare, and what drawings must be prepared under the auspices of a licensed architect or engineer.

Protecting your "Bathroom Design Plans"

After drafting the design plans for your client, you should insure that they will not be copied or used by a competitor. This may be done by copyrighting the design plan that you prepare.

Copyright is an International form of protection/exclusivity provided by law to authors of original works, despite whether the work is published or not. Original works of authorship include any literary, pictorial, graphic, or sculptured works, such as your design plans, provided they are original works done by you.

Copyright protection exists from the moment the work is created in its final form and will endure fifty years after your death.

Naturally, if two or more persons are authors of an original work, they will be deemed *co-owners* of its copyright. For example; if you as the Bathroom Specialist collaborate with an Interior Designer, you will both be co-owners of the design copyright.

An original work generated by two or more authors is referred to as a *"joint work"*. Generally, a *"joint work"* results if the authors collaborated on the work or if each prepared a segment of it with the knowledge and intent that it would be incorporated with the contributions submitted by other authors. Accordingly, a *"joint work"* will only be found when each co-author intended his respective contribution to be combined into a larger, integrated piece. There is no requirement that each of the co-authors work together or even be acquainted with one another.

A work created by an employee within the scope of his employment is regarded as *"work made for hire"*, and is normally owned by the employer, unless the parties explicitly stipulate in a written agreement, signed by both, that the copyright will be owned by the employee. If you are an independent contractor, the *"works made for hire"* statutes do not include architectural drawings or other design plans, therefore, the copyright in any bathroom design created by you will remain vested with you until you contractually agree to relinquish ownership.

To secure copyright protection for your plans, you are required to give notice of copyright on all publicly distributed copies. The use of the copyright notice is your responsibility as the copyright owner and does not require advance permission from, or registration with, the Copyright Office in Washington, DC.

Copyright © Notice

A proper copyright notice must include the following three items:

- 1. The symbol ©, or the word "Copyright", or the abbreviation "Copy";
  (© is considered as the International symbol for copyright)

- 2. The year of the first publication of the work; and

- 3. The name of the owner of the copyright in the work, or an abbreviation by which the name can be recognized, or a generally known alternative designation of the owner.

An example of a proper copyright notice would be:

Copyright © 1995 Joe Smith

The notice should be affixed to copies of your design plan in such a manner and location as to give reasonable notice of the claim of copyright.

As mentioned previously, you or your firm continue to retain copyright protection of your design plan even if the plan is given to the client after he has paid for it. Although the copyright ownership may be transferred, such transfer must be in writing and signed by you as the owner of the copyright conveyed. Normally, the transfer of a copyright is made by contract. In order to protect your exclusive rights, however, you should include a clause in your contract which reads:

> Design plans are provided for the fair use by the client or his agent in completing the project as listed within this contract. Design plans remain the property of (your name) and cannot be used or reused without permission of (your name).

This clause should also be in any agreement between you and a client who requests that you prepare a design plan for his review. Such a design plan usually serves as the basis for a subsequent contract between you and the client for the actual installation of the kitchen. This type of agreement will prevent the client from obtaining a design plan from you and then taking that plan to a competitor who may simply copy your plan.

So long as you retain the copyright in the design plan, you will be able to sue any party who has copied your design plan for infringement.

Glossary - Graphic Terms

Architects Scale: A measuring tool used to draw at a determined unit of measure ratio accurately; ie. 1/2" = 1', in which each half inch represents one foot.

3/32" = 1'	1/4" = 1'	1" = 1'
3/16" = 1'	3/8" = 1'	1 1/2" = 1'
1/8" = 1'	3/4" = 1'	3" = 1'

It is equally acceptable to use the metric equivalents. (inches x 2.54)

Break Symbol: Indicated by (⤝) and used to end wall lines on a drawing which actually continue or to break off parts of the drawing.

Color: A visual sensation which is a result of light reflecting off objects and creating various wavelengths which when reaching the retina produces the appearance of various hues.

Copyright: Is an International form of protection/exclusivity provided by law to authors of original works, despite whether the work is published or not. Original works of authorship include any literary, pictorial, graphic, or sculptured works such as design plans that are your own original works. The symbol (©) is considered as the International symbol for copyright exclusivity.

Dimension Lines: Solid lines terminating with arrows, dots or slashes which run parallel with the object it represents and includes the actual length of the line written in inches or centimeters inside or on top of the line. Whenever possible, dimension lines should be located outside of the actual walls of the floor plan or elevation.

Dimetric: A dimetric drawing is similar to oblique, with the exception that the object is rotated so that only one of its corners touches the picture plane. The most frequently used angle for the projecting line is an equal division of 45° on either side of the leading edge. A 15° angle is sometimes used when it is less important to show the *"roof view"* of the object.

Elevation: A drawing representing a vertical view of a space taken from a preselected reference plane. There is no depth indicated in an elevation, rather everything appears very flat and is drawn in scale.

Floor Plan: A drawing representing a horizontal view of a space taken from a preselected reference plane (often the ceiling). There is no depth indicated in a floor plan, rather everything appears very flat and is drawn in a reduced scale.

Isometric: The isometric, a special type of dimetric drawing, is the easiest and most popular paraline (three-dimensional) drawing. All axes of the object are simultaneously rotated away from the picture plane and kept at the same angle of projection (30° from the picture plane). All legs are equally distorted in length at a given scale and therefore maintain an exact proportion of 1:1:1.

Kroy Lettering Tape: Translucent sticky backed tape, which after running it through a special typing machine, creates a stick on lettering ideal for labeling drawing title blocks.

Lead: A graphite and clay mixture which is used for drawing and drafting in combination with a lead holder. Similar to a pencil without the wooden outer portion. Available in various degrees of hardness, providing various line weights.

Legend: An explanatory list of the symbols and their descriptions as used on a mechanical plan or other graphic representation.

Matte Board: A by product of wood pulp with a paper surface which has been chemically treated in order to be acid free and fade resistent. The use of matte board will protect drawings from fading, becoming brittle and bending or creasing.

Oblique: In an oblique drawing one face (either plan or elevation) of the object is drawn directly on the picture plane. Projected lines are drawn at a 30° or 45° angle to the picture plane.

Owners Agent: That person or persons responsible for mediating the clients requests with the designer and acting as the interpretor on any area the client is unsure of or in question on.

Ozalid Prints: More commonly referred to as "*Blueprints*", are a method of duplicating drawings in which special paper coated with light sensitive diazo is used. This paper with drawing on transparent paper, is exposed to ultra violet light creating a negative, then the print is exposed again to the developer which produces the "*blackline*", "*blueline*" or "*sepia print*" depending upon the paper used.

Perspective: The art of representing a space in a drawing form which appears to have depth by indicating the relationship of various objects as they appear to the human eye or through the lens of a camera.

Photocopy: A method of duplicating drawings in which light causes toner to adhere to paper of various sizes, typically *(8 1/2" x 11"), (11" x 14")* or *(11" x 17")*, producing prints in high contrast, which are similar to blackline ozalid prints.

Quadrille Paper: White ledger paper base with blue, non-reproducible ruling lines which all carry the same weight. *** NOTE: This is not an acceptable type of drafting paper for project documentation.**

Section: Often referred to as a *"cut-view"*, these drawings are defined as an imaginary cut made through an object and used to show construction details and materials which are not obvious in standard plan or elevational views.

Technical Rapidograph Pens: Provides for a smooth flow of ink with stainless steel points or *"Tungsten Carbide"* point of various sizes, again providing various line weights.

Tracing Paper: Thin semi-transparent paper used for sketching. Also called *"bumwad"* paper.

Transfer Type: Sometimes referred to as *"Press-Type"* or *"Rub-on-Type"*, is a translucent film with lettering or dot screen images which may be transferred to a drawing by rubbing the image after it is positioned on the drawing paper. When the film is lifted, the image remains on the drawing paper and the film is left blank.

Trimetric: The trimetric drawing is similar to the dimetric, except that the plan of the object is rotated so that the two exposed sides of the object are not at equal angles to the picture plane. The plan is usually positioned at 30/60° angle to the ground plane. The height of the object is reduced proportionately as illustrated (similar to the 45° dimetric).

Vellum: Rag stock which has been transparentized with synthetic resin resulting in medium weight transparent paper with a medium-fine grain or *"tooth"* which holds lead to the surface.

Witness Lines: Solid lines which run perpendicular to the dimension line and cross the dimension line at the exact location of its termination. These lines should begin approximately 1/16" outside of the walls of the floor plan and end approximately 1/16" beyond the dimension line.

Appendix C
Imperial/Metric Comparison Chart

Kitchen and bath floor plans should be drawn to a scale of
1/2" equals 1' (1/2 =1'-0"). An equally acceptable metric scale
would be a ratio of 1 to 20 (ie. 1cm to 20cm)

	INCHES	MILLIMETERS	CENTIMETERS
* Actual metric conversion to millimeters is	1/8"	3 mm	.32 cm
1" = 25.4mm. To facilitate conversions	1/4"	6	.64
between imperial + metric dimensioning for	1/2"	12	1.27
calculations under 1", 24 mm is used.	3/4"	18	1.91
	1" →	→ 24	2.54
* To facilitate conversions between			
imperial + metric for calculations			
over 1", 25 mm is typically used.	3" →	75	7.62
	6" →	→ 150	15.24
* Actual metric conversion to	9"	225	22.86
centimeters is 1"= 2.54 cm.	12"	300	30.48
	15"	375	38.1
	18"	450	45.72
	21"	525	53.34
	24"	600	60.96
	27"	675	68.58
	30	750	76.2
	33"	825	83.82
	36"	900	91.44
	39"	975	99.06
	42"	1050	106.68
	45"	1125	114.3
	48"	1200	121.92
	51"	1275	129.54
	54"	1350	137.16
	57"	1425	144.78
	60"	1500	152.4
	63"	1575	160.02
	66"	1650	167.64
	69"	1725	175.26
	72"	1800	182.88
	75"	1875	190.5
	78"	1950	198.12
	81"	2025	205.74
	84"	2100	213.36
	87"	2175	220.98
	90"	2250	228.6
	93"	2325	236.22
	96"	2400	243.84
	99"	2475	251.46
	102"	2475	259.08
	105"	2625	266.7
	108"	2700	274.32
	111"	2775	281.94
	114"	2850	289.56
	117"	2925	297.18
	120"	3000	304.8
	123"	3075	312.42
	126"	3150	320.04
	129"	3225	327.66
	132"	3300	335.28
	135"	3375	342.9
	138"	3450	350.52
	141"	3525	358.14
	144"	3600	365.76

Metric Conversion Chart

Length

10 millimeters = 1 centimeter (cm)
10 centimeters = 1 decimeter
10 decimeters = 1 meter (m)
10 meters = 1 dekameter
100 meters = 1 hectometer
1,000 meters = 1 kilometer

Area

100 sq. millimeters = 1 sq. centimeter
100 sq. centimeter = 1 sq. decimeter
100 sq. decimeters = 1 sq. meter
100 sq. meters = 1 are
10,000 sq. meters = 1 hectare
100 hectares = 1 sq. kilometer

Linear Drawing Measurements

1 millimeter (mm) = .03937   1" = 25.4 mm   12" = 304.8 mm
1 centimeter (cm) = .3937   1" = 2.54 cm   12" = 30.48 cm
1 meter (m) = 39.37   1" = .0254 m   12" = .3048 m

Square Measure

1 sq. inch = 6.4516 sq. centimeters
1 sq. foot = 9.29034 sq. decimeters
1 sq. yard = .836131 sq. meter
1 acre = .40469 hectare
1 sq. mile = 2.59 sq. kilometers

Dry Measure

1 pint = .550599 liter
1 quart = 1.101197 liter
1 peck = 8.80958 liter
1 bushel = .35238 hectoliter

Cubic Measure

1 cu. inch = 16.3872 cu. centimeters
1 cu. foot = .028317 cu. meters
1 cu. yard = .76456 cu. meters

Liquid Measure

1 pint = .473167 liter
1 quart = .946332 liter
1 gallon = 3.785329 liter

Long Measure

1 inch = 25.4 millimeters
1 foot = .3 meter
1 yard = .914401 meter
1 mile = 1.609347

Glossary of Terms

Accessory: Towel bars, handrails, toilet paper holders and various other items that complement the fixtures and fittings and are an important part of each bathroom center.

Active Solar: In solar heating, active solar means that collectors and pumps that distribute heat are needed.

Aerator: A device used on the end of a faucet that mixes air with water so splashback is minimized.

Aluminum, Anodized: Aluminum that has been sealed/coated by an electro-chemical process to provide corrosion resistance and color.

Ampere (Amps): The measurement of the rate of flow of electricty.

Angle, Acute: An angle which is less that 90 degrees.

Angle, Obtuse: An angle which is more than 90 degrees.

Angle, Right: An angle equal to 90 degrees or two perpendicular legs.

Auger: A tool used to mechanically break free and move a clog.

Backflow: The term used for negative pressure.

Ballast: A device that limits the electric current flowing into a fluorescent or high intensity discharge lamp.

Bidet: A fixture designed for personal cleanliness; used to wash the perineal area.

Brightness: Intensity of light from an object or surface that directly reaches the eye of the viewer.

Candela: The light produced from one candle in one direction.

Carbon Filter System: Removes contaminants from water as the water passes through a filter containing particles of carbon. The carbon absorbs the contaminants.

Cast Iron: A manufacturing process used to mold metal when it is so hot it is in a liquid state.

Cast Polymer: A fixture and surfacing material created by pouring a mixture of ground marble and polyester resin into a treated mold, where curing takes place at room temperature or in a curing oven.

Centerlines: A designation noting a point equally distant from all points of a surface and/or object.

CFM: Cubic feet per minute.

CFM Rating: Cubic feet per minute a fan is capable of moving.

Color Rendition Index (CRI): A scale which refers to the extent which a perceived color of an object under a light source matches the perceived color of that object under another source (such as daylight or incandescent lighting).

Comfort Zone: The range of temperatures and humidities that humans are comfortable at.

Conduit: A hollow metal tube that contains electrical wiring.

Console Lavatory: A separate or integral fixture that is installed above or below a countertop material that is supported by decorative legs, creating a console piece of furniture.

Contrast: The brightness difference between surfaces in the field of view.

Convection Heat: Heat which is air heated by an element and then circulated.

Countertop Lavatory: A separate fixture installed above or below the level of the countertop material. Plumbing lines are concealed in the cabinetry.

Cross Lighting: Task lighting which provides even illumination from side to side and top to bottom.

Dielectric Union: Union used to join two pipes of different materials in order to prevent the pipe materials from reacting chemically with each other and causing corrosion.

Diffuser: A device used to deflect air from an outlet in various directions. Also a device for distributing the light of a lamp evenly.

Distiller: A heating element which boils water and as the steam condenses, impurities are removed.

Diverter: A knob, handle or button that is moved, pushed or turned to provide water output selections.

Drain/Waste/Vent (DWV) System: A system which carries water and waste out of the house.

Drawing: The term used to describe a press operation which involves the forming of a shape with at least some depth.

Drawings, Elevations: True, scaled drawings in both height and width, however they have no depth.

Drawings, Interpretive: Elevations, paraline drawings and perspectives which illustrate the vertical elements in a design that are not shown in a floor plan.

Drawings, Paraline: Drawings which are similar to orthographic drawings and remain in a true scale format, yet offer a three dimensional view of the space.

Enclosure: A sliding, folding or swinging door/panel system.

Energy Efficiency Rating (EER): The efficiency of room air conditioners is measured by the ratio of the cooling output in BTUs divided by the power consumption.

Escutcheon: A protective plate used to enclose pipe or fitting at wall or floor covering.

Fitting: The term used for any device that controls water entering or leaving a fixture. Faucets, spouts, drain controls, water supply lines and diverter valves all come under this category.

Fixture: A bathtub, shower, lavatory, toilet, bidet or urinal that receives water.

Flue Gas: A toxic gas produced during the combustion of fossil fuels.

Flush-mounted: Installed completely even with the surrounding deck.

Focal Glow: A small area highlighted with a high brightness to provide sensory stimulation.

Foot Candle: The unit of illumination when the foot is the unit of length; the illumination on a surface one square foot in area on which there is a uniformly distributed flux of one lumen.

Furring: The creation of space by using thin strips of wood or metal.

Granite: An igneous rock with visible coarse grains used for countertops in bathrooms.

Glass, Safety/Tempered: Glass tempered or altered in such a manner to enhance its strength significantly over ordinary glass.

GPM: Gallons per minute. An abbreviation used to describe water flow ratings.

Grab bars: Safety bars installed in bathtubs and showers to prevent falls. A device, usually installed on a wall, that provides support while rising from, sitting in, entering or exiting a bathtub or shower.

Ground Fault Circuit Interrupter (GFCI): A device that monitors the electrical circuit at all times and, upon detecting a ground fault (a leakage on the line to ground), removes power to the circuit.

Ground Wire: A bare copper wire or a coated green wire which does not carry current.

Hammer, Water: A shock wave, sounding like a hammer being banged on the pipes, which is caused by the water supply being turned off quickly.

"Hard Water": Water that contains scale-forming minerals, such as calcium and magnesium.

Home Run Supply Line: A supply line which goes all the way back to the main and the water heater.

Homogeneous: The term used when color goes all the way through an object.

Human Ergonomics: An Applied Science concerned with the characteristics of people that need to be considered in designing and arranging things that they use in order that people and things will interact most effectively and safely.

Hydronic Heat: A form of central heat which carries its heat in water and circulates the hot water in pipes.

Integral Lavatory: A fixture that is fabricated from the same pice of material as the countertop material. Plumbing is concealed in the cabinetry.

Junction Boxes: Rectangular, octagonal or circular boxes made of plastic or metal which house connections between wires.

Laminates: A surfacing material used on bathroom wall areas, countertops, cabinet interiors, cabinet doors and bathtub platforms.

Lamp: An artificial light source, such as an incandescent bulb or fluorescent tube.

Lavatory: A fixture with running water and drain pipe for washing, shaving, etc. Sometimes called a "wash basin", but not to be confused with "sink" which always refers to a kitchen fixture.

Lighting, Fluorescent: A tubular lamp which produces heat by the absorption of radiation from another source.

Lighting, Incandescent: Produced when the filament is subjected to intense heat.

Lumens: The amount of light measured at the light source.

Luminaires: Term for lighting fixtures in the lighting industry.

Marble: Recrystallized limestone, marble is brittle. A stone used for countertops and flooring in bathrooms.

Overflow: A second outlet for water in a bathtub or lavatory, to prevent flooding if water is left running.

Passive Solar: In solar heating, passive solar means that the building itself is designed to capture the sun's heat.

Pedestal Lavatory: A free-standing fixture. The water supply lines are visible. The trap is partially concealed by the base.

Pipe, Fixture Supply: The pipe bringing water from behind a wall to a fixture.

Pipe, Vent: The pipe installed to provide air flow to or from a drainage system or to provide air circulation within the system.

Pipe, Waste: The line that carries away the discharge from any fixture, except toilets, conveying it to building drain.

Plenum: A large, sheet-metal enclosure either above or below the furnace which distributes heated air.

Pythagorean Theorem: In a right-angled triangle, the sum of the squares of the legs is equal to the square of the hypotenuse.

Radiant Heat: Heat which is transferred through invisible electromagnetic waves from an infrared energy source.

Recovery Rate: The length of time required for the water heater to bring the temperature of the cold, stored water up to the temperature set on the dial.

Rough-in: The installation of piping concealed in walls and floor to which supply lines and drain from a plumbing fixture are attached.

Self-rimming: A lavatory that is designed to sit on top of the countertop.

Soil Line: Term for the toilet discharge pipe.

Sone Rating: A measurement of sound level.

Stack: General term for the main vertical pipe of soil, waste or vent pipe system.

Stack, Vent: Vertical pipe providing circulation of air to and from any part of a drainage system.

Stamping: The term used to describe the cutting or forming of products from sheet-metal in a cold state.

Supply Branches: The two sets of pipes that run horizontally through the floor joists or concrete slab and deliver water from the supply main.

Supply Risers: Supply branches that run vertically in the wall to an upper story.

Surround: The material used to finish the wet wall surface surrounding a fixture.

Terrazzo: A slurry mixture of stone chips consisting of marble and cement. Used as a flooring surface or wall treatment in bathrooms.

Toilet: A bowl-shaped plumbing fixture fitting with a device to flush out sanitary waste. Also known as a water closet, commode, hopper, john, etc.

Trap: Bent pipe section or device that holds a water deposit and forms a seal against the passage of sewer gases from the waste pipe into the room.

Urinal: A plumbing fixture designed specifically for male urination/disposal.

Under-mounted: Installed from below the counter surfaces.

Urinal: A plumbing fixture designed specifically for male urination/disposal.

Vacuum Breaker: A device to prevent waste water backflow into a water supply line.

Valve, Diverter: A spring-loaded push or lift type used to divert or open secondary channels.

Valve, Pressure Balance: Shower control that eliminates hot or cold surges of water by reacting to pressure changes in the water supply line.

Vitreous China: A form of ceramics/porcelain that is "glass-like".

Volt: The measurement of electrical pressure.

Wall-hung Lavatory: A fixture that hangs from the wall. Plumbing lines and trap are visible unless a shroud is used to cover them.

Water Closet: A term used for the bathroom which comes from a European home design that featured the toilet and a small lavatory in one room separated from a larger room housing the bathtub.

Water Supply System: Carries water from the municipal water system or well into the house and around to fixtures and appliances.

Watts (Wattage): The measurement of the amount of energy consumed by a light source.

Wet Wall: A wall containing supply lines and soil and waste lines.

Whirlpool: A therapeutic bath in which all or part of the body is exposed to whirling currents of hot water.

Zoned Heat: A division of the house into two or more parts with a separate heat source for each part.

Index